T0256345

# SYSTEM INNOVATION FOR A TROUBLED WORLD: APPLIED SYSTEM INNOVATION IX

**System Innovation for a Troubled World: Applied System Innovation IX,** includes the contributions presented at the IEEE 9th International Conference on Applied System Innovation (ICASI 2023, Chiba, Japan, 21-25 April 2023). The conference received more than 600 submitted papers from 12 different countries, whereby roughly one quarter of these papers was selected to present at ICASI 2023. The book aims to provide an integrated communication platform for researchers from a wide range of topics including information technology, communication science, applied mathematics, computer science, advanced material science, and engineering. Hopefully, it will enhance interdisciplinary collaborations between science and engineering technologists in the fields of academics and related industries.

# Smart Science, Design and Technology

ISSN: 2640-5504
eISSN: 2640-5512

*Book Series Editors*

Stephen D. Prior
*Faculty of Engineering and Physical Sciences*
*University of Southampton*
*Southampton*
*UK*

Siu-Tsen Shen
*Department of Multimedia Design*
*National Formosa University*
*Taiwan, R.O.C.*Volume 7

PROCEEDINGS OF THE IEEE 9TH INTERNATIONAL CONFERENCE ON APPLIED SYSTEM INNOVATION (ICASI 2023), CHIBA, JAPAN, APRIL 21–25, 2023

# System Innovation for a Troubled World
## Applied System Innovation IX

*Edited by*

Artde Donald Kin-Tak Lam
*Fujian University of Technology, P.R. China*

Stephen D. Prior
*University of Southampton, Southampton, United Kingdom*

Siu-Tsen Shen
*National Formosa University, Taiwan, R.O.C.*

Sheng-Joue Young
*National United University, Taiwan*

Liang-Wen Ji
*National Formosa University, Huwei District, Taiwan*

**CRC Press**
Taylor & Francis Group
Boca Raton   London   New York   Leiden

CRC Press is an imprint of the
Taylor & Francis Group, an **informa** business

A BALKEMA BOOK

First published 2024
by CRC Press/Balkema
4 Park Square, Milton Park, Abingdon, Oxon, OX14 4RN

and by CRC Press/Balkema
2385 NW Executive Center Drive, Suite 320, Boca Raton FL 33431

*CRC Press/Balkema is an imprint of the Taylor & Francis Group, an informa business*

*British Library Cataloguing-in-Publication Data*
*A catalogue record for this book is available from the British Library*

*Library of Congress Cataloging-in-Publication Data*
A catalog record has been requested for this book

ISBN: 978-1-032-60846-4 (hbk)
ISBN: 978-1-032-60853-2 (pbk)
ISBN: 978-1-003-46076-3 (ebk)

DOI: 10.1201/9781003460763

Typeset in Times New Roman
by MPS Limited, Chennai, India

*System Innovation for a Troubled World – Lam et al. (Eds)*
© 2024 the Editor(s), ISBN: 978-1-032-60846-4

# Table of Contents

# Preface

We have great pleasure in presenting this conference proceeding for technology applications in engineering science and mechanics from the selected articles of the International Conference on Applied System Innovation (ICASI 2023), organized by the International (Taiwanese) Institute of Knowledge Innovation and the IEEE, held in Chiba, Japan April 21-25, 2023.

The ICASI 2023 conference was a forum that brought together users, manufacturers, designers, and researchers involved in the structures or structural components manufactured using smart science. The forum provided an opportunity for exchange of the research and insights from scientists and scholars thereby promoting research, development and use of computational science and materials. The conference theme for ICASI 2023 was: "System Innovation for a Troubled World" and tried to explore the important role of innovation in the development of the technology applications, including articles dealing with design, research, and development studies, experimental investigations, theoretical analysis and fabrication techniques relevant to the application of technology in various assemblies, ranging from individual to components to complete structure were presented at the conference. The major themes on technology included Materials Science & Engineering, Communication Science & Engineering, Computer Science & Engineering, Electrical & Electronic Engineering, Mechanical & Automation Engineering, Architecture Engineering, IOT Technology, and Innovation Design. About 400 participants, representing 12 countries came together for the 2023 conference and made it a highly successful event. We would like to thank all those who directly or indirectly contributed to the organization of the conference.

Selected articles presented at the ICASI 2023 conference will be published as a series of special issues in various journals. In this conference proceeding we have some selected articles from various themes. A committee consisting of experts from leading academic institutions, laboratories, and industrial research centres was formed to shortlist and review the articles. The articles in this conference proceedings have been peer reviewed to maintain a high standard. We are extremely happy to bring out this conference proceeding and dedicate it to all those who have made their best efforts to contribute to this publication.

Professor Siu-Tsen Shen & Dr Stephen D. Prior

# Editorial Board

*System Innovation for a Troubled World – Lam et al. (Eds)*
*© 2024 the Author(s), ISBN: 978-1-032-60846-4*

# Stackable band pass filter: A numerical simulation

Shin-Ku Lee
*Research Center for Energy Technology and Strategy, National Cheng Kung University, Taiwan*

Mingtsu Ho*
*Department of Electrical Engineering, WuFeng University, Chia-Yi, Taiwan*

ABSTRACT: In this paper, a stackable band pass filter is proposed and reported with supporting numerical results. The numerical simulation is an application of the method of characteristics in one dimension which yields the computational solutions of Maxwell's equations and validates that the proposed structure enhances the transmission (minimizes the reflection) a specific spectral band. The proposed unit structure consists of five layers of transparent thin sheets that are made of three different dielectric materials each of which has a particular thickness and is symmetric in formation and stackable for broader bandwidth if necessary. These transparent dielectric materials ($\varepsilon_{ra}$, $\varepsilon_{rb}$, $\varepsilon_{rc}$) are assumed uniform, non-magnetic, and lossless. When a ray of light moves from $\varepsilon_{ra}$ through $\varepsilon_{rb}$ to $\varepsilon_{rc}$ and since the strength of the reflection depends on the dielectric constant of the three media, the maximum total transmittance requires the following: $\varepsilon_{ra} < \varepsilon_{rb} < \varepsilon_{rc}$ and $\varepsilon_{rb} = \sqrt{\varepsilon_{ra}\varepsilon_{rc}}$ which is known as the Rayleigh's film. The proposed unit structure is $\varepsilon_{ra}$-$\varepsilon_{rb}$-$\varepsilon_{rc}$-$\varepsilon_{rb}$-$\varepsilon_{ra}$ where each dielectric material is equivalent to 90° in optical path length. The spectral band of interest is assuming visible light whose wavelengths range from 400 nm (750 THz) to 550 nm (545.5 THz). The numerical results strongly support the proposed stackable band pass filter.

## 1 INTRODUCTION

The main purpose of this paper is to report a proposal for a stackable bandpass filter. The unit structure of the proposed bandpass filter is composed of three various transparent dielectric materials in which the two materials with less dielectric constants are equally divided into two pieces and then rearranged in a symmetric formation. Each unit consists of five layers of three kinds of materials with three different thicknesses and passes frequencies within a certain range while rejecting frequencies outside that range. Moreover, it can be stacked up to enhance the bandwidth of the pass band. The idea of the proposed structure is supported by the computational results through the application of the method of characteristics (MOC).

In early 1995, MOC was developed for the numerical solutions of Maxwell's equations of the electromagnetic (EM) scattering problem from an infinitely long perfect electric conductor (PEC) strip and produced computational results that are compatible with those generated by the finite-difference time-domain (FDTD) technique [1,2]. MOC then was applied to the several EM scattering problems listed below and yielded results that

were found in good agreement with the theoretical values or demonstrating reasonable trends. They are as follows: EM reflections from PEC surfaces that are either traveling or vibrating or both [3,4] where EM relativistic relationships were added to complete the EM boundary conditions. EM scattering from rotating dielectric circular cylinders where MOC combined with the passing center swing back grids technique and the modified O-type grid system [5–8]. The reflection and transmission of EM fields from lossless nonuniform dielectric slabs [9]. EM pulse propagates onto a dielectric half-space of finite conductivity [10].

The proposed structure was inspired by fiber Bragg grating (FBG). An FBG is made of multiple materials with various refractive indices arranged in a periodic pattern and built in an optical fiber core that acts as an optical filter [11,12]. The FBG can perform many primary functions, such as reflection and filtering [13–20].

## 2 MAXWELL'S EQUATIONS AND EM BOUNDARY CONDITIONS

In the present one-dimensional numerical simulation, the governing equations are Maxwell's equations; the numerical method employed is MOC which gives the computational solutions of

---

*Corresponding Author: homt@wfu.edu.tw

DOI: 10.1201/9781003460763-1

Maxwell's equations. We build the numerical model in free space; the numerical excitation source is a Gaussian EM pulse that propagates onto the proposed structure.

For the current numerical simulation in one dimension, the incident Gaussian EM pulse is transverse electromagnetic (TEM) mode and propagates in the positive-x direction toward the proposed structure. The TEM mode propagation employed in the model has its electric field direction along the z-axis (i.e., $\mathbf{E} = -\hat{z}\mathbf{E}_z$) and its magnetic fields along the negative-y direction (i.e., $\mathbf{B} = -\hat{y}\mathbf{B}_y$).

There are two types of EM boundary conditions for the current simulation. Since the incident Gaussian EM pulse is propagating normally onto the proposed structure, on the air-to-dielectric, dielectric-to-air, and dielectric-to-dielectric interfaces, the boundary conditions between media are that the electric fields and the magnetic fields of both sides are continuous. At both truncated ends of the one-dimensional numerical model, the boundary condition requires that these two numerical boundaries are transparent to the EM fields.

## 3   THE PROPOSED STRUCTURE

A schematic diagram of the proposed unit structure is given in Figure 1 where it is surrounded by air. It is symmetric in formation and consists of three kinds of dielectric material ($\varepsilon_{ra}$, $\varepsilon_{rb}$, $\varepsilon_{rc}$) with three different thicknesses ($d_a$, $d_b$, $d_c$). The idea of Rayleigh's film and for a maximum total transmittance requires $\varepsilon_{ra} < \varepsilon_{rb} < \varepsilon_{rc}$ and $\varepsilon_{rb} = \sqrt{\varepsilon_{ra}\varepsilon_{rc}}$ [21,22]. The proposed unit structure is numerically proved to function as a band pass filter. It is also found that if several units are stacked up as shown in Figure 2 the width of pass band is broadened. Figure 2 illustrates a structure of three folds. Note that there exists a thin air gap between units.

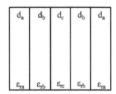

Figure 1.   Schematic diagram of the proposed unit structure.

Figure 2.   Schematic diagram of three-fold structure.

Table 1 summarizes the specifications of the proposed structure where the differences between the design values and the numerical values have resulted from the spatial discretization. Note that all three dielectric constants follow Rayleigh's film rule while that of air is taken as one, that every material is designed to have a 90° in the optical path length, and that materials $\varepsilon_{ra}$ and $\varepsilon_{rb}$ are evenly divided into two pieces to form a symmetric configuration. The term "working wavelength" refers to the one on which the definition of the thickness of the transparent material is based. It is shown that when materials $\varepsilon_{ra}$ and $\varepsilon_{rc}$ have 800 nm as working wavelength and material $\varepsilon_{rb}$ 300 nm, the structure functions as a band-pass filter allowing EM fields through with wavelength ranging from 400 nm to 550 nm.

Table 1.   Design specifications (band-pass: 400 ~ 550 nm).

| Material | a | b | c |
|---|---|---|---|
| Dielectric constant ($\varepsilon_r$) | 1.5 | 2.25 | 3.375 |
| Design o. p. l.* (°) | 90 | 90 | 90 |
| Working wavelength (nm) | 800 | 300 | 800 |
| Numerical thickness (nm) | 163.299 | 50.000 | 108.866 |
| Number of pieces | 2 | 2 | 1 |
| Numerical o. p. l.* (°) | 90.055 | 90.180 | 90.028 |
| Numerical thickness (nm) | 163.4 | 50.0 | 108.9 |
| Numerical wavelength (nm) | 800.49 | 300.00 | 800.25 |

* o. p. l. = optical path length

## 4   NUMERICAL RESULTS

The computational results of the band-pass filter whose dimensions are listed in Table 1 are plotted in Figure 3. In the graph spectrum, the reflected electric fields along with that of the incident Gaussian pulse as a reference are given. Both axes are logarithmic and both spectra are normalized based on the incidence. The coordinate axis y is the normalized magnitude and axis x is in the units of nanometers (nm). Note that the figure legend indicates that the working wavelengths are 300 and 800 nm and the design optical path length is 90°. The two vertical dashed lines stand for 400 nm and 550 nm, respectively. Within that range the following are observed: there exists a relatively low reflectance between the two working wavelengths that consists of two small lobes having levels below one hundredth and three minima at about 400, 475, and 550 nm.

According to the experimental results, the extension of the working wavelengths to 200 and 900 nm can suppress the magnitude of reflectance

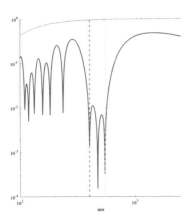

Figure 3. Reflected electric field spectrum (300 ~ 800 nm, 90°).

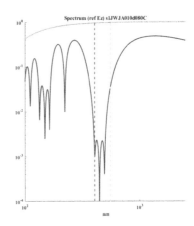

Figure 5. Reflected electric field spectrum (200 ~ 900 nm, 80°).

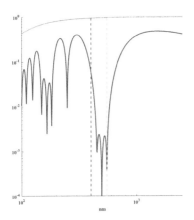

Figure 4. Reflected electric field spectrum (200 ~ 900 nm, 90°).

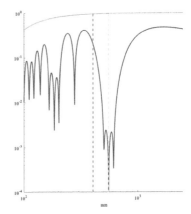

Figure 6. Reflected electric field spectrum (200 ~ 900 nm, 100°).

within the band-pass bandwidth as shown in Figure 4. A comparison of the difference within the band-pass region of Figures 3 and 4 revealed that the levels of the two small lobes drop from one hundredth to two thousandths but in the cost of narrowing the bandwidth from 400 ~550 nm to 450 ~ 550 nm and that the center minimum between shifts from 475 nm to 496 nm. As expected, the computational results also show that the decrease in thickness or the optical path length shifts the pass band toward the shorter wavelength end (as shown in Figure 5) while increasing toward the longer end (as shown in Figure 6).

More experiments were carried out for stacking up multiple units. Figures 7 and 8 illustrate two and three units with working wavelengths of 300 and 800 nm, respectively, where the air gap between units is 10 nm. As can be pointed out from Figure 7, the pass band width is wider yet the cost of introducing two more lobes within that pass band ranges from about 383 nm to 629 nm.

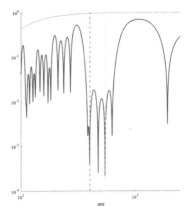

Figure 7. Reflected electric field spectrum (300 ~ 800 nm, 90°, 2 units).

The bandpass width of the three-unit structure measured from about 358 nm to 700 nm and one more lobe than that of the two-unit structure.

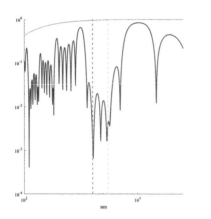

Figure 8. Reflected electric field spectrum (300 ~ 800 nm, 90°, 3 units).

## 6 CONCLUSION

The computational results of the proposed stackable bandpass filter made of three different materials are presented in this paper. The following are demonstrated and observed: changing the optical path lengths and the working wavelengths can adjust the locations of minima of reflectance, and by stacking up unit structures the width of the passband can be widened, however, extra lobes within the passband are introduced. The numerical results produced by the method of characteristics strongly support the idea of the proposed structure. The proposed structure is symmetric and simple in formation and stackable to broaden the pass bandwidth.

## REFERENCES

[1] Taflove A., *Computational Electrodynamics, The Finite-Difference Time-Domain Method*, Artech House, Boston, 1995.

[2] Donohoe J.P., Beggs J.H., Mingtsu Ho, "Comparison of finite-difference time-domain results for scattered EM fields: Yee algorithm vs. a characteristic based algorithm," *27th IEEE Southeastern Symposium on System Theory*, March 1995.

[3] Mingtsu Ho, "Scattering of EM waves from traveling and/or vibrating perfect surface: numerical simulation," *IEEE Transactions on Antennas and Propagation*, 54(1): 152–156, January 2006.

[4] Mingtsu Ho "EM Scattering from PEC plane moving at extremely high speed: simulation in one dimension," *Journal of Applied Science and Engineering (JASE)*, 17(4): 429–436, December 2014.

[5] Mingtsu Ho, Numerically solving scattered electromagnetic fields from rotating objects using passing center swing back grid technique: a proposal," *Journal of Electromagnetic Waves and Applications (JEMWA)*, 23(23): 389–394, January 2009.

[6] Mingtsu Ho, "Simulation of scattered fields from rotating cylinder in 2D: under illumination of TE and TM gaussian pulses," *Progress in Electromagnetics Research Symposium (PIERS Proceedings, 1646 – 1651, 2009) in Moscow, Russia, August 18–21, 2009.

[7] Mingtsu Ho, "Simulation of scattered EM fields from rotating cylinder using passing center swing back grids technique in two dimensions," *Progress in Electromagnetic Research*, PIER 92, pp 79–90, April 2009.

[8] Mingtsu Ho, Li-An Tsai, and Cheng-Jr Tsai "EM fields inside a rotating circular hollow dielectric cylinder: numerical simulation in 2Ds," *Progress in Electromagnetics Research (PIER) M*, 45: 1–8, January 2016.

[9] Mingtsu Ho, Fu-Shun Lai, Shun-Wen Tan, & Pi-Wei Chen, "Numerical simulation of propagation of EM pulse through lossless non-uniform dielectric slab using characteristic-based method," *progress in electromagnetic research*, PIER 81, pp. 197–212, January 2008.

[10] Mingtsu Ho & F.-S. Lai, "Effects of medium conductivity on electromagnetic pulse propagation onto dielectric half space: one-dimensional simulation using characteristic-based method," *Journal of Electromagnetic Waves and Applications (JEMWA)*, 21(13): 1773–1785, 2007.

[11] Meltz, *et al.* (1989). "Formation of bragg gratings in optical fibers by a transverse holographic method". *Opt. Lett.* 14 (15): 823–5.

[12] Canning J., Fiber gratings and devices for sensors and lasers, *Lasers and Photonics Reviews*, 2 (4), 275–289, Wiley, USA (2008)

[13] Hill K.O., Fujii Y., Johnson D.C., and Kawasaki B.S., "Photosensitivity in optical fiber waveguides: Application to reflection filter fabrication," *Appl. Phys. Lett.* (32): 647–649, 1978.

[14] Kawasaki B.S., Hill K.O., Johnson D.C., and Fujii Y., "Narrow-band bragg reflectors in optical fibers," *Opt. Lett.*, vol. 3, pp. 66–68, 1978.

[15] Hill K.O. and Meltz G., "Fiber bragg grating technology fundamentals and overview," *Journal of Lightwave Technology* (15)8, 1263–1276, Aug 1997.

[16] Lord Rayleigh (Strutt J.W.), *Proc. London Math. Soc.* 17, 4 (1887).

[17] Othonos A. (2000) Bragg gratings in optical fibers: fundamentals and applications, *Optical Fiber Sensor Technology*.

[18] Othonos A. and Kalli K. (1999) *Fiber Bragg Gratings: Fundamentals and Applications in Telecommunications and Sensing*, Artech House.

[19] Bennion I., Williams J.A.R., Zhang L., Sugden K. and Doran N. J. (1996) UV-written in-fibre bragg gratings. *Optical and Quantum Electronics*, 28, 93–135.

[20] Othonos A. (1997) Fiber bragg gratings. *Review of Scientific Instruments*, 68, 4309–41.

[21] Moreno I., Araiza J., Avendano-Alejo M. (2005) "Thin-film spatial filters," *Optics Letters*. 30 (8): 914–916.

[22] Krepelka J. (1992) "Maximally flat antireflection coatings," *Jemná Mechanika A Optika* (3–5): 53.

System Innovation for a Troubled World – Lam et al. (Eds)
© 2024 the Author(s), ISBN: 978-1-032-60846-4

# Effect of brinewater curing on the compressive strength of concrete incorporating high-volume fly ash/blast furnace slag

Chung-Hao Wu*
*Department of Civil Engineering, National Kaohsiung University of Science and Technology, Kaohsiung, Taiwan*

Yu-Feng Lin
*Department of Civil Engineering, Chienkuo Technology University, Changhua, Taiwan*

Shu-Ken Lin & How-Ji Chen
*Department of Civil Engineering, National Chung Hsing University, Taichung, Taiwan*

ABSTRACT: This research aimed to study the effect of brinewater curing on the compressive strength of concrete containing fly ash (FA) and blast furnace slag (BFS). The water-cementitious ratio was 0.4, The FA and BFS replaced 0%, 30%, and 60% of cement weight, respectively. The concrete specimens were cured by freshwater and brinewater till the ages of 28 and 56 days for testing. Test results showed that the compressive strength of concrete cured by brinewater was higher than that of concrete cured by freshwater, and the compressive strength at 56-day was higher than their strength at 28-day. The compressive strength of concrete with FA was lower than other concretes, and the compressive strength of concrete cured by freshwater or brinewater presented not much difference on 28-day. The strength of concrete with FA cured by brinewater was significantly higher than that of concrete cured by freshwater on 56-day. The BFS concrete had the highest strength, however, it showed no obvious effect for freshwater or brinewater curing on its compressive strength. The compressive strength of concrete with FA/BFS was lower than that of concrete with BFS, but higher than that of control concrete (F00B00). Adding FA and BFS in concrete at the same time can enhance the compressive strength of concrete with sole FA at the age of 28 days.

## 1 INTRODUCTION

The production of Portland cement concrete will emit a large amount of carbon dioxide, which will have an adverse impact on the natural environment. Therefore, reducing the emission of carbon dioxide and producing environmentally friendly concrete has become an important research issue. The current practice is to use mineral admixtures, like fly ash or blast furnace slag, to replace part of cement for producing concrete, thus reducing the usage of cement [1]. Due to the small size and large specific surface area of the mineral admixture, the pozzolanic reaction can be accelerated to form calcium silicate hydrate (C-S-H) and calcium aluminate hydrate (C-A-H), which effectively consumes the calcium hydroxide crystals (CH), fills the microspores inside the concrete and improves the microstructure of the concrete, resulting in improving the later strength and durability of concrete [2].

Seawater is not particularly harmful to pure concrete, and several underwater pure concrete blocks and structures exposed to different marine environments for years are still in relatively good condition. The only chemical limit generally recommended for cement used in marine environments is related to its $C_3A$ content, which should not exceed 8% [3]. However, seawater is very harmful to reinforced concrete because chloride ions can induce the steel to rust, causing the covering of reinforced concrete to peel off quickly. All corrosion mechanisms are related to the ease with which harmful substances attack the concrete, so having very dense and impermeable concrete may provide better protection [4].

Many studies have pointed out that adding FA, BFS, and other mineral admixtures can increase the density of concrete. However, due to the reduction in the amount of cement, the hydration reaction is slowed down, while the strength of concrete can be improved at a late age, especially for the concrete with high-volume FA (FA replaces more than 50% of cement) [5]. Selin et al. [6] explored the feasibility of replacing freshwater with seawater, using FA to replace 25%, 30%, and 35% cement, and tested the compressive strength at 3, 7, and 28 days. The results showed that the concrete strength was increased by about 30%; the proportion

*Corresponding Author: chunghaowu@nkust.edu.tw

DOI: 10.1201/9781003460763-2

5

of cement replaced by BFS was 40%, 50%, and 60%, and the compressive strength was increased by about 50%. Ibrahim et al. [7] used waste ceramic powder to replace part of the cement to study the effect of brinewater curing on the compressive strength of concrete. It presented that the compressive strength of concrete cured in brine water is higher than that of concrete cured in freshwater.

From the above research results, it can be seen that the strength of concrete mixed with brinewater can be higher than that of concrete mixed with freshwater, but the amount of materials used, especially the proportion of FA to replace cement is only discussed to 35%, and the case of mixing addition of FA and BFS is also not discussed. Therefore, this study investigates mainly the compressive strength of the concrete incorporating high-volume FA/BFS cured by brinewater.

## 2 EXPERIMENTAL PROGRAM

### 2.1 *Materials*

The general tap water, Portland cement, fly ash, blast furnace slag, natural coarse aggregate, fine aggregate, and superplasticizer were used. The basic properties of each material are summarized below:

1. Water: Tap water.
2. Cement: Type I Portland cement in accordance with CNS 15286.
3. Natural coarse aggregate (NCA): The maximum size of coarse aggregates is 19 mm, the specific gravity is 2.72, and the water absorption is 2.16%.
4. Natural fine aggregate (NFA): The specific gravity of fine aggregates is 2.70, the water absorption is 1.35%, and the fineness modulus is 2.62.
5. Fly ash (FA): Low-calcium class F fly ash, whose basic properties meet the requirement of CNS 3036.
6. Blast furnace slag (BFS): Grade 120 of ground granulated blast furnace slag, whose basic properties meet the requirement of CNS 12549.
7. Superplasticizer (SP): The composition meets the requirements of ASTM C 494-81 Type G.

### 2.2 *Mix proportion, specimen preparation, and test method*

Table 1 shows the mix proportion of concretes. The water-cementitious ratio (w/cm) was 0.40 for producing the target compressive strength of 42 MPa on 28th day, and the superplasticizer was appropriately added to attain the slump of concrete around 250 ± 20 mm, and slump flow around 500 ± 100 mm. Cylinder specimens ($\varphi$ 100 × 200 mm) were cast for compressive strength test according to the requirement of ASTM C39. All specimens were subjected to freshwater curing

Table 1. Mix the proportion of concrete per cubic meter.

| Specimen no. | w/ cm | Water | Cement | FA | BFS | NFA | NCA | SP |
|---|---|---|---|---|---|---|---|---|
| | | | | kg/m³ | | | | |
| F00B00 | 0.40 | 180 | 450 | 0 | 0 | 855 | 855 | 4.5 |
| F60B00 | 0.40 | 180 | 180 | 270 | 0 | 810 | 810 | 4.5 |
| F00B60 | 0.40 | 180 | 180 | 0 | 270 | 845 | 845 | 4.5 |
| F30B30 | 0.40 | 180 | 180 | 135 | 135 | 828 | 828 | 4.5 |

* Taking F30B30 as an example, F30 is the 30% replacement ratio of cement weight by FA, and B30 is the 30% replacement ratio by BFS.

(Figure 1) and brinewater curing (Figure 2) till the test ages of 28 and 56 days.

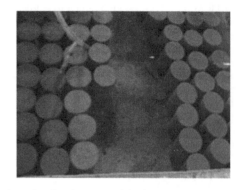

Figure 1. Specimens cured by freshwater.

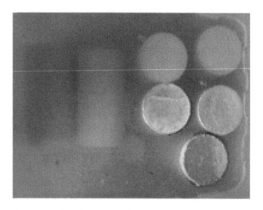

Figure 2. Specimens cured by brinewater.

## 3 RESULTS AND DISCUSSION

### 3.1 *Slump and slump flow of concrete*

Table 2 shows the slump and slump flow test results of the fresh concrete. It can be seen that the measured slump ranges from 230 to 275mm, and

Table 2. Measured the workability of concrete.

| Specimen no. | Slump | Slump flow | Specimen no. | Slump | Slump flow |
|---|---|---|---|---|---|
| | mm | | | mm | |
| F00B00 | 245 | 460/480 | F60B00 | 275 | 640/660 |
| F00B60 | 230 | 450/460 | F30B30 | 260 | 570/580 |

the slump flow ranges from 455 to 650mm. In order to improve the workability of concrete, an appropriate amount of superplasticizer (1% of the weight of the cementitious material) was added to the concrete in this study. In addition, comparing the effect of adding a high amount of fly ash on the workability of concrete, it is found that the slump and slump flow of concrete with FA are higher than other types of concrete. This is due to the fact that the particle of FA presents a spherical morphology that is beneficial to the workability of concrete.

## 3.2 Compressive strength of concrete

The compressive strength tests were carried out for all concretes at the ages of 28 and 56 days. The test results are shown in Table 3 and Figures 3 and 4. It can be seen from Figures 3 and 4 that the compressive strength of control concrete F00B00 cured by brinewater at 28 days is higher than that of concrete cured by freshwater. This is because the water in the concrete will be absorbed by the high concentration of brinewater, reducing the water in the concrete, resulting in a decrease in the water-binder ratio and an increase in the strength of the concrete. At the age of 56 days, the compressive strengths of all concrete cured by brinewater are higher than their compressive strengths at 28 days. The strength of concrete with FA (F60B00) is lower than that of other concretes, and the strength of concrete with FA/BFS (F30B30) after brinewater curing is close to that of concrete with BFS (F00B60), but higher than that of control concrete. The strength of concrete with FA/BFS

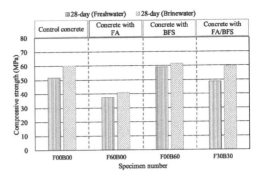

Figure 3. Compressive strength (28-day).

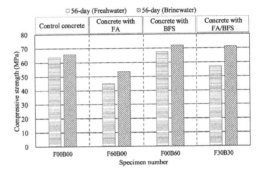

Figure 4. Compressive strength (56-day).

cured by brinewater is higher than its strength cured by freshwater, which has a difference of about 12MPa. This is the largest increase in strength among the four kinds of concrete cured by brinewater.

Observing the strength development of concrete with FA in Figures 3 and 4, it is found that the compressive strength of concrete with FA at 28 days and 56 days is lower than that of the other concretes. The replacement ratio of FA in concrete is up to 60% of the cement weight, which belongs to the grade of high-volume. Hence, it is reasonable that the compressive strength develops slowly. In addition, comparing the effects of freshwater curing and brinewater curing, it can be seen that the compressive strength of concrete of the two curing methods is not much different at the age of 28 days, the strength of concrete cured by brinewater is slightly higher than that of concrete cured by freshwater. However, the strength of the concrete cured in brinewater is obviously higher than that of concrete cured in freshwater at the age of 56 days. It seems that the brinewater curing can accelerate the hydration reaction and pozzolanic reaction of concrete incorporating high-volume fly ash, and its strength increase is significantly higher than that of other concretes.

From the analysis of the development of the compressive strength of the concrete with BFS in

Table 3. Compressive strength of concrete.

| | Freshwater curing | | Brinewater curing | |
|---|---|---|---|---|
| | 28-day | 56-day | 28-day | 56-day |
| Specimen no. | MPa | | | |
| F00B00 | 51.6 | 63.8 | 60.0 | 66.0 |
| F60B00 | 37.3 | 44.9 | 40.8 | 53.6 |
| F00B60 | 59.0 | 67.4 | 61.3 | 72.0 |
| F30B30 | 48.5 | 57.1 | 59.3 | 71.2 |

Figures 3 and 4, it is seen that this concrete has the highest strength among the four kinds of concrete. The compressive strengths of concrete with BFS at 28 days and 56 days are higher than those of other concretes. Moreover, the strength of concrete with BFS is already much higher than that of control concrete and concrete with FA at the age of 28 days, indicating that the strength of concrete with BFS mostly developed at the age of 28 days. The development of compressive strength of concrete with FA/BFS can also be observed in Figures 3 and 4. The compressive strength of the concrete with FA/BFS is only lower than that of control concrete and concrete with BFS. Because the pozzolanic reaction of FA can be effectively produced at a later age, the 28-day strength of concrete with FA is lower; the fineness and hydrate reaction of BFS are higher than that of FA, which leads to the acceleration of the pozzolanic reaction. Therefore, adding FA and BFS in concrete at the same time may increase the compressive strength of concrete with FA at the age of 28 days.

## 4 CONCLUSION

Based on the results of the experimental work, the following conclusions can be drawn:

1. The compressive strength of concrete cured by brinewater is higher than that of concrete cured by freshwater.
2. For the concrete with FA, its compressive strength is lower than the other concretes. The compressive strength of concrete cured by freshwater or brinewater has not much difference at the age of 28 days. However, the strength of concrete cured by brinewater is significantly higher than that of concrete cured in freshwater at the age of 56 days.
3. Concrete with BFS has the highest strength among the three kinds of concretes. The effect of freshwater or brinewater curing on its compressive strength is not obvious at the ages of 28 and 56 days.
4. The compressive strength of concrete with FA/BFS is lower than that of concrete with BFS, but higher than that of control concrete and concrete with FA. Adding FA and BFS in concrete at the same time may enhance the compressive strength of concrete with FA at the age of 28 days.

## REFERENCES

[1] Jhonatan A.B.-D, Diana R.-A., 2022. *Eng. Appl. Sci. Res.* 49(4) 495–504.
[2] Paiva H., Silva A.S., Velosa A., Cachim P., Ferreira V.M., 2017, *Constr. Build. Mater.* 140(1) 374–384.
[3] ACI CODE-318-19, Building Code Requirements for Structural Concrete and Commentary (Reapproved 2022), Reported by ACI Committee 318 (2022).
[4] Amadou S.S., Toshiyuki K., 2022, *Materials* 15 7016.
[5] Wu C.-H., Chen C.-J., Lin Y.-F., Lin S.-K., 2021. *Adv. Concr. Constr.* 12(5) 367–375.
[6] Selin B., Smitha M.S., Elson J., 2016. *Int. J. Innov. Sci. Eng. Technol.* 5(9) 17084–17090.
[7] Ibrahim A.-B., Oladimeji O., Festus O., 2017. *Am. J. Eng. Res.* 6(4) 158–163.

*System Innovation for a Troubled World – Lam et al. (Eds)*
© 2024 the Author(s), ISBN: 978-1-032-60846-4

# Correlation analysis of the online courses video style and video watching rate

Lien-Chi Lai* & Nien-Lin Hsueh*
*Department of Information Engineering and Computer Science, Feng Chia University, Taichung, Taiwan*

ABSTRACT: Massive Open Online Courses (MOOCs) have gained popularity for their flexibility in learning anytime and anywhere. However, many students fail to complete the course, and it has been found that low video-watching rates may be a contributing factor. In this study, we aim to investigate the relationship between video style (slide-based, studio-based, or code-based) and video-watching rates. We designed an automatic approach to classify videos using transfer learning techniques and built an Education Video Classifier model (EVC) based on VGG16, a CNN-based image classifier. We also analyzed the rate of video watching for each student and conducted statistical analysis to explore the correlation between video style and student watching rates. Decision trees were used to investigate the factors influencing learners' willingness to watch videos to completion. Our experiment analyzed 9,552 course videos across 556 courses in a real OpenEdu learning system. According to our research, the video style does not strongly influence the video-watching rate, but the length of the video does. These findings can serve as a guide for educators creating course videos.

## 1 INTRODUCTION

Massive Open Online Courses (MOOCs) are online courses designed for the general public. Learners can access courses online without being limited by time or location, and can even take courses from prestigious universities. A large number of learners are attracted because MOOCs are designed and structured similarly to university courses, and completing a course can receive a certificate or other credential.

MOOCs have two key features:

- Open access: Their participants do not need to be registered learners and do not have to pay tuition fees.
- Scalability: They are designed to accommodate an uncertain number of learners with varying levels of proficiency.

Resources for learning in MOOCs usually include videos, exercises, and interactive discussions on forums. Videos are the most direct resource for obtaining course content, and learners typically watch videos and complete exercises and practice questions as part of the course design.

The characteristics of MOOCs make it easy for learners to enroll in courses. However, course teams usually faced the common challenge of increasing the course completion rate. In MOOCs, learners typically watch videos, complete exercises provided by the course, and participate in discussions with teachers and other learners in order to learn course content. Video-watching is the primary channel for delivering knowledge in courses, so observing learners' video-watching behavior may know the learners' thinking.

Many researchers have proposed the styles of videos contained in MOOCs. Chen used the method of affective engineering to investigate whether video styles are related to learners' emotions (Chen et al.); Hansch categorized videos into 18 styles by interviewing MOOC course designers and instructors (Hansch et al.); Guo mentioned that online course learning videos can be divided into six styles. Each style has its own characteristics, and each video may contain more than one style, such as the use of slides with headshot videos. The above researchers have their own criteria for classifying video styles, which can be roughly divided into three categories: Slides that use slides, Studio with pre-recorded videos, and Code with actual operations. Other classifications can also be classified into these three categories based on the characteristics of the screen.

This study explores whether there is a correlation between the style of videos and learners' watching behavior. Factors that influence video watching are listed, and eliminating the relevant influences, statistical calculations are performed to explore the relationship between video and watching rates. The data is also clustered hierarchically to investigate whether the style of videos affects learners' watching behavior.

*Corresponding Authors:
p1000433@mail.fcu.edu.tw and nlhsueh@fcu.edu.tw

DOI: 10.1201/9781003460763-3

## 2 LITERATURE REVIEW

The MOOC course involves watching course videos, answering questions, and completing assignments based on the course contents. Learners can also discuss with teachers and other learners on the forum. The main way of acquiring knowledge is through watching videos, so the learning effectiveness is closely related to video watching. In order to investigate the factors related to video watching that affect learners, we explore the related research on video length, video style, and quiz in video in relation to learning effectiveness.

Guo pointed out that learners' engagement was highest when the video length was between 6 and 9 minutes, indicating that shorter videos are preferable when creating course videos (Guo *et al.*). Kim's peak analysis of activity records and time for 862 videos found that the dropout rate of learners increased with the video length. The dropout rate for a 5-minute video was 53%, while that for a 20-minute video increased to 73% (Yu *et al.*).

Kovacs mentioned that 74% of users attempt to answer the quiz in video, and it was observed that users would rewind the video or go back to the previous section of the video to find answers (Kovacs *et al.*). Kim noted that learners would rewind the video when encountering Quiz in Video to search for the part of the video that explains the knowledge points to find answers or retry the questions.

Chen used the method of Kansei Engineering to investigate whether video style is related to learners' emotions, and the results showed that video styles with richer content are more likely to arouse learners' interest (Chen *et al.*). Hansch interviewed MOOC course designers and instructors to categorize videos into 18 styles, some of which are recordings of classroom lectures or instructional videos on practical activities, among others (Hansch *et al.*). Guo mentioned that online course learning videos can be categorized into six styles, and each video may contain more than one style. For example, the Slide type can also be filmed in conjunction with the Talking Head type.

## 3 EXPERIMENTAL

First, we integrated OpenEdu log data with video styles. OpenEdu logs record learners' video-watching behavior, and we calculate a learner's watching situation in a single video by analyzing the time points of their play, pause, and stop behavior while watching the video, thereby obtaining the learner's watching time. On the other hand, we extracted course videos from OpenEdu and used a VGG16 transfer learning trained image classification model to classify the

video styles of the course videos. We used the style with the highest proportion as the video style of the course, then calculated the styles of all the videos in the course, and classified the course into the style category with the highest number of videos.

The data on video style and watching rates were analyzed using one-way ANOVA. We first calculated the watching rate for each learner who watched the videos and then calculated the average watching rate for all courses and videos. Then, we analyzed the relationship between the mean watching rates of individual videos and courses and three different styles. Decision tree analysis was conducted to group data containing factors that influence video watching, such as video style, length, course type, Quiz in Video question count, and video position in the course, and calculate the importance of each factor. We queried the database for each record related to course videos, listed the factors to be analyzed, and calculated the average watching rate. Then, we divided the mean watching rate into two clusters—high and low— with videos having a rate above 90% classified as high and those below 90% as low.

The reason for using 90% as a threshold is to determine whether these factors affect learners' willingness to watch the video to completion.

## 4 RESULTS AND DISCUSSION

Section 4.1 will use ANOVA to analyze the relationship between learners' watching rates, course style, and video style. Section 4.2 will use decision tree analysis to explore the importance of factors influencing learners' watching rates and analyze the relationship between video style and learner's watching rates under fixed factors. In Section 4.3, the position of the course when the watching rate drops by 50% will be calculated for various course styles to understand whether course style affects the decline in viewership.

### 4.1 *The correlation between video style and watching rate*

The purpose of this statistical analysis is to examine the correlation between OpenEdu course video styles and learners' watching behavior. We analyzed the relationship between course video style and learners' watching rates of the videos. The sampling method used was stratified sampling, where each cluster was sampled based on its actual proportion.

#### 4.1.1 *Course style and watching rate*
To test the hypothesis that there is no significant difference in the learners' watching rates between the different styles, we conducted a one-way ANOVA. The null hypothesis states that the

learners' watching rates of the course style are equal, while the alternative hypothesis states that there is a significant difference in learners' watching rates between the three styles.

We employed a stratified sampling method to select our sample of courses. We randomly selected courses from each stratum in proportion to their representation in the courses. The final sample consisted of 109 courses, with 14 samples from the Code style, 35 samples from Slide style, and 60 samples from the Studio style. The use of stratified sampling allowed us to ensure that our sample was representative of the courses on OpenEdu and that we had a sufficient number of courses from each style to examine the relationship between different styles.

The descriptive statistics of the samples are shown in Table 1, and the box plots of the samples are shown in Figure 1. The homogeneity test passed and the p-value is 0.425, which is not less than 0.05, indicating that the null hypothesis cannot be rejected. As there was no significant difference found, post hoc tests weren't conducted.

Table 1. Descriptive statistics table of course styles.

|  | N | Mean | SD | Range |
|---|---|---|---|---|
| **Code** | 14 | 0.166 | 0.137 | 0–0.663 |
| **Slide** | 35 | 0.210 | 0.155 | 0.015–0.597 |
| **Studio** | 60 | 0.176 | 0.102 | 0.034–0.410 |

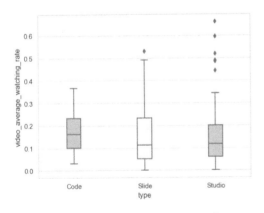

Figure 1. Box-and-whisker plot of course styles.

### 4.1.2 Video style and watching rate

We still used ANOVA to test the difference between video style and watching rates. The null hypothesis states that the learners' watching rates of the video style are equal, while the alternative hypothesis states that there is a significant difference in learners' watching rates among the three styles.

We randomly selected videos from each stratum in proportion to their representation in the videos as same as the analysis of the difference between course style and learners' watching rate. The final sample consisted of 9552 videos, with 1090 samples from the Code style, 2690 samples from the Slide style, and 5502 samples from the Studio style.

The descriptive statistics of the samples are shown in Table 2, and the box plots of the samples are shown in Figure 2. The homogeneity test passed and the p-value is 0.493, which is not less than 0.05, indicating that the null hypothesis cannot be rejected. As there was no significant difference found, post hoc tests weren't conducted.

Table 2. Descriptive statistics table of video styles.

|  | N | Mean | SD | Range |
|---|---|---|---|---|
| **Code** | 54 | 0.714 | 0.194 | 0.006–0.973 |
| **Slide** | 148 | 0.720 | 0.212 | 0.001–0.983 |
| **Studio** | 275 | 0.714 | 0.222 | 0.001–0.976 |

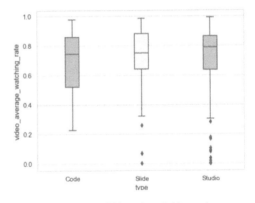

Figure 2. Box-and-whisker plot of video styles.

### 4.2 Analysis of factors affecting video watching rate

We obtained factors such as video style, course type, video length, number of quiz in video, and where the video is located within the course, and added the video completion rate to obtain data that can be analyzed using decision tree analysis. We used these column data to build decision tree clusters, allowing them to group based on important column data to uncover hidden meanings in the data.

The completion rate is divided into high and low categories based on a 90% completion threshold. Data from videos that were not watched have already been excluded during the calculation of the watching rate. This data emphasizes the relationship between video style and watching rate, so only data relevant to watched videos is included.

11

According to the results of the decision tree, the video style has some influence on the completion rate. The factors that affect the watching according to the importance ranking given by the decision tree are video length, normal, quiz in video, position, code, studio, slide, special, and self. The most important factor is the length of the video, followed by the normal course format. The video style is not the most important feature that affects the watching rate.

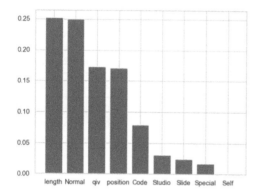

Figure 3. Feature importance from decision tree analysis.

### 4.3 *Analysis of factors affecting video watching rate*

We calculated the decay rate of video watching in the course. The views of online course videos decrease as the course progresses. We calculated the position of the video with half the highest views in the course and then calculated the position of this video in the course progression. We counted the watching decay rate of 50% or more at one-third and one-half of the course progress for each style and plotted the data in Figures 4 and 5.

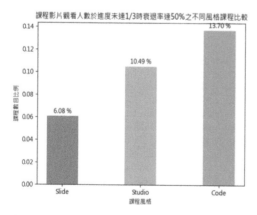

Figure 4. The proportions of the course that the decay rate higher than 50% while at one-half of the course progress.

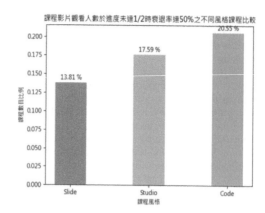

Figure 5. The proportions of the course that the decay rate higher than 50% while at one-third of the course progress.

The courses with a decay rate of 50% at one-third of the course progress are 11 Slide courses, 34 Studio courses, and 10 Code courses. While at one-half of the course progress, there are 25 Slide courses, 57 Studio courses, and 15 Code courses with a decay rate of 50%. After calculating the decay rate, at one-third of the course progress, the proportions of Slide, Studio, and Code courses are 6.08%, 10.49%, and 13.7%, and at one-half of the course progress, the proportions are 13.7%, 17.59%, and 20.55%.

## 5 CONCLUSION

In this study, the Slide, Studio, and Code styles were used to investigate the differences in watching rates resulting from different video styles. However, these three styles cannot represent all the design styles of online course videos. Additionally, the Code style emphasizes programming or computer-operated experiments, which cannot fully represent all video styles related to practical operations or drills. Some courses with richer design content are not just a single style but rather a mix of multiple styles, which were not investigated in detail in this study. OpenEdu offers courses for credit, which greatly affects the watching situation of learners and differs from the watching situation on general traditional online course platforms.

In the one-way ANOVA analysis, no significant difference was found between video style and watching rates. Therefore, decision tree analysis was used to identify the factors that influence watching rates. The results revealed that video length is the most important factor among all the factors, and the impact of video style on watching rates is significant, but not very important.

Based on the conclusions of this study, some suggestions are offered for course development teams. For example, for general courses, the Slide type can be chosen, which can maintain the proportion of learners' watching rate and shorter videos can increase the proportion of learners who complete the videos. In the future, courses or videos with mixed styles can be classified into more detailed styles for analysis. This can provide suggestions that are more in line with online learning trends for learners and course development teams, making online learning more diverse and interesting.

# REFERENCES

Chen, C.J., *et al.* "MOOC videos-derived emotions." *Journal of Telecommunication, Electronic and Computer Engineering (JTEC)* 9.2–9 (2017): 137–140.

Guo, Philip J., Juho Kim, and Rob Rubin. "*How Video Production Affects Student Engagement: An Empirical Study of MOOC Videos.*" Proceedings of the first ACM conference on Learning@ scale conference. 2014.

Hansch, Anna, *et al.* "Video and online learning: Critical reflections and findings from the field." *HIIG Discussion Paper Series No. 2015–02*

Kim, Juho, *et al.* "*Understanding In-Video Dropouts and Interaction Peaks in Online Lecture Videos.*" Proceedings of the first ACM conference on Learning@ scale conference. 2014.

Kovacs, Geza. "*Effects Of In-Video Quizzes on MOOC Lecture Viewing.*" Proceedings of the third (2016) ACM conference on Learning@ Scale. 2016.

Giannakos, Michail N., Letizia Jaccheri, and John Krogstie. "How video usage styles affect student engagement? implications for video-based learning environments." *State-of-the-Art and Future Directions of Smart Learning*. Springer, Singapore, 2016. 157–163.

System Innovation for a Troubled World – Lam et al. (Eds)
© 2024 the Author(s), ISBN: 978-1-032-60846-4

# The effect of graphene oxide-polyvinyl alcohol (GO-PVA) on insulin detection

Yaw-Jen Chang* & Chun-Yi Hsieh
*Department of Mechanical Engineering, Chung Yuan Christian University, Chung Li District, Taoyuan City, Taiwan*

ABSTRACT: Abnormal insulin secretion or a lack of effective insulin may lead to hyperglycemia and even diabetes. The detection of insulin can enable better glucose control. This study presents a three-electrode chip fabricated using a printed circuit board for the detection of insulin. The surface of the working electrode was modified with graphene oxide and polyvinyl alcohol (GO-PVA) for electroplating nickel-cobalt alloy. Cyclic voltammetry (CV) measurements were performed using 0.5 μM recombinant human insulin. From the comparison of surface modification methods of electrodes, the CV measurements showed no redox peaks using the bare copper electrode and the Ni-Co electrodeposited copper electrode in the detection of insulin. In contrast, GO-PVA-modified chips, with or without electrodeposited Ni-Co alloy, had redox peaks. This result indicated that GO-PVA promoted the redox reaction, resulting in distinct oxidation and reduction peaks. Moreover, $O_2$-plasma treatment affected the catalytic effect of GO-PVA on insulin. Prior to coating GO-PVA on the working electrode, the bare copper electrode was treated with $O_2$ plasma. The experimental results showed that the electrodeposited Ni-Co alloy chip had a better catalytic effect than the chip without Ni-Co alloy deposited. However, the chip treated again with $O_2$ plasma before electroplating Ni-Co alloy had the best catalytic effect on insulin.

## 1 INTRODUCTION

Human insulin is a peptide hormone that regulates the metabolism of carbohydrates in the human body. It triggers the transport of glucose to the liver, muscle, and other tissue cells and controls glucose levels in the blood. A deficiency of insulin secretion or a lack of effective insulin may lead to hyperglycemia and even diabetes. It is estimated that approximately 463 million people were suffering from diabetes in 2019, and the prevalence had risen to 9.3% from 4.7% in 1980 (P. Saeedi *et al.* 2019). The World Health Organization predicts that diabetes will become one of the leading causes of death in the world by 2030. Therefore, accurate determination of insulin is of great significance for the clinical diagnosis of diabetes.

Up to the present, a variety of analytical methods for insulin determination have been developed and commonly used, including luminescent immunoassay, radioimmunoassay, enzyme-linked immunosorbent assays, high-performance liquid chromatography (HPLC), capillary electrophoresis, etc. Recently, various nanomaterials have been reported for modifying microelectrodes of biosensors, such as nickel (oxide) nanoparticles (Y. Yu *et al.* 2016, J. Shepa *et al.* 2021), cobalt oxide

nanostructures (H. Razmi *et al.* 2019), carbon nanotubes (I. Šišoláková *et al.* 2020), and graphene oxide nanosheets (A. Noorbakhsh *et al.* 2016, A.K. Yagati *et al.* 2016, M.S. Khan *et al.* 2020).

In this study, a three-electrode chip was fabricated using a printed circuit board (PCB) for the detection of insulin. The surface of the working electrode (WE) was modified with graphene oxide and polyvinyl alcohol (GO-PVA) for electroplating nickel-cobalt alloy. Electrochemical characterization of GO-PVA containing electrodeposited Ni-Co species has been investigated (Coviello and Casella 2018). The effect of GO-PVA with an electrodeposited Ni-Co alloy on insulin detection was studied in this paper.

## 2 EXPERIMENTAL

The analyte to be detected was recombinant human insulin purchased from BioGems International, Inc. The powder of recombinant human insulin was dissolved in phosphate-buffered saline (PBS) containing 0.1 M NaOH to obtain a 0.5 μM analyte solution. The chemicals required for Ni-Co electrodeposition, including Ni $(NH_2SO_3)_2 \cdot 4H_2O$, $Co(NH_2SO_3)_2 \cdot 4H_2O$, etc., were obtained from Blue Giant Inc. (Taiwan).

---

*Corresponding Author: justin@cycu.edu.tw

DOI: 10.1201/9781003460763-4

Graphene oxide (GO) was synthesized from graphite powder using a modified Hammer's method. Then, GO and polyvinyl alcohol (PVA) were added to deionized water and stirred with an ultrasonic oscillator to prepare the GO-PVA aqueous solution with a weight percentage of 5%.

This insulin sensor was a three-electrode chip composed of a WE, a counter electrode, and a reference electrode. Its dimensions are shown in Figure 1. The structure of the three-electrode chip was formed by etching the copper foil of the PCB using conventional PCB processing technology. The chip was first treated with $O_2$ plasma for 30 seconds. Then, 10 $\mu$L of GO-PVA aqueous solution was drop-cast on the WE, followed by dehydration baking in a 37°C hot circulator oven for 1.5 hours. The chip was again treated with $O_2$ plasma for 30 seconds. After surface modification, a layer of nickel-cobalt alloy was electroplated on the GO-PVA with a plating current of 5 A/dm$^2$. Finally, the chip was dried in a 37°C circulator oven for 1.5 hours.

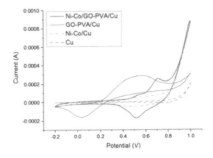

Figure 2. Comparison of surface modification methods of electrodes: GO-PVA/Cu and Ni-Co/GO-PVA/Cu electrodes had redox peaks.

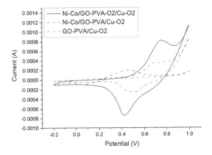

Figure 3. Comparison of $O_2$-plasma treatment: The peak oxidation current increased significantly when the chip was treated with $O_2$ plasma twice.

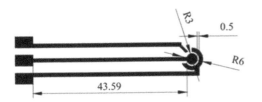

Figure 1. Dimensions of the three-electrode chip. Unit: mm

## 3 RESULTS AND DISCUSSION

Detection of 0.5 $\mu$M recombinant human insulin was performed using cyclic voltammetry (CV) measurement between $-0.2$ and $+1.0$ V at a scan rate of 50 mV/s. The effect of GO-PVA on insulin detection was studied.

Different surface modification methods of electrodes were first compared, including bare copper electrodes, Ni-Co electrodeposited copper electrodes (Ni-Co/Cu), and GO-PVA modified electrodes (GO-PVA/Cu and Ni-Co/GO-PVA/Cu). As shown in Figure 2, CV measurements indicate no redox peaks for insulin detection using the bare copper electrode and the Ni-Co/Cu electrode. In contrast, both GO-PVA/Cu and Ni-Co/GO-PVA/Cu electrodes had redox peaks. This result explained that GO-PVA promoted the redox reaction, resulting in distinct oxidation and reduction peaks. Without surface modification of GO-PVA, the chip was difficult to catalyze and detect insulin. Moreover, the Ni-Co/GO-PVA/Cu electrode exhibited a peak oxidation current of 0.25215 mA at 0.708 V.

In this study, the GO-PVA coating was prone to peeling off due to the hydrophobic surface of the copper electrode. Since $O_2$ plasma can clean the electrode surface and increase hydrophilicity, it was used to treat the copper WE before coating GO-PVA. The experimental results demonstrated that, with $O_2$-plasma treatment, the peak oxidation current of the Ni-Co/GO-PVA/Cu electrode was increased to 0.3581 mA, as shown in Figure 3. Furthermore, the peak oxidation current increased significantly to 0.82065 mA when the chip was treated with $O_2$ plasma again before electroplating the Ni-Co alloy. Obviously, $O_2$-plasma treatment affected the catalytic effect of GO-PVA on insulin.

Next, CV measurements were observed for 4 consecutive potential cycles between $-0.2$ and $+1.0$ V at a scan rate of 50 mV/s. The experimental results are shown in Figure 4. For the GO-PVA/Cu-$O_2$ electrode, the oxidation current decreased continuously during the CV measurement of 4 consecutive potential cycles, as shown in Figure 4 (a). The peak current dropped by 33.6%. A similar situation occurred for the Ni-Co/GO-PVA/Cu-$O_2$ electrode with a 3.12% reduction in the peak current, as shown in Figure 4(b). The electrode using

15

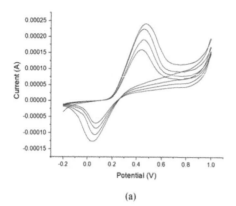

(a)

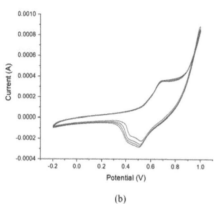

(b)

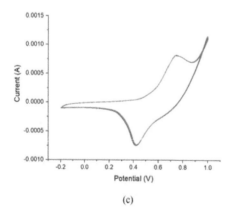

(c)

Figure 4. Comparison of CV measurement of 4 consecutive potential cycles: (a) GO-PVA/Cu-O$_2$ electrode. (b) Ni-Co/GO-PVA/Cu-O$_2$ electrode. (c) Ni-Co/GO-PVA-O$_2$/Cu-O$_2$ electrode.

GO-PVA with Ni-Co alloy yielded better stability in CV measurements. As shown in Figure 4(c), the peak oxidation current of the Ni-Co/GO-PVA-O$_2$/ Cu-O$_2$ electrode, which was treated with O$_2$

plasma twice, was only reduced by 1.25%. This electrode had not only the largest peak redox currents but also the best stability in CV measurements. That is, O$_2$-plasma treatment can assist GO-PVA with Ni-Co alloy to produce a better catalytic effect on insulin.

## 4 CONCLUSION

Diabetes is one of the most prevalent chronic metabolic diseases. Accurate determination of insulin is of great significance for the clinical diagnosis of diabetes, enabling better glucose control. In this paper, the catalytic effect of GO-PVA with an electrodeposited Ni-Co alloy on insulin is discussed in depth. In addition to Ni-Co alloy, GO-PVA coating and O$_2$ plasma treatment both promote the catalytic effect. Moreover, this three-electrode chip has a low cost and is easy to fabricate.

## ACKNOWLEDGEMENT

This work was supported by the National Science and Technology Council (NSTC) of Taiwan, R.O.C. [grant number MOST 110-2221-E-033-024-MY2]

## REFERENCES

Coviello D., Casella I.G., 2018. *Electrochim. Acta* 261 104–112.
Khan M.S., Ameer H., Ali A., Manzoor R., Yang L., Feng R., Jiang N., Wei Q., 2020. *Biosens. Bioelectron.* 147 111767.
Noorbakhsh A., Alnajar A.I.K., 2016. *Microchem. J.* 129 310–317.
Razmi H., Ezzati L., Khorablou Z., 2019. *J. Electrochem. Soc.* 166 B961.
Saeedi P., Petersohn I., Salpea P., Malanda B., Karuranga S., Unwin N., Colagiuri S., Guariguata L., Motala A.A., Ogurtsova K., Shaw J.E., Bright D., Williams R., 2019. *Diabetes Res. Clin. Pract.* 157 107843.
Shepa J., Šišoláková I., Vojtko M., Trnková L., Nagy G., Maskaľová I., Oriňak A., Oriňaková R., 2021. *Sensors* 21 5063.
Šišoláková I., Hovancová J., Oriňaková R., Oriňak A., Trnková L., Třísková I., Farka Z., Pastucha M., Radoňák J., 2020. *J. Electroanal. Chem.* 860 113881.
Yagati A.K., Choi Y., Park J., Choi J.-W., Jun H.-S., Cho S., 2016. *Biosens. Bioelectron.* 80 307–314.
Yu Y., Guo M., Yuan M., Liu W., Hu J., 2016. *Biosens. Bioelectron.* 77 215–219.

# Greener thermal insulation material production of foam glass from bottle glass using silicon cutting waste as a foaming agent

Li-Pang Wang*, Pin-Wei Tseng, Kai-Jyun Huang & Yan-Jhang Chen
*Institute of Environmental Engineering and Management, National Taipei University of Technology, Taipei, Taiwan*

ABSTRACT:  A thermal insulation material made from foam glass was produced from waste bottle glass using silicon cutting waste (SCW) as a foaming agent. The influence of affecting factors, including sintering temperature, glass powder particle size, SCW dosage, heating rate, and holding time, was investigated. The produced foam glass was characterized to examine its microstructure, bulk density, compressive strength, porosity, and thermal conductivity. The results indicated that under the optimal conditions of sintering temperature of 775°C, glass powder particle size of 0.15 mm, SCW dosage of 1 wt.%, heating rate of 10°C/min, and holding time of 30 min, the produced foam glass had a compressive strength of 4.1 MPa, bulk density of 0.56 g/cm$^3$, porosity of 78%, and thermal conductivity of 0.16 W/m·k; these properties meet standards for thermal insulation materials. By using SCW as the foaming agent, foam glass is able to be produced at a comparatively low temperature and has favorable properties. In addition, the simultaneous waste valorization of waste bottle glass and SCW can be achieved.

## 1 INTRODUCTION

Foam glass is a glass material that has uniform porosity, low weight, high strength, low thermal conductivity, incombustibility, and corrosion resistance and is thus often used as a construction material for thermal insulation (D'Amore *et al.* 2017). Foam glass is mainly produced through the powder sintering method, in which glass powder is blended with a foaming agent and subjected to sintering treatment. During the sintering process, the glass softens, and the foaming agent creates bubbles inside the glass. Several chemical reagents have been researched as the foaming agent, including carbonates (Fang *et al.* 2017), sulfates (Yan *et al.* 2015), silicates (Owoeye *et al.* 2020), and various carbon-based materials, such as coke, anthracite, soot, graphite (da Silva *et al.* 2021), and silicon carbide (SiC) (Wang *et al.* 2018). In addition, various waste materials have been proposed as alternatives to chemical reagents for foam glass production, including aluminum dross (El-Amir *et al.* 2021), ark clam shell (Hisham *et al.* 2022), eggshell (Saparuddin *et al.* 2020; Souza *et al.* 2017), oyster shell (Teixeira *et al.* 2017), and marble cutting sludge (Fernandes *et al.* 2009).

In this study, silicon cutting waste (SCW), a solid waste produced from the slicing procedure of silicon ingots for the fabrication of silicon wafer that contains polished silicon (Si) powders and SiC powders, was used as the foaming agent and mixed with waste bottle glass to produce foam glass. The influence of affecting factors, including sintering temperature, glass powder particle size, SCW dosage, heating rate, and holding time, was investigated. The produced foam glass was characterized to examine its bulk density, compressive strength, porosity, and thermal conductivity.

## 2 EXPERIMENTAL

A waste wine bottle glass sample containing $SiO_2$ of 72.0 wt.%, sodium oxide ($Na_2O$) of 17.3 wt.%, and calcium oxide (CaO) of 8.3 wt.% was used as the waste bottle glass. An SCW sample obtained from a silicon wafer fabrication corporation in Taiwan containing Fe filings of 3.0 wt.%, Si powders of 47.3 wt.%, and SiC powders of 49.7 wt.% was used as the foaming agent. The particle size distribution of the SCW foaming agent indicated that the particles in the SCW foaming agent were distributed between 0.115 μm ($D_{10}$) and 19.91 μm ($D_{90}$), and the median particle size ($D_{50}$) was 3.512 μm. Two peaks around 0.1 μm and 10 μm were observed, which implied the $D_{50}$ of Si powders and SiC powders, respectively.

The waste bottle glass sample was crushed and ground by using a stainless-steel mortar and an automatic agate mortar (ANM1000, Nittokagaku Co., Ltd., Japan), respectively, to the determined particle size range, and uniformly mixed with the

*Corresponding Author: kuniwang@ntut.edu.tw

DOI: 10.1201/9781003460763-5

determined dosage of SCW foaming agent in a 43 mm x 43 mm x 25 mm stainless rectangle mold. The mold containing waste bottle glass and foaming agent was then moved to a muffle furnace (HS-3, Yi-Feng Instrument Co., Ltd., Taipei, Taiwan) and heated at the determined heating rate to the determined sintering temperature. When the determined holding time was reached, the mold was air-cooled to room temperature and then released to obtain the sintered product. Referring to the CNS 13481 Method of Test for Autoclaved Lightweight Aerated Concrete Blocks, the sintered product was cut into a 20 mm x 20 mm × 20 mm foam glass specimen for subsequent physical and mechanical characteristic analyses, including bulk density, compressive strength, and porosity. In addition, thermal conductivity was analyzed for the foam glass specimen obtained under optimal conditions. The bulk density was measured according to the CNS 8647 A3146 method by dividing the mass of the specimen by its volume. The porosity was calculated according to the formula reported by Bai et al. and Owoeye et al. (Bai et al. 2014; Owoeye et al. 2020), in which the powder density of the specimen powder was measured by the pycnometer method. The compressive strength was measured using Standard Automatic Compression Testers for Cylinders, Wizard Auto (50-A22W02, Controls Co., Ltd., MI, Italy). The thermal conductivity was measured according to the CNS 7333 method of Test for Thermal Conductivity of Thermal Insulation Material using a Quick Thermal Conductivity Meter (QTM-500) made by Kyoto Electronics Manufacturing Co., Ltd., Kyoto, Japan.

## 3 RESULTS AND DISCUSSION

Figure 1 presents the morphology of foam glass specimens produced at various sintering temperatures. The particle size of the glass powder was 75 μm, the SCW dosage was 1.0 wt.%, the heating rate was 10°C/min, and the holding time was 30 min. The results reveal that increasing the sintering temperature increased the pore size of the produced foam glass. This increase was attributable to the gas produced from the decomposition of the SCW foaming agent, which was trapped in the softened glass. In addition, the increase in sintering temperature increased the intensity of the foaming agent reaction, causing small pores to merge and form large pores. Therefore, the walls between the pores of the foam glass created at 700°C were thick, and the pore size was small. When sintered at 800°C, pore walls became thinner, and pore size increased because small pores combined into large pores.

Figure 2 presents the bulk density, compressive strength, and porosity of the produced foam glass

under various sintering temperatures. The bulk density decreased with the increase in sintering temperature. When the sintering temperature was 700, 725, 750, 775, and 800°C, the bulk density was 0.88, 0.72, 0.63, 0.56, and 0.46 g/cm³, respectively. The compressive strength and porosity decreased and increased, respectively, with increasing sintering temperatures. For sintering temperatures of 700, 725, 750, 775, and 800°C, the compressive strength was 17.5, 10.2, 6.3, 4.1, and 2.1 MPa, respectively, and the porosity was 64.8%, 71.3%, 75%, 77.7%, and 81.7%, respectively. Increasing the sintering temperature increased the pressure in foam glass pores, thereby enlarging these pores. Thus, the highest porosity (81.7%) was obtained when sintered at the highest temperature of 800°C. However, the pores in the foam glass created at 800°C had thin walls and an uneven distribution. Consequently, the resulting compressive strength was the lowest (2.1 MPa). Accordingly, a sintering temperature of 775°C was selected for subsequent experiments.

Figure 3 presents the bulk density, compressive strength, and porosity of foam glass produced from

Figure 1. Morphology of foam glass specimens produced at various sintering temperatures (a) 700°C; (b) 725°C; (c) 750°C; (d) 775°C; (e) 800°C (Experimental conditions: glass power particle size 75 μm, SCW dosage 1.0 wt.%, heating rate 10°C/min, and holding time 30 min).

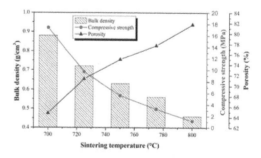

Figure 2. Bulk density, compressive strength, and porosity of produced foam glass specimens under various sintering temperatures (Experimental conditions: glass power particle size 75 μm, SCW dosage 1.0 wt.%, heating rate 10°C/min, and holding time 30 min).

various glass powder particle sizes. The results revealed that reducing the particle size decreased the bulk density. For particles with size of 0.27–0.83, 0.15–0.27, 0.075–0.15, and 0.038–0.075 mm, the bulk density was 0.8, 0.63, 0.56, and 0.56 g/cm³, respectively. Increasing the porosity reduced the compressive strength. When the porosity was 68.3%, 74.9%, 77.7%, and 78%, the compressive strength was 10, 4.7, 4.1, and 4.1 MPa, respectively. When the glass powder particle size was ≥ 0.15 mm, the compressive strength and bulk density decreased with the decrease in the particle size of the glass powder. This result was attributed to the fact that smaller particles had a higher specific surface area, facilitating their softening. In addition, the gas released from the foaming agent and its subsequent expansion were also improved. By contrast, glass powder with a larger size had a smaller specific surface area and did not soften easily, impeding the movement of the foaming agent and its decomposition in the glass. If the glass powder particle size was <0.15 mm, the foam glasses exhibited similar bulk density, compressive strength, and porosity. In general, small particle sizes are conducive to producing foam glass with favorable properties, but producing glass of small size requires the grinding of waste bottle glass, which substantially consumes energy. Therefore, a glass powder particle size of <0.15 mm was selected for the subsequent experiment.

Figure 4 presents the bulk density, compressive strength, and porosity of the produced foam glass

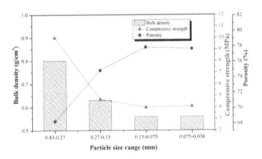

Figure 3. Bulk density, compressive strength, and porosity of foam glass specimens produced from various glass powder particle sizes (Experimental conditions: sintering temperature of 775°C, SCW dosage 1.0 wt.%, heating rate 10°C/min, and holding time 30 min).

specimens at various SCW dosages. The results revealed that increasing the SWC dosage reduced the bulk density and compressive strength but increased the porosity. At SCW dosages of 0.1, 0.3, 0.5, 1.0, 1.5, and 2.0 wt.%, the bulk density was 1.05, 0.67, 0.59, 0.56, 0.56, and 0.58 g/cm³, respectively; the compressive strength was 19, 6.9, 5.8, 4.1, 4.7, and 4.9 MPa, respectively; and the

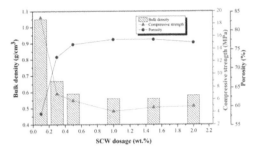

Figure 4. Bulk density, compressive strength, and porosity of produced foam glass specimens at various SCW dosages (Experimental conditions: sintering temperature of 775°C, glass powder particle size of <150 μm, heating rate 10°C/min, and holding time 30 min).

porosity was 58.1%, 73.1%, 76.4%, 77.7%, 77.7%, and 76.9%, respectively. When an SCW dosage of <1.0 wt.% was used as the foaming agent, increasing the SCW dosage reduced the bulk density and the compressive strength but increased the porosity. This phenomenon was caused by the increased gas generated from the SCW, which reduced the bulk density and enabled glass pores to merge more easily. This in turn thinned the pore walls of the foam glass and thus reduced the overall compressive strength. When the SCW dosage was ≥ 1.0 wt.%, the bulk density did not change substantially. Therefore, 1.0 wt.% was selected as the SCW dosage for the subsequent experiments.

Figure 5 presents the bulk density, compressive strength, and porosity of the produced foam glass specimens at heating rates of 5, 10, and 15°C/min. The bulk density was 0.46, 0.56, and 0.58 g/cm³, respectively; the compressive strength was 7.7, 4.1, and 4.3 MPa, respectively; and the porosity was 74.5%, 77.7%, and 76.9%, respectively. Foam glass with the lowest bulk density and highest porosity was yielded at a heating rate of 10°C/min. In general, an overly fast heating rate causes temperature differences between the surface and interior of a foam glass, resulting in uneven pore distributions. By contrast, an overly slow heating rate causes excessive foaming agents to be consumed, reducing the amount of gas and pores generated in the glass. However, slower heating rates require additional energy consumption and reduce production efficiency.

Figure 6 presents the bulk density, compressive strength, and porosity of the produced foam glass specimens at a holding time of 15, 30, 45, and 60 min, respectively. The bulk density was 0.61, 0.56, 0.53, and 0.56 g/cm³, and the compressive strength was 7.9, 4.1, 3.0, and 3.5 MPa; the porosity was 75.6%, 77.7%, 78.79%, and 77.7%. If the holding time was ≤ 45 min, the bulk density and compressive strength decreased with the increase

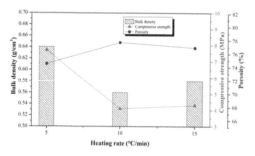

Figure 5. Bulk density, compressive strength, and porosity of produced foam glass specimens at various heating rates (Experimental conditions: sintering temperature of 775°C, glass powder particle size of <150 μm, SCW dosage of 1.0 wt.%, and holding time of 30 min).

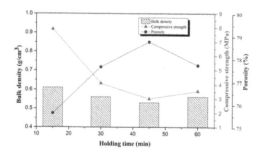

Figure 6. Bulk density, compressive strength, and porosity of produced foam glass specimens at various holding times (Experimental conditions: sintering temperature of 775°C, glass powder particle size of <150 μm, SCW dosage of 1.0 wt.%, and heating rate of 10°C/min).

in holding time because longer holding times enabled gas to be trapped in the softened glass, leading to the pores merging and increasing the porosity. Moreover, this process reduced the glass's viscosity, enabling the gas to expand. The bulk density did not decrease if the holding time lengthened to 60 minutes because the low glass viscosity enabled the escape of the generated gas. The compressive strength also decreased because the pore size increased and the walls thinned. Overall, samples held for 45 minutes had the highest porosity and lowest compressive strength, whereas those held for 30 minutes had similar porosity but higher compressive strength. Therefore, 30 minutes was selected as the holding time for subsequent experiments.

Based on the foregoing experiments, the optimal parameter configuration for foam glass production was as follows: sintering temperature of 775°C, glass powder particle size of <150 μm, SCW dosage of 1.0 wt.%, heating rate of 10°C/min, and holding time of 30 min. A foam glass

Table 1. Properties of produced foam glass with optimal parameter configuration (sintering temperature 775°C, glass powder particle size <150 μm, SCW dosage 1.0 wt.%, heating rate 10°C/min, holding time 30 min)

| Bulk density | Compressive strength | Porosity | Thermal conductivity |
|---|---|---|---|
| 0.56 g/cm$^3$ | 4.1 MPa | 77.7% | 0.16 W/m K |

sample was created with this configuration to perform thermal conductivity testing. Table 1 lists the properties of the created sample, which were a bulk density of 0.56 g/cm$^3$, a compressive strength of 4.1 MPa, a porosity of 77.7%, and a thermal conductivity coefficient of 0.16 W/m·K. Generally, thermal insulation materials have a bulk density of <0.6 g/cm$^3$, a compressive strength of >0.3 MPa, and a thermal conductivity coefficient of <0.23 W/m·K (Zhang 2011). Foam glass applied for thermal insulation should have a lower thermal conductivity coefficient. Thus, the produced foam glass is suitable to be used as a building material for thermal insulation.

In previous studies, foam glass produced using graphite (da Silva et al. 2021), aluminum dross (El-Amir et al. 2021), ark clam shell (Hisham et al. 2022), oyster shell (Teixeira et al. 2017), water glass (Owoeye et al. 2020), eggshell (Saparuddin et al. 2020; Souza et al. 2017), limestone (Jeong et al. 2019), and dolomite (Ercenk 2017) as the foaming agent were sintered at 800–1,075°C and exhibited a bulk density of 0.42–1.4 g/cm$^3$, compressive strength of 0.15–4.1 MPa, and thermal conductivity of 0.055–0.177 W/m·K. Compared with the foam glass produced in previous studies, the foam glass produced using SCW as the foaming agent with the optimal configuration proposed in this study required the lowest sintering temperature, had slightly higher compressive strength, and had comparable thermal conductivity.

## 4 CONCLUSION

In this study, SCW was used as a foaming agent and mixed with waste bottle glass to produce foam glass. The optimal conditions for foam glass production from waste bottle glass and SCW were a sintering temperature of 775°C, a glass powder particle size of <150 μm, an SCW dosage of 1.0 wt.% (with a SiC content of 49.7 wt.%), a heating rate of 10°C/min, and a holding time of 30 min. The resulting foam glass had a bulk density of 0.56 g/cm$^3$, a compressive strength of 4.1 MPa, a porosity of 78%, and a thermal conductivity coefficient of 0.16 W/m·k.

These properties are in accordance with standards for thermal insulation materials.

The study results confirmed that by using SCW as a foaming agent, cleaner foam glass production from waste bottle glass could be fulfilled at a lower sintering temperature and had favorable properties. In addition, the simultaneous waste valorization of waste bottle glass and the SCW of loose abrasive slurry sawing could be achieved.

## ACKNOWLEDGEMENTS

The authors appreciate the R.O.C. Ministry of Science and Technology for financially supporting this research under Grant Nos. MOST 111-2221-E-027-016 and MOST 110-2221-E-027-038.

## REFERENCES

Bai J., Yang X., Xu S., Jing W., Yang J., 2014. *Mater. Lett.* 136 52–54.

da Silva R.C., Puglieri F.N., de Genaro Chiroli D.M., Bart meyer G.A., Kubaski E.T., Tebcherani S.M., 2021. *Sci. Total Environ.* 771 145276.

D'Amore G.K.O, Caniato M., Travan A., Turco G., Marsich L., Ferluga A., Schmid C., 2017. *J. Clean. Prod.* 165 1306–1315.

El-Amir A.A., Attia M.A., Newishy M., Fend T., Ewais E.M., 2021. *J. Mater. Res. Technol.* 15 4940–4948.

Ercenk E., 2017. *J. Therm. Anal. Calorim.* 127, 137–146.

Fang X., Li Q., Yang T., Li Z., Zhu Y., 2017. *Constr. Build. Mater.* 134 358–363.

Fernandes H.R., Tulyaganov D.U., Ferreira J.M.F, 2009. *Ceram. Int.* 35 229–235.

Hisham N.A.N., Zaid M.H.M., Matori K.A., Shabdin M.K., 2022. *Mater. Sci. Eng. B* 281 115730.

Jeong T.U, Chu K.H., Kim S.J., Lee J., Chae K.J., Hwang M.H., 2019. *J. Environ. Manage.* 239 159–166.

Owoeye S.S, Matthew G.O., Ovienmhanda F.O., Tunmilayo S.O., 2020. *Ceram. Int.* 46 11770–11775.

Saparuddin D.I., Hisham N.A.N., Ab Aziz S., Matori K.A., Honda S., Iwamoto Y., Zaid M.H.M., 2020. *J. Mater. Res. Technol.* 9 5640–5647.

Souza M.T., Maia B.G., Teixeira L.B., de Oliveira K.G., Teixeira A.H., de Oliveira A.P.N., 2017. *Process Saf. Environ.* 111 60–64.

Teixeira L.B., Fernandes V.K., Maia B.G.O., Arcaro S., de Oliveira A.P.N., 2017. *Ceram. Int.* 43 6730–6737.

Wang H., Chen Z., Liu L., Ji R., Wang X., 2018. *Ceram. Int.* 44 10078–10086.

Yan Z., Wang Z., Liu H., Tu Y., Yang W., Zeng H., Qiu J., 2015. *J. Anal. Appl. Pyrolysis* 113 491–498.

Zhang H., 2011. *Building Materials in Civil Engineering.* Cambridge: Woodhead Publishing.

*System Innovation for a Troubled World – Lam et al. (Eds)*
© 2024 the Author(s), ISBN: 978-1-032-60846-4

# Development and application of clay sculpture cultural relics cleaning materials – take room temperature ionic molten salt and self-made gel as examples

Han-Chung Wu
*Conservation Center, Cheng Shu University, Kaohsiung, Taiwan*

He-Jing Cai
*Institute of Creative Cultural Design & Art Preservation Techniques, Cheng Shu University, Kaohsiung, Taiwan*

Wu-Shan Chu & I-Cheng Li*
*Conservation Center, Cheng Shu University, Kaohsiung, Taiwan*

ABSTRACT: Clay sculptures are made of clay and are kneaded by hand, so the materials are more convenient to obtain and the conditions of application are relatively easy. Taiwanese clay sculptures are deeply rooted in folklore and religion. There are many objects made of clay sculptures in religious sacrificial vessels, statues, and relief sculptures on building walls. This technique records the belief and aesthetic evolution of folk religious culture and is one of the important traditional crafts. Because clay sculptures are more sensitive to humid environments, it is easy to pulverize the clay sculptures or produce molds. Most of the skeletons in the early clay sculptures were composed of wood and some organic materials, which were easily damaged. Most of the preserved clay sculpture cultural relics are concentrated in temples and monasteries. During the preservation process, they are often easily damaged and destroyed by insects, mildew, light, temperature and humidity and human factors. The production method itself also easily affects the difficulty of subsequent preservation. The surface pores of clay sculptures are large, and the liquid has a good penetration effect on this, so great attention should be paid to the use of solvents. On the other hand, ionic molten salt is a good and stable synthetic material tool and has a wide range of applications. Its low permeability and non-volatility are very good characteristics in the restoration of cultural relics. However, the current research on ionic molten salt in the field of cultural relic restoration has less application. The chemical stability and adjustable physical and chemical properties of ionic molten salts can better protect the environment and protect the health and safety of employees.

## 1 INTRODUCTION

Clay sculpture artifacts had long appeared in the Stone Age, with the earliest ones dating back to 10,000 years ago. The predecessors used the readily available clay to simulate the images they saw in life as well as the necessities they used every day. Therefore, the clay sculptures made by them were close to human life and beliefs. The clay sculpture is a type of sculpture. From ancient times to the present, with cultural development, clay sculptures still retain the original craftsmanship, and record the changes of each period. Ever since the Taiwan government promulgated implementation of the Cultural Heritage Preservation Act[1] in 1982,

cultural heritages[2] have been divided into tangible and intangible cultural heritages. For clay sculpture artifacts, the sculptures themselves belong to tangible cultural heritages, whereas the craftsmanship belongs to intangible cultural heritages. Regarding the saying "paper first, soil second, wood third, stone fourth, and gold fifth" commonly said by Taiwanese folks, the "soil second" refers to clay sculpture. The clay sculptures commonly seen by us are mostly the statues of gods in temples. If a clay sculpture artifact not glazed and burned is in contact with liquid, its porous surface will make it easily absorb the

---

*Corresponding Author: plastic@gcloud.csu.edu.tw
[1]Laws and Regulations Database of the Republic of China (Taiwan) — Cultural Heritage Preservation Act,

Search: https://law.moj.gov.tw/LawClass/LawHistory.aspx?pcode=h0170001
[2]National Cultural Heritage Database Management System, Search: https://nchdb.boch.gov.tw/

DOI: 10.1201/9781003460763-6

liquid, which will penetrate the sculpture, and eventually, the clay sculpture will disintegrate.

Clay sculpture artifacts are often found to be chemically, physically, and biologically deteriorated. Chemical deterioration is mainly caused by the aging of materials or qualitative changes produced by external factors; physical deterioration is caused by the impacts of external forces, resulting in the situations of scratch, deformation, break or defect; and biological deterioration is caused by the impacts from insects and fungi, which lead to insect excretion, bites, as well as infestation and mold damages. To deal with these kinds of deterioration on clay sculptures, cleaning can be done and is divided into mechanical cleaning and solvent cleaning. The latter is an irreversible step. Users of cleaning solvent must be familiar with the materials of the artifacts as well as the characteristics of the solvent, and have to evaluate carefully artifact restoration before carrying out solvent cleaning. In order to avoid the situation mentioned above, this paper attempts to use room-temperature molten ionic salt and self-made gel, which are less volatile and less permeable, to take cleaning tests, and discuss the feasibility of applying them to clay sculpture artifacts.

## 2 EXPERIMENTAL

In order to simulate the repair and restoration site, the researcher applied no/oil-based/water-based protective paints on the painted layers of the clay sculpture artifacts. The source of contamination, mainly the deterioration by temple smoke, was taken as the simulation object. The cleaning procedure was to use aqueous solution and organic solvents of different polarities to conduct cleaning tests, and to analyze the cleaning effects of the pure solvent as well as those added with gel and ionic solution. As to samples of clay sculptures, clay, and terra cotta were used as the base materials. For the coating, special pigments exclusively for painting of god statues were used. The finish paint was divided into two types: water-based and oil-based finish paints, as shown in Figure 1. To simulate the deterioration, smoke was created by burning the incense sticks available on the market.

| Inside the experimental environment | Before and after deterioration |
|---|---|

Figure 2. Deterioration process of sample.

The samples were hung in a special smoking box placed with incense sticks, with 30 incense sticks as a bundle, as shown in Figure 2.

Cleaning Material:

1. Aqueous solvent: $KOH_{(aq)}$ and $NaOH_{(aq)}$, 1 M.
2. Low-polarity solvents: Toluene and petroleum ether.
3. High-polarity solvents: Ethanol and acetone.
4. Self-made gels: Methylcellulose and $SiO_2$. The weight ratios of self-made gels in grams are shown below:
   - 1 M of KOH aqueous solution: Methyl cellulose = 100 : 3
   - 1 M of NaOH aqueous solution: Methyl cellulose = 100 : 3
   - Toluene : $SiO_2$ = 40 : 12
   - Petroleum ether : $SiO_2$ = 40 : 14
   - Ethanol : 3% Methylcellulose gel = 10 : 50
   - Acetone : 3% Methylcellulose gel = 10 : 50
5. Molten ionic salt
   - 1-Ethyl-3-methylimidazolium tetrafluoroborate [BMIM][$BF_4$]
   - 1-n-Butyl-3-methylimidazolium hexafluorophosphate [BMIM][$PF_6$]

After synthesis of [BMIM][$BF_4$] and [BMIM][$PF_6$], 6 solvents were added in a ratio of 20:1. When $KOH_{(aq)}$, $NaOH_{(aq)}$ and toluene were added with [BMIM][$PF_6$], they were found to be immiscible with each other. Thus, no follow-up test was taken.

Numbering of Samples:
After cross-numbering, the following sample numbers are obtained and shown in Table 1.

| Colorful paints applied | Protective paint applied |
|---|---|

Figure 1. Production process of samples.

Table 1. Sample numbers.

| | Aqueous solution W | | Low-polarity L | | High-polarity L | |
|---|---|---|---|---|---|---|
| | NaOH | KOH | Toluene | Petroleum ether | Ethanol | Acetone |
| | 1 | 2 | 3 | 4 | 5 | 6 |
| Solvents A0 | A0W1 | A0W2 | A0L3 | A0L4 | A0H5 | A0H6 |
| Gels B0 | B0W1 | B0W2 | B0L3 | B0L4 | B0H5 | B0H6 |
| [BMIM][BF4] C1 | C1W1 | C1W2 | C1L3 | C1L4 | C1H5 | C1H6 |
| [BMIM][PF6] C2 | C2W1 | C2W2 | C2L3 | C2L4 | C2H5 | C2H6 |

Sample Tests:

The solution group is used in wet applications to carry out cleaning tests. Let the solution cover the tested area for 30 seconds, and then remove the solution. For the gel group, let the gel be directly applied to the sample and remove the gel after 30 seconds. Regarding the B0W1 group and the B0W2 group, since there was a quick reaction after application of the gels, the gels were removed after application for 15 seconds. For the molten ionic salt group, it was used in drip coating. In terms of proportion, molten ionic salt contains 5% solvent only, so the time of drip coating is 10 minutes.

## 3 RESULTS AND DISCUSSION

Cleaning with an alkaline aqueous solution achieved a remarkable effect on the part without protective paint and the part with oil-based or water-based protective paints. Just in the process of wet application, the pollutants were found to be dissolved in the sculpture cleaning materials. After the removal of the sculpture cleaning materials as well as the removal of the residual lye with pure water, no significant difference in cleaning effect was found between the two parts aforesaid. The coating was not discolored; the water-based protective paint, as observed in the photometric aspect, still existed; but the oil-based protective paint had lost its luster.

Low-polarity solvents mostly do not have an obvious cleaning effect on the coating without protective paint. Regarding cleaning a surface with water-based protective paint, the cleaning effect of A0L4 was better than A0L3, but for oil-based protective paint, the cleaning effect was the opposite. During operation, A0L3 volatilized more quickly; and during removal of sculpture cleaning materials, efflorescence was produced on part of the surface of the oil-based protective paint.

When cleaning with high-polarity solvents, both of them had obvious effects in cleaning the contaminated surfaces without protective paint and with water-based protective paint. As to the surface with oil-based protective paint, after removal of the sculpture cleaning materials, efflorescence was found on both A0H5 and A0H6, but the removal effect was only found on A0H6. After the tests of the cleaning effect of the 3 groups, the alkaline aqueous solution had the best cleaning effect, and the low-polarity organic solvent had the worst cleaning effect.

When the gel was added to an alkaline aqueous solution, we needed to apply it for 10~15 seconds only, and a significant cleaning effect could be found on 3 different surfaces. Especially for the removal of contamination from an oil-based protective layer, the cleaning effect was even greater. But on the part without protective paint, it would be discolored. In the group of gel/low-polarity

solvent, when toluene volatilized, $SiO_2$ was quickly agglomerated on the surface. Although petroleum ether volatilized more slowly, it was just the same as toluene after drying that there was residue of $SiO_2$, and the protective paint on the oil-based protective paint layer was eroded. During the wet application of the group of gel/high-polarity solvents, we could see that the contaminants were dissolved. But on the coating without protective paint, efflorescence was produced.

In the molten ionic salt group, when the dropper was dripping solvent, C1W1, C1W2, and C1L4 were found to maintain a higher viscosity, but C1L3, C1H5, and C1H6 were of a lower viscosity. On the surface with water-based protective paint, [BMIM]$BF_4$ had a higher cohesion. When it was placed still, the dripping solvent could be observed to have dissolving contaminants coming out. When [BMIM]$BF_4$ was combined with 3 groups of different solvents, the cleaning effects were all very obvious. But for the parts without protective paint, they were all discolored. It was speculated that this was related to the adhesive of the material itself. Any of the solvents being added to [BMIM]$PF_6$ had no cleaning effect at all but had an obvious water-repellent effect on the water-based protective paint. After comprehensive comparison among solvents, alkaline aqueous solution has a good cleaning effect in different operation methods. However, if it is not operated properly, it can easily damage the coating of the painting. As can be seen from the research results of this paper, the cleaning effect in the molten ionic salt group is related to the properties of the ionic liquid itself. The related collation results are shown in Table 2.

After cleaning the sample deteriorated due to smoke, it was rather difficult to restore its original luster. However, after comparison, the restoration degree of both the gel group and the molten ionic salt groups was higher. Of the two groups, the group added with high-polarity solvent had a better effect.

## 4 CONCLUSION

In the solvent group, since the cause of deterioration was smoke, which could be cleaned with water, the effect of the aqueous solvent group was the most significant, and so was the high-polarity group that was miscible with water. As to the parts without a protective layer, obvious effects were found on all of them. In the low-polarity group, there were more options. According to the nature of the protective layer, there were three obvious differences, which were related to the solvent itself.

In the gel group, due to the raw material properties of the gel part in the low-polarity group, no comparison could be made with the low-polarity group. However, it was found that when the two groups of solvents prepared with SiO2 were

Table 2. Comparison of cleaning effects (table made by the researcher).

| | Water/Solvent | | | Methylcellulose | | |
|---|---|---|---|---|---|---|
| Protective paint | Nil | Water | Oil | Nil | Water | Oil |
| No addition | ● | ○ | ○ | ● | ◊ | ◎ |
| NaOH | ◎ | ◎ | ◎ | ◎ | ◎ | ◎ |
| KOH | ◎ | ◎ | ◎ | ◎ | ◎ | ◎ |
| Toluene | ● | ◊ | ○ | ● | ● | ● |
| Petroleum ether | ● | ○ | ○ | ◊ | ● | ● |
| Ethanol | ○ | ○ | ◊ | ◊ | ◎ | ◎ |
| Acetone | ○ | ○ | ○ | ◊ | ◎ | ◎ |

| | [BMIM] BF$_4$ | | | [BMIM] PF$_6$ | | |
|---|---|---|---|---|---|---|
| Protective paint | Nil | Water | Oil | Nil | Water | Oil |
| No addition | ◎ | ◎ | ◎ | ● | ● | ● |
| NaOH | ◎ | ◎ | ◎ | | — | |
| KOH | ◎ | ◎ | ◎ | | — | |
| Toluene | ◎ | ◎ | ◎ | | — | |
| Petroleum ether | ◎ | ◎ | ◎ | ● | ● | ● |
| Ethanol | ◎ | ◎ | ◎ | ● | ● | ● |
| Acetone | ◎ | ◎ | ◎ | ● | ● | ● |

◎: Having significant effect
○: Having obvious effect
◊: Having effect
●: Having no obvious effect/cannot be used in the aqueous solvent group, gel helps retain more luster than the solution. But for the part with no protective paint, there will be discoloring.

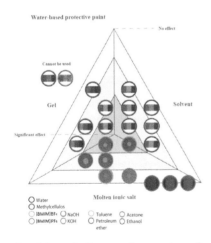

Figure 3. Schematic diagram of comparison of water-based protective paint layer.

semi-dried, the protective layer was removed altogether. Nevertheless, the solvent evaporated too quickly that the removal could not be completely done. However, the pigment layer was not removed, so the test could be taken a few more times. As to the effect of the other two groups, the visual effect after cleaning with the solution group was more uniform.

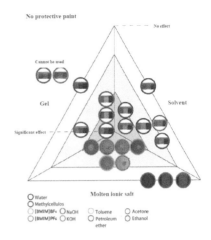

Figure 4. Schematic diagram of comparison of oil-based protective paint layer.

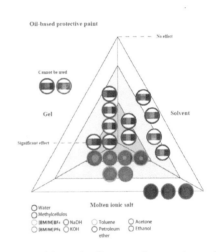

Figure 5. Schematic diagram of comparison of no protective paint layer.

The percentages of the prepared solvents of [BMIM]BF$_4$ and [BMIM]PF$_6$ are smaller. There are even fewer types that are miscible with [BMIM] PF$_6$. For [BMIM]PF$_6$, it was just tested that the cleaning effect was not obvious. As to [BMIM]BF$_4$ itself, the cleaning effect was obvious, and there was no obvious residue visually found after cleaning and removal, more tests can be done.

REFERENCES

BOOKS:

Bao-Chung Zhou (2007), *The Complete Works of Chinese Traditional Craft Arts: Cultural Conservation and Distinguishing*, Zhengzhou, Elephant Press.

Cheng-Xing Wang, Hui-Dao Yin (2005), *Wenwu Baohu Jishu (Techniques of Cultural Conservation)*, Hefei City, China, Anhui Normal University Press.

Chi-Feng Xie (2016), *The Research of Tainan "Zhuang Fo" Techniques*, Tainan, Cultural Affairs Bureau, Tainan City Government.

Ching-Wang Shao (2022), *Book of Conservation and Restoration for Paintings on Traditional Wooden Architecture*, Bureau of Cultural Heritage, Ministry of Culture, Taiwan.

Daniel Rhodes (2016), *Clay and Glazes for the Potter*, New Taipei City, Xushi Culture & Education Foundation

Ding-Li Wang (1993), *The Application and Produce of Chinese Painting Color*, Taipei, Artist Publishing.

Dong-Yu Shi (2019), *Illustrations of Chinese Painting Pigments*, Beijing, China Science and Technology Press.

Fei-Wen, Tsai (2018), *The Book of the Management and Conservation for Cultural Relics*, Taichung City, Taiwan, Bureau of Cultural Heritage, Ministry of Culture (BOCH).

Han-Chung Wu (2018), *Research Report of the Conservation Strategy of Ye Wang's Koji Pottery at Tainan Syuejia Chihjih Temple*, Bureau of Cultural Heritage, Ministry of Culture, Taiwan.

Han-Chung Wu (2021), *Development and Application on Cleaning Materials for Textile Cultural Relics*, Bureau of Cultural Heritage, Ministry of Culture, Taiwan

Huey-Cheng Lin (1995), *Book of Taiwan Traditional Architecture: Form and Practice*, Taipei, Artist Publishing.

Huey-Jiun Wang (2000), *Bricks and Earthen Bricks (I)*, NTUST Department of Architecture.

Lin He (2017), *Analysis and Identification of Chinese Ancient Paintings*, Beijing, Science Press.

National Taxation Bureau of Kaohsiung, Ministry of Finance (2008), *Survey Report on the Usual Level of Raw Material Consumption in the Manufacturing Industry/Chemical Industry (Ink Industry)*, Kaohsiung, National Taxation Bureau of Kaohsiung, Ministry of Finance, Taiwan.

Neng-Lin Cheng (2021), *Manual of Solvents*, Beijing, Chemical Industry Press.

Qi-Tai Wang (2012), *The Conservation and Restoration of Pottery Cultural Relics*, Beijing, China Publishing.

San-Tsai Xi (1999), *Techniques and Materials of Cultural Conservation*, Tainan, Press of Tainan National University of the Arts.

Shih-Hui Huang (2019), *The Research and Conservation Project Report of the "Zhuang Fo" Technique of Jui-Yi Chang*, Chiayi, Cultural Affairs Bureau.

Shin-Jie Tsen (2017), *Manual for Safe Keepers of Collections*, Tainan, Cultural Affairs Bureau, Tainan City Government.

Wan-Bao Yang (1996), *Talking About Traditional Clay Buddha Sculptures*, Nantou, Cultural Affairs Bureau of Nantou County Government

Wen-Zhung Gu (2000), *The Conservation of Antiques*, Beijing, Beijing Publishing.

Xing-Chen Zhang (2009), *Ionic Liquids: From Basic Theory to Research*, Beijing, Chemical Industry Press.

Yuan Zhang, Yang Zao (2005), *Art Materials: The Q&A on Painting Application*, Beijing, Higher Education Press.

Yu-Zen Kao (2001), *Conference Proceeding of Cultural Conservation and Restoration Between Taiwan and China*, Taipei, National Museum of History, Taiwan.

Zheng-Zhong Huang (2009), *Cleaning Cultural Property-Philosophy and Practices in Preventive Conservation*, Kaohsiung, National Science and Technology Museum.

Zui-Hsung Li (2005), *Preservation of Painted Sculptures on Silk Road Grottoes Murals*, Beijing, Science Press.

## JOURNAL AND CONFERENCE ARTICLES:

Chia-Jin He, Bi-Yen Xu, Yung-Kuan Tsen (2014, Sept), A study of materials and solvents for poultice cleaning of incense stains in temples, *IIC 2014 Hong Kong Congress*.

Chien-Hui Lin, (2009), Discussion of sol-gel preparation of nanoscaled SiO2 particles, *Chemical Monthly*, Vol.78, p.80–88

Cornell University Department of College of Agriculture and Life Sciences (2007), *Soil Texture*, Agronomy Fact Sheet Seri Fact Sheet 29.

Danyang Wang, Bingjian Zhang, Guofeng Wei (2014), A critical review of the handicraft techniques of ancient chinese painted clay sculpture, *Chinese Traditional Culture*, Vol.2, p.46–54.

Fei Huang, Zhengjia Li, Jing Bai, Tetsai Kung (2014), Research on materials and technology of painted sculpture in manjusri hall of yanshan temple, *Shanxi, World of Antiquity*, Vol.2, p.3–8

Jinsong Gui and Kaimei Zhu (2010, Dec), Synthesis of room temperature ionic liquid [Bmim][䃿䃿6]. *Chinese Scientific Papers Online*, Vol.5, No.12, p.963–966.

K.R. Seddon, A. Stark, M.-J. Torres (2000), Influence of chloride, water, and organic solvents on the physical properties of ionic liquids, *Pure Appl. Chem*, Vol. 72, No. 12, p.2275–2287.

Po-Yu Chen (2006, June), The developments of ionic liquids and their applications in electrochemistry and other fields – the unique solvents, *Chemistry (The Chinese Chem. Soc., Taipei)*, Vol.64, No.2, p.235–259.

Seda Keskin, Defne Kayrak-Talay, Uğur Akman, Ö ner Hortaçsu (2007), *A review of ionic liquids towards supercritical fluid applications*, J. of Supercritical Fluids, 2007(43), p.150–180.

Shinyu Wang, Chunyang Wu, Chingyang Chen, Yao Lu, Meilin Yen, Ning Zhang, Peng Tian (2019), Green solvent – the synthesis and properties of ionic liquids, *SHANDONG Chemical Industry*, Vol.48, No.7, p.63–65.

Tang Hongguo, Li Tao, Lu Zhaopo, Wei Lingchao, Ren Baozeng (2016), *Research progress on recovery methods of ionic liquids*, Henan Chemical Industry, Vol.33, Issue 5.

Wei Shuya, Li Qianqian, Fu Yingchun (2016), *Organic glued materials in cultural heritage*, Beijing, Science, Issue 6, p.36–39.

Wu Xin (2017), Research on the production techniques of ancient Chinese Buddhist painted sculptures, *Hunan, Literary and Artistic Life*.

Xiao-Ping Wu, Zhi-Ping Liu (2005), Computer simulation study of the mixtures of room temperature ionic liquid [bmim][BF4] and water, *Acta Physico-Chimica Sinica*, 21(09), p1036–1041.

Yangang Huang and Mei Xu, (2005). Cleaning solvent in chemical synthesis, *Chemical Engineer*, Issue 2, p48–50.

Yulan Song (2019), A review on the study of cementing materials for ancient murals, *Shanxi, Identification and Appreciation of Cultural Relics*, Issue 14

Yung-Mei Shao (2016), Analysis on the produce of a color-painted clay maid statue, *Shaanxi*, Wenbo, Vol.4, p.97–104.


## MASTER DISSERTATIONS:

Chia-Shuang Chen (2009), *The Change of Joss's form and material Using*, Master Dissertation, College of Design, Chaoyang University of Technology.

Jheng-Yu Wu (2013), *Density and Viscosity Measurements for Eight Binary Mixtures of Organic Solvents with a Room Temperature Ionic Liquid [Bmim][BF4]*, Master Dissertation, Chemical Engineering and Biotechnology Department, National Taipei University of Technology.

Yi-Ting Hsieh (2021), *Solvent Gels for the Cleaning of Taiwanese Temples Contamination of the Stone Objects – A Case Study of the Granite Stone*, Master Dissertation, Graduate Institute of Conservation of Cultural Relics and Museology, Tainan National University of the Arts.

## WEBPAGES:

*Soil Texture*, Website: https://urbanfarmer-story.tw/2017/09/24/soil-irrigation-note1/

*National Cultural Heritage Network*, Website: https://nchdb.boch.gov.tw/

*National Religion Information Network*, Website: https://religion.moi.gov.tw/Knowledge/Content?ci=2&cid=156

*Chemistry Center-Ionic Liquids*, Website: https://gc.chem.sinica.edu.tw/new-no-ionic.html

*Laws and Regulations Database of Taiwan – Cultural Heritage Preservation Act*, Website: https://law.moj.gov.tw/LawClass/LawHistory.aspx?pcode=h0170001

*Qingdao Ionike Ltd.*, Website: http://www.ionike.com/product/Imidazolium/MIm/2014-03-27/23.html

*Science Paper Online*, Website: http://www.paper.edu.cn/releasepaper/content/201108-161

*Science Online*, Website: https://highscope.ch.ntu.edu.tw/wordpress/?p=4613

*National Academy for Educational Research*, Website: https://www.naer.edu.tw/

*Conservation of Mazu Sculpture*, Website: http://library.taiwanschoolnet.org/cyberfair2008/artc/3.htm

*Encyclopedia Taiwan*, Website: https://nrch.culture.tw/twpedia.aspx?id=2596

*E-news of LANYANG Museum*, Website: https://www.lym.gov.tw/ch/collection/epaper/epaper-detail/e14437a6-1271-11ea-8482-2760f1289ae7/

*System Innovation for a Troubled World – Lam et al. (Eds)*
*© 2024 the Author(s), ISBN: 978-1-032-60846-4*

# The effect of heat treatment and rapid drying on the adhesion of oriental lacquer

Han-Chung Wu
*Conservation Center, Cheng Shu University, Kaohsiung, Taiwan*

Yao-Wen Hong
*Institute of Creative Cultural Design and Art Preservation Techniques, Cheng Shu University, Kaohsiung, Taiwan*

Wu-Shan Chu & I-Cheng Li*
*Conservation Center, Cheng Shu University, Kaohsiung, Taiwan*

ABSTRACT: More than 100,000 years ago, the Neanderthals used tree sap to stick spearhead stones and hunt wild beasts for food. According to this, an 8,000-year-old bow painted with oriental lacquer was discovered at the site of the Kuahu Bridge in Zhejiang, and its bowstring has decayed. It is speculated that humans understood the adhesiveness and the properties of protecting woodware of sap a long time ago. Lacquer art originated in China and spread eastward to Japan. Lacquer was introduced to Taiwan during the Japanese occupation period and laid the foundation for Taiwan's lacquer art. However, with the rapid development of the petrochemical industry, handmade has become expensive, and it takes too much time to paint lacquerware. It has become a traditional technique and turned to artistic creation by losing the daily necessities markets. In this study, oriental lacquer was used to repair the adhesion after simulating the ceramic fracture. There were 6 combinations of different temperatures and time was set to bake the oriental lacquer to solve the problem including the oriental lacquer surface needing to dry and cure for a week, and the adhesion and hardening took more than a year. The heat treatment test samples of this experiment were Taiwan Oriental lacquer, Japanese lacquer, and Japanese red lacquer; and the first one as the control samples were naturally cured for one year under normal temperature and high humidity. Both that control samples and the others which had completed the heat treatment were carried out an anti-push-pull test comparison. The data results show that the adhesive force is the most stable when the heat treatment temperature is 150°C; Japanese lacquer has the best push-pull resistance after baking, and Taiwan Oriental lacquer performs slightly better than Japanese red lacquer in the tensile tests but worse in the pressure tests. The overall adhesive forces of heat treatment samples were better than those of the natural maturation samples. According to the results of this research, the heat treatment method can reduce the adhesion time of Oriental lacquer to the shortest half an hour. It is obvious that the feasibility of the Oriental lacquer to accelerate the curing by heat treatment. The time course of the lacquer art technique is simplified, and there is experimental data for reference.

## 1 INTRODUCTION

The development of lacquer art has gradually changed to an artistic form. Generally, lacquerware for people's daily life is rare on the market due to the high price or the increase of substitutes. Although East Asian countries continue to promote lacquer art and lacquerware production, it is still unable to change the gradual decline of lacquer art. The changing of lacquer art represents that the lacquer is getting farther and farther away from the daily use, without daily needs, lacquer art is not easy to be popular among the public, and the skills cannot be reached and understood.

Therefore, it should be one of the future development directions of lacquer art to carry out research, experiment, and analysis in a scientific way, simplify the process of lacquer art, increase the application of raw lacquer, and make the price affordable and popularize it to the public.

## 2 EXPERIMENTAL

### 2.1 *Motivation and purpose*

Apart from the Western countries, where the buildings are mainly built with stones, every detail of the buildings of Eastern countries is related to wood materials. In order to make wooden

*Corresponding Author: plastic@gcloud.csu.edu.tw

DOI: 10.1201/9781003460763-7

products last longer and avoid climate change, insect damage, and decay, humans invented the lacquer technique about 8,000 years ago (A-Hua Luo 2015). It can be seen everywhere in daily necessities, and even lacquering techniques on ceramics and metals have emerged as the times require. When various techniques compete for the front, lacquerware and lacquer art are now able to be seen everywhere in people's daily life. After the Industrial Revolution, with the rapid progress of human beings in material science, lacquer art quickly disappeared from daily life, and it was barely spread in the form of artistic works, which urgently needed to be passed on from generation to generation.

To improve the lacquer process time, this study plans to use heat treatment to see whether the raw lacquer can be controlled by heat treatment and reduce the ripening time. Then proceed with the anti-push-pull test after the heat treatment of the raw lacquer to the ceramic film, and compared with the natural maturing conditions of raw lacquer optimization under different temperature and time conditions.

## 2.2  Research architecture

After generalizing the four reasons for the decline of lacquer art, this study is expected to improve the processing time of lacquer art as the main research purpose and take the acceleration of the drying of mature raw lacquer as the research architecture, then use experimental data to support the feasibility of heat treatment to accelerate ripening. It is expected to reduce the ripening time of raw lacquer, simplify the lacquer process, and facilitate promotion. The architecture is shown in Figure 1.

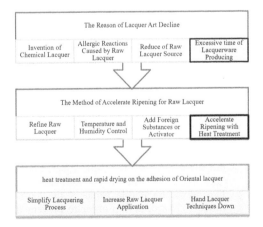

Figure 1.   Research architecture.

## 2.3  Methods

Lacquerware is made by repeatedly painting raw lacquer, grinding and polishing, and adding enzymes to make it oxidize and polymerize to form a film, which takes a long period to produce. In order to accelerate the ripening of raw lacquer, this study simulates the bonding with raw lacquer when the ceramic breaks, and ripen the raw lacquer by the oven with a timer and thermostat. They then carry out the push-pull test to understand the feasibility of heat treatment of raw lacquer to accelerate ripening.

Lacquer samples were tested in three types: Taiwan Oriental Lacquer, Japanese Lacquer, and Japanese Red Lacquer. Set 6 baking time courses, 100°C/480 min, 120°C/300 min, 150°C/180 min, 150°C/60 min, 180°C/60 min, 180°C/30 min, for the bonded test pieces to accelerate their ripening by heat treatment. Then set the bonded test piece that has been naturally aged for up to 1 year as the control group, and carry out the anti-push-pull test. Each test piece sample was at least 10 pieces, so as to find the average value with the least error. Finally, compare the data of the experimental group and the control group, and make a bar graph to visualize the test results between the raw lacquer heat treatment experimental group and the natural aging control group, as shown in Figure 2.

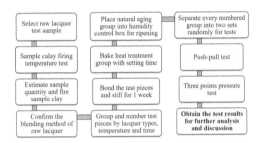

Figure 2.   Experiment process.

The total number of 40 mm clay test pieces used in this experiment is about 1,000 pieces. Because the test pieces are small and difficult to control, the shrinkage rate of the test pieces after firing is uneven, and some of the edges are slightly warped. In this experiment, the test pieces were randomly bonded without sieving, and at least 10 sets of test samples were used for each push-pull test to reduce errors.

Randomly select test pieces, and apply raw lacquer to the short sides of the 40 mm clay test pieces to be bonded, then join them by hand and squeeze slightly. After scraping off the overflowing varnish, the 80 mm push-pull test piece was completed.

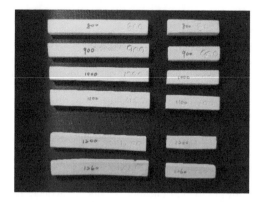

Figure 3.    Clay test pieces after firing.

Figure 4.    Raw lacquer samples.

### 2.3.1    Heat treatment samples
Still the test pieces for 1 week after bonding, when the test pieces are stable, heat treatment and baking are carried out according to the set temperature and time. Start timing when the temperature is ready, and when the time is up, keep them in the oven for cooling down to room temperature before taking them out. This is to prevent embrittlement of the test pieces and raw lacquer due to excessive temperature differences. After heat treatment and baking, the test pieces can be finished by standing still for 1 week. Then randomly separate the 3 groups of raw lacquer test pieces into 2 sets after heat treatment, and process three-point pressure and push-pull tests.

### 2.3.2    Natural ripening samples
The bonded test piece must be placed in a suitable environment where the raw lacquer is oxidized and formed into a film. This experiment was simulated in a sealed box. Wet towels and water cups are spread on the bottom of the sealed box to maintain a relative humidity of 100% RH; iron grids are spread on the towels, and the test pieces are placed on the iron grids evenly and

flatly, and the raw lacquer is allowed to ripen naturally. Stored at room temperature, it was divided into 90 days, 180 days, 270 days, and 365 days according to the test time and taken out for the anti-push-pull test. The test pieces were taken out at random and then separated into two sets for three-point pressure and tension tests.

### 2.4    Other variable control during the experiment
In the process of the experiment, in addition to the controllable variables of raw lacquer type, temperature, and time, the following situations may also occur in the experiment, so to assume those situations are fixed factors, and not to consider the differences. In order to prevent other unpredictable differences that may occur during the experiment, the test pieces are increased to 10 pieces in 1 group to obtain the best test results.

(a)    In this study, the clay test samples were tested and fired at 1200°C, which is a temperature not easily cause deformation. However, because the size of the test sample is too small, and the plane firing is easy to cause distortion and deformation, the shrinkage of many samples is unable to show uniformity. Also, the bonded side of the test piece is a smooth surface, which is different from the cross-sectional shape of the actual damaged ceramic.

(b)    The source of raw lacquer purchased is available tube products on the market; it is not easy to know the proportion of ingredients or whether other substances and catalysts have been added.

(c)    Taiwan's climate is between subtropical and tropical climates, and the average indoor temperature can meet the lacquer oxidation film formation reaction temperature of 20°C to 30°C, and the relative humidity RH is 80%.

(d)    First, manually apply raw lacquer on the test pieces, then bond two test pieces together, and slightly squeeze, and scrape off the overflowing lacquer, so as to make the amount of raw lacquer coated on each test piece equal.

(e)    Because the tension test fixture is made of metal, and the test piece is a smooth surface, too tight force on the fixture will easily cause the test piece to break; however, loose force will also cause the test piece to slip off. Therefore, rubber pads are used to prevent slipping and the tension value affected by the rubber pads or fixture is preset to zero.

(f)    The maximum tensile value of the tension gauge is 50 kgf, and in order to prevent the test piece from breaking, the fixture should not be set too tight. During the tensile test, even if the fixture has a rubber pad to prevent slipping, it still slips occasionally. It is speculated that the adhesion of the same test piece will be affected in the next test, but it is unpredictable and the tensile strength of the test pieces is greater than 20 kgf, which has reached the ideal value. Therefore, it is assumed that the test sample is still unaffected during the 2nd and 3rd tensile tests. The upper limit of the test for the same test piece is 3 slippages. Although it is known that the tensile test value exceeds 50 kgf, the average value and standard deviation in the group will be reduced, but the tensile test result is still greater than that of the control group.

(g) The clay test samples in this experiment are fired at 1200°C. During the lacquer baking process, the maximum temperature is 180°C, and the deformation coefficient of the clay matrix should be very small, so the paint body will not be deformed during the lacquer baking process.

## 3 CONCLUSION

For the analysis of experimental data, Taiwan Oriental Lacquer, Japanese Lacquer, and Japanese Red Lacquer will be used to evaluate the anti-push-pull test in sequence. In addition to tabulating each test data and making bar charts, the experimental group and the control group will also be combined to form a graph, to compare and analyze the results in a bar graph for better understanding the results. Also, based on the experimental results, discuss the most favorable temperature and time schedule for heat treatment in various procedures of lacquer art, for evaluation and use by craftsmen or artists.

According to the pressure and tensile test results, Japanese Red Lacquer shows the most stability at 120°C/300min. Although it had the best compression resistance at 180°C/60min, the push-pull values were not performing well. As the heat treatment time increases, the push-pull performance becomes worse, yet the pressure performance becomes better. Based on this, it is obvious that the color lacquer is unstable at high temperatures, and the push-pull resistance value at 100°C and 150°C is slightly worse, but it tends to become better with the heat treatment time increasing.

The Japanese Red Lacquer is relatively fluid, which is the characteristic of transparent lacquer, because it is needed to fill the capillary pores of each paint layer at the final finishing layer, to make the lacquer film transparent and smooth. In order to prevent fogging and cracking of the lacquer film at high temperatures, it is recommended to use 120°C as the most appropriate heat treatment temperature, and then increase or decrease the heat treatment time according to the amount or thickness of the lacquer coating.

The data of Japanese Lacquer after various heat treatments are much better than those of Japanese Red Lacquer and Taiwan raw lacquer. It is obvious that Japanese Lacquer has a very excellent effect in the use of adhesion with heat treatment. Generally, the lacquer layer should be applied more than 3 times on the lacquerware and it must have good adhesion. Some craftsmen will even add bone ashes, pig blood, or shellac to increase its adhesion, which is the foundation of lacquerware. Whether the body is good or bad, it will definitely affect the preservation and usability of lacquerware in the future.

The test data of Taiwan Oriental Lacquer is between Japanese Red Lacquer and Japanese Lacquer. In terms of non-special firing lacquer, the data presented is inevitably slightly worse if compared with Japanese Lacquer. Also, because of the large amount of rubber contained in it, the tension performance is better than the pressure performance, as long as the temperature and time are controlled at about 150°C. Taiwan Oriental Lacquer has a cheaper price, and is relatively fresh, so it can be used in various construction methods.

The results of this experiment show that the proportion of rubber contained in raw lacquer varies greatly, and the proportion has a great influence on the heat treatment temperature and time. Although there are fired raw lacquer products in the market, the relationship between rubber content and temperature time course is still unknown. If we can further analyze, to understand the influence of the proportion of rubber on the accelerated aging of raw lacquer heat treatment, in-depth analysis of the rubber proportion of each raw lacquer, whether cracks occur in the lacquer film after heat treatment, and the size of microscopic cracks, which will be a beneficial reference data for the accelerated aging of raw lacquer by heat treatment.

## REFERENCES

BOOKS:

Akiyoshi Totoki, Shigeki Kudo, Takaaki Nishikawa (2015), *Techniques of Lacquer Painting: Easy-to-understand explanations of lacquer characteristics, basic knowledge, and various techniques*, Tokyo City, Japan, SEIBUNDO SHINKOSHA Publishing Co., LTD.

Cheng-Xing Wang, Hui-Dao Yin (2005), *Wenwu Baohu Jishu (Techniques of Cultural Conservation)*, Hefei City, China, Anhui Normal University Press.

Fei-Wen, Tsai (2018), *The Book of the Management and Conservation for Cultural Relics*, Taichung City, Taiwan, Bureau of Cultural Heritage, Ministry of Culture (BOCH).

Kai Yeh, (2017), *The Example of Kintsukuroi Conservation and Restoration*, Zhejiang City, China, Ningbo Makie Kintsukuroi Cultural Creativity Ltd.

Li-Shu Huang (2010), *Exuberance: The Splendor World of Lacquer Art*, Kaohsiung City, Taiwan, Kaohsiung Museum of History.

Mari Kobayashi (2017), *How to See Lacquer Art: Understand Traditional Japanese Masterpieces at a Glance*, Tokyo City, Japan, SEIBUNDO SHINKOSHA Publishing Co.,LTD.

Shi-Xiang Wang (1987), *Ancient Chinese Lacquer*, Beijing City, China, Cultural Relics Press.

Xu-De Weng, Li-Shu Huang, (2000), *Retrospect and Prospect: The Lacquerware of Taiwan*, Taipei City, Taiwan, National Center for Traditional Arts.

Yanagi Muneyoshi (2014), *The Way of Craftsmanship*, Taipei City, Taiwan, BIGART Press.

Yanagi Muneyoshi (2018), *Tea and Beauty*, Taipei City, Taiwan, Always Studying Cultural.

Yanagi Muneyoshi (2019), *Handcrafted Japan*, New Taipei City, Taiwan, Walkers Cultural Enterprise Ltd.

Yi-Miao Chen, Xian-Min Wang, Xian-Zhi Wang, Pei-Qin Wang, Tian-Yin Wang (2018), *Wang Qingshuang: the Beautiful Life of Lacquer Masters*, Taichung City, Taiwan, Bureau of Cultural Heritage, Ministry of Culture (BOCH).

Zhang Li (2018), *Lacquer Art Tutorial*, Chongqing City, Chongqing University Press.


JOURNAL ARTICLES:

Chang Bei (2010), Investigation on the current situation of taiwan lacquer art, *Journal of Chinese Lacquer*, Vol.30, No.1.

Chang Bei (2011), Different local lacquer art – taiwan and hong kong lacquer art, *Journal of Chinese Lacquer*, Vol.30, No.1.

Dong-Xu Li, Cheng-Min Wang (2015), A brief probe of lacquer culture in taiwan, *Journal of Chinese Lacquer*, Vol.34, No.1, p.18–21.

Guang-Long Zou (2002), Chemical origin of ancient chinese lacquerware, *Journal of Chinese Lacquer*, No.2.

Hisatoshi Ueda (2005), Study on lacquer sculpture technique, *Research and Development Center for Educational Practice*, Okayama University, Volume 5, p.99–108.

Hiroshi Oyabu, Toru Asami, Toshio Ogawa (1997), Deterioration process of urushi films by accelerated weathering test, *Materials Life*, Vol. 10, No. 1, p.43–51.

Hsiu-Ling Lee, Chia-Wei Chang, Kun-Tsung Lu (2016), Effect of refining time to the curing properties of oriental lacquer, *Quarterly Journal of Chinese Forestry*, Vol.49, No.1, p.13–22

Hsuan-Hong Lin (2009), Research on the origin of taiwan lacquerware development, *Journal of Chinese Lacquer*, Vol.28, No.1.

Masanobu Kobayashi (2007), Strength of lacquer in iwate prefecture by baking finish, *Journal of Local Independent Administrative Agency Iwate Industrial Research Institute*, Vol.14, p.97–99.

Lu Hao, The renovation way of contemporary lacquer arts, *Journal of Chinese Lacquer*, Vol.34, No.1, p.30–35.

Li Xin, Shi Yu, Fei-Long Zhang (2006), Research on the effect of refining chinese lacquer on its rheological property, *Journal of Chinese Lacquer*, Vol.25, No.2, p.6–10.

Mei-Chen, Lin (2000), Lacquer high temperature hardening coating, *Taiwan Craft Arts*, Vol.2, p.19–24.


MASTER DISSERTATIONS:

Hsiu-Ling Lee (2015), *Modification and refining of oriental lacquer*, Master Dissertation, Department of Forestry, National Chung Hsing University, Taiwan.

Lee Lin (2008), *Study on Bark Structure and Chemical Composition of Bark and Raw Lacquer*, Master Dissertation, Department of Botany, Northwest University, China.

Sheng-Yu Tsai (2016), *Reduction of drying time for raw oriental lacquer*, Master Dissertation, Department of Forestry, National Chung Hsing University, Taiwan.


WEBPAGES:

*Lacquer Vase of Whale Hunting with Taku-Nan-Maru Boat*, Kaohsiung Museum of History, http://collection.khm.gov.tw/detail.aspx?ID=5818

*Shikata Urushi*,https://www.shikataurushi.com/products/list.php?category_id=221

*Taiwan Lacquer Art History*,Taiwan Lacquerware Art Electronic School, Misitry of Culture, https://lacquer.moc.gov.tw/home/zh-tw/ASD

System Innovation for a Troubled World – Lam et al. (Eds)
© 2024 the Author(s), ISBN: 978-1-032-60846-4

# Resource allocation and client association in mmWave 5G networks using stochastic geometry

Jeng-Ji Huang* & Po-Chen Chen
*Department of Electrical Engineering, National Taiwan Normal University, Taipei, Taiwan*

ABSTRACT: A 5G millimeter wave (mmWave) network, which operates at frequency bands above 24 GHz, is able to deliver speeds of Gbps through the use of beam-forming and the dense deployment of small cell access points (APs). In order to achieve load balancing among APs and fair allocations of channel resources among clients, a distributed algorithm based on dual decomposition has been proposed in the literature to deal with the problem of the associations of clients with APs and the allocations of channel resources. In order to obtain the overall throughput performance of a mmWave 5G network, clients are generally assumed to be evenly distributed over a service area, and a point Poisson process (PPP) is performed to generate the locations of clients and APs in each simulation run. In this paper, a different approach is adopted, in which stochastic geometry is employed to estimate the theoretical average throughput performance, without having to resort to a large number of simulations.

## 1 INTRODUCTION

In this paper, a millimeter wave (mmWave) network is considered, where clients are assumed to be uniformly distributed in a service area and access points (APs) are deployed for clients to associate with. Let $\mathcal{C}$ be the set including all clients, and $\mathcal{A}$ be the set consisting of all APs. A client is associated with a single AP, and resources are allocated by an AP to all the clients that are associated with it.

## 2 CHANNEL MODEL

Instead of relying on received signal strengths (RSSs) between clients and APs, the speeds of connections are often used in the determination of the associations of clients and APs. To calculate the speed of the connection between a client and an AP, we refer to the channel model suggested in [1]. According to the distance between a client and an AP, the signal-to-noise ratio (SNR) can be obtained through the following calculation. Then, using Shannon's theorem, the channel rate can be calculated. In addition, based on 3GPP specification, the potential connection between an AP and a client can only be in either of two possible states: line of sight (LOS) and non-line of sight (NLOS). From data collected from measurement results in [1], the probability of the states of a potential connection is a function of the distance $d$ (m), as

shown in Figure 1. In [1], an additional outage state is added in mmWave networks. According to Figure 1, the state probabilities can be found as:

$$P_{out}(d) = max\left(0, 1 - e^{-a_{out}d + b_{out}}\right), \quad (1)$$

$$P_{LOS}(d) = (1 - P_{out}(d))e^{-a_{los}d}, \quad (2)$$

$$P_{NLOS}(d) = 1 - P_{out}(d) - P_{LOS}(d), \quad (3)$$

where the values of $a_{out}$, $b_{out}$, and $a_{los}$ are related to the frequency band used, and can be found in [1]. As can be seen in Figure 1, when $d$ increases, the probability of LOS decreases whereas the probability of NLOS increases; when $d > 200$ m, the probability of a signal blockage is 100%. The state

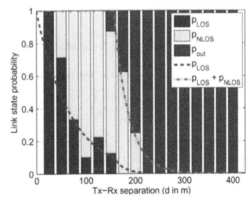

Figure 1. Relationship between link state probability and transmission distance [1].

*Corresponding Author: hjj2005@ntnu.edu.tw

DOI: 10.1201/9781003460763-8

of a link between a client and an AP can then be determined by using a uniform distribution of random numbers.

After the link state of a potential connection between a client and an AP is determined, the path loss (PL) of the potential connection can be calculated as follows:

$$PL \ [dB] = a + 10\beta log(d) + \xi, \qquad (4)$$

where $\xi$ is lognormally distributed with an average value of 0 and a variance of $\sigma^2$. For the values of $a, \beta, \sigma^2$, please refer to [2]. The received power can then be calculated as:

$$PL = P_{TX} - P_{RX} + G_{TX} + G_{RX}, \qquad (5)$$

where $P_{TX}$ is the transmission power in dBm, $P_{RX}$ is the received power, and $G_{TX}$ and $P_{RX}$ are the gains of the transmitting and receiving antenna, respectively. For example, in [2], $P_{TX} = 30$ dBm, $G_{TX} = G_{RX} = 24.5$ dBi. Lastly, the SNR can be obtained as:

$$SNR = P_{RX} - (P_{noise} + NF), \qquad (6)$$

where $P_{noise}$ is the noise power, which equals the noise power spectral density ($-174$ dBm/Hz [2]) multiplied by the bandwidth (1 GHz [2]), and $NF$ is the noise figure at the receiving end, which is 6 dB in [2].

## 3 THE DISTRIBUTED ALGORITHM

Denote by $x_{ik}$ a binary association indicator. If client $i$ is associated with AP $k$, $x_{ik} = 1$; otherwise, $x_{ik} = 0$. Denote by $y_{ik}$ the resource allocated by AP $k$ to client $i$, which amounts to the portion of time that AP $k$ will direct its antenna to client $i$. Let $r_{ik}$ be the bit rate between client $i$ and AP $k$, which is basically calculated by $r_{ik} = B \cdot \log_2(1 + SNR_{ik})$, where $B$ is the bandwidth and $SNR_{ik}$ is the signal-to-noise ratio of client $i$ seen at AP $k$.

When proportional fairness is taken into account, the problem can be formulated as [2]

$$\begin{aligned} &\max_{x,y} \sum_{i \in C} \sum_{k \in A} x_{ik} \cdot log(r_{ik} y_{ik}) \\ s.t. \quad &\sum_{k \in A} x_{ik} = 1, \quad x_{ik} \in \{0,1\}, \quad \forall i \in C, k \in A, \\ &\sum_{i \in C} x_{ik} \leq 1, \quad y_{ik} \geq 0, \quad \forall i \in C, k \in A, \end{aligned} \qquad (7)$$

where $x, y$ are vectors of $x_{ik}, y_{ik}$, respectively.

$y$ in (7) can be solved by first letting $x_{ik}$ is known. That is, by assuming $x$ a feasible solution, $y$ can then be found from $r_{ik}$. The steps of finding $y$ are illustrated as follows. First of all, the objective function in (7) can be rewritten as:

$$\begin{aligned} &\max_y \sum_{i \in C} \sum_{k \in A} x_{ik} log(r_{ik} y_{ik}) \\ &= \max_y \sum_{i \in C} \sum_{k \in A} x_{ik} (log r_{ik} + log y_{ik}) \\ &= \max_y \sum_{i \in C} \sum_{k \in A} x_{ik} log r_{ik} + x_{ik} log y_{ik} \qquad (8) \end{aligned}$$

Let $n_k = \sum_{i \in C} x_{ik}$. As $x_{ik}$ is known, (8) is equivalent to

$$\begin{aligned} &\max_y \sum_{i \in C} \sum_{k \in A} x_{ik} log y_{ik} \\ &= \max_y \sum_{i \in C_k} \sum_{k \in A} log y_{ik}, \end{aligned} \qquad (9)$$

where $C_k = \{i|, x_{ik} = 1\}$ is the set consisting of those clients that are associated with AP $k$. (9) can further be expressed as:

$$\max_y \sum_{k \in A} log \left( \prod_{i=1}^{n_k} y_{ik} \right). \qquad (10)$$

As $log(\cdot)$ is an increasing function, (10) can be rewritten as:

$$\begin{aligned} &\max_y \prod_{i=1}^{n_k} y_{ik} \\ &s.t. \quad \sum_{i \in C_k} y_{ik} \leq 1. \end{aligned} \qquad (11)$$

According to arithmetic-geometric mean inequality, $\prod_{i=1}^{n_k} y_{ik}$ is maximized when $y_{ik} = 1/n_k$. From this and (8), (7) can be rewritten as:

$$\begin{aligned} &\max_{x,n} \sum_{i \in C} \sum_{k \in A} x_{ik} b_{ik} - \sum_{k \in A} n_k log n_k \\ s.t. \quad &\sum_{k \in A} x_{ik} = 1, \quad x_{ik} \in \{0,1\}, \quad \forall i \in C, k \in A, \\ &\sum_{i \in C} x_{ik} = n_k, \qquad\qquad\qquad \forall k \in A, \end{aligned} \qquad (12)$$

where $b_{ik} = log r_{ik}$, $n$ is a vector formed by $n_k$.

In order to solve (12), Lagrange multipliers are utilized. Furthermore, $x_{ik}$ is relaxed to be a real number between 0 and 1. Let $\lambda$ be a vector formed by $\lambda_k$, where $k \in A$. The Lagrangian function can then be expressed as:

$$\begin{aligned} &\mathcal{L}(x,n,\lambda) \\ &= \sum_{i \in C} \sum_{k \in A} x_{ik}(b_{ik} - \lambda_k) + \sum_{k \in A} n_k(\lambda_k - log n_k) \end{aligned} \qquad (13)$$

(13) can be solved by using the dual decomposition method. First, (13) is rewritten into its Lagrangian dual function as:

$$\min_\lambda \mathcal{L}(x,n,\lambda) = \min_\lambda f(n,\lambda) + g(x,\lambda), \qquad (14)$$

where

$$f(n, \lambda) = \sum_{k \in \mathcal{A}} n_k(\lambda_k - \log n_k), \quad (15)$$

$$g(x, \lambda) = \sum_{i \in \mathcal{C}} \sum_{k \in \mathcal{A}} x_{ik}(b_{ik} - \lambda_k), \quad (16)$$

By using the dual decomposition method, the minimization of (13) can be implemented in a distributed manner. That is, according to current $\lambda$, (15) and (16) seek to search for an optimal solution for $n$ and an optimal solution for $x$, respectively, in each round. Since

$$\frac{\partial \mathcal{L}}{\partial \lambda_k} = n_k - \sum_{i \in \mathcal{C}} x_{ik}, \quad (17)$$

$\lambda$ is updated for the next round by

$$\lambda_{k+1} = \lambda_k - \delta \cdot \left( n_k - \sum_{i \in \mathcal{C}} x_{ik} \right). \quad (18)$$

where $\delta$ is a predefined step size. Note that the term $-\delta \cdot \left( n_k - \sum_{i \in \mathcal{C}} x_{ik} \right)$ is in the reverse direction of $\partial \mathcal{L}/(\partial \lambda_k)$ in (17), meaning that in each round a new $\lambda$ lets $\mathcal{L}$ get smaller. The algorithm stops when $n_k = \sum_{i \in \mathcal{C}} x_{ik}, \forall k \in \mathcal{A}$.

The optimization of (15) is found by:

$$\frac{\partial f}{\partial n_k} = \lambda_k - (\log n_k + 1), \quad (19)$$

or

$$n_k = e^{(\lambda_k - 1)}, \forall k \in \mathcal{A}, \quad (20)$$

On the other hand, the optimization of (16) is given as:

$$\frac{\partial g}{\partial x_{ik}} = b_{ik} - \lambda_k, \forall i \in \mathcal{C}., \quad (21)$$

Note that (21) is calculated using the current $\lambda_k$ at each client $i$. Since each client $i$ has its own limited capacity to contribute to the maximization of (16), it is clear that the best policy for client $i$ is to let $x_{ik} = 1$ and $x_{ik'} = 0$ for $k' \neq k$. It is because

$\partial g/(\partial x_{ik})$ is the steepest, and, by doing so, client $i$ has done its utmost to maximize (16).

After (21) is performed at each client $i$, $x_{ik}$ is then determined, which can be made known to each AP $k$. Then, at AP $k$, $n_k = e^{(\lambda_k - 1)}$ calculated by (20) for current $\lambda_k$. When the calculated $n_k$ is different than the actual number of associated clients, i.e., $\sum_{i \in \mathcal{C}} x_{ik}$, the algorithm is yet to finish and has to continue its next round by updating $\lambda_k$ in (18).

## 4 NUMERICAL RESULTS

In this section, our numerical result is shown in Figure 2.

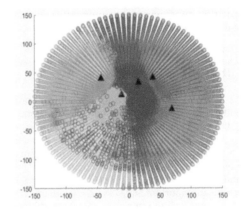

Figure 2. Results of clients' associations with APs.

## REFERENCES

[1] Rappaport T.S., MacCartney G.R., Samimi M. K. and Sun S., "Wideband millimeter-wave propagation measurements and channel models for future wireless communication system design," *IEEE Transactions on Communications*, vol. 63, no. 9, pp. 3029–3056, 2015.

[2] Xu Y., Shokri-Ghadikolaei H. and Fischione C., "Distributed association and relaying with fairness in millimeter wave networks," *IEEE Transactions on Wireless Communications*, vol. 15, no. 12, pp. 7955–7970, 2016.

*System Innovation for a Troubled World – Lam et al. (Eds)*
*© 2024 the Author(s), ISBN: 978-1-032-60846-4*

# Progressive image feature matching based on vector field consensus

Chin-Hung Teng*

*Department of Information Communication, Yuan Ze University, Chung-Li, Taiwan*

ABSTRACT: Image feature matching is a critical task in computer vision. Traditionally, feature matching is processed independently for each feature. However, matched features can provide constraints for subsequent matches, thus improving overall matching efficiency. In this paper, we propose employing the vector field consensus (VFC) model to restrict subsequent feature matching. We incorporate the concept of the Gaussian process with VFC to estimate the covariance of the vector field of a new feature. This covariance allows us to determine the search range of this new feature in the second image. As the VFC model is progressively updated, the search range is further reduced, making the matching process more efficient. To evaluate our proposed framework, we conducted an experiment. The results demonstrate that our framework is more efficient than the traditional nearest-neighbor approach and the original vector field consensus algorithm.

## 1 INTRODUCTION

The detection and matching of image feature points is a critical topic in computer vision. As digital cameras advance, image resolution has continuously increased, resulting in the detection of a significant number of image feature points in images. Consequently, quickly matching a large number of image feature points in two images has become an important subject in the academic field.

One approach to improving matching efficiency is to restrict the range of feature matching. Epipolar geometry is the most well-known image constraint used for this purpose (Hartley & Zisserman 2003; Shah et al. 2015), and this method is also referred to as guided image feature matching. While epipolar geometry can reduce the area of feature matching from the entire image to a single line, it is not applicable to all image conditions. Specifically, when the scene displays non-rigid motion, epipolar geometry is not valid and cannot effectively speed up the matching process.

Guided feature matching can be approached in different ways, including using the matched features to create a triangle mesh (Zhu et al. 2005, 2007). By doing this, when a new feature falls within a triangle in the first image, its correspondence will also fall within the corresponding triangle in the second image, limiting the range of feature point matching. The more points that are successfully matched, the smaller the size of the triangles, further improving the matching efficiency. However, this approach is not suitable when there are multiple objects with

different motions, as the true correspondence may lie outside the triangle. Additionally, an incorrect match can lead to an incorrect triangle mesh, resulting in error accumulation.

In the field of SLAM, a concept called active search was proposed (Davison 2005, 2007), which can also be considered a form of guided matching. This approach detects a feature in a specified area by using the probability distribution of the device's position to predict the potential locations of image features. However, this method is only applicable to the SLAM domain and cannot be used to match features when only two images are available since it requires the location of the device and the three-dimensional coordinates of the reconstructed feature points.

Teng and Dong proposed an additional method for guided feature matching, which uses the spatial order of feature points to restrict the matching range (Teng & Dong 2019). This approach builds a spatial order model using the matched features, dividing the image domain into intervals. For a new feature, the probabilities of correspondences falling in these intervals are calculated. The features in the intervals with probabilities below a certain threshold are filtered out, effectively guiding the feature matching. However, this method assumes that the correct matches maintain a consistent spatial order, which is not the case when images have rotation. Therefore, this method is not applicable when dealing with rotated images.

To address the limitations of epipolar geometry, the vector field consensus (VFC) algorithm was proposed (Ma et al. 2014). This method uses a nonparametric vector field function to predict the vector field values of corresponding points and

---

*Corresponding Author: chteng@saturn.yzu.edu.tw

DOI: 10.1201/9781003460763-9

identify incorrectly matched feature points (the outliers). Since VFC does not rely on two-view geometric constraints, such as epipolar geometry, it is more widely applicable. However, VFC is primarily designed to eliminate outliers by initially matching all features and then creating and using VFC to identify the points that do not obey the vector field. It is not originally intended to perform guided matching in the image domain during the feature matching process.

In this study, we propose a novel approach to guided feature matching by employing the Gaussian process to transform the application mode of the VFC algorithm. The vector field function is progressively built during the matching process, and for a new feature, the covariance of its vector field is estimated to determine its matching range in the second image. By using VFC-based guided matching, we can improve the matching efficiency. Since our method is based on the nonparametric VFC model, it is more widely applicable than the traditional epipolar geometry-based guided matching.

## 2 SYSTEM ARCHITECTURE

The architecture of the system used in this study is depicted in Figure 1. Initially, two input images (I and J) are processed using a feature detection algorithm. Our framework does not restrict the type of feature detection method used, meaning any algorithm can be employed.

To apply the VFC algorithm, the coordinates of feature points in both images need to be normalized. This normalization step involves adjusting the mean to 0 and the standard deviation to 1.

After normalization, we partition the first image into several regular cells and group feature points in each cell. We then select feature points sequentially from each cell for subsequent matching. This partitioning ensures that the matched features are evenly distributed throughout the image, preventing them from clustering in specific areas and

potentially reducing the effectiveness of our progressive feature-matching approach.

After accumulating a certain number of feature points, we use them to compute the VFC model. To employ the Gaussian process theory, we then use the VFC model to eliminate outliers and reformulate the vector field function by using the inliers as the basis functions. Then, for a new feature $\mathbf{x}^*$, we substitute it into the vector field function to obtain its corresponding vector field value $\mathbf{f}(\mathbf{x}^*)$. Additionally, we use Gaussian process theory to compute the covariance of $(\mathbf{x}^*)$, which enables us to determine the feature search range in the second image. By utilizing this range, we can filter out unreasonable matches, thereby improving matching efficiency.

We repeat the above procedures to match more features, and as we accumulate more matches, we build a more accurate and effective VFC model that guides subsequent feature matching. To balance the overall computing efficiency of the system, we avoid calculating the VFC model for every new feature. Instead, we activate the update of the VFC after accumulating a certain number of points.

## 3 COMPUTING THE VECTOR FIELD CONSENSUS MODEL

In this study, we compute the VFC model based on the method proposed by Ma *et al.* (2014). Given a set of normalized matched feature pairs: $(\mathbf{u}_i, \mathbf{v}_i), i = 1, \cdots, N$, where $\mathbf{u}_i$ and $\mathbf{v}_i$ are the feature points in the first and second images, respectively, we define $\mathbf{x}_i = \mathbf{u}_i$, $\mathbf{y}_i = \mathbf{v}_i - \mathbf{u}_i$. Here, $\mathbf{y}_i$ is the corresponding vector field value of $\mathbf{x}_i$. The goal of the VFC model is to find a vector field function $\mathbf{f}(\mathbf{x})$ such that $\mathbf{y}_i = \mathbf{f}(\mathbf{x}_i)$. However, since measurement errors are inevitable, we assume that the vector field of a correct match is only disturbed by the white Gaussian noise, i.e.,

$$\mathbf{y}_i = \mathbf{f}(\mathbf{x}_i) + \boldsymbol{\varepsilon}, \tag{1}$$

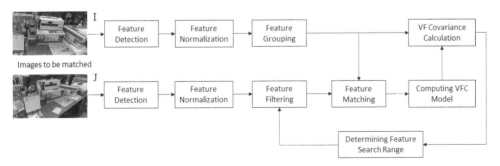

Figure 1. System Architecture.

where $\boldsymbol{\varepsilon} \sim \mathcal{N}(0, \sigma^2 \mathbf{I})$ and $\sigma^2$ is noise variance. For an incorrect match, the vector field value $\mathbf{y}_i$ usually exhibits random characteristics, so it is reasonable to assume that it follows a uniform distribution with a probability density function of $1/a$, where $a$ is the area of the space of feature points. To distinguish correct and incorrect matches, a hidden variable $z_i$ is introduced with a value of 1 for a correct match and a value of 0 for an incorrect match. Assuming that these $N$ points are independent, we can express the joint probability density function for these points as:

$$p(\mathbf{Y}|,\mathbf{X},\boldsymbol{\theta}) = \prod_{i=1}^{N} \left( \frac{\gamma}{(2\pi\sigma^2)^{D/2}} e^{-\frac{||\mathbf{y}_i - \mathbf{f}(\mathbf{x}_i)||^2}{2\sigma^2}} + \frac{1-\gamma}{a} \right), \tag{2}$$

where $\mathbf{X} = [\mathbf{x}_1^T \quad \cdots \quad \mathbf{x}_N^T]^T, \mathbf{Y} = [\mathbf{y}_1^T \quad \cdots \quad \mathbf{y}_N^T]^T$, $\gamma = p(z_i = 1)$ represents the prior probability that a pair of matching points is a correct match, $D$ represents the dimension of the vector field, and $\boldsymbol{\theta} = \{\mathbf{f}, \sigma^2, \gamma\}$. The purpose of VFC is to find an optimal $\boldsymbol{\theta}$ and based on Bayes' rule, the optimal $\boldsymbol{\theta}$ can be obtained by maximizing the following function:

$$\boldsymbol{\theta}^* = \arg\max_{\boldsymbol{\theta}} p(\boldsymbol{\theta}|, \mathbf{X}, \mathbf{Y}) = \arg\max_{\boldsymbol{\theta}} p(\mathbf{Y}|\mathbf{X}, \boldsymbol{\theta}) p(\mathbf{f}). \tag{3}$$

The optimal solution of Eq. (3) can be realized by the EM algorithm, which consists of two steps: the E-step and the M-step:
E-step:

$$P(z_i = 1|, \mathbf{x}_i, \mathbf{y}_i, \boldsymbol{\theta})$$
$$= \frac{\gamma \exp\left(-\frac{||\mathbf{y}_i - \mathbf{f}(\mathbf{x}_i)||^2}{2\sigma^2}\right)}{(1-\gamma)\frac{(2\pi\sigma^2)^{D/2}}{a} + \gamma \exp\left(-\frac{\mathbf{y}_i - \mathbf{f}(\mathbf{x}_i)^2}{2\sigma^2}\right)}. \tag{4}$$

This equation calculates the probability that a match is correct. In the M-step, the optimal $\gamma$ and $\sigma^2$ are estimated as follows:
M-step:

$$\gamma = \frac{\text{tr}(\mathbf{P})}{N}, \tag{5}$$

$$\sigma^2 = \frac{(\mathbf{Y} - \mathbf{V})^T \tilde{\mathbf{P}} (\mathbf{Y} - \mathbf{V})}{D \cdot \text{tr}(\mathbf{P})}, \tag{6}$$

where $\mathbf{P}$ is a diagonal matrix with diagonal entries $p_i = P(z_i = 1|, \mathbf{x}_i, \mathbf{y}_i, \boldsymbol{\theta})$, $\mathbf{V} = [\mathbf{f}(\mathbf{x}_1)^T \quad \cdots \quad \mathbf{f}(\mathbf{x}_N)^T]^T$, and $\tilde{\mathbf{P}} = \mathbf{P} \otimes \mathbf{I}_D$, where $\otimes$ denotes the Kronecker product. In addition to finding $\gamma$ and $\sigma^2$, we also need to determine the corresponding vector field

function $\mathbf{f}(\mathbf{x})$. In VFC, $\mathbf{f}(\mathbf{x})$ is assumed from a reproducing kernel Hilbert space (RKHS), and according to the representer theorem (Alvarez et al. 2012), $\mathbf{f}(\mathbf{x})$ can be expressed as a linear combination of a set of kernel functions, as follows:

$$\mathbf{f}(\mathbf{x}) = [\Gamma(\mathbf{x}, \mathbf{x}_1) \quad \cdots \quad \Gamma(\mathbf{x}, \mathbf{x}_N)] \begin{bmatrix} \mathbf{c}_1 \\ \vdots \\ \mathbf{c}_N \end{bmatrix} = \Gamma_{\mathbf{x}}^T \tilde{\mathbf{C}}, \tag{7}$$

where $\tilde{\mathbf{C}} = [\mathbf{c}_1^T \quad \cdots \quad \mathbf{c}_N^T]^T$, $\Gamma_{\mathbf{x}}^T = [\Gamma(\mathbf{x}, \mathbf{x}_1) \quad \cdots \quad \Gamma(\mathbf{x}, \mathbf{x}_N)]$, and $\Gamma(\mathbf{x}_i, \mathbf{x}_j)$ is the kernel function of this RKHS. Finally, the optimal $\tilde{\mathbf{C}}$ can be obtained by solving the following system of linear equations (Ma et al. 2014):

$$\left(\tilde{\Gamma} + \lambda \sigma^2 \tilde{\mathbf{P}}^{-1}\right) \tilde{\mathbf{C}} = \mathbf{Y}, \tag{8}$$

where

$$\tilde{\Gamma} = \begin{bmatrix} \Gamma(\mathbf{x}_1, \mathbf{x}_1) & \cdots & \Gamma(\mathbf{x}_1, \mathbf{x}_N) \\ \vdots & & \vdots \\ \Gamma(\mathbf{x}_N, \mathbf{x}_1) & \cdots & \Gamma(\mathbf{x}_N, \mathbf{x}_N) \end{bmatrix} \in R^{ND \times ND}. \tag{9}$$

In this study, we choose the following matrix as the kernel function:

$$\Gamma(\mathbf{x}_i, \mathbf{x}_j) = \exp\left\{-\frac{||\mathbf{x}_i - \mathbf{x}_j||^2}{\beta}\right\} \mathbf{I}_D. \tag{10}$$

In summary, the VFC is calculated as follows: First, the initial values of $\gamma$ and $\sigma^2$ are given. Then, the EM algorithm is performed. The probability of a match being correct is calculated using Eq. (4), and the matrix $\mathbf{P}$ is formed. Next, the values of $\gamma$ and $\sigma^2$ are updated using Eqs. (5) and (6), respectively. The vector $\tilde{\mathbf{C}}$ is obtained by solving Eq. (8) and the corresponding vector field function $\mathbf{f}(\mathbf{x})$ is obtained from Eq. (7). These steps are repeated until the EM algorithm converges. Once the VFC model is computed, the correctness of a match can be determined by thresholding $P(z_i = 1|, \mathbf{x}_i, \mathbf{y}_i, \boldsymbol{\theta})$.

## 4 CALCULATING THE COVARIANCE OF VECTOR FIELD

The VFC algorithm described above can determine the correctness of a match, but it does not provide the variation of the vector field. To address this issue, we can use the Gaussian process (Rasmussen and Williams 2006) to calculate the covariance of the vector field for a new feature. This covariance provides information on the

38

variation of the vector field, which can be used to determine the matching range of a new feature.

However, because Eq. (2) contains incorrect matches, it is not possible to apply the Gaussian process theorem. To address this issue, we need to extract the correct matches from $(\mathbf{x}_i, \mathbf{y}_i)$ to form a new set $(\tilde{\mathbf{x}}_i, \tilde{\mathbf{y}}_i)$, $i = 1, \cdots, M$, where $M$ is the number of correct matches. This new set can then be used to form a new vector field function $\mathbf{f}_s(\mathbf{x})$ as follows:

$$\mathbf{f}_s(\mathbf{x}) = [\Gamma(\mathbf{x}, \tilde{\mathbf{x}}_1) \quad \cdots \quad \Gamma(\mathbf{x}, \tilde{\mathbf{x}}_M)] \begin{bmatrix} \tilde{\mathbf{c}}_1 \\ \vdots \\ \tilde{\mathbf{c}}_M \end{bmatrix} = \Gamma_{\mathbf{x},s}^T \tilde{\mathbf{C}}, \tag{11}$$

where $\Gamma_{\mathbf{x},s}^T = [\Gamma(\mathbf{x}, \tilde{\mathbf{x}}_1) \quad \cdots \quad \Gamma(\mathbf{x}, \tilde{\mathbf{x}}_M)]$ and $\tilde{\mathbf{C}} = [\tilde{\mathbf{c}}_1^T \quad \cdots \quad \tilde{\mathbf{c}}_M^T]^T$. Because $\tilde{\mathbf{y}}_i$ is only disturbed by white Gaussian noise, the joint probability density function $p(\tilde{\mathbf{Y}} | \tilde{\mathbf{X}}, \tilde{\mathbf{C}})$ is also a Gaussian distribution, where $\tilde{\mathbf{X}} = [\tilde{\mathbf{x}}_1^T \quad \cdots \quad \tilde{\mathbf{x}}_M^T]^T$ and $\tilde{\mathbf{Y}} = [\tilde{\mathbf{y}}_1^T \quad \cdots \quad \tilde{\mathbf{y}}_M^T]^T$. By applying Bayes' theorem, we can obtain $p(\tilde{\mathbf{C}} | \tilde{\mathbf{X}}, \tilde{\mathbf{Y}})$ as follows:

$$p(\tilde{\mathbf{C}} | \tilde{\mathbf{X}}, \tilde{\mathbf{Y}}) \propto p(\tilde{\mathbf{Y}} | \tilde{\mathbf{X}}, \tilde{\mathbf{C}}) p(\tilde{\mathbf{C}}). \tag{12}$$

Here, we assume that $\tilde{\mathbf{C}}$ follows a zero mean Gaussian distribution with covariance matrix $\boldsymbol{\Sigma}_{\mathbf{C}}$. Then, Eq. (12) can be written as:

$$p(\tilde{\mathbf{C}} | \tilde{\mathbf{X}}, \tilde{\mathbf{Y}}) \propto$$
$$\exp\left(-\frac{1}{2}(\tilde{\mathbf{C}} - \overline{\mathbf{C}})^T \left(\tilde{\Gamma}_{\mathbf{X},s}^T \boldsymbol{\Sigma}^{-1} \tilde{\Gamma}_{\mathbf{X},s} + \boldsymbol{\Sigma}_{\mathbf{C}}^{-1}\right)(\tilde{\mathbf{C}} - \overline{\mathbf{C}})\right)$$
$$\cdot N_{others}, \tag{13}$$

where $\tilde{\Gamma}_{\mathbf{X},s} = [\Gamma_{\mathbf{x}_1,s} \quad \cdots \quad \Gamma_{\mathbf{x}_M,s}]^T$, $\boldsymbol{\Sigma}^{-1} = \mathbf{I}_M \otimes \boldsymbol{\Sigma}_n^{-1}$, $\boldsymbol{\Sigma}_n = \sigma^2 \mathbf{I}$, $\overline{\mathbf{C}} = \left(\tilde{\Gamma}_{\mathbf{X},s}^T \boldsymbol{\Sigma}^{-1} \tilde{\Gamma}_{\mathbf{X},s} + \boldsymbol{\Sigma}_{\mathbf{C}}^{-1}\right)^{-1} \tilde{\Gamma}_{\mathbf{X},s}^T \boldsymbol{\Sigma}^{-1} \tilde{\mathbf{Y}}$, and $N_{others}$ represents a term irrelevant to $\tilde{\mathbf{C}}$. In fact, Eq. (13) is a form of Gaussian distribution with $N_{others}$ just a normalization constant. Therefore, the posterior probability of $\tilde{\mathbf{C}}$ is a Gaussian distribution with mean $\left(\tilde{\Gamma}_{\mathbf{X},s}^T \boldsymbol{\Sigma}^{-1} \tilde{\Gamma}_{\mathbf{X},s} + \boldsymbol{\Sigma}_{\mathbf{C}}^{-1}\right)^{-1} \tilde{\Gamma}_{\mathbf{X},s}^T \boldsymbol{\Sigma}^{-1} \tilde{\mathbf{Y}}$ and covariance $\left(\tilde{\Gamma}_{\mathbf{X},s}^T \boldsymbol{\Sigma}^{-1} \tilde{\Gamma}_{\mathbf{X},s} + \boldsymbol{\Sigma}_{\mathbf{C}}^{-1}\right)^{-1}$.

Suppose now we have a new feature point $\mathbf{x}^*$ on the first image. Then, we can calculate the corresponding vector field $\mathbf{f}_s(\mathbf{x}^*) = \sum_{m=1}^{M} \Gamma(\mathbf{x}^*, \tilde{\mathbf{x}}_m) \mathbf{c}_m$ by Eq. (11). Since $\mathbf{f}_s(\mathbf{x}^*)$ is a linear combination of $\tilde{\mathbf{c}}_i$, it also follows a Gaussian distribution with mean and covariance given by:

$$\overline{\mathbf{f}}^* \overset{\Delta}{=} E(\mathbf{f}_s(\mathbf{x}^*)) = E\left(\Gamma_{\mathbf{x}^*,s}^T \tilde{\mathbf{C}}\right) = \Gamma_{\mathbf{x}^*,s}^T E(\tilde{\mathbf{C}})$$
$$= \Gamma_{\mathbf{x}^*,s}^T \overline{\mathbf{C}}, \tag{14}$$

$$\boldsymbol{\Sigma}_{\mathbf{f}^*} = \Gamma_{\mathbf{x}^*,s}^T \left(\tilde{\Gamma}_{\mathbf{X},s}^T \boldsymbol{\Sigma}^{-1} \tilde{\Gamma}_{\mathbf{X},s} + \boldsymbol{\Sigma}_{\mathbf{C}}^{-1}\right)^{-1} \Gamma_{\mathbf{x}^*,s}, \tag{15}$$

where $\Gamma_{\mathbf{x}^*,s}^T = [\Gamma(\mathbf{x}^*, \tilde{\mathbf{x}}_1) \quad \cdots \quad \Gamma(\mathbf{x}^*, \tilde{\mathbf{x}}_M)]$.

## 5 DETERMINING THE SEARCH RANGE OF A FEATURE

In the previous section, it was shown that $\mathbf{f}_s(\mathbf{x}^*)$ follows a Gaussian distribution with mean $\overline{\mathbf{f}}^*$ and covariance $\boldsymbol{\Sigma}_{\mathbf{f}^*}$, i.e., $\mathbf{f}_s(\mathbf{x}^*) \sim \mathcal{N}(\overline{\mathbf{f}}^*, \boldsymbol{\Sigma}_{\mathbf{f}^*})$. According to probability theory, the quantity $\left(\mathbf{f}^* - \overline{\mathbf{f}}^*\right)^T \boldsymbol{\Sigma}_{\mathbf{f}^*}^{-1} \left(\mathbf{f}^* - \overline{\mathbf{f}}^*\right)$ follows a chi-square distribution. Thus, given a confidence level $\alpha$, the range of possible values of $\mathbf{f}^*$ can be obtained by referencing the chi-square distribution table. For example, if $\alpha = 99.9\%$, the corresponding chi-square value is 13.82. Therefore, the search range of a feature can be determined using the following equation:

$$\left(\mathbf{f}^* - \overline{\mathbf{f}}^*\right)^T \boldsymbol{\Sigma}_{\mathbf{f}^*}^{-1} \left(\mathbf{f}^* - \overline{\mathbf{f}}^*\right) \le 13.82. \tag{16}$$

That is, we have 99.9% confidence that the vector field of a correct match will meet this constraint. Figure 2 illustrates the feature search range, where × represents the expected position of correspondence of a feature in the second image and the ellipse around it indicates the possible search range for matching this feature point.

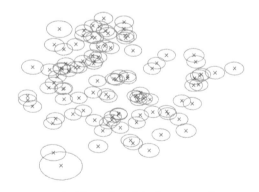

Figure 2. An illustration of the feature search range.

## 6 EXPERIMENTAL RESULTS

To validate the efficacy of the proposed method, a set of simulated images was generated for testing purposes. We selected 100 images from the ImageNet dataset and then applied image transformations on each image to generate a corresponding target image for matching. The image transformation approach was based on the method proposed by Dosovitskiy et al. (Dosovitskiy et al. 2016), with minor modifications. In addition, we incorporated a perspective transformation to diversify the range of image variations.

Our experimental environment is a desktop PC running on the Microsoft 64-bit Windows 10 operating system, equipped with an AMD Ryzen 9 3900 12-Core Processor @ 3.79GHz CPU, and 64GB RAM. We utilized SURF (Bay et al. 2008) for image feature detection and the accompanying descriptor for feature similarity calculation. Since the image used in our experiment underwent a known transformation, we can determine the exact position of the corresponding point in the second image for each feature in the first image. However, due to the presence of inherent computational errors in detecting image features, we deemed a match correct if the distance between the position of a matched point and its true position is within 3 pixels.

Table 1 presents the experimental results for the 100 images. The Nearest Neighbor method indicates that we compute the similarities of each feature in the first image with all features in the second image. A match was deemed successful if the most similar feature pair had a similarity less than a predefined threshold value.

Table 1. Experimental results of 100 ImageNet images

| | Nearest Neighbor | SparseVFC | Proposed Method |
|---|---|---|---|
| # Matches | 71386852178 | 71386852178 | 1494736402 |
| # Inliers | 351986 | 351725 | 367334 |
| Precision | 0.457459 | 0.726954 | 0.813586 |
| Matching Time (s) | 2310.86 | 2338.26 | 402.30 |

SparseVFC is a method proposed by the authors of VFC, where the term "sparse" refers to the use of a limited number of points to generate the vector field function. According to the authors, SparseVFC achieves comparable accuracy to the original VFC, but with significantly faster computational speed.

In our proposed progressive matching framework, we update the VFC model every 40 accumulated points, with a total of 3 updates. In order to compare with SparseVFC on an equal basis, we also perform SparseVFC in our framework after matching all the features to remove outliers.

Table 1 presents several performance metrics of the proposed progressive matching framework. The #Matches indicates the total number of feature matches that were computed. The #Inliers shows the number of feature matches that were considered correct according to the applied image transformation. The Precision shows the percentage of inliers among all matched feature pairs. The Matching Time denotes the time required for feature matches, excluding feature detection time. Except for Precision, which represents the overall precision of these 100 images, the values in Table 1 represent the cumulative results of 100 images.

Since SparseVFC is executed after all feature matches are completed by Nearest Neighbor, it requires the same number of matches as Nearest Neighbor. Its matching time is also slightly higher than that of the Nearest Neighbor. However, SparseVFC can significantly improve precision by removing outliers. In contrast, among the three methods reported in Table 1, our VFC-based progressive matching framework produces the minimum number of matches to obtain the maximum number of inliers and the highest precision in the shortest time.

## 7 CONCLUSION

Image feature detection and matching play a crucial role in image processing and computer vision. Despite the availability of numerous reliable techniques, mismatches remain a common issue in feature point matching. Therefore, eliminating incorrect matches (or outliers) is a crucial challenge in this field. Typically, robust algorithms like RANSAC are used for removing outliers using geometric constraints such as epipolar geometry. However, this approach requires a parametric model and holds only under certain conditions, which may limit its practical applications.

The VFC algorithm offers an alternative solution to the limitations of epipolar geometry-based approaches. However, it requires an initial matching of feature points in both images and aims to remove outliers from the initial matches. To address this, we propose a VFC-based progressive image feature-matching framework. This framework incrementally builds a model during the feature-matching process, which can be used to limit the search range of subsequent matching attempts. By doing so, we can significantly reduce the number of matches required and improve matching efficiency. Furthermore, by constraining matching to more likely areas, the framework is capable of identifying correct matches that may not have the highest similarity scores.

To assess the effectiveness of the proposed framework, we conducted an experiment and the results are encouraging. Our method demonstrated improved precision with higher matching efficiency. In the future, we plan to conduct more comprehensive experiments to further evaluate the performance of the proposed method.

## ACKNOWLEDGEMENT

This work was supported by the National Science and Technology Council, Taiwan, under Grant No. MOST 110-2221-E-155-048.

## REFERENCES

Alvarez M.A., Rosasco L. and Lawrence N.D., "Kernels for vector-valued functions: a review," arXiv:1106.6251, 2012.

Bay H., Ess A., Tuytelaars T. and van Gool L., "Speeded-up robust features (SURF)," *Computer Vision and Image Understanding*, vol. 110, no. 3, pp. 346–359, 2008.

Davison A.J., "Active search of real-time vision," *IEEE International Conference on Computer Vision*, 2005.

Davison A.J., Reid I.D., Molton N.D. and Stasse O., "MonoSLAM: Real-time single camera SLAM," *IEEE Transactions on Pattern Analysis and Machine Intelligence*, vol. 29, no. 6, pp. 1052–1067, 2007.

Dosovitskiy A., Fischer P., Springenberg J.T., Riedmiller M. and Brox T., "Discriminative unsupervised feature learning with exemplar convolutional neural networks," *IEEE Transactions on Pattern Analysis and Machine Intelligence*, vol. 38, no. 9, pp. 1734–1747, 2016.

Hartley R.I. and Zisserman A., *Multiple View Geometry in Computer Vision*, Cambridge University Press, 2nd edition, ISBN: 0521540518, 2003.

Ma J., Zhao J., Tian J., Yuille A.L. and Tu Z. "Robust point matching via vector field consensus," *IEEE Transactions on Image Processing*, vol. 23, no. 4, pp. 1706–1721, 2014.

Rasmussen C. E. and Williams C.K.I., *Gaussian Processes for Machine Learning*, the MIT Press, 2006, ISBN 026218253X.

Shah R., Srivastava V. and Narayanan P.J., "Geometry-aware feature matching for structure from motion applications," *IEEE Winter Conference on Applications of Computer Vision*, pp. 278–285, 2015.

Teng C.-H.and Dong B.-J., "Using feature spatial order in progressive image feature matching," *International Conference on Machine Learning and Cybernetics*, July 7–10, Kobe, Japan, 2019, pp. 31–36.

Zhu Q., Zhao J., Lin H. and Gong J., "Triangulation of well-defined points as a constraint for reliable image matching," *Photogrammetric Engineering & Remote Sensing*, vol. 71, no. 9, pp. 1063–1069, 2005.

Zhu Q., Wu B. and Tian Y., "Propagation strategies for stereo image matching based on the dynamic triangle constraint," *ISPRS Journal of Photogrammetry & Remote Sensing*, vol. 62, pp. 295–308, 2007.

System Innovation for a Troubled World – Lam et al. (Eds)
© 2024 the Author(s), ISBN: 978-1-032-60846-4

# An energy consumption estimation method for Linux-based embedded real-time systems[†]

Jun Wu* & Han-Sheng Shih

*Department of Computer Science and Information Engineering, National Pingtung University, Pingtung, Taiwan*

ABSTRACT: In this paper, an energy consumption estimation method is proposed for Linux-based embedded real-time systems. We consider the energy consumption of a system mainly from CPU computations. In order to obtain the power consumption data, a series of measurements have been conducted at the run-time. We then apply a linear regression on the measurement data to generate power and energy consumption functions of CPU utilization. Based on the estimated energy consumption function, the system lifetime is also derived. An experiment was conducted to collect the actual CPU utilization, battery capacity, and system lifetime. The results have been compared to the estimated lifetime for which encouraged results were achieved.

## 1 INTRODUCTION

In recent decades, embedded systems have become increasingly popular in many application domains, such as transportation, aerospace, robotics, medical, automation control, surveillance, etc. Using Linux as the operating system is undoubtedly gaining popularity due to its high customizability and scalability that meet the vast requirements of different application domains. Moreover, Linux supports many device drivers, making it easy to use any peripheral device. However, the major drawback of using Linux is that there is no timing guarantee for task execution. To overcome the drawback, many embedded systems have installed a Linux patch (such as PREEMPT RT (Linux Foundation 2023), RTLinux (Yodaiken 1999), and RTAI (RTAI 2023)) for handling tasks with strict timing constraints. We call such a system a *Linux-based embedded real-time system* (LERTS).

In addition to providing the timing guarantee, energy efficiency is another critical design issue for LERTS. It is because most LERTS'es are energy-constrained systems (powered by batteries) with only a finite amount of energy. Therefore, the primary design goal of an energy-constrained LERTS is to meet the timing constraints of tasks and to minimize energy consumption such that the system's lifetime can be prolonged.[1] For reducing the energy consumption of embedded real-time systems, many excellent works have been

proposed. Interested readers can refer to Chen and Kuo (2007) and Wu (2017) based on various energy-efficient techniques and approaches (Mittal 2014) during the past two decades.

In this paper, we are interested in energy consumption measurement and estimation, which are vital for providing insights to develop or conduct energy-efficient approaches for embedded systems. In other words, accurate measurement and estimation are the fundamentals of the energy efficiency of embedded systems. Unfortunately, only comparably little work has been done in this direction, which motivates this research. We will propose an energy consumption estimation method for LERTS'es, and apply it to the estimation of the remaining lifetime of an energy-constrained LERTS. We believe that the accuracy of the energy consumption estimation is proportional to the degree of energy efficiency. The results of this research could benefit the research community in the energy-efficient design of embedded systems.

Since the primary objective of this research is to provide an accurate estimation method, we have conducted a series of experiments to measure the energy consumption of tasks running on a Linux-based single-board computer. We then apply a linear regression on the measurement data to generate an energy consumption function of CPU utilization and I/O activity. Based on the proposed estimation method, the estimated remaining system lifetime of the system is also derived.

---

[†]This work was supported in part by the National Science and Technology Council (NSTC) of Taiwan under grants 110-2221-E-153-001-MY3 and 111-2813-C-153-011-E.
*Corresponding Author: junwu@mail.nptu.edu.tw

---

[1]For mains-powered embedded systems, energy efficiency is also vital since it relates to carbon emissions and the bill amount.

DOI: 10.1201/9781003460763-10

Moreover, estimated energy consumption is compared to the actual energy consumption measured from a series of experiments for which we have encouraged results.

## 2 RELATED WORK

In the field of energy consumption measurement, direct measurement (Carroll & Heiser 2010; Rice & Hay 2010; Gurun et al. 2006; Flinn and Satyanarayanan 1999; Aras et al. 2015) is the way to obtain the most accurate measurement data. It uses external instruments (such as a digital multimeter (DMM), memory recorder (MR), oscilloscope, and data acquisition (DAQ) card) to sample the voltage across them regularly such that the corresponding current and power consumption can be calculated accordingly. However, direct measurement is not flexible enough to conduct a measurement on an embedded system since the hardware circuit needs to be modified to connect to the external instruments (Guo et al. 2021). In the literature, there are some measurement platforms such as FlockLab (Lim et al. 2013), PowerBench (Haratcherev et al. 2008), and Nemo (Zhou & Xing 2013) have been proposed such that the flexibility of conducting measurements on an embedded system is improved. Furthermore, some researchers have conducted and reported energy consumption measurements of Raspberry Pi (Kaup et al. 2014; Kesrouani et al. 2020; Ardito & Torchiano 2018) since it is getting popular in many application domains.

After obtaining measurement data, it can be analyzed with statistical data collected at the run-time (such as CPU utilization and battery capacity) to generate an energy consumption model. Šimunić *et al.* have pointed out that an accurate energy consumption model is crucial for building energy-efficient embedded systems (Šimunić et al. 2001). This is because an energy consumption model can estimate/predict the amount of energy consumed by the execution of tasks. Therefore, it provides valuable insights into the design of an energy-efficient embedded system. Researchers have proposed various energy consumption models (e.g., Shye et al. 2009; Nash et al. 2005; Xiao et al. 2010; You et al. 2010) for embedded systems with different software and hardware environments.

Along with this research direction, we will conduct a series of experiments to measure the energy consumption of tasks running on an LERTS. Based on the measurement data, we will propose an energy consumption model and estimation method for LERTS'es. Based on the proposed methods, we will derive a system lifetime (i.e., battery lifetime) estimation method for which energy-efficient designs of an LETRS can be realized.

## 3 SYSTEM AND TASK MODELS

This paper focuses on the energy consumption measurement and estimation of a Linux-based embedded real-time system (LERTS) that runs on a Raspberry Pi since it is the most popular Linux-based single-board computer (SBC). Specifically, we consider a set of real-time tasks that are executed on an application platform, called yet another platform for embedded real-time systems (*Y*apers) (Wu et al. 2023). At the current stage, *Y*apers is operating on a Raspberry Pi 4B SBC with Raspberry Pi OS[2].

Based on the well-known periodic real-time task models (Liu & Layland 1973), *Y*apers support a set of N periodic tasks $T = \{\tau_i | 1 \le i \le N\}$ running on the system. At the run-time, a task $\tau_i$ will instantiate its instances regularly, i.e., instantiate its first instance $\tau_i^1$ at its arrival time (denoted by *ArrivalTime*$_i$), and instantiate the remaining instances $\tau_i^j$ (for j > 1) for every period of time (i.e., instantiate $\tau_i^j$ at *ArrivalTime*$_i$ + *Period*$_i$ × (j − 1). A task instance $\tau_i^j$ has to be executed on the CPU for no longer than its worst-case execution time (denoted by *WCET*$_i$). We define the fraction of CPU execution time spent for executing the task set $T$ as the overall system utilization,

$$U = \sum_{\tau_i \in \tau} U_i = \sum_{\tau_i \in \tau} \frac{WCET_i}{Period_i}$$

where $U_i$ is the utilization factor of task $\tau_i$. Note that the execution of a task instance $\tau_i^j$ has to be completed no later than *ArrivalTime*$_i$ + *Period*$_i$ × (j − 1) + *Deadline*$_i$, where *Deadline*$_i$ is the relative deadline of task $\tau_i$'s instances. We say a task instance meets the deadline if its completion time is no later than the deadline; otherwise, it misses the deadline.

## 4 ENERGY CONSUMPTION AND CPU UTILIZATION

As the evidence shown in Fan et al. (2007), power consumption increases linearly as CPU utilization. In this section, we conducted a series of experiments to measure the power consumption of varied workload real-time tasks and then derived power and energy consumption estimation functions of CPU utilization.

### 4.1 *Measurement setup*

In our experiments, a Raspberry Pi 4B SBC is the device under test. As shown in Figure 1, the test

---

[2]Raspberry Pi OS is the official Linux distribution for Raspberry Pi SBC, formerly called Raspbian.

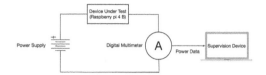

Figure 1. Electrical wiring diagram of the measurement setup.

device (i.e., a Raspberry Pi 4B SBC) is powered by a GW Instek GPS-1830D power supply (through GPIO pins) in order to provide a stable 5V DC voltage. Note that GPS-1830D can provide up to 18V/3A which is higher than that of a Raspberry Pi 4B (5V/3A).

Furthermore, an external digital multimeter, GW Instek GDM-8342, is used to obtain the power consumption data. Both ends of the digital multimeter are connected to the power supply and the device under test, respectively. Notice that a shunt resistor is connected to the circuit typically to protect the potential overloading or, even worse, the short circuit situations. However, we didn't use a shunt resistor in our experiments since the GDM-8342 can measure current across it up to 10A which is higher than the maximum output current of a Raspberry Pi 4B (i.e., 3A). At the run-time, GDM-8342 will measure the current across it and periodically return the data to a backend supervision device (a Windows 10 PC) through USB.

Figure 2 shows the physical setup of our experiments. Astute readers might point out that the supply voltage is 5.7V in the figure. It is because we considered the potential voltage drop. The supply voltage must be higher than 5V in order to guarantee that the Rasberry Pi 4B SBC is powered stable. We have observed that the digital multimeter (GDM-8342) has a voltage drop of 0.5V. We set the supply voltage as 5.7V so that it can provide 5.2V to the Raspberry Pi 4B SBC.

Figure 2. Physical measurement setup.

## 4.2 Measurement task sets and results

The primary objective of our experiments is to explore the relationship between power consumption and CPU utilization. In our experiments, a large number of task sets have been generated and measured. In particular, we generated task sets with the utilization factor from 1% to 100% stepped by 1%.

Note that task sets with specific utilization factors were generated by lookbusy (Carraway. 2023) which is an application for generating workload (i.e., tasks) on Linux systems. Over 30 task sets per utilization factor have been executed and their power consumptions were measured on the $\mathcal{Y}$apers platform. Figures 3 and 4 show the raw and filtered data (95% confidence interval) of the measurement power consumption data.

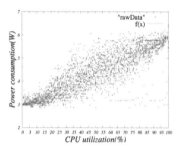

Figure 3. The measurement of power consumption (raw data).

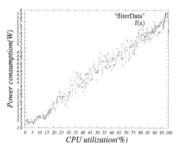

Figure 4. The measurement of power consumption (filtered data).

## 4.3 Estimated power consumption

Based on the measurement data obtained from our experiments, the filtered power consumption data (i.e., the results in Figure 4) is used to generate an estimated power consumption function of CPU utilization (i.e., $EPC(u)$) by using linear regression. The power consumption estimation function is as follows:

$$EPC(u) = 2.6051 \times u + 2.68\,Watt \qquad (1)$$

Note that the root-mean-square-error (RMSE) of Equation 1 is 0.1423, which is accurate enough. The function can be used to estimate the power consumption for various CPU utilization, i.e., the estimation power consumption is $EPC(0.8) = 2.6051 \times 0.8 + 2.68\,Watt = 4.76408\,W$ when the CPU utilization is 80%.

### 4.4 Energy consumption estimation

Let $PC(t)$ and $EC_{(t1,t2)}$ be the power consumption at time $t$ and the energy consumption for a given time interval $(t_1, t_2]$, respectively.

$$EC_{(t_1,t_2)} = \int_{t_1}^{t_2} PC(t)\, dt \qquad (2)$$

However, it is impossible to obtain the power consumption at every time instant $t$ within the interval$(t_1, t_2]$. In this paper, we will calculate the estimated energy consumption (denoted as $EEC$) by using estimated power consumption instead of the measured one.

$$EEC_{(t_1,t_2)} = \int_{t_1}^{t_2} EPC(t)\, dt \qquad (3)$$

Unfortunately, obtaining the estimated power consumption at every instant is still impossible. For a given set of periodic real-time tasks $T$, its CPU utilization $U(T)$ can be calculated:

$$U(\tau) = \sum_{\tau_i \in \tau} \frac{WCET_i}{Period_i} \qquad (4)$$

By replacing the estimated power consumption of time with the estimated power consumption of CPU utilization, the estimated energy consumption can be calculated as follows:

$$EEC_{(t_1,t_2)} \leq EPC(U(\tau)) \times (t_2 - t_1) \qquad (5)$$

### 4.5 Lifetime estimation

According to Equation 5, the estimated system lifetime (denoted as $ELT$) can be calculated as follows:

$$ELT = \frac{EBC \times V_{dd}}{EPC(U(\tau))} \qquad (6)$$

Where $EBC$ and $V_{dd}$ are the effective battery capacity and the supply voltage (i.e., 5.2V). Note that the effective battery capacity is usually lower than the nominal battery capacity. For example, we have observed from many experiments that a 4000 mAh battery can only provide stable 5.2V output while its remaining capacity is no less than 1500 mAh. Suppose that a set of real-time tasks is

running on a Raspberry Pi 4B SBC powered by a 4000mAh fully charged battery (with 2500mAh effective battery capacity, i.e., $EBC = 2500$mAh). Assume that the CPU utilization of tasks is 0.8, the estimated system lifetime can be calculated as follows:

$$ELT = \frac{2500mAh \times 5.2V}{EPC(U(0.8))}$$

$$= \frac{2500mAh \times 5.2V}{4.76408\,W} \qquad (7)$$

$$= 2.7287535h \cong 2 : 43'43$$

## 5 EVALUATION

In order to verify the accuracy of our proposed estimated power consumption function and the estimated system lifetime. We have conducted a long-lasting experiment based on $\mathcal{Y}$apers platform in which a set of real-time tasks with 80% CPU utilization has been generated and executed on a Raspberry Pi 4B SBC. A fully charged 4000mAh battery is installed on an RPi UPSPack V3 to power the Raspberry Pi 4B SBC. Note that it can provide up to 2500mAh effective battery capacity.

We also implement a monitoring program to get information about the actual CPU utilization and the remaining battery capacity regularly during the run-time. Figures 5 and 6 show the actual CPU utilization and the remaining battery capacity during the run-time, respectively. The results show that the tasks use about 80% CPU utilization during the run-time, and the battery capacity has been consumed accordingly. The experiment was executed for 2.7016 hours (i.e., 2:42'06) before the battery was fully exhausted. Compared to our estimated lifetime (i.e., 2.7287535 hours), the error is less than 0.0271 hours (i.e., less than 1 minute and 37.5 seconds). It implies that our estimation method is accurate and the error is ignorable.

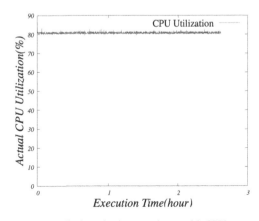

Figure 5.    The long-lasting experiment with CPU usage.

45

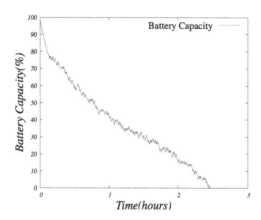

**Figure 6.** The long-lasting experiment with the remaining battery capacity.

## 6 CONCLUSION

In this paper, a power consumption estimation method and an energy consumption estimation method have been proposed based on a series of measurements. The estimated system lifetime can be derived based on our proposed energy consumption estimation method. It was shown that our estimation is accurate and the error is ignorable. For future work, we will measure and analyze the energy consumption of I/O activities which is another important source of power consumption. We will also extend the results to $y$apers platform such that some energy-efficient designs can be achieved by using the accurate estimation of the energy consumption and the system lifetime.

## REFERENCES

Aras S., Johnson T., Cabulong K., and Gniady C. , "Greenmonitor: Extending battery life for continuous heart rate monitoring in smart-watches," in *Proceedings of the 17th International Conference on E-health Networking*, Application & Services, 2015.

Ardito L. and Torchiano M., "Creating and evaluating a software power model for linux single board computers," *in 2018 IEEE/ACM 6th International Workshop on Green And Sustainable Software (GREENS)*, 2018, pp. 1–8.

Carraway D., "Lookbusy-A Synthetic Load Generator," Availableonline at http://www.devin.com/lookbusy/ (visited on March 28, 2023.), 2023.

Carroll A. and Heiser G., "An analysis of power consumption in a smartphone," in *Proceedings of the 2010 USENIX Annual Technical Conference*, 2010.

Chen J.-J. and Kuo C.-F., "Energy-efficient scheduling for real-time systems on dynamic voltage scheduling (DVS) platforms," in *Proceedings of the 13th IEEE International Conference on Embedded and Real-Time Computing Systems and Applications (RTCSA2007)*, 2007.

Fan X., Weber W.-D., and Barroso L.A., "Power provisioning for a warehouse-sized computer," in *Proceedings of the 34th ACM Annual International Symposium on Computer Architecture*, September 2007, pp. 13–23.

Flinn J. and Satyanarayanan M., "Powerscope: A tool for profiling the energy usage of mobile applications," in *Proceedings of the 2nd IEEE Workshop on Mobile Computing Systems and Applications*, 1999.

Guo C., Ci S., Zhou Y., and Yang Y., "A survey of energy consumption measurement in embedded systems," *IEEE Access*, vol. 9, pp. 60 516–60 530, 2021.

Gurun S., Nagpurkar P., and Zhao B.Y., "Energy consumption and conservation in mobile peer-to-peer systems," in *Proceedings of the 1st International Workshop Decentralized Resource Sharing Mobile Computing*, 2006.

Haratcherev I., Halkes G., Parker T., Visser O., and Langendoen K., "PowerBench: A scalable testbed infrastructure for benchmarking power consumption," in *Proceedings of the Intl Workshop on Sensor Network Engineering (IWSNE)*, 2008.

Kaup F., Gottschling P., and Hausheer D., "Powerpi: Measuring and modeling the power consumption of the raspberry pi," in *39th Annual IEEE Conference on Local Computer Networks*, 2014, pp. 236–243.

Kesrouani K., Kanso H., and Noureddine A., "A preliminary study of the energy impact of software in raspberry pi devices," in *2020 IEEE 29th International Conference on Enabling Technologies: Infrastructure for Collaborative Enterprises (WETICE)*, 2020, pp. 231–234.

Lim R., Ferrari F., Zimmerling M., Walser C., 'sommer P.and Beutel J, "FlockLab: A testbed for distributed, synchronized tracing and profiling of wireless embedded systems," in *Proceedings of the 12th International Symposium on Information Processing in Sensor Networks*, 2013.

Linux Foundation, "PREEMPT RT Patch Versions," Available online at https://wiki.linuxfoundation.org/realtime/preem pt rt versions (visited on March 16, 2023.), 2023.

Liu C. L. and Layland J.W., "Scheduling Algorithms for Multiprogramming in a Hard-Real-Time Environment Scheduling Algorithms for Multiprogramming," *Journal of the ACM*, vol. 20, no. 1, pp. 46–61, 1973.

Mittal S., "A survey of techniques for improving energy efficiency in embedded computing systems," *International Journal of Computer Aided Engineering and Technology*, vol. 6, no. 4, pp. 440–459, 2014.

Nash D., Martin T., Ha D. and Hsiao M., "Towards an intrusion detection system for battery exhaustion attacks on mobile computing devices," in *Proceedings of the 3rd IEEE International Conference on Pervasive Computing and Communications Workshops*, 2005, pp. 141–145

RTAI, "*RTAI – Real Time Application Interface Official Website*," Available online at https://www.rtai.org/ (visited on March 16, 2023.), 2023.

Rice A. and Hay S., "Decomposing power measurements for mobile devices," in *2010 IEEE Intl. Conf Conference on Pervasive Computing and Communications (PerCom)*, 2010, pp. 70–78.

Shye A., Scholbrock B. and Memik G., "Into the wild: Studying real user activity patterns to guide power optimizations for mobile architectures," in *Proceedings of the 42nd Annual IEEE/ACM*

International Symposium on Microarchitecture (MICRO), 2009, pp. 168–178.

Šimunić T., Benini L. and Micheli G.D., "Survey: Embedded linux ahead of the pack," *IEEE Transactions on Very Large Scale Integration Systems*, vol. 9, no. 1, pp. 15–28, 2001.

Wu J., "A survey of energy-efficient task synchronization for real-time embedded systems," in *Proceedings of the 23rd IEEE RTCSA*, Hsinchu, Taiwan, August 16–18 2017.

Wu J., Hwang C.-S., Liau J.-Y., Hwang J.-L. and Kuo M.-I., "Yapers: An novel application platform for embedded real-time systems," *Submitted to 2023 Information Technology and Applications Symposium*, June 2023.

Xiao Y., Bhaumik R., Yang Z., Siekkinen M., Savolainen P. and Yl-Jski A., "A system-level model for runtime power estimation on mobile devices," in *Proceedings of the 2010 IEEE/ACM International Conference on Green Computing and Communications and International Conference on Cyber, Physical and Social Computing*, 2010, pp. 27–34.

You D.-C., Hwang Y.-S., Ahn Y.-H., and Chung K.-S., "Energy consumption prediction technique for embedded mobile device by using battery discharging pattern," in *Proceedings of the 2nd IEEE Intl Conference on Network Infrastructure & Digitial Content*, September 2010, pp. 907–910.

Yodaiken V., *"The RTLinux Manifesto,"* in Proceedings of the 5th Linux Expo, 1999.

Zhou R. and Xing G., "Nemo: A high-fidelity non-invasive power meter system for wireless sensor networks," *in Proceedings of the 12th ACM/IEEE Conference on Information Processing in Sensor Networks*, 2013.

System Innovation for a Troubled World – Lam et al. (Eds)
© 2024 the Author(s), ISBN: 978-1-032-60846-4

# Semi-quantum private comparison protocol with graph state

Chia-Wei Tsai, Jyun-Jie Hong & Yun-Hao Lee
*Department of Computer Science and Engineering, National Taichung University of Science and Technology, North Dist., Taichung, Taiwan*

Jason Lin
*Department of Computer Science and Engineering, National Chung Hsing University, South Dist., Taichung, Taiwan*

Chun-Wei Yang\*
*Master Program for Digital Health Innovation, College of Humanities and Sciences, China Medical University, Beitun Dist., Taichung, Taiwan*

ABSTRACT: The quantum private comparison (QPC) protocol is an important research issue in the quantum secure computation field. The participants obtain the relational comparison between each other private messages without leaking any secret information by QPC protocol. In order to improve the practicality of quantum secure communication protocol, the semi-quantum concept was proposed to let the users who only have limited quantum capabilities (called the classical users) can also achieve the quantum secure communication protocol. According to the semi-quantum concept, this study proposes a semi-quantum private comparison (SQPC) protocol using a measurement property of a graph state $|G\rangle_{123} = \frac{1}{2\sqrt{2}}(|000\rangle + |001\rangle + |010\rangle - |011\rangle + |100\rangle - |101\rangle - |110\rangle - |111\rangle)_{123}$. The proposed SQPC protocol lets the two classical users can compare whether their private messages are equal or not with the assistance of a dishonest three-party quantum user (TP), in which TP owns the complete quantum capabilities and the classical users only equip the two quantum devices including (1) Hadamard operation and (2) Z-basis $\{|0\rangle, |1\rangle\}$ measurement. Because the one-way qubit transmission is adopted, the proposed SQPC protocol is free from quantum Trojan horse attack. Moreover, a security analysis also is given to prove that the proposed SQPC is robust under the collective attack.

## 1 INTRODUCTION

Since Yao [1] proposed the first secure computation problem, known as the millionaires' problem, in 1982, the scholar focused on this issue. Secure computation is a general technology that allows two or more parties to jointly compute a function without revealing their inputs to each other. In the real world, secure computation has various applications, such as in finance, healthcare, and online voting, where multiple parties must collaborate and compute over private data without revealing that data to others. By using secure computation techniques, these parties can work together to achieve their goals while maintaining privacy and confidentiality.

Various classical mathematical technologies have been adopted to propose solutions for the millionaires' problem [2–7]. Due to the rapid development of quantum computing technologies, certain classical cryptography algorithms may be broken. In view of this challenge, quantum cryptography, which uses quantum mechanics and properties to design secure protocols, has been proposed to ensure information-theoretical security and provide long-term security, in which the quantum private comparison is an important branch of quantum cryptography. In 2009, Yang and Wen [8] proposed the first quantum private comparison (QPC) protocol, and then various QPC protocols [10–28] have been proposed by using different quantum states or methods continually. However, these QPC protocols always assume that the protocol participants own complete quantum capabilities. So far, certain quantum technologies (e.g., storing qubits in the long-term, generating complex entanglement states, and so on) are still difficult to implement. For this issue, Boyer et al. [29] proposed a semi-quantum quantum environment with two types of users, quantum users and classical users. The quantum user has complete quantum capabilities, but the classical user is equipped with only limited quantum capabilities. According to the concept of a semi-quantum environment, this study proposes a semi-quantum private comparison (SQPC)

---
\*Corresponding Author: cwyang@mail.cmu.edu.tw

DOI: 10.1201/9781003460763-11

protocol using the measurement property of a triangle graph state $|G\rangle_{123} = \frac{1}{2\sqrt{2}}(|000\rangle + |001\rangle + |010\rangle - |011\rangle + |100\rangle - |101\rangle - |110\rangle - |111\rangle)_{123}$. The proposed SQPC protocol allows the two classical participants to compare their private messages with each other and evaluate whether their private messages are equal or not with the help of a dishonest third-party (TP). Here, TP owns complete quantum capabilities, and the classical participants only equip (1) Hadamard operation and (2) Z-basis $\{|0\rangle, |1\rangle\}$ measurement. This study also gives the analyses to prove that the proposed SQPC protocol is robust under collective attack and is free from quantum Trojan horse attacks.

The remainder of this paper is organized as follows: Section 2 describes the measurement property of the triangle graph state, Section 3 proposes our SQPC protocol, and then gives the security analyses for the proposed QSPC protocol in Section 4. Finally, conclusions are presented in Section 5.

## 2 MEASUREMENT PROPERTY

Before describing the proposed SQPC protocol, this study briefly explains the graph state and its measurement properties. A graph state can be represented as a $G = (V, E)$, where the node set $V$ denotes the qubits in this state and the edge set $E$ denotes the entanglement relationship among these qubits [30]. Here, this study uses the following quantum state (**Eq. (1)**) to show the graph state with $G = (V, E)$.

$$|G\rangle = \prod_{(a,b)\in E} CZ^{\{a,b\}}|+\rangle^{\otimes n}, \quad (1)$$

where $|+\rangle = \frac{1}{\sqrt{2}}(|0\rangle + |1\rangle)$ and $CZ_{(i,j)}$ means performing the control-Z operation on vertices $a$ and $b$ if there is an edge between $a$ and $b$. The control Z-operation is given by **Eq. (2)**.

$$CZ^{\{a,b\}} = \begin{bmatrix} 1 & 0 & 0 & 0 \\ 0 & 1 & 0 & 0 \\ 0 & 0 & 1 & 0 \\ 0 & 0 & 0 & -1 \end{bmatrix} \quad (2)$$
$$= |00\rangle\langle00| + |01\rangle\langle01| + |10\rangle\langle10| - |11\rangle\langle11|$$

To design SQPC protocol, this study proposes a measurement property for a 3-qubit triangle graph state. The quantum state of the 3-qubit triangle graph state is expressed as follows:

$$|G\rangle_{123} = \frac{1}{2\sqrt{2}}(|000\rangle + |001\rangle + |010\rangle - |011\rangle$$
$$+ |100\rangle - |101\rangle - |110\rangle - |111\rangle)_{123}$$

$$= \frac{1}{2}(|+\rangle_i \otimes (|00\rangle - |11\rangle)_{\{1,2,3\}-i}$$
$$+ |-\rangle_i \otimes (|01\rangle + |10\rangle)_{\{1,2,3\}-i}) \quad (3)$$

According to **Eq. (3)**, we can find out a specific measurement property when measuring one qubit and others on X-basis $\{|+\rangle = \frac{1}{\sqrt{2}}(|0\rangle + |1\rangle)$, $|-\rangle = \frac{1}{\sqrt{2}}(|0\rangle - |1\rangle)\}$ and Z-basis $\{|0\rangle, |1\rangle\}$, respectively. This specific measurement result is that the result of performing the XOR operation on each measurement result must be 0, where this study encodes $|0\rangle$ $(|+\rangle)$ and $|1\rangle$ $(|-\rangle)$ as the classical bits 0 and 1, respectively. Taking Eq. 3 as an example, $\oplus_{i=1}^{3} MR_i$ must be equal to 0 in any measurement situation shown in Figure 1, where $\oplus_{i=1}^{3} MR_i$ denotes $MR_1 \oplus MR2 \oplus MR_3$.

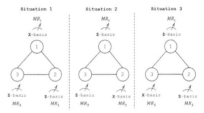

Figure 1. Measurement property of 3-qubit triangle state.

## 3 PROPOSED PROTOCOL

There are two classical participants (i.e., Alice and Bob) who want to compare the $n$-bit classical private messages (i.e., $M_A = \{m_A^1, m_A^2, \ldots, m_A^n\}$ and $M_B = \{m_B^1, m_B^2, \ldots, m_B^n\}$, where $m_A^i \in \{0, 1\}$ and $m_B^i \in \{0, 1\}$) between each other with the proposed SQPC assistance of the quantum participant TP in the protocol. Here, this study assumes that the classical participants only equip the two quantum capabilities including (1) performing Hadamard operation (shown in **Eq. (4)**), and (2) measuring single qubits in Z-basis $\{|0\rangle, |1\rangle\}$, but TP can own the complete quantum capabilities.

$$H = \frac{1}{\sqrt{2}} \begin{bmatrix} 1 & 1 \\ 1 & -1 \end{bmatrix} \quad (4)$$

Moreover, the honestness of TP is assumed as semi-honest; that is, TP can launch any possible attack but cannot conspire with Alice or Bob. The processes of the proposed SPQC protocol are described as follows:

**Step 1.** TP generates the triangle graph state $|G\rangle_{123}$ and then TP keeps the 1st qubit and sends the 2nd and 3rd qubits to Alice and Bob, respectively.

**Step 2.** After receiving the qubit sent from TP, Alice (Bob) selects CHK or CALC mode randomly. If she (he) selects CALC mode, she (he) will perform $H$ operation on the received qubit and then measure it on a Z-basis;

49

otherwise, she (he) measures the qubit on the Z-basis. Then, she (he) records the selected mode and the measurement result in this session. Finally, she (he) returns a classical message "ACK" through the classical channel. When TP receives acknowledgments from Alice and Bob, TP also selects CHK or CALC mode randomly and then performs the same operations as the classical participants.

TP and the classical participants repeat the above steps a sufficient number of times to let Alice and Bob can reach the private comparison for the $n$-bit messages.

**Step 3.** TP and the classical participants publicly discuss the selected modes in each session, and they only keep the measurement results in the valid sessions in which only one participant selects **CALC** mode.

**Step 4.** Assuming that there are $n + m$ valid sessions. Alice (and Bob) mark each corresponding measurement result as $mr_A^i$ ($mr_B^i$), where $i = 1$ to $m + n$. Alice and Bob select $m$ sessions randomly and then they request TP to announce the measurement results in the $m$ sessions. Then, Alice and Bob use their corresponding measurement results to check whether these measurement results conform with the entanglement property of the triangle graph state or not; that is, they calculate $mr_A^i \oplus mr_B^i \oplus mr_T^i$ and verify whether the result is equal to 0 or not. If the error rate is higher than the default threshold (i.e., the noise rate of the quantum channel), the participants will abort this execution and restart the protocol; otherwise, they continue the following processes.

**Step 5.** Alice, Bob, and TP take $n$ remaining measurement result as the secret bit sequences, $S_A = \{s_A^1, s_A^2, \ldots, s_A^n\}$, $S_B = \{s_B^1, s_B^2, \ldots, s_B^n\}$, and $S_T = \{s_T^1, s_T^2, \ldots, s_T^n\}$, respectively. Then, Alice (Bob) calculates $x^i = m_A^i \oplus s_A^i$ ($y^i = m_B^i \oplus s_B^i$) from $i = 1$ to $n$, and then she (he) sends $X = \{x^1, x^2, \ldots, x^n\}$ ($Y = \{y^1, y^2, \ldots, y^n\}$) to TP through the authenticated classical channel.

Figure 2. The processes of the proposed SQPC protocol.

**Step 6.** TP calculates $o_{AB}^i = x_A^i \oplus y_B^i \oplus s_T^i$ from $i = 0$ to $n$. If $o_{AB}^i = 0 | \forall i \in \{1, 2, \ldots, n\}$, TP will announce that Alice's and Bob's private messages are the same; otherwise, TP will announce that they have different private messages.

## 4  SECURITY ANALYSIS

To prove the security of the proposed SQPC protocol, this study proposes the security analyses for the collective attack and the quantum Trojan horse attack in this section. In the quantum private comparison protocol, TP has the greatest advantage over other inside or outside attackers because TP owns the most important, generating and distributing the quantum resources. Therefore, this study proves that the proposed SQPC protocol is robust under the collective attack launched by TP.

**Theorem 1**: Assume that TP performs a collective attack on the qubit sent to Alice and Bob. To achieve the attack, TP performs an attack unitary operation $U_e$ on a quantum state to insert a probe qubit $|E\rangle$ into the quantum state, and then TP wants to steal the secret information of any participant by measuring the probe qubits, where $U_e$ must comply with the theorems of quantum mechanics. However, there is no unitary operation to allow TP to obtain information on the participants' private messages without being detected. That is, if TP can steal the participants' private messages by using the collective attack, the participants can detect TP's attack behavior with a non-zero probability.

**Proof:** After TP generates the triangle graph state, it applies $U_e$ to insert the probe qubit $|E\rangle$ into the graph state, keeps the probe qubit in its quantum memory, and then executes the follow-up processes of the SQPC protocol. According to the theorems of quantum mechanics, the quantum system state is converted to **Eq. (5)**.

$$U_e |G\rangle_{123} \otimes |E\rangle = |G'\rangle_{123E}$$

$$= a_1 |000\rangle |e_1\rangle + a_2 |001\rangle |e_2\rangle$$

$$+ a_3 |010\rangle |e_3\rangle + a_4 |011\rangle |e_4\rangle$$

$$+ a_5 |100\rangle |e_5\rangle + a_6 |101\rangle |e_6\rangle$$

$$+ a_7 |110\rangle |e_7\rangle + a_8 |111\rangle |e_8\rangle, \quad (5)$$

where $\sum_{j=1}^{8} |a_j|^2 = 1$. The state of the probe qubit $|e_j\rangle$ for $\forall j \in \{1, 2, \ldots, 8\}$ can be distinguished by TP because $|e_x\rangle$ and $|e_y\rangle$ are orthogonal if $x \neq y$. If TP wants to pass the secret check in **Step 4** of the proposed protocol, it must adjust the parameters of $U_e$ to let the quantum state of **Eq. (5)** conform to the measurement results of the triangle graph states. Here, this study analyzes the three situations as follows:

- Situation 1: Alice selects **CALC** mode

After Alice performs Hadamard operation on the 1st qubit of the graph state, the quantum state will become **Eq. (6)**.

$$H \otimes I \otimes I \cdot |G'\rangle_{123E} = |000\rangle(a_1|e_1\rangle + a_5|e_5\rangle)$$

$$+ |001\rangle(a_2|e_2\rangle + a_6|e_6\rangle)$$

$$+ |010\rangle(a_3|e_3\rangle + a_7|e_7\rangle)$$

$$+ |011\rangle(a_4|e_4\rangle + a_8|e_8\rangle)$$

$$+ |100\rangle(a_1|e_1\rangle - a_5|e_5\rangle)$$

$$+ |101\rangle(a_2|e_2\rangle - a_6|e_6\rangle)$$

$$+ |110\rangle(a_3|e_3\rangle - a_7|e_7\rangle)$$

$$+ |111\rangle(a_4|e_4\rangle - a_8|e_8\rangle) \quad (6)$$

To pass through the participants' security check, TP must set $a_2|e_2\rangle + a_6|e_6\rangle = -0$, $a_3|e_3\rangle + a_7|e_7\rangle = \vec{0}$, $a_1|e_1\rangle - a_5|e_5\rangle = 0$, and $a_4|e_4\rangle - a_8|e_8\rangle = \vec{0}$.

- Situation 2: Bob selects **CALC** mode

Similar to situation 1, the quantum state will change to **Eq. (7)** after Bob performs the Hadamard operation on the 2nd qubit.

$$H \otimes H \otimes I \cdot |G'\rangle_{123E} = |000\rangle(a_1|e_1\rangle + a_3|e_3\rangle)$$

$$+ |001\rangle(a_2|e_2\rangle + a_4|e_4\rangle)$$

$$+ |010\rangle(a_1|e_1\rangle - a_3|e_3\rangle)$$

$$+ |011\rangle(a_2|e_2\rangle - a_4|e_4\rangle)$$

$$+ |100\rangle(a_5|e_5\rangle + a_7|e_7\rangle)$$

$$+ |101\rangle(a_6|e_6\rangle + a_8|e_8\rangle)$$

$$+ |110\rangle(a_5|e_5\rangle - a_7|e_7\rangle)$$

$$+ |111\rangle(a_6|e_6\rangle - a_8|e_8\rangle) \quad (7)$$

Here, TP needs to set $a_2|e_2\rangle + a_4|e_4\rangle = \vec{0}$, $a_1|e_1\rangle - a_3|e_3\rangle = \vec{0}$, $a_5|e_5\rangle + a_7|e_7\rangle = \vec{0}$, and $a_6|e_6\rangle - a_8|e_8\rangle = \vec{0}$.

- Situation 3: TP selects **CALC** mode

When TP performs Hadamard operation on the 3rd qubit of the graph state, the quantum state will become **Eq. (8)**.

$$I \otimes I \otimes H \cdot |G'\rangle_{123E} = |000\rangle(a_1|e_1\rangle + a_2|e_2\rangle)$$

$$+ |001\rangle(a_1|e_1\rangle - a_2|e_2\rangle)$$

$$+ |010\rangle(a_3|e_3\rangle + a_4|e_4\rangle)$$

$$+ |011\rangle(a_3|e_3\rangle - a_4|e_4\rangle)$$

$$+ |100\rangle(a_5|e_5\rangle + a_6|e_6\rangle)$$

$$+ |101\rangle(a_5|e_5\rangle - a_6|e_6\rangle)$$

$$+ |110\rangle(a_7|e_7\rangle + a_8|e_8\rangle)$$

$$+ |111\rangle(a_7|e_7\rangle - a_8|e_8\rangle) \quad (8)$$

Similar to the above situations, TP must set $a_1|e_1\rangle - a_2|e_2\rangle = \vec{0}$, $a_3|e_3\rangle + a_4|e_4\rangle = \vec{0}$, $a_5|e_5\rangle + a_6|e_6\rangle = 0$, and $a_7|e_7\rangle - a_8|e_8\rangle = 0$.

From the above-mentioned parameter settings, we can find out that TP must set $a_1|e_1\rangle = a_2|e_2\rangle = a_3|e_3\rangle = a_5|e_5\rangle$, $a_4|e_4\rangle = a_6|e_6\rangle = a_7|e_7\rangle = a_8|e_8\rangle$, and $a_4|e_4\rangle = -a_1|e_1\rangle$ when TP wants to pass through the classical participants' secret check. If TP adopts the settings, the state of Eq. (5) will become the following state:

$$|G'\rangle_{123E} = a_1|000\rangle|e_1\rangle + a_1|001\rangle|e_1\rangle + a_1|010\rangle|e_1\rangle$$

$$- a_1|011\rangle|e_1\rangle + a_1|100\rangle|e_1\rangle$$

$$- a_1|101\rangle|e_1\rangle - a_1|110\rangle|e_1\rangle$$

$$- a_1|111\rangle|e_1\rangle = \frac{1}{2\sqrt{2}}(|000\rangle + |001\rangle$$

$$+ |010\rangle - |011\rangle + |100\rangle - |101\rangle - |110\rangle$$

$$- |111\rangle)_{123} \otimes |e_1\rangle_E \quad (9)$$

Although TP's collective attack cannot be detected by Alice and Bob, TP also cannot steal any private messages by measuring the probe qubits due to the non-entanglement relationship between the graph state and the probe state. That is to say, if TP wants to obtain private messages, TP's attack behavior will be detected by the classical participants with a non-zero probability.

Furthermore, this study analyzes the quantum Trojan horse attacks, which are common implementation-dependent attack strategies. However, the attacker can steal secret information about the participants only when the participants return the qubits, depending on the attacking manners of the quantum Trojan horse attacks. Because the qubit transmission in the proposed SQPC protocol is one-way, TP or any attacker cannot obtain any private message by using the quantum Trojan horse attacks. Therefore, the proposed SQPC protocol is free from quantum Trojan horse attacks.

## 5  CONCLUSION

This study uses the measurement property of the triangle graph state to propose a semi-quantum private comparison protocol that lets the two classical participants compare their private messages securely with the assistance of the semi-dishonest TP. The proposed SQPC protocol is lightweight and practical because the classical participants only equip two quantum capabilities, i.e., Hadamard operation and Z-basis measurement. Further, our future research issues will be whether to extend the proposed measurement

51

property to the n-qubit graph state and how to design an efficient multiparty semi-quantum private comparison protocol.

Acknowledgments

This research was partially supported by the National Science and Technology Council, Taiwan, R.O.C. (NSTC 111-2221-E-039-014, NSTC 110-2221-E-143-003, NSTC 110-2221-E-259-001, NSTC 110-2221-E-143-004, NSTC 110-2222-E-005-006, NSTC 110-2634-F-005-006, NSTC 111-2218-E-005-007-MBK, NSTC 111-2221-E-005-048, and NSTC 111-2221-E-025-010), Bureau of Energy, Ministry of Economic Affairs, Taiwan (Grant No. 111-E0208), and China Medical University, Taiwan (Grant No. CMU111-S-28).

# REFERENCES

[1] Yao A.C.: Protocols for secure computations. In: *Proceedings of 23rd IEEE Symposium on Foundations of Computer Science* (FOCS'82), p. 160. Washington, D.C. (1982)

[2] Boudot F., Schoenmakers B., Traoré J.: A fair and efficient solution to the socialist millionaires' problem. *Discrete Appl. Math.* 111(1–2), 23–36 (2001)

[3] Ioannis Ioannidis and Ananth Grama. An efficient protocol for Yao's millionaires' problem. In *Proceedings of the 36th Hawaii International Conference on System Sciences* 2003.

[4] Marc Fischlin. A cost-effective pay-per-multiplication comparison method for millionaires. In *Proceedings of the 2001 Conference on Topics in Cryptology: The Cryptographer's Track at RSA*, volume 2020 of LNCS, pages 457–472. Springer-Verlag, 2001.

[5] Berry Schoenmakers and Pim Tuyls. Practical two-party computation based on the conditional gate. In *Proceedings of Advances in Cryptology – ASIACRYPT '04*, volume 3329 of LNCS, pages 119–136. Springer-Verlag, 2004.

[6] Christian Cachin. Efficient private bidding and auctions with an oblivious third party. In *Proceedings of the 6th ACM conference on Computer and communications security-CCS '99*, pages 120–127. ACM Press, 1999.

[7] Lin, Hsiao-Ying, and Wen-Guey Tzeng. "An efficient solution to the millionaires' problem based on homomorphic encryption." *International Conference on Applied Cryptography and Network Security. Springer*, Berlin, Heidelberg, 2005.

[8] Yang Y.-G., Wen Q.-Y.: An efficient two-party quantum private comparison protocol with decoy photons and two-photon entanglement. *J. Phys. A Math. Theor.* 42(5), 055305 (2009)

[9] Yang Y.-G., Cao W.-F., Wen Q.-Y.: Secure quantum private comparison. *Phys. Scr.* 80(6), 065002 (2009)

[10] Chen X.B., Xu G., Niu X.X., Wen Q.Y., & Yang Y.X.: An efficient protocol for the private comparison of equal information based on the triplet entangled state and single-particle measurement. *Optics Communications*, 283(7), 1561–1565 (2010).

[11] Lin J., Tseng H.Y., & Hwang T. (2011). Intercept–resend attacks on Chen et al.'s quantum private comparison protocol and the improvements. *Optics Communications*, 284(9), 2412–2414.

[12] Jia H.-Y., Wen Q.-Y., Song T.-T., Gao F.: Quantum protocol for millionaire problem. *Opt. Commun.* 284(1), 545–549 (2011)

[13] Liu, W., Wang Y.-B., Jiang Z.-T.: An efficient protocol for the quantum private comparison of equality with W state. *Opt. Commun.* 284(12), 3160–3163 (2011)

[14] Luo Q.-B., Yang G.-W., She K., Niu W.-N., Wang, Y.-Q.: Multi-party quantum private comparison protocol based on d-dimensional entangled states. *Quantum Inf. Process.* 13(10), 2343–2352 (2014)

[15] Tseng H.-Y., Lin J., Hwang T.: New quantum private comparison protocol using EPR pairs. *Quantum Inf. Process.* 11(2), 373–384 (2012)

[16] Wen L., Yong-BinW., Wei C.: Quantum private comparison protocol based on Bell entangled states.Commun. *Theor. Phys.* 57(4), 583 (2012)

[17] Yang Y.-G., Xia J., Jia X., Shi L.: New quantum private comparison protocol without entanglement. *Int. J. Quantum Inf.* 10(06), 1250065 (2012)

[18] Chang Y.-J., Tsai C.-W., Hwang T.: Multi-user private comparison protocol using GHZ class states. *Quantum Inf. Process.* 12(2), 1077–1088 (2013)

[19] Zhang W.-W., Zhang K.-J.: Cryptanalysis and improvement of the quantum private comparison protocol with semi-honest third party. *Quantum Inf. Process.* 12(5), 1981–1990 (2013)

[20] Huang S.-L., Hwang T., Gope P.: Multi-party quantum private comparison protocol with an almost dishonest third party using GHZ states. *Int. J. Theor. Phys.* 55(6), 2969–2976 (2016)

[21] Hung S.-M., Hwang S.-L., Hwang T., Kao, S.-H.: Multiparty quantum private comparison with almost dishonest third parties for strangers. *Quantum Inf. Process.* 16(2), 36 (2017)

[22] Ye T.-Y., Ji Z.-X.: Multi-user quantum private comparison with scattered preparation and one-way convergent transmission of quantum states. *Sci. China Phys. Mech. Astron.* 60(9), 090312 (2017)

[23] Ting Xu, and Ye Tian-Yu. "Cryptanalysis and improvement for the quantum private comparison protocol based on triplet entangled state and single-particle measurement." *International Journal of Theoretical Physics* 56.3 (2017): 771–780.

[24] Liu B., Gao F., Jia H.-y., Huang W., Zhang, W.-W., Wen, Q.-Y.: Efficient quantum private comparison employing single photons and collective detection. *Quantum Inf. Process.* 12(2), 887–897 (2013)

[25] Ji, ZhaoXu, HuanGuo Zhang, and PeiRu Fan. "Two-party quantum private comparison protocol with maximally entangled seven-qubit state." *Modern Physics Letters A* 34.28:1950229 (2019)

[26] Fan, Peiru, *et al.* "Two-party quantum private comparison based on eight-qubit entangled state." *Modern Physics Letters A*: 2250026 (2022)

[27] Sun, Qi. "Quantum private comparison with six-particle maximally entangled states." *Modern Physics Letters A* (2022): 2250149.

[28] Boyer, M., Kenigsberg, D., Mor, T.: Quantum key distribution with classical Bob. *Phys. Rev. Lett.* 99, 140501 (2007)

[29] Hein, Marc, Jens Eisert, and Hans J. Briegel.: Multiparty entanglement in graph states. *Phys. Rev. A* 69.6 (2004): 062311.

System Innovation for a Troubled World – Lam et al. (Eds)
© 2024 the Author(s), ISBN: 978-1-032-60846-4

# Implementation of TISM and fuzzy MICMAC analysis in Jupyter notebook with Python

Weerapat Pookkaman & Taweesak Samanchuen*
*Technology of Information System Management Division, Faculty of Engineering, Mahidol University, Nakhon Pathom, Thailand*

Siriphong Sirisawat & Kotchaphun Boonkong
*Computer Department, Faculty of Science and Technology, Chiang Mai Rajabhat, Thailand*

ABSTRACT: Total Interpretive Structural Modeling (TISM) and fuzzy Matrixed Impacts Croisés Multiplication Appliquée á a Classement (fuzzy MICMAC) are factor analysis techniques to evaluate the relationships among the factors on one interest topic. More works have started to use these techniques as the primary analysis tool. This paper introduces a new implementation of TISM and fuzzy MICMAC analysis using Jupyter Notebook and Python. The motivation behind this implementation is the limited availability of suitable software tools for conducting this type of analysis. The methodology used to implement the function is detailed in the paper. The TISM analysis function is implemented using an iterative algorithm approach, while the fuzzy MICMAC function is implemented using a matrix approach. The function allows for user input of criteria and factors, and outputs interpretive structural modeling and cross-impact matrix calculations, as well as a stability graph for fuzzy MICMAC analysis. To validate the implementation, the results generated by the function were compared to those obtained in previous research. The comparison showed that our implementation provides accurate results that align with those generated by the previous research. Furthermore, the function was found to be easy to use and allowed researchers to input their data and obtain results quickly.

## 1 INTRODUCTION

Total Interpretive Structural Modeling (TISM) and fuzzy Matrixed Impacts Croisés Multiplication Appliquée á a Classement (fuzzy MICMAC) have established factor analysis techniques utilized in various research fields. They explicate the characteristic role of each factor relative to others and can identify significant factors for future system development. In industrial research, these techniques were applied to rank the factors affecting performance in the oil and automotive supply chain sectors (Bari 2022; Mathivathanan et al. 2022; Ray 2020). In the manufacturing sector, they were used to categorize factors related to intelligent production systems, environmentally friendly practices, and remanufacturing (Khan et al. 2022; Shukla *et al.* 2022; Ullah *et al.* 2021). In healthcare, TISM and fuzzy MICMAC were employed to identify critical success factors for medical cannabis traceability and clinical decision support systems using machine learning (Abujaber et al. 2022; Pookkaman *et al.* 2022), as well as to investigate variables impacting the success of e-learning (Ahmad et al. 2018).

There are several well-known model equations in use, including SEM and AHP. However, TISM and fuzzy MICMAC have been shown to outperform these methods. A key strength of these techniques is their ability to analyze relationships between factors. This requires specialized knowledge and expertise in the field, but can lead to more accurate and robust relationships. TISM, in particular, can identify the reasons for relationships between factors, while fuzzy MICMAC categorizes factors based on their interdependence and driving power. However, the detailed and complex analysis required by TISM and fuzzy MICMAC has led to incomplete studies of their theoretical variables. To address this issue, this article presents a methodology and pseudocode for computer-assisted analytical processes, reducing analytical mistakes and saving time for researchers. The key contribution of this paper is that it presents the first analytical process program for analyzing relationships using TISM and fuzzy MICMAC techniques.

The paper is structured into five sections. The first section provides an overview of the steps involved in using TISM and fuzzy MICMAC. Section 2 explains the details and significance of these methods. Section 3, the primary focus of this

*Corresponding Author: taweesak.sam@mahidol.ac.th

DOI: 10.1201/9781003460763-12

53

study, presents pseudocode for developers interested in evaluating this approach. Section 4 presents the results of the transitivity matrix and stabilized matrix processes. Finally, the paper concludes with a discussion and conclusion.

## 2 TISM AND FUZZY MICMAC PROCESS

In this section, we will outline the thirteen steps involved in the TISM and fuzzy MICMAC analysis processes, as shown in Figure 1. The TISM analysis operations are presented first, consisting of eight processes enclosed in black frames. This is followed by the fuzzy MICMAC processes, shown in blue frames.

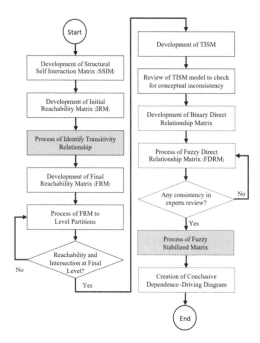

Figure 1.    TISM and fuzzy MICMAC processes.

This paper focuses on two critical processes: the identify transitivity relationship process and the fuzzy stabilized matrix process, highlighted in gray. These processes require careful analysis and can take a considerable amount of time to complete. However, omitting these steps can lead to inaccurate relationship analysis, which can result in incorrect conclusions. Therefore, these two processes are crucial for conducting a comprehensive and accurate TISM and fuzzy MICMAC analysis.

### 2.1   TISM

TISM is a hierarchical structural equation modeling method that was developed from Interpretive

Structural Modeling (ISM) (Shankar et al. 2018). However, one significant limitation of ISM is that it cannot provide operational interpretations for its links. To overcome this limitation, TISM was developed to provide precise interpretations for both links and nodes (Jena et al. 2016). The TISM model aims to improve the decision-making process by defining the explanations of all relationships along the respective links that connect each pair of elements. The TISM model was developed using expert interviews in which they were asked to agree using a pairwise comparison method on the relationships between the identified factors.

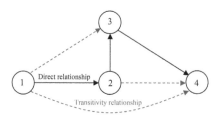

Figure 2.    Transitivity relationship.

### 2.2   Process of fuzzy MICMAC

Fuzzy MICMAC is a systematic assessment approach used to create complex structural equation modeling that utilizes the output of TISM as input. It is an indirect method for classifying factors based on their driving and dependent powers. Conventional MICMAC analysis uses a binary number to account for the parity of the relations between factors to categorize them. However, analyzing the relationship between factors in depth reveals a more complex level of relationship beyond the binary. Some relationships may be weak, strong, or very powerful (Hasanuzzaman et al. 2019). Therefore, fuzzy MICMAC analysis considers the strength of the connection between direct relationships in the binary direct reachability matrix. This approach increases the possibility of correctly analyzing the relationships between factors (Sushil 2012).

## 3   PROGRAMMING FOR TISM AND FUZZY MICMAC

This section discusses the significance of the process and pseudocode in program development. It is explained in two sections: the Identify Transitivity Relationship Process in TISM and the fuzzy stabilized matrix process in fuzzy MICMAC.

Overall, the development of computer-assisted analytical processes with pseudocode for these two processes will reduce the time required for analysis, decrease the likelihood of errors, and provide clear interpretations of the results. It will also make it easier for researchers to replicate the analysis and compare results across studies.

## 3.1 *Identify transitivity relationships process*

The first process, the identification of a transitivity relationship, is a crucial step in TISM. It identifies the transitive relationships between factors and determines their levels of interdependence, as shown in Figure 2. This process involves a series of calculations that are time-consuming and can be mistaken if done manually. Therefore, developing a computer-assisted analytical process with pseudocode will reduce the time and risk of mistakes in the analysis. It is a subprocess of TISM for finding transitivity relationships between factors. This process is carried out after a direct correlation between the factors has been established based on the experts' opinions.

In this section, we present the pseudocode for identifying transitivity relationships. Our proposed method uses the Floyd-Warshall algorithm, which was introduced by Floyd (Floyd 1962) and is based on Warshall's algorithm (Warshall 1962), to detect transitive relationships. This algorithm has been widely accepted and frequently employed for identifying relationships between variables due to its reliability.

---

**Algorithm 1:** Identifying Transitivity Relationships

---

INPUT: A matrix of direct relationship (**R**)
OUTPUT: A transitivity matrix (**T**)
Start
    n = size of R
    for k=0 to n-1
        for i=0 to n-1
            for j=0 to n-1
                R[i][j] = R[i][j] or (R[i][k] and R[k][j])
    T = R
    return T
End

---

## 3.2 *Fuzzy stabilized matrix process*

The second process is the fuzzy stabilized matrix process in fuzzy MICMAC. It is a complex process that involves categorizing factors based on their driving and dependent powers. This process can be prone to errors if not done carefully, and the results can be difficult to interpret. Therefore, developing a computer-assisted analytical process with pseudocode will reduce the risk of errors and provide a clear interpretation of the results.

A fuzzy MICMAC stabilized matrix was used to put together fuzzy relationships to figure out how the direct and indirect relationships between

the factors affected the whole (Hasanuzzaman *et al.* 2019). This process, if the complex matrix, number of factors, and their relationships are large, will be very tough. Thus, using the programming will make matrix stabilization simple, quick, and accurate. The formula used to calculate the stabilized matrix is as follows:

$$m_c(i,j) = \max_{k=1}^{n}[\min\{m_1(i,k), m_{c-1}(k),j)\}],$$

$$i, j = 1, 2, \ldots, n; c = 2, 3, \ldots$$

where $m_c(i,k)$ represents the direct relationship strength between parameters $i$ and $k$.

In this section, we provide the pseudocode for the fuzzy stabilized matrix based on a review of several literature sources, with a particular emphasis on research in framework development (Hasanuzzaman *et al.* 2019). The pseudocode outlines the steps involved in computing the fuzzy MICMAC and is presented below for clarity:

---

**Algorithm 2:** Fuzzy Stabilized Matrix

---

INPUT: A fuzzy matrix (**F**)
OUTPUT: A fuzzy stabilized matrix (**FS**)
Start
    n = size of F
    Initialize F_PREV matrix of size (n, n) with 0
    while F != F_PREV
        F_PREV = F
        for i=0 to n-1
            for j=0 to n-1
            num_arr = []
            for k=0 to n-1
                num_arr.append(min(F[i][k], F[k][j]))
            F[i][j] = max(num_arr)
    FS = F
    return FS
End

---

# 4 RESULT

The results of TISM and fuzzy MICMAC processing on the stabilized matrix are demonstrated in this section using a program developed from the pseudocode discussed in the previous section. This program facilitates the fast and accurate processing of outcomes.

## 4.1 *TISM result*

This section includes two figures: Figure 3 depicts the input matrix used to identify transitivity relationships, while Figure 4 displays the output after applying the pseudocode to generate transitivity relationships between factors. The data presented is derived from a study that examined the factors

Input data:
```
[[1 1 0 1 0 1 0 1 0 1 0 1 0 0 0 0]
 [0 1 0 0 0 0 0 0 0 0 1 0 0 0 0 0]
 [0 0 1 1 0 0 1 0 1 0 1 0 0 0 0 0]
 [0 0 1 1 0 0 0 0 1 0 0 0 0 0 0 0]
 [0 0 0 0 1 0 0 0 1 0 0 0 0 0 0 0]
 [0 0 0 0 0 1 0 1 0 1 1 1 1 1 1]
 [0 0 1 0 1 0 1 0 1 0 0 0 0 0 0 0]
 [0 0 0 0 0 0 0 0 1 1 0 0 0 0 0 0]
 [0 0 0 0 0 0 0 0 1 0 0 0 0 0 0 0]
 [0 0 0 0 0 0 1 1 1 1 0 0 0 0 0]
 [1 0 0 0 0 0 0 0 0 0 0 1 0 0 0]
 [1 0 0 0 0 1 0 0 0 0 0 0 1 1 0]
 [0 0 0 0 0 0 0 0 0 0 1 0 0 1 0]
 [1 0 0 0 0 1 0 1 0 0 0 0 0 0 1]]
```

Figure 3.   Matrix for identify transitivity relationship.

Trasitivity matrix:
```
[[1 1 1 1 1 1 1 1 1 1 1 1 1 1]
 [0 1 1 1 1 0 1 1 1 0 0 0 0]
 [0 0 1 1 1 0 1 0 1 0 0 0 0 0]
 [0 0 1 1 1 0 1 0 1 0 0 0 0 0]
 [0 0 0 0 1 0 0 0 1 0 0 0 0 0]
 [1 1 1 1 1 1 1 1 1 1 1 1 1 1]
 [0 0 1 1 1 0 1 0 1 0 0 0 0 0]
 [0 0 0 0 0 0 0 0 1 1 0 0 0 0]
 [0 0 0 0 0 0 0 0 1 0 0 0 0 0]
 [0 0 1 1 1 0 1 1 1 0 0 0 0]
 [1 1 1 1 1 1 1 1 1 1 1 1 1 1]
 [1 1 1 1 1 1 1 1 1 1 1 1 1 1]
 [0 0 1 1 1 0 1 1 1 0 0 1 0]
 [1 1 1 1 1 1 1 1 1 1 1 1 1 1]]
```

Figure 4.   Transitivity matrix.

influencing the medicinal cannabis traceability system (Pookkaman et al. 2022).

### 4.2   *Fuzzy stabilized matrix result*

We utilized expert assessments from a journal that investigated the factors affecting consumers' beef purchasing behavior (Mishra et al. 2017) as the initial value for our analysis, as shown in Figure 5. The results of the stabilized matrix analysis are presented in Figure 6. We also developed software that can identify stable values occurring in each cycle and present them in a graph, as shown in Figure 7. The graph fluctuates slightly, with a cumulative value of either 23.1 or 23.5, depending on whether an even or odd number of cycles was

```
[[0.  0.9 0.  0.7 0.  0.  0.  0.  0.7 0.  0.5]
 [0.9 0.  0.  0.5 0.  0.  0.  0.  0.  0.  0. ]
 [0.5 0.3 0.  0.5 0.  0.  0.  0.7 0.  0.  0. ]
 [0.  0.  0.  0.  0.  0.  0.  0.  0.  0.  0. ]
 [0.  0.  0.  0.1 0.  0.  0.1 0.  0.  0.  0. ]
 [0.5 0.5 0.  0.5 0.  0.  0.  0.  0.  0.  0.7]
 [0.  0.  0.  0.  0.1 0.  0.  0.  0.  0.  0. ]
 [0.  0.  0.  0.1 0.  0.  0.  0.  0.  0.  0. ]
 [0.5 0.  0.  0.5 0.  0.  0.  0.  0.  0.  0. ]
 [0.7 0.  0.  0.9 0.  0.  0.  0.  0.  0.  0. ]
 [0.5 0.  0.  0.3 0.  0.7 0.  0.  0.  0.  0. ]]
```

Figure 5.   Initial value of processing.

```
[[0.9 0.5 0.  0.5 0.  0.5 0.  0.  0.5 0.  0.5]
 [0.5 0.9 0.  0.7 0.  0.5 0.  0.  0.7 0.  0.5]
 [0.5 0.5 0.  0.5 0.  0.5 0.  0.  0.5 0.  0.5]
 [0.  0.  0.  0.  0.  0.  0.  0.  0.  0.  0. ]
 [0.  0.  0.  0.  0.1 0.  0.  0.  0.  0.  0. ]
 [0.5 0.5 0.  0.5 0.  0.7 0.  0.  0.5 0.  0.5]
 [0.  0.  0.  0.1 0.  0.  0.1 0.  0.  0.  0. ]
 [0.  0.  0.  0.  0.  0.  0.  0.  0.  0.  0. ]
 [0.5 0.5 0.  0.5 0.  0.5 0.  0.  0.5 0.  0.5]
 [0.5 0.7 0.  0.7 0.  0.5 0.  0.  0.7 0.  0.5]
 [0.5 0.5 0.  0.5 0.  0.5 0.  0.  0.5 0.  0.7]]
```

Figure 6.   Stabilized matrix result.

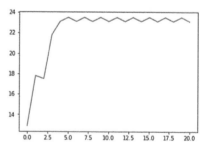

Figure 7.   Stability check graph of the stabilized process.

conducted. However, this difference did not significantly impact the expression of the variables' relationships, as it was very small.

## 5   DISCUSS AND CONCLUSION

This paper introduces a new implementation of TISM and fuzzy MICMAC analysis using Jupyter Notebook and Python. These analysis techniques are used to evaluate the relationships among factors on a given topic, and their use has become increasingly prevalent in recent years. The motivation behind this implementation is the limited availability of suitable software tools for conducting this type of analysis.

The methodology used to implement the function is detailed in the paper, with the TISM analysis function implemented using an iterative algorithm approach and the fuzzy MICMAC function implemented using a matrix approach. The function allows for user input of criteria and factors and outputs interpretive structural modeling and cross-impact matrix calculations, as well as a stability graph for fuzzy MICMAC analysis. To validate the implementation, the results generated by the function were compared to those obtained in previous research. The comparison demonstrated that our implementation provides accurate results that align with those generated by previous research. Furthermore, the function was found to be user-friendly, enabling researchers to input their data and obtain results quickly.

Overall, this study presents a valuable contribution to the field of analysis techniques, providing an easy-to-use implementation of TISM and fuzzy MICMAC analysis that can generate accurate results. The availability of this tool is expected to facilitate the use of these analysis techniques in future research.

## ACKNOWLEDGMENT

This work was supported in part by a Ph.D. scholarship from the Ministry of Higher Education, Science, Research, and Innovation (MHESI) of the Royal Thai Government.

## REFERENCES

Abujaber A.A., Nashwan A.J. and Fadlalla A., "Enabling the adoption of machine learning in clinical decision support: A total interpretive structural modeling approach," *Informatics in Medicine Unlocked*, vol. 33, pp. 101090, 2022.

Ahmad N., Quadri N.N., Qureshi M.R.N. and Alam M.M., "Relationship modeling of critical success factors for enhancing sustainability and performance in e-learning," *Sustainability*, vol. 10, no. 12, pp. 4776, 2018.

Bari A.M., Siraj M.T., Paul S.K. and Khan S.A., "A hybrid multi-criteria decision-making approach for analysing operational hazards in heavy fuel oil-based power plants," *Decision Analytics Journal*, vol. 3, pp. 100069, 2022.

Floyd R.W., "Algorithm 97: shortest path," *Communications of the ACM*, vol. 5, no. 6, pp. 345, 1962.

Hasanuzzaman and Bhar C., "Development of a framework for sustainable improvement in performance of coal mining operations," *Clean Technologies and Environmental Policy*, vol. 21, pp. 1091–1113, 2019.

Jena J., Fulzele V., Gupta R., Sherwani F., Shankar R. and Sidharth S., "A TISM modeling of critical success factors of smartphone manufacturing ecosystem in India," *Journal of Advances in Management Research*, vol. 13, no. 2, pp. 203–224, 2016.

Khan S., Haleem A. and Fatma N., "Effective adoption of remanufacturing practices: a step towards circular economy," *Journal of Remanufacturing*, vol. 12, no. 2, pp. 167–185, 2022.

Mathivathanan D., Agarwal V., Mathiyazhagan K., Saikouk T. and Appolloni A., "Modeling the pressures for sustainability adoption in the Indian automotive context," *Journal of Cleaner Production*, vol. 342, pp. 130972, 2022.

Mishra N., Singh A., Rana N.P. and Dwivedi Y.K., "Interpretive structural modelling and fuzzy MICMAC approaches for customer centric beef supply chain: application of a big data technique," *Production Planning & Control*, vol. 28, no. 11–12, pp. 945–963, 2017.

Pookkaman W. and Samanchuen T., "An innovation framework of medical organic cannabis traceability in digital supply chain," *Journal of Open Innovation: Technology, Market, and Complexity*, vol. 8, no. 4, pp. 196, 2022.

Ray A. and Khaba S., "Study of ethical issues of green procurement in Indian automobile industry using integrated ISM-fuzzy MICMAC–AHP–VIKOR," *Journal of Global Operations and Strategic Sourcing*, vol. 13, no. 3, pp. 251–274, 2020.

Shankar R., Gupta R. and Pathak D. K. "Modeling critical success factors of traceability for food logistics system," *Transportation Research Part E: Logistics and Transportation Review*, vol. 119, pp. 205–222, 2018.

Shukla M. and Shankar R., "An extended technology-organization-environment framework to investigate smart manufacturing system implementation in small and medium enterprises," *Computers & Industrial Engineering*, vol. 163, pp. 107865, 2022.

Sushil S., "Interpreting the interpretive structural model," *Global Journal of Flexible Systems Management*, vol. 13, no. 2, pp. 87–106, 2012.

Ullah S., Khan F. U. and Ahmad N., "Promoting sustainability through green innovation adoption: a case of manufacturing industry," *Environmental Science and Pollution Research*, pp. 1–21, 2022.

Warshall S., "A theorem on boolean matrices," *Journal of the ACM (JACM)*, vol. 9, no. 1, pp. 11–12, 1962.

System Innovation for a Troubled World – Lam et al. (Eds)
© 2024 the Author(s), ISBN: 978-1-032-60846-4

# Alpha-boost: A fast algorithm for mining workflow nets

Yu-Xiang Zou & Jason Lin*
*Department of Computer Science and Engineering, National Chung Hsing University, Taichung, Taiwan*

Chia-Wei Tsai
*Department of Computer Science and Information Engineering, National Taichung University of Science and Technology, Taichung, Taiwan*

Chun-Wei Yang
*Master Program for Digital Health Innovation, College of Humanities and Sciences, China Medical University, Taichung, Taiwan*

ABSTRACT: Process mining is significant for visualizing the workflow structure of event logs stored in information systems. However, nearly no existing works have discussed the efficiency of executing the process mining algorithm on large datasets of event logs. In this paper, we present an enhancement to the Alpha algorithm proposed by Aalst et al. in 2004. The Alpha algorithm is the first and one of the most popular techniques for converting event logs into Petri nets in the process mining field. This study discovered that when analyzing the synthesis relations between events, the Alpha algorithm first enumerates all possible sets and then deletes unnecessary sets one by one. This approach repeatedly enumerates many redundant sets that increase the time cost during execution and is not suitable for big data analysis. Therefore, we propose a so-called Alpha-boost algorithm that applies the Bron-Kerbosch algorithm in graph theory to address this issue. The proposed algorithm directly generates the local maximum sets, thereby mitigating the need for superfluous enumeration. Compared to the original Alpha algorithm, the time complexity of the proposed Alpha-boost algorithm requires only $\left(\frac{3}{8}\right)^{\frac{n}{3}}$ times of the original Alpha algorithm, resulting in a significant reduction in execution time. Furthermore, experimental results have shown that the Alpha-boost algorithm consistently performs shorter execution times than the baseline Alpha algorithm on both the synthetic and the real-life datasets. These results align with the theoretical analysis of time complexity.

*Keywords*: Process mining, Alpha algorithm, Petri net, Bron–Kerbosch algorithm

## 1 INTRODUCTION

Process mining is a critical discipline that enables the comprehensive understanding of workflows and the auditing of operational activities within businesses. Due to their concurrent property, Petri nets are very suitable for the representation of business models. The $\alpha$-series algorithms [1–3] are the first to provide theoretical proof to recover workflow nets from complete logs. However, it takes more than 10 minutes to create Petri nets on real-world logs where there are about 400 event types. The most computationally expansive operation is the places synthesis process, which is formulated as the enumeration of the local maximal constrained independent set pair (LMCISP) in this paper.

The existing solution is a growing-based method, where there are many unnecessary non-maximal enumerations to get the maximal LMCISP. Besides, the existing solution faces the challenge of duplication enumeration. Adding duplication-checking will have side effects of overhead since the candidate set is very large, while no duplication-checking will result in unnecessary calculation. Instead, we propose a procedure to first enumerate the left independent sets and generate corresponding local maximal right independent sets through the existing maximal clique enumeration (MCE) solution. The MCE solution, Bron–Kerbosh algorithm [4], mitigates the unnecessary non-maximal enumeration. Our framework for enumerating the left independent sets does not exhibit any issues of duplication. The superiority of the proposed algorithm has also been demonstrated through experiments conducted on both simulated and real-world data.

The remainder of this paper is organized as follows: Section 2 provides an overview of existing research relevant to the background of this work, while Section 3 elucidates the formulation of the

---

*Corresponding Author: jasonlin@nchu.edu.tw

DOI: 10.1201/9781003460763-13

LMCISP enumeration problem. In Section 4, we further introduce our algorithm and its implementation, and the experiment results and analysis are presented in Section 5. Finally, we briefly summarize our findings and contributions in this paper.

## 2 RELATED WORK

In this section, we survey two related domains: the MCE and the biclique set enumeration. Then, we present the related applications of our work.

A survey on the MCE problem can be found in [5]. The Bron–Kerbosh (BK) algorithm [4] is a backtracking algorithm that is more efficient than any other alternatives [6]. Kose [7] also proposed a growing algorithm that uses the cliques of size $k$ to generate cliques of size $k + 1$. We apply similar concepts in the enumeration of independent sets for different sizes, which is like checking the maximal property from a larger clique (pair) to a smaller clique (pair) by redefining the edges as those undirected relations.

The biclique set enumeration problem [8] differs from our problem in that it involves only one type of undirected relation, where every element of the first independent set is connected to every element of the second independent set. This is in contrast to our problem, which may involve multiple types of undirected relations. The two sets made up of the biclique set are also independent sets with no relation between any pair of elements within each set. However, using biclique set enumeration exclusively with the between independent set relation will make it difficult to satisfy the undirected relations within the independent set while maintaining maximality at the same time.

LMCISP is the core of the alpha series algorithm [1–3] for place synthesis of Petri nets. Petri nets is a very useful mathematical framework to describe concurrent, asynchronous, distributed, parallel, and stochastic systems [9]. The Petri nets is widely used in applications such as distributed database system, performance evaluation, communication protocol, programmable logic, and VLSI arrays [9].

## 3 PROBLEM FORMULATION

Given an element set $\mathcal{E}$, the independent set $\mathcal{S} \subset \mathcal{E}$ is a set of elements such that every two elements $s, s' \in \mathcal{S}$ satisfy the non-connected relation $r_n(s, s')$. Another important structure is the constrained independent set pairs (CISP) $(\mathcal{S}_1, \mathcal{S}_2)$, with every element pair constructed from one element $s_1 \in \mathcal{S}_1$ and the other element $s_2 \in \mathcal{S}_2$, satisfying the precede (follow) relation $r_p(s_1, s_2)$. $\mathcal{S}_1$ and $\mathcal{S}_2$ are called the left independent set (LIS) and the right

independent set (RIS), respectively. We further constrain that no element pair can satisfy both the non-connected relation and the precede (follow) relation at the same time.

Given a CISP $(\mathcal{S}_1, \mathcal{S}_2)$, it has the property that $(\mathcal{S}_1', \mathcal{S}_2')$ with $\mathcal{S}_1' \subseteq \mathcal{S}_1$ and $\mathcal{S}_2' \subseteq \mathcal{S}_2$ is also a CISP. This property leads to the attempt to find the local maximal CISPs (LMCISP), from which all the CISPs could be enumerated. The LMCISP is defined as a CISP $(\mathcal{S}_1, \mathcal{S}_2)$ with $\mathcal{S}_1 \subseteq \mathcal{S}_1'$, $\mathcal{S}_2 \subseteq \mathcal{S}_2'$, and $\left(\mathcal{S}_1', \mathcal{S}_2'\right)$ is a CISP such that $(\mathcal{S}_1, \mathcal{S}_2) = \left(\mathcal{S}_1', \mathcal{S}_2'\right)$. Since LMCISP is not unique, it makes the searching process more difficult.

Figure 1 shows an example to illustrate the definition of LMCISP. The element set is defined as $\mathcal{E} = \{a, b, c, d, e\}$. On the top two blocks, all pairs satisfying the non-connected relation and the precede (follow) relation are enumerated. Based on the non-connected relation, we could enumerate all independent sets as shown in the left-bottom block. Since each element $\alpha$ satisfies $r_n(\alpha, \alpha)$, every set consisting of one element $\{\alpha\}$ is an independent set. The set consisting of two elements $\{a, d\}$ in Figure 1 is an independent set because it has the following four relations: $r_n\{a, a\}$, $r_n\{a, d\}$, $r_n\{d, a\}$, and $r_n\{d, d\}$. CISPs are constructed based on the independent sets and the precede (follow) relation. For example, the pair $(\{a\}, \{b, e\})$ in Figure 1 is a CISP because of $r_p(a, b)$ and $r_p(a, e)$. The maximal CISP can be further discovered by checking the relation between CISPs as shown in the gray area. Note that $(\{a\}, \{b\})$ is not maximal due to $(\{a\}, \{b, e\})$ is a CISP.

Event Log $= \{abcd, acbd, aed\}$

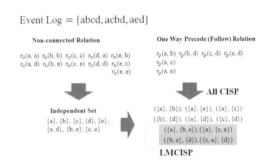

Figure 1. Example of local maximal CISP generation.

The LMCISP is useful in the Petri-Nets place synthesis process of $\alpha$-series algorithms, with many applications in business process mining and concurrent modeling. The existing algorithm needs to enumerate all CISPs, and each CISP needs to check whether they are maximal among a large subset of all CISPs in a dynamic queue. In this paper, the acceleration for the enumeration of LMCISP has been proposed from two aspects. First, we reduce unnecessary enumeration by only enumerating the left set and find the corresponding maximal right independent set (MRIS). This process guarantees all LMCISPs are included. Second, we limit the subset of CISP to be checked to determine the local maximal property of a CISP, thus, reducing the computational complexity.

# 4 ALGORITHM DESCRIPTION

This section will first introduce the local maximal RIS (LMRIS). The LMRIS is useful for reducing the enumeration given an LIS. We will then introduce the LMCISP enumeration algorithm, which is based on the LMRIS enumeration approach and incorporates efficient local maximum checking. Finally, we provide proof that our algorithm guarantees complete enumeration of all LMCISPs. To facilitate the introduction of the algorithm, Table 1 lists the internal data when the LIS algorithm is applied to the example in Figure 1. Detailed explanations will be provided in the following sections.

Table 1.    The enumeration process of Figure 1.

|  | LIS | LMRIS | LMCISP |
|---|---|---|---|
|  | {a} | {b, e}, {c, e} | ({a}, {b, e})<br>({a}, {c, e}) |
| $k = 1$ | →{b} | {d} |  |
|  | {c}← | {d} |  |
|  | {d} | Empty |  |
|  | →{e}← | {d} |  |
| $k = 2$ | {a, d} | Empty |  |
|  | {b, e} | {d} | ({b, e}, {d}) |
|  | {c, e}← | {d} | ({c, e}, {d}) |

$\vdots$

## 4.1 Local maximal right independent set

For an independent set $S_1$, we will call $S_2$ the LMRIS of $S_1$ if the following conditions hold:

- $(S_1, S_2)$ is a CISP.
- $!\exists S'$ satisfying $S_2 \subset S'$ (strict subset) such that $(S_1, S')$ is also CISP.

Consider an independent set $S_2$ as one of the LMRIS of $S_1$, then the pair $(S_1, S_2)$ is called the right local maximal CISP (RLMCISP). Note that the term "local maximal" implies there might be multiple LMRISs for each LIS.

In the example of Figure 1, there are two LMRISs {b, e} and {c, e} for a LIS {a}. This LMRIS concept has two useful properties. First, by only enumerating the MRIS, we don't leave out any LMCISPs. This property will be proved later. Second, the number of enumerations could be reduced. By enumerating the LMRISs for the LIS {a}, we only need to enumerate two LMRISs to find the two candidates ({a}, {b, e}) and ({a}, {c, e}) for LMCISP, instead of five CISP

candidates: ({a}, {b}),  ({a}, {e}),  ({a}, {c}), ({a}, {b, e}), and ({a}, {c, e}). This advantage is more evident when the size of the independent set is large. Given one LMRIS of size $n$, we needed $2^n$ enumeration in the past.

## 4.2 LMCISP enumeration

The workflow of the LMCISP enumeration process is as shown in Algorithm 1. It has four parts: the generation of LISs (line 2), loop terminate condition (lines 3-4), LMRIS creation (lines 5-8), local maximum checking (lines 10-14), and the collection of LMCISP (lines 15-22). We will explain the algorithm in the following paragraphs with illustrations using the example in Figure 1.

---

**Algorithm 1:** LMCISP Enumeration

---

1.   For $k = 1 : |E|$
2.     $\mathbb{S}_k$ = Independent Sets of size $k$
3.     If $\mathbb{S}_k$ is empty:
4.       break
5.     For S in $\mathbb{S}_k$:
6.       $LIS2LMRISs(S)$ = LMRISs of Independent Set S
7.       For LMRIS in $LIS2LMRISs(S)$:
8.         $Mark((S, \text{LMRIS}))$ = True
9.     If $k > 1$:
10.      For S in $\mathbb{S}_k$
11.        For $\epsilon \in$ S:
12.          For LMRIS in $LIS2LMRISs(S \backslash \{\epsilon\})$
13.            If LMRIS in $LIS2LMRISs(S)$:
14.              $Mark((S \backslash \{\epsilon\}, \text{LMRIS}))$ = False
15.      For S in $\mathbb{S}_{k-1}$:
16.        For LMRIS in $LIS2LMRISs(S)$:
17.          If $Mark((S, \text{LMRIS}))$ is True:
18.            Add (S, LMRIS) as LMCISP
19.    For S in $\mathbb{S}_k$:
20.      For LMRIS in $LIS2LMRISs(S)$:
21.        If $Mark((S, \text{LMRIS}))$ is True:
22.          Add (S, LMRIS) as LMCISP

---

We first iterate $k$ from 1 to $\mathcal{E}$ as the size of the LIS. In each iteration, we enumerate independent sets of size $k$, $\mathbb{S}_k$, as the LISs. For the example in Figure 1, when $k = 1$, the independent sets are {a}, {b}, {c}, {d}, and {e}. For each LIS $S \in \mathbb{S}_k$, the corresponding set LIS2LMRIS($S$) of LMRISs is obtained. For example, given the set {a} as the LIS, we have {b, e} and {c, e} as the LMRISs.

The further step in lines 10-13 in each iteration is to check the local maximum of the independent set pairs with size $k - 1$ LIS. We skip the condition $k = 1$ since the size of LIS would be zero. In lines 2-8, we enumerated all LISs of size $k$ and constructed the corresponding LMRISs. This information is used to determine whether an LIS with size $k - 1$ and its corresponding LMRIS are not

60

LMCISP. For each size $k$ LIS, the LISs with size $k-1$ are obtained by removing one element in the original set as shown in lines 10-11. Then, for each size $k-1$ LIS, we check whether each LMRIS is not feasible to construct LMCISP and the condition is that the LMRIS of size $k-1$ LIS is also the LMRIS of size $k$ LIS. All pairs that are not marked as invalid are considered LMCISP. Let us take the LIS $\{b, e\}$ as an example. One of its subsets of size $k-1$, $\{b\}$, has only one LMRIS, $\{d\}$. However, since $\{d\}$ is also the LMRIS of the LIS $\{b, e\}$, this makes the CISP $(\{b\}, \{e\})$ not local maximal, and it will be marked as an invalid pair. All LMCISPs will eventually be extracted at the final stage (lines 15-22), and the code snippet (lines 19-22) is used for handling the boundary condition.

### 4.3 Implementation details

In this section, we will introduce some notations to facilitate a better explanation. Then, we will present the independent set enumeration procedure as the algorithm for generating the LIS and LMRIS for the enumeration of LMCISP.

To make the algorithm easier to understand, an arbitrary order relation "$<$" is defined over a pair of elements $(x, y)$, where $< (x, y)$ represents event $x$ followed by event $y$ in the event log. Let element $\epsilon \in \mathcal{E}$. The set $P(\epsilon) = \{\epsilon' | r_p(\epsilon, \epsilon')\}$ contains all elements satisfying the precede (follow) relation. Given a set $\mathcal{S}$, we define $\mathbb{P}(\mathcal{S}) = \{\epsilon' | \forall \epsilon \in \mathcal{S}, r_p(\epsilon, \epsilon')\}$. To avoid duplicate enumeration, we consider the order relation and define the set $P_<(\epsilon) = \{\epsilon' | r_p(\epsilon, \epsilon') \wedge < (\epsilon, \epsilon')\}$. Similarly, the set of elements satisfying the precede (follow) relation and order relation with respect to a set of elements $\mathcal{S}$ is defined as $\mathbb{P}_<(\mathcal{S}) = \{\epsilon' | \forall \epsilon \in \mathcal{S}, r_p(\epsilon, \epsilon') \wedge < (\epsilon, \epsilon')\}$.

#### 4.3.1 Enumeration of size $k$ LISs

To enumerate the LISs with increasing size, we follow a strategy similar to Kose [7] et al.'s method, which enumerates a maximal clique of size $k+1$ from a clique of size $k$. The pseudocode in Algorithm 2 will first be presented with explanations, followed by formal proof of the enumeration's correctness and completeness.

---

**Algorithm 2:** LIS Enumeration

---

1. For $\epsilon \in \mathcal{E}$:
2.     Add $\{\epsilon\}$ to $\mathbb{S}_1$
3.     Initialize $\mathbb{N}(\{\epsilon\}) = N(\epsilon)$
4. For $k = 2: |\mathcal{E}|$
5.     For $\mathcal{S} \in \mathbb{S}_{k-1}$:
6.         For $\epsilon \in \mathbb{N}(\mathcal{S})$:
7.             Add $\mathcal{S} \cup \{\epsilon\}$ to $\mathbb{S}_k$
8.             $\mathbb{N}(\mathcal{S} \cup \{\epsilon\}) \leftarrow \mathbb{N}(\mathcal{S}) \cap N(\{\epsilon\})$

---

Initially, each element is considered an independent set in lines 1-3. From lines 4-8, we construct an independent set of size $k$ by combining independent sets of size $k-1$.

Since there are no duplicates at the initial setting, we only add elements with higher order to an existing independent set, and the added element will have the highest order in the newly created independent set. If two independent sets are duplicated, their highest order element is the same, which indicates the independent sets they construct from are the same. Note that given an independent set, we will not create duplicated independent sets of larger sizes.

Our next step is to prove that all independent sets have been enumerated using mathematical induction. It can be proven by showing all independent sets of size $k$ are enumerated. For $k = 1$, a base case has satisfied the condition. Suppose all independent set of size $k-1$ have been enumerated. We want to prove that all independent sets have been enumerated for size $k$ as well. If there is an independent set of size $k$ that is not enumerated. By removing the highest-order element $\epsilon_h$, it is an independent set of size $k-1$ $\mathcal{S}_{k-1}$, and $\epsilon_h \in \mathbb{P}_<(\mathcal{S}_{k-1})$. Given that all size $k-1$ independent sets should already be enumerated. That is, $\mathcal{S}_{k-1}$ should be in $\mathbb{S}_{k-1}$. According to the construction rule, the independent set of size $k$ should be enumerated as well, which leads to a contradiction.

#### 4.3.2 LMRIS generation

The enumeration of LMRIS has two constraints: (1) it must have the precede (follow) relation with LIS; (2) it should be a maximal independent set. Given a LIS $\mathcal{S}$, we first get all elements $\mathbb{P}(\mathcal{S})$ satisfying the precede (follow) relation. Then, we apply the BK algorithm with pivot vertex to find the maximal independent sets in the $\mathbb{P}(\mathcal{S})$. The BK algorithm is a recursive algorithm with three sets as the parameters: R, P, and X. Given the three sets, the algorithm finds the maximal independent sets that include all elements in R, some of the elements in P, and none of the elements in X. Therefore, the function call BronKerbosch $(\varnothing, \mathbb{P}(\mathcal{S}), \varnothing)$ will gain all maximal independent sets from $\mathbb{P}(\mathcal{S})$ as shown in Algorithm 3. The notation $N(u)$ in the algorithm indicates the neighbor of $u$, which are the elements satisfying the non-connected relation with respect to $u$.

---

**Algorithm 3:** LMRIS Enumeration

---

1. BronKerbosch(R, P, X) :
2.     If (P is $\varnothing$ and X is $\varnothing$)
3.         Report R as maximal independent set
4.     Choose a pivot vertex $u \in$ P $\cup$ X

---

5. For each vertex $v \in P \backslash N(u)$:
6. BronKerbosch($R \cup \{v\}, P \cap N(v), X \cap N(v)$)
7. $P = P \backslash \{v\}$
8. $X = X \cup \{v\}$

## 5 EXPERIMENT AND PERFORMANCE ANALYSIS

This section first introduces the datasets used for experiments, followed by the performance criteria used for evaluation. We then present and analyze the empirical results obtained by evaluating our algorithm on both simulated and real-world datasets.

### 5.1 Data preparation

For the simulated data, we create a scenario where there is only one LMCISP with a size of both LIS and RIS as $n$, where $n \in$. [3,11] This test case will demonstrate the superiority of our algorithm for handling large LMCISP. This dataset is relatively simple to validate the correctness of the theoretical analysis.

We also tested our algorithm on the real data from BPI 2017, BPI 2019 challenges[1], and the sample dataset from Disco [10]. The information on these datasets is shown in Table 2.

Table 2. The information of real-life datasets.

|  | Event Classes | Total Events | Traces |
|---|---|---|---|
| BPI 2019 | 40 | 1048575 | 3545 |
| BPI 2017 | 26 | 1048575 | 144 |
| Purchasing Example | 24 | 9119 | 608 |

### 5.2 Performance measurement and execution environment

The experimental part of this paper compares the existing Alpha miner [1] and the proposed Alpha-boost algorithms, focusing on the execution time. The experiments were conducted on a Mac OS computer system with a dual-core processor running at 2.3 GHz, 8 GB of memory, and an Intel Iris Plus Graphics 640 graphics card. Both algorithms were executed using a single process and a single thread, and the first execution time was recorded as the result.

### 5.3 Experimental results

Figure 2 shows the performance comparison results for the simulated dataset. As the size of the independent set increases, there is a significant improvement in the execution efficiency, and the rate of improvement is exponential. At an independent set size of 11, Alpha-boost is over 1000 milliseconds faster than Alpha miner. While Alpha miner enumerates all sets using a brute force approach, it may be faster than Alpha-boost for very small datasets. However, as the dataset size increases slightly, the time advantage of Alpha-boost becomes evident.

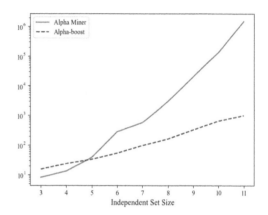

Figure 2. Comparison of execution times (simulation dataset).

Figures 3–5 show the execution results of real-life datasets, where the y-axis represents the execution time, and the x-axis represents the number of traces in the dataset. The solid line represents Alpha miner, and the dashed line represents Alpha-boost. From the three figures, it is evident that Alpha-boost outperforms Alpha miner in terms of execution efficiency for all datasets.

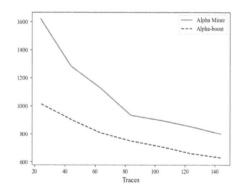

Figure 3. Comparison of execution times (BPI 2017 dataset).

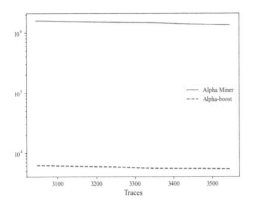

Figure 4. Comparison of execution times (BPI 2019 dataset).

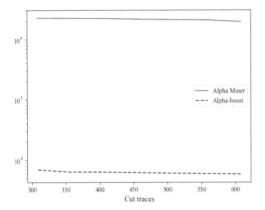

Figure 5. Comparison of execution times (Disco example dataset).

## 5.4 *Analysis of results*

From the simulated dataset, it can be observed that there is a significant increase in execution time as the size of the independent set increases. This is because as the size of a single independent set increases, the number of non-connected relations also increases, resulting in a larger number of overall independent sets. For Alpha miner, this means that more CISP will be generated, resulting in a longer time spent filtering out redundant CISP. On the other hand, for Alpha-boost, there is no need to filter out these redundant CISPs, resulting in a much faster execution speed.

In the real-life dataset, it is noticeable that the execution time decreases as the number of traces increases. This trend can be attributed to the fact that a higher number of traces corresponds to a larger number of interconnected events. Conversely, when there are fewer traces, it tends to result in more non-connected relationships, which in turn leads to longer processing times. In this context, it becomes evident that Alpha-boost

consistently demonstrates significant improvements in execution speed.

The approach of Alpha miner is to first generate the power set of all events, then filter out the non-independent sets, and finally compare the remaining independent sets pairwise to produce the final LMCISP. If there are $n$ events, then the power set will have $2^n$ elements. In the worst-case scenario, if all the elements in the power set are independent sets, then the time required to compare them pairwise will be $2^n \times 2^n$, which is $O(4^n)$.

The most time-consuming aspect of Alpha-boost is the identification of LMRIS. Once LMRIS is found, the execution time of the remaining parts does not exceed that of the initial identification process. Thus, the time required to process the BK algorithm in Alpha-boost represents a significant portion of the overall time complexity, as expressed in Big-O notation. However, the execution time of the BK algorithm may vary depending on the initial construction settings. Fortunately, according to the theory proposed by Moon and Moser [11], a graph with $n$ nodes can produce at most $3^{\frac{n}{3}}$ cliques, so the worst case of the BK algorithm is $O(3^{\frac{n}{3}})$. Additionally, since Alpha-boost executes this algorithm for all left maximal independent sets, which can have up to $2^n$, the worst case of Alpha-boost execution time is $O(3^{\frac{n}{3}} \times 2^n)$. As a result, the worst case of Alpha miner is $4^n = 64^{\frac{n}{3}}$, while the worst case of Alpha-boost is $3^{\frac{n}{3}} \times 2^n = 3^{\frac{n}{3}} \times 8^{\frac{n}{3}} = 24^{\frac{n}{3}}$, which shows that the execution time of Alpha-boost is consistently shorter than that of Alpha miner.

## 6 CONCLUSION

This study proposes a boost in the time complexity of the well-known alpha algorithm in process mining. We incorporate the BK clique-finding algorithm to discover the local maximal constrained independent set pairs for the event logs. Since the original design of the existing alpha algorithm could create duplicated candidate pairs, our approach utilizes a top-down process such that the right independent sets for each left independent set are only enumerated once. Empirical results show speed up over the alpha algorithm in both simulated data and real data.

ACKNOWLEDGEMENTS

This research was partially supported by the National Science and Technology Council, Taiwan, R.O.C. (Grant Nos. NSTC 111-2218-E-005-007-MBK, NSTC 111-2221-E-005-048, NSTC 111-2221-E-025-010, and NSTC 111-2221-E-039-014).

# REFERENCES

[1] Van der Aalst W., Weijters T. and Maruster L. (2004), "Workflow mining: Discovering process models from event logs," *IEEE Transactions on Knowledge and Data Engineering*, 16(9), 1128–1142.

[2] Wen L., Wang J., van der Aalst W.M., Huang B., and Sun J. (2009), "A novel approach for process mining based on event types," *Journal of Intelligent Information Systems*, 32, 163–190.

[3] Corallo A., Lazoi M. and Striani F. (2020), "Process mining and industrial applications: A systematic literature review," *Knowledge and Process Management*, 27(3), 225–233.

[4] Bron C. and Kerbosch J. (1973), "Algorithm 457: finding all cliques of an undirected graph," *Communications of the ACM*, 16(9), 575–577.

[5] Eblen J.D., Phillips C.A., Rogers G.L. and Langston M.A. (2012), "The maximum clique enumeration problem: algorithms, applications, and implementations," *BMC Bioinformatics*, 13 (Suppl 10), S5.

[6] Cazals F. and Chinmay K. (2008), "A note on the problem of reporting maximal cliques," *Theoretical Computer Science*, 407(1), 564–568.

[7] Kose F., Weckwerth W., Linke T. and Fiehn O. (2001), "Visualizing plant metabolomic correlation networks using clique–metabolite matrices," *Bioinformatics*, 17(12), 1198–1208.

[8] Gély A., Nourine L. and Sadi B. (2009), "Enumeration aspects of maximal cliques and bicliques," *Discrete Applied Mathematics*, 157(7), 1447–1459.

[9] Murata T. (1989), "Petri nets: properties, analysis and applications," *Proceedings of the IEEE*, 77(4), 541–580.

[10] Günther C.W. and Rozinat A. (2012), "Disco: discover your processes," *Proceedings of the Demonstration Track of the 10th International Conference on Business Process Management*, 940 (1), 40–44.

[11] Moon J.W. and Moser L. (1965), "On cliques in graphs," *Israel Journal of Mathematics*, 3(1), 23–28.

System Innovation for a Troubled World – Lam et al. (Eds)
© 2024 the Author(s), ISBN: 978-1-032-60846-4

# Application effects of AI text mining and ChatGPT as a content analysis for developmental trends in leisure and recreation industries

Li-Shiue Gau*
*Department of Leisure and Recreation Management, Asia University, Taichung, Taiwan*

Hsiu-Tan Chu
*Doctoral student, Department of Business Administration, Asia University, Taichung, Taiwan*

Meng-I Chen
*Mingdao University, Pitou, ChangHua County, Taiwan*

Chiung-Hsien Huang
*Department of Electronic Engineering, National Formosa University, Hu-Wei, Yunlin, Taiwan*

ABSTRACT: A knowledge gap exists in the application effects of AI-based text mining and ChatGPT as a content analysis tool, which motivates this research. The study utilized four research cases to assess the application effects of AI-powered Text Mining (AITM), compared to the traditional time-consuming content analysis process. The AITM procedure involved four steps: crawling, generating a word cloud, editing codes, and categorizing codes using ChatGPT. AITM in the first case on the daylily tour in Huatan Township found four out of six themes, compared to traditional content analysis. Similarly, the second case on Taiwanese elements in spectator sports yielded two-thirds of the six themes. The third case, which examined the impact of 5G on the travel and tourism industry, demonstrated the effectiveness of automated AI-powered text mining in capturing almost all seven themes. In contrast, the fourth case on travel trends in the metaverse showed that AITM identified seven themes out of nine identified by traditional content analysis. In conclusion, AITM's effects were approximately 78%. This was quite good but still had difficulty identifying themes with subtle and subjective labels, such as authentic experiences, food and agricultural education, nostalgia, art and culture, stakeholders, and triggering factors.

## 1 INTRODUCTION

The development of artificial intelligence (AI) has recently helped revolutionize the way data is processed and analyzed in text mining to provide insights into the underlying themes and patterns within the text data. Particularly, one such AI-based tool, ChatGPT, is useful in content analyses to inductively identify trends. However, the lack of knowledge about the application effects of AI-based text mining and ChatGPT as a content analysis tool has motivated research in this area.

Typically conducted in a qualitative inquiry with rigor, a traditional time-consuming content analysis includes four steps (Patton 2002; Auerbach & Silverstein 2003; Gau & James 2013). The first step is to get the text and attain relevant text. Then, the next step is to separate text into meaningful units, give codes, and find repeating ideas. The third step involves categorizing recurring ideas into distinct themes (Auerbach & Silverstein 2003). The final step involves consulting relevant literature to aid in interpreting and labeling each theme. This entails crafting a theoretical narrative for each theme by utilising selected textual excerpts as evidence to support the theme.

Compared to the traditional content analysis, the automated AI-powered text mining along with the AI-based tool, ChatGPT, can greatly expedite the procedure by crawling text, generating codes, and categorizing themes. However, a knowledge gap exists in its application effects, compared to the traditional time-consuming content analysis process. This research attempts to fill the gap.

## 2 EXPERIMENTAL

Four research cases were used to evaluate the application effects, compared to the results obtained through traditional step-by-step time-consuming content analysis typically conducted in a qualitative inquiry with rigor. The procedure of AI-powered text mining involves four steps. The

---

*Corresponding Author: lsgau@asia.edu.tw

DOI: 10.1201/9781003460763-14

first step is to crawl the text by applying Python or using software such as PolyAnalyst (Megaputer 2023). The second step simply copies and pastes the text into HTML5 Word Cloud (Chien et al. 2019) to generate a word cloud and produce a list of codes.

In the third step, the "Edit List" function of HTML5 Word Cloud is employed to refine the codes by either deleting or adding certain codes. Subjective judgment is inevitably involved in deciding whether to move or add certain codes, based on researchers' understanding of the topic. The final step involves requesting ChatGPT for assistance in categorizing the codes and labeling each group of codes as themes. A typical inquiry made to ChatGPT was similar to: "The following list contains codes and their respective frequencies on the left. Please categorize these codes into different groups." The categorization may not include codes with frequencies that are too low to be considered significant. Here again, researchers have their own discretion to decide the threshold value of a code frequency for entering the categorization step.

At the same time, the traditional content analyses were conducted independently by different groups of researchers. Subsequently, the outcomes obtained through AI text mining with ChatGPT and the traditional content analysis were compared. The juxtaposition primarily sought to identify consistent themes that were extracted using these two different methods.

## 3 RESULTS AND DISCUSSION

### 3.1 Daylily tour at Huatan township

Using AI text mining, the first study (Gau et al. 2020) on the daylily tour at Huatan Township, Changhua County, in the middle of Taiwan, found four out of six themes, compared to traditional content analysis. Using the Chinese term "花壇金針花" (Huatan daylily), a search was conducted on Google to find relevant Chinese text. This search yielded a total of 82 articles, comprising 49 blogs, 31 news articles, and 2 governmental announcements. The PolyAnalyst software was employed to assist in the process of downloading the text. Next, the traditional way of content analysis revealed six themes: fads and trends, community-based small tours, aesthetic tours, authentic experiences, family activities, and food and agricultural education (Table 1).

However, automated text mining powered by AI and the AI-based tool ChatGPT (abbreviated as AITM) was only able to yield four corresponding themes (Table 1). AITM appeared to have difficulty identifying themes with subjective or nuanced labels such as authentic experiences, and food and agricultural education. According to these results, the application of AITM would have a 67% effect (that is, equivalent to 4 themes out of 6 themes).

Table 1. Themes of daylily tour in huatan township.

| Traditional method | AI-Powered |
| --- | --- |
| Fads and trends | Related to popularity and check-in |
| Community-based small tour | Related to travel and destination |
| Aesthetic tour | Related to good food and attraction |
| Authentic experience | |
| Family activities | Parents-children activities |
| Food and agricultural education | |

### 3.2 Taiwanese elements in spectator sports

Similarly, using automated AI-powered text mining, the second study on Taiwanese elements in spectator sports (Gau & Chu 2021) yielded two-thirds of the six themes, compared to the traditional content analysis. Two primary keywords, Taiwanese elements and sports (in traditional Chinese "台灣味" and "運動"), were used in the Google search; and 98 articles or texts were extracted to be considered relevant during this decade. The rigorous and comprehensive procedure of the traditional content analysis found six themes: Types of sports, delicious food, cultural identification, nostalgia, experiences, and art and culture (Table 2).

Table 2. Themes of taiwanese elements in spectator sports.

| Traditional method | AI-Powered |
| --- | --- |
| Types of sports | Related to sports such as baseball |
| Delicious food | Related to Taiwan specialty food and sport restaurant |
| Cultural identification | Related to Taiwan's geography culture |
| Nostalgia | |
| Experiences | Related to perceived feeling and social experiences with affection |
| Art and culture | |

On the other hand, AITM performed exploratory content analyses including word frequency, word cloud, and code clustering, which revealed four themes that were consistent with those found through the traditional method. Two themes in the results of traditional analysis were not identified by AITM. First, AITM did not identify the theme of "nostalgia" due to its implicit and subtle labeling.

Second, another theme, "art and culture", refers to a sports movie, Kano (2014), for entertainment, and an installation art exhibition in swinging skirts golf tournament created by Taiwanese artist Hung Yi (Formosa TV, 2014; River Art Gallery, 2023). Although its occurrences were not high, this theme possesses distinctiveness and impressiveness that merits its classification as an independent and representative category. Nevertheless, the extraction of this theme by AITM through the literal meaning or connotation of codes in clustering seemed to be challenging. As a result, AITM's contribution could be calculated as 67%, which is equivalent to 4 out of the 6 themes (Table 2), and is the same as that of the first study.

### 3.3 Impact of 5G on travel and tourism industry

The third study, which examined the impact of 5G on the travel and tourism industry (Gau *et al.* 2021), demonstrated the effectiveness of AI text mining in capturing almost all seven themes. Keywords such as 5G, influence, impact, trend, travel, and tourism in English were used to search relevant reports online after 2019. Exploratory coding and categorization were executed by HTML5 Word Cloud (Chien et al. 2019) and ChatGPT in AITM, while subjective open coding was conducted by four researchers in the traditional content analysis to find repeating ideas and organize them into groups or categories that expressed different themes.

Valid 30 reports were acquired, and more than 500 codes were indexed. With raters' reliability and cross-confirmation, the traditional content analyses showed seven categories as major themes: Characteristics of 5G, related technology, possible and potential services and products, stakeholders, travel and tourism industries, suppliers' benefits, and customers' perception and experiences (Table 3) In AITM, ChatGPT was requested by the

Table 3. Themes of 5G impact on travel and tourism industries.

| Traditional method | AI-Powered |
| --- | --- |
| Characteristics of 5G | Telecommunications, networking, and connectivity |
| Related technology | Technology and innovation such as AR, VR, and AI |
| Possible and potential services and products | Service, solution, and support |
| Stakeholders | Sector, company, city, and infrastructure |
| Travel and tourism industries | Travel, tourism, and transportation |
| Suppliers' benefits | Mobility, improvement, interaction |
| Customers' perception and experiences | Customer immersive experience |

instructions: "The number indicates the frequency of the word after the number. Please use the following list to make some, seven, or eight major meaningful categories." Remarkably, this AI-powered approach generally produced outcomes (as shown in Table 3) that encompassed nearly all the themes extracted by the traditional method.

### 3.4 Travel trends caused by the metaverse

The fourth study on travel trends in the metaverse (Gau 2023) showed that AI text mining identified seven themes out of nine identified by traditional content analysis. The keywords "metaverse, tourism or travel" ("元宇宙, 觀光, 旅遊" in Chinese) were used to search on Google and find 30 articles as texts for content analysis. Inductive reasoning behind the traditional content analysis was used to extract nine tourism trend development themes related to the metaverse: Triggering factors, characteristics of the metaverse, related technology, stakeholders, industries, applied areas, potential products and services, customers' perceived experiences, and future development (Table 4).

Table 4. Travel trends caused by metaverse.

| Traditional method | AI-Powered |
| --- | --- |
| Triggering factors | |
| Characteristics of metaverse | Virtual world and metaverse related |
| Related technology | Technology development |
| Stakeholders | |
| Industries | Industry related |
| Applied areas | Travel, tourism, geography, art, culture, entertainment, destination |
| Potential products and services | Services and products |
| Customers' perceived experiences | Reality-related and virtual experience-related |
| Future development | Future related |

As for AITM outcomes, seven themes were identified out of nine themes through traditional analysis. Although the theme of "triggering factors" was not detected in AITM analysis, it did receive attention in detailed traditional analysis as it required critical system thinking in an interdisciplinary sense. The emergence of the metaverse, along with the development of blockchain and NFT (non-fungible token), is believed to be the next evolutionary stage of the Internet of Things (IoT). The COVID-19 pandemic has also played a significant role in pushing this trend, as people have gradually become more used to adopt digital means to solve problems and fulfill their needs during the pandemic (Cheng 2022). This trend raises an interesting debate about whether the metaverse would negatively or positively impact the travel industry. On the one hand, Metaverse would offer immersive experiences without leaving one's living room, while on the other hand, these virtual experiences could motivate people to travel to real-life attractions or destinations. Since these "triggering factors" were thought-provoking, this theme was suggested by traditional analysis. Nevertheless, AITM faced difficulty in extracting this theme due to the complex reasoning behind it.

When comparing AITM outcomes to those obtained through traditional content analysis, the overlap was observed among three themes: stakeholders, industry-related, and applied areas. In traditional content analysis, the theme of stakeholders was recognized and labeled because it was essential to highlight different perspectives or various roles in the value chain or environmental trend analysis. The label of stakeholders tended to be an all-encompassing and abstract term, which would be hard for AITM to identify. Nevertheless, upon closer examination and careful comparison, it can be argued that the theme of "industry-related" partially overlaps with a subset of stakeholders.

The theme of "industry-related" is also partially covered by a subset of "applied areas", and can be removed. Additionally, the theme of "potential products and services" can be merged with "applied areas" to form a new theme called "applied areas and potential products." Consequently, similar to a theoretical framework of analysis that demonstrates influences on supply and demand through environmental and industrial analyses of factors, Figure 1 (Gau 2023) can offer a more concise conceptual framework for the travel trend driven by metaverse technology. This framework connects all themes from triggering factors, metaverse characteristics, and related technology to stakeholders, applied areas and potential products, and customers' perceived experiences.

## 4 CONCLUSION

In conclusion, AITM demonstrated effects of around 67% in the first and second studies, 100% in the third case, and 78% in the fourth study. The average of these four effect percentages was approximately 78%. This was quite good but still had difficulty identifying themes with subtle and subjective labels, such as authentic experiences, food and agricultural education, nostalgia, art and culture, stakeholders, and triggering factors.

Despite aiming to examine the impact and the application effects of AI text mining and ChatGPT on analyzing developmental trends in leisure and recreation industries, compared to traditional content analysis, this study suggests that AITM can serve as a valuable and effective complementary approach to enhance the quality of inquiry during the traditional analysis process. For researchers or managers who require a quick overview of the text, AITM can offer sufficient evidence and adequate outcomes. In future research, AI-powered association analysis of themes can be applied to aid in constructing a model for developing grounded theory (Strauss & Corbin 1998).

Further research is also required to examine whether English text outperforms Chinese text when conducting AITM. The third study in this research, which was the only one with English text, performed better in AITM than the other three studies with Chinese texts. However, the limited number of cases in this research prohibited definitive conclusions to be drawn.

## ACKNOWLEDGMENT

This study appreciates some funding support partly and indirectly from the Ministry of Education (PHE1080049) and the National Science and Technology Council (MOST 111-2410-H-468-016).

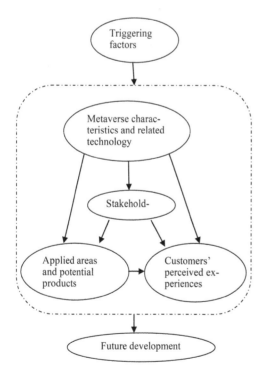

Figure 1. A framework of travel trend driven by metaverse.

## REFERENCES

Auerbach C. F. & Silverstein L.B. (2003). *Qualitative Data: An Introduction to Coding and Analysis*. New York: New York University.

Cheng S. (Ed.). (November 8, 2022). What is metaverse? (in Chinese). *ELLE*. From https://www.elle.com/tw/life/tech/a41881417/what-is-metaverse/.

Chien T.G.T. & other contributors (2019). *HTML5 Word Cloud*. Released under the MIT license. From https://wordcloud.timdream.org/.

Formosa TV (2014). Art Installations Give Extra Dose of Character to Swing Skirts Golf tournament. From https://youtu.be/mOalN4S159Y.

Gau L.S. (2023). Exploring metaverse and travel trend (in Chinese). *2023 Shih Hsin University Tourism Conference*, Taipei, Taiwan: Shih Hsin Uinversity, March 4, 2023.

Gau L.S., & Chu H.T. (2021). Explore business opportunities of service innovation using Taiwanese elements in spectator sports. (Poster presentation) *NVivo Virtual Conference 2021* (Virtual). USA. November 3–4, 2021.

Gau L.S., Layson P.T., Chu H.T., & Yeh W.K. (2021). Application of AI text mining into innovative teaching: 5G impact in travel and tourism industry. (Online oral presentation) *2021 China Asia Associated University Teaching Practice Research and Innovation Online Conference* (中亞聯大教學實踐研究與創新線上研討會), Taichung, Taiwan: Asia University. July 26, 2021.

Gau L. S., & James J. D. (2013). A Ten-Value-Type Framework Associated with Spectator Sports: A Qualitative Inquiry. *Sage Open (April-June)*, *3*(2). DOI: 10.1177/2158244013485580.

Gau L.S., Yeh W.K., & Hsu Y.Y. (2020). Reviewing the development trend of leisure and recreation from a scientific viewpoint (in Chinese). *The Journal of Chinese Public Administration*, *27*, 59–74.

Kano (2014). From https://youtu.be/pmG6LuRxilw.

Megaputer (2023). *PolyAnalyst Software*. From https://www.megaputer.com/polyanalyst/.

Patton M.Q. (2002). *Qualitative Evaluation and Research Methods* (3rd ed.). Newbury Park, CA: SAGE.

River Art Gallery (2023). *HUNG Yi*. From https://www.riverart.com.tw/artists-hung-yi.

Strauss A., & Corbin J. (1998). *Basics of Qualitative Research: Techniques and Procedures for Developing Grounded Theory* (3rd ed.). Los Angeles, CA: SAGE.

*System Innovation for a Troubled World – Lam et al. (Eds)*
© 2024 the Author(s), ISBN: 978-1-032-60846-4

# Semi-supervised cyber-attack detection for industrial control system of water storage

Fu-Nie Loo & Chia-Wei Tsai*

*Department of Computer Science and Information Engineering, National Taichung University of Science and Technology, North District, Taichung City, Taiwan*

ABSTRACT: An Industrial Control System (ICS) is a computerized control system that manages and automates industrial processes. Because ICS plays a crucial role in the modern industrial infrastructure and cyber-attacks in the ICS area not only leak private information but also endanger human life and safety, how to let it be free from cyber-attack is an important issue. The cyber-attack detection that is used to detect and analyze malicious attacks is one of ICS's cybersecurity solutions. Although the existing studies and literature have proposed the corresponding solutions for ICS cyber-attacks, these methods could not capture the zero-day attacks efficiently because they all use supervised learning models. With this in mind, this study uses the one-class support vector machine (SVM) model to build an ICS cyber-attack detector using the semi-supervised learning strategy. This study also used WUSTL-IIOT 2018 dataset to train the proposed detector. The experiment result shows that (1) the proposed ICS cyber-attack detector is feasible, and (2) its performance also approaches the other detectors using supervised learning models.

*Keywords*: cyber-attacks, cybersecurity, cyber-attack detector, semi-supervised learning, industrial control system

## 1 INTRODUCTION

In the modern era, automation control is the main topic. Because the industries continue to develop and grow, factory process control has become a critical issue. For this issue, Supervisory Control and Data Acquisition (SCADA) was designed to efficiently control industrial processes such as traffic light systems, electrical power systems, and manufacturing. SCADA also controls and monitors equipment by collecting data from sensors and using actuators to control processes [1,2]. Although the SCADA system improves the efficiency of industrial processes, has also become high risk and vulnerable to confidential data loss with malicious attacks [2].

Cyber-attack detection on ICS/SCADA has been widely developed in recent years. Different tools and algorithms are available to simplify the development of cyber-attack detectors, including machine learning algorithms, anomaly detection, and intrusion detection systems (IDS) [9,14], These tools and algorithms are able to improve the performance of cyber-attacks detector with great efficiency and accuracy. However, as sophisticated cyber-attacks on ICS/SCADA continue to develop and grow, we need to keep up with the latest tools and algorithms continuously updating to enhance the cyber-attack detector [2,4].

The current approaches to studying cyber-attack detection on ICS/SCADA primarily depend on supervised learning methods. However, supervised learning has limitations in detecting zero-day attacks due to a lack of labeled data about the zero-day attacks. Moreover, the detector using the supervised learning method is also unable to detect new patterns of cyber-attacks, because the supervised learning model is only trained with the information about known attacks [5,11]. Additionally, collecting and processing labeled data for the new cyber-attack information is a time-consuming process, which is one of the crucial limitations of supervised learning in cyber-attack detection.

This study aims to propose a method for cyber-attack detection method using a semi-supervised learning manner, which only uses the party-labeled data to improve the practicality of cyber-attack detection [14,15]. The proposed semi-supervised detector can overcome the limitations of supervised learning methods. Moreover, the proposed method also enables the capability for detecting zero-day attacks, which are difficult to detect by using the supervised learning methods.

In the semi-supervised learning method, this study implements the cyber-attack detector by utilizing the one-class SVM which is a semi-supervised

---

*Corresponding Author: cwTsai@nutc.edu.tw

DOI: 10.1201/9781003460763-15

machine learning algorithm that can be used to learn a decision boundary around the normal data, and then it can classify the anomaly data depending on the boundary [4,9].

In the feature selection process, this study uses the Pearson correlation coefficient (PCC) to filter the features [5,6]. Moreover, this study also uses f1-score (Equation (3)), recall (Equation (2)), precision (Equation (1)), accuracy (Equation (4)), false alarm rate (FAR) (Equation (5)), and undetection rate (UND) (Equation (6)) to evaluate the performance of the proposed cyber-attack model detection [1,3,5]. This study achieves the following contributions:

1) This study uses the WUSTL-IIOT 2018 dataset to implement the proposed semi-supervised model. The experiment results show that the proposed model has a similar performance to the supervised learning methods.
2) This study proves the feasibility and effectiveness of the semi-supervised detector for cyber-attacks in ICS/SCADA systems. This contribution has the potential to enhance the security of ICS/SCADA systems for zero-day attacks.

The remainder of this paper is organized as follows: Section 2 presents the background, and then the proposed semi-supervised cyber-attack detection method is described in Section 4. Section 4 shows the experiment processes and results. Finally, conclusions are presented in Section 5.

## 2 BACKGROUND

In recent years, cyber-attacks on ICS/SCADA systems have become a major concern due to the serious damage they can cause, including damage to infrastructure, operational breakdowns, and leakage of sensitive data. Furthermore, cyber-attacks can affect basic infrastructure facilities, such as water storage systems, electrical power systems, and manufacturing systems, which are critical to human necessities. Thus, enhancing cyber-attack detection is our main goal to achieve, and further improve the security of ICS/SCADA [3,5,8,9].

To fulfill this goal, we utilize the WUSTL-IIOT 2018 dataset for training and testing, which was originally developed for ICS (SCADA) Cybersecurity. This dataset was built using a SCADA system testbed to emulate real-world water storage tank control systems. This testbed consists of a variety of control components such as programmable logic controllers (PLC), sensors, and actuators that connect and interact with each other to control the process of the water storage system. Additionally, the authors created various cyber-attack scenarios, which were gathered by the testbed [1,2].

According to the details, the raw data has 25 networking features. A total of 6 features was carried out by the authors for the proposed model training, testing, and performance evaluation. These selected features are a port number of the source (sport), total transaction packet count (TotPkts), total transaction bytes (TotBytes), source/destination packet count (SrcPkts), destination/source packet count (DstPkts), and source/destination transaction bytes (SrcBytes). Moreover, the dataset contains 93.93% normal traffic (no attacks) and 6.07% abnormal traffic (attack traffic) [1,2,5,13].

By using this dataset, we are able to capture various patterns of cyber-attacks on ICS/SCADA using a semi-supervised learning approach. The effectiveness of using semi-supervised learning allows us to detect zero-day attacks or new patterns of cyber-attacks without prior knowledge. This experiment enhances the security of ICS/SCADA and protects critical infrastructure, contributing to a safer society [4,11]. Furthermore, this study utilizes one-class classifiers, specifically the one-class SVM from scikit-learn, to train the proposed method. This study utilizes the pearson correlation coefficient to identify the key features, aiming to improve the performance of the proposed cyber-attack detector.

One-class SVM is an unsupervised machine learning algorithm used for anomaly detection, it is a type of SVM that is trained only on one class of data, which is the normal class. One-class SVM learns decision boundaries around the normal data and classifies anomaly data that falls outside the boundary. The main advantage of one-class SVM is its ability to detect anomalies without requiring labeled data. One-class SVM is commonly used in various fields, including anomaly detection and cybersecurity. Furthermore, one-class SVM has the ability to handle high-dimensional data and handle non-linear decision boundaries, making it capable of capturing complex patterns in the data [4,9].

During the model training phase, adjusting hyperparameters is a crucial step for achieving optimal model performance. To achieve this, finding the optimal parameters is necessary. This study introduces Optuna, a state-of-the-art machine learning tool that speeds up optimization time and improves performance [12].

To enhance the performance of the proposed model, the Pearson correlation coefficient is commonly used to evaluate the strength and direction of the relationship between two variables, such as the correlation between two features. Pearson correlation coefficient ranges from −1 to 1, where −1 indicates a perfect negative correlation, 0 indicates no correlation, and 1 indicates a perfect positive correlation. In machine learning, the Pearson correlation coefficient can be utilized for tasks such as feature selection, data preprocessing, and model evaluation.

To evaluate the performance of the proposed model, we use the confusion matrix, which is a metric to evaluate the performance of a classification model by showing the number of true positives (TP), true negatives (TN), false positives (FP), and false negatives (FN) predicted by the model. The confusion matrix is a valuable tool for evaluating the performance of a classification model and identifying the sources of misclassification [1,3,5,7].

Another approach to evaluate the performance is by utilizing precision, as shown in Equation (1). Precision represents the fraction of correctly classified positive instances among all instances that the model predicted as positive. Recall, as indicated in Equation (2), is the fraction of correctly classified positive instances among all the true positive instances. F1-score, as described in Equation (3), is the harmonic mean of precision and recall, and it provides a single score that balances both metrics. Accuracy, as shown in Equation (4), is the fraction of correctly classified instances (both positive and negative) among all the instances. FAR also known as false alarm rate as shown in Equation (5), represents the fraction of negative instances that were incorrectly classified as positive. Undetected error rate (UND), as mentioned in Equation (6), represents the fraction of positive instances that were incorrectly classified as negative, for both FAR and UND, a lower value indicates better performance [1,5].

Precision, recall, f1-score, accuracy, FAR, UND are given as (1), (2), (3), (4), (5) and (6):

$$1)\ \text{Precision} = \frac{TP}{(TP + FP)}, \tag{1}$$

$$2)\ \text{Recall} = \frac{TP}{(TP + FN)}, \tag{2}$$

$$3)\ \text{F1} - \text{score} = 2\frac{\text{Precision} * \text{Recall}}{\text{Precision} + \text{Recall}}, \tag{3}$$

$$4)\ \text{Accuracy} = \frac{TP + TN}{(TP + TN + FP + FN)}, \tag{4}$$

$$5)\ \text{FAR} = \frac{FP}{(TN + FP)}, \tag{5}$$

$$6)\ \text{UND} = \frac{FN}{(FN + TP)}, \tag{6}$$

## 3 PROPOSED METHOD

In this section, we present an overview of the proposed method for cyber-attack detection using semi-supervised model. To improve previous studies in detecting cyber-attacks, we review many studies and find that most of them rely on a supervised learning approach [1,3,5,6]. However, this approach has limitations in detecting zero-day attacks. Zero-day attacks are previously unknown attacks that can make it difficult to detect using traditional supervised learning approaches on ICS/ SCADA systems [11].

After several discussions, we decided to continue this study and use one-class SVM, which is a semi-supervised approach capable of detecting new attack patterns, including zero-day attacks. One-class SVM is able to detect anomalous behavior based on a defined decision boundary that separates anomalous behavior from normal behavior.

### 3.1 The dataset

As mentioned earlier in the background section, we utilize the WUSTL-IIOT 2018 dataset, which was originally developed for ICS (SCADA) cybersecurity research and emulates the real-world testbed water storage tank control system. The size of this dataset is 7,037,983 rows after data cleaning by the author. Moreover, this dataset is highly reliable as it was collected using scan tools to inspect the topology of the victim network and identify devices and their weaknesses, making it highly suitable for our further studies on detecting cyber-attacks.

This dataset initially had 25 networking features, which were later cleaned and classified by the authors, leaving only 6 features. These 6 features are Sport, TotPkts, TotBytes, SrcPkts, DstPkts, and SrcBytes. These 6 features are the real-world cyber-attack features that were selected by the authors as usable, and reliable for the proposed model training. In addition, this dataset has 93.93% correspondence with normal traffic and 6.07% correspondence with anomaly traffic [1,13]. The dataset's column and data are shown in Figure 1.

|  | Sport | TotPkts | TotBytes | SrcPkts | DstPkts | SrcBytes | Target |
|---|---|---|---|---|---|---|---|
| 0 | 143 | 2 | 180 | 2 | 0 | 180 | 0 |
| 1 | 68 | 2 | 684 | 2 | 0 | 684 | 0 |
| 2 | 0 | 1 | 60 | 1 | 0 | 60 | 0 |
| 3 | 54949 | 10 | 628 | 4 | 6 | 248 | 0 |
| 4 | 54943 | 8 | 496 | 4 | 4 | 248 | 0 |
| ... | ... | ... | ... | ... | ... | ... | ... |
| 7037978 | 49317 | 14 | 904 | 8 | 6 | 520 | 0 |
| 7037979 | 49318 | 14 | 904 | 8 | 6 | 520 | 0 |
| 7037980 | 49319 | 12 | 780 | 8 | 4 | 520 | 0 |
| 7037981 | 49320 | 12 | 780 | 8 | 4 | 520 | 0 |
| 7037982 | 132186 | 82169 | 1655422536 | 82169 | 4585 | 5939202 | 0 |

```
[7037983 rows x 7 columns]
0    6634581
1     403402
Name: Target, dtype: int64
```

Figure 1. The columns and data in the dataset WUSTL-IIOT 2018.

### 3.2 Feature selection

Feature selection is an important preprocessing step in machine learning. As discussed in the background section, the Pearson correlation coefficient measures the strength and direction of the relationship between two variables, with a range of −1 to 1. A value of −1 indicates a perfect negative correlation, 0 indicates no correlation and 1 indicates a perfect positive correlation. To implement this method on the WUSTL-IIOT 2018 dataset, we define a scope of column names and use a nested loop to compute the Pearson correlation coefficient between each pair of features. We obtain the top two features, TotPkts and SrcPkts, with the highest correlation coefficients and assign them to the variable "best_features". These two features will be used to train and test the proposed model. Figure 1 shows the scope of the column names used in our implementation, except for the column target.

### 3.3 Data slitting

This section presents data preprocessing in the proposed method. In this study, the dataset is separated into two parties depending on the labels, where one of the sub-dataset is the normal dataset and the other is the anomaly dataset. The normal dataset is used as the training set, and the anomaly dataset is used as the testing set. As shown in Figure 2, the proposed method separates the data flow into two streams, one for the normal dataset and the other for the anomaly dataset.

The separation of the normal class and anomaly class is done based on the feature name called "Target" in the dataset. According to the documentation of the WUSTL-IIOT-2018 Dataset for ICS (SCADA) Cybersecurity Research, 0 represents normal traffic, while 1 represents attack traffic. We filter the data by "Target" 0 and assign it to a new list for normal traffic, while "Target" 1 is assigned to another new list for anomaly traffic, as shown in Figure 2 [13].

A common technique used in machine learning before the training phase is data splitting. The proposed method uses an 80/20 rule for data splitting, where the entire dataset is split 80% for training data and 20% for testing data. This train-test-split method from the sklearn library helps to minimize the risk of overfitting or underfitting the model [10].

To split the normal data, we use the 80/20 rule as mentioned above as our data splitting method, where the entire normal class data is split into 80% training data and 20% testing data, as shown in Figure 2. After that, we use 80% of the training data to proceed into the training phase by using one-class SVM.

Another data splitting process is applied to the anomaly data, where we use the 20% testing set that is separated from normal class data using the 80/20 rule, as mentioned previously. Then we combine the 20% testing set with the anomaly class data, which is filtered by "Target" 1, and randomly shuffling it to create a testing data set, as shown in Figure 2. By combining the 20% dataset from the normal class data with the anomaly class data, the testing dataset becomes more representative and accurate for evaluating the model's performance. This process is referred to as data preprocessing.

### 3.4 Data training and testing

In this section, we feed 80% of training data to a one-class SVM algorithm during the training phase. In this phase, we determine the range of the model's hyperparameters that we will use for model training. To speed up optimization time and improve performance, we utilize a state-of-the-art machine learning hyperparameter optimization tool called Optuna [12]. Compared to traditional methods such as GridSearch, Optuna significantly improves optimization time and performance. Moreover, Optuna automates the process of finding the optimal hyperparameter, massively improving the performance of the model.

During our training stages, we use both the classic one-class SVM and another variant of the one-class SVM algorithm known as SGDOneClassSVM from sklearn [16]. In the classic one-class SVM, the basic hyperparameters are nu, kernel, and gamma. Nu controls the trade-off between having a flexible decision boundary; a small value of nu lets the decision boundary be more flexible but easily causes overfitting. A high value of nu means lets the decision boundary be

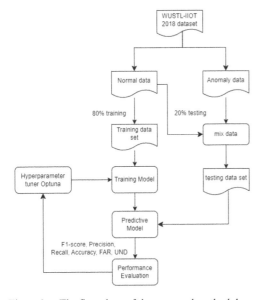

Figure 2.   The flow chart of the proposed methodology.

73

less flexible but can result in underfitting. Both linear and RBF kernels are used in the training phase [9,14,15]. The Linear kernel is used for linearly separable data as shown in Figure 3, while the RBF kernel is used for non-linearly separable data as shown in Figure 4 [14,15]. The RBF kernel transforms the input data into higher-dimensional space using a Gaussian function. Gamma controls the width of the Gaussian function, and a large value of gamma results in a more complex decision boundary, while a small value of gamma results in a simpler decision boundary [14].

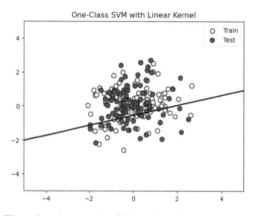

Figure 3.    An example of Linear kernel.

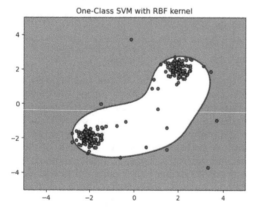

Figure 4.    An example of RBF kernel.

In SGDOneClassSVM, stochastic gradient descent (SGD) is used to optimize the hyperparameters of the model. This algorithm is designed for large-scale datasets. The hyperparameters used for training are nu, eta0, and learning rate. Both eta0 and learning rate are the initial learning rate and determine the update rule for the learning rate during training. By adjusting both parameters, we can optimize the learning process to find the best

model parameters and achieve the best performance [16].

In the training phase, we utilize Optuna and automate the process of finding the optimal value of hyperparameters such as nu, eta0, and learning rate in SGDOneClassSVM. Due to the time complexity of classic one-class SVM, we choose to train the model with fewer iterations instead of using Optuna. By providing a range of values, this process allows us to find the best parameters within the given range. Thus, Optuna greatly helps to reduce optimization time, making the training phase more efficient and effective. Furthermore, we create a study with 500 trials using Optuna to train the proposed model using SGDOneClassSVM, which allows Optuna to have more opportunities to find the best parameters. In the classic one-class SVM, due to the large resources and training time, we only run 5 iterations for the training phase.

Moving on to the testing phase, we feed the trained model with mixed data that includes 20% testing from both normal and anomaly data. By doing this, we obtain a list of predictions that we use to evaluate the model in the next step. In the dataset, the value of the column 'target' 0 represents normal traffic, while 1 represents attack traffic as shown in Figure 1 [13]. However, in the one-class SVM, the predictions return $-1$ for outliers and 1 for inliers [9], which is the opposite of the dataset's representation. To solve this issue, we map all the values in the list of predictions from one-class SVM from $-1$ to 1 and 1 to 0. This allows us to evaluate the model correctly using confusion metrics, which provide a measure of the model's accuracy (4), precision (1), recall (2), and F1 score (3).

### 3.5    Evaluation metrics

In this section, we describe how we evaluate the performance of the proposed using evaluation metrics. Model evaluation is crucial as it allows us to assess the performance of the machine learning model after the training and testing phases, and helps us to identify areas for further improvement.

As discussed in the background section, we use confusion matrices to summarize the performance of the classification model by showing the number of TP, TN, FP, and FN predicted by the model. Based on these values, we calculate the F1 score (3), recall (2) score, and precision (1) score using the calculation formulas mentioned in the background section.

Additionally, we use the TP, TN, FP, and FN values generated by the confusion matrix to calculate other performance metrics such as accuracy (4), false alarm rate, and undetected error rate, as mentioned in the background section for the proposed model. These metrics help us assess the overall performance of the proposed model in terms of its accuracy (4), false alarm rate, and undetected error rate, which are important indicators of the model's effectiveness in identifying normal and anomaly instances.

By employing this evaluation process, we gain a comprehensive understanding of how well the proposed model is performing in terms of accuracy, false alarm rate, and undetected error rate, allowing us to make informed decisions about the performance of the proposed model and identify areas for improvement.

## 4   EXPERIMENT AND RESULTS

This section presents the experiment results, performance evaluation, and execution time of the proposed semi-supervised learning model based on one-class SVM. One of the contributions of our study is to compare the performance of supervised and semi-supervised learning approaches.

Figure 5 shows the performance comparison of the proposed model using one-class SVM with six different techniques: Adaboost (AD), decision tree (DT), gradient boosting (GB), random forest (RF), extreme gradient boosting (XGB) and the recurrent neural network (RNN), as reported in a previous study [5]. The authors of the previous study train and test the models on three datasets, which are WUSTL-IIOT-2018, ICS-SCADA, and CICIDS2019. However, in our study, we specifically focus on evaluating the performance of the proposed model on the WUSTL-IIOT-2018 dataset [13].

Figure 5 presents the performance of the techniques used in the previous study in terms of accuracy (4) and precision (1), with all achieving a score of 99.8%. The recall (2) and f1-score (3) for all techniques are also nearly identical, achieving 99.97%, with only a slight difference in XGB. However, the RNN technique achieves lower scores in all evaluation metrics [5]. Only random forest and decision trees achieve 0.1% and 0.0% in FAR and UND, respectively, as reported in the previous studies.

As shown in Figure 5, we train the proposed model using the classic one-class SVM with a linear kernel. The results indicate an accuracy of 99.35%, a precision of 97.77%, a recall of 99.50%, an f1-score of 98.63%, a FAR of 0.68%, and a UND of 0.49%. We observe that the precision (1) is slightly lower than the recall (2), f1-score (3), and accuracy (4) scores.

Next, we evaluate the RBF kernel of the classic one-class SVM. The results show an accuracy of 63%, a precision of 38.65%, a recall of 100%, an f1-score of 55.76%, a FAR of 48.23%, and a UND of 0. As shown in Figure 5, the accuracy (4), precision (1), f1-score (3), and FAR (5) are lower than when using the linear kernel. Especially, The UND (6) score of 0 is an abnormal condition.

After training using both linear and RBF kernel in classic one-class SVM, we realize that the performance does not achieve better scores compared to the previous study that uses a supervised learning approach. In particular, the time complexity of classic one-class SVM is not optimal for training and testing the proposed model, as listed in Table 1 and Table 2. After some discussion and further research, we use another variant of the one-class SVM algorithm known as SGDOneClassSVM. Using this algorithm, we are able to achieve better performance scores and speed up training time and testing time compared to the classic one-class SVM.

Figure 5 shows that the proposed trained model achieves high performance using SGDOneClassSVM, with an accuracy of 99.35%, precision of 99.85%, recall of 99.31%, f1-score of 99.57%, FAR of 0.68%, and UND of 0.49%. As we can see both FAR (5) and UND (6) achieve low-performance scores, indicating that the model is able to detect very few false alarm and undetected errors. Although the performance scores are very similar compared to the linear kernel, the significant difference is in the time complexity of training and testing. SGDOneClassSVM is much faster in both training and testing, as listed in Tables 1, 2 and 3, lists the amount of training and prediction sets.

Table 1.   The usage time under the training phase.

| Algorithm | Training Time (S) |
| --- | --- |
| Linear kernel | 11,342.23 |
| RBF kernel | 7,150.29 |
| SGDOneclassSVM | 6.13 |

Table 2.   The usage time under the prediction phase.

| Algorithm | Prediction Time (S) |
| --- | --- |
| Linear kernel | 730.87 |
| RBF kernel | 1,043.38 |
| SGDOneclassSVM | 0.04 |

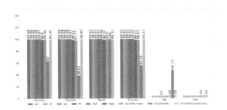

Figure 5.   Model performance of the previous study using supervised learning compared to the proposed model using semi-supervised learning.

Table 3. The amount of training and prediction sets.

| Phase | Amount |
|---|---|
| Training | 5,307,664 |
| Prediction | 1,703,039 |

## 4.1 Experiment setup

In this experiment, this study implements these models in a single PC with the following specifications:

1. Gen Intel® Core ™ i9-11900 @ 2.50GHz processor, 94Gi RAM.
2. Ubuntu 20.04 operating system.
3. Python 3.9.7 using Jupyterlab.

## 5 CONCLUSION

This paper proposes a new cyber-attack detector using a semi-supervised learning strategy for the ICS system. The experiment results show that the model using SGDOneClassSVM has better performance than the models training by the standard one-class SVM with linear and RBF kernels, and this model also has equal performance compared to the supervised model. According to the experiment result, this study proves that the proposed detector is feasible for detecting cyber-attacks in ICS systems. Additionally, because the semi-supervised model is more sensitive than the supervised models in terms of detecting zero-day attacks, the proposed ICS cyber-attack detector is more practical than the existing solutions.

## REFERENCES

[1] Teixeira M.A., Salman T., Zolanvari M., Jain R., Meskin N. and Samaka M., "SCADA system testbed for cybersecurity research using machine learning approach," *Future Internet*, vol. 10, no. 8, p. 76, 2018.

[2] Illy P., Kaddoum G., de Araujo-Filho P.F., Kaur K. & Garg, S. (2022). "A hybrid multistage DNN-based collaborative IDPS for high-risk smart factory networks," *IEEE Transactions on Network and Service Management*.

[3] Alani M.M., Damiani E. & Ghosh U. (2022, July). "DeepIIoT: An explainable deep learning based intrusion detection system for industrial IOT," In *2022 IEEE 42nd International Conference on Distributed Computing Systems Workshops (ICDCSW)* (pp. 169–174). IEEE.

[4] Bui, Cong Thanh, Minh Hoang, and Quang Uy Nguyen. "One-class fusion-based learning model for anomaly detection," *Journal of Computer Science and Cybernetics* (2023).

[5] Nwakanma, Cosmas Ifeanyi, *et al.* "Effective industrial internet of things vulnerability detection using machine learning."

[6] Ahakonye, Love Allen Chijioke, *et al.* "Agnostic CH-DT technique for SCADA network high-dimensional data-aware intrusion detection system," *IEEE Internet of Things Journal* (2023).

[7] Awajan, Albara. "A novel deep learning-based intrusion detection system for iot networks," *Computers* 12.2 (2023): 34.

[8] Anthi, Eirini, *et al.* "Adversarial attacks on machine learning cybersecurity defences in industrial control systems," *Journal of Information Security and Applications* 58 (2021), p. 102717.

[9] Catillo, Marta, Antonio Pecchia, and Umberto Villano. "CPS-GUARD: Intrusion detection for cyber-physical systems and IoT devices using outlier-aware deep autoencoders." *Computers & Security* (2023): 103210.

[10] Naz, Naila, *et al.* "A comparison of ensemble learning for intrusion detection in telemetry data."

[11] Verkerken, Miel, *et al.* "Unsupervised machine learning techniques for network intrusion detection on modern data." *2020 4th Cyber Security in Networking Conference (CSNet)*. IEEE, 2020.

[12] Akiba, Takuya, *et al.* "Optuna: A next-generation hyperparameter optimization framework." *Proceedings of the 25th ACM SIGKDD International Conference on Knowledge Discovery & Data Mining*. 2019.

[13] "WUSTL-IIOT-2018 Dataset for ICS (SCADA) Cybersecurity Research," Mar 2023. [Online; accessed 3. Mar. 2023], https://www.cse.wustl.edu/~jain/iiot/index.html.

[14] Chandola, Varun, Arindam Banerjee, and Vipin Kumar. "Anomaly detection: A survey." *ACM Computing Surveys (CSUR)* 41.3 (2009): 1–58.

[15] Perera, Pramuditha, Poojan Oza, and Vishal M. Patel. "One-class classification: A survey." *arXiv preprint arXiv:2101.03064* (2021).

[16] Zhang, Jiuqi Elise, Di Wu, and Benoit Boulet. "Time series anomaly detection via reinforcement learning-based model selection." *2022 IEEE Canadian Conference on Electrical and Computer Engineering (CCECE)*. IEEE, 2022.

*System Innovation for a Troubled World – Lam et al. (Eds)*
© 2024 the Author(s), ISBN: 978-1-032-60846-4

# Development of an interactive surgical robot training system

Yu-Chieh Chiang, Tick-Huat Lee & Kuu-young Young*
*Department of Electrical Engineering, National Yang Ming Chiao Tung University, Hsinchu, Taiwan*

Chun-Hsu Ko
*Department of Electrical Engineering, I-Shou University, Kaohsiung, Taiwan*

Shu-Ling Cheng
*Department of Finance and International Business, Fu-Jen Catholic University, New Taipei City, Taiwan*

ABSTRACT: Nowadays, more robots have been introduced for medical applications, including surgery, rehabilitation, walking assistance, among others. It thus motivates us to develop a robot surgical system that can provide assistance for the surgeons during surgery. As a continuing research for building such a system, this paper focuses on the development of its training system, including a realistic simulator and experimental platform. To achieve more precise control and higher safety during surgery, we gather both position and force information, and propose making use of the force feedback for developing virtual fixtures as an assistive tool during surgery emulation and thus design an interactive VR-based system that can closely emulate the surgical environment. Virtual fixtures intended for guidance and restriction are both designed to generate appropriate force for guidance or protection according to different task requirements. An experimental platform is developed to validate this assistive surgical robot training system. For demonstration, experiments based on the treatment of soft tissue in the abdominal cavity are conducted. The experimental results show that the VFs serving as the assistive tool are effective, implicating the proposed system is a step further toward its testing on a real surgical robot platform.

## 1 INTRODUCTION

Nowadays, more robots have been introduced for medical applications, including surgery, rehabilitation, and walking assistance, among others. It thus motivates us to develop a robot manipulation system that can provide assistance for the surgeons during surgery. In this research, we focus on the development of a surgical robot training system that can emulate the actual environment closely, so that more practical training can be achieved.

As it is of interest to not only the academics but also the industry, many training systems have been developed by leading companies in surgical robots, such as Mimic RobotiX Mentor from Surgical Science, Sweden, and da Vinci skill simulator from da Vinci Surgery, USA [1,2]. Among them, the technique of virtual reality is widely utilized, along with assistive strategies to help the surgeon during the process of the operation [3]. Following this trend, we also develop a training system based on virtual reality and propose our assistive strategies, which make use of both visual and tactile feedback [4] to realize virtual fixture (VF) [5,6].

VF is basically a kind of constraint generated by software, which can be divided into (1) guidance virtual fixtures (GVF), which guide the robot to move along a predetermined path, and (2) forbidden-region virtual fixtures (FRVF), which restricts robot movement to a specific area. In previous research, Moccia et al. [5] proposed the use of FRVF in minimally invasive surgery to avoid the collision between surgical tools. Zheng et al. [6] proposed a hyperboloid VF used in robot-assisted endoscopic sinus surgery to guide surgical instruments in the nasal cavity.

The realization of both FRVF and GVF demands the use of force information, which has also been demonstrated to be able to improve the muscle memory of novices to strengthen their surgical ability [7]. In addition to force feedback itself, we also integrate it with the visual feedback to let the user be better immersed in the simulated environment [8,9]. Altogether, the proposed system can yield the user a realistic sense of the interaction between the surgical instrument and tissue, and the VFs can generate appropriate force for guidance or protection according to different task requirements. Consequently, the training via this system may lead to higher safety and efficiency when the surgeons conduct actual surgeries later

*Corresponding Author: kyoung@nycu.edu.tw

DOI: 10.1201/9781003460763-16

on. Experiments based on the puncturing and cutting of soft tissue in the abdominal cavity are conducted for demonstration. System performance with and without the virtual fixture involved is then evaluated.

## 2 PROPOSED SYSTEM

Figure 1(a) shows the system block diagram of the proposed VR-based surgical robot training system, with the VR-based simulator serving for training. The experimental platform, shown in Figure 1(b), is used to evaluate the training effect of the simulator, which allows the user to govern a real robot with force formation fed back from the equipped force sensor. During the process shown in Figure 1(a), the user utilizes the head-mounted display (HMD) to experience a realistic visual effect and then manipulates the haptic device to govern the robot. He/she then follows the clue from the generated VFs (FRVF and GVF) for surgery conduction.

To simplify the modeling of the organs, muscles, and tissues of the human body for simulation, we adopted the well-known mass-spring-damping formulation, which can achieve the linear response of the soft tissue in about 2 ms [7]. We consider the common actions during surgery, including puncturing, cutting, and pulling [10].

### 2.1 VF generation

Among various strategies for surgery assistance, this study focuses on the development of virtual fixture (VF), including GVF and FRVF), described below.

#### 2.1.1 Guidance Virtual Fixture (GVF)

The GVF is designed to provide guidance so that the user can better manipulate the tool for task execution. It is especially helpful for the novice to be acquainted with the unfamiliar procedures during training. The design will start from planning a path according to specific surgical require-ments. The GVF will then generate the corresponding attractive force to guide the user to follow that path. To respond to various conditions that may happen during surgery, we propose to generate the GVF in three ways.

One straightforward approach is to have the system to generate a path consisting of the basic geometric line(s), for example, horizontal or vertical line, circle, etc., as the example of straight-line GVF shown in Figure 2(a). Second, the users may also generate a path of their own via the manipulative device, an example is shown in Figure 2(b). This approach is suitable for the experts to provide reference paths based on their specialty. Third, the user may only need to specify some key locations and let the system take over the planning of the entire path, for example, via the use of the Bezier curve for interpolation.

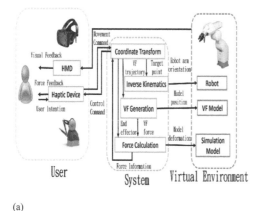

(a)

(b)

Figure 1. (a) Proposed VR-based surgical robot training system with (b) an experimental platform.

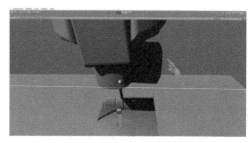

(a) Straight-line GVF

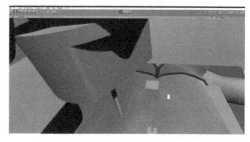

(b) GVF generated by the user

Figure 2. Illustrion of GVF generation: (a) straight-line GVF and (b) GVF generated by the user.

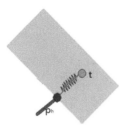

Figure 3.    Illustration of FRVF generation.

### 2.1.2  Forbidden-region virtual fixture (FRVF)

The use of FRVF is mainly to prohibit the tool manipulated by the user to reach certain regions to avoid damage to human organs and others. The FRVFs can be realized as virtual walls of various shapes. When the surgical tool moves close to the FRVF, a corresponding repulsive force $F_{rf}$ will be generated according to the distance of penetration, derived as Eq. (1):

$$F_{rf} = -k_{rf}(p_h - t) \qquad (1)$$

where $p_h$ is the position of the manipulative device, $k_{rf}$ is the selected stiffness, and $t$ is the starting point of the virtual spring. For safety concerns, the virtual wall may maintain a small distance from the region to be protected.

## 3  EXPERIMENT

To evaluate the effect of GVF and FRVF, two sets of experiments for the training system and one for the experimental platform were conducted. The first set of experiments was intended for surgical training of puncture and cutting, which were executed with or without GVF, the second one was for laparoscopic surgical training, which was designed to investigate the effect of FRVF, and the third set was conducted on the experimental platform for the user to govern a real robot.

In experiment 1, the users were asked to conduct the actions of puncture, straight cutting, and curve cutting, as shown in Figure 4. The results are listed in Table 1, including the cases with or without GVF. We observed that the errors along the

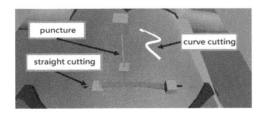

Figure 4.    Experimental scene for experiment 1.

Table 1.    Average path errors for experiment 1.

|  | Puncture | Straight cutting | Curve cutting |
| --- | --- | --- | --- |
| Without GVF | 0.486cm | 0.487cm | 0.597cm |
| With GVF | 0.351cm | 0.306cm | 0.454cm |

path were less when the GVF was employed for all these three actions, while that for curve cutting was more evident. It demonstrates that the use of GVFs was indeed helpful, especially for more complicated manipulation.

In experiment 2, the user was asked to conduct training for the laparoscopic surgery, including tissue pulling, Fallopian tube electrosurgery, and membrane tissue electrosurgery, as shown in Figure 5. The results are listed in Table 2, including the cases with or without FRVF. The total time spent for these three operations was less when the FRVF was employed. It shows that the presence of FRVF did help the user to avoid contact with the issues unrelated to the surgery, and thus increased the efficiency. Especially, it was still effective even when the field of view was blocked.

Figure 5.    Experimental scene for experiment 2: left: tissue pulling training; middle: Fallopian tube electrosurgery training; right: membrane tissue electrosurgery training.

Table 2.    Average time for experiment 2.

|  | Without FRVF | With FRVF |
| --- | --- | --- |
| Time | 54.10s | 38.38s |

The third set of experiments was conducted on the experimental platform, during which the user was asked to cut chicken meat along a specified path by governing a real robot with force feedback from the force sensor, as shown in Figure 1(b). Six subjects, 5 males and 1 female, were invited for the experiments. The results are listed in Table 3, including the cases with or without GVF. The smaller path errors for all six subjects indicates that the GVF was also effective for motion governing of a real robot.

Table 3. Average path errors for experiment 3.

| Gender | Without VF(0.1cm) | With VF(0.1cm) |
|---|---|---|
| M | 2.119978 | 0.983142 |
| M | 2.336096 | 0.517923 |
| M | 6.273976 | 0.925676 |
| F | 20.71319 | 3.827468 |
| M | 15.21708 | 3.142379 |
| M | 2.478352 | 1.573995 |
| Average | 8.1898 | 1.8284 |

In summary, the experimental results demonstrate that the developed GVFs and FRVFs were helpful in conducting surgical types of tasks. Compared with conventional force feedback methods, the proposed VFs are more modular and flexible, so that they can be easily designed to meet the task requirements more systematically.

## 4 CONCLUSION

In this paper, we have proposed a VR-based surgical robot training system, along with an experimental platform. To provide assistive tools for the user during robot manipulation, we utilize force information to develop virtual fixtures, including both GVF and FRVF. Their effectiveness has been demonstrated by the experimental results. In future works, we intend to develop more assistive tools and apply them for various types of surgeries, so that the system can be prepared for test on a real surgical robot platform.

## ACKNOWLEDGMENT

This work was financially supported in part by the Ministry of Science and Technology, Taiwan.

## REFERENCES

[1] surgicalscience 2022 Website, https://surgicalscience.com/

[2] da Vinci Surgery 2022 Website, https://www.davincisurgerycommunity.com/Systems_I_A/Skills_Simulator/

[3] Guo J. and Guo S., "A haptic interface design for a vr-based unskilled doctor training system in vascular interventional surgery," IEEE International Conference on Mechatronics and Automation, pp. 1259–1963, 2014.

[4] Okamura A., "Methods for haptic feedback in teleoperated robot-assisted surgery," Industrial Robot, vol. 31, no. 6, pp. 499–508, 2004.

[5] Moccia R., Iacono C., Siciliano B. and Ficuciello F., "Vision-based dynamic virtual fixtures for tools collision avoidance in robotic surgery," IEEE Robotics and Automation Letters, vol. 5, no. 2, pp. 1650–1655, 2020.

[6] Zheng Q., He Y., Qi X., Zhang P., Hu Y. and Li B., "Safety tracking motion control based on forbidden virtual fixtures in robot assisted nasal surgery," IEEE Access, vol. 6, pp. 44905–44916, 2018.

[7] Vafai N. M. and Payandeh S., "Toward the development of interactive virtual dissection with haptic feedback," Virtual Reality, vol. 14, pp. 85–103, 2010.

[8] Tai Y., Wei L., Zhou H., Peng J., Shi J., Li Q. and Nahavandi S., "Development of haptic-enabled virtual reality simulator for video-assisted thoracoscopic right upper lobectomy," IEEE International Conference on Systems Systems, Man and Cybernetics, 2018.

[9] Gerovich O., Marayong P. and Okamura A. M., "The effect of visual and haptic feedback on computer-assisted needle insertion," Computer Aided Surgery, vol. 9, no. 6, pp. 243–249, 2004.

[10] Takacs A., Tar J., Haidegger T. and Rudas I., "Applicability of the maxwell-kelvin model in soft tissue parameter estimation," IEEE International Symposium on Intelligent Systems and Informatics, 2014.

*System Innovation for a Troubled World – Lam et al. (Eds)*
© 2024 the Author(s), ISBN: 978-1-032-60846-4

# Guidance assistance control of upper-limb exoskeleton robot using EMG signal

Hsin-Chieh Chien
*Department of Electrical Engineering, I-Shou University, Kaohsiung, Taiwan*

Kuu-Young Young
*Department of Electrical Engineering, National Yang Ming Chiao Tung University, Hsinchu, Taiwan*

Chun-Hsu Ko*
*Department of Electrical Engineering, I-Shou University, Kaohsiung, Taiwan*

ABSTRACT: This paper proposes a guidance assistance control approach of upper-limb exoskeleton robot using electromyogram (EMG) signal. The user's torque model is first built with the detected motion state and EMG signal by using the fuzzy method. The robot assistance torque for guidance is then calculated with the guidance assistance method. The user can intuitively manipulate the upper-limb exoskeleton robot to complete tasks. Simulation and experiments are conducted to verify the effectiveness of the proposed upper-limb exoskeleton robot system.

## 1 INTRODUCTION

With the advent of the aging society, the number of people with mobility impairments is increasing. The exoskeleton robots are thus developed for rehabilitation and daily activities of the elderly and patients with limited mobility. Among them, the upper-limb exoskeleton robot is designed to be worn on the user's upper-limb and move together with the user (Gopura et al. 2016). Since the robot needs to provide the movement assistance based on human upper-limb motions, it is important to control the robot to effectively assist the user.

Many upper-limb exoskeleton robots have been proposed to assist the arm movement of the user. Kooren *et al.* presented a wearable five-degree-of-freedom exoskeleton to assist people with Duchenne muscular dystrophy in the performance of activities of daily living (Kooren et al. 2016). Chen *et al.* proposed an assistive control system for an upper-limb rehabilitation robot with 7-DOF (Chen et al. 2016). Cui *et al.* designed a 7-degree-of-freedom cable-driven arm exoskeleton for dexterous motion training or assistance of the whole-arm (Cui et al. 2017). Kiguchi *et al.* used an electromyogram (EMG)-based impedance control method for an upper-limb power-assist exoskeleton robot to control the robot in accordance with the user's motion intention (Kiguchi et al. 2012). Zeiaee *et al.* developed a lightweight and compact exoskeleton for upper-limb rehabilitation (Zeiaee et al. 2022). Ko *et al.* presented

the design and control of an upper-limb exoskeleton robot with visual sensing (Ko *et al.* 2022). Effective approaches for guidance assistance control based on user-applied torque are still in demand.

This paper proposes the guidance assistance control of an upper-limb exoskeleton robot using an EMG signal. We present the developed upper-limb exoskeleton robot and establish its dynamic model. By detecting the motion state and EMG signal of the user's upper-limb, the fuzzy method is utilized to establish the user's torque model. To assist the user's arm in reaching the target, we propose a guidance assistance method for computing robot control torque. The user can intuitively manipulate the upper-limb exoskeleton robot to complete tasks. Finally, simulations and experiments are conducted to verify the effectiveness of the developed upper-limb exoskeleton robot system.

The remainder of this paper is organized as follows. Section II describes the developed upper-limb exoskeleton robot system. Section III presents the simulation and experimental results. Finally, concluding remarks are given in Section IV.

## 2 DEVELOPED UPPER-LIMB EXOSKELETON ROBOT SYSTEM

The developed two-DOF upper-limb exoskeleton robot is shown in Figure 1. Two brushless DC motors along with reduction gears are used to provide the assistance torque for the flexion and

*Corresponding Author: chko@isu.edu.tw

DOI: 10.1201/9781003460763-17

Figure 1.    The upper-limb exoskeleton robot.

extension of the shoulder and elbow, respectively. The incremental encoders are used to detect the shoulder and elbow angles. The robot state is given by

$$\theta = [\,\theta_1 \quad \theta_2\,]^T \qquad (1)$$

where $\theta_1$ and $\theta_2$ are the shoulder and elbow angles, respectively. By applying the Euler-Lagrange equation, the robot dynamic equation is obtained as

$$\tau_h + \tau_r + \tau_g = M(\theta)\ddot{\theta} + V(\dot{\theta},\theta) + G(\theta) \qquad (2)$$

where $\tau_h$ is the human applied torque, $\tau_r$ is the robot torque for moving assistance, $\tau_g$ is the robot torque for gravity compensation, $M$ is the mass matrix, $V$ is the vector of the Coriolis and centrifugal forces, and $G$ is the vector of the gravitational force. Here, $\tau_g$ is set to be equal to $G(\theta)$.

The position of the exoskeleton robot can be obtained with the robot angles and expressed as $x = f(\theta)$. On differentiating this equation of the position twice, it leads to

$$a = J\ddot{\theta} + \dot{J}\dot{\theta} \qquad (3)$$

where $a$ is the acceleration, and $J$ is the Jacobian matrix. From Eqs. (2) and (3), we get

$$\tau_r = M(\theta)J^{-1}(a - \dot{J}\dot{\theta}) + V(\dot{\theta},\theta) - \tau_h \qquad (4)$$

Figure 2 shows the guidance assistance control system of the exoskeleton robot. The user moves

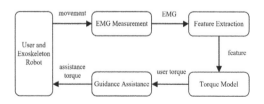

Figure 2.    Guidance assistance control system.

upper-limb based on the intention and the EMG signal is detected by the measurement device. The torque model is built with the extracted EMG feature and the robot angles by using an adaptive-network-based fuzzy inference system (ANFIS) (Jang 1993). The user-applied torque is then obtained with the torque model. The assistance torque can be calculated with the guidance assistance controller and applied for controlling the robot to approach the target. The procedure is repeated until the stop criterion is satisfied.

To obtain the robot assistance torque, we plan a smooth path that passes from the initial position to the final position. The exoskeleton robot can thus follow the path with the assistance of torque. The acceleration $a$ of the endpoint can be expressed as:

$$a = a_t\hat{t} + \kappa v^2\hat{n} \qquad (5)$$

where $a_t$ is the tangent acceleration, $\kappa$ is the path curvature, $v$ is the speed, $\hat{t}$ is the unit vector of the tangent direction, and $\hat{n}$ is the unit vector of the normal direction. From Eqs. (4) and (5), the robot torque $\tau_r$ for moving assistance can be obtained by selecting a tangent acceleration $a_t$. Here, we set the maximum speed and the maximum tangent acceleration for tangent acceleration selection.

## 3 RESULTS

For performance evaluation, the simulation and experiment are performed by applying the proposed approach for exoskeleton robot guidance. The maximum speed and the maximum tangent acceleration are set as 0.2 $m/s$ and 0.4 $m/s^2$, respectively.

In the simulation, the initial and the final angles $(\theta_1, \theta_2)$ are set to be $(0, 0.2\pi)$ and $(0.2\pi, 0.4\pi)$, respectively. The user-applied torques were

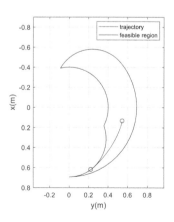

Figure 3.    The guidance assistance trajectory.

82

assumed to follow the function $\tau_p(1 + 0.2\sin2\pi t)$ with the mean torque $\tau_p = [0.2\ 0.2]^T$ Nm. Figure 3 shows the trajectory of the guidance assistance. The exoskeleton robot can assist the upper-limb of the user to accurately reach the target. The trajectories of speed, angle, angular speed, user-applied torques, and robot torques are shown in Figure 4. The speed was kept within 0.2 $m/s$, and the trajectories of the angle and angular speed were all smooth. The robot torques show oscillations to compensate for the oscillating torques applied by the user in guidance.

In the experiment, the user raised the arm to the target angle (0.873 $rad$, 1.047 $rad$). The experimental results are shown in Figures 5–7. In Figure 5, it can be observed that the EMG of the user's anterior deltoid and biceps brachii increases, indicating that the system can detect the user's intention to lift the arm. The guided trajectory in Figure 6 shows that the exoskeleton robot can assist the user's upper-limb to approach the target angle (0.873 $rad$, 1.047 $rad$) with a small angle error (0.03 $rad$, 0.016 $rad$). In Figure 7, the trajectory of the angle was smooth. The speed $v$, angular speed $\omega_1$, and $\omega_2$ were maintained within 0.24 $m/s$, 0.39 $rad/s$, 0.14 $rad/s$, respectively. The robot can provide the appropriate torques for guidance based on the user-applied torques. The results

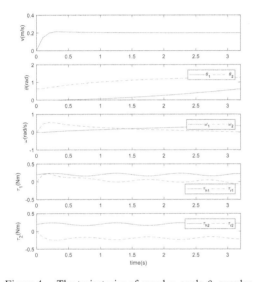

Figure 4.    The trajectories of speed $v$, angle $\theta$, angular speed $\omega$, user-applied torques $\tau_{h1}$, $\tau_{h2}$, and robot torques $\tau_{r1}$, $\tau_{r2}$.

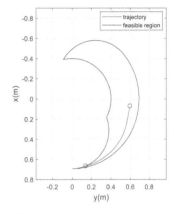

Figure 6.    The guidance trajectory.

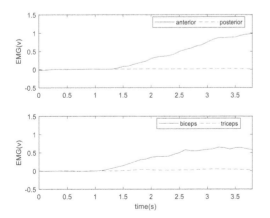

Figure 5.    The EMG signal.

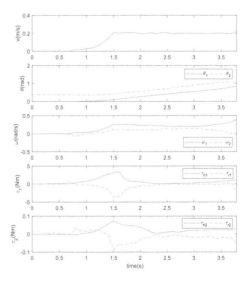

Figure 7.    The trajectories of speed $v$, angle $\theta$, angular speed $\omega$, user-applied torques $\tau_{h1}$, $\tau_{h2}$, and robot torques $\tau_{r1}$, $\tau_{r2}$.

demonstrate that the proposed approach can assist the user's upper-limb to approach the target.

## 4 CONCLUSION

In this paper, we have proposed a guidance assistance control approach for the upper-limb exoskeleton robot. The user torque model was built with the upper-limb angles and EMG signal by using the fuzzy method. The user's intention of arm motion was detected with the torque model. The appropriate assistance torque for guidance can be obtained with the proposed method. The simulation and experimental results show that the proposed exoskeleton robot system can assist the user's upper-limb to approach a target, demonstrating the effectiveness of the proposed approach.

## ACKNOWLEDGMENTS

This work was supported in part by the National Science and Technology Council, Taiwan, under the Grants MOST 111-2221-E-214-021.

## REFERENCES

Chen S.H., Lien W.M., Wang W.W., Lee G.D., Hsu L. C., Lee K.W., Lin S.Y., Lin C.H., Fu L.C., Lai J.S., Luh J.J., Chen W.S., 2016. *IEEE Trans. Neural Syst. Rehab. Eng.* 24 1199–1209.

Cui X., Chen W., Jin X., Agrawal S. K., 2017. *IEEE/ ASME Trans. Mechatron.* 22 161–172.

Gopura R.A.R.C., Bandara D.S.V., Kiguchi K., Mann G.K.I., 2016. *Rob. Auton. Syst.* 75 203–220.

Jang J.S.R., 1993. *IEEE Trans. Syst. Man Cybern.* 23 665–685.

Kiguchi K., Hayashi Y., 2012. *IEEE Trans. Syst. Man Cybern.* 42 1064–1071.

Kooren P.N., Lobo-Prat J., Keemink A.Q.L., Janssen M.M., Stienen A.H.A., de Groot I.J.M., Paalman M. I., Verdaasdonk R., Koopman B.F.J.M., 2016. *IEEE Int. Conf. Biomed. Robot. Biomech.* 637–642.

Ko C.H., Cheng S.L., Young K.Y., Huang J.B., Lin I. Y., Young S.Y., 2020. *iRobotics* 3 10–17.

Zeiaee A., Zarrin R.S., Eib A., Langari R., Tafreshi R., 2022. *IEEE Robot. Autom. Lett.* 7 1880–1887.

*System Innovation for a Troubled World – Lam et al. (Eds)*
© 2024 the Author(s), ISBN: 978-1-032-60846-4

# The transformation of 3D printing parameters under sustainable manufacturing

Ching-Chia Huang & Hua-Chen Shih
*Program in Interdisciplinary Studies, National Sun Yat-sen University, Kaohsiung, Taiwan*

Tim de Ancos
*Industrial Engineering, Technische Hochschule Mittelhessen, Friedberg, Germany*

Cheng-Jung Yang*
*Program in Interdisciplinary Studies, National Sun Yat-sen University, Kaohsiung, Taiwan*

ABSTRACT: Three-dimensional (3D) printing is a novel product creation process. Although it is convenient for human life, it generates large amounts of greenhouse gases and air pollutants, which cause global warming and adversely affect human health. This study used fusion deposition molding technology as an example to investigate the multi-target optimization results of mechanical properties (dimensional accuracy and surface roughness), manufacturing costs, $CO_2$ emissions (electricity consumption generation), and air pollution (PM2.5), which represent the quality of manufactured products to achieve a win-win situation for both economic and environmental aspects in the process of mechanical manufacturing. The multi-target optimization results obtained by desirable analysis are without heat bed and fan, 185°C of extrusion temperature, 10 mm/s of printing speed, 50% filled Tri-hexagon pattern, lying flat on the printing platform, two-layer shell with 0 mm height per layer, two outer shells with a layer height of 0.2 mm each, and blue filament.

*Keywords*: 3D printing, fusion deposition molding, multi-target optimization, desirable analysis

## 1 INTRODUCTION

Fusion deposition molding (FDM) is a popular 3D printing manufacturing technology with advantages such as low cost, ease of operation, and ease of equipment maintenance. Numerous studies conducted in the past investigated the mechanical properties (e.g., surface roughness and dimensional accuracy), manufacturing costs, and air pollution (including PM2.5 and VOCs—Volatile organic compounds) of plastic filaments.

Different printing planes (XY, YZ, and XZ) affect the energy consumption and dimensional accuracy of the sample thickness. (Carmita Camposeco-Negrete 2020) The printing speed has a smaller effect on the mechanical properties of polylactic acid (PLA) parts (Farazin & Mohammadimehr 2022). Regarding manufacturing costs, energy consumption decreased when the printing speed increased (Vincenzo Lunetto, Paolo C. Priarone, Manuela Galati & Paolo Minetola. 2020). When the filament width increased, the percentage change in length and width in dimensional accuracy increased, however, the percentage change

in thickness decreased (Omar Ahmed Mohamed, Syed Hasan Masood and Jahar Lal Bhowmik. 2016). Regarding cost, the larger the layer thickness, the shorter the printing time and the lower the energy consumption (Carmita Camposeco-Negrete. 2020). The power consumption is strongly related to heating (bed and extrusion temperatures), which is considerably higher than the power consumption of the stepper motor. Therefore, the power consumption is primarily related to the printing time rather than the complexity of printing; therefore, the shorter the printing time, the lower the power consumption (Hunter James Hinshaw, Shane Terry, and Ismail Fidan, 2020). The higher the infill density and extrusion temperature, the higher the number of PM particles emitted (Shirin Khaki, Emer Duffy, Alan F. Smeaton, Aoife Morrin. 2021). During 3D printing, PLA released VOCs in the liquid state, and these compounds condensed upon contact with air (Timothy R. Simon, Wo Jae Lee, Benjamin E. Spurgeon, Brandon E. Boor, Fu Zhao. 2018). In addition, different filament colors produce different amounts of suspended PM particles for the same printed item. Therefore, 3D printing emits air pollutants such as PM particles and VOCs during the manufacturing process, and the amount of these pollutants is affected by

*Corresponding Author: cjyang0521@mail.nsysu.edu.tw

DOI: 10.1201/9781003460763-18

different factors such as printing parameters and filament color (Haejoon Jeon, Jihoon Park, Sunju Kim, Kyungho Park, Chungsik Yoon. 2020).

However, most of these studies were conducted on a single target, and comprehensive analysis results are missing. Therefore, this study aims to determine the best parameters for optimizing the total performance of FDM while simultaneously considering the mechanical properties, manu-facturing cost, and air pollution. This study will conduct experimental planning using the Taguchi method; 36 sets of experiments will be designed using 10 factors, and each set of experiments will be conducted three times; the best results of the single target will be analyzed by the S/N ratio and ANOVA after the experiments. In addition, this study investigates the best combination of printing parameters of 10 factors for multiple targets by a desirable analysis, and the optimization of the best combination is measured empirically.

## 2 EXPERIMENTAL

In this experiment, an XYZ-type FDM 3D printer (Original Prusa i3 MK3S) and a 1.75 mm diameter filament of PLA were used for printing; all three filament colors were produced by the same fac-tory. The surface roughness was measured using a Mitutoyo surface roughness meter (SJ-210), and the dimensional accuracy was measured using a Vernier caliper (TESA – CCMA-M – 0.01 mm). The energy consumption and air quality data of the printer were collected using Python (Figure 1). When the program detected that the printer was printing, it automatically collected the values of

Figure 1.   Python data collection.

energy consumption, PM 2.5, VOCs, and CO2 and saved the data as CSV files after printing was completed.

The experiment had different objectives for different aspects. The first is the total weight and power consumption of the prints for

manufacturing costs. Second, manufacturing emissions of PM2.5, CO2, and VOCs affect human health. Finally, the surface roughness and dimensional accuracy (Wi, Wo, OL, & T in Figure 2) for the mechanical properties of the prints. Ten single objectives were summarized from these three aspects. The main factors affecting these objectives are the manufacturing parameters: bed temperature, fan speed, extrusion temperature, print speed, infill density, infill pattern, color, layer height, number of contours, and build orientation. The print object specification standard is ASTM-1708, as shown in Figure 2. Referring to the orthogonal arrays invented by Dr. Taguchi, L36 was selected for the experimental design, and the ten factors are in the order of A–J in Table 1. Three experiments were performed for each group, and the average calcula-tion was used to understand the influence of each parameter on different single objectives using the S/N ratio. The S/N ratio was used to determine the influence of each parameter on the different single targets. The results of the ANOVA were used to determine whether the influence of each parameter was significant. Finally, a desirable analysis and Taguchi's prediction were used to obtain the optimal combination of all the single objectives. The improvement rate of the difference between

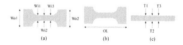

Figure 2.   ASTM-1708.

Table 1.   Factors and their corresponding levels and codes.

| Code | Factors | Levels | | |
|---|---|---|---|---|
| | | 1 | 2 | 3 |
| A | Bed tempera-ture | 25°C | 50°C | - |
| B | Fan speed | 0% | 100% | - |
| C | Extrusion temperature | 185°C | 195°C | 205°C |
| D | Print speed | 10 mm/s | 20 mm/s | 40 mm/s |
| E | Infill density | 20% | 50% | 80% |
| F | Infill pattern | Grid | Triangles | Tri-hexagon |
| G | Color | Green | Blue | Black |
| H | Layer height | 0.1 mm | 0.2 mm | 0.3 mm |
| I | Number of contours | 1 | 2 | 3 |
| J | Build orienta-tion | 0° | 45° | 90° |

Taguchi's prediction and the actual value was calculated.

As shown in Figure 2, the dimensional accuracies of Wi (inner width of the specimen), Wo (outer width of the specimen), OL (length of the specimen), and T (thickness of the specimen) were 5 cm, 15 cm, 38 cm, and 3 cm, respectively, according to ASTM-1708. Wi and T are the averages of three measurements (1 to 3), and Wo is the average of Wo1 and Wo2.

The better the accuracy of the single target size in this experiment, the better the actual geometry is close to the ideal geometry, which belongs to the Taguchi method (Vincenzo Lunetto, Paolo C. Priarone, Manuela Galati and Paolo Minetola. 2020). The smaller the measured value is, the better it belongs to the Taguchi method. The relevant analytical formula for Signal Noise Ratio (SNR), standard deviation, sum of squares, and contribution rate is sequentially described as equation (1) to (5).

$$SNR = -10 \cdot \log\left(\sum Y^2/n\right) \quad (1)$$

$$SNR = 10 \cdot \log\left(1/\left(\overline{Y}^2 * S^2\right)\right) \quad (2)$$

$$S = \left(\sum_{i=1}^{n} (y_i - \overline{y})^2/n\right)^{0.5} \quad (3)$$

$$SS_A = \frac{(A_1)^2}{m} + \frac{(A_2)^2}{m} + \ldots + \frac{(A_p)^2}{m} - CF \quad (4)$$

$$\rho\,(\%) = (SS/TSS) \times 100\% \quad (5)$$

Note: k is the constant of proportionality, y is the measurement value of product quality characteristics, n is the number of measurement values, S is the standard deviation, and $\overline{y}$ is the average of n measurements, $CF = \left(\sum \eta_i\right)^2/N$.

The desirability function calculates the best reconciliation result for multiple targets. The target value is the value of the smallest of the 36 groups for the lookahead characteristics. However, for the lookahead characteristics, the target value is the value defined in Figure 2. Equations (6) to (8) can be used to minimize response desirability. The targets of the response desirability are (9) to (12). Composite desirability is given by Equation (13).

Minimize the Response Desirability:

$$Di = 0 \qquad\qquad \text{if} \quad yi > Ui \quad (6)$$

$$Di = ((Ui - yi)/(Ui - Ti))ri \quad \text{if} \quad Ti \le yi \le Ui \quad (7)$$

$$Di = 1 \qquad\qquad \text{if} \quad yi < Ti \quad (8)$$

Target the Response Desirability:

$$Di = ((yi - Li)/(Ti - Li))ri \quad \text{if} \quad Li \le yi \le Ti \quad (9)$$

$$Di = ((Ui - yi)/(Ui - Ti))ri \quad \text{If} \quad Ti \le yi \le Ui \quad (10)$$

$$Di = 0 \quad \text{if} \quad yi < Li \quad (11)$$

$$Di = 0 \quad \text{if} \quad yi > Ui \quad (12)$$

Composite desirability:

$$D = (d1 \times d2 \times d3 \times \ldots\ldots \times dn)^{1/n} \quad (13)$$

Note: Di = Desirability of individual responses, D = Composite desirability, n = the total number of responses, yi = experimentally produced value, Ti = Target value of response under consideration, Li = Lowest value of response under consideration, Ui = Highest value of response under consideration, and ri = weight value.

## 3 RESULTS AND DISCUSSION

Through the S/N ratio and ANOVA analysis, this study found that the build orientation parameter had a significant effect on all single targets except for Wi and Wo. The second most significant

Table 2. Optimal combination of single objectives and ranking of the influence of each factor.

| Response | Optimal factors | Factor importance |
|---|---|---|
| Wi | A1,B2,C3,D1,E3, F3,G1,H2,I2,J1 | G>I>E>B>F>D>J>H>C>A |
| Wo | A1,B2,C1,D2,E3, F2,G3,H1,I1,J1 | E>F>I>H>G>J>D>C>B>A |
| OL | A1,B2,C3,D3,E1, F3,G1,H3,I3,J3 | J>G>B>C>E>I>F>D>A>H |
| T | A2,B2,C2,D2,E1, F3,G2,H2,I3,J3 | B>J>H>G>E>I>D>C>F>A |
| Ra | A2,B1,C3,D3,E2, F3,G3,H1,I3,J1 | J>H>A>F>C>G>I>B>E>D |
| Weight | A1,B1,C1,D3,E1, F3,G2,H1,I1,J1 | J>H>E>B>I>C>D>F>A>G |
| Power | A1,B1,C1,D1,E1, F3,G1,H3,I1,J1 | A>J>H>B>G>C>E>F>I>D |
| PM2.5 | A2,B2,C1,D1,E1, F3,G1,H3,I3,J1 | J>H>G>E>F>D>B>C>I>A |
| CO2 | A1,B1,C3,D1,E3, F1,G2,H3,I3,J3 | J>H>A>G>D>I>E>B>C>F |
| VOCs | A1,B1,C3,D1,E1, F2,G1,H3,I1,J1 | J>H>A>G>E>I>D>B>F>C |

87

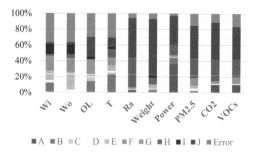

■A ■B ▨C  D ▨E ■F ▨G ■H ■I ■J ■Error

Figure 3. The contribution of different factors to each single objective.

Table 3. Comparison between the results achieved using the desirability analysis and the taguchi methodology.

| Group | Composite Desirability | Rank |
|---|---|---|
| Best | 0.988434 | – |
| 1 | 0.982454 | 1 |
| 8 | 0.974883 | 3 |
| 33 | 0.980556 | 2 |

roughness, energy consumption, CO2, and VOCs. Table 2 shows the detailed correlation of all the parameters with each target. Figure 3 shows the contributions of different factors to each objective.

The optimal combination of multiple targets obtained by Desirable analysis and Taguchi's prediction is indicated by the code A1B1C1D 3E2F3G2H2I2J1, which stands for no fan, no hotbed, 185° of extrusion temperature, 10 mm/s of printing speed, 50% filled tri-hexagon pattern, lying flat on the printing platform, and a two-layer shell with 0 mm height per layer, two outer shells with a layer height of 0.2 mm each, and blue filament. This Taguchi-derived best solution was not included in L36, so additional experiments were required. Analyzing the results of the best solution experiments revealed that, the performance of the derived best solution for multiple targets was indeed the best when compared to the original 36 sets of experiments. The improvement rate compared with the best combination of multiple targets in the original 36 groups, was 0.6%.

## 4 CONCLUSION

This study investigated the effects of various parameters on the mechanical properties, manufacturing cost, and air pollution of FDM 3D printing through a multi-objective analysis and used the Taguchi method to determine the best formulation for the combined manufacturing parameters. In addition, this study also analyzed the influence of every single objective and found that three parameters—orientation, layer height,

parameter affecting most of the single targets was the layer height, except for Wi and OL. The bed temperature parameter had no significant effect on dimensional accuracy, total grammage, and PM2.5 but had a significant effect on surface

Table 4. Comparison between the results achieved using the desirability analysis and the Taguchi methodology.

| Response | Scenarios | | | | | | | | | | |
|---|---|---|---|---|---|---|---|---|---|---|---|
| | Best | 1 | 2 | 3 | 4 | 5 | 6 | 7 | 8 | 9 | 10 |
| Wi(cm) | 5.03 | 5.00 | | | | | | | | | |
| Wo(cm) | 15.14 | | 15.07 | | | | | | | | |
| OL(cm) | 38.05 | | | 37.99 | | | | | | | |
| T(cm) | 3.00 | | | | 3.18 | | | | | | |
| Ra($\mu$m) | 8.062 | | | | | 4.474 | | | | | |
| weight(g) | 1.50 | | | | | | 1.2 | | | | |
| Power(W) | 15911 | | | | | | | 10904 | | | |
| PM2.5(ug/m3) | 3943 | | | | | | | | 334 | | |
| CO2(g) | 231963 | | | | | | | | | 148400 | |
| VOCs(ppb) | 84129 | | | | | | | | | | 50036 |
| Difference between scenarios | – | 0.67% | 0.44% | 0.17% | −5.77% | 45.92% | 80.19% | 25.00% | 1080.44% | 56.31% | 68.14% |

and bed temperature—play key roles in weight, power, and surface roughness. In the future, obtaining good product quality while reducing energy use and environmental pollution should be a priority when setting printing parameters. In terms of environmental impact, future research can focus on the life-cycle assessment of 3D printing and explore the possibility of optimizing carbon emissions while optimizing energy consumption, air quality, and mechanical properties.

# REFERENCES

Carmita Camposeco-Negrete. 2020. Optimization of FDM parameters for improving part quality, productivity, and sustainability of the process using Taguchi methodology and desirability approach. *Progress in Additive Manufacturing.* 5:59–65

Carmita Camposeco-Negrete. 2020. Optimization of printing parameters in fused deposition modeling for improving part quality and process sustainability. *Advanced Manufacturing Technology.* 108:2131–2147

D'Addona D.M., Raykar S.J., Singh D. & Kramar D. 2021. Multi-objective optimization of fused deposition modeling process parameters with desirability function. *Procedia CIRP.* 99:707–710.

EDIMAX AI-2002W *Smart Wireless Indoor Air Quality Detector with 7-in-1 Multi-Sensor,* https://www.edimax.com/edimax/merchandise/merchandise_detail/data/edimax/tw/air_quality_monitoring_indoor/ai-2002w.

Farazin A., & Mohammadimehr M. 2022. Effect of different parameters on the tensile properties of printed Polylactic acid samples by FDM: Experimental design tested with MDs simulation. *The International Journal of Advanced Manufacturing Technology,* 118(1), 103–118. doi:10.1007/s00170-021-07330-w

Haejoon Jeon, Jihoon Park, Sunju Kim, Kyungho Park, Chungsik Yoon. 2020. Effect of nozzle temperature on the emission rate of ultrafine particles during 3D printing. *Indoor Air,* 2020 Mar; 30(2): 306–314.

Hunter James Hinshaw, Shane Terry and Ismail Fidan. 2020. Power consumption investigation for fused filament fabricated specimen. *Rapid Manufacturing.* 9. Nos. 2/3.

Heidari-Rarani M., Ezati N., Sadeghi P. and Badrossamay M.R. 2020. Optimization of FDM process parameters for tensile properties of polylactic acid specimens using Taguchi design of experiment method. *Journal of Thermoplastic Composite Materials.* 1–18.

Mitutoyo SJ-210 *Portable Surface Roughness Tester.* (n.d.). https://www.mitutoyo.com/products/form-measurement-machine/surface-roughness/sj-210-portable-surface-roughness-tester-2/

Omar Ahmed Mohamed, Syed Hasan Masood and Jahar Lal Bhowmik. 2016. Optimization of fused deposition modeling process parameters for dimensional accuracy using I-optimality criterion. *Measurement.* 81:174–196

*Original Prusa i3 MK3S+,* https://www.prusa3d.com/category/original-prusa-i3-mk3s.

Shirin Khaki, Emer Duffy, Alan F. Smeaton, Aoife Morrin. 2021. Monitoring of Particulate Matter Emissions from 3D Printing Activity in the Home Setting. *Sensors (Basel).* 21(9): 3247.

*TESA – CCMA-M – 0.01mm* (n.d.). Greatest Idea Strategy Co., Ltd., http://www.gch-lab.com.tw/web/product/product_in.jsp?pd_no=PD1532427574593

Timothy R. Simon, Wo Jae Lee, Benjamin E. Spurgeon, Brandon E. Boor, Fu Zhao. 2018. An experimental study on the energy consumption and emission profile of fused deposition modeling process. *Procedia Manufacturing.* 26:920–928.

*TP-LINK HS110 Kasa Smart Wi-Fi Plug with Energy Monitoring,* https://www.tp-link.com/us/home-networking/smart-plug/hs110.

Vincenzo Lunetto, Paolo C. Priarone, Manuela Galati and Paolo Minetola. 2020. On the correlation between process parameters and specific energy consumption in

*System Innovation for a Troubled World – Lam et al. (Eds)*
© 2024 the Author(s), ISBN: 978-1-032-60846-4

# Numerical analysis of using phononic crystal on quartz oscillators

Nugraha Merdekawan & Yi-Mei Huang*
*Department of Mechanical Engineering, National Central University, Taiwan*

Shih-Yung Pao
*R&D Center, TXC Corporation, Taiwan*

ABSTRACT: This paper discusses the possibility of using the concept of phononic crystal on a quartz oscillator for increasing the Q factor, enhancing the designated mode, and diminishing unwanted modes. Phononic crystal is a type of metamaterial with small holes arranged in a repeated pattern for scattering elastic waves. The numerical data on the dynamic features of the quartz oscillator with phononic holes were generated by using the finite element software, COMSOL. Discussions include the effects of increasing Q and rejecting unwanted modes. In addition, some trends between phononic crystal arrangement and device performance are presented.

*Keywords*: quartz oscillator, phononic crystal, simulation, COMSOL

## 1 INTRODUCTION

The piezoelectric effect was first discovered by Piere Curie and Jacques Pure in 1880 (Mould 2017). The quartz oscillator (Figure 1(a)) is an important electrical component within each electrical device. The oscillator is composed of a quartz plate with electrodes fixed to both surfaces. Applying an appropriate alternating voltage signal to the gold electrodes can lead to continuous vibration of the quartz oscillator. The frequency of vibration is generally its natural frequency, which is determined by the cut, shape, and size of the quartz plate and the electrodes. The efficiency of a quartz oscillator can be evaluated by examining the value of the Q factor since a larger Q usually provides a more reliable design with less energy loss. The mode shape of the vibration is also considered because the appointed mode should be relatively strong to achieve a good temperature-frequency effect.

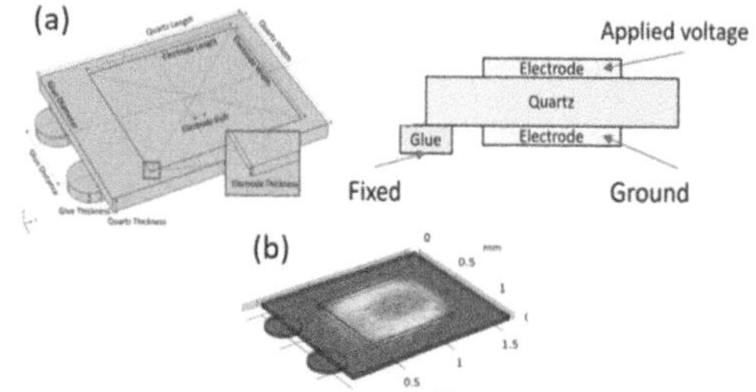

Phononic crystal is artificially made, periodically arranged, and embedded in a structure. With the appropriate material and crystal lattice arrangement, the phononic structure can be customized for blocking waves with a specific frequency range. A typical plate with the phononic crystal arrangement (Chen *et al.* 2015) is given in Figure 2(a), where the phononic lattice is between the electrode and the attachment glue. The low Q phenomenon usually comes from the small difference in frequencies between the appointed and unwanted modes.

Phononic crystal is usually used for blocking the appointed mode and dissipating the energy of unwanted modes. The analysis of phononic crystals usually starts by studying floquet periodicity (Degirmenci and Landais, 2013; Hakoda *et al.*, 2018) by the finite element method. A floquet plate (Figure 2(b)) is an infinitely large plate with holes in a repetitive pattern. A band gap of frequency is found, and motion with any frequency within this range theoretically cannot propagate. Therefore,

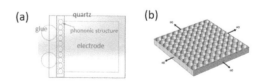

Figure 1. The quartz oscillator. (2) quartz oscillator, (b) thickness shear mode.

*Corresponding Author: t330005@cc.ncu.edu.tw

Figure 2. (a) Phononic structure on an oscillator, (b) Floquet plate.

DOI: 10.1201/9781003460763-19

the wave cannot transmit out of the structure, and the specific vibration is blocked. This research then attempted to use the blocking effect of phononic crystals on quartz oscillators. The materials in this paper are based on the reference (Merdekawan 2023).

## 2 QUARTZ OSCILLATORS

The quartz oscillator (Figure 1(a)) consists of a small quartz plate, thin electrode sheets on the top and bottom of the quartz, and two pieces of glue for fixing the oscillator. An AC voltage is applied to excite the oscillation. The quartz, in our study, was designed to vibrate in the Thickness Shear Mode (TSM), as given in Figure 1(b).

Figure 3(a) is the figure of conductance versus frequency obtained from the simulation, where the frequencies corresponding to the points with maximum conductance (a, b, and c in Figure 3(a)) are the natural frequencies. The mode shapes corresponding to these natural frequencies are given in Figure 3(b). Although we expect TSM, the modes in Figure 3(b) are not TSM but a combination of unwanted modes and TSM. The occurrence of the coupling is because of the close values of natural frequencies. This phenomenon should be avoided to reduce the temperature-frequency effect (Lee & Yong 1984). Usually, the high conductance, or Q factor, of TSM is an indication of a good design.

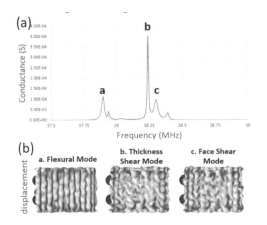

Figure 3. Conductance and modes from simulation. (a) Conductance of quartz oscillator, (b) different modes.

## 3 RESULTS AND DISCUSSIONS

In the present study, we chose the design of a quartz oscillator with a frequency of around 38.2 MHz. The use of the concept of phononic crystal in the design of quartz is an innovation for eliminating the influence of unwanted modes and increasing the Q factor.

To properly arrange phononic structure in quartz, one needs to work on the infinite Floquet plate (Figure 2(b)) first. In the analysis procedure, a unit cell (Figure 4(a)) is defined, and only the first Brillouin zone (Du et al. 2017) (Figure 4(b)) is considered. In this zone, the computation starts from the point "0"($\Gamma$), then "1"(X), "2"(M), "3"(Y), and then returns to point "4"($\Gamma$) for finding the dispersive diagram. The dispersive diagram (given in Figure 5) shows the relationship between wave propagation directions and the natural frequencies of the floquet plate, where the horizontal axis is the wave number $k$ and the vertical axis is the frequency of the wave. One can observe a frequency band gap in this figure. In other words, there is no frequency curve in the band, from 36.1 to 46.4 MHz, for every $k$, and this indicates the corresponding waves cannot propagate in the floquet plate. Our quartz oscillator has a natural frequency in the band gap. Therefore, this particular phononic design in the oscillator may result in a good effect by trapping the energy of TSM, scattering unwanted modes, and increasing the Q factor.

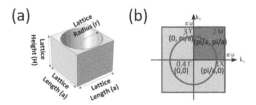

Figure 4. Unit cell. (a) the cell, (b) first Brillouin zone.

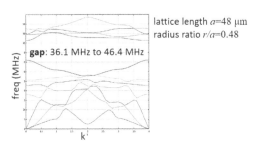

Figure 5. Dispersive diagram.

Different dimensions of phononic structure on the floquet plate yield different frequency ranges of band gaps, as shown in Figure 6, where the red dashed line is the designated natural frequency, 38.2 MHz, of the quartz oscillator. The purple arrows, for $r/a = 0.48$, indicate the corresponding band gaps for various lattice values of $a$. Figure 6 shows that, with $a > 40$ μm and $r/a = 0.48$, the frequency of 38.2 MHz is within the frequency band gap. Figure 7 illustrates the oscillation modes for several designs of oscillators. The mode of quartz with no phononic structure is in Figure 7 (a), where the mode is TSM combined with another stronger unwanted flexible mode, hence with a rather small Q factor. A row of phononic through holes was then arranged between the glue and the electrode, as shown in Figure 7(b) and (c). These two figures give modes of quartz plates with phononic holes, and their modes are more like TSM. In Figure 7(c), the frequency of quartz, 38.2 MHz, is in the band gap of the floquet plate, and this design yields a strong TSM and a 27-fold increase in Q. In another case shown in Figure 7 (b), the quartz's frequency is located slightly outside the band gap, and this design can still result in TSM but with a lower Q compared with Figure 7 (c). Note that in Figure 7, three different cases have similar natural frequencies.

motion is closer to TSM, the displacement ratios y/z and z/x should be much smaller than 1. In case A with a large Q, two displacement ratios correspond to this saturation. In case B with a small Q, displacement ratios are apparently large and indicate the combination of TSM and other unwanted modes. Figure 10(b) illustrates the modes for cases A and B, where the mode of case A shows a motion near TSM and that of case B shows the opposite.

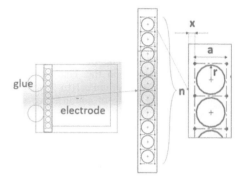

Figure 8. Geometric parameters in arrangement of phononic holes.

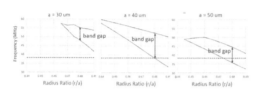

Figure 6. Floquet plate. (a) unit cell, (b) first Brillouin zone.

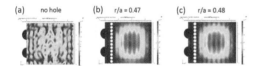

Figure 7. Oscillation modes of quartz oscillators. (a) no hole, (b) r/a = 0.47, (b) r/a = 0.48.

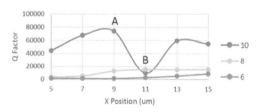

Figure 9. Q factors by varying geometric parameters $n$ and $X$.

Besides the arrangement of the phononic structure discussed before, there are also other parameters affecting the results. We will investigate the effects of changing the number of holes $n$ and the distance of lattices from the glue $X$. The definition of these two geometric parameters is illustrated in Figure 8. The numerical results of Q factors using various $n$ and $X$ are given in Figure 9. In general, quartz oscillators with phononic structure have Q factors greater than those without a hole. More holes seem to have a higher Q. This is because the blocking effect of phononic holes is stronger for a longer row of holes. On the other hand, the resulting value of Q nonlinearly depends on the distance $X$. For $n$ = 10 and $X$ = 11 μm (case B in Figure 9), the corresponding Q factor has a sudden drop. Figure 10 then shows the results using a phononic structure with $n$ = 10. Figure 10(a) gives Q factors and displacement ratios, where x motion is in the thickness direction and y and z are the other two directions of the quartz plate. If the total

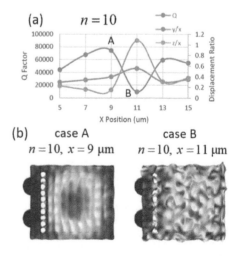

Figure 10. Results using a phononic structure with $n$ = 10. (a) Q and frequency ratios, (b) modes.

# 4  CONCLUSIONS

This research investigated the influence of embedding phononic structure in a quartz oscillator on increasing its Q factor, enhancing TSM, and eliminating unwanted modes beside TSM. One row of phononic holes is placed between the attachment glue and the electrode. Numerical results by the finite element method, using COMSOL, were obtained and discussed. Our main conclusions are listed below:

(1) The phononic structure in an infinitely large floquet plate results in the band gap in the dispersive diagram.
(2) For excellent effects of blocking the designated mode and increasing Q, the natural frequency of the oscillator should be within the band gap of the corresponding floquet plate.
(3) In the case of a quartz oscillator with a natural frequency not far away from the band gap, a satisfactory effect of increasing Q could still be obtained.
(4) A long row of holes, covering the entire width of the quartz plate, can usually give maximum effects.
(5) Another geometric parameter is the distance from the phononic holes to the glue. This parameter gives nonlinear and complicated effects to the results.

## ACKNOWLEDGEMENT

This work was supported by the funding NSC-111-2622-E-008-018 "Development of Key Technologies for Fabricating Advanced Quartz Oscillator" of the Taiwan Government.

## REFERENCES

Chen Y.Y, Lin Y.R., Wu T.T. and Pao S.Y., 2015, *IEEE International Ultrasonics Symposium Proceedings.*
Degirmenci E. and Landais P, 2013, *Applied Optics*, V. 52, 7367–7375.
Du Q., Zeng Y., Huang G. and Yang, H., 2017, *AIP Advances*, V. 7, 075015.
Hakoda C., Rose J, Shokouhi P. and Lissenden C., 2018, *AIP Conference Proceedings*, V. 1949, 020016.
Lee P.C.Y. and Yong, Y.K., 1984, *Journal of Applied Physics*, V. 56, pp. 1514–1521.
Merdekawan N., 2023, *Master Thesis*, Dept. of Mechanical Engineering, National Central University, Taiwan.
Mould R.F., 2007, *Current Oncology*, V. 14, 74–82.

System Innovation for a Troubled World – Lam et al. (Eds)
© 2024 the Author(s), ISBN: 978-1-032-60846-4

# Research on the development and popular factors of short video—taking TikTok as an example

Hsin-Yi Yu
*Department of Digital Multimedia Arts, Shih Hsin University, Taipei, Taiwan*

Jiun-Ting Chen*
*Department of Information and Communication/Department of Digital Multimedia Arts, Shih Hsin University, Taipei, Taiwan*

ABSTRACT: With the progress of science and technology, mobile devices are becoming increasingly popular. Consumers' dependence on smart devices is growing as well. TikTok has risen with this wave and has won the number one download in the world for four consecutive years. With over one billion users worldwide, short videos have become a trend on the Internet trend. At the same time, a large amount of information and AI technology lead to an increase in false information and fraud. Information security issues are very important in the Internet age. The research intends to explore how the trust of generation X, Y, and Z users in audio-visual information affects user satisfaction and willingness to use. The study used an online questionnaire for investigation and conducted sampling to study factors such as source credibility, information credibility, personal identity, professionalism, trustworthiness, and degree of liking. Analyzing the correlation between the information credibility of short videos and audio, user satisfaction, and usage intention of different generations. The research seeks to clarify the needs and preferences of users from different generations and provide more precise reference suggestions for short video creators in the future.

*Keywords*: short videos, personal identification, information credibility, user satisfaction, behavioral intention

## 1 INTRODUCTION

Mobile devices are gradually popularized with the advancement of technology. According to the survey conducted by the Communication Survey Database (2020) of the Ministry of Science and Technology, the users of mobile phones in Taiwan has reached 93.4%, with an average daily usage of nearly 4 hours. The social media algorithm will push relevant content to users according to their preferences to catch the audience's eyes. As a result, users passively acquire information and hardly come into contact with different opinions. Meanwhile, short videos quickly became a fad online due to their convenience and low cost. Self-operated media, such as short videos and videos, contain various forms of information. Users share short videos and video content through links to quickly spread information on the Internet. Innovative push also creates ideological separation in audio-visual media, and users will connect with users with characteristics and ideologies, thereby expanding the influence of misinformation (Brummette et al., 2018).

### 1.1 *Purposes*

TikTok, an App based on short videos, has grown and developed astonishingly, attracting academic attention. With the rapid development of short videos as an emerging model, related research has also produced different concerns, mainly focusing on development status, customer satisfaction, information content, and development risks. This study combs through the literature to explore the factors that affect the user willingness of TikTok and to understand the public's satisfaction with TikTok, which contains the following three points:

(1) Explore whether there are differences in the degreen of trust in TikTok among different age groups.
(2) Discuss how satisfied each age group is while using TikTok.
(3) Explore whether there are differences in the usage intentions of TikTok among different age groups.

## 2 LITERATURE REVIEW

Short videos are a type of video content with a shorter duration, usually within a few minutes. In

*Corresponding Author: andy@mail.shu.edu.tw

DOI: 10.1201/9781003460763-20

recent years, short videos have become popular on the internet and can be shared on various online platforms such as TikTok, Instagram, and YouTube. Because of their concise and impactful nature, short videos can quickly convey information and capture users' attention. The following is some information and literature about short videos.

## 2.1 The origin and development of TikTok

Officially launched in 2016, TikTok is a social app developed by the Chinese company Byte Dance and has gained popularity in the global market. Its most prominent feature is a short video-based social platform where users can show their creative life by shooting and sharing 15-second to 3-minute videos (TikTok 2022). According to the (Digital 2022) data report, as of September 2021, TikTok has a total of 1 billion monthly active users worldwide, 54.1% of global female users and 45.9% of global male users, of which 18–24 Young people under ten years old are the main user groups as shown in Figure 1.

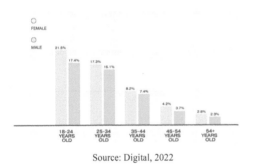

Source: Digital, 2022

Figure 1. TikTok users of different age groups in 2022. Source: Digital, 2022

## 2.2 Generation X

Generation X refers to people born between 1965 and 1980. They are the first generation to grow up in the information age and have a unique experience and perception of technological products and digital life. Generation X pays more attention to personal autonomy and balance and pursues a balance between career and family. In the workplace, Generation X is described as an autonomous, innovative, and visionary generation (Bock et al. 2020).

## 2.3 Generation Y

Generation Y, or Millennial Generation, was born between 1981 and 1994. Deloitte (2014) analyzed the habits of millennials in terms of work, consumption, and social media usage, pointing out that they pay more attention to personal development and work balance, and pay more attention to

issues such as corporate social responsibility and environmental protection.

## 2.4 Generation Z

Generation Z refers to people born between 1995 and 2010. They grew up in the era of rapid development of digital technology and had a high degree of acceptance of technology, social media, and the digital lifestyle. Generation Z spends much time using the Internet, mobile devices, and social media. They are the generation most closely connected through the Internet (Kunja & Gvrk 2018).

## 2.5 Information credibility

The source of information must be credible, and objective, scientific, and professional information is the most credible. Emotional and visual elements also affect the credibility of the information (Li & Suh 2015). To increase the credibility of information, subjective, emotional, and biased elements should be avoided, and positive emotions and high-quality visual elements should be appropriately used when disseminating information.

## 2.6 User satisfaction

A research report on user satisfaction (Zhao et al. 2018) indicates that website security and brand image also have a positive and significant impact on satisfaction. If the actual user experience meets or exceeds user expectations, it may lead to continued usage intention and higher levels of satisfaction (Bhattacherjee 2001).

## 2.7 Behavioral intention

Behavioral intention is an essential concept in behavioral psychology, which refers to the intention or tendency of a person to perform a particular behavior. Specifically, behavioral intention refers to a person's subjective judgment on whether a specific behavior will be performed at a specific time and situation. Research on behavioral intentions helps companies better understand consumer needs and decisions to formulate more effective marketing strategies and plans.

## 3 RESEARCH METHODS

Based on the literature review, we can find a correlation between information trust, usage satisfaction, and behavioral intentions for each generation. This study extends this research based on literature theories such as information credibility, user satisfaction, and behavioral intentions, and develops the research architecture of this study is shown in Figure 2.

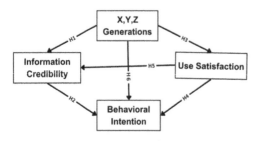

Figure 2.  Research structure diagram

The following hypotheses are drawn based on the discussion of the literature mentioned above and the correlation of each aspect. Through the analysis of questionnaire data, these hypotheses will be further tested to determine whether they are supported or not, and conclusions will be drawn.

H1::Generation X, Y, and Z have different emphases on the credibility of information content.
H2::Differences in information credibility will lead to differences in behavioral intentions.
H3::Generations X, Y, and Z have different satisfaction levels with using short videos.
H4::User satisfaction will directly affect behavioral intention.
H5::User satisfaction will affect the trust in information content.
H6::Generations X, Y, and Z have different behavioral intentions for short videos.

### 3.1  Operational definition and measurement

This section discusses the aspects of the research framework. The primary measurement aspects include information credibility, user satisfaction, and behavioral intentions. The operational definition of this study is defined as shown in Table 1.

Table 1.  Operation definition comparison.

| Dimensions | Details | Operation definition | Source |
|---|---|---|---|
| Information credibility | Professional | Professional sources can affect the credibility of information. | Kleiman's et al. (2015) |
| Information credibility | Degree of trust | And if there are many people endorsed at the same time and the content is highly consistent, it will give people a sense of trust, which will affect their original views. When the number of messages is large, the per- | Chung (2012) |

(continued)

Table 1.  Continued

| Dimensions | Details | Operation definition | Source |
|---|---|---|---|
| | | suasive effect is more effective. | |
| User satisfaction | Ease of use | Ease of use has a significant correlation with brand loyalty, which will increase consumers' willingness to use. | Chang (2016) |
| User satisfaction | Satisfaction level | Information content design has a greater impact on satisfaction. | Zhao (2018) |
| Behavioral intention | Loyalty | Behavioral loyalty may lead to a brand's higher market share, while attitudinal loyalty increases a brand's relative brand value. | Ebrahim (2020) |
| Behavioral intention | Degree of preference | Brand attachment can more correctly predict behavioral intention, and it is also an indicator that brand attitude strength can more strongly predict actual consumer behavior. | Park (2010) |

### 3.2  Questionnaire

In this study, the relevant literature on the aspects and variables proposed by the referenced scholars was rectified, and the test questions on the aspects were modified, and the parts of information trust, user satisfaction, and behavioral intentions were moderately corrected; using structural Questionnaires used to explore the relationship between information trust, user satisfaction, and behavioral intentions among users of generations X, Y, and Z; Scores of 5 points, 4 points, 3 points, 2 points, and 1 point are given sequentially, divided into five scales: "5 strongly agree", "4 agree", "3 moderate", "2 disagree", "1 strongly disagree".

The research questionnaire setting is divided into four parts: the first part is "demographic analysis," which is the basic information and usage status of the subjects to facilitate the cross-comparison of each generation after the study; the second part is "information credibility" to see how much different generations of users value it. The third part is "Usage Satisfaction" to understand the user satisfaction of users of different generations. The fourth part is "Behavioral Intention" Related research will help companies better understand consumer needs and decision-making.

### 3.3 Questionnaire facets and questions

The test questions of each research dimension variable are explained in the following Table 2.

Table 2. Test item table.

| Dimensions | Test topic content |
|---|---|
| Information credibility | 1. I think the information provided on TikTok is professional. |
| | 2. I will use the shopping guide on TikTok with peace of mind. |
| | 3. I think TikTok is a trustworthy platform. |
| | 4. I have doubts about the accuracy of repeated and relevant information on TikTok. |
| | 5. The information I saw on TikTok will be verified again. |
| | 6. Whether TikTok information is professional or not will affect my willingness to use it. |
| | 7. I doubt the authenticity of the content when watching TikTok short videos. |
| | 8. I will collect short knowledge-based videos on TikTok. |
| | 9. Comments on short videos and videos will affect my opinion. |
| | 10. Creator subscriber count affects my trust level. |
| User satisfaction | 1. I have good reviews on TikTok. |
| | 2. Overall, TikTok meets my needs. |
| | 3. I am satisfied with TikTok's user interface. |
| | 4. I am satisfied with the kind of content TikTok offers. |
| | 5. I am satisfied with TikTok's smart push function. |
| | 6. I am satisfied with the ease of use of the overall interface of TikTok. |
| Behavioral intention | 1. I use TikTok a lot. |
| | 2. I will use TikTok as a conduit for knowledge. |
| | 3. My main purpose of using TikTok is entertainment. |
| | 4. I am the creator of TikTok short videos. |
| | 5. There is an increasing trend in the amount of time I use TikTok. |
| | 6. Most of my relatives and friends use TikTok. |
| | 7. I will recommend or share this APP to my relatives and friends. |
| | 8. Sharing TikTok to other platforms is a function I often use. |
| | 9. I use TikTok a lot to find out what's trending right now. |

## 4 EXPECTED RESULTS

The study expects to gain a deeper understanding of the trust degree of users of different generations in short audio-visual information and its impact on user satisfaction and willingness to use through questionnaire analysis and the analysis of source credibility, information credibility, personal identity, professionalism, and trustworthiness, to understand the needs and preferences of users of different generations, finding out how much each generation values the authenticity of information. In addition, this research provides more accurate reference suggestions for short video creators to improve users' satisfaction and willingness and put forward relevant suggestions for short video information on mobile devices to ensure information security. Ultimately, the result of this study provides references for relevant industries, government units, and academic researchers to promote the further development and improvement of the short video industry on mobile devices.

## REFERENCES

Bhattacherjee A., 2001. Understanding information systems continuance: an expectation confirmation model. *MIS Quarterly*, 351–370.

Bock G.W., Kim Y.G. & Lee J.N. 2020. The effects of perceived cognitive load on technology acceptance: A meta-analysis. *Information & Management*, 57(1), 103168. https://datareportal.com/reports/digital-2022-taiwan https://www.tiktok.com/zh-Hant-TW/

Brummette J., Distaso M., Vafeiadis M. & Messner M., 2018. Read all about it: The politicization of fake news on twitter. *Journalism & Mass Communication Quarterly*, 95(2), 497–517.

Chang W.H., 2016. The Relationship Among Perceived Ease of Use, User Experience and Loyalty of Mobile Banking.

Ebrahim R.S., 2020. The role of trust in understanding the impact of social media marketing on brand equity and brand loyalty. *Journal of Relationship Marketing*, 19(4), 287–308.

Kleiman's M., Schaad G., & Hermans L., 2015. Citizen sources in the news: above and beyond the vox pop? *Journalism*, 18(4), 464–481.

Kunja S.R. & Gvrk A., 2018. Examining the effect of ewom on the customer purchase intention through value co-creation (vcc) in social networking sites (snss): a study of select facebook fan pages of smartphone brands in india. *Management Research Review*, 43(3), 245–269.

Li R. & Suh A., 2015. Factors influencing information credibility on social media platforms: evidence from faceook pages. *Procedia Computer Science*, 72, 314–328.

Park C.W., MacGinnis D., Priester J.R., Eisingerich A. B. & Iacobacci D., 2010. Brand attachment and brand attitude strength: conceptual and empirical differentiation of two critical brand equity drivers, *Journal of Marketing*. 74(11), 1–17.

Wang R.Y. & Wang J.H. & Chuang C.J., 2012. *The Influence of Electronic Word-of-Mouth to Online Collective Purchasing Intention*, 10(1), 26.

Zhao Y., Ni Q. & Mao Q., 2018. Investigating the impact of website quality on user satisfaction in the context of online shopping. *Journal of Retailing and Consumer Services*, 40, 139–148.

*System Innovation for a Troubled World – Lam et al. (Eds)*
© 2024 the Author(s), ISBN: 978-1-032-60846-4

# A simulation framework for V2X autonomous vehicles based on cyber physical vehicle systems technologies

Ming-Jui Ho & Tsung-Ying Sun
*Department of Electrical Engineering, National Dong Hwa University, Hualien, Taiwan*

Shiow-yang Wu*
*Department of Computer Science and Information Engineering, National Dong Hwa University, Hualien, Taiwan*

ABSTRACT: Autonomous vehicle technology has been advancing rapidly. Comprehensive testing is essential before road deployment. However, no test can cover every possible situation. Thus, a good simulation system is necessary. Most existing systems are restricted to limited aspects that fail to correspond with reality in complex and volatile environments. Cyber-Physical Vehicle System (CPVS) technology enables the simulation systems to integrate more closely with actual vehicles. Nevertheless, the behavior analysis and decision-making capabilities are still far from perfect. The proposed framework is based on CPVS that integrates physical sensors and mechanical components on a vehicle with a ROS2-based cyber-system receiving messages through WAN for cooperative optimization. The messages conform to IEEE and SAE standards integrated with RealSense, Lidar, IMU sensor data and mechanical components information to display the vehicle status with Unity graphics in two modes: real-time scene rendering and vehicle monitoring mode for vehicle monitoring, and scene restoring mode for error analysis. We emphasize the cyber-physical interaction in which the physical system serves feedback data for model building and scene construction while the cyber system tests the controller with various simulated scenes. A scene editor subsystem is provided to visually layout static/moving objects on a virtual plane to construct any desired scene and trigger Unity to generate simulated sensor data for evaluating the reactions of simulated or physical vehicles. The CPVS is used in the design of an autonomous ground vehicle (AGV) simulated and tested using serval situations layout with the scene editor. Compared with testing the AGV in real environments, the result is highly satisfactory.

*Keywords*: Cyber-Physical Vehicle System, V2X, autonomous vehicles, digital simulation, Robot Operate System

## 1 INTRODUCTION

Computer simulations are indispensable in the design and analysis of complex dynamic systems, especially for the testing and validation of structural and functional behavior at different levels of detail (Žlajpah 2008). It is even more important for autonomous vehicle design as the vehicle status along with all possible interactions with surrounding objects must be taken into consideration. Most existing systems are restricted to limited aspects such as lane keeping, driving patterns, electronic systems, fleet control, etc. but fail to correspond with reality in complex and volatile environments (Gelbal et al. 2017; Nilsson et al. 2017; Li et al. 2012; Marjovi et al. 2015). We proposed a CPVS-based simulation framework for V2X and driving control in autonomous vehicles. The framework is built on top of ROS2 which integrates the physical system, navigation control,

and sensor data on the vehicle with a cyber system on Unity for scene generation, test data provisioning, and vehicle status visualization. The simulation can be conducted in two modes: **real-time scene rendering and vehicle monitoring mode** for online simulation and visualization, as well as **scene restoring mode** for error analysis. A scene editor subsystem is provided to layout any desired scene and trigger the generation of simulated data for the testing and evaluation of simulated or physical vehicles. With special emphasis on cyber-physical interactions, the framework facilitates tight correspondence between simulated environment and reality which is the key to effective design, testing, and co-optimization.

The paper is organized as follows. Section 2 presents existing cyber-physical vehicle systems (CPVSs) and related systems for autonomous vehicles, especially ROS2 and Unity-based systems. Section 3 describes the architectural design and system components of our CPVS-based simulation system. Section 4 continues with a detailed analysis of the key characteristics and main

*Corresponding Author: showyang@gms.ndhu.edu.tw

DOI: 10.1201/9781003460763-21

advantages. In Section 5, we discuss the implementation and evaluation of our framework. Section 6 concludes the paper.

## 2 LITERATURE REVIEW

CPS facilitates tight integration of virtual and physical systems on computing, communication, and control to achieve stability, performance, reliability, robustness, and efficiency in many application domains (Wang et al. 2018). CPVS is the extension of CPS on ground, aerial, and maritime vehicles. It is more challenging due to the need to deal with not only surrounding objects but also complex issues such as weather, regulations, and social interactions. The size and resource limits on vehicles make everything trickier. On-road deployment brings even more uncertainty. With tight integration of all modules and components between cyber and physical systems, CPVS facilitates close coordination and co-optimization in both design and operation to meet the demanding requirements of autonomy, adaptability, reliability, effectiveness, robustness, and safety as illustrated in Figure 1 (Bradley & Atkins 2015).

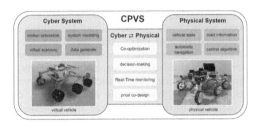

Figure 1. Cyber-Physical Vehicle System concepts.

In our framework, ROS2 is chosen as the kernel of the physical system. ROS2 is a meta operating system and a set of tools for robots. It has been highly versatile and very popular among roboticists ever since its first release (Macenski et al. 2022). With its concise yet comprehensive considerations of embedded systems, diverse networks, real-time processing, security, and product readiness, it is now widely used in autonomous systems such as robots and AGVs. The cross-platform support of ROS2 allows us to integrate seamlessly with Unity for the cyber system part of our CPVS framework. However, our framework is flexible enough to adopt other 3D simulation tools such as Gazebo and CoppelizSim (formerly V-Rep). Most existing systems that integrate Unity and ROS2 are restricted to limited functionalities or one-way communication (Sita et al. 2017; Hussein et al. 2018). Our CPVS-based framework achieves tight integration of cyber and physical systems for the design, simulation, testing, and optimization of autonomous vehicles.

The scope of autonomous ground vehicle (AGV) control has been extended from vehicle control to V2V (communicating with surrounding vehicles) to V2X (interacting with all objects on the road such as traffic signals and pedestrians). With the increasing need for V2X communication, the interoperability of vehicles and objects of different nations, brands, and models must be established. International standards such as IEEE 802.11p and SEA J2735 are becoming more mature and popular (SAE 2022). Our system abides by the international standards above to cover V2X.

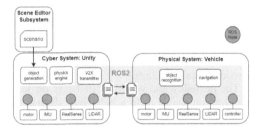

Figure 2. The proposed CPVS system architecture.

## 3 SYSTEM DESCRIPTION

### 3.1 *Framework*

The CPVS-based framework we proposed and implemented is built on top of ROS2 and Unity as illustrated in Figure 2. ROS2 is the operation platform of the physical system to support navigation control, object recognition, and all sensor modules. The cyber system is modeled and visualized by Unity. A common ROS2 substrate is used for the connection and message exchange between the two. A scene editor subsystem is provided to design test scenarios and trigger the object generator in Unity to construct corresponding simulated scenes for testing and evaluation. More details are in the following sections.

#### 3.1.1 *ROS2*
The physical system (vehicle) is composed of multiple ROS2 nodes to manage underlying mechanical components as well as different types of on-vehicle sensors for camera image capturing, IMU data collection and filtering, voltage measurement, wheel speed detection/control, etc. The information feedback from the physical system is crucial. After applying the control commands, the ROS2 nodes can capture vehicle status information such as wheel speed, turning angle, acceleration, and other data for the cyber system to reconstruct the vehicle state dynamically on the simulator GUI. This can be used for system modeling and monitoring to facilitate system design, decision-making, testing, and co-optimization.

### 3.1.2 Unity game engine

The cyber system is driven by the Unity game engine. Upon receiving the data captured and transmitted from ROS2, the Unity engine compares and adjusts the cyber vehicle state to truthfully represent the physical vehicle so that the simulation and analysis results can be more reliable and useful.

For more comprehensive simulation, our system can reconstruct not only the dynamic vehicle state—such as coordinate, orientation, acceleration, and trajectory—but also the interactions of the vehicle with surrounding objects. This is achieved by a set of virtual sensors provided by our CPVS system. For example, a virtual RealSense camera can simulate and render the image and depth data similar to a real camera. A virtual LiDAR can reflect the distance between objects in the simulated scene and render it with PhysicsRaycast in Unity.

The flexibility and versatility of Unity on scene construction enable us to achieve high diversity in simulation. Simple scenes can be constructed with built-in obstacles in Unity for initial testing. For complex scenes in the real world, we can import 3D models built by tools such as AutoCAD, Blander, etc. as well as the rich 3D model resources provided by the open-source community. With the model importing function, our system can potentially simulate any real-world scene to significantly extend the coverage of testing at a very low cost.

### 3.1.3 ROS2 and UNITY Connection

The connection between cyber and physical systems is done through message exchange between ROS2 and Unity. The message header contains information such as ID, timestamp, data format, encoding, etc. Control and sensing data such as motor control commands, data from various sensors, and calculated output are transmitted in the message payload. The message transmission is through the LAN using the official Unity-Robotics-Hub (Unity Technologies, 2022).

### 3.2 V2X

Compared with the information collected by sensors, the data provided by V2X is richer and more accurate, which is of great value to the prediction and decision-making in AGV. V2X can also provide a field of vision of obscured objects and blind spots through intermediate vehicles. Most existing V2X simulators are aimed at the testing and verification of communication protocols. To test the operation of the AGV control system in a V2X environment, existing test sites are very rare and expensive, and almost all of them are closed sites. As an important feature of our framework, we introduce V2X into our system to test the AGV control responses on V2X events. Our message format is defined based on the Basic Safety

Message format released by SEA, without the fields that are not used in our system, such as Brake Applied Status as presented in Table 1.

Table 1. V2X Message Packet Definition

| Data Element | Format | unit |
| --- | --- | --- |
| Vehicle ID | Text | |
| Position | Vector3 | m |
| Position accuracy | Float | m |
| Liner Speed | Vector3 | m/sec |
| Liner acceleration | Float | m/sec |
| Heading | Float | rad |
| Turn angle | Float | rad |
| Turn rate | Float | rad/sec |
| Control status | Text | |
| Vehicle size | Vector3 | m |

### 3.3 Real-time scenes rendering and vehicle monitoring mode

This is one of the two primary operation modes provided by the cyber system. When Unity receives the physical-system data provided by ROS2, it restores the current state of the vehicle and surrounding scenes in the simulator. The speed, acceleration, and attitude of the vehicle are determined by the IMU, and the wheel speed, battery voltage, system power, temperature, etc. can be obtained from corresponding sensors. Driving environment data, including other vehicles, pedestrians, traffic signs, obstacles, etc., can be detected not only by cameras and LiDAR but also from V2X information which allows us to create more accurate scenes.

It is essential to correctly model and simulate the interactions of the AGV control system with all other objects in the driving environment so as to make proper decisions. Under this mode, the cyber system can present the users with detailed physical data of the vehicle as well as all interactions with other objects in real-time. In addition to facilitating remote real-time monitoring, a great opportunity for the optimization of the AGV decision-making system is at hand.

### 3.4 Scene restoring mode

The second primary mode of the cyber system is to record and store essential data during real-time simulation and rendering so that critical scenarios can be reconstructed repeatedly for controller adjustment and system optimization. The stored information can also be used on other controllers for the purposes of comparison and evaluation. System optimization is not limited to the current controller on the vehicle. It can be applied to test the controllers in all stages of system design, even on the optimization of mechanical structure.

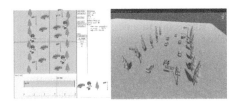

Figure 3. Scene editor subsystem (left) and scenes construction in Unity (right).

## 3.5 *Scene editor subsystem*

To achieve comprehensive testing of the control system, solely relying on the test data recorded by actual vehicles is not enough. The cost of collecting test data for all possible scenarios is prohibitively high. Some experimental vehicles may not even be allowed to test on the road without legal approval.

For this reason, we propose a Scene Editor Subsystem that can design and edit test scenarios. Through this system, a scene containing multiple dynamic and static objects, such as an intersection with cars and pedestrians, can be edited with a concise and friendly user interface to generate a corresponding script. Unity engine can simulate the test scenario by running the script and analyzing if the simulated AGV meets the expected control results.

As illustrated in Figure 3, after designing the layout and arranging the movement of all objects in the scene editor subsystem, the generated script can be executed by Unity to create the scene dynamically. They provide the driving environment data for the simulated vehicle on ROS2 for further simulation and control. Simulation results can be visualized in different ways as demonstrated in Figure 4.

Figure 4. ROS2 visualization. Pointcloud (left), camera (top right) and object ID (bottom right).

## 4 SYSTEM CHARACTERISTICS

### 4.1 *Control system evaluation*

When testing on the simulator, the focus is often on whether it can truthfully reflect the actual running state and provide reference information for optimization. During the testing of the controller,

if the thresholds of proper responses can be determined according to the test data, then an evaluation function can be devised to measure the controller performance. To the best of our knowledge, neither the current simulation software nor the test equipment for self-driving cars can offer this function.

The advantage of CPVS is that the physical and cyber systems are closely integrated, and various information in both systems can be exchanged comprehensively. For example, if we want to test the decision-making of an AGV control system in response to a sudden obstacle in a V2X environment. Existing simulation software can only simulate roads with different types of traffic flow or generate V2X information independently on the road. The proposed CPVS architecture can record the sensing time of the control system, the control commands output, vehicle movement data, etc. during the execution of the script. Upon judging whether the controller achieves the designated task, it can also evaluate the quality of the decision process. For the above-mentioned case, we can evaluate if the vehicle always stops at a certain distance before the obstacle. Other metrics such as the time point when the object is recognized, the time and cost of calculation, and the vehicle deceleration behavior, etc. also need to be analyzed to set proper thresholds. By obtaining this detailed information, the system components can be optimized separately and as a whole.

### 4.2 *Cooperative optimization*

The main purpose of using a traditional simulator is to investigate and evaluate control system behavior for controller optimization through simulated system operation and data analysis. In our CPVS architecture, however, not only the control system and mechanical structure on the physical system can be optimized, but also the restoration of the simulated vehicle and the generation of the simulated environment in the cyber system.

Take the development process of an AGV as an example. After setting the vehicle mission, the target driving environment and terrain can be generated in the cyber system. Then the designated vehicle model can be tested and adjusted to meet the requirements. After model adjustment, various simulated sensors can also be configured and installed on the virtual model. With satisfactory simulation results, the actual vehicle can be built based on the successful model in the cyber system. In addition to cost savings, the simulations also ensure a certain level of applicability and reliability of the physical vehicle. After vehicle construction is completed, the physical system can provide true data with loaded sensors and compare it with that of a simulated vehicle. System identification is used to ensure the consistency between the simulated vehicle with the actual vehicle, so as to match simulation to reality. This makes the subsequent design and optimization of the control system in the simulator more compatible with the actual vehicle. After the deployment of the vehicle loaded with the control system, the operating environment data collected by the vehicle can be used to further optimize the cyber system, such as introducing real-world noise to the sensors and V2X data of the simulator or making the characteristics of generated scenes more similar to real-world environments and so on.

The above is a legitimate development process using our CPVS framework but not the only one. Our system can offer invaluable assistance to many AGV design, testing, and manufacturing tasks. In particular, the physical system and cyber system can be continuously improved at different stages and layers to achieve cooperative optimization.

### 4.3 Decision-making

In addition to the cooperation of the cyber and physical systems, our system can also generate possible future scenes dynamically based on certain conditions and parameter changes, then predict the decision in advance according to the situation at hand or ahead of time. This allows the system to make more resourceful and reliable decisions.

## 5 EXPERIMENTS

### 5.1 Platform description

#### 5.1.1 Physical system
The physical system includes the physical vehicle with ROS2 kernel for the control system. The controller consists of upper-level calculation and control algorithms with lower-level motor control and sensor receptors. The ROS2 employed is the Foxy Fitzroy release. NVIDIA Jetson Nano Developer Kit is chosen as the development platform. Each component is modeled by a ROS2 node including each sensor, remote control, navigation, and Unity connector. The sensors include RealSense, 2D LiDAR, IMU, wheel-speed sensor, voltage sensor, and power sensors.

#### 5.1.2 Cyber system
The cyber system consists of a Unity 20203.11f kernel on Win10 driven by an Intel i7-7700 CPU with 16 GB RAM. The simulator consists of two parts, a simulated vehicle and an object generator.

The simulated vehicle is the 3D model of the target vehicle under simulation. They have the same structure and simulated components with the same set of simulated sensors: a virtual RealSense, virtual 2D LiDAR, and virtual IMU.

The object generator generates static and dynamic objects based on the script exported from the Scene Editor Subsystem. The script is an XML

file with object definitions, object types, coordinates, size, and the designed scenes along the timeline. Each scene contains all the objects in the scene and where/when/how each object moves. Unity executes the script and renders the objects accordingly to create the scene dynamically.

To simulate the V2X environment, each object in the running scene, including pedestrians, vehicles, traffic signals, trees, and obstacles, has a corresponding data publisher to publish data according to Table 1.

The simulated vehicle receives commands from the remote control or autonomous controller on the physical vehicle to determine how to move. When both the simulated vehicle and the physical vehicle receive the commands and act accordingly, the system is in real-time monitoring mode. If only the simulated vehicle is operating without the corresponding physical vehicle, it is in scene-restoring mode. With various scene editing, restoration, and simulation, we can test the vehicle system comprehensively at a very low cost.

### 5.2 Validation use cases

We design a test scene on the Scene Editor Subsystem and export the script to Unity. The simulated vehicle accepts control commands and sensor data from Unity without a corresponding physical vehicle. With cyber-only vehicle, we can easily and repeatedly test the controller and modify the code if necessary. The initial controller and corresponding AGV trajectory are depicted as blue lines in Figure 5.

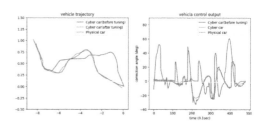

Figure 5. Simulated AGV trajectory and control output.

To correspond closely with the physical vehicle, a calibration process is necessary so that the control properties of both systems can be consistent. In this case, we need to calibrate wheel speed, DC motor response time, and the PI control parameters of the servo motor. After calibration, the cyber vehicle and physical vehicle are now in line with each other as illustrated by the orange and green lines in Figure 5.

We now apply the controller on the cyber vehicle to the physical vehicle and arrange a real-world scene that mimics the script scene. The trajectory and control output of the physical vehicle coincide closely with that of the cyber vehicle as illustrated in Figure 6. The controller designed and optimized in the cyber system can be used directly on the physical system without modification or adjustment, which demonstrates the effectiveness of our CPVS-based simulation framework.

Figure 6. Scenario for demonstrating the close correspondence between cyber and physical vehicle in our system.

The integration of V2X information is an important feature of our framework. As illustrated in Figure 7, upon traversing on a target path (blue line), the on-vehicle LiDAR can only detect visible obstacles within sensing range (the purple circle) and trigger dynamic obstacle avoidance locally (the green line). With V2X information (the orange dots), the control system can recognize obstacles along the target path far ahead of local sensing range to facilitate global optimal path planning instead of local adjustment.

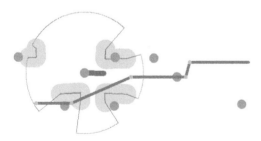

Figure 7. V2X information for the control system to plan ahead.

## 6 CONCLUSIONS

We proposed and implemented a CPVS-based framework for autonomous vehicle development and simulation. The framework integrates a ROS2-based physical system with a Unity-based cyber system such that the control system developed, simulated, and tested on the cyber system can be used directly on the physical system without

modification yet still exhibits almost identical behavior. A scene editor subsystem makes the framework even more versatile and useful.

The framework can be extended with more tools for validation and performance evaluation. We plan to devise precise metrics to measure the effectiveness of simulation and the quality of control system.

## REFERENCES

Bradley J.M. and Atkins E.M., "Optimization and Control of Cyber-Physical Vehicle Systems," *Sensors*, vol. 15, no. 9, pages 23020–23049, 2015.

Gelbal Ş.Y., Tamilarasan S., Cantaş M.R., Güvenç L., and Aksun-Güvenç B., "A connected and autonomous vehicle hardware-in-the-loop simulator for developing automated driving algorithms," *in 2017 IEEE International Conference on Systems, Man, and Cybernetics (SMC)*, 2017, pp. 3397–3402.

Hussein A., García F. and Olaverri-Monreal C., "ROS and Unity Based Framework for Intelligent Vehicles Control and Simulation," in *IEEE International Conference on Vehicular Electronics and Safety (ICVES)*, 2018, pp. 1–6.

Li Q., Chen W., Li Y., Liu S., and Huang J., "Energy management strategy for fuel cell/battery/ultra-capacitor hybrid vehicle based on fuzzy logic," *International Journal of Electrical Power & Energy Systems*, vol. 43, no. 1, pages 514–525, 2012.

Macenski S., Foote T., Gerkey B., Lalancette C., and Woodall W., "Robot Operating System 2: Design, architecture, and uses in the wild," *Science Robotics*, vol. 7, no. 66, pages eabm6074, 2022.

Marjovi A., Vasic M., Lemaitre J., and Martinoli A., "Distributed graph-based convoy control for networked intelligent vehicles," in 2015 IEEE Intelligent Vehicles Symposium (IV), 2015, pp. 138–143.

Nilsson P., Laine L., and Jacobson B., "A simulator study comparing characteristics of manual and automated driving during lane changes of long combination vehicles," *IEEE Transactions on Intelligent Transportation Systems*, vol. 18, no. 9, pages 2514–2524, 2017.

Sita E., Horváth C.M., Thomessen T., Korondi P. and Pipe A.G., "ROS-Unity3D based system for monitoring of an industrial robotic process," in *IEEE/ SICE International Symposium on System Integration (SII)*, 2017, pp. 1047–1052.

*Soc. Automotive Eng.J2735 V2X Communications Message Set Dictionary*, 2022–11. [Online]. Available: http://www.sae.org

*Unity Technologies*. (2022). Unity-Robotics-Hub. [Online]. Available: https://github.com/Unity-Technologies/Unity-Robotics-Hub

Wang H., Xu M., Zhu F., Deng Z., Li Y., and Zhou B., "Shadow traffic: A unified model for abnormal traffic behavior simulation," *Computers & Graphics*, vol. 70, no. pages 235–241, 2018.

Žlajpah L., "Simulation in robotics," *Mathematics and Computers in Simulation*, vol. 79, no. 4, pages 879–897, 2008.

*System Innovation for a Troubled World – Lam et al. (Eds)*
© 2024 the Author(s), ISBN: 978-1-032-60846-4

# The impact of digital networks on the shoe-buying process

Chia-An Chou* & Huang-Yu Che
*Department of Industrial Design, Chaoyang University of Technology, Taiwan*

ABSTRACT: In today's world, digital networking has become such an integral part of people's lives, that it's impossible to ignore its impact on the way people buy goods and services. In this study, we explore the impact of digital networks on the shoe-buying process. There is a wealth of information on the Internet, and consumers can easily compare different brands, styles, and prices, as well as search for reviews from other customers. Having this information helps to make an informed decision. Additionally, digital networks have made it easier for footwear retailers to market their products to potential customers. Social media platforms, in particular, enable retailers to reach a wider audience through targeted advertising and promotions. This study wants to explore whether there is a significant correlation between digital networks and buying shoes and whether digital networks play an important role in the growth of online footwear sales. The current situation of the shoe makes recommendations with total.

## 1 INTRODUCTION

Research has shown that there is a correlation between digital networks and buying shoes. As more people spend time on digital networks, the number of people buying shoes online has increased. Digital networks provide consumers with easy access to shoe retailers, allowing them to browse a wide range of styles and prices from the comfort of their own homes. This convenience has led to a significant increase in online shoe sales. In addition, digital networks provide consumers with access to user reviews and ratings, allowing them to make more informed decisions when buying shoes. This transparency has increased consumer confidence in online shopping, further contributing to the rise in online shoe sales. Furthermore, digital networks have made it easier for shoe retailers to market their products to potential customers. Social media platforms, in particular, have allowed retailers to reach a wider audience with targeted advertising and promotions. Overall, digital networks play a significant role in the growth of online shoe sales.

## 2 EXPERIMENTAL

Based on the purpose of the research, this chapter focuses on the literature to understand consumer purchasing behavior, online shopping service models, and the impact of today's digital networks. The following is divided into three parts,

the first introduces the relevant literature on the importance of the current shopping model, the second consumption intention, the third service model and the business model, which is required for future research.

### 2.1 Today's shopping model

Since the current lifestyle online store has the advantage of 24-hour operation and no regional restrictions, providing consumers with a shopping mode anytime, anywhere has high convenience, saving consumers valuable time. Forsythe and Shi (2003) pointed out that the convenience of the Internet is the main reason for consumers to choose online shopping. And, as Rayport and Sviokla (1994) argue, the advent of the Internet has shifted business competition from physical marketplaces to marketspaces, where consumers can shop through a computer screen instead of having to shop in stores. Li Yichen (2022) According to the survey results of the Market Intelligence and Consulting Institute (MIC) of the Taiwan Information and Policy Council, 52.9% of Taiwanese consumers shopped online and offline in 2020, and the proportion of 18- to 25-year-olds is nearly 60%. It can be seen that in recent years, more than half of young people have chosen to use the Internet to shop online, and more and more merchants will set up online stores to attract more young consumers to shop.

### 2.2 Willingness to spend

Dodds, Monroe, and Grewal (1991) hold that willingness to purchase refers to the likelihood of

---
*Corresponding Author: cga890406@gmail.com

DOI: 10.1201/9781003460763-22

an intention to purchase a product or service. Sherif and Cantril (1947) proposed that consumers judge product information based on their product knowledge. When the product is more important to consumers, the higher the degree of consumer involvement and their willingness to buy. Product diversity is one of the product strategies for sellers, and the product choices provided by enterprises to consumers include differences in brand, size, color, production technology, or other characteristics of the product, as well as differences in delivery requirements, delivery time, after-sales service, and guarantee services.

## 2.3 Service model and the importance of service model

Engel, Blackwell, and Kollat (1982) in their EKB model mentioned that information is an important factor in consumer purchasing behavior, and when consumers obtain more diverse information about goods or services, the willingness to purchase will be relatively increased. Conversely, when the information about the product or service is insufficient, the higher the consumer's uncertainty about the product or service, the lower the willingness to buy. Among the online respondents surveyed by TWNIC, 61.23% had an online shopping experience, with the highest proportion of online shopping at least once per quarter, accounting for 20.85%. As consumers compare prices, online stores will attract consumers with low-price strategies and promotions, resulting in a decline in profits Cai Minghe (2010). Therefore, Zeithaml, Parasuraman, and Molthotra (2002) argue that for online stores to succeed, they must focus on quality of service rather than providing low-priced products. Albert & Leyland (1997) has mentioned a similar concept, arguing that service quality is the degree to which the service provided meets the expectations of customers. Parasuraman *et al.* (1985) pointed out that a high level of service quality cognition will effectively improve consumer satisfaction, and his service quality model has been cited many times in the academic community. In 1988, the original ten determinants of service quality were reduced to five, as follows: 1. Tangible: refers to the physical part of the service process, including the grooming of the service personnel and the building and hardware equipment. 2. Reliability: refers to whether the performance measurement index of the service has the ability to fulfill the promise. 3. Responsiveness: refers to the ability of service personnel to provide timely assistance in solving customer problems. 4. Assurance: refers to the professional knowledge, ability, etiquette required by service personnel, and the ability to inspire customer confidence such as paying attention to customer privacy in the past. 5. Empathy: refers to providing special care for customers while considering their interests, that is,

putting themselves in their shoes and empathizing with empathy. In addition, Wang Junkai (2005) uses the concept of technology readiness to explore the impact of consumer technology readiness on online service quality measurement, combining several components with similar definitions into six aspects: "security", "reliability", "ease of use", "transaction function", "website aesthetics", and "resilience". These aspects are related to the items that consumers attach importance to when using online shopping, which is not only safe to use, but also beautiful and practical, which is the beautiful online consumer experience that consumers hope to achieve.

## 3 RESEARCH METHODS

According to the motivation and literature review of this study, the research process is divided into the following five steps:

1. Set the research objective: to investigate the impact of consumers on the process of buying shoes through the digital network, and to compare the two website service design models to the current situation of buying shoes on the digital network.
2. Collect data: Collect relevant literature from these years and cite the required research information.
3. Literature Integration: Integrate the collected data.
4. Literature analysis: Analyze the integrated data to obtain the required important information.
5. Summary: Finally, the above information is collated and presented (Figure 1).

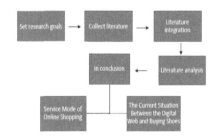

Figure 1.   Research flow chart.

## 4 CONCLUSION

### 4.1 Is there a correlation between digital networks and shoe buying?

There may be a correlation between digital networks and shoe buying. The relationship between the two can be influenced by a variety of factors, including personal preferences, advertising, marketing strategies, and cultural trends. However, digital networks can influence consumer behavior, including their propensity to buy shoes. Digital networks, especially social media, have become a ubiquitous part of modern life. Many people use social media platforms to connect with friends and family, as well as discover new products and services. Social media can keep users informed about various fashion trends, including shoes, which can influence their purchasing decisions. In addition, digital networks can provide consumers with access to online marketplaces such as Amazon or Zappos, where they can easily browse and buy shoes. Social media platforms also provide advertising opportunities for shoe brands, enabling them to target specific audiences and potentially drive more sales. However, it's worth noting that digital networks are just one of many factors influencing shoe-buying behavior. Other factors, such as personal style, budget, and seasonal trends, also play an important role in influencing consumer decisions. Overall, while there may be some relationship between digital networks and shoe-buying behavior, it is difficult to make a definitive statement without further analysis and data.

## 4.2 Does digital networking play an important role in online footwear sales growth?

Digital networks play an important role in the growth of online footwear sales. The rise of e-commerce and digital technologies has greatly impacted the way consumers buy footwear. Digital networks such as social media platforms, search engines, and e-commerce sites provide consumers with access to a wide range of footwear products and enable them to make purchases from the comfort of their homes. Social media platforms such as Facebook, Instagram, and Twitter provide footwear brands with a platform to showcase their products and interact directly with consumers. These platforms allow brands to create targeted advertising campaigns, reach new audiences, and build brand loyalty through personalized content. Search engines like Google have also played a vital role in the growth of online footwear sales. Consumers can easily search for footwear products, compare prices and features, and read reviews before making a purchase decision. This accessibility and convenience have made online shopping the first choice for many consumers. E-commerce sites like Amazon, Zappos, and Foot Locker offer consumers a seamless shopping experience, including easy navigation, secure payment options, and fast shipping. These platforms also offer a wide variety of footwear products, often at competitive prices. Overall, digital networks have played an important role in the growth of online footwear sales by providing consumers with easy access to a wide range of footwear products, personalized experiences, and convenient shopping options.

## 4.3 What is the future of footwear in digital networks?

The future of footwear and digital networks is likely to be driven by technological advances and consumer demand for more powerful and connected products. In the footwear sector, we can expect to see continued innovation in materials and construction technologies that lead to footwear that is more durable, comfortable, and sustainable. This could include the use of 3D printing and other advanced manufacturing techniques to make custom shoes and more efficient production processes. We may also see the integration of smart technologies, such as sensors and wearable computing devices, to provide real-time feedback on performance and health. Regarding digital networks, we can expect to see continued growth and expansion of the Internet of Things (IoT), which will enable better connectivity and communication between devices, including shoes. This could include the development of shoe-to-shoe communication and enhanced interaction between shoes and other wearable devices such as smartwatches and fitness trackers. We may also see advances in augmented and virtual reality technologies that allow consumers to experience and interact with shoes in new, immersive ways. In summary, the future of footwear and digital networks, driven by technological advances and changing consumer needs and preferences, is likely to be characterized by increased functionality, connectivity, and innovation.

## REFERENCES

Albert & Leyland, 1997, *Service Loyalty: The Effects of Service Quality and the Mediating Role of Customer Satisfaction*

Cai Minghe (2010). Research on the correlation between online shopping service quality, trust, perceived risk and loyalty: Taking sneakers as an example. *Unpublished Master's Thesis*, Institute of Physical Education, National Taiwan Normal University, Taipei.

Dodds W. B., Monroe K. B. & Grewal, D. (1991). Effects of price, brand, and store information on buyers' product evaluations. *Journal of Marketing Research*, 28(3), 307–319.

Engel J.F., Kollat D.T. & Blackwell, R.D. (1982). *Consumer Behavior*, (4th ed.). New York: Dryden Press.

Forsythe, S.M. and Shi, B. (2003) Consumer patronage and risk perceptions in internet shopping. *Journal of Business Research*, 56, 867–875.

Li Yichen (2022). *Exploring the antecedent of sneakers consumers' purchase intention*, National Changhua Normal University.

Parasuraman A., Zeithaml V. A. & Berry, L. L. (1998). A conceptual model of service quality and its implications for future research. *Joural of Marketing*, 49(3),41–50.

Parasuraman *et al.*, 1985, *Reproduced with permission of the A Conceptual Model of Service Quality and Its Implications for Future Research*, Vol. 49, 41–50.

Ramdas, K.(2003).Managing product variety: An integrative review and research directions. *Production and Operations Management*,12(1),79–101.

Sherif, Cantril, *The Psychology of Ego-involvements*, New York, 1947

Through Web Sites: A critical review of extant knowledge. *Journal of the Academy of Marketing Service*, 30 (4), 362–375.

Wang Junkai (2005). A study on the impact of consumer technology readiness on online service quality measurement. *Unpublished Master's Thesis*, Institute of Information Management, National Taiwan University, Taipei City.

Zeithaml, V. A., Parasuraman, A. & Malhotra, A. (2002). *Service Quality Delivery.*

*System Innovation for a Troubled World – Lam et al. (Eds)*
*© 2024 the Author(s), ISBN: 978-1-032-60846-4*

# Virtual fashion brand IoT platform: A study of shopping architecture based on consumer demand

Lin I-Hsuan & Huang Yu-Che*

*Department of Industrial Design, Chaoyang University of Technology, Taichung, Taiwan*

ABSTRACT: This thesis aims to explore the operation process of the shopping IoT platforms for virtual fashion clothing brands The Fabricant and Dress-X, as well as the factors influencing consumers' willingness to purchase clothing designs. It provides a certain reference value for the IoT management of virtual fashion clothing brands and consumer behavior. This study starts from aspects such as brand image, design style, price, and service experience, and deeply explores the motivation and psychological factors of consumers' purchase of virtual fashion clothing. It analyzes the design of the shopping IoT platform for virtual fashion clothing and compares the characteristics and advantages and disadvantages of the platform shopping process of the two brands The Fabricant and Dress-X. The research results show that consumers' willingness to purchase virtual fashion clothing is influenced by brand image and design style, while price and service experience also have a certain impact on purchase decisions. The results of this study provide certain inspiration and reference value for the design, shopping, IoT architecture, and management strategy of virtual fashion clothing.

## 1 INTRODUCTION

### 1.1 Research background

In recent years, with the maturity of virtual fashion technology, virtual fashion clothing brands have gradually emerged as a new force in the fashion industry. Among them, The Fabricant and Dress-X have attracted widespread attention from consumers for their unique design styles and innovative shopping modes, providing different shopping experiences and services. However, there has not been a deep exploration of the platform shopping process of these two brands and the factors that affect consumers' purchasing willingness. This is also the motivation for this research.

### 1.2 Research motivation

With the rise of virtual fashion, consumers' willingness to purchase and consumer behavior toward virtual fashion clothing is gradually changing. However, there is still a lack of consumer research on virtual fashion brands, especially The Fabricant and Dress-X. Therefore, this study aims to explore the comparison of the platform shopping process of these two brands, as well as the factors that influence consumers' willingness to purchase clothing designs, to provide some reference value for the operation of virtual fashion clothing brands and consumer behavior.

Through research, we can gain a deep understanding of the position and advantages of these two brands in the virtual fashion market, explore consumers' motives and psychological factors for purchasing virtual fashion clothing, and provide better direction and inspiration for future clothing designs.

### 1.3 Research objectives

The purpose of this study is to compare the platform shopping processes of The Fabricant and Dress-X, two virtual fashion brands, analyze their respective characteristics and advantages and disadvantages, and explore the factors that influence consumers' willingness to purchase clothing designs, including brand image, design style, price, and service experience. Additionally, this study will analyze the business strategies and consumer behavior of virtual fashion clothing brands, and provide insights and references for future virtual fashion clothing design.

The study will also delve into the shopping experiences and factors influencing consumer purchasing intentions of The Fabricant and Dress-X, with the aim of providing useful insights and recommendations for the future development of virtual fashion clothing design and the market.

The specific research objectives are as follows:

- Compare the similarities and differences in the platform shopping processes of The Fabricant and Dress-X virtual fashion clothing brands.

*Corresponding Author: doris10713075@gmail.com

DOI: 10.1201/9781003460763-23

- Study the factors influencing consumers' willingness to purchase clothing designs.
- Explore the future development trends of this type of brand's clothing designs.

### 1.4 Research scope

This research will focus on the comparison of the shopping process of the two virtual fashion brands: The Fabricant and Dress-X, and the factors that affect consumers' purchase intentions for clothing design. The goal of the study is to understand the online shopping platforms of these two brands and the factors that affect consumers' purchase intentions for virtual fashion brands and to explore the possible impact of these factors on future clothing design.

## 2 LITERATURE REVIEW

### 2.1 Virtual reality

Augmented Reality (AR) is an augmented interactive reality environment realized through holographic technology through digital visual elements, sound, and other sensory stimuli. AR has three characteristics: integration of digital and physical worlds, real-time interaction, and accurate 3D recognition of virtual and real objects [1]. AR technology can increase and strengthen the real world by combining the virtual and the real world, and improve people's cognition and transformation ability of the real world in a new way [2]. The main features of AR include a combination of reality and reality, real-time interaction, and 3D positioning. The application of AR covers a wide range, including education, games, cultural heritage, healthcare, e-commerce, entertainment, and other fields [3]. AR can be classified according to application scenarios, such as marker-based AR, location-based AR, facial recognition-based AR, etc. In the future, AR technology will continue to innovate and develop under the integration of artificial intelligence, machine learning, and big data. Based on the above literature, we can conclude that augmented reality technology has many characteristics, such as the combination of virtual and real, virtual and real synchronization, and natural interaction, and can be classified according to different application scenarios. At the same time, augmented reality technology has a wide range of applications and can be applied in many fields. Therefore, the research and application of augmented reality technology will have a positive impact on future technological development and social progress.

### 2.2 The rise of virtual fashion

Virtual fashion refers to the digitization of clothing design and production process through 3D modeling, computer animation, and augmented reality technologies, so as to create fashion that only exists in the virtual world. In recent years, virtual fashion has gradually attracted the attention of the fashion industry and researchers. According to related literature [4,7], the design and production process of virtual fashion has many advantages compared with traditional fashion, such as being more environmentally friendly, and saving time and cost. Designers can use virtual fashion technology to quickly and more sustainably create a variety of fashion designs and provide fashion that consumers can own in a virtual world. At the same time, virtual fashion is also supported by sustainable fashion, as it can reduce the production and waste of physical samples and thus be more environmentally friendly. Recent studies have shown that virtual fashion has become a trend for many fashion brands and e-commerce sites [4]. In addition, virtual fashion has also received attention in the research field. Some researchers use virtual fashion technology to conduct research on sustainable fashion, such as environmentally friendly fashion design, the market prospect of virtual fashion, etc. [6]. Therefore, virtual fashion, as an emerging way of fashion design and production, is attracting more and more attention and research. In the future, virtual fashion will play an increasingly important role in the fashion industry [8]. In recent years, with the development of technology and the popularization of the Internet, virtual fashion has become an emerging field in the fashion industry and has attracted widespread attention. Virtual fashion refers to the use of 3D design, virtual reality technology, and digital technology to create fashion designs that can be worn in the virtual world, which has higher creativity and sustainability [4]. Through virtual fashion, people can fully display their own style in the virtual reality world, and at the same time, it can promote the sustainable development of the fashion industry. At present, scholars at home and abroad have also begun to pay attention to issues related to virtual fashion, and have conducted systematic research on the development trend, market opportunities, design methods, and cultural significance of virtual fashion [5,6].

### 2.3 Interaction and thinking between fashion designers and consumers [8]

As a fashion designer, the interaction with consumers is very important, because consumers are the final users and buyers. The following are a few important aspects of interaction and thinking with consumers:

- *Understand consumer needs and preferences:* When designing clothing, designers should take into account the needs and preferences of consumers to ensure that the designed products meet market demand. Therefore, it is very important to conduct market research and interviews with consumers to understand their needs, preferences, styles, and trends.

- *Consider consumers' body shape:* Everyone's body shape is different, so consumers' body shape should be considered when designing clothing, and styles and sizes suitable for different body shapes should be designed to meet consumers' needs.
- *Listen to consumer feedback:* Consumer feedback is very important because it can provide valuable opinions and suggestions about the product. Therefore, designers should pay attention to consumer feedback, and make adjustments and improvements based on feedback.
- *Provide good customer service:* Good customer service can increase consumers' loyalty and trust in the brand. Therefore, designers should provide good customer service, including answering consumers' questions and providing solutions.
- *Consider sustainability and social responsibility:* Now more and more consumers are concerned about sustainability and social responsibility, so designers should take these aspects into consideration and design products that comply with sustainability and social responsibility.
- The interaction between designers and consumers is very important because it can ensure that the designed products meet the needs and preferences of consumers, and increase consumers' loyalty and trust in the brand.

## 3 RESEARCH METHOD

This study aims to explore the impact of the digital fashion services provided by The Fabricant and Dress-X on consumers and analyze their marketing strategies.

### 3.1 *Defining the scope of the research*

The scope of this study focuses on The Fabricant and Dress-X companies to explore the impact of their digital fashion services on consumers and analyze their market strategies. Specifically, the study will delve into their service characteristics, consumer usage experiences, market response, competitive advantages, and other aspects.

### 3.2 *Literature review*

The researcher will conduct relevant literature reviews, including professional journals, academic papers, business reports, internet resources, etc., to gain a deeper understanding of the market trends, consumer behavior, competitive environment, and other related knowledge of digital fashion services.

### 3.3 *Determining research methods*

This study will use methods such as literature review, historical research, and inductive summarization to conduct research. A literature review will be used to collect relevant information on market research, consumer behavior analysis, competitive environment, etc. Historical research will be used to understand the development process, service characteristics, market strategies, and the impact on consumers of The Fabricant and Dress-X companies. Inductive summarization will be used to analyze research results, summarize main findings, and research conclusions, and provide relevant recommendations.

### 3.4 *Conclusion*

In the final stage of the study, the researcher will conduct a summary of the research results and compare them with the research objectives. The main findings and conclusions will be summarized, relevant recommendations will be provided to promote the development of the digital fashion service industry.

## 4 RESEARCH ANALYSIS

### 4.1 *Overview of the fabricant [9]*

The Fabricant is a digital fashion house that specializes in creating virtual clothing and fashion accessories. The company was founded in 2018 by Kerry Murphy, a former fashion designer and entrepreneur, and Amber Slooten, a digital fashion designer and 3D artist.

The Fabricant's goal is to revolutionize the fashion industry by using digital design and technology to create sustainable, zero-waste fashion that can be experienced and enjoyed online. The company creates 3D digital garments that are designed to fit and move realistically on virtual models and can be used in virtual fashion shows, social media campaigns, and online marketing.

The Fabricant has collaborated with several fashion brands, including Puma, Adidas, and

Figure 1.   The Fabricant website [9].

110

Tommy Hilfiger, to create digital fashion collections and campaigns. The company has also partnered with blockchain technology companies to create digital fashion items that can be sold as unique, one-of-a-kind digital assets.

Overall, The Fabricant is at the forefront of a new movement in the fashion industry that combines digital technology, sustainability, and creativity to create innovative and engaging fashion experiences.

## 4.2   *Overview of dress-X [10]*

Dress-X is an online platform that allows users to design and create virtual fashion garments that can be worn in virtual and augmented reality environments. The platform provides users with a library of pre-made designs and tools to customize and create their own unique virtual garments. Once the garment is created, users can wear it in various virtual environments such as online gaming, social media, or virtual events.

Dress-X uses 3D modeling technology and digital printing to create virtual garments that are realistic and high-quality. The platform also offers a marketplace where users can buy and sell virtual garments. The garments can be purchased using cryptocurrencies or traditional payment methods.

Dress-X aims to provide a sustainable and eco-friendly alternative to traditional fashion. By creating virtual garments, Dress-X eliminates the need for physical production, shipping, and storage, which reduces the environmental impact of fashion production.

Overall, Dress-X is an innovative platform that combines fashion and technology to create a new form of fashion consumption.

Figure 2.    Dress-X website [10].

## 4.3   *The Fabricant shopping process*

The Fabricant is a digital fashion house that creates and sells virtual clothing and accessories. The company uses 3D modeling and digital design software to create unique digital garments and then markets them to consumers who can use them in virtual environments such as video games, augmented reality applications, and social media platforms.

The Fabricant's process typically involves the following steps:

- Conceptualization: The Fabricant's designers work with clients to create a concept for a digital garment or accessory. This can involve sketching out ideas or using 3D modeling software to create a rough prototype.
- 3D modeling: Once the concept is approved, The Fabricant's designers use 3D modeling software to create a detailed digital version of the garment or accessory. They consider factors such as texture, color, and lighting to make the garment as realistic as possible.
- Rendering: The 3D model is then rendered into high-quality images or videos that showcase the garment in various poses or environments. The Fabricant's marketing team uses these images to promote the garment to potential buyers.
- Distribution: Once a garment is sold, The Fabricant delivers it to the customer in the form of a 3D file that can be used in a variety of digital environments. Customers can use the garment in video games, virtual reality experiences, or even as part of their social media presence.

The Fabricant has been at the forefront of the digital fashion industry, offering an environmentally sustainable alternative to traditional fashion production while also catering to the growing demand for unique digital experiences.

## 4.4   *Dress-X shopping process*

Dress-X is an online platform that allows users to create and wear virtual clothing. Here's how it works:

- Choose a design: Dress-X offers a variety of designs created by independent designers. Users can browse through the available designs and choose the one they like.
- Customize the design: Once a design is selected, users can customize it according to their preferences. They can choose the color, texture, and other details to make the virtual clothing look exactly how they want it.
- Upload a photo: Users can then upload a photo of themselves to the Dress-X platform. The platform uses advanced technology to map the photo onto a 3D model of the user's body.
- Try on the virtual clothing: Once the 3D model is created, users can see how the virtual clothing looks on them. They can adjust the fit and make additional changes to the design if necessary.
- Purchase the virtual clothing: If the user is happy with the design, they can purchase the virtual clothing. Dress-X will provide the user with a high-quality image of the virtual clothing that they can use on social media or other platforms.

Overall, Dress-X allows users to experience the joy of wearing unique and customized clothing without having to buy physical garments. It's a fun and innovative way to explore fashion and express oneself creatively.

## 4.5  Comparative analysis

The Fabricant and Dress-X are both digital fashion platforms that offer users the opportunity to design and purchase virtual clothing. Here are some general advantages and disadvantages of each platform:

### 4.5.1  Advantages of the fabricant:

- High-Quality Designs: The Fabricant's digital clothing is known for its high-quality designs and realistic visuals, which have earned the platform recognition and accolades in the fashion industry.
- Industry Expertise: The Fabricant is run by industry experts who have extensive knowledge and experience in fashion design, marketing, and technology.
- Customization: The Fabricant offers customization options for customers who want to personalize their virtual clothing designs.
- Collaboration: The Fabricant collaborates with fashion brands and designers to create digital collections and campaigns, providing opportunities for exposure and collaborations.

### 4.5.2  Disadvantages of the fabricant:

- Expensive: The Fabricant's virtual clothing can be expensive, and the platform is geared toward high-end fashion brands and customers.
- Limited Availability: The Fabricant offers limited styles and designs, and it may not be accessible to customers who do not have a specific vision in mind.
- Technical Requirements: Creating designs on The Fabricant may require technical skills and specialized software that not everyone may possess.

### 4.5.3  Advantages of dress-X:

- Accessibility: Dress-X is more accessible than The Fabricant, as it offers a wider range of styles and designs at a lower price point.
- User-Friendly: Dress-X's platform is user-friendly and easy to navigate, making it accessible to people who may not have design experience.
- Sustainability: Dress-X promotes sustainable fashion by creating virtual clothes that reduce textile waste and pollution.
- Customization: Dress-X allows customers to customize their designs to their liking, providing a unique and personalized experience.

### 4.5.4  Disadvantages of dress-X:

- Limited Realism: Dress-X's digital clothing may not have the same level of realism and quality as The Fabricant's designs.
- Technical Skills: Dress-X's platform may still require some technical skills and knowledge of design software.
- Uncertainty: As a newer platform, there is no guarantee that Dress-X will have long-term success in the digital fashion industry.
- Lack of Tangibility: Like The Fabricant, Dress-X's virtual clothing does not have a tangible, physical presence, which some customers may find unappealing.

## 4.6  Consumer behavior analysis

There are six main business models for virtual product offerings in the market:

Selling points or virtual currency: This type of business model is usually found in online games or social media platforms, where users can purchase points or virtual currency to unlock more game content or increase virtual props to enhance the user experience.

Selling visuals or character growth: This type of business model is usually found in online games or social media platforms, where users can purchase artwork or clothing to create their favorite virtual characters and increase visual satisfaction.

Selling features or content: This type of business model is usually found in online services or applications, where users can purchase features or content to increase convenience or add value to the application.

Selling exposure or user traffic: This type of business model is usually found on online platforms, where companies can sell advertising exposure or user traffic to increase brand exposure or promote user conversion.

Selling content or service experience: This type of business model is usually found on online platforms, where companies provide high-quality content or service experience to attract users to pay for related virtual products and enhance the user experience.

Selling vanity or community status: This type of business model is usually found on social media or online gaming platforms, where companies offer users ways to obtain a sense of vanity or community status to increase user loyalty or engagement.

The Fabricant and Dress-X are two companies that specialize in digital fashion services. On their platforms, users can purchase and use digital fashion garments to showcase their fashion style through virtual character displays. The design and production of these garments are based on 3D technology, which can present a high degree of realism and visual effects to provide users with a better experience of virtual fashion services.

Additionally, these garments can be used in various scenarios, such as virtual fashion shows, e-commerce, and advertising, with broad application prospects. Therefore, The Fabricant and Dress-X's business model belongs to "selling visuals or character growth," with its core value lying in providing high-quality virtual fashion service experiences to enhance users' visual satisfaction and the charm of their virtual characters.

## 5 CONCLUSION

Based on the comprehensive research and analysis, it can be concluded that The Fabricant and Dress-X, as virtual fashion brands, have different characteristics and advantages and disadvantages in clothing design, platform shopping process, and consumer behavior. In this era, as IoT technology gradually matures, it also brings new opportunities for virtual fashion brands. For example, through technologies such as smart wearables, IoT sensors, etc., it is possible to achieve real-time virtual clothing try-on, network live broadcasts, and other interactive experiences, enhancing consumer shopping experiences and satisfaction.

Therefore, for the business strategy and future development of virtual fashion brands, it is recommended to combine IoT technology to develop more interactive and experiential virtual clothing products. At the same time, in the process of operating virtual fashion brands, it is necessary to focus on shaping and enhancing brand image, providing clothing designs that match consumer preferences, and formulating targeted business strategies based on consumer psychological needs and behaviors, thereby enhancing brand competitiveness and market influence.

In conclusion, with the continuous development and popularization of IoT technology, virtual fashion brands also need to innovate and progress constantly, in order to adapt to the constantly changing consumer demands and the intense competition in the market, achieving better business benefits and social value.

## REFERENCES

[1] Microsoft Dynamics 365. (n.d.). *What is Augmented Reality (AR)?* Retrieved April 5, 2023, from https://dynamics.microsoft.com/en-us/mixed-reality/guides/what-is-augmented-reality-ar/

[2] VRNEW. (n.d.). *What is Virtual Reality (VR)?* Retrieved April 5, 2023, from https://www.vrnew.com/index/index/xinwena/id/168.html

[3] Apple. (n.d.). *Augmented Reality on iOS.* Retrieved April 5, 2023, from https://www.apple.com.cn/augmented-reality/

[4] Fashinza. (2022, September 15). *What is Virtual Fashion? Definition, Examples and Virtual Fashion Events.* Retrieved April 5, 2023, from https://fashinza.com/textile/technology/what-is-virtual-fashion-definition-examples-and-virtual-fashion-events/

[5] Luxiders. (n.d.). *Virtual Fashion Design.* Retrieved April 5, 2023, from https://luxiders.com/virtual-fashion-design/

[6] Puri, K. (2020, August 21). *Learn Everything About Virtual Fashion and How Indian Brands are Diving Into the Trend. HERZ.* Retrieved April 5, 2023, from https://www.herzindagi.com/fashion/learn-everything-about-virtual-fashion-and-how-indian-brands-are-diving-into-the-trend-article-202018

[7] The List. (2022, November 4). *The Truth About Virtual Fashion.* Retrieved April 5, 2023, from https://www.thelist.com/474873/the-truth-about-virtual-fashion/

[8] Li Xueqin (2016). Interaction and thinking between fash-ion designers and consumers. *Journal of Textile Science,* Volume 37, Issue 2, Pages 72–78.

[9] The Fabricant. (n.d.). *Fashion goes digital.* Retrieved April 5, 2023, from https://www.the-fabricant.com/

[10] DressX. (n.d.). *Digital Fashion Marketplace.* Retrieved April 5, 2023, from https://dressx.com/

System Innovation for a Troubled World – Lam et al. (Eds)
© 2024 the Author(s), ISBN: 978-1-032-60846-4

# Research on the application of digital visual art in the internet

Huang-Mei Chen & Huang-Yu Che*
*Department of Industrial Design, Chaoyang University of Technology, Taiwan*

ABSTRACT: Virtual clothing product design has become a popular trend in recent years, especially with the impact of online shopping and the inability to go out due to the epidemic. Many Internet sites now offer virtual apparel product design tools that allow customers to create their own custom apparel designs and make them available for purchase online. One of the main benefits of virtual clothing product design is that it allows customers to personalize their clothing according to their preferences and tastes. This is especially attractive to consumers who are looking for unique clothing not available in traditional stores. Therefore, this study will conduct a survey and research on The Fabricant and Tribute Brand, two virtual clothing design websites, to find out the current situation of virtual visual clothing product design under the current situation of the Internet and the visual map of virtual product design websites under the Internet. Like design guidelines and countermeasures, put forward suggestions and summarize internally.

## 1 INTRODUCTION

Digital visual art and the Internet are closely intertwined. The Internet provides a platform for digital visual artists to showcase their work to a global audience, and it has also enabled new forms of digital art to emerge. The Internet has created new opportunities for digital visual artists to display their work through online galleries, websites, and social media platforms. This has allowed artists to reach a much larger audience than they would have been able to before the advent of the Internet. In addition, the Internet has enabled new forms of digital art to emerge, such as net art and interactive installations. These forms of art often rely on the Internet as a medium, and they are designed to engage with audiences in unique ways. Furthermore, the Internet has also facilitated the creation of collaborative digital art projects, as artists from around the world can work together on a single project despite being in different locations. This has led to the creation of new and innovative forms of digital art. Overall, the relationship between digital visual art and the Internet is a symbiotic one, with the Internet providing a platform for artists to display their work and enabling new forms of digital art to emerge.

## 2 EXPERIMENTAL

For the thesis, I want to explore the influence of the art of web design on the Internet, so I studied some domestic literature to collect and read relevant materials. Yan Chunhuang and Guo Qiutian (2004) proposed that several web pages can form a

website. Although the development time of webpage design technology is not long compared with other computer technologies, and in the past webpage design was quite simple, usually all the content is put into the format of the Internet industry for typesetting and decoration, and the prepared webpage is thrown on the Internet for users all over the world to browse. Then commercial websites began to appear, and the scale of the website gradually expanded, and its influence continued to spread in daily life. Gradually growing in China, Strauss & Frost (2002) included the method of making webpages in their research. In recent years, making web pages has become easier. Initially, webpages were made using Hyper Text Markup Language (HTML) programs. The language construction was simple, but now many companies have developed more operable writing tools, making programming more complicated. Visual art design is a focus of this research to explore whether it has an impact on the utilization rate of the Internet. The application of digital art is to integrate the basic elements that appear on the website, such as text design, content resonance, and image placement. The collocation of colors, the way of content layout, and the design and placement of logos make the webpage more attractive and also make the content presented by the website more perfect. The navigation design of the webpage needs to be built in a fairly complete structure. Among them, it can speed up the user to get the desired information, whether the richness of the website and whether the content can be clearly presented to the viewer are all very important in the browsing design Newman & Landay (2000). Lin Peiyi (2000) pointed out the key points of website design in her research, including

---

*Corresponding Author: judy.070649@gmail.com

DOI: 10.1201/9781003460763-24

comfortable and easy-to-understand viewing, clear classification of items and information, easy-to-understand search tools to find content, clear transaction assistance design, loading speed, and design requirements. It can attract viewers to buy, among which the information classification is clear, and there are easy-to-understand search tools to find content. These two items will affect the use satisfaction of viewers. In his research, Norman (1998) proposed to design each page on the website with the same theme. The same page should not have too many items, and the theme should not be too complicated. One page only needs to convey the information of one topic. Try to make the screen clear and simple, which can reduce the discomfort in use and facilitate operation. Liao Pengwen and Lu Kangyu (2004) mentioned a very important thing in their research. At that time, the website had gradually become a media platform, which was very different from the traditional print media (newspapers and magazines). The designers of the website must collect the information needed for the website content, the design style of the exclusive website, and the interaction method that the website wants to give the viewer, etc., according to the appearance that the website wants to present to the viewers in the future. These are the key tasks of the website design. The job content of designing a website is divided into these projects: (1) Content design: systematically process all information, and distinguish different themes or categories for easy browsing; (2) Organizational structure: systematically divide and design, use the content to find out the relevance, and then according to Content design information process; (3) Navigation system: it can lead the viewer to easily explore the structure of the entire webpage, the design of the navigation must be clear enough, and the content must also have consistency; (4) Page Design: The four principles of visual balance, rhythm, web page grids, and graphic arrangement must be given considerable attention when designing a website; (5) Interface design: designed to conform to the habits of most viewers Considering and emphasizing the practicality of functions, the four principles of simplicity, readability, consistent style and smooth functions are required; (6) Interactive design: Make the viewer feel that he is in charge of the use process easily when using it. This design allows the viewer to browse the entire website unconsciously. information to provide. Therefore, the browsing method required by website visitors is "intuitive". It only needs to plan a complete set of web page navigation, which can not only enable visitors to quickly obtain the information they want but also continuously improve the website according to the past experience of visitors. Various items were designed. It is a relatively abstract part to set the visual art style of the website in the process of website construction. The research of Huang Chaomeng and Zhao Meihui (2001) shows that the successful websites that are popular with everyone have one thing in common because they have their own unique style; An environment that is comfortable to look at and reluctant to leave the line of sight may be what a good website should have, including the main colors used in the website, image layout, navigation design, applications, information delivery, etc. factors are indispensable. In addition to noticing the images and functions on the website, it is more important for the viewer to experience the overall service provided by the website. Many literatures have recorded that the style of the website should be based on the goals and demands it wants to present, to choose the appropriate main style route or color tone, etc. Huang Chaomeng and Zhao Meihui's (2001) research suggests that streamlined important information is more suitable for the main content of the website than lengthy and meaningless content. The focus of website design is to allow most visitors to obtain the information they want simply and quickly, so as to achieve the purpose of real use. Wang Kaili (2000) research pointed out that people go through life constantly bombarding their consciousness with a lot of information. Cognitive ability will filter the large amount of information we have read in order to make the information more meaningful and only keep the part that attracts the attention of the viewer. Therefore, when planning and designing the operation interface, several points need to be considered to ensure the quality of using the webpage: (1) In the design of the interface, every operation action must be carefully considered to use images to focus the viewer's attention. (2) Provide information logically and systematically to increase the chances of successful browsing for visitors. (3) Visual Markers must be used at the end part in a timely manner, for example, hyperlink change the way of text presentation, such as adding a bottom line, bold font, animation flashing, and other effects to get the attention of viewers. Many of the above-mentioned documents prove that web design has grown in each process under the continuous development of the Internet. In order to be more suitable for presenting on the Internet and provide suitable browsers with the information they want to search for, they are always constantly making adjustments. In the beginning, it provided a large amount of information; it began to pay attention to the visual presentation of the webpage; it began to design navigation based on the usage habits of most of the viewers; and now it can record the usage habits of each viewer and provide customized calculations. Information and digital visual art are gradually growing under the development of the Internet. Digital visual art and the Internet are inseparable. At present, most digital art still relies on the use of the Internet for exposure and presentation. Without the Internet, how can there be digital art? The production of art.

## 3 RESEARCH METHODS

The research process of this study is divided into the following five steps:

1. Set research goals: I investigated some virtual clothing design and manufacturing platforms, and selected two as my research goals to compare whether visual images, interfaces, and visual styles on the Internet can affect users' use.
2. Collecting literature: Use the literature in recent years to read and cite positive research information.
3. Literature integration: Integrate and organize all positive research information.
4. Analysis of literature data: Analyze the consolidated literature data and absorb the essence of them.
5. Induction and summary: Make a statement after sorting out the above information (Figure 1).

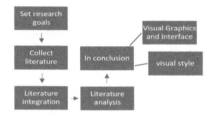

Figure 1. Research flow chart.

## 4 CONCLUSION

1. What is the visual art of the five clothing companies' clothing on their website?

   All five of these companies have distinctive visual art styles, but based on their general approach to visual arts, The Fabricant and Tribute Brand are the most distinctive. The Fabricant is known for its use of 3D graphics and animation to create virtual fashion items, which are often presented in a minimalistic and futuristic style. Their focus on creating realistic and visually stunning images of their virtual items through the use of lighting, shading, and texture mapping techniques sets them apart from other companies. Tribute Brand, on the other hand, uses photography to showcase their sustainable fashion items on their website, often featuring natural lighting and a rustic aesthetic to create a warm and inviting atmosphere. Their use of hand-drawn illustrations and patterns to create a unique and rustic aesthetic on their website is also distinctive. While all the other companies have unique visual art styles, they

may not be as distinctive as The Fabricant and Tribute Brand. For example, Dress-X and Hanifa also use 3D graphics and animation, and Carling uses photography, but they do not have the same level of focus on advanced techniques or unique aesthetics as The Fabricant and Tribute Brand. 2. Compare the differences in the visual art of these clothing designs. design styles and aesthetics. (1) The Fabricant: It is a digital fashion house that creates virtual fashion items. Their website has a minimalistic design with black and white color tones. The website features high-quality 3D renders of their virtual fashion items, which are showcased in a visually pleasing way. The website's design is futuristic and minimalistic, with a strong emphasis on the 3D graphics of the virtual items.

Figure 2. The Fabricant's website.

2. Dress-X: Dress-X is another digital fashion company that creates virtual clothing items. The website's design features bright colors and a clean, modern design. The website has a fun and playful vibe, with animated elements that enhance the user experience. The virtual clothing items are showcased in a visually engaging way, with a strong emphasis on the vibrant colors and textures of the virtual items.

Figure 3. The Fabricant's website.

Figure 4. Dress-X website.

3. Tribute Brand: Tribute Brand is a sustainable fashion company that creates clothing items made from recycled materials. The website's design has a rustic, vintage feel, with muted colors and a natural aesthetic. The website features high-quality images of their sustainable clothing items, which are showcased in a visually pleasing way. The website's design highlights the brand's commitment to sustainability and ethical fashion.

Figure 7. Tribute Brand website.

Figure 5. Dress-X website.

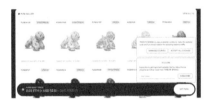

Figure 6. Tribute Brand website.

Figure 8. Hanifa website.

4. Hanifa: Hanifa is a fashion brand that creates clothing items for women. The website's design features bold colors and a clean, modern design. The website has a chic and stylish vibe, with high-quality images of their clothing items showcased in a visually engaging way. The website's design emphasizes the brand's commitment to empowering women through fashion.

5. Carling: Carling is a fashion brand that creates clothing items for women. The website's design features a minimalistic, modern design with a monochromatic color scheme. The website has a sophisticated and elegant vibe, with high-quality images of their clothing items showcased in a visually pleasing way. The website's design emphasizes the brand's commitment to timeless, classic fashion. Overall, these five companies have unique website designs that showcase their individual aesthetics and brand identities. Each website's design highlights the brand's commitment to its specific area of expertise, whether it be virtual fashion, sustainable fashion, or classic fashion, This study will conduct a survey and research on two virtual clothing design websites, The Fabricant and Tribute Brand.3. When should digital visual design be paid attention to in clothing design? Digital clothing design has already made significant strides in recent years, with the use of 3D modeling, animation, and other advanced technologies. However, there are several areas of potential development in the future of digital clothing design. Improved realism. While current digital clothing design tools are already quite advanced, there is still room for improvement in terms of creating more realistic and detailed virtual garments. Future technologies may involve even more advanced 3D modeling and rendering techniques, as well as the incorporation of physics-based simulations for more realistic movement and draping. Customization: As digital clothing design becomes more prevalent, there may be an increased focus on customization and personalization. This could involve the use of AI and machine learning algorithms to create personalized garments based on individual preferences and measurements. Sustainability: As the fashion industry faces increasing pressure to become more sustainable, digital clothing design could play a significant role in reducing waste and environmental impact. Future technologies may involve the use of 3D printing and other additive manufacturing techniques to create garments on demand, reducing the need for mass production and excess inventory. Virtual try-on: As e-commerce continues to grow, there is a need for better ways to visualize and try on clothing online. Future technologies could involve the use of augmented reality and virtual reality to create realistic virtual try-on experiences, allowing customers to see how

garments will look and fit before making a purchase. Overall, the future of digital clothing design is likely to involve continued innovation and advancement in the use of 3D modeling, simulation, AI, and other technologies. As these technologies improve, they could have a significant impact on the fashion industry, leading to more sustainable and personalized garments, as well as new and innovative ways to shop for and experience fashion. The future development of digital visual art clothing design on the internet is likely to continue to evolve and grow. With the increasing popularity of e-commerce and online shopping, there is a growing demand for unique and personalized clothing designs. Advances in technology, such as 3D printing and augmented reality, are also likely to have a significant impact on the way digital visual art clothing design is created and consumed. These technologies will allow for more efficient and cost-effective production of customized clothing designs. In addition, social media platforms and online marketplaces are providing new avenues for digital visual art clothing designers to showcase their work and reach a broader audience. This is likely to result in an increased focus on creating designs that are visually appealing and shareable on social media. Overall, the future of digital visual art clothing design on the internet is exciting and full of potential. As technology continues to advance and new platforms emerge, we can expect to see continued growth and innovation in this field.

# REFERENCES

Anderson D *et al.* (1994). Professional collaboration: Empowering school personnel through peer coaching. (ERIC Document Reproduction Service No. ED 371496)

Aladwani A.M. & Palvia C.P. (2002). Developing and validating an instrument for measuring user-perceived web quality. *Information & Management*, 39, 467–476.

Cohan (1999) Peter S., *Net Profit*, Jossey-Bass Publishers.

Eighmey J. and McCord L (1998). Adding value in the information age: Uses and gratifications of sites on the world wide web, *Journal of Business Research*, 41, 187–194.

Feser E. J. and Bergman, E. M. (2000). National industry cluster templates: a framework for applied regional cluster analysis. *Regional Studies*, vol. 34.

Huizingh E.K.R.E. (2000).The content and design of websites: An empirical study. *Information & Management*, 37, 123–134.

Horton & Lynch J.P. (1999). *Web Style Guide: Basic Design Principles for Creating Web Sites*, Yale, New Haven and London.

Huang Chaomeng, Zhao Meihui (2001). *.com Strategic Planning and Design*. Taipei: Shang Ding Culture Publishing House.

Johanson, J. & L.G. Mattsson (1988) "Interorganizational relations in industrial systems A network approach compared with the transaction-cost approach", *International Studies of Management and Organization*, 17. 34–48.

Kim J. (1997). Toward the construction of customer interfaces for cyber shopping malls-HCl research for Electronic commerce, *EM-Electronic Markets*, 7, 012–015.

Kotler, Philip (1994). *Marketing Management: Analysis, Planning and Control*, (5th ed). Englewood Cliffs, New Jersey: Pretice-Hall.

Krauss, M. (1998) How the web is changing the customers, *Marketing News*, 32, Iss. 10 10

Liu, C. & Arnett, K. P., 2000, Exploring the factors associated with website success in the context of electronic commerce. *Information & Management*, 38, 23–33.

Liu C., Arnett K.P., Capella, L.M., & Beatty R.C. (1997) Web sites of the fortune 500 companies: Facing customers through home pages. *Information & Management*, 3, 335–345.

Liao C., To P., & Shin M.L. (2006) Website Practices: A comparison between the top 1000 companies in the U. S. and Taiwan. *International Journal of Information Management*, 26, 196–211.

Lin Peiyi (2000). *The relationship between website design and user satisfaction – a cluster study of Internet users and shopping experience*. Department of Information Management, National Chengchi University.

Liao Pengwen, Lu Kangyu (2004). *Don't Let my Mouse Get Lost*. Taipei: Digital Human Information.

Norman D.A. (1998). *The Design of Everyday Things*. Doubleday. New York.

Pairin K. (2002). Framework of Effective Web Site Design for Business–to–Consumer Internet Commerce, *INFOR*, 40, No. 1 57–70.

Pearrow, M. (2000). *Web Site Usability Handbook*, Charles River Media, Inc. Rockland, Massachusetts.

Powell, Thomas A. (2000). *Web design:the complete reference, Berkeley*. Calif.: Osborne/McGraw-Hill.

Porter M. E. (1990). *The Cometitive Advantage of Nations*, Free Press: New York.

Robbins, S. S., & Stylianou, A. C. (2003). Global Corporate Web Sites. *Information & Management*, 40, 205–212.

Steinle, C. and H. Schiele (2002) When Do Industries Cluster? A Proposal on How to Assess an Industry's Propensity to Concentrate at a Single Region or Nation, *Research Policy*, 31, 849–859.

Whitaker, G.P. (1980), Coproduction: Citizen Participation in Service Delivery. *Public Administration Review*, May/June, 2–4.

Wonlisky, H. & Wonlisky, J. (1997). Form Print to the Web with Roger Black. *Digital Chicago*.

Whitaker, L.A. (1998). *Human Navigation, Human Factors and Web Development*, Lawrence Erlbaum Associates, Inc., 63–71.

Wang Kaili (2000). The communicative meaning of images in web design. *Symposium on Design and Management*, pp. 269–276.

Yan Chunhuang, Guo Qiutian (2004). *The practice of web design*. Taipei: National Air University.

System Innovation for a Troubled World – Lam et al. (Eds)
© 2024 the Author(s), ISBN: 978-1-032-60846-4

# Paired domination in extended hypergrid graphs

Ruo-Wei Hung*
*Department of Computer Science and Information Engineering, Chaoyang University of Technology, Wufeng, Taichung, Taiwan*

Yuh-Min Tseng
*Department of Mathematics, National Changhua University of Education, Changhua, Taiwan*

Hung-Yu Chien
*Department of Information Management, National Chi Nan University, PuLi, Nantou, Taiwan*

ABSTRACT: A subset of vertices of a graph is a dominating set if every vertex is in the set or is adjacent to one of the vertices of the set. A dominating set is said to be paired if its induced subgraph contains a perfect matching. The domination and paired domination problems are to compute a dominating set and a paired dominating set, respectively, of a graph with minimum cardinality. Domination and its variants have applications in many fields, including network center allocation, very-large-scale integration (VLSI) layout, guard location systems, and more. In the past, we have proposed a generalization of hypergrid graphs called extended hypergrid graphs, including grid graphs, triangular grid graphs, and hypergrid graphs as their subclasses. The domination and independent domination problems for hypergrid and grid graphs were known to be NP-complete. However, the complexity of the paired domination problem for these two graph classes remains unknown. In this paper, we will prove that the paired domination problem on hypergrid graphs is NP-complete

## 1 INTRODUCTION

For a graph $G$, we will use $V(G)$ and $E(G)$ to represent the set of vertices and edges, respectively. Let $v$ be a vertex in $V(G)$. The degree of $v$ in $G$, denoted by $deg_G(v)$, is the number of vertices adjacent to $v$. The neighborhood of v is denoted as $N_G(v) = \{u \in V(G) \mid (u, v) \in E(G)\}$, and its closed neighborhood is represented as $N_G[v] = N_G(v) \cup \{v\}$. Let $S, D \subseteq V(G)$. A subgraph induced from S is denoted as $G[S]$. A set $S$ is called an independent set if $G[S]$ contains $|S|$ isolated vertices. Also, two edges are called independent edges if they do not share a common vertex. Generally, $N_G(S) = \cup_{v \in S} N_G(v)$ and $N_G[S] = \cup_{v \in S} N_G[v]$. If $N_G[v] \cap D \neq \phi$, then $D$ is said to dominate $v$. If $D$ dominates all vertices of set $S$, then we call that $D$ dominates $S$. The subset $D$ of vertices in a graph $G$ is called a dominating set of $G$ if and only if $D$ dominates $V$ $(G)$. The domination number, denoted $\gamma(G)$, of a graph $G$ is equal to the minimum cardinality of a dominating set of $G$. A minimum dominating set of G is a dominating set with cardinality $\gamma(G)$. The domination problem is to compute a minimum dominating set of a graph, which is NP-complete for general graphs (Garey *et al.* 1979).

In the past, many variants of the dominating set have been proposed. These variants are to compute a minimum dominating set of a graph for satisfying certain conditions. For instance, the independent dominating set satisfies the condition that the dominating set is independent; the connected dominating set satisfies the condition that the induced subgraph by the dominating set forms a connected graph. The dominating set problem and its variants have many applications. For example, in a network, the dominating set is a set of computer centers that can be built so that these centers can monitor other computers. For related problems and applications, we recommend readers to refer two survey books (Haynes *et al.* 1998).

In this paper, we will study a variant of the domination problem called the paired domination problem. A dominating set $S$ of a graph $G$ is called paired if the subgraph $G[S]$ induced by $S$ contains a perfect matching $M$. That is, any vertex in the dominating set can be paired exactly with another vertex. Two vertices of a paired dominating set are connected by an edge of such a perfect matching and are called paired. In this paper, we will denote two paired vertices $u$, $v$ in $M$ by $\langle u, v \rangle$. Every graph without isolated vertices has a paired dominating set since any maximal matching of it forms such a set (Haynes *et al.* 1998). The paired domination number of graph $G$ is the size of the smallest paired dominating set on it and is expressed as $\gamma_{rp}(G)$. The paired domination problem is to find a paired dominating set of a graph $G$ with cardinality $\gamma_{rp}(G)$.

*Corresponding Author: rwhung@cyut.edu.tw

DOI: 10.1201/9781003460763-25

Haynes and Slater (Haynes *et al.* 1998) introduced the concept of paired domination in graphs and considered the following applications. If, in graph $G$, we consider each vertex as a possible guard position capable of guarding every vertex adjacent to it, then the "dominant set" is the set guarding all vertices. In pair domination, each defender is assigned to another adjacent defender who is designed to provide backup to each other for enhanced protection. The paired domination problem for general graphs was known to be NP-complete (Haynes *et al.* 1998). For some special classes of graphs, such as bipartite graphs, chordal graphs, and split graphs (Chen *et al.* 2010), undirected path graphs (Chang *et al.* 2012), and perfect elimination bipartite graphs (Panda *et al.* 2013), it is still NP-complete. For more related researches and applications of paired domination, readers can refer to the survey conducted by Desormeaux *et al.* (2014).

In this paper, we will study the problem of paired domination on extended hypergrid graphs. Hypergrid graphs were proposed for computing stitches for computerized embroidery machines (Hung *et al.* 2015) in which hypergrid graphs are called supergrid graphs. We (Chen *et al.* 2022) have proposed extended hypergrid graphs, which is a generalization of hypergrid graphs and are also called extended supergrid graphs. Extended hypergrid graphs include grid, triangular grid, and hypergrid graphs as subclasses of graphs. Rectangular hypergrid graphs, grid graphs, and triangular-grid graphs form subclasses of hypergrid graphs, grid graphs, and triangular grid graphs, respectively. Generally, hypergrid graphs, triangular grid graphs, and grid graphs are three different classes of graphs, among which, hypergrid graphs include triangular grid graphs and grid graphs as their subgraphs. Also, the intersection of rectangular hypergrid graphs and rectangular grid graphs is empty generally. The Hamiltonian problems for hypergrid graphs were verified to be NP-complete (Hung *et al.* 2015). In the past, the Hamiltonian and longest path problems for some special classes of hypergrid graphs have been studied (Hung *et al.* 2017; Keshavarz *et al.* 2022). Related researches on domination problems for these graph classes are as follows. The domination problem for grid graphs was known to be NP-complete (Clark *et al.* 1990). Recently, the domination, independent domination, and restrained domination problems for hypergrid graphs have been proven to be NP-complete (Chen *et al.* 2022). Recently, we proved that the restrained domination problem on supergrid graphs is NP-complete (Hung 2023).

In this paper, we will study the complexity of the paired domination problem for extended hypergrid graphs and their one subclass. We will show that the paired domination problem for hypergrid graphs is NP-complete. Therefore, the investigated problem is also NP-complete for extended hypergrid graphs.

The paper is organized as follows. In Section 2, some notations are introduced. In Section 3, the paired domination problem for hypergrid graphs is proved to be NP-complete. Finally, we make some concluding remarks in Section 4.

## 2 PRELIMINARIES

In this section, we will introduce some notations and some results in the literature. A path $P$ on a graph $G$ is composed of a sequence of different adjacent vertices. If the starting vertex of $P$ is $v_1$ and the end vertex is $v_k$, then we will express it as $(v_1, v_k)$-path. If there exists no confusion, we will denote the path of $n$ vertices as $P_n$. Since a pair of vertices in a path can dominate at most 4 vertices (2 vertices and itself), the following lemma can be easy to verify by mathematic induction.

Lemma 1 (Sangeetha *et al.* 2019): $\gamma_{rp}(P_n) = 2 \times \frac{n}{4}$.

Since the paired domination problem for paths can be easily solved (as in the lemma above), the classes of graphs introduced below will not include paths. Consider points on a plane with integer coordinates, where the x- and y-coordinates of point $v$ are denoted as $v_x$, respectively and $v_y$, and denoted as $v = (v_x, v_y)$. Let $V^\infty$ denote the set of all integer coordinate points on the plane, then $|V^\infty| = \infty$. Consider any vertex $v$ in $V^\infty$. If the vertex $u$ adjacent to $v$ satisfies the distance between $u$ and $v$ is 1, then the set formed by these edges is called $E^\infty{}_g$. On the other hand, if the distance between vertices adjacent to $u$ and $v$ is not larger than sqrt (2) ($\sqrt{2}$), then the set formed by these edges is called $E^\infty{}_s$. There are three types of edges on $E^\infty{}_s$: For $(u, v) \in E^\infty{}_s$, if $u_x = v_x$, the edge is called a vertical edge, and when $u_y = v_y$, the edge is called a horizontal edge, otherwise, it is called a diagonal edge. The 2-D integer grid $G^\infty$ is an infinite graph satisfying $V(G^\infty) = V^\infty$ and $E(G^\infty) = E^\infty{}_g$; while the 2-D integer hypergrid $S^\infty$ is an infinite graph satisfying $V(S^\infty) = V^\infty$ and $E(S^\infty) = E^\infty{}_s$. In addition, the 2-D integer triangular grid $T^\infty$ is an infinite graph by adding the upper-left to lower-right diagonal edge to each square in $G^\infty$. For example, Figure 1(a)-(c) shows a partial fragment of $G^\infty$, $T^\infty$ and $S^\infty$, respectively.

Figure 1. The partial fragment of (a) $G^\infty$, (b) $T^\infty$, and (b) $S^\infty$.

Grid graphs, triangular grid graphs, and hypergrid graphs are finitely connected and vertex-induced subgraphs of $G^\infty$, $T^\infty$ and $S^\infty$, respectively. These graph classes are different and have no mutual subordinate relationship, that is, the intersection of these graph classes is an empty set generally. However, an extended hypergrid graph is a finitely connected subgraph of $S^\infty$ and need not be a vertex-induced subgraph of $S^\infty$. Therefore, a grid graph, triangular grid graph, or hypergrid graph will be an extended hypergrid graph. Then, extended hypergrid graphs will contain grid graphs, triangular grid graphs, and hypergrid graphs as graph subclasses. On the other hand, we can easily see that all grid and triangular grid graphs are planar graphs, and each grid graph is a bipartite graph (Itai *et al.* 1982). However, hypergrid graphs may not be planar or bipartite graphs. Figure 2 lists the affiliations of these graph classes above.

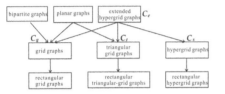

Figure 2. The containment relationship among extended hypergrid, grid, triangular grid, and hypergrid graph classes.

A path on an extended hypergrid graph, if the edges on it are all horizontal, the path is called a horizontal path; and if the edges on it are all vertical, then the path is called a vertical path.

## 3 NP-COMPLETENESS RESULT

In this section, we will prove that the paired domination problem on hypergrid graphs is NP-complete. In (Chen *et al.* 2022), the domination and independent domination problems in this graph class were proved to be NP-complete. We will use a similar technique to prove the result of this NP-complete. Clark *et al.* (1990) have proved that the domination problem on grid graphs is NP-complete as follows:

Theorem 2 (Clark *et al.* 1990): *The domination problem on grid graphs is NP-complete.*

As follows, we will reduce the domination problem on grid graphs to the paired domination problem on hypergrid graphs to prove that the paired domination problem on hypergrid graphs is NP-complete. We first start from a grid graph $G_g$ to construct a hypergrid graph $G_s$, and then prove that $G_g$ has a dominating set of size $\leq k$ iff $G_s$ has a paired dominating set of size $\leq 2k+4|E(G_g)|$. In this way, it can be verified by Theorem 2 that the paired domination problem for hypergrid graphs is NP-complete. Given a grid graph $G_g$, a corresponding hypergrid graph $G_s$ is constructed as follows:

Step 1: Convert every edge of $G_g$ to a vertical or horizontal path $P_{10}$ with 9 edges, i.e., every edge of $G_g$ is enlarged by 9 times; let this enlarged graph be

$G'_g$, which is also a grid graph. For instance, Figure 3(b) is the grid graph $G'_g$ after $G_g$ is enlarged;

Step 2: Replace each enlarged path $(u, v)$-path of $G'_g$ with a $(u, v)$-component as shown in Figure 3 (c), and the replaced graph is a hypergrid graph $G_s$.

The $(u, v)$-component shown in Figure 3(c) is called crab $(u, v)$-tentacle and denoted as $C_t(u, v)$, where $u, v \in V(G_g)$ is called connectors of $C_t(u, v)$. For example, given a grid graph $G_g$, as shown in Figure 3 (a), Figure 3(d), is the hypergrid graph $G_s$ constructed by the above steps.

With the method of our published paper (Chen *et al.* 2022), we can arrange all the crab tentacles to ensure that these tentacles except connectors are vertex disjoint. For the placement rules of crab tentacles, please refer to Chen *et al.* (2022). Because of space constraints, the proof of the following lemma is omitted.

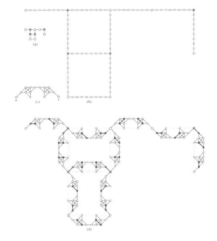

Figure 3. (a) A grid graph $G_g$, (b) a grid graph $G'_g$ by enlarging every edge of $G_g$ 9 times, (c) a crab $(u, v)$-tentacle $C_t(u, v)$ for replacing every enlarged path of $G'_g$, and (d) a hypergrid graph $G_s$ constructed from the enlarged grid graph $G'_g$, where solid lines depict edges of $G_g$ and $G_s$, double circles represent the vertices of $G_g$, and solid circles represent the vertices in a (paired) dominating set of $G_g$ or $G_s$.

Lemma 3 (Chen *et al.* 2022): *The crab tentacles of $G_s$ can be arranged to satisfy that they are vertex disjoint except connectors.*

Given a grid graph $G_g$, the hypergrid graph $G_s$ can be easily constructed in $|V(G_g)|+|E(G_g)|$-linear time. Thus, we have the following lemma.

Lemma 4: *Given a grid graph $G_g$, hypergrid graph $G_s$ can be constructed in $|V(G_g)|+|E(G_g)|$-linear time.*

In the following, we will prove that grid graph $G_g$ has a dominating set $D$ with $|D| \leq k$ if and only if hypergrid graph $G_s$ contains a paired dominating set $D'$ with $|D'| \leq 2k+4|E(G_g)|$. First, we prove that if $G_g$ has a dominating set $D$ whose size is less than or equal to $k$, then a paired dominating set $D'$ of $G_s$ whose size is less than or equal to $2k+4|E(G_g)|$ can be obtained. The process of constructing

$D'$ is stated below. For each $u \in D$, we find one vertex of the corresponding crab tentacle to pair it; and in each crab tentacle, we find 2 pairs to dominate the crab tentacle. Due to space limitations, we will not prove it, and an example is given as follows: for a dominating set $D$ in grid graph $G_g$ of Figure 3(a) having a size of 4, we construct a paired dominating set $D'$ of the hypergrid graph $G_s$ in Figure 3(d) whose size is $2|D|+4\|E(G_g)\| = 2 \times 4 + 4 \times 13 = 60$. Next, we will prove the if part that if $G_s$ contains a paired dominating set $D'$ with $|D'| \leq 2k+4|E(G_g)|$, then $G_g$ has a dominating set $D$ of size $\leq k$. Given a paired dominating set $D'$ of hypergrid graph $G_s$, we first reconstruct a paired dominating set $D^*$ of hypergrid graph $G_s$ satisfying that the following properties holds for $D^*$:

(p1) $|D^*| \leq |D'|$;

(p2) any vertex in $D^*$ is paired with exactly one vertex of $D^*$;

(p3) for any crab $(u, v)$-tentacle satisfying that $u, v \notin D^*$, there exist two crab tentacles, called crab $(z_1, u)$-tentacle and crab $(z_2, v)$-tentacle, such that $z_1, z_2 \in D^*$;

(p4) every crab tentacle in $D^*$ contains exactly two pairs of vertices not in $G_g$;

(p5) for each crab $(u, v)$-tentacle $C_t(u, v)$ satisfying that $deg_{Gg}(v) = 1$ and $v \notin D^*$, $u \in D^*$.

For instance, given a paired dominating set $D'$ of $G_s$ with size 40 and 20 pairs in Figure 4(a), the re-constructed paired dominating set $D^*$ of $G_s$ with size 38 and 19 pairs from $D'$ is shown in Figure 4 (b). We then obtain a dominating set $D$ of $G_g$ from $D^*$ by removing all vertices of $D^*$ not in $G_g$ from $D^*$. For instance, by removing all vertices of $D^*$-$V(G_g)$ for Figure 4(a), we obtain a dominating set $D$ of $G_g$ with size 3, Because of space constraints, the proofs of the following lemma will be omitted.

Lemma 5: *Let $G_g$ be a grid graph, and let $G_s$ be the hypergrid graph constructed from $G_g$. Then, $G_g$ has a dominating set $D$ of size $|D| \leq k$ if and only if $G_s$ contains a paired dominating set $D'$ of size $|D'| \leq 2k+4|E(G_g)|$.*

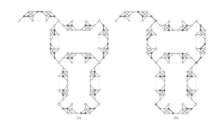

Figure 4. (a) The paired dominating set $D'$ of $G_s$ with size 40 and 20 pairs, and (b) a re-constructed paired dominating set $D^*$ of $G_s$ with size 38 ($\leq |D'|$) and 19 pairs, where bold solid lines indicate the pairs in $D'$ and $D^*$}, double circles represent the vertices of $G_g$, and solid circles represent the vertices in a paired dominating set of hypergrid graph $G_s$.

Clearly, the paired domination problem on hypergrid graphs is in NP. Through Theorem 2 and Lemma 5, we obtain the following theorem.

Theorem 6: *The paired domination problem for hypergrid graphs is NP-complete.*

# 4 CONCLUSION

In this paper, we prove that the paired domination problem for hypergrid graphs is NP-complete. It is interesting to find the complexities of the paired domination problem on the subclasses of extended hypergrid graphs. We would like to post it as an open problem to interested readers.

# ACKNOWLEDGMENTS

This work is partly supported by the National Science and Technology Council, Taiwan, under grant no. MOST 110-2221-E-324-007-MY3, MOST 110-2221-E-018-006-MY2, MOST 111-2221-E-260-009-MY3.

# REFERENCES

Chang G.J., Panda B.S., Pradhan D., 2012. *Theor. Comput. Sci.* 459 89–99.

Chen L., Lu C., Zeng Z., 2010. *J. Comb. Optim.* 19 457–470.

Chen J.S., Hung R.W., Keshavarz-Kohjerdi F., Huang Y.F., 2022. *Algorithms* 15(11) #402.

Clark B.N., Colbourn C.J., Johnson D.S., 1990. *Discrete Math.* 86 165–177.

Desormeaux W.J., Henning M.A., 2014. *Util. Math* 94 101–166.

Garey M.R., Johnson D.S., 1979. *Freeman,* San Francisco, CA.

Haynes T.W., Hedetniemi S.T., Slater P.J., 1998. *Marcel Dekker,* New York.

Haynes T.W., Slater P.J., 1998. *Networks* 32 199–206.

Hung R.W., Yao C.C., Chan S.J., 2015. *Theor. Comput. Sci.* 602 132–148.

Hung R.W., Li C.F., Chen J.S., Su Q.S., 2017. *Discrete Optim.* 26 41–65.

Hung R.W., 2023. *Theor. Comput. Sci.* 956 #113832.

Itai A., Papadimitriou C.H., Szwarcfiter J.L., *SIAM J. Comput.* 11(4) 676–686.

Keshavarz-Kohjerdi F., Hung R.W., 2022. *Algorithms* 15 (2) #61.

Panda B.S. and Pradhan D., 2013. *J. Comb. Optim.* 26 770–785.

Sangeetha S., Swarnamalya M., 2019. The 11th National Cconference on Mathematical Techniques and Applications, *AIP Conference Proceedings* 2112 #020068.

# The Relationship between managerial optimism and the long-term operating performance of start-ups

Jung-Ho Lai*
*Department of Finance, National Taipei University of Business, Taipei, Taiwan*

ABSTRACT: This study investigates the relationship between managerial optimism and the three-year operating performance of start-ups postinitial public offerings (IPOs). The result of the data of 1320 US young start-ups over the 2010–2020 period shows a contingent effect of managerial optimism, where the effect of managerial optimism significantly interacts with the effect of uncertainties from different sources in distinct ways. Specifically, uncertainties due to external environmental factors negatively interact with the effect of managerial optimism such that under a higher external uncertainty environment managerial optimism negatively affects the three-year operating performance of start-ups. On the other hand, uncertainties due to internal organizational factors generate a positive interaction effect with managerial optimism such that under a higher organizational uncertainty context managerial optimism enhances the three-year operating performance of start-ups. The factors of external environmental uncertainty are measured by the level of international diversification, and the level of industrial diversification, respectively. The factors of internal organizational uncertainty are measured by the levels of a firm's internal growth opportunity, and the level of R&D intensity, respectively. The findings of the present study suggest that managerial optimism can be a double-edged sword, where the net effect of managerial optimism is contingent upon the source of uncertainties in quite different ways.

*Keywords*: managerial optimism, operating performance, start-ups, initial public offerings, corporate governance.

## 1 INTRODUCTION

The link between managerial optimism and poor firm performance is a well-established phenomenon in the academic literature. Over-optimistic CEOs tend to set overly ambitious goals and pursue strategies that may be beyond their capabilities, resulting in poor decision-making and negative outcomes for the firm (Chen & Lin 2013). Despite this evidence, many companies continue to hire and promote over-optimistic executives.

One explanation for this disparity between theory and practice is that overconfidence is often seen as a desirable trait in leaders, particularly in the corporate world. Over-optimistic individuals are often perceived as more charismatic, persuasive, and confident, which can make them more effective in negotiations, networking, and other aspects of business over-investment (Ben-David, Graham, & Harvey, 2010).

Moreover, the selection of CEOs is a complex process that involves many factors beyond just their level of confidence. For example, companies may prioritize experience, education, industry knowledge, or other objective criteria over

subjective traits like confidence. Additionally, the selection of a CEO often involves input from multiple stakeholders, including shareholders, board members, and other executives, each of whom may have their own preferences and biases (Hribar an Yang 2015).

Finally, it is important to note that not all forms of overconfidence are necessarily harmful. While excessive overconfidence can lead to poor decision-making, a moderate level of confidence can be beneficial for leaders. For example, confident CEOs may be more willing to take risks and pursue bold strategies that can lead to innovation and growth for their firms (Picone et al. 2014).

In summary, the persistence of over-optimistic CEOs in the corporate world despite evidence of their negative impact on firm performance is a complex phenomenon that likely involves a combination of factors. While overconfidence can be detrimental in some cases, it is also a valued trait in many contexts.

The objective of our study is to address the paradoxical effects of overconfidence in the context of entrepreneurial firms that have recently completed initial public offerings (IPOs) in the high-technology industry. While overconfidence has been associated with positive outcomes such as improved

*Corresponding Author: julialai@ntub.edu.tw

DOI: 10.1201/9781003460763-26

decision implementation and commitment, risk mitigation, innovation output, and product introduction acceleration, it can also have negative impacts on a firm's prospects. Hence, we propose a scenario-based examination of overconfidence to account for these contradictory effects.

We selected entrepreneurial firms that have recently completed IPOs in the high-tech industry for our study for several reasons. First, these firms offer top executives considerable discretion and freedom in decision-making, which is typically not found in mature firms with established governance systems. This indicates a more dominant role of the CEO in decision-making. Second, most startup ventures exhibit high risk-taking, innovativeness, and proactiveness, which are also characteristic of over-optimistic managerial behavior. Third, the high-tech industry is characterized by high uncertainty, short technology and product life cycles, and a significant risk of failure, which may exacerbate the negative effects of managerial optimism related to overestimation of one's own abilities in controlling event outcomes (Tang et al. 2015). Finally, the high-tech industry offers great profit potential, which is largely based on a firm's ability to innovate and develop expertise to facilitate future competition in the market. Thus, a firm's risk tolerance and ability to innovate appear advantageous for prosperity in the high-tech environment.

Our study aims to explicitly examine the value of managerial optimism in the high-tech IPO context, despite its prospective great impact, which has not been explicitly explored in the literature. Overall, our research highlights the need for a nuanced understanding of the effects of overconfidence and the importance of considering contextual factors in assessing its impact on firm performance outcomes.

## 2 LITERATURE AND HYPOTHESES

The conventional view suggests that managerial optimism has a negative impact on firm performance due to the overestimation of managers' abilities, the utility of firm resources, and information about the external environment, known as overprecision (Roll 1986). This phenomenon is particularly evident in merger and acquisition activities, where over-optimistic CEOs tend to maintain excessively optimistic expectations regarding potential synergies and their ability to manage target firms (Chen). Research has also shown that over-optimistic CEOs tend to overestimate the validity of their information when making M&A decisions, which can lead to erroneous assessments of the target's value (Malmendier & Tate 2005, 2008).

Given that the bias caused by managerial optimism is exacerbated in highly information-asymmetric environments, the authors predict a negative interaction effect between the level of external environmental unpredictability and managerial optimism on firm performance outcomes. The study examines external environmental uncertainty using the degree of international diversification and corporate business diversification.

Internationalization offers numerous advantages to entrepreneurial firms, including continued growth, enlargement of the customer base, and greater technological learning (Zahra et al. 2000). However, firms must also overcome unfamiliarity with host institutional environments, which can be challenging due to differences in national culture, law and tax regulations, accounting systems, and business practices forces (Barroso et al. 2011). Additionally, international expansions can increase the volume and variety of information that managers must process, thereby enhancing management complexity and difficulty. For entrepreneurial firms with limited history, smaller size, and poor resources, these challenges can be especially tough. Over-optimistic CEOs can exacerbate these challenges by overestimating their ability to control environmental chaos and underestimating the potential downsides and uncertainties their firms face in the internationalization process (Johanson and Vahlne 2009). As a result, highly optimistic CEOs may underperform moderate CEOs as the degree of internationalization increases, particularly in highly uncertain environmental conditions where managerial hubris can be especially detrimental.

*Hypothesis 1: There exists a negative interaction effect between managerial optimism and the degree of international diversification on start-up firm performance.*

Business diversification can also be used as a measure of the threat posed by environmental information asymmetry. When firms enter different business domains, they face a certain level of "liability of newness," as they are not familiar with the prevailing market conditions in the target industry, such as customer preferences, competitors' competencies, barriers to entry, and intensity of rivalry (George and Kabir 2012). This can be especially challenging for entrepreneurial firms, which typically have limited business networks and information access.

However, cross-business investment also has inherent advantages, such as economies of scope through knowledge and resource spillovers across different segments, and the creation of an internal capital market that allows for cross-subsidization of less profitable segments (Kor 2003). Over-optimistic CEOs, motivated by the potential synergies of cross-business investments, may overestimate their own knowledge and understanding of different industries and inflate their ability to achieve synergies from economies of scope. Therefore, the authors predict that:

*Hypothesis 2: There exists a negative interaction effect between managerial optimism and the degree of industrial diversification on start-up firm performance.*

Internal corporate factors, such as growth opportunities and internal R&D development, can create uncertainties that are more controllable by firm executives than external environmental uncertainties. While these uncertainties may still pose challenges for firms, they also have the potential to create positive synergies with the effect of managerial optimism. The agency problem between shareholders and managers is an ongoing challenge in corporate governance. Managers have a responsibility to act in the best interest of shareholders and maximize shareholder value, but they also have their own personal interests to consider, such as job security and career advancement. This can lead to conflicts of interest, where managers may act in ways that benefit themselves at the expense of shareholders (Lang et al. 1991).

One of the main sources of this conflict is the difference in risk attitudes between managers and shareholders. Managers are typically more risk-averse than shareholders because they have more at stake in the success or failure of the company. Their compensation and wealth are closely tied to the company's prospects, which can make them hesitant to take on risky projects that could jeopardize their position. Shareholders, on the other hand, are more risk-tolerant because they can diversify their wealth across multiple companies. They are not as directly affected by the success or failure of any one company and can therefore afford to take on more risk in pursuit of higher returns.

This difference in risk attitudes can lead to a situation where managers are reluctant to pursue high-expected-return projects that would benefit shareholders. Instead, they may choose to play it safe and pursue lower-risk, lower-return projects that are less likely to put their own positions in jeopardy (Jensen 1993). This is known as the agency problem in corporate governance.

However, overconfident managers are less prone to this conservatism as they underestimate the risks incurred and strongly believe in their problem-solving skills; thus, they are more willing to pursue risky but positive net-present-value (NPV) projects on behalf of risk-neutral shareholders (Goel & Thakor 2008; Engelen et al. 2014). The efficacy of optimism in encouraging desirable risk-taking and mitigating underinvestment may be crucial for firms to engage in high-growth opportunities, as the opportunity cost of missing out on positive NPV projects is higher than for firms with low-growth opportunities (Englmaier 2007).

Over-optimistic CEOs may exhibit proactive attitudes, which can be beneficial in a high-growth environment. Their strong belief in their abilities can lead them to take risks and pursue new ideas earlier than their competitors, which can give them a competitive advantage. They may also be more willing to make quick decisions and recognize the potential in ideas before a complete roadmap is outlined, which can help them stay ahead of the curve.

Moreover, over-optimistic CEOs are more likely to ignore the uncertainties in the market and actively search for projects with high investment potential. They may keep pursuing these projects despite unforeseen challenges, which can help them capitalize on growth opportunities that others may miss (Simon & Shrader 2012). This can help them grow their businesses quickly and achieve greater success in the long run.

*Hypothesis 3: There exists a positive interaction effect between managerial optimism and the degree of firm growth opportunities on start-up firm performance.*

Overconfidence can also have positive effects on a firm's R&D activities. The willingness of over-optimistic managers to take risks can help facilitate innovation, which is essential for successful R&D. Over-optimistic CEOs are willing to accept the high risks inherent in innovative activities that have greater earnings potential relative to projects with lower potential. This can help a firm to explore new ideas and take necessary risks to drive innovation (Galasso & Simcoe 2011).

Moreover, overconfidence can elicit higher effort from managers in order to meet their own over-optimistic forecasts. Over-optimistic agents, who overestimate the degree to which their effort contributes to the firm's success, can make firms more valuable under conditions of high project difficulty by overcoming the usual effort-aversion agency problem characterizing general managers (Landier, Augustin, & David Thesmar, 2009). Since successful R&D requires persistent managerial effort to explore a variety of potential projects, the extra drive and commitment associated with overconfidence are thus valuable (Hirshleifer et al. 2012).

High optimism can also arouse positive emotions, allowing firms to sustain and rebound from numerous trial failures and continue with the innovation process. This can help firms to persevere through setbacks and continue to pursue innovative ideas, which is essential for long-term success in R&D. Finally, CEOs with strong belief in their insights and competence are less likely to imitate their peers and tend to be more creative. Over-optimistic individuals can add fresh information to group decisions and lead a creative discussion by prompting other team members to investigate focal issues using multiple perspectives, thereby driving more innovative initiatives (Hayward et al. 2010). This can help a firm to generate more innovative ideas and stay ahead of the competition.

*H4: There exists a positive interaction effect between managerial optimism and firm R&D intensity on start-up firm performance.*

# 3 SAMPLE AND METHODOLOGY

## 3.1 Data

The initial IPO sample set is collected from the Taiwan Stock Exchange (TWSE) and Taipei Exchange (TPEx) databases, covering the 2010–2020 period. We target entrepreneurial firms that have recently completed IPOs (young post-IPO firms within ten years of their founding. The selected IPO firms are then matched with their accounting and financial information available from the Taiwan Economic Journal (TEJ) Data Bank. IPO firms with complete data comprise the final sample.

## 3.2 Dependent variable

The dependent variable in this study is the post-IPO long-run stock performance, which is measured by the difference between the sample IPO firm's three-year compounding monthly stock returns and the matching firm's three-year compounding monthly stock returns. The matching firm is a firm with the same industry code as the IPO firm and has the closest size, which is measured by the year-end market capitalization of equity of the IPO year.

To compute the buy-and-hold returns (BHRs) over a relevant window, the cumulative return over the window is computed by compounding the monthly returns on the IPO firm's stock during this period. The cumulative market return for the matching firm is computed in a similar way. The difference between the two returns provides the BHRs for the IPO firm in the three-year event window. If any of the matching firms is delisted prior to the end of the sample firm's holding period, the Taiwan Stock Index (Taiwan Capitalization Weighted Stock Index) returns are spliced into the calculation of the returns from the delisting date of the matching firm.

This method measures the total returns from a buy-and-hold strategy where a stock is purchased at the end of the month following IPO and held until its third anniversary. This approach is commonly used in IPO literature to measure long-term stock performance and is a useful way to assess the effectiveness of an IPO investment strategy.

The following equation models this construct, where $R_{it}$ denotes the ith monthly return of the focal IPO firm and $Rmt$ denotes that of the matching firm, respectively.

$$BHRs_i = \prod_{t=1}^{36} (1 + R_{it}) - \prod_{t=1}^{36} (1 + R_{mt})$$

## 3.3 Independent variables

We follow the recent overconfidence literature by measuring executive overconfidence using an overconfidence score that incorporates multiple measures of overconfidence (Schrand & Zechman, 2012; Boulton & Campbell, 2016). The first measure investigates executive personal portfolio investment decisions, specifically the purchases and sales of stocks in their firms. This measure exploits the tendency of over-optimistic CEOs to "purchase additional company stock despite their already high exposure to company risk" (Malmendier & Tate 2005: 2672). Following Malmendier & Tate (2005, 2008) and Campbell et al. (2011), etc., we denote CEOs as over-optimistic if they are net buyers of firm equity during the 5-year period prior to the IPO formation; that is, if they buy shares of their firms (on net) in more years than they sell (on net) during the past five years. Next, it is conceivable that over-optimistic managers would seek to retain a larger portion of their firm's stock, as they would expect company stock to be worth more in the future under their leadership. We use a dummy variable that equals 1 for CEOs if their annual dividend-adjusted shareholding rates increase for at least two of the three years prior to the IPO event, and zero otherwise (Lin et al. 2008). The third measure exploits over-optimistic CEOs' tendency to invest aggressively, leading to a much higher level of firm investment relative to industry rivals (Boulton & Campbell, 2016; Campbell et al. 2011). Following Schrand & Zechman (2012) and Lu & Chen (2017), we calculate a firm's industry-adjusted excess investment by using the firm's residual from a regression of total asset growth on sales growth less the industry median residual. The idea of overinvestment induced by overconfidence suggests a further alternative indicator, which serves as our fourth overconfidence measure. Here we assess corporate excess capital expenditure, measured by capital expenditures as a ratio of beginning-of-year property, plant, and equipment (PP&E) less the industry median value (Boulton & Campbell 2016). Fifth, since overconfidence causes an optimistic assessment of investment payoffs, firms led by over-optimistic managers are more likely to choose risky debt and have longer debt duration (Malmendier et al, 2011). We assess a firm's industry-adjusted debt-to-equity ratio by long-term debt scaled by the market value of the firm, less the industry median value. We assess the overconfidence indicators of debt-to-equity ratio, excess capital expenditure, and excess investment using the annual data of the IPO year, and denote those with values higher than the industry median as exemplifying overconfidence (Malmendier et al. 2011; Schrand & Zechman 2012). Finally, executives are determined to be over-optimistic if three or more than five indicators exhibit overconfidence (Schrand & Zechman 2012).

# 4 RESULTS AND DISCUSSION

Table 1 presents the results of the regression analyses of post-IPO performance of high-tech entrepreneurial firms. Model 1 is the baseline model, which includes only the control variables. Three of the control variables, including Underwriter Reputation, IPO proceeds, and Underpricing show significant association with post-IPO performance, consistent with prior literature. Models 2 to 5 test the moderating effects of four separate contingency factors. Model 2 tests the influence of the degree of international diversification measured by an entropy index. This measure considers both the number of geographic segments in which a firm operates and the relative importance in sales contributed by each geographic segment, formulated as where Pi is the percentage of sales in geographic segment i and $\ln(1/P_i)$ is the weight of each geographic segment. As shown, the coefficient of this interaction term (International Diversification X CEO optimism) is negatively significant at the 1% level, which is consistent with Hypothesis 1. This result suggests that there exists a negative interaction effect between corporate international diversification and CEO overconfidence, such that managerial optimism has an adverse effect as the level of international diversification increases. Model 3 tests the moderating effect of Business Diversification measured by the number of business segments (Business_segments) across the different industries in which a firm operates. This is operationalized by taking the logarithm of one plus the number of industry segments in which a firm is involved. This measure controls for sectoral diversification (e.g., Elango & Pattnaik 2007). Consistent with the prediction of Hypothesis 2, a negatively significant interaction effect ($p < 0.05$) is observed between business diversification and CEO overconfidence. This suggests that the negative impact of managerial optimism is amplified as a firm operates across a greater number of business segments.

Next, we test the moderating effect induced by factors associated with internal development uncertainty from the perspectives of internal growth opportunities (Model 4) and R&D intensity (Model 5). We calculate a firm's Growth Opportunity by first partitioning the value of the firm (V) into the value of assets in place (VAIP) and the value of growth options (VGO). A firm's growth opportunity (VGO) is then measured as a percentage of the firm's market value (V). We follow the IPO literature (Kester 1984) to estimate an IPO firm's Growth Opportunity (GOV) by applying a 20% discount rate to capitalize the firm's current earnings to obtain its value of assets in place (VAIP), and measure firm value (V) by the market value of its common stock plus the book value of its preferred stock and debt (Alessandri *et al.*, 2007; Reuer & Koza 2006). Finally, a firm's

R&D Intensity is calculated as the underlying firm's three-year R&D expenditure divided by its corresponding net sales. The results of both Models 4 and 5 support the positive interaction effect between a firm's internal development uncertainty and CEO overconfidence, such that managerial optimism has a positive influence on performance when firms have greater growth opportunities (as predicted by Hypothesis 3) and a higher level of R&D intensity (predicted by Hypothesis 4). Finally, in Model 6, we incorporate all of the variables simultaneously in a full model. The results are qualitatively similar to those in Models 2 through 5, with the impact of separate interaction effects remaining statistically significant when considered in the same model.

Table 1. Cross-Sectional Regression Analyses of BHRs of Start-Up Firm Performance.

| Table Cross-Sectional Regression Analyses of BHRs of Start-Up Firm Performance | | | | | | |
|---|---|---|---|---|---|---|
| Variables | Model 1 | Model 2 | Model 3 | Model 4 | Model 5 | Model 6 |
| Intercept | 1.338 (3.12)**** | 1.321 (1.77)* | 1.339 (2.65)*** | 1.313 (2.67)*** | 1.339 (1.81)* | 1.306 (2.58)*** |
| Industrial Diversification x Managerial Optimism | | -3.160 (-2.92)*** | | | | -3.164 (-3.54)*** |
| International Diversification x Managerial Optimism | | | -3.725*** (-2.75) | | | -1.143 (-2.36)** |
| Growth Opportunity x Managerial Optimism | | | | 2.210 (2.18)** | | 2.365 (2.69)*** |
| R&D Intensity x Managerial Optimism | | | | | 2.467 (2.02)** | 3.132 (2.05)** |
| Underwriter Reputation | 2.156 (3.21)*** | 1.225 (1.76)** | 1.245 (2.13)*** | 1.272 (1.89)** | 1.415 (2.35)*** | 2.325 (2.67)*** |
| VC-back | -0.015 (-0.55) | 0.091 (1.03) | 0.057 (0.76) | 0.038 (0.58) | 0.064 (0.47) | 0.097 (0.39) |
| IPO proceeds | -0.808 (-1.72)* | -0.176 (-2.02)*** | -0.021 (-0.32) | -0.232 (-2.96)*** | 0.012 (0.03) | -0.285 (-1.67)* |
| Ln Issuer Age | 0.048 (0.23) | -0.022 (-0.56) | -0.012 (-0.20) | 0.015 (0.19) | -0.092 (-1.25) | 0.070 (0.43) |
| Underpricing | 0.357 (2.376)*** | 0.275 (2.376)*** | 0.356 (3.086)*** | 0.346 (1.750)* | 0.351 (2.336)** | 0.344 (2.265)*** |
| Year and Industry Dummies | Yes | Yes | Yes | Yes | Yes | Yes |
| F value | 2.78*** | 2.31*** | 2.36*** | 2.16*** | 2.41*** | 2.69*** |
| Adjusted R² | 0.145 | 0.178 | 0.131 | 0.156 | 0.058 | 0.045 |
| n | 1320 | 1121 | 1010 | 951 | 1069 | 951 |

The parentheses contain t-statistics based on standard errors adjusted for heteroskedasticity (White, 1980).

# 5 CONCLUSION

In summary, the study found that managerial optimism has different effects on internal R&D activities and external cross-country and cross-industry investments. managerial optimism was found to boost internal R&D activities, but not external investments, which may be due to the unique mechanisms that create different synergy effects with CEO overconfidence. The study suggests that over-optimistic CEOs may struggle in unfamiliar heterogeneous environments, where they may overstate their possession of information about target markets. However, in the context of internal R&D activities, managerial optimism can facilitate emotional resilience, which is more beneficial than the negative aspects of overconfidence, such as overestimating assessment of the external environment, existing intelligence, and established market conditions.

The effects of managerial optimism on firm performance are not straightforward and depend on various contextual factors. Our study found that overconfidence has a positive effect on internal R&D activities but not on external cross-country and cross-industry investments, and its effect on firm growth opportunities can be both positive and negative. These results highlight the importance of considering contextual factors when examining the relationship between managerial optimism and firm performance. Moreover, the study suggests that overconfidence can be a double-edged sword, with its positive or negative effects depending on the contingency factors that interact with it.

Overall, our study highlights the importance of considering the context in which managerial optimism may have a positive or negative impact on firm performance. This suggests that firms should carefully consider the potential risks and benefits of appointing an over-optimistic CEO, and assess the fit between the CEO's personality and the firm's strategic goals and industry environment. Additionally, our study contributes to the growing literature on managerial optimism and its implications for firm outcomes, while also calling for further empirical research to better understand the complex relationships between CEO overconfidence, contextual factors, and firm performance.

# REFERENCES

Barroso, C., Villegas, M.M., & Pérez-Calero, L. (2011). Board influence on a firm's internationalization. *Corporate Governance: An International Review*, 19 (4), 351–367.

Ben-David, I., Graham, J. R., & Harvey, C. R. (2010). *Managerial Miscalibration (No. w16215)*. National Bureau of Economic Research.

Chen, H. J., & Lin, S. H. (2013). Managerial optimism, investment efficiency, and firm valuation. *Multinational Finance Journal*, 17(3/4), 295–340.

Engelen, A., Neumann, C., & Schwens, C. (2014). "Of Course I Can": The effect of CEO overconfidence on entrepreneurially oriented firms. *Entrepreneurship Theory and Practice*,

Englmaier, F., 2007. 'A strategic rationale of having overoptimistic managers'. *Discussion Paper Series in Economics and Management*, No.07-27.

Galasso, A., & Simcoe, T. S. (2011). CEO overconfidence and innovation. *Management Science*, 57 (8), 1469–1484.

George, R., & Kabir, R. (2012). Heterogeneity in business groups and the corporate diversification–firm performance relationship. *Journal of Business Research*, 65(3), 412–420.

Gervais, S., Heaton, J. B., & Odean, T. (2011). Overconfidence, compensation contracts, and capital budgeting. *Journal of Finance*, 66(5), 1735–1777.

Goel, A. M., & Thakor, A. V. (2008). Overconfidence, CEO selection, and corporate governance. *The Journal of Finance*, 63(6), 2737–2784.

Hayward, M. L., Forster, W. R., Sarasvathy, S. D., & Fredrickson, B. L. (2010). Beyond hubris: How highly confident entrepreneurs rebound to venture again. *Journal of Business Venturing*, 25(6), 569–578.

Hirshleifer, D., Low, A., & Teoh, S. H. (2012). Are overconfident CEOs better innovators? *The Journal of Finance*, 67(4), 1457–1498.

Hribar, P., & Yang, H. (2015). *CEO overconfidence and management forecasting*. Contemporary Accounting Research.

Jensen, M.C. (1993). The modern industrial revolution, exit, and the failure of internal control systems. *Journal of Finance* 48(3), 831–880.

Johanson, J., & Vahlne, J. E. (2009). The Uppsala internationalization process model revisited: From liability of foreignness to liability of outsidership. *Journal of International Business Studies*, 40(9), 1411–1431.

Kor, Y. Y. (2003). Experience-based top management team competence and sustained growth. *Organization Science*, 14(6), 707–719.

Landier, Augustin, and David Thesmar, (2009). Financial contracting with optimistic entrepreneurs, *Review of Financial Studies* 22, 117–150.

Lang, L. H., Stulz, R., & Walkling, R. A. (1991). A test of the free cash flow hypothesis: The case of bidder returns. *Journal of Financial Economics*, 29(2), 315–335.

Malmendier, U., & Tate, G. (2005). CEO overconfidence and corporate investment. *The Journal of Finance*, 60 (6), 2661–2700.

Malmendier, U., & Tate, G. (2008). Who makes acquisitions? CEO overconfidence and the market's reaction. *Journal of Financial Economics*, 89(1), 20–43.

Picone, P. M., Dagnino, G. B., & Minà, A. (2014). The origin of failure: A multidisciplinary appraisal of the hubris hypothesis and proposed research agenda. *The Academy of Management Perspectives*, 28(4), 447–468.

Reuer, J. J., & Koza, M. P. (2000). Asymmetric information and joint venture performance: theory and evidence for domestic and international joint ventures. *Strategic Management Journal*, 21(1), 81–88.

Roll, R. (1986). The Hubris Hypothesis of Corporate Takeovers. *The Journal of Business*, 59(2), 197–216.

Simon, M. & Shrader, R. (2012). Entrepreneurial actions and optimistic overconfidence: The role of motivated reasoning in new product introductions. *Journal of Business Venturing*, 27(3), 291–309.

Tang, Y., Li, J., & Yang, H. (2015). What I see, what I do: How executive hubris affects firm innovation. *Journal of Management*, 41(6), 1698–1723.

Zahra, S. A., Ireland, R. D., & Hitt, M. A. (2000). International expansion by new venture firms: International diversity, mode of market entry, technological learning, and performance. *Academy of Management Journal*, 43(5), 925–950.

*System Innovation for a Troubled World – Lam et al. (Eds)*
© 2024 the Author(s), ISBN: 978-1-032-60846-4

# Discuss the development and the design of the cultural and creative products with visual elements of Tainan temple architecture and their application

Chiu-Ling Hsieh* & Shang-Chia Chiou
*Graduate School of Design National Yunlin University of Science & Technology, Douliou, Taiwan*

ABSTRACT: Aiming at the ancient buildings of the Nanmiao, this paper studies the meaning and use of the system and makes use of and carries out visual research and locates the feeling and stability of the Zhongshi scientific public opinion in the building, so as to play a role, add modern elements, and shape the architectural image design. In the teaching form of architectural form, the new theme of architecture is deconstructed into a new theme, and the new theme of architecture is launched in view of vitality. Course design such as extended application shows Tianhou's iconic architectural form. To create a work of art with the relevant design meaning. A deep dive into the study of sex and how to use it together. Look for features and design inspirations in buildings, represent the visual experience of people, represent the visual experience of people, and use the form of creation to extend the architectural shape of people to create the design meaning in modern cultural commodities, and carry out new targeted designs.

## 1 INTRODUCTION

The architectural concept of ancient architectural forms has always been the goal of appreciation and research by later generations. Due to the wisdom of the ancestors, many amazing technologies are hidden in the details of the architecture. For example, the incredible knowledge of how to use a single nail as the tenon to construct the structure of the whole building is what still makes future generations feel extraordinary about the wisdom of the old ancestors. Moreover, the wisdom of the ancestors is easily lost over time. "Education" plays an important role. How to pass on important knowledge requires the combination of innovative concepts and elements, in order to successfully achieve a professional, innovative, and traditional way.

### 1.1 Research background

Tainan, the capital city in the old days, is a cultural and historic site with abundant historical stories and legends, most of which can stand for the different dynasties. The spirit and touching stories of the ancient architectural form of Tainan Grand Matsu Temple located near downtown Chikan Cultural Park have affected the local residents for more than 300 years.

### 1.2 Research motivation

In recent years, national consciousness has risen, and research fields such as "Taiwan Studies" and

"Ethnology" have become more and more extensive. In such a situation where hundreds of flowers are blooming and flourishing, a question arises how to explore the level of cultural spirit and activate the life value of culture? In addition, how to achieve cultural learning and inheritance is an important topic and the basic motivation of this research.

In the domestic design professional education development research, most of the research is based on the combination of professional practice, and the type of certification examination is mostly research. The related research also focuses on the overall development.

In the combination of extension design and traditional concepts, it focuses on discussing of goods development mode, the integrating the design effect, the observing goods selling effect, surveying customer satisfaction, the researching consumers' background and purchasing willingness, etc., so that merchandise designed professionally can be on the market and accepted by the public.

### 1.3 Research purpose

Regarding the theme of this thesis, the researcher will focus on the ancient architectural form of Datianhou Palace, study the meaning symbols, and uses contained in the building, and discuss the visual experience and stability effect brought to people by its architecture at the level of visual elements, and then incorporate modern science. Elements, extending to the photography course of the researcher's school, integrating the "visual image" of photography teaching, exploring the "subjectivity of photography and the nature of the

---

*Corresponding Author: ami.artidea@gmail.com

DOI: 10.1201/9781003460763-27

medium" through the training category of photography course education, and integrating the product design course of architectural images, guide students to gradually pass through photography activities, explore cultural connotations, integrate visual elements of cultural connotations, draw design drawings of cultural and creative works, and innovate the way of use, to give new vitality to the tradition, so that it can be passed on.

Based on the above, we expect to achieve the following three goals:

(1) Determine and discuss the historical architecture and space-time background of Datianhou Palace through literature, and then explain the symbolic meaning of the building item by item, and review and understand the development process of ancient architecture.
(2) For the cultural design that may be applied to the extension of architectural form, select the representative architectural form and create the pattern.
(3) How to extend the meaning represented in traditional architecture to the analysis and discussion of curriculum design, and develop a series of merchandise.

### 1.4  Research scope

At present, there are numerous varieties of historic sites, and the researches on the Datianhou Palace is quite a lot. Each of them has their own features and goals, which make it difficult to present the specific information. Hence, this research focuses on the historical buildings and buildings inside the Datianhou Palace and selects the main buildings that existed in the palace of King Ningjing in the early Ming Dynasty as the research representative. At the very beginning, the domain was the residence of the princes of the Ming Dynasty. Its architectural structure was different from that of the private houses. It was equivalent to a lot of architectural decorations in the palace. Therefore, it is necessary to study the buildings remaining in the Ming Dynasty. Selecting the representative architectural decoration that can represent the spirit of this historic building in the building, and extending other research and design, is a modest contribution to the preservation and continuation of culture, and it is also helpful for inheritance.

### 1.5  Research object

The object of this study is the old constructure of the Datianhou Palace. It uses various visual, image, aesthetics, architectural art, and architectural implications to analyze the historical buildings of the Datianhou Palace. As the research object, after many visits and researches, the historic building was chosen as the representative of the early stage of architecture—"Dragon Pillar of the Ming Dynasty", It was used as the symbol of

the extended design of cultural goods, to study the form, shape, and meaning of the remaining buildings, and to study the feasibility of developing cultural goods and the value that can be used. In addition, it studied how to maintain the original architectural aesthetics and combine them with the design characteristics of cultural goods, and what elements and methods are used. Furthermore, the design was extended by adding dragon-related nine dragon elements, in order to increase the richness and feasibility of cultural goods. Attempting to develop creative and historic goods with specific and practical features that are handy and useful, is aimed at achieving the ultimate goal of inheriting the culture of research.

### 1.6  Research design creation process

This research is divided into six stages, and its architecture diagram is shown in Figure 1.

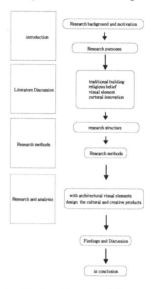

Figure 1.  Architecture diagram of this research.

## 2  DISCUSSION ON RELEVANT LITERATURE

Mazu is one of the mainstream beliefs with the largest number of believers, the largest mobilization force, and the widest distribution in Taiwan's traditional beliefs. Residential space is the most closely spaced and the most mysterious research subject.

### 2.1  About architecture (Related references review)

As for the wisdom of ancestors handed down from ancient times, understanding how it is constructed and its representative meaning requires that, as a latecomer, one must learn its important essence through countless documents and materials. Only thinking and exploration can integrate subsequent research into the wisdom left by our ancestors.

## 2.2 *Faith*

In the books "The Records of the Tainan Datianhou Palace" and "Research on the Shape of Dragon Columns in Tainan Temples", it is mentioned that the dragon columns of the four town temples handed down from the Qing Dynasty three hundred years ago are the most preserved among the temples at present. A complete building, the legendary image represented by the dragon column is lofty and sacred, almost the same as the emperor, so this study is based on the dragon column as the first and primary element in the design of subsequent courses and activities. The shape of the dragon column was conceived through activities, and other extendable lesson plans were developed. Furthermore, there are many types and quantities of sculptures in the temple. This study selected the architectural structure of the dragon-related nine sons and carried out other related cultural goods designs.

## 2.3 *Characteristics and elements of visual presentation*

Visual elements are ubiquitous in our lives, and we are used to forming them into nature. We may not be able to perceive them and assimilate them without mentioning them. Before studying visual elements, we must first understand vision. Since architecture is also rich in many visual elements, it must also be integrated into the next cultural and creative design, so that relevant cultural and creative works can be reasonably interpreted and represented. Just like entering the spacious hall after entering the Sanchuan Gate, the visual sense is quiet, comfortable, and solemn. The Qing Dynasty dragon pillar stands tall in the sky, visually majestic and impenetrable. However, the sculpture is round and full, making people feel kind and kind. Many shapes and visual elements are matched with each other and are closely related. If the curriculum design is carried out in the future, the visual elements must be taken into account in the design direction.

## 3 RESEARCH AND ANALYSIS

In terms of the application of data, Taiwanese local literature and history are mainly based on the local chronicles of Taiwan or related stele data compiled in the Qing Dynasty, modern scholars' investigations and research are used as the research reference of this article, and the rationality of its theory is studied in detail and researched in-depth. After understanding the historical connotation of its architectural art, extract the elements of architectural form and design a series of cultural goods related to it.

### 3.1 *Research methods and theoretical discussion and analysis*

In this research, we discuss the history of Tainan Datianhou Palace. Besides realizing the process, the important records, and the preserved relics of hundreds of history, we create new goods with vision elements, the art, and the meanings of the construction, soaking into people's lives and making them connect with the meanings of the culture.

In the research, we use "document research" for document collection and analysis, "field research" for observation and interviews, and "observation research" for recording methods to conduct more in-depth discussions to understand the current teaching phenomenon of domestic design education, aiming at architectural form, visual elements, lesson plan design of course activities, as the main part of this research.

The research methods such as literature analysis, field investigation, and observational research that will be applied in this study are described as follows.

### 3.1.1 *Literature analysis*
Based on literature collection and analysis, this paper finds that the main building structure of the Datianhou Palace is the official residence of the Ming Dynasty. It has been restored for several generations, and the key points of its architectural details are relatively complicated. "Taiwan Ancient Architectural Illustrated Dictionary" should be verified, and then collated by this study, and its architectural form related to the dragon is selected as the key to the curriculum design content.

By studying literature related to the current development of design professional education in China,, analyzing core courses and teaching modes of design education, the background of each department, teaching objectives, operation direction, number of credits, course hours, course characteristics, teachers and students, teaching and practice space, class situation, grading method, etc., this study provides a systematic summary and compares the differences.

### 3.1.2 *Fieldwork and observational research*
In Tainan Datianhou Palace, the tradition and the memory of the history are not the lost legends but still the presentation of the new and old histories with their powerful influence on people.

In Tainan Datianhou Palace, three pairs of Dragon Pillar, which went through from the Ming Dynasty to the period of the Republic of China, have been the representative parts. As long as people pray at Tainan Datianhou Palace, they will stand in front of the dragon pillars observing the differences between one another. Although they are old monuments, they are even shiny after being touched by the followers within generations. After visiting it, I decided to take Dragon Pillars and nine sons of Dragon to be the design concept and the foundation.

### 3.1.2.1 Dragon

The Chinese dragon has been deeply legendary and impressive in Chinese culture and tradition since ancient times. Although people never see any real dragons, in the legend, Chinese dragons have many animal-like forms such as fish scales, antlers, Dragon feelers, fishtail, fins, and paws. These combinations stand for its spirits, extraordinary power, and supreme majesty. In the Chinese ancient books, The Book of Changes, a flying dragon was mentioned in Qiangua. Dragons are also the representative of the four spiritual creatures. According to these powers of dragons, the Emperor of China added this quality to himself for the sake of ruling the subjects and people efficiently. As a result, the Emperor of China usually used the dragon as a symbol of his imperial strength and power. That is, the clothing and accessories of the Emperor with dragon motifs were called dragon robes. Moreover, they even decorated their palaces with dragons. Because this kind of culture has been formed for so long, dragons have become a symbol of the Emperor of China.

### 3.1.2.2 *Pillars in the house*

Pillars, one kind of building material, carry the weight of the constructures.

- Pillars in different parts include Dian-Jin Pillars, Fu-Dian Pillars, General Pillars, Feng Pillars, and Yan Pillars.
- The most popular building materials include stones, wood, and brass.
- Different shapes of pillars include cylinder pillars, square pillars, octagonal pillars, shuttle-shaped pillars, dragon pillars, flower and bird carving pillars, and bamboo pillars.

Due to the various pillar types, we only introduce the representative pillars, dragon pillars, in Tainan Datianhou Palace.

### 3.1.2.3 *Dragon pillars*

The dragon pillars in Taiwan temples are also called coiled dragon pillars, which means the dragons before going to heaven. They are decorated spirally on the pillars with a magnificent state welcoming the visitors. In the legend, dragons were the spirits, also the representative of the four spiritual creatures. As mentioned above, China emperors regarded themselves as *reincarnation* of dragons. As a result, after the Yuan dynasty, only emperors could use the gold dragon pattern with five paws, while temples in the folk could only use the gold dragon pattern with three or four paws, called python. Therefore, the dragon pillars in temples should be called python pillars. However, they are still called dragon pillars because it's quite hard to tell the differences between dragons and pythons.

People can realize the features of each dynasty from the style of dragon pillars in temples. In the early ages, the diameter of dragon pillars with simple carvings was smaller than those with complex carvings in the late ages.

Dragon pillars are stated in four periods:

① **Simple period:** Before the mid-Qing Dynasty, only one dragon was carved on one pillar. Overall, pillars are thin and simple cylinders with few clouds carved, such as the Ming Dynasty dragon pillars at Tainan Datianhou Palace and the dragon pillars at the Guan Yin Palace.

② **Worldly period:** During the mid-Qing Dynasty, each pillar was a cylinder with one single dragon spiraled. The dragon's body is part of the pillar; yet, its paws are fretwork, being away from the pillar. The dragon spiraled with big curvature and the style is getting mature, such as the dragon pillars at the Longshan Temple in Lukang.

③ **Mature period:** During the late ages of the Qing Dynasty, people used octagonal columns to replace the cylinders. But still maintained one dragon on one pillar. The diameter of dragon pillars is bigger, whereas the dragon fretwork is quite out of the surface of the pillar. Besides clouds carving, people, flowers, birds, and sea creatures were added to the decoration vividly, such as the Qing Dynasty dragon pillars at Tainan Datianhou Palace and the dragon pillars at Taipei Wanhua Sansia Tzushr Temple.

④ **Gorgeous period:** During the Japanese colonial period, the carving of the dragon pillars became gorgeous. The upper part appeared in **Corinthian Order, and the** diameters of the dragon pillars are two times bigger than the original ones with too much detail, such as the dragon pillars at Taipei Confucius Temple Dacheng Hall.

## 4 CURRICULUM IMPLEMENTATION PLANNING AND REVIEW

In any building, every architectural form and form reveals many signals, and these signals guide every movement of people and also form a "ceremonial space" in the temple. In a narrow sense, ritual space refers to all kinds of ritual activities within the scope of common people's cognition. It is an event ceremony that must be held or held in a specific space, and participants play various roles in its activities.

### 4.1 *Content and form*

Because most elements of construction are pictures and patterns, architects are usually presented with simplified patterns. Moreover, they chose the elements of construction to redesign the representative patterns, hoping to turn the old constructures into new life. This research finds out the characteristics of the ancient architectural form from the architectural space composition. Design elements for an activity course have been taken from parts of a lesson plan. Primarily, a photography course was chosen as the main activity concept, and the treasure hunt mode was made to participate in the activities on the spot so that students could learn easily. The main axis of this activity is to be closer to the inheritance of history in daily life and to guide students in other courses to design related image totems and make them suitable products, to promote the effect of cultural and creative products.

At present, the architectural form of the planned extension design for Datianhou Palace is as follows:

1. Qing Dynasty Dragon Pillar
2. Nine Dragons

The goods design extends to camera belts, cell phone back covers, clothing, and other handy objects in daily life, to integrate ancient architectural elements into the modern design and promote the handy goods into the markets.

### 4.2 *Applicable methods and techniques*

The materials on the market are nothing more than plastic, paper, logs, metal, silicone, glass, acrylic, etc., and the techniques are becoming more and more diverse due to the progress of the times, such as hollowing out, sculpture, round sculpture, relief etc., the researcher will choose the materials and techniques suitable for the designed images to cooperate with each other, so that the cultural and creative products can exert their own value and presentation effect.

In view of the increasingly serious environmental pollution and the increasing importance of environmental protection issues, this study decided to use eco-friendly materials, mainly decomposable and recyclable, as the design products and production guidelines.

1. Wood: Try to pick up dead branches and design the hand-carved pen according to the selected shape, which is eco-friendly and does not lose the antique flavor.
2. Recycled paper: The hand-sewn notebook is made of recycled paper, which is integrated into the wonderful door opening and closing design, which is rich in antiques and eco-friendly.
3. Gypsum sculpture: Imitate the reliefs in the building, guide students to make sculptures with rich stories, and encourage creativity and innovation.
4. FRP fiberglass: Imitate the selected style, make related models with daily practical items, and extend creative works.
5. Ceramics: Taiwan's Yingge Ceramics is famous for its origin and production, and because ceramics are also natural products, they can be used in their works. Students can be guided to shape the Q-shaped pattern out of clay and send them to make. into a complete work.

6. Photography: Design treasure-hunting or puzzle-solving games, take students to the research field to carry out on-site puzzle-solving activities, and photograph designated objects and architectural shapes to achieve the effect of learning.

## 5 CONCLUSION

This research is based on three parts: history, society, and space.

Through deeply realizing the features and the history of the Datianhou Palace, the researcher as a cultural scholar discussed the history literature and documents so as to solve parts of the riddles in the architectural space composition.

### 5.1 *Result and contribution*

1. Discuss and research the architectural forms, vision elements, and folk beliefs, from which numerous architectural elements can be used to design cultural creative goods. Both the totems and sculptures have their own styles.
2. We extend the architectural forms of the Datianhou Palace to cultural creative goods. At present, the representative architectural forms of the Datianhou Palace are the official buildings of the Ming Dynasty. As a result of that, it is really appropriate to use these elements within ancient buildings to create cultural creative goods.
3. We first discussed the history and the background of the era of the Datianhou Palace. Afterward, we explained the features of the architectural forms. Eventually, we made sure that we could promote cultural creative goods from here.
4. We consult the ideas from the cultural creative products in the present markets, which can also help us to analyze and discuss the extending meanings of the cultural creative goods we want to create, making our products perfect.

According to the above-mentioned approach, we treat it as a main factor to melt the architectural elements of the Ming Dynasty into cultural creative goods, making them rich in historic elements, in order to protect the ancient buildings and maintain the generation inheritance.

### 5.2 *Expectations of the pattern design for developing culture industry*

#### 5.2.1 *Create the brand image*

Create various cultural creative goods from life and create a unique brand image. Only when people build up their own features and the positioning of the brand, can they promote the cultural creative goods to every level of the users and everywhere to approach the goal of sustainable development.

### 5.2.2  Build up the strategic alliance

It is easier to approach success by team building than by working alone. We attempt to build the network of the design and the manufacturing process. With different productions and marketing units combined, people can develop more different cultural creative goods and promote them into the markets, making a new design notion with the traditional culture.

### 5.2.3  Redevelopment of cultural creative goods

Combine the nine-dragon patterns, the historic architecture, and the legend meanings to create practical and fashionable goods. In the future, we will attempt to design new architectural forms, making old buildings alive and creating new value.

## REFERENCES

## BOOKS:

[1] Li Qianlang (1993). *"Taiwan Architecture History"*. Taipei: Lions Books Co., Ltd.

[2] Li Qianlang (1999). *"Introduction to Traditional Architecture"*. Taipei: Cultural Construction Committee, Executive Yuan.

[3] Li Qianlang (2002). *"Taiwan Architecture Review"*. Taipei: Yushan Society.

[4] Li Qianlang (2010). *"Taiwan Ancient Architecture Illustrated Dictionary"*. Taipei: Yuanliu Publishing Co., Ltd.

[5] Zhou Liqiang (1994). *"Our Lady of Heaven"*. Taipei: Cultural Publishing Department of Zili Evening News.

[6] Lin Huicheng (1995). *"Taiwan Traditional Architecture Manual/Form and Practice"*. Taipei: Artist Press.

[7] The Management Committee of Tainan Datianhou Temple (2001). *"Sacrificing Tainan Datianhou Palace Chronicles"* Tainan: Sacrificing Tainan Datianhou Palace.

[8] Gao Mingshi, editor-in-chief (2004). *"Historical Studies in Post-War Taiwan 1945→2000"*. Taipei: National Taiwan University Publishing Center.

[9] Gao Canrong (1989). *"Swallowtail Horseback Tile Town"*. Taipei: Nantian Book Co., Ltd.

[10] Shaorong Kang (2010). *"Story of Painted Paintings in Nanying Temples"*. Tainan: Tainan County Government.

[11] Zhang Yunshu (2013). *"Research on Mazu Beliefs in Tainan"*. Tainan: Cultural Bureau of Tainan City Government.

[12] Huang Dingsheng (2007). *"Travel with Mazu"*. Taipei: Red Ant Books Co., Ltd.

[13] Liang Zhenming (2010). *"Study on the Formation of Dragon Columns in Taiwanese Temples"*. Taipei: National Institute of Compilation and Translation.

[14] Edited by Cheng Wanli (2008). *"Chinese Architectural Form and Decoration"*. Taipei: Nantian Book Co., Ltd.

[15] Yang Fei, Xu Mingzhu / ed. (2008). *"Fucheng historical monuments and architectural first-class monuments"*. Taipei: Wenjin Publishing House Co., Ltd.

[16] Dong Fangyuan (1996). *"Exploring Taiwanese Folk Beliefs"*. Taipei: Changmin Cultural Enterprise Co., Ltd.

[17] Yuanliu Publishing House (2003). *"Taiwan Heritage Tour"*. Taipei: Yuanliu Publishing House.

[18] Cai Taishan ed. (2006). *"A Collection of Academic Papers on Mazu Culture"*. Taipei: Lide Publishing House.

[19] Zhong Mingyuan (1993). *"Graphic Understanding of Temples"*. Taipei: World Buddhist Publishing House.

[20] Ji Ning Taoist, Guo Ruiyun/edited (1988). *"Fucheng Taoist Temple Cultural Relic Collection"*. Tainan: Autumn Rain Printing Company.

[21] Fujishima Kaijiro / Author, Li Yirong / Translator (2002). *"Taiwan Original Architecture"*. Taipei: Aboriginal Culture.

*System Innovation for a Troubled World – Lam et al. (Eds)*

# The influence of principles and elastic concepts existing in rituals on the inheritance of ceremonies—taking thanksgiving ceremony in Zhanghu village as an example

Chiu-Mei Lai*
*Graduate School of Design, National Yunlin University of Science and Technology, Yunlin, Taiwan*

Shyh-Huei Hwang
*College of Design, National Yunlin University of Science and Technology, Yunlin, Taiwan*

ABSTRACT: Zhanghu Village, located in the Gukeng Mountain area, preserves the Thanksgiving Ceremony, which has been inherited from ancestors for more than a hundred years. Since the pilgrimage project in the festival cannot be completed in one day in the mountainous area, it is divided into two settlements every year to carry out the ceremonies at staggered times. However, in the inheritance of the festival, due to the migration and aging of the population in mountainous areas, the manpower for the festival is becoming increasingly insufficient. In addition, the residents mainly rely on agriculture for their livelihood, and their income is affected by the weather and is not sufficient. The details and the scale of sacrifices may be flexibly adjusted according to the current situation by the Censer Keeper who was in charge of the festival. This research took two years to collect data through in-depth interviews with local residents and participating observations, and compared and analyzed four times Thanksgiving ceremonies. It was found that there were "principles" and "elasticity" in the implementation of Thanksgiving ceremonies. The principal part is to preserve each item of the ceremony according to the routine, which is enough to preserve the appearance of the ceremony. The flexible part is mostly about the details of the execution of the ceremony, which is greatly influenced by the attitude and ideas of the Censer Keeper. This study found that there are many meanings in the details of the Thanksgiving ceremony in Zhanghu Village, but in the process of inheritance, the residents only knew the superficial practices but did not know the meaning behind them, so they were not taken seriously and easily became the object of elastic simplification.

*Keywords*: Thanksgiving, Zhanghu Village, Gukeng mountainous area, ceremonies

## 1 INTRODUCTION

### 1.1 *Research motives and purposes*

Zhanghu Village, which holds an annual Thanksgiving ceremony, is in the Gukeng mountainous area. There are four ritual activities, including "rewarding the soldiers and generals[1] (賞兵犒將)," "door worship[2] (拜門~)," "worshipping the Jade Emperor (拜天公)," and the "pilgrimage (遶境)." Every 12th year of Thanksgiving, the Village will expand the door worship, thus, the 12th year of Thanksgiving is also called "Xiaopu[3]

(小普)." During the Xiaopu, due to the expansion of the pudu[4] activities, more ghosts came to participate, so a ritual item of "Zhong Kui Expelling the Spirits" was added at the end of the pudu. It takes approximately two days to complete the aforementioned ritual, which is different from the Thanksgiving activities in ordinary plain townships, where it takes approximately two hours to complete the Thanksgiving activities (Yang 2015).

Currently, the total population of Zhanghu Village is less than 500 residents, and they are scattered in the mountainous area to form several small settlements. A century ago, because the pilgrimage could not be completed in one day, the Village was divided into two settlements for the

---

*Corresponding Author: a0912190626@gmail.com

[1]The soldiers and generals here refer to the invisible soldiers and generals in the Jiangye Temple . Their task is to guard the village and prevent ghosts from entering the village.
[2]Door worship refers to worshipping various ghosts at the entrance of one's own home or at a ceremonial place.

[3]"Xiaopu" is the meaning of "small Pudu", which is a modest way for residents to speak of Pudu.
[4]Pudu is a ritual that exorcise solitary spirits, prepares offerings, and performs a series of rituals.

DOI: 10.1201/9781003460763-28

Thanksgiving Ceremony. To date, although the Village still maintains the ceremony tradition every year, according to the participant observations in this study, there are several differences in the annual practices of the Thanksgiving Ceremony. Therefore, the two purposes of this study are, as follows:

(1) To investigate whether there are any rules that the staff must follow when performing the rituals.
(2) To investigate whether the staff can adjust their own practices when performing the rituals.

## 1.2  Research method

This study mainly used in-depth interviews to collect data on the research topic. From March 2021 to December 2022, this study focused on the topic of Thanksgiving Ceremonies and performed in-depth interviews with local elders, Censer Keepers, and enthusiastic residents. This study gradually summarized the details of Zhanghu Village's beliefs and rituals.

In addition, this study participated in the observation of every Thanksgiving Ceremony event in Zhanghu Village in 2021 and 2022. The multiple participant observations helped this research to verify whether the details of the said ceremony, as described by the residents during the interviews before the ceremony, were correctly understood. The observations of the ceremonies of the northern and southern settlements helped compare the differences in the preservation of traditional ceremonies, as well as the efforts made when facing changes between the two settlements, which originally held the ceremony together (Hwang & Lai 2022). Furthermore, based on the observations of the ceremonies held by the same settlements the years before and after, this study found that artificial factors affected the details of the ceremonies.

## 1.3  Taiwanese folk thanksgiving belief

The Thanksgiving Ceremony in Taiwan is to convert a series of gratitude into a ceremony. The concept of such gratitude originated from the expectations of the farming, fishery, and animal husbandry communities for a good harvest from God. In order to thank God for the food during the harvest (Lee nd), farmers will prepare rich sacrifices after the autumn harvest to thank the gods of heaven and earth. Therefore, the meaning of Thanksgiving is to express gratitude to God. On the one hand, people will express gratitude for a good harvest. On the other hand, people will pray for a safe and good harvest in the coming year (Zhuang 2019). One of the most important rituals in the Thanksgiving Ceremony is worshiping The God of Heaven, which refers to the Jade Emperor in folk belief (Lin 2009). The Jade Emperor is in charge of all gods, and his status is higher than that of other gods. Due to his noble status, the earlier people worship the Jade Emperor, the greater their gratitude; therefore, residents usually choose to worship the Jade Emperor in the early morning or at the beginning of the day (Lee 2015). However, the folk beliefs in Taiwan are very free, and there are often unique ways of holding Thanksgiving ceremonies according to different geographical environments (Liu 2000).

## 2  THANKSGIVING CEREMONY OF ZHANGHU VILLAGE

### 2.1  Thanksgiving in Zhanghu Village is divided into two scales

The annual Thanksgiving ceremonies of Zhanghu Village are held around November of the lunar calendar and are conducted on different dates by the two settlements of North Zhanghu Village and South Zhanghu Village. If Thanksgiving Ceremonies are distinguished by scale, there are two types of Thanksgiving ceremonies:

(1) Annual Thanksgiving Ceremonies.
(2) The Peace Dharma Ritual is conducted once every twelve years. The local residents used to call the peace dharma ritual "Xiaopu."

### 2.2  Detailed rituals and process design in the ceremony

#### 2.2.1  Rituals on day 1

##### 2.2.1.1  Rewarding soldiers and generals

The residents will thank soldiers and generals of five barracks for keeping evil spirits out of the village. During the Thanksgiving Ceremony every year, some rituals reward the soldiers and generals of the five barrack for their hard work over the past year. On the morning of the day of the ceremony, the boss[5] will collect the five barracks flags, which represent that the soldiers and generals of the five barracks are called back to receive rewards. Another important representation of collecting the five barracks flags is to call the soldiers and generals back to maintain order at the door of worship or pudu ceremony.

##### 2.2.1.2  Door worship or pudu[6]

Taiwan is an immigrant society, and the bachelors who came to Taiwan alone had the custom of taking care of each other. During the door worship or pudu period, residents will prepare sacrifices

---

[5]Boss refers to one of the staff titles of Thanksgiving work team, there are 1 censer keeper, 1 vice censer keeper and 4 boss in the Thanksgiving work team.
[6]In Zhanghu Village, door worship is synonymous with Pudu In the sacrificial field, because the scale is relatively small in normal years, the locals call it door worship, and the large scale in Xiaopu is called Pudu.

and come to the sacrifice site to call for the souls of the nearby mountains to enjoy the meals. On one hand, the purpose of door worship is to appease the souls of the dead in the mountains; on the other hand, people hope that the dead won't create trouble when people worship the Jade Emperor.

### 2.2.1.3 Zhong kui[7] expelling the spirits

The Expelling the Spirits ritual is only available in the Xiaopu. After the pudu is ended, the Taoist priest will play the role of Zhong Kui and perform the Expelling the Spirits ritual. Ordinary people are not allowed to approach or watch this ritual, of which the purpose is: *"After the completion of offering meals, the act of helping the spirits return to where they were, prevents wandering ghosts from lingering in the world."* (20211126, Interviewee SXA10-11).

### 2.2.2 *Rituals on day 2*

### 2.2.2.1 *Worshipping the jade emperor*

Worshipping the Jade Emperor is the most important ritual in the entire Thanksgiving Ceremony. The time selection of worshiping the Jade Emperor involves choosing an auspicious time based on the birthday of the Censer Keeper, and then, launching the schedule of the day before and after the ceremony based on that time.

### 2.2.2.2 *Pilgrimage*

The pilgrimage is the key event on Day 2 of the Thanksgiving Ceremony. The purpose of the pilgrimage is to enable the gods to patrol the realm and keep the residents safe. During the pilgrimage, the black flag is the leader and sweeps along the pilgrimage route to expel the wandering ghosts lingering in the world, the gods go on pilgrimage in sedan chairs or cars, and the censer keeper holds the censer and goes door-to-door to distribute peace talismans.

## 3 PRINCIPLES AND FLEXIBILITY FOR RITUAL PERFORMERS

### 3.1 *Ritual performers*

While Zhanghu Village holds the Thanksgiving Ceremony every year, the Censer Keeper team is the main personnel performing rituals and is responsible for various details and preparations. However, since the execution of various rituals requires the Taoist priest to act as an intermediary to communicate and convey the mind to the worshipped, the Taoist priest is also an important ritual performer:

---

[7]Zhong Kui is a god in Chinese mythology who can drive away evil spirits.

### 3.1.1 *Externally hired Taoist priest*

The residents depend on a Taoist priest in the Thanksgiving Ceremony, including (1) choosing the date for the Thanksgiving Ceremony; (2) purchasing the different types and quantities of gold paper incense required in the ceremony; (3) commanding the altar arrangement and offering placement; (4) performing chants sutras to guide the three rituals: "rewarding soldiers and generals," "door worship," and "worshipping the Jade Emperor." Moreover, in the year of Xiaopu, a Taoist priest is also required to (5) play the role of Zhong Kui to perform the Expelling the Spirits ritual. Taoist priest is the one with the heaviest workload during the ceremony.

### 3.1.2 *Censer keeper team*

The Thanksgiving ceremony activities in Zhanghu Village are implemented based on the Censer Keeper system, and traditional beliefs are passed down according to the annual rotation of the Censer Keeper who must perform the Thanksgiving ceremony tasks. While the Censer Keeper is responsible for organizing the ceremony, the Bosses will assist the Censer Keeper in "book down number of participants," "collecting barrack flags," "put back the barrack flags," and "collecting charge share from participants." The preparations before the ceremony by the whole Censer Keeper team include deciding the date of the ceremony, erecting the altar, erecting the Jade Emperor altar, preparing the sacrifices required for various rituals, contacting the gong and drum performers, hand puppetry performers, catering operators, and drivers of vehicles participating in pilgrimages. During the ceremony, the team follows the Taoist priest to perform relevant rituals. In other words, the Censer Keeper team is responsible for whether or not the ceremony is successfully completed and whether the residents can achieve peace due to the ceremony.

### 3.2 *Principles and flexibility of performing rituals*

The rituals in the ceremony are performed by people, thus, due to human factors, the ceremony will be slightly different with the working attitudes of the ritual performers every year. Based on the participant observations of the 4 Thanksgiving Ceremonies held by Zhanghu Village during the 2 years of observation, this study concluded that there are principles and flexibility for the ceremony rituals. In principle, the rituals of rewarding soldiers and generals, the door worship (pudu), Zhong Kui Expelling the Spirits, worshiping the Jade Emperor, and the pilgrimage must be performed and cannot be changed, as the above-mentioned rituals are the traditions handed down by ancestors. One interviewee said, *"No one dares to change the rituals because they are related to the safety of the whole village."* What can be flexible is the method and sacrifice of the rituals. When the Censer Keeper team faces difficulties in performing rituals, such as a manpower shortage or a lack of financial resources, he often adopts simplified methods to overcome problems. One interviewee said, *"We follow the tradition to perform rituals. However, the procedures can be simplified."* (2021.11.26, Interviewee SXA01-17). This flexibility in performing rituals is possible for Taoist priests or Censer Keepers. This study observed that because of the differences in human attitudes towards "flexibility" or "seriousness" in their ways of doing things do indeed lead to differences in ritual details between different years or settlements. Examples are as follows:

1. The same Taoist priest uses different approaches for the black flags in different settlements in the same year

   The black flag is the command flag of the gods. During the pilgrimage, the black flag must be the leader to open the way for the gods and sweep away the unclean (Yu 2009). One interviewee said that the black flag must be reconsecrated every year. Consecration is equivalent to drawing a talisman, and because any talisman is only valid for one year, before the start of each year's pilgrimage, the black flag must be consecrated again to have the cleaning function. In 2022, the black flag of North Zhanghu Village was consecrated (Figure 1), while that of South Zhanghu Village was not consecrated, which seemed to be ignored due to simplification.

Figure 1. In 2022, the black flag of North Zhanghu was consecrated. (photo taken by this research)

Figure 2. In north Zhanghu, the meat wine in 2021 (left) and 2022 (right). (photo taken by this research).

2. Different Censer Keeper teams use slightly different approaches to perform the pilgrimage and offer sacrifices
   (1) In 2021, North Zhanghu Village used 108 bowls of raw meat wine[8] to reward the soldiers and generals, then, in 2022, it used longan pulp to replace raw pork (Figure 2), which shows that different Censer Keepers in the same settlement had different approaches.
   (2) In 2021, South Zhanghu Village used one sedan chair for the pilgrimage, while it used four sedan chairs for the pilgrimage in 2022. In North Zhanghu Village, the Xuanwu God took the sedan chair in 2021 for the pilgrimage, while Nezha took the sedan chair in 2022. Although it is the same settlement, different censer keepers have different practices (Figure 3).

Figure 3. In south Zhanghu, the sedan chair numbers in 2021 (left) and 2022 (right). (photo taken by this research).

Figure 4. In 2022, a ritual of crossing the fire was performed, but not in 2021. (photo taken by this research)

[8]Raw meat wine is made by putting small pieces of raw pork in a bowl or cup, and then adding wine. Eating raw meat wine can increase energy and increase the ability to protect the village. Thirty-six heavenly soldiers and seventy-two earth generals will add up to 108, so a total of 108 bowls are needed.

Figure 5.    There are still six loads and twelve baskets of Xiaopu in South Zhanghu in 2009 (left, photo provided

(3) In South Zhanghu in 2021, the pilgrimage returned to the altar place without a ritual of crossing the fire, but a ritual of crossing the fire was performed in 2022, which shows that different Censer Keepers in the same settlement had different degrees of seriousness and simplification.

(4) Regarding the Xiaopu of South Zhanghu in 2021, the Censer Keeper decided to change the traditional sacrifice of "six loads total twelve baskets" per household to one table per household, which directly removed the traditional requirement for sacrifices. If this decision is followed by the Censer Keeper of the Xiaopu next time (after twelve years), the traditional sacrifices of "six loads total twelve baskets" may soon become history.

## 4    CONCLUSION

The residents in Zhanghu Village have maintained the concept of "The tradition is passed down from the ancestors and cannot be changed," and have preserved the rituals for more than a century. However, although the ceremony is preserved, many details are flexible.

From the perspective of principle and flexibility for performing rituals, in principle, ritual performers follow traditional rituals, but in terms of flexibility, they can adjust their approaches according to social changes, changes in ceremony manpower, and economic conditions. This practice flexibility considers traditional etiquette and adapts to contemporary social and cultural changes, thus, meeting the needs of beliefs and the acceptance of residents.

Although the presence of flexible approaches is a way to adapt to social changes under various conditions, it cannot be ignored that rituals have their connotations and significance. Only when the connotations of the ceremony are understood can the details of the ceremony be correctly executed, and the thoughts expressed in the ceremony be preserved and passed down (Handelman, 2004). From the perspective of a sustainable culture, exploring the connotations of rituals and recording and inheriting them are necessary approaches to prevent traditional rituals from being overly simplified and avoid losing traditional practices. Only by deliberately preserving the details of the ceremony can arbitrary simplifications be avoided, which is also an important approach to preserving the traditional ceremony culture, thus, future studies are advised to explore the details of traditional ceremonies.

## REFERENCES

Handelman, D. (2004). Introduction: Why ritual in its own right? How so? *Social Analysis*, 48(2), 1–32.

Hwang Shyhhuei; Lai Chiumei. (2022). *A Study on the Differences of Xie Pingan Ceremony in the North and South of Zhanghu Village*. Yunlin Regional Culture Research and Design Symposium, Douliu City, Yunlin County.

Li Xiu'e. (2015). *Illustrating Taiwan Folk Festivals*. Morning Star Publishing House.

Li Fengmao. (nd). Xie Ping'an. 2022. 04. 25 Retrieved from: National Religion Information Network https://religion.moi.gov.tw/Knowledge/Content?ci=2&cid=8

Lin Meirong. (2009). Jade Emperor. https://nrch.culture.tw/twpedia.aspx?id=4414

Liu Huanyue. (2000). *Gods and Sacrificial Rituals of the Taiwanese*. Taiwan·Common Culture, 277.

Yang Chaojie (2015). Folklore and Local Society, *A Survey of "Xie Ping'an"* Ceremony in Xiluo Area, Yunlin, Field Minutes of the 11th Issue of Common People's Culture Studies, pp. 156-200.

Yu Weihao. (2009). *Black Order Flag* (2009). https://nrch.culture.tw/twpedia.aspx?id=12093

Zhuang Maode. (2019). *Research on the Impact of Local Festivals on Cultural Industry——Taking Jiande Palace in Budai Town as an Example*. Nanhua University. Chiayi County. https://hdl.handle.net/11296/kgp64t

System Innovation for a Troubled World – Lam et al. (Eds)
© 2024 the Author(s), ISBN: 978-1-032-60846-4

# Research on the empathy design of community long-term care – An example of Juren community in Beidou

Shu-Huei Wang* & Shyh-Huei Hwang
*Department of Digital Design, MingDan University, Wen-Hua, ChangHua, Taiwan*
*Graduate School of Design, Master and Doctoral Program, National Yunlin University of Science and Technology, University, Yunlin, Taiwan*

ABSTRACT: The sub-replacement fertility and aging population problems imposed impact on all walks of life. Under the influence of the pandemic in 2019, the first year of the metaverse began in 2021 and human life was going to be digitized completely. At the 11th National Science Technology Conference held by the Executive Yuan in December 2020, the human-oriented core value was proposed and the policy of tolerance was to be implemented. Taiwan became an aged society in 2018 with an aging population rate of 14.5% (343.4 million people) and was going to be a super-aged society in 2025. As a result, the Ministry of Health and Welfare presented the ten-year long-term care 2.0 project in Taiwan (2017–2026) to construct a community-based holistic community care service system, which was divided into three levels of A, B, and C. The LTC stations for level C were established everywhere to provide convenient care service. An initial exploration of applying empathic design to the C-level long-term care (LTC) station in Juren Community, Beidou Township was made through a literature review and case study. The case profile was analyzed by SWOT. The concept of designers as users in empathic design was obtained from the literature and developed to establish the user value chart. This empathic design system needs to create values to become a business model and the operation of this system will be maintained through these values.

## 1 INTRODUCTION

At the 11th National Science Technology Conference held by the Executive Yuan in December 2020, the human-oriented core value was proposed and the policy of tolerance was to be implemented. The science and technology visions for 2030 in Taiwan are innovation, inclusion, and sustainability. Precision health development, industrial application of big data, and establishment of a living environment that is friendly to all ages via applying technology are the goals of this plan (Executive Yuan 2020). According to the report estimating the population in Taiwan (2022-2070) published in August 2022, Taiwan, was going to be a super-aged society in two years (2025). Over 30% of the elder people will be more than 85 years old in 2070. The advent of a super-aged society and the sub-replacement of fertility can be predicted. Current solutions are to apply digital technology to replace and solve problems of human resources, including issues related to food, clothes, living, transportation, entertainment, etc. The Super-Intelligent Society (Society 5.0) was proposed in Japan to cope with the changes in the population structure through digital technology. The Ministry of Health and Welfare presented the ten-year long-term care 2.0 project in Taiwan (2017~2026) to construct a community-based holistic community care service system. Taiwan had met the standard of an aging society defined by the WHO in 1993 and the aging index in 2015 was 92.18% (Ministry of Health and Welfare, Dec. 2016).

## 2 LITERATURE REVIEW

According to the National Development Council, Executive Yuan (hereinafter referred to as the NDC), Taiwan will become an aged society in 2018 with an aging population ratio of 14.5% (3.434 million people), a super-aged society in 2026 with an aging population ratio of 20.6% (4.881 million people) and the aging population ratio would keep growing to 38.9% (7.152 million people) in 2061. The demand for long-term care resulting from chronic diseases, disability, dementia, and functional disorders due to the rapid growth of the aging population would increase with time (Ministry of Health and Welfare, Dec. 2016). Consequently, the author expected that technology might bring convenient benefits for the elderly and disadvantaged people and that the effect of empathy and caring for society through technology could be brought into full play.

*Corresponding Author: wangsh@mdu.edu.tw

DOI: 10.1201/9781003460763-29

## 2.1 Community long-term care

Stone considered that long-term care included an extensive assistance net to provide service of helping the chronically disabled patients with their daily life needs since these people were required to be taken care of for a longer period of time. Basically, such long-term care was low-tech services. The rehabilitation service made up for lost physical and mental functions and fundamental daily life assistance was included as well as service with tools. OECD (2011) indicated long-term care refers to a series of services required for a person when his/her physical or cognitive function declines. Consequently, it took more time to help with his/her basic daily activities, such as taking a shower, putting on clothes, eating, getting on/off the bed (or a chair), walking around and using the bathroom, etc. The Ministry of Health and Welfare of Taiwan deemed that long-term care meant to provide comprehensive and continual services to people who needed long-term care and these services included prevention, diagnosis, treatment, and rehabilitation in a supportive, maintenance, and social manner. The object to serve was not only the patient himself/herself, but also the need of the caregiver. In the ten-year long-term care 2.0 project, a community-based holistic community care service system would be constructed to develop a community-based service system with multiple goals, which was further divided into three levels: A, B and C. Level A would provide technical support and integration service to Levels B and C. Besides, Level A also motivated general establishment of compound service centers of Level B and the LTC stations of Level C to provide convenient care services (Ministry of Health and Welfare, Dec. 2016).

## 2.2 Empathic society

In the book titled Connect: Design for an Empathic Society (2013), design for connectedness refers to the creation of a general environment to support, enhance, and motivate those important things that could improve the benefits of human beings (Wildevuur et al. 2013). As the global aging population grows gradually, people who retire from their work feel lonely and isolated due to a decreasing connection to people. As a result, connectedness is a brand-new field to be excavated (Wildevuur et al. 2013). The so-called connectedness was the belonging emotions that a person felt in a social connection or network (Colombo et al. 2011). The scholar George Levinger developed five stages of interpersonal relationships (Figure 1).

Figure 1. Interpersonal Relationship Development (amended and adopted from Levinger, G. 1980).

## 2.3 Empathy design

In the book titled Well-Designed: How to Use Empathy to Create Products People Love, empathy was the acquisition of a sensation to put yourself in another's shoes. If you want to feel how an 85-year-old lady feels, you need to place yourself in all kinds of situations that she might face (Kolko, J., 2014). An instinctive response or interaction could be triggered by touching a certain object, which imposes a physical and cognitive impact (Wildevuur et al. 2013). Friendship or a pleasant atmosphere could be created through interaction; a positive experience that could influence human behavior might be developed further and then an empathic system could be constructed (Wildevuur et al. 2013). This empathic system could create values and form a business model and the operation of this system was maintained through these values. The user value chart was developed on the basis of users as designers and ethnographic research by combining customer participation with empathic design principles (Wildevuur et al. 2013), as shown in Figure 2.

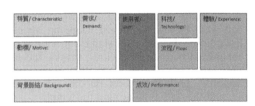

Figure 2. User Value Chart (amended and adopted from Wildevuur, S., etc., 2013).

## 3 METHODOLOGY

### 3.1 Case study

Case studies belong to exploratory research and they are individual with respective characteristics that can't be repeated. A researcher needs to do an in-depth exploration and understanding to see and measure facts clearly for objective analysis and verification so that the truth of the case can be located for others to know. Various data collection methods can be applied such as in-depth interviews, questionnaire surveys, literature information, secondary data, and field observations (Chang Shao-xun, 2000).

## 3.2 Document analysis

In compliance with a certain research purpose or issue, documents related to market data, survey reports, and industrial information are collected through different channels and integrated via analysis and induction. There are four analysis steps: reading and arrangement, description, classification, and interpretation (Herzog, T., 1996; Yeh Li-cheng and Yeh Zhi-cheng, 1999).

## 4 JUREN COMMUNITY IN BEIDOU

### 4.1 Community profile

The population growth rate in Juren Village is low and most of the local residents are businessmen, office workers, teachers, and retired civil servants. Guangren Street was called Yezihung in the early days because it was the center of trading a variety of merchandise, including beetle nuts. Baolang Temple located at 332 on Dizheng Road is the faith center for local people. It was built in the 23rd year of Emperor Jiaqing of the Qing Dynasty with a history of over 201 years. The major gods in this temple for people to worship are Xing Wang Ye, Zhu Wang Ye, and Li Wang Ye (three Royal Lords), which is a unique feature. Juren Children's Park was completed due to the hard work of Lin Zheng-rong, the village head, as well as the contribution of the construction company. It has a parking lot and excellent public facilities and is praised as the cleanest place in town. Douyuan Road and Fusing Road are shopping streets. Clinics, hospitals, and snack stands concentrate on Zhonghua Road and delicious snacks include Taiwanese meatball (Ba Wan), fried dumplings, sesame oil, pork jerks, beef noodles, clay oven rolls, and the tasty food around the temple.

### 4.2 Population of Juren Village

There were 1,479 people in Juren Village, Beidou Township (2022) and 156 aged 0–11, 91 aged 12–18, 81 aged 19–24, 398 aged 25–44, 404 aged 45–64, and 350 aged over 65, which accounted for 23.66% of total population (provided by Juren Community Development Association, Beidou Township, 2022).

Table 1. Population Distribution Chart of Juren Village(2022).

| Age | Aged 0-11 (Children) | Aged 12-18 (Teenagers) | Aged 19-24 (Youths) | Aged 25-44 (Middle-agers) | Aged 45-64 (Prime of life) | Aged over 65 (Elders) | Total No. of People |
|---|---|---|---|---|---|---|---|
| No. of People | 156 people | 91 people | 80 people | 398 À 398 people | 404 people | 350 people | 1,479 people |
| Ratio | 10.54% | 6.15% | 5.4% | 26.92% | 27.33% | 23.66% | 100% |

### 4.3 Geographic location

Juren Community is situated in the administrative region of Juren Village, Beidou Township. Dongguang Village is on the east, Guangfu Village on the west, Chihsing Village on the south, and Wenchang Village on the north. It is a plain with an area of 0.11 square meters and serves as the administrative center of Beidou Township.

### 4.4 SWOT analysis of C-level LTC stations in Juren Community

The C-class alley stations mainly provide the following services: 1. Preventing disability or delaying disability deterioration; 2. Care for a few hours or respite care (short-term breaks); 3. Nutritious food (community meals or meal delivery); and 4. Places for social participation and community activities. The major functions of C-level LTC stations are: (1) to provide convenient care service and respite care, and (2) to further extend and strengthen the primary prevention function of the community (Ministry of Health and Welfare, Dec. 2016). The SWOT analysis of C-level LTC stations in Juren Community was as follows:

(A) Strengths (internal): 1. Excellent convenience of connecting to resources due to its location in downtown Beidou; 2. The Chairman's familiarity with things related to the community; 3. The C-class LTC station takes care of 30 elder people by providing lunches from Mondays through Fridays; 4. A special administrator designated to deal with the matters in the LTC station; 5. The Chairman and the association were active in participating in project application and the activities of Changhua County, helping the elderly to move and learn and promoting community care service in the disadvantaged families; and 6. Helping pupils with their homework after school twice a week.

(B) Weaknesses (internal): 1. Residents nearby didn't know activities were held in the C-class LTC station due to the remote location of the community; 2. Unfamiliarity with the things related to the community except the Chairman; 3. Currently, only one full-time person and the Chairman propose projects and support the expenses of internal and external activities; 4. Other activities supported by volunteers merely; 5. Future challenges include how to motivate more residents of Juren Village to take part in; 6. How to get an exclusive place for the C-class LTC station since it is rented presently.

(C) Opportunities (external): 1. Good development potential for a burgeoning community; 2. This C-class LTC station is a model in Beidou; 3. Outgoing elders are active in participating in external activities like a performance in the flower festival of Changhua in 2023, a show at Tianhua Lecture Hall and making an income for the station by selling healthy steamed buns; 4. A variety of activities such as the light clay class, aromatherapy with dōTERRA essential oils, painting class, and physical fitness exercise were held for the elders; 5. Maintaining a good relationship with the Changhua County Government and Beidou Administration Office; for example, tour cars for Bone Mass Density (BMD) measurement sent by the Public Health Bureau of Changhua County to Juren Village.

(D) Threats (external): 1. Unfamiliarity with the communities in the neighborhood causing fewer opportunities for exchanging resources; 2. Much emulation of the example community resulted in similar classes without many changes; 3. Participation in external activities required enthusiasm and positiveness from the elders; 4. Difficulty in obtaining external resources.

## 5 CONCLUSION

1. More community activities should be held so that more local residents can know and like their community. 2. The team of volunteers should work together to be helpmates of the chairman (Chairman of Jurenli Community Development Association). 3. A special mascot and relevant products of the Juren Community should be developed. 4. Take the initiative in understanding the needs of the elderly and creating opportunities for interaction. 5. A positive experience that may influence human behavior should be developed by applying the user value chart and an empathic design system can be further built. Finally, this empathic design system needs to create values to become a business model and the operation of this system will be maintained through these values.

## REFERENCES

Chang Shao-xun (2000), *Research Method.* Taichung city: Canghai Book Company.

Community Profile. *Juren Community Development Association*, Beidou Township, 2022.

Colombo, F., Llena-Nozal, A., Mercier, J., & Tjadens, F.(2011). OECD health policy studies help waned. *Providing and Paying for Long-term Care: Providing and Paying for Long-term Care: OECD Publishing.*

Herzog, T. (1996). Translated by Zhu Rou-ruo. *Research Methods and Data Analysis in the Social Sciences.* Yang-Chih Book Co., Ltd.

Kolko, J. (2014). *Well-designed: How to Use Empathy to Create Products People Love.* Harvard Business Press.

Levinger, G. (1980). Toward the analysis of close relationships. *Journal of Experimental Social Psychology,* 16(6), 510–544.

Stone, R. (2001). Research on frontline workers in long-term care. *Generations,* 25(1), 49–57.

Wildevuur, S., Van Dijk, D., Hammer-Jakobsen, T., Bjerre, M., Äyväri, A., & Lund, J. (2013). *Connect: Design for an Empathic Society.* BIS Publishers.

Yeh Li-cheng & Yeh Zhi-cheng (1999). Edit, *Research Methods and Thesis Writing.* Taipei: scbooks.

## WEBSITES

*Ministry of Health and Welfare* (Dec. 2016). The Ten-Year Long-Term Care Project 2.0 in Taiwan (2017~2026). Date of reference: Jan. 23 2023. Reference website: https://www.ey.gov.tw/Page/448DE008087A1971/aa69f5ba-4fc4-4825-9ba8-c93588dcbc86

*Report of estimating the population in Taiwan* (2022-2070) published in August 2022. National Development Council. ISBN: 978-626-7162-20-0, P:10. Date of reference: Jan. 23 2023. Reference website: https://pop-proj.ndc.gov.tw/download.aspx?uid=70&pid=70

*Summary of the 11th National Science Technology Conference, the Executive Yuan (2020).* Date of reference: Jan. 23 2023. https://www.ey.gov.tw/Page/448DE008087A1971/b316701e-c0fa-40c8-bed6-08c5150b7d0a

*System Innovation for a Troubled World – Lam et al. (Eds)*
© 2024 the Author(s), ISBN: 978-1-032-60846-4

# Interactive new media installations of the human-computer dynamic relationship

Yun-Ju Chen
*Department of Creative Technologies and Product Design, National Taipei University of Business, Taoyuan, Taiwan*

Yueh-Tuan Li
*Department of Creative Technologies and Product Design, National Taipei University of Business, Taoyuan, Taiwan*
*Department of Marketing, Feng Chia University*

Chen-Wei Chiang*
*Department of Creative Technologies and Product Design, National Taipei University of Business, Taoyuan, Taiwan*

ABSTRACT:  This study utilized Don Ihde's Human-Technology Relations Theory within the framework of the Phenomenology of Technology as the methodology and incorporated related concepts from Phenomenology and Hermeneutics Theory to establish its research context. The focus was on exploring the creativity and discourse of new media art based on the idea of perception and bodily engagement. The thesis highlights the need for four types of human-computer dynamic structures and provides an analysis of these structures in the context of new media interactive installations. The aim of this study, which also serves as its main contribution, is to offer new media artists potential considerations for designing interactive installations, including interactive processes and dynamic system creative structures.

## 1 INTRODUCTION

This study explores the phenomenon of the "Human - Technology" relationship in new media interactive installations, focusing on the relationship between technology and human experience and culture, and investigating a certain special dynamic structure in the relationship between humans and technology, people and the world. It attempts to start from a perspective of technological phenomenology and takes new media art interactive installations as the main analysis object and explains its development context. In addition to analyzing and exploring the meaning of dynamic structure relationships derived from new media interactive installations, the study also examines the technology and perception linkages displayed in new media interactive installations. This study examines the development process and historical significance of the dynamic structure between humans and technology in new media art interactive installations. The study uses new media artworks as research texts and the method is based on Don Ihde's phenomenology of technology, with an emphasis on the dynamic structure relationship between humans and technology in new media art interactive

installations, with a further analysis of relevant phenomenology and hermeneutic theories.

Interactive installations are one of the forms of expression in New Media Art, which invites the audience to interact with the artwork interactively, changing the artwork's structure and the audience's physical sensory experience. The term "New Media Art" has had many different names since the 1970s, and with the development of computer technology, art that was applied to emerging computer media was called Computer Art, later replaced by Multimedia Art with multiple sensory stimulations and Net Art with hypertext links (from the 1960s to the 90s). Nowadays, New Media Art and Digital Art are interchangeable concepts that have become a huge umbrella, encompassing all forms of emerging art creation (Christiane Paul, 2015). Today, New Media Art is dealing with the invisible, transforming systems and interactivity, an art that emerges from multiple interactive processes in the electronic space. Roy Ascott (Roy Ascott, 2003) defines five characteristics of this type of new media art: (1) Connectivity: of the part to part, person to person, mind to mind; (2) Immersion: into the whole, and the dissolution thereby of subject and ground; (3) Interaction: as the very form of art, such that art as the behavior of forms has become art as a form of behavior; (4) Transformation: perpetual

_____
*Corresponding Author: chenwei@ntub.edu.tw

DOI: 10.1201/9781003460763-30

flux of image, surface, and identity; (5) Emergence: the perpetual coming into being of meaning, matter, and mind. These five characteristics of "connectivity," "immersion," "interaction," "transformation," and "emergence" will serve as the cornerstone for the research of the dynamic structure between humans and technology in interactive new media art installations.

In general, new media interactive works emphasize the collaboration between the viewer and data, structure, interface, systems, and new forms through technology. Therefore, establishing interactive works has become an important path for developing new media art. This study aims to analyze the thinking and transformation in the creation of new media art through the relationship theory between "human-technology" and the characteristics of new media art creation and to view new media artworks through the perspectives of creators and researchers. The dynamic structure that expands under the "human-technology" relationship in interactive works will be analyzed and classified and the human-machine dynamic structure that interactive works possess will be summarized, which can more comprehensively discuss the perspectives of creators and researchers. In exploring the issues of "perception" and "body activity", this study provides new media art creators with a technological phenomenology perspective to conceptualize the dynamic structure system and creative path in interactive works.

## 2   HUMAN-TECHNOLOGY RELATIONSHIP

The main focus of the "human-technology" relationship theory is on how people form relationships with technology through their bodily experiences or by using technology to interact with the environment. Four characteristics are analyzed and deduced from the mutual experiences between people and technological products, instruments, and other forms of technology. This perspective, which analyzes the relationship between human perceptual and bodily activities and technology, is similar to that of new media art, which uses various new media and technologies as means of creating interactive environments and devices that invite participation. The artworks are changed by the participants' bodily actions and behaviors, and the relationship between the artworks and the participants evolves accordingly. In the late 21st century, new media art has become a field that aims to integrate technology and art, with both forms and media being essential components of the integration. Therefore, this paper will delve deeper into the four relationships in the "human-technology" relationship phenomenology, analyzing how people from different perceptual experiences through technology intermediation and how

different technologies have different impacts on perceptual and bodily experiences, using new media art as an example.

### 2.1   Embodiment relations

Don Idhe described the "Embodiment relations" as "(I-Technology)→World" using the formula of intentionality formula. This relationship can be expressed as humans and technology merging to intend the world. Technology, in essence, transforms our perception and in this relationship, technology acts as a mediator between humanity and the world, expanding human perception and allowing people to experience the world through technology. People's experiences are changed by technology's in-between and people and technology merge into one entity. In the process of creating new media interactive installations, the participation of human beings becomes one of the crucial elements. By creating dynamic situational worlds through technological intermediaries, new media artists expand the perception of the participants, extending their senses. Participants experience the dynamic situational world through the interactive installations. Through technological intermediation, "human (participants) and technology products (new media interactive installations) can co-shape or co-constitute the subjective and objective world in any situation. (Robert Rosenberger and Peter-Paul Verbeek, 2015)" "We take the technologies into our experience in a particular way by way of perceiving through such technologies and through the reflexive transformation of our perceptual and body senses. (Don Ihde, 1990)"

### 2.2   Hermeneutic relations

Embodiment relations are the extension of the human body, while hermeneutic relations are the extension of human language. According to Don Ihde, "In hermeneutic relations, the technology is not so much experienced-through as experienced-with. The perceptual act directed toward the technology is a specialized interpretive act. (Don Ihde, 1991)" The hermeneutic relations can be expressed by the intentional formula: "I→(Technology-World)". This relationship can be understood as the world presented in the technological text that the person intends. Technology is an extension of human language - a form of "reading" that involves interpreting technology in a technical context and revealing some aspect of the world to the human interpreter. This kind of interpretation requires a special mode of behavior and perception that is similar to "reading," in which the text affects our bodies in a particular way. For example, on a very hot day, you use your smartphone to check the temperature outside and find out its 39 degrees Celsius. You know that it's very hot outside, but you don't feel the heat indoors. However, if you step outside, you will personally experience the scorching heat of 39 degrees. This kind of interpretation that allows you to know that it's hot outside has a sense of immediacy, and it points to the represented object in a special way. This means that the relationship between numbers/data and the things they represent is the key to visualizing numbers/data and fully analyzing and interpreting them. Computers can convert numbers into different visual graphics and colors, but you must establish the connection between numbers/data and the real world, that is, pointing to the things and world they represent through numbers/data.

## 2.3 *Alterity relations*

The concept of Alterity Relations exists beyond the relations of embodiment and hermeneutics. Alterity Relations refer to the situation where technology becomes an independent entity in use, becoming an "other." Automated machinery is a representative of this relationship, characterized by its ability to make decisions and function autonomously. The intentional formula used by Don Ihde is expressed as I→Technology-(-World). This relationship can be expressed as the relationship between a person and technology, where technology becomes an other or quasi-other in relation to me, and the world becomes the context and background. These devices seem to operate automatically, and their appearance or behavior, full of vitality, resembles some kind of animal, creature, or human, making them fascinating and more closely resembling quasi-life. A very important manifestation of its alterity relation is the personification perspective, that is, artificial intelligence and machine learning. The focus of new media interactive installation creation is on the dynamic structure between the body and technology, making its creation directly or indirectly generate potential similar to the human body.

## 2.4 *Background relations*

With Background Relations, "this phenomenological survey turns from attending to technologies in the foreground to those which remain in the background or become a kind of near-technological environment itself. (Don Ihde, 1990)" In the background relation, Don Ihde did not provide a specific intentional formula, but it is commonly described by researchers as "I-(-Technology)→World". This relationship can be expressed as technology receding into the background of the human-world relationship, with humans intending the world within the context of technology as a backer The background relation is at work when technology is operating but not drawing attention to itself work. However, it is still shaping people and their surrounding environment. It also refers to the fact that we cannot live without technology in our daily lives. Technological products have become an essential part of our daily lives, and as technology products gradually recede into the background, the world returns to the foreground position of focus. Technology has infiltrated daily life and merged with the living environment and landscape. Public art installations featuring lighting have become part of the street view, seemingly receding to the background as an unobtrusive element of everyday experience and an integral part of the current environment and residents' emotions. Technology has become part of our bodily perception, and we bracketing bracket out our awareness of it. In other words, the existence of technology has become a background element of our living space or environment.

## 3 HUMAN-COMPUTER DYNAMIC STRUCTURE RELATIONSHIP

In the interactive process of new media installation, interaction is not only a driving behavior of sense but also a necessary process and way to construct the entire dynamic system. Technology is an essential structure in new media art creation. New media artists transform programming languages and data into the interactive installation in the form of modules and structures. In other words, a human-computer dynamic structure is generated as an automatic algorithmic interactive system through programming languages, data, or new technologies. This interactive system itself is a human-computer dynamic structure, and by inviting viewers to engage in interactive behavior, they become the providers, co-constructors, or decision-makers of the meaning of the interactive system. In such an open, non-static, and non-fixed dynamic structure, constantly interacting and adding new elements, the dynamic structure becomes an important structure of the interactive installation work, and the viewer and the work co-shape or co-constitute the dynamic structure system. In other words, this human-computer dynamic structure focuses on how to co-shape the specific dynamic world (objectivity) and the specific participants (subjectivity) in the dynamic world created by the interactive device work. This human-computer dynamic structure can be seen as a method and basic framework for experimental phenomena of the relationship between humans and technology. The dynamic world created by the interactive device work is a dynamic system jointly constructed by participants and the work itself. In this case, the structure relationship of "Viewer/ Participant (Human)-Interactive Installation (Technology)-Dynamic System (World)" in interactive installation is studied [Figure 1], to provide an analysis of the four types of human-computer dynamic structure in interactive dynamic processes, which will be further explained below.

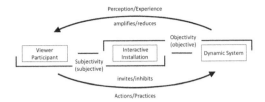

Figure 1. "Human-Technology-World" structure in interactive installation.

## 3.1 Dynamic passive structure

This type of interactive installation is a dynamic and continuous environment created by artists through program calculations, mechanical devices, or virtual technology simulations. The viewing experience is similar to watching a movie in that once a movie is completed, it can only be played according to the original narrative structure and cannot be changed in real-time. However, with the rise of artificial intelligence, the fixed narrative structure can be broken, and the closed image can be transformed into an open, random, and variable narrative structure. Although artificial intelligence technology can convert the fixed image structure into a randomly generated one, viewers still do not have control over the content and elements of the work through interactive behavior. Viewers participate in the dynamic world created by the artist in the form of observation, generating connections and interpretations of the work through each viewing. Therefore, in the "Dynamic Passive Structure" [Figure 2], new media artists create interactive installations that establish a situational atmosphere. The system of this work is dynamically flowing with the environment and time through program calculations, mechanical devices, or virtual technology simulations. In this passive structure, viewers do not have control and cannot drive or modify any content in the interactive installation. However, through the virtual dynamic world created by the artist, viewers' participation in their thoughts extends the "passive" construction of subtle emotional connections and imagination in the process of body perception, creating a unique sensory experience through viewing.

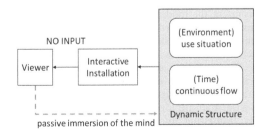

Figure 2. Dynamic passive structure.

## 3.2 Dynamic interactive structure

The completion of an interactive installation artwork requires the viewer to participate in some form of action or behavior in order for the artwork concept to be operational and executed. The interactive process transforms the viewer into a participant, who collaboratively creates the interactive experience through their actual engagement in the process. This shift from passive observer to active participant involves the participant's interaction behavior being guided into the interactive installation artwork. This type of human-computer dynamic structure is called a "dynamic interactive structure," where the viewer must become a participant to enter the dynamic structure and engage in dialogue with the artwork. This structure refers to the behavior of the participant linking with the computer/machine, with their mutual interaction being conveyed through programming and execution messages, transforming behavior into commands and descriptions, allowing for dynamic processes that can be controlled and automatically run. In essence, within the "dynamic interactive structure" (as shown in Figure 3), the artist creates a feedback loop system that responds in real-time, establishing a relationship between the participant and the interactive installation artwork through communication within the dynamic system of the artwork. The participant's engagement behavior through physical activity, such as using hands, limbs, or objects, drives the artwork and changes its content, making the participant a part of the interactive installation artwork as a whole.

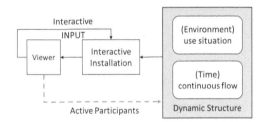

Figure 3. Dynamic interactive structure.

## 3.3 Dynamic interactive crossing structure

So far, interactive installations discussed are considered to be a dynamic system that undergoes further changes with the introduction of interaction. The role of the viewer has evolved from being a mere spectator to becoming an active participant. As the content of the work is rewritten with each iteration, the overall meaning of the piece is also constantly rewritten. Whether through programming or as contained within the work, the work gradually moves towards a mathematical description of images or shapes through algorithmic computation. "Through appropriate algorithmic manipulation, media becomes programmable. (Lev Manovich, 2001)" The result is a dynamic system that is more open, two-way, and non-linear in structure, creating a continuous, dynamic, and open appearance of the work that generates real-time changes and unpredictable dynamic patterns and forms based on differences in participants, time points, and elements. This type of human-computer dynamic structure is called a "dynamic interactive crossing structure" [Figure 4]. In this structure, artists not only create a system that can respond and provide feedback in real-time but also emphasize programming coding, detection and recognition, procedures, and logical systems, and focus on the interaction between participants' physical activities, message transmission, actions, responses, and feedback. They attach great importance to the interdependence and co-construction between the elements provided by the participants and the overall dynamic system, and use computer computation to modify, simulate, and reproduce participants' data, deriving an interactive structure with real-time changes, unpredictable, and varied forms. The emphasis of this dynamic interactive crossing structure lies in the participation and interaction of participants, which is considered part of the work's element. This element's concept is an important part of the work, and if it is removed from the work, not only does it lose its completeness, but it also loses its spirit and meaning.

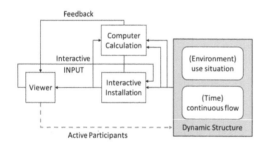

Figure 4.   Dynamic interactive crossing structure.

### 3.4  *Dynamic intelligence structure*

With the development of artificial intelligence, robots have become more human-like, and computer technology provides a field for interaction between humans and artificial intelligence, involving the integration of symbiosis, thinking, imagination, and creativity. From an artistic perspective, this can lead to a transformation of social and cultural diversity and produce rich interpretations and definitions in science, art, and philosophy. In short, artificial intelligence responds to humans' desire for something beyond the deep psyche, that is, to achieve an intelligent system that is non-material, spiritual, beyond the

body and mind, and beyond the limitations of time and space. This intelligent system, which is achieved through artificial intelligence and learning systems, is called the "dynamic intelligence structure". This structure has a system that can transform behavior and cognitive abilities and covers the procedures and architecture of biological evolution, which is a form of the artificial intelligence system. This system structure has an open-mindedness, based on the ideas of information, feedback, and learning, which influences the decisions and behaviors of subsequent machine development. In the "dynamic intelligence structure" [Figure 5], the artist constructs a system with machine learning, which provides a way to input elements into the work. This input method comes not only from images, videos, sounds, texts, and data on the Internet but also from elements that may come from the participants who are present at the moment. Through each audience participation, each computer calculation, each machine learning, and each feedback, a dynamic artwork form that is endlessly algorithmically generated is collectively formed.

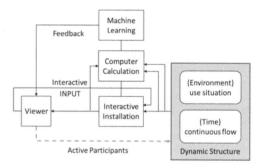

Figure 5.   Dynamic intelligence structure.

## 4  CONCLUSION

This study summarizes four human-computer dynamic structures of new media interactive installations: "Dynamic Passive Structure," "Dynamic Interactive Structure," "Dynamic Interactive Crossing Structure," and "Dynamic Intelligence Structure." These structures not only represent the modes of human-computer interaction but also provide a foundation for creating unique dynamic structures in new media interactive installations.

The researchers argue that digital technology is a medium for new media artists to transform programming languages and data into interactive devices that are logical, modular, and structured. By translating information transmission, bodily activity, and memory into programming code, coding language becomes another form of perception and body activity that exists within dynamic systems. The dynamic system, which aggregates people's perception and body activity, becomes an element of interactive installation works. Through random and algorithmic logic processes, participants are invited to interact with the work and become providers, co-constructors, or decision-makers of the dynamic system meaning. In this open, non-static, and non-fixed dynamic structure, participants continuously interact and immerse themselves, adding new elements that become important dynamic structure content. The data content of people's perception and body activity is transformed and emerges as a dynamic structural element that participants and artworks co-create.

New media art interactive installation works combine images, devices, and space to create different pathways of perception for participants, immersing them in dynamic situations. The work is transformed into a field of communication through participant and work interaction, creating a dynamic structural relationship. This study only examines the dynamic structural relationship of new media art interactive installation works that use computer technology, programming, mechanical devices, or virtual technology. With the development of digital technology, the media form and dynamic system of new media art interactive installations are becoming increasingly diverse and complex. However, due to the research focus and length limitations, not all interactive installations

are suitable for the "four dynamic structures" classification. This is a research limitation, and future research directions can explore more interactive procedures and dynamic system structure aspects of interactive installations. It is hoped that new media researchers and creative practitioners can further consider the deconstruction of the human-machine dynamic system of new media interactive installations, reflecting on the potential of technological dynamic aesthetics and expanding the contemporary meaning of new media interactive installation art through a comprehensive understanding of technology and its applications.

## REFERENCES

Ascott, Roy. 2003. *Telematic Embrace: Visionary Theories of Art, Technology, and Consciousness.* London: University Of California Press, Ltd.

Ihde, Don. 1990. *Technology and the Lifeworld: From Garden to Earth*. USA: Indiana University Press.

Ihde, Don. 1991. *Instrumental Realism: The Interface between Philosophy of Science and Philosophy of Technology*. Bloominton: Indiana University Press.

Manovich, Lev. 2001. *The Language of New Media.* Cambridge: MIT Press, 2001.

Paul, Christiane. 2015. *Digital Art Third edition.* London: Thames & Hudson Ltd.

Rosenberger, Robert and Verbeek, Peter-Paul. 2015. A Field Guide to Postphenomenology. In *Postphenomenological investigations: essays on human-technology relations*. USA: Lexington Books.

*System Innovation for a Troubled World – Lam et al. (Eds)*
*© 2024 the Author(s), ISBN: 978-1-032-60846-4*

# Exploring the effect of peer assessment on lacquer art learners' discussion promotion and motivation

Shun-Yao Chiang*
*Graduate School of Design, Doctoral Program Graduate Student, National Yunlin University of Science and Technology, Yunlin, Taiwan*

Shyh-Huei Hwang
*Professor, National Yunlin University of Science and Technology, Yunlin, Taiwan*

ABSTRACT: Traditional craft education, although teaching learners the techniques, often fails to teach them how to apply those techniques, especially in the case of lacquer crafts, which involve complex materials and diverse techniques. Based on traditional teaching methods, students simply learn what the teacher teaches them, and thus, they rely on the teacher's instructions to complete their work step by step. This study attempts to apply peer assessment in the teaching of traditional lacquer crafts, where students engage in mutual commenting, suggesting, discussing, thinking, and inspiring one another, allowing learners to express their own opinions and provide constructive feedback on their peers' works. The study targets learners in the lacquer painting class at a community college in Nantou County, Taiwan, with their works as the primary focus. The study has two objectives: (1) to explore the expansion and transfer of lacquer learners' commenting focus in peer assessment; (2) to analyze the motivating effects of peer assessment on lacquer learners. First, learners engage in lacquer painting creation with the theme of "hometown." Second, in monthly discussions, learners provide suggestions and discuss the themes, compositions, techniques, and colors of their own and their peers' works. The researcher records the opinions provided in each discussion. Third, in-depth interviews are conducted with the learners to document their learning status. Finally, coding analysis is carried out using grounded theory. The results show that: (1) commenting on works and sharing life experiences are equally important: the learners in this study are middle-aged and elderly, and while they have many concerns when evaluating their peers' works, they are also able to provide personal life experiences to expand effective concepts for creation; (2) self-reflection on one's own creations through peer assessment: traditional craft education often involves teachers demonstrating techniques and learners imitating them, which means that even senior learners may lack the confidence to express their own work styles clearly; (3) peer motivation effects: during the course, learners not only focus on their own works but also provide various opinions to others during discussions, resulting in mutual motivation and drive.

*Keywords*: Traditional crafts, Instructional design, Peer assessment, Creativity teaching, Lacquer art creation

## 1 INTRODUCTION

Learning traditional crafts places great emphasis on processes and techniques, especially in lacquer art. There are strict steps, diverse and intricate materials, and constantly changing techniques, which often confuse and frighten beginners. Some people cannot create independently even after studying for several years. In addition, early education in Taiwan was more focused on rote learning, emphasizing memorization, and lacking opportunities for independent thinking. Sometimes, learners may not want to comment on other people's works, in addition to

being unable to express their opinions. Traditional craft education still adopts the "apprenticeship system" of teaching. The apprentice only needs to follow the teacher's instructions without the need for independent thinking. Sometimes, teachers do not encourage too many personal opinions. For learners, besides cultivating skills, they often do not know how to use the techniques they have learned well, cannot surpass the methods taught by teachers, and dare not attempt to innovate. With the progress of the times, more and more people are learning traditional crafts. Many people also begin to think about whether they should completely imitate the teacher's work style or develop their unique artistic style.

Therefore, it is challenging for ordinary people to convey their artistic style and creative ideas through

*Corresponding Author: jonamai@gmail.com

 DOI: 10.1201/9781003460763-31

lacquer art. During the learning period, not only is there no sense of accomplishment, but it also makes the creator feel difficult, which will consume the learners' enthusiasm for learning. Therefore, lacquer artists who are willing to learn for a long time and be able to work independently are rare.

The participants in this study who engaged in peer assessment were mainly ten students from the lacquer painting class of Nantou County Community College in Taiwan. They have been learning lacquer techniques for about two to three years, with an average age of about 58.8 years. They are people who have experienced Taiwan's early education system. Some even learned their skills from traditional apprenticeship education during their job-seeking phase.

This study attempted to use the innovative teaching design of peer assessment in traditional lacquer craft teaching. By commenting, suggesting, discussing, thinking, and inspiring works and creative themes, learners are encouraged to set themes, compositions, and techniques before creating. Through presenting and discussing their creations and ideas, they can mutually discuss and stimulate each other, promote their ideas on artwork creation, and provide appropriate feedback.

Learners express their own opinions on their own works and provide comments and feedback on peer works. The study explored whether adopting a new teaching method could enhance learners' discourse ability on artwork and the feedback from peers.

## 2 CASE STUDY

### 2.1 *Artistic concept communication*

Liu Guangxia (2021) once quoted American art education scholar Elliot Wayne Eisne (1933-2014) theory, stating that *"Most American teachers can only teach technical aspects and cannot address issues related to art, aesthetics, and other different levels. Artistic creation involves creativity and self-perception, which is difficult to have a clear answer like a math test."* In other words, when it comes to art evaluation, there is no correct answer or standard, and what the creator wants to express is usually unclear and cannot be fully understood by others. Art and creativity rely on intuition and feeling, which cannot be precisely predicted. Therefore, when guiding the creative process, the instructor can only offer their opinion based on their own professional training and cannot determine the quality of the work. This is also why art and design works are not evaluated and discussed in a quantitative manner, but rather through qualitative commentary on the viewer's perspective.

### 2.2 *Metacognition and introspection in peer assessment*

Although creation is subjective, can discussing and presenting one's subjective work produce objective

feedback? Can peers not only examine others' works but also reflect on their own blind spots? Metacognition refers to the self-awareness and evaluation of one's own cognitive processes and results, as well as the knowledge and ability to self-adjust. Knowing what one is doing and how to learn to acquire this knowledge. Through this learning process, one can understand oneself and one's work. Therefore, if the original cognition is "knowing it," then metacognition is "knowing why," deepening the level of cognition and being able to digest old knowledge to produce new or suitable knowledge for oneself (Chang & Tsai, 2018, as cited in Chang, 1995). This will create conscious thoughts about oneself, which is introspection. However, this introspection needs to be generated under the effect of epistemology,[1] which brings together perception, memory, and knowledge thinking. When self-reflection and external observation interact, learners can continuously examine the internal concepts and external expressions of their own work.

### 2.3 *Social cognitive theory (SCT)*

The social psychology foundational theory proposed by Canadian psychologist Albert Bandura (1925-2021) involves learning through direct or indirect observation of others' behavior and performance. This process starts with imitation and later becomes the object of imitation by others. In this process, learners set their own standards and norms to evaluate themselves, which is known as "Observational Learning".[2] Also known as "vicarious experience", the object of learning is the "model" and the process of learning is "modeling". In the process of peer assessment, learners are both commentators and models, observers and imitators, and can achieve learning outcomes by constantly observing their peers' creations (Chang & Tsai, 2018).

## 3 RESEARCH PURPOSE AND METHODS

### 3.1 *Research purpose*

The purpose is to:

• investigate the expansion and transfer of key comments in peer assessment among lacquer art learners;

---

[1]Trying to understand what knowledge is and how it can be beneficial to the knower, Plato's epistemology is employed. Knowledge, according to Plato, is not mere true opinion, but a justified true belief.
[2]Social cognitive theory : https://lefthand1001.pixnet.net/blog/post/12144245-%E7%A4%BE%E6%9C%83%E8%AA%8D%E7%9F%A5%E7%90%86%E8%AB%96(retrieve date : 2023.3.27)

- analyze the motivational effects of peer assessment methods on lacquer art learners.

## 3.2 Research design

This study used action research to plan the curriculum in line with the spirit of instructional practice. The teaching design incorporated peer assessment, with traditional lacquer craft as the carrier. Through discussion, reflection, and inspiration, students were encouraged to express their opinions and provide comments and feedback on their peers' works. The cycle phases of action research included planning, action, observation, and reflection, with each phase serving as a reflection point to seek research starting points, identify problems, clarify issues and current challenges, and then develop feasible practical strategies. Monthly discussions were held, and in-depth interviews with research subjects were conducted by the researcher to encode grounded theory during the study period. The researcher (teacher) recorded the discussion without providing a decisive opinion, allowing students to adjust the most suitable plan through a continuous cycle of reviewing and reflection (Figure 1).

## 3.3 Subject and field of study

The main members of this study are students of the lacquer painting class at a community college in Nantou County, Taiwan. Currently, there are a total of 21 students in the class, and 10 of them (coded as A-HYG, B-CJW, C-THF, D-LG, E-WSG, F-LYJ, G-WWC, H-LSH, I-YJJ, J-JLI, detailed information can be found in Table 1) participated in the interviews. In addition to the basic weekly courses at the community college, the students also have regular monthly meetings one to two times for progress discussions and problem-solving, while the rest of the time they work on their creations at home.

The discussion topic of the first interview was "Hometown." Most of the participating students are married women who have moved to Nantou from other counties or cities decades ago and have already integrated into the local community. However, they still have fond memories or concerns about their original families. This topic was chosen as it is the most emotional and touching for them.

In terms of teaching design, the researcher encouraged the students to discuss their work. During the monthly discussions, the students provided suggestions and discussed their own and others' topics, compositions, techniques, and

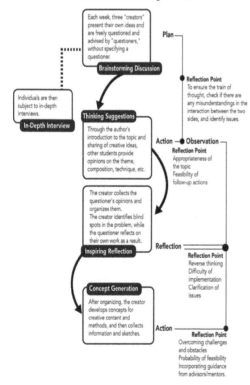

Figure 1. Flowchart for creative brainstorming discussionthe research was produced/made.

Table 1. Basic information of participating students.

| Code | Gender | Age | Artistic Learning | Occupation Type |
|---|---|---|---|---|
| A-HYG | F | 68 | Oil painting | Supervisor retiring |
| B-CJW | M | 48 | Sculpture | Sculpture artist |
| C-THF | F | 55 | Knitting, dyeing/weaving | Fabric art creator |
| D-LG | F | 65 | Ceramics | Ceramic painter |
| E-WSG | F | 58 | Ink painting watercolor | Tea master |
| F-LYJ | F | 63 | Bamboo weaving ink painting | Tea master, bamboo craft artist |
| G-WWC | F | 53 | Weaving pottery | Weaving, dessert-making teacher |
| H-LSH | M | 38 | Acrylic photography | Horticulture stone carving |
| I-YJJ | F | 75 | Ink painting oil painting | Teacher retiring |
| J-JLI | F | 65 | Bamboo weaving dyeing/weaving | Self-employed |

The research was produced/made.

colors. The researcher recorded the feedback from the students and analyzed their feasibility and acceptance. The third step was to conduct in-depth interviews with the students, record their learning status implement assessments, and finally conduct coding analysis based on grounded theory.

## 4 RESULTS AND DISCUSSION

### 4.1 Collaboration and observation

In this study, the creator's creative context was determined by sharing, and feedback was collected and organized by the creator, who timely provided feedback and opinions.[3]

*"My children have grown up and are starting their careers, and I am preparing for retirement. So, I started looking for a teacher to learn how to paint. But the teacher said that I was always uncontrollable and would draw whatever I wanted, scribbling randomly. However, each of my drawings has meaning and reflects my philosophy of life. Every day, I think about what I should paint to make it interesting. I can't sleep at night, thinking about painting something meaningful. But if I don't make it clear, no one will understand what I'm trying to express."* (Student A-HYG); *"I think A-HYG's work is very open, and it doesn't look like lacquer art. Does it need adjustment? Which is more important, the lacquer art technique or the creative method?"* (Student C-THF responded to A-HYG) *"Is it meaningful to create art under the lacquer art technique, otherwise it's just painting.* (Student E-WSG responded to A-HYG) *"Your drawing is very interesting, and it feels like a novice painter. Whether it's oil painting or lacquer painting, this can obviously help you establish your style."* (Student I-YJJ responded to A-HYG) *"Using people as the theme of one's hometown is unique. It seems that everyone emphasizes natural landscapes more."* (Student J-JLI responded to A-HYG).

Through open discussions, feedback providers not only identify and support the creator's creative concepts but also often identify any misunderstandings in their interaction. This may be the initial period of collaboration, where both parties can provide more constructive suggestions after clarifying their thoughts. Although the study participants were biased towards the middle-aged and elderly, with strong subjective awareness, after several rounds of collaboration, both the creator and the feedback providers can assist in providing opinions on the creative theme.

### 4.2 Reflection and inspiration from peers

As artworks often focus on things around us, creators will propose their own ideas, but feedback is often provided in a reverse-thinking manner. Of course, this is not to oppose the creator's ideas, but it often points out blind spots in the creator's work.

*"The environment is constantly changing. The place where I grew up used to be a vast expanse of golden rice paddies and tobacco fields. It was a place where I played and helped my parents work. This is Bird's Beak Pond, but now it has been developed and everywhere is sand and gravel, like a desert. I have a deep feeling about this! So I want to use the Yakumo-nuri technique and also try to use circular lacquer boards to paint."* (Student E-WSG)

*"If the Yakumo-nuri color tone is too deep, it will fall into a feeling of 'memories.' But it seems like it's difficult to create a feeling of past beauty and present sand and gravel. Is it too weak and not strong enough?"* (Student C-THF replied to E-WSG)

*"The composition looks majestic enough now. It is Ninety-nine Peak after the earthquake. Can we use bald mountains and golden rice to contrast with it? The composition is the same... one is a vibrant golden color scheme, and the other is a silver-gray scheme. Use gold and silver foils as color schemes to create strong contrast."* (Student H-LSH replied to E-WSG)

*"If E-WSG wants to show an endless view, a square composition would be better. Using circles would create more focus, but it would be too soft. A horizontal rectangle would be more shocking for this composition."* (Student B-CJW replied to E-WSG)

### 4.3 Overcoming challenges and improving feasibility

The students not only focused on completing their own work but also provided feedback on the feasibility of each other's ideas, which resulted in different positive and negative opinions from their peers. Through the creators' organization, they gradually focused on forming their creative concepts and strengthening the probability of feasibility. In addition, this process also had a mutually motivating effect and generated momentum.

*"Walking my dog after work every day is what I look forward to the most, so this time I set the theme as my dog and his favorite garden with a more relaxed mindset,"* (Student B-CJW): *"The technique I used this time is more special. I plan to use aluminum plate to create my artwork, and after it's completed, I'll use a needle to scrape off the paint, which is similar to the technique of Japanese shinkin. Because my job is sculpting copper, I have a special emotional attachment to metal, so I want to create a paint piece using aluminum plates,"* (Student B-CJW) *"Metal plate art should be very cool. I also wanted to create using the technique of shinkin, but I feel like I can't control it well,"*

---

[3]The participants are both creators and feedback providers who engage in peer assessment. To avoid confusion of roles and positions, this study uniformly refers to them as *"creators"* and *"feedback providers."*

(Student C-THF responded to B-CJW) ; *"I think using dogs and flowers as the theme is quite special, with a yin and yang harmonious feeling. Dogs are animals and flowers are plants, which also complement each other as a "contrast". However, are you worried that there might be too many colors and chaos? Would it be better to consider the proportion or technique?"* (Student D-LG responded to B-CJW).

Student C-THF and D-LG's replies on the use of technique and color were also mentioned in the subsequent discussion: *"But this time, I want to put new and old, traditional and innovative, with a bit of conflict in the picture. Seeing B-CJW's theme of dogs and flowers seems to make the concept of "conflict" more clear to me."* said student C-THF.

## 5  CONCLUSION

This study utilized an open and public approach to encourage peers to take on the roles of creators and questioners simultaneously. Through four stages of interactive discussion (brainstorming, suggestion, reflection, and concept generation), creators could refer to the helpful suggestions provided by questioners in a moderate manner. Regardless of the final outcome of the work, the process of creative inspiration and discussion broke away from the traditional learning mode of craft, eliminating concerns of non-artistic backgrounds. The study investigated the effects of peer evaluation on discourse promotion and motivation for lacquer learners. The results showed:

### 5.1  *The balance between work comments and life experience sharing*

The learners in this study had many concerns about judging their peers' work, but through open discussions and personal sharing, they could provide useful suggestions for the creation of the works. Although the age range of the participants was relatively high, and they initially had many concerns about judging their peers' work, after several rounds of discussions, both evaluators and evaluatees could provide personal opinions and experiences that contributed to the expansion of effective concepts for creating.

### 5.2  *Reflecting on one's own creations and style through peer evaluation*

Traditional craft teaching often involves the teacher demonstrating while the students imitate, resulting in many experienced students who understand techniques but have difficulty applying them. Peer evaluation helped promote learners' confidence in their own work and helped them better understand their work style through discussion.

### 5.3  *Mutual motivation between peers*

During the course, learners not only focused on completing their own work but also needed to provide multi-faceted opinions to their peers during discussions, which generated mutual motivation and momentum. Encouraging learners to speak out about their own ideas for their works and to bravely propose feasible ideas for their peers' works created sparks in the process, and open-minded thinking helped learners better understand the strengths and weaknesses of their works and further interpret their works. Traditional craft techniques require solid step-by-step learning, but as individual creators, if they cannot break away from the teacher's style, they may become mere copying machines. Therefore, in the face of the gradual decline of traditional crafts, encouraging creators to propose their own creative contexts may be a way for teachers and learners of traditional crafts to try to interact.

## REFERENCES

Chang J.H., & Tsai M.H. (2018). A brief discussion on peer assignment mutual evaluation and implementation suggestions. *Taiwan Education Review Monthly*, 7 (8), 212–218.

Chu L. (2016, 9). The development and evolution of lacquerware during the japanese colonization period. *Journal of Art Forum, 10*, pp. 1–38.

Kuang-Hsia Liu. (2021). Beyond subjectivity: The practice research of web-based peer assessment for college art and design courses. *Journal of Design*, 26(2).

Web site://lefthand1001.pixnet.net/blog/post/12144245-%E7%A4%BE%E6%9C%83%E8%AA%8D%E7%9F%A5%E7%90%86%E8%AB%96

Web site:https://sites.google.com/site/prac328/fang-fa?tmpl=%2Fsystem%2Fapp%2Ftemplates%2Fprint%2F&showPrintDialog=1

System Innovation for a Troubled World – Lam et al. (Eds)
© 2024 the Author(s), ISBN: 978-1-032-60846-4

# Introducing design thinking into university social responsibility program instruction: A case study of the local care practice program at national Formosa university

Chia-Wei Wang* & Shyh-Huei Hwang
*Graduate School of Design, National Yunlin University of Science and Technology, Douliu, Yunlin, Taiwan*

ABSTRACT: University social responsibility (USR) has become an increasingly significant trend in global higher education. Beyond their current educational position, universities wish to emphasize their social responsibility and morality. In addition, this motivates universities to pursue community support and communication. Incorporating social responsibility into the program poses numerous challenges, including how to align the profession with the issues in the field, cultivate students' awareness of problems, and integrate students' knowledge and practice. Therefore, there is a critical need for a modernized strategy to address the complex issues in teaching practice. As a systematic and innovative method of thinking, design thinking has been widely adopted in a variety of fields for creative problem-solving. This study has utilized a USR course from Taiwan's National Formosa University as a case study. Five local cultural institutions in the Dounan region served as teaching venues for introducing design thinking concepts and conducting case studies. This study has aimed to investigate the evolution and function of design thinking in the USR program, as well as the patterns of innovative student team behavior. As research methodologies, participatory action research and semi-structured interviews have been utilized. The investigation has reached two conclusions. First, three models for stimulating innovative action have been proposed: (1) a model of action that attaches to the needs of stakeholders; (2) a model of action that begins with team expertise; and (3) a model of action that is inspired by an interactive process. This study has concluded by introducing design thinking into the USR program and elaborating on its role in providing a viable pedagogical practice for the field.

## 1 INTRODUCTION

The function of universities in modern society extends far beyond the fundamental assumptions of knowledge production and dissemination (Ali et al. 2021). Inheriting the concept of corporate social responsibility, the government and society are demanding that universities assume their societal responsibilities (Yang 2019). As a result, universities are progressively transcending their traditional educational stance and emphasizing their social responsibility and ethics, which has prompted them to seek community support and communication. Consequently, a growing number of universities around the world have incorporated the concept of university social responsibility (USR) into their institutional priorities, including incorporating the concept of social responsibility into their curricula with features such as field practice, issue-oriented teaching, application orientation, and cross-disciplinary collaboration, which numerous studies have shown to be advantageous to learning. According to Larrán Jorge et al. (2017) on USR education, despite the fact that some universities incorporate the concept of social responsibility into their curricula, USR operates in a limited manner, and there are still obstacles such as a lack of resources and resistance to change. This study has focused on the challenges associated with teaching practice, such as how to align the profession with field issues, how to cultivate students' problem awareness, and how to integrate students' knowledge and practice. As a result, this study has employed design thinking as an approach to address challenging issues in USR teaching practice. As a systematic and innovative method of thinking, design thinking has been widely adopted for creative problem-solving in a variety of fields. This study has used a USR course at the National Formosa University in Taiwan as a case study, introducing the concept of design thinking at a local cultural institution in the Dounan region and conducting a case study. This study has aimed to investigate the evolution and function of design thinking in the USR program, as well as the patterns of innovative student team behavior.

*Corresponding Author:
d10930013@gmail.yuntech.edu.tw

DOI: 10.1201/9781003460763-32

## 2 LITERATURE REVIEW

### 2.1 The development context of USR

Before the existence of the term USR, a similar concept emerged in 1862 with the establishment of the Cooperative Extension Service for U.S. land-grant universities, which used education as a social policy instrument for issues such as food production and distribution in U.S. agriculture (Hoag 2005; Sellers & Markham 2012; Su et al. 2020). As a result of their political and economic integration, European nations signed the "Bologna Declaration" in June 1999, in which the social dimension of higher education was emphasized multiple times during biennial meetings (Liu & Chu 2019). The Decade of Education for Sustainable Development, which was endorsed by the United Nations General Assembly in 2002, articulates the role of universities in society by emphasizing the interrelationship between universities, society, and the economy (UNESCO, 2005). In 2015, the Japanese government also proposed the "Center of Innovation" and "Center of Community +" programs, which have reaffirmed the close connection between universities and local development (Yang et al. 2018). Between 2012 and 2014, the European Union USR (EU-USR) framework was introduced in the European Union (EU-USR, 2018). The Ministry of Education of Taiwan introduced the USR Practice Program in 2017 to promote a people-centered approach based on local needs to guide universities in carrying out their social responsibilities (Ministry of Education of Taiwan, 2018). It is evident that USR has become a significant global trend, and universities are gradually moving beyond their established educational stance to emphasize their moral and ethical stance on social responsibility and to make positive changes to cultivate the talents needed by society in the future. This has prompted universities to abandon their academic ivory towers and begin to seek community support and communication.

### 2.2 USR program

Several studies have demonstrated the learning benefits of USR programs, such as Ting et al.'s (2021) utilization of problem-based learning as a design and strategy for USR courses that address complex structural issues and help students comprehend their social responsibilities. In addition, MacVaugh and Norton (2011) have investigated the incorporation of social responsibility topics into business-related degree programs. Their research has revealed that an active learning approach enables students to become independent of their instructors and instead develop a sense of personal responsibility. According to Chen (2020), the USR program facilitates early community engagement and paves the way for future employment. Moreover, it allows instructors to contribute to the community by exposing them to issues in the field. This study participated in the 2022 USR Expo in Taiwan and observed the "Local Care" pavilion to comprehend the current operation of USR programs in Taiwan. By establishing special programs or credits, a number of these universities would enhance the relevance of their curriculum to social issues. Such programs include Pingtung University's "Innovative Industries in Adult Care for the Physically and Mentally Challenged Credit Program," Chung Shan Medical University's "USR Slash Micro Credit Courses," and National Tsing Hua University's "Program of Urban-Rural Revitalization Education (PURRE)". The National Formosa University, where the institute is located, has established two required courses to support the USR program: "Local Care Practice" in the first semester and "Knowledge of Innovation and Entrepreneurship" in the second. National Chi Nan University in Nantou established the "Shui Sha Lian College" in March 2022 to cultivate the talents required by the local community through a more proactive and innovative approach. Nevertheless, although some universities do incorporate the concept of social responsibility into their curricula, they do so in a limited manner, and obstacles such as a lack of resources and resistance to change remain (Larrán Jorge et al. 2017). The focus of the study has been the challenges of teaching practice.

### 2.3 Design thinking as a guide for the USR program

The objective of the USR program is to instill in students a sense of social responsibility, and it is a method of education based on actual social issues. In terms of teaching methodology, it differs from courses in which knowledge is imparted unilaterally. The USR program places greater emphasis on the so-called unity of knowledge and action, which is the teaching process from the cultivation of problem awareness to the application of the profession to generate actions to solve problems and implement them in the field, and ultimately to comprehend the meaning of social responsibility through this process. However, social issues are frequently complex. For instance, Chan (2017) argues that when significant knowledge is tasked with resolving social issues, it is challenging for students to align their knowledge with the issues. Design thinking is a collection of constructive techniques for creative thinking that cultivates the mentality of not being frightened of failure and putting ideas into action (Editorial Parenting of Common Wealth, 2017). Design thinking is a systematic and innovative way of thinking. Originally developed at Stanford University in the late 1950s as an innovative management approach to education, it was later expanded by IDEO, a design firm founded in the 1990s, for use in a variety of business projects and has since gained widespread recognition (Auernhammer & Roth 2021). Brown argues that creative thinking is a human-centered process of exploration that repeats through the so-called 3I space (inspiration, ideation, and implementation) and follows three major criteria (feasibility, viability, and desirability) to solve the constraints in the design environment. The common approach to design thinking can be summed up in five iterative stages: empathize, define, ideate, prototype, and test. In terms of implementation education, the "assess" phase can be added to evaluate the design thinking implementation outcomes (Berto et al., 2023). Moreover, Kimbell (2012) defines design thinking as a general theory of design, a cognitive approach, and an organizational innovation resource. It is evident that design thinking is utilized not only by designers for design projects but also as a framework for thinking and can be implemented within organizations for member training and organizational innovation. In various industries, design thinking has been implemented as a strategy for pursuing innovation (Brown 2008). In conclusion, the preceding arguments suggest that design thinking can serve as a guide for teachers in preparing lessons (training strategies) and for students in addressing issues on the field (innovative actions) in the face of complex issues and uncertainties in the USR program.

# 3  CASE STUDY

## 3.1  Research design

This study investigated the role of design thinking in introducing social responsibility courses in universities through a case study of a USR course titled "Local Care Practice" in the College of Arts and Sciences of the National Formosa University, participatory action research, and semi-structured interviews. This study followed the stages of action research, including planning, action, observation, and reflection, to address issues in the teaching practice of USR programs. The following are the stages of the research process:

### 3.1.1  Defining the question
Establishing a theoretical framework through literature research and developing implementation strategies and plans for integrating design thinking into teaching and learning.

### 3.1.2  Teaching implementation
Implementing the teaching process and resolving practical challenges in a cycle of action and reflection.

### 3.1.3  Collecting feedback
Observing and documenting students' responses to the course, followed by interviewing them about their experiences.

### 3.1.4  Analysis
The analysis of oral, visual, and documentary data gathered during the teaching practice to conclude,

iterate upon them, and establish a foundation for future research.

## 3.2  Data collection

This institute's courses were attended by students from five distinct departments: multimedia design, leisure and recreation, applied foreign languages, biotechnology, and agricultural technology. Thirty students were divided into five groups, and semi-structured group interviews were conducted using a semi-structured interviewing method. Additionally, two students were selected from each group for individual interviews, and a total of fifteen oral interviews were collected. The study also included video recordings of the course, documentation of student work, and photographs of the prototypes and completed products that resulted.

# 4  CASE DESCRIPTION AND ANALYSIS

## 4.1  The development and function of introducing design thinking into USR programs

### 4.1.1  Curriculum development incorporating design thinking
This study has adopted the design thinking iterative process of Stanford University's d.school (2013) as the theoretical framework (empathize, define, ideate, prototype, and test & iteration) for the instructional design of the USR program. The course lasted 18 weeks and consisted of two class hours per week. After deducting the first week of class introduction and the last week of grade review, the actual course duration was 16 weeks and 32 hours, with the following teaching stages:

Figure 1.  Design thinking into USR curriculum development.

#### 4.1.1.1 Knowledge construction period

It would last three weeks and be primarily taught by instructors to construct the course's necessary knowledge and to invite teachers to share their experiences.

#### 4.1.1.2 Field entry

The first week would consist of a general tour, and the students would be divided into groups to adopt the operation sites; the second week would consist of groups interviewing the curators of individual sites to comprehend the field issues.

#### 4.1.1.3 Design thinking and planning

This three-week course would first concentrate on the problems using methods of design thinking such as brainstorming, mind mapping, and the KJ method, and then attempt to devise solutions.

#### 4.1.1.4 Field practice phase

This would be a four-week period during which small group members would organize their own time to practice in the field according to the proposal and take turns discussing it with the instructor. In the third week, a class-wide progress report will be distributed.

#### 4.1.1.5 Preparation for the results showcase

In the sixteenth week, the course would conduct a competition for the results showcase, which would be judged alongside nine other classes at the local care practice. Therefore, three weeks have been allotted to prepare for the results exhibition and to evaluate and provide feedback on the competition.

#### 4.1.2 *The role of design thinking training*

The specific function of design thinking in the USR program can be illustrated through two components: teacher preparation and student fieldwork. The subsequent subparagraphs shall explain:

1. Teacher's Preparation: Consider the teaching as an innovative project.

Table 1. The role of design thinking in teacher preparation.

| Step | Teacher's Preparation |
| --- | --- |
| Empathize | Identify through prior experience the challenges students may face in USR programs and comprehend the direction of issues in the practice field, such as the communication split between students and the community. |
| Define | The identified problems would be defined and grouped to identify behavioral patterns and investigate potential solutions, such as designating the problem as "communication skills." |

*(continued)*

Table 1. Continued

| Step | Teacher's Preparation |
| --- | --- |
| Ideate | After defining the framework of the problem, potential resources and solutions would be identified and conceptualized for the course's content design. For instance, the ORID interviewing method would be incorporated into the program to improve students' conversational abilities. |
| Prototype | Considering the teaching strategies and course outline as prototypes, and simultaneously creating prototypes of course teaching aids, such as the design of ORID form materials. |
| Test and Iteration | With an open and exploratory perspective, the actual teaching process would be adjusted continuously to meet the challenges of the teaching process. |
| Assess | Assessing the effectiveness of instruction and learning is a prerequisite for a new curriculum cycle. |

(Source: conducted by this study)

(2) Students' field practice: The section on developing innovative solutions to field-specific problems.

Table 2. The role of design thinking in students' field practice.

| Step | Students' Field Practice |
| --- | --- |
| Empathize | Through previous learning experiences, field tours, and interviews with key individuals, students would develop an understanding of the issues facing the field of practice. |
| Define | After comprehending the issues in the field and the expertise of the group members, students would define the problems by designing thinking methods, such as mind maps, to concentrate on particular operational directions. |
| Ideate | Combining the requirements of the field with the expertise of the members, the students would create innovative solutions and submit proposals. |
| Prototype | Developing prototypes based on the solution's content. |
| Test and iteration | Implementing innovative solutions in the field would yield learning benefits through practical outcomes and iterative process experience. |
| Assess | Through the presentation and showcasing of results, as well as peer-to-peer interactions, feedback would be obtained as a basis for evaluating the efficacy of the actions and, consequently, for learning reflection. |

(Source: conducted by this study)

## 4.2 Practical case analysis

The six iterative stages of design thinking—empathize, define, ideate, prototype, test, and assess—were utilized as the analytical framework for the analysis of the practice cases in this study. Due to page constraints, only one of five sets of analysis results will be presented:

### 4.2.1 Case description

The discussion topic for the student group (code: Group E) was the Taliwu Library of Illustrated Story Books in Dounan Township. In addition to perusing and promoting illustrated books, the library offers craft classes. The primary audience is made up of parents and children. Two members of the Department of Leisure and Recreation and four members of the Department of Biotechnology formed the group. The final innovative action proposed by the group was to transform the museum's bookmarks using discarded picture books and to engage local parents and children in the transformation by conducting craft activities. The deeper meaning of the activity was to "promote environmental awareness," "give discarded picture books a second chance at life," and "strengthen the bond and identity between museum visitors and the institution." The activity, in which 50 individuals participated, was awarded first place by the jury at the final results showcase.

### 4.2.1 Empathize stage

During the fourth and fifth weeks of the course, through on-site observations and interviews with the director, students were able to acquire knowledge and comprehension of the operating conditions and difficulties. The director mentioned the large number of discarded picture books, the desire to increase the parent-child customer base, and the structure of previous activities at the facility. The student group observed space and outdated equipment issues in the field.

### 4.2.2 Define stage

The students used the KJ method to define the key elements of the field issue, the function of the field, and the expertise of the members, as well as the venue problem, such as an old building, insufficient funding, and fixed target customers, during the definition stage. In contrast, the venue's space includes a classroom for handicrafts, a reading area, and a viewing window. The group's expertise consists of graphic design, computer graphics, planning ability, and integration skills.

### 4.2.3 Ideate stage

During the ideation stage, the student group and the director stimulated each other, made associations, and stimulated creativity through the definition stage's summary of keywords. While the students observed the old bookmarks through the eyes of an outsider, the project director shared his experience in handicraft courses and his desire to repurpose the discarded picture books. As a result of the free-flowing exchange of ideas, creativity was stimulated, and several elements were interconnected to produce the bookmark renovation activity.

### 4.2.4 Prototype stage

The primary attempt during the prototype stage was the bookmark renovation module. Through repeated hands-on work and testing, the student group determined the appropriate materials and established a standardized production procedure for the handcraft course's lesson plan.

### 4.2.5 Test and iteration (Action practice)

The test stage was a rehearsal and preliminary testing phase in which the student group visited the field before the official event and tested the viability of the lesson plans during the event. The iterative process was insufficient, however, due to the limited time allocated for the course.

### 4.2.6 Access

Through feedback from stakeholders such as the public, the director, peer-to-peer interaction, and showcase jury members, the initiative's efficacy will be determined.

## 4.3 Three models to stimulate innovative actions

The initial inspiration for innovative action occurs primarily during the design thinking process of empathizing, defining, and ideating, which is stimulated and influenced by students (the composition of members), teachers' guidance, the ideas of field partners, the primary axis of the issue, and even the environment and space. Consequently, the methods of soliciting proposals may diverge. To understand the role of design thinking in stimulating and developing innovative actions, this study has investigated the models of generating innovative actions with students as the primary subjects; the analysis is summarized below.

### 4.3.1 A model of action that attaches to the needs of stakeholders

In the process of ideation, student groups base their actions on the ideas or needs of stakeholders. In this model, students would be the passive implementers, opting to follow the advice of instructors or field partners in the conception and structure of the action, and the student group would be minimally innovative or creative in terms of performance style or specifics.

Table 3. Corresponding description of the case.

| Group | Description |
|---|---|
| Group A | The practice field for Group A is a small local exhibition hall. Following the director's suggestion to develop creative experience activities for an exhibition lecture, the group decided to develop ink-blowing badges as a DIY project. |
| Group C | The practice field for Group C is a local museum devoted to film, and the proposal relies on the direction of the director and the teachers. It was more of a project executor than an innovator, and the final product was a booklet and illustrated postcards. |

(Source: conducted by this study)

### 4.3.2 *A model of action that begins with team expertise*

In the process of ideation, students initiate actions based on the expertise of their group members. Students are active action leaders in this model. Because the objective is based on the student's own area of expertise, the ideation and structure of the action are relatively straightforward, and students are more dominant. However, if the empathy stage is insufficiently precise, it is easy to disregard the requirements of stakeholders, or the form of innovation is constrained by the members' expertise.

Table 4. Corresponding description of the case.

| Group | Description |
|---|---|
| Group B | The practice field of Group B is the local environmental education center. The majority of this group's members are from the Department of Biotechnology and the Department of Agricultural Technology; consequently, they chose this sector on purpose at the outset, resulting in the creation of aquaponics experience activities. |
| Group D | Group D, a collaboration between the Department of Multimedia Design and the Department of Applied Foreign Languages, chose the Comics Theme Museum as its field of practice, with Multimedia Design students taking the lead in creating a series of bilingual comics with local themes. |

(Source: conducted by this study)

### 4.3.3 *A Model of Action that is Inspired by An Interactive Process*

The basis for action in the process of ideation is an interaction between the student team and the subject matter experts. In this model, the environment, the requirements of the stakeholders, the guidance of the teacher, and the expertise of the team members inspire innovative actions among student groups. This model enables students to consider beyond a singular perspective and to be innovative and open-minded in ways unimaginable.

Table 5. Corresponding description of the case.

| Group | Description |
|---|---|
| Group B | The students in Group B chose aquaponics based on their expertise and initially envisioned a static display design. After active communication with the director and incorporation of his experience, the design was implemented as an experiential activity. |
| Group E | The practice field of Group E is a local illustrated book library. The bookmark renovation activity was the result of a proposal to stimulate the environment, the librarian's requirements, the expertise of the members, and the creativity of a few teachers. |

(Source: conducted by this study)

## 5 RESEARCH CONCLUSIONS AND LIMITATIONS

### 5.1 *Research conclusions*

USR courses are based on learning in real-world social contexts and issues, and they stimulate students' social responsibility throughout the learning process. Consequently, USR programs are frequently influenced by the requirements of stakeholders, the interpersonal skills of students, and the complexity of problems in the field. In contrast to programs of unidirectional knowledge transfer, instructors no longer have authority over instruction. In addition, students transition from being passive recipients to active participants, and at the conclusion of the course, students (and possibly teachers) will individually summarize the skills acquired. Before the course begins, no one can be certain of the skills that will be acquired; only the location of practice and the social issues that may arise are known. As a result, design thinking provides teachers and students with methods and steps to follow when preparing lessons and coping with complex and unpredictable situations encountered in the field. Design thinking is, in brief, a framework for thinking about reflexive practice that can serve as a guide for instructors and students when confronting unknown issues. The program facilitates communication between faculty, students, and stakeholders, helps students extend their imaginations, and encourages them to integrate field issues with their own profession to produce more creative design solutions.

The purpose of this study is to address challenging issues in the teaching practice of the USR program by introducing design thinking into the USR program, the development and role of which are explored in this study; additionally, the model of innovative student team action generation is explored. First, this study has proposed three models for stimulating innovative actions that are as follows: (1) a model of action that attaches to the needs of stakeholders; (2) a model of action that begins with team expertise; and (3) a model of action that is inspired by an interactive process. The third of these modes is the superior mode of action initiation, as well as the state in which design thinking operates most efficiently. The second contribution of this study is the incorporation of design thinking into the USR curriculum and the elucidation of its function in providing a viable pedagogical practice for the field.

## 5.2 *Research limitations*

Due to the limited course time, the student team did not have sufficient time to operate in the "iterate and test" stage of design thinking, resulting in an insufficient number of iterations that may have affected the innovative actions' outcomes. In addition, the impact of students' individual psychological and cognitive states on learning was not investigated. Due to limitations in space, the case has only been described in a limited manner. These are the limitations of this study, which are anticipated to be addressed by future research.

## REFERENCES

Ali M., Mustapha I., Osman S. & Hassan, U.(2021). University social responsibility: A review of conceptual evolution and its thematic analysis. *Journal of Cleaner Production*, 286, 124931.

Auernhammer J. & Roth, B. (2021). The origin and evolution of Stanford University's design thinking: From product design to design thinking in innovation management. *Journal of Product Innovation Management*, 38(6), 623–644.

Bertão R.A., Jung C.H., Chung J. & Joo J. (2023). Design thinking: a customized blueprint to train R & D personnel in creative problem-solving. *Thinking Skills and Creativity*, 101253.

Brown T. (2008). Design thinking. *Harvard Business Review*, 86(6), 84.

d.school & Hasso Plattner Institute of Design at Stanford. (2013). *Design thinking bootleg* (p. 90). https://dschool.stanford.edu/resources/the-bootcamp-bootleg

EU-USR (2018). Social responsibility of universities in Europe and development of a community reference framework. Retrieved from http://www.eu-usr.eu/wp-content/uploads/2014/05/2013_EU-USR_e-leaflet.pdf

Hoag D.L. (2005). Economic principles for saving the Cooperative Extension Service. *Journal of Agricultural and Resource Economics*, 30(1835-2016-148930), 396–410.

Kimbell L. (2012). Rethinking design thinking: Part II. *Design and Culture*, 4(2), 129–148.

Larrán Jorge M., Andrades Peña F.J. (2017). Analysing the literature on university social responsibility: A review of selected higher education journals. *Higher Education Quarterly*, 71(4), 302–319.

MacVaugh J. & Norton M. (2011). Introducing sustainability into business education contexts using active learning. *Higher Education Policy*, 24, 439–457.

Sellers D.M. & Markham M.S. (2012). Raising awareness of assistive technology in older adults through a community-based, cooperative extension program. *Gerontology & Geriatrics Education*, 33(3), 287–301.

Ting K.H., Cheng C.T. & Ting H.Y. (2021). Introducing the problem/project based learning as a learning strategy in University social responsibility program-A study of local revitalization of coastal area, yong-an District of kaohsiung city. *Marine Policy*, 131, 104546.

Unesco U. (2005). Decade of education for sustainable development: 2005-2014. *Draft International Implementation Scheme*.

Brown T. (2021)。設計思考改造世界(十周年增訂新版)。臺北市：聯經出版事業公司。

刘爱玲、褚欣维(2019)。博洛尼亚进程20年:欧盟高等教育一体化过程，经验与趋势。首都师范大学学报(社会科学版), 3, 160-170.

教育部（2018）。107 教育部推動大學社會責任實踐計畫一般大學徵件須知。2022年7月15日，取自：https://reurl.cc/ZXEOy6

陳信宏 (2020)。從USR探討課堂中社會影響力之行動研究。高等教育研究紀要, 12, 25-46.

楊正誠(2019)。大學社會責任發展的國內外趨勢。評鑑雙月刊, (79), 32-36.

楊玉惠 等（2018）。訪問日本國家推動地方創生與大學社會責任實踐計畫出國報告書。2022年7月15日，取自：https://reurl.cc/9VxExj

親子天下編輯部、台大創新設計學院、Design for Change台灣團隊 (2017)。設計思考：從教育開始的破框思維。臺北市：親子天下股份有限公司。

蘇良委、郭瑞坤、謝政勳 (2020)。推動大學社會責任對學生社會參與行為意願影響研究。國立中山大學公共事務管理研究所(碩士論文)。

System Innovation for a Troubled World – Lam et al. (Eds)
© 2024 the Author(s), ISBN: 978-1-032-60846-4

# Drawing as an influence to regulate mood

Huang Yunching* & Dengchuan Tsai
*National Yunlin University of Science and Technology, Yuntech Graduate School of Design,
Doctoral Program, Pingtung, Taiwan*

Li-Hsun Peng
*Yuntech GRAD School and Department of Creative Design, National Yunlin University of Science and
Technology, Taichung, Taiwan*

ABSTRACT: The development of contemporary society is rapidly changing, and the pressure on modern people's life is increasing rapidly. Improving psychological adaptability and achieving physical and mental health is an important issue. This study explores painting as a carrier for regulating the mind to relieve people's body and mind, improve the regulation of emotions, and keep the mind elastic and healthy.

In the study, students from Taiwan Community College were taken as the research objects. The participants were aged 45–70. A total of 20 students participated in the test. They received painting lessons for 3 months. Practice drawing one piece weekly and continue practicing for a long time. The theme of the painting is to express the painter's mind and emotions as an exercise. During the research, monthly interview questionnaires and data are used as records, and the results of the research questionnaires are analyzed.

After research and analysis, it is found that long-term participation in art practice - painting courses, research questionnaires and data descriptions of participating students, the results of research factor analysis show that the percentage of variation is 66.32%, the research questions are divided into four factors: Meditation and focus enhance the sense of meaning, creating balance enhances the sense of health, pleasure enhances the sense of existence, and freedom enhances the sense of reinforcement. Research has shown that drawing practice has a positive effect on emotion regulation.

*Keywords*: drawing practice, human factors design, regulating emotions, physical and mental balance

## 1 INTRODUCTION

With the rapid development of modern technology, changes in climate and environment, and the sharp increase in life pressure, everyone faces different challenges and problems in life. Therefore, how to enhance the ability of self-regulation in time to maintain the flexibility of life and the balance of body and mind has become a key issue for the future of human beings.

This study aims to explore painting as a method of regulating inner emotions, transforming and soothing emotions and perceptions through painting. Art can be the carrier of the soul, and painting is a medium to soothe and transform the mood. Creation helps soothe and balance an individual's mind and emotions. The journey of life is a process of continuous learning and continuous growth. Drawing can be a way to strengthen the mind and soothe the mood.

When we paint, we can transform our inner emotions and perceptions through painting. This is a cyclic process of imagination, perception, and creation, and it is also a spiritual activity with rich physical and mental experience and far-reaching significance. Creation is the presentation of an individual's inner soul, which can be transformed from the inside out, while painting practice can activate the heart, hands, and brain, and promote the development of the inner spirit.

## 2 LITERATURE REVIEW

The creative process can be used as a means of spiritual sublimation by iteratively processing emotions and translating emotional imagery into images of concrete form. Art can also help people "concrete emotions" through body perception and manipulation of materials, which helps to think about life creatively (Xu Wenling, 2021: 28). Painting, as a way of self-expression, allows people to transform their

---

*Corresponding Author: D11030018@yuntech.edu.tw

DOI: 10.1201/9781003460763-33

psychological feelings and deeply personal emotions into image expression, and it becomes a positive way to regulate emotions and obtain a sense of joy in life in the process of painting.

Everyone can benefit from drawing as a positive way of life to feel more comfortable and express themselves. Dr. Pat B. Allen proposed that self-transformation through practice and creation can lead to a deep inner journey. Painting has become a way of expressing the soul and emotion, purifying and precipitating the inner soul, and bringing relief and new insights into emotions. The drawing process can help individuals understand and process emotions more deeply and find emotional balance and liberation.

Carl Rogers, an American psychologist stated, "Really having creative adaptation seems to be the only possible way to coexist with the ever-changing world"; indeed, art is closely related to freedom. The most essential foundation of existentialism in philosophy is that the artistic process makes people aware, artistic expression makes people aware, and awareness produces creative anxiety, and then change and action, expression, and awareness become a circular and relative relationship (Moom, 2011: 46). Therefore, the art experience process allows people to perceive, create, act, and express, to release the subconscious mind, maintain flexibility and creativity, and experience perception, perception and emotional expression from the art creation process.

## 3 RESEARCH METHODS

At present, many advanced countries have community colleges. Community colleges provide local community residents with more diverse and more flexible learning spaces. They are the third learning space between formal school and family environment, so that people can maintain lifelong The spirit of learning allows local residents to have an alternative and sustainable space for learning knowledge and multiple arts in community colleges (Peng Lixun, 2008).

In this study, the students of Taiwan Community University and the composite media creation course were taken as the research objects. The students who participated in the painting research were 45–70 years old, and a total of 20 students participated in the test. They were invited to participate in the painting course regularly for 3 months' practice. Participate in painting practice regularly every week, each class has two hours of continuous painting practice.

Community college students regularly participate in painting courses. The theme of painting is to express the soul and emotion of the painter. The painting process allows people to experience creation and expression. During the study, interview questionnaires and data will be conducted every month as records, as research questionnaires and to analyze the research to explore the emotional perception and practice experience of the students participating in the practice of painting.

◎ 2023 Community College Composite Media Creation Course Design Chart:

| Painting study Course Design | Lesson 01–03 Geometric Modeling Exercises | Lesson 03–06 Natural Image Practice | Lesson 06–09 aesthetic form exercise | Lesson 10–12 Comprehensive creative exercises |
|---|---|---|---|---|
| Guide content | Geometry application (triangle, circle, square, rhombus, etc.) | Natural Image Applications (Flowers, leaves, natural materials, animal and plant shapes, etc.) | Aesthetic form (Principles of Form of Beauty – Repetition, Contrast, Gradients … ) | Integrating geometric shapes, natural totems, aesthetic form principles, and creativity) |
| Class time | 2 hours | 2 hours | 2 hours | 2 hours |
| Use media | Mixed media | Colored pencils, pencils | Scratch paper, bamboo pen | Mixed media |
| teaching time | 30 minutes | 30 minutes | 30 minutes | 30 minutes |
| References | Handouts, examples | Handouts, examples | Handouts, examples | Students play freely |

Figure 1. Records of the mixed media art creation course in community colleges.

A questionnaire survey was administered to 20 respondents. There were 12 questions in the questionnaire, as follows: sense of love, concentration, balance, pleasure, meditation, health, continuity, meaning, presence, strengthening, creativity, and

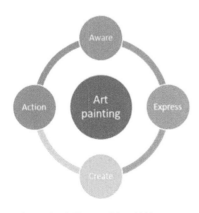

Art Experience Cycle Process Map 2023

freedom. A questionnaire was administered to the participants at the end of each month of painting and the results were recorded. Three surveys were conducted for this study.

## 4  RESEARCH RESULTS AND ANALYSIS

Through three months of drawing practice, 12 questions from the interview questionnaire were used: sense of love, concentration, balance, joy, meditation, health, continuity, meaning, presence, strengthening, creativity, and freedom. The results of each questionnaire are described below.

The results of the ANOVA analysis of the three-month responses to the Favorite question are shown in Table 1. The table shows that there was a significant difference between the three months' responses (F = 5.869, p = 0.005) and the results of the SNK post-hoc test are shown in Table 2. The table shows that the second and third months were more positive than the first month.

Table 1.  ANOVA table of favorite.

| Source of Var. | SS | DF | MS | F | Sig. |
|---|---|---|---|---|---|
| Between Grp. | 3.233 | 2 | 1.617 | 5.869 | 0.005 |
| Error | 15.700 | 57 | 0.275 | | |
| Total | 18.933 | 59 | | | |

Table 2.  Result of SNK tests of favorite of three months.

| Month | N | Means | SNK groups |
|---|---|---|---|
| 1 | 20 | 4.15 | A |
| 2 | 20 | 4.55 | B |
| 3 | 20 | 4.70 | B |

The results of the ANOVA analysis of the subjects' responses to the Concentration question at three months are presented in Table 3. The table shows that there was a significant difference between the three months' responses (F = 9.385, p < 0.001), and the results of the SNK post-hoc tests are shown in Table 4. The table shows that the second and third months were more positive than the first month.

Table 3.  ANOVA table of concentration.

| Source of Var. | SS | DF | MS | F | Sig. |
|---|---|---|---|---|---|
| Between Grp. | 5.433 | 2 | 2.717 | 9.385 | 0.000 |
| Error | 16.500 | 57 | 0.289 | | |
| Total | 21.933 | 59 | | | |

Table 4.  Result of SNK tests of concentration of three months.

| Month | N | Means | SNK groups |
|---|---|---|---|
| 1 | 20 | 3.95 | A |
| 2 | 20 | 4.50 | B |
| 3 | 20 | 4.65 | B |

The results of the ANOVA analysis of the three-month responses to the Sense of balance question are presented in Table 5. The table shows a significant difference between the three-month responses (F = 12.626, p < 0.001), and the results of the SNK post-hoc check are presented in Table 6. The table shows that the second and third months were more positive than the first month.

Table 5.  ANOVA table of sense of balance.

| Source of Var. | SS | DF | MS | F | Sig. |
|---|---|---|---|---|---|
| Between Grp. | 6.933 | 2 | 3.467 | 12.626 | 0.000 |
| Error | 15.650 | 57 | 0.275 | | |
| Total | 22.583 | 59 | | | |

Table 6.  Result of SNK tests of sense of balance of three months.

| Month | N | Means | SNK groups |
|---|---|---|---|
| 1 | 20 | 3.95 | A |
| 2 | 20 | 4.55 | B |
| 3 | 20 | 4.75 | B |

The results of the ANOVA analysis of the three-month responses to the Pleasure question are presented in Table 7. The table shows a significant difference between the three-month responses (F = 8.408, p = 0.001), and the results of the SNK post-hoc validation are shown in Table 8.

Table 7.  ANOVA table of pleasure.

| Source of Var. | SS | DF | MS | F | Sig. |
|---|---|---|---|---|---|
| Between Grp. | 4.233 | 2 | 2.117 | 8.408 | 0.001 |
| Error | 14.350 | 57 | 0.252 | | |
| Total | 18.583 | 59 | | | |

Table 8.  Result of SNK tests of pleasure of three months.

| Month | N | Means | SNK groups |
|---|---|---|---|
| 1 | 20 | 4.10 | A |
| 2 | 20 | 4.40 | A |
| 3 | 20 | 4.75 | B |

The results of the ANOVA analysis of the three-month responses to the Serenity question are presented in Table 9. The table shows a significant difference between the three-month responses (F = 3.246, p = 0.046), and the results of the SNK post hoc test are shown in Table 10. The table shows that the second and third months were more positive than the first month.

Table 9.   ANOVA table of serenity.

| Source of Var. | SS | DF | MS | F | Sig. |
|---|---|---|---|---|---|
| Between Grp. | 1.600 | 2 | 0.800 | 3.246 | 0.046 |
| Error | 14.050 | 57 | 0.246 | | |
| Total | 15.650 | 59 | | | |

Table 10.   Result of SNK tests of serenity of three months.

| Month | N | Means | SNK groups |
|---|---|---|---|
| 1 | 20 | 4.15 | A |
| 2 | 20 | 4.35 | A B |
| 3 | 20 | 4.55 | B |

The results of the ANOVA analysis of the three-month responses to the Health question are presented in Table 11. The table shows that there was a significant difference between the three-month responses (F = 14.755, p = 0.000), and the results of the SNK post-hoc validation are shown in Table 12. The table shows that both the second and third months were more positive than the first month.

Table 11.   ANOVA table of health.

| Source of Var. | SS | DF | MS | F | Sig. |
|---|---|---|---|---|---|
| Between Grp. | 7.300 | 2 | 3.650 | 14.755 | 0.000 |
| Error | 14.100 | 57 | 0.247 | | |
| Total | 21.400 | 59 | | | |

Table 12.   Result of SNK tests of health of three months.

| Month | N | Means | SNK groups |
|---|---|---|---|
| 1 | 20 | 3.65 | A |
| 2 | 20 | 4.15 | B |
| 3 | 20 | 4.50 | C |

The results of the ANOVA analysis of the three-month responses to the Sustainability question are presented in Table 13. The table shows a

significant difference in the responses between the three months (F = 14.956, p = 0.000), and the results of the SNK post hoc test are shown in Table 14.

Table 13.   ANOVA table of sustainability.

| Source of Var. | SS | DF | MS | F | Sig. |
|---|---|---|---|---|---|
| Between Grp. | 6.533 | 2 | 3.267 | 14.956 | 0.000 |
| Error | 12.450 | 57 | 0.218 | | |
| Total | 18.983 | 59 | | | |

Table 14.   Result of SNK tests of sustainability of three months.

| Month | N | Means | SNK groups |
|---|---|---|---|
| 1 | 20 | 3.75 | A |
| 2 | 20 | 4.25 | B |
| 3 | 20 | 4.55 | C |

The results of the ANOVA analysis of the three-month responses to the Sense of meaning question are presented in Table 15. The table shows a significant difference in the responses between the three months (F =8.033, p < 0.001), and the results of the SNK post-hoc check are shown in Table 16.

Table 15.   ANOVA table of sense of meaning.

| Source of Var. | SS | DF | MS | F | Sig. |
|---|---|---|---|---|---|
| Between Grp. | 5.200 | 2 | 2.600 | 8.033 | 0.001 |
| Error | 18.450 | 57 | 0.324 | | |
| Total | 23.650 | 59 | | | |

Table 16.   Result of SNK tests of sense of meaning of three months.

| Month | N | Means | SNK groups |
|---|---|---|---|
| 1 | 20 | 3.95 | A |
| 2 | 20 | 4.45 | B |
| 3 | 20 | 4.65 | B |

The results of the ANOVA analysis of the three-month responses to the Presence question are presented in Table 17. The table shows a significant difference in the responses between the three months (F = 15.363, p = 0.000), and the results of the SNK post-hoc test are presented in Table 18. The table shows that both the second and third months were more positive than the first month.

165

Table 17.   ANOVA table of presence.

| Source of Var. | SS | DF | MS | F | Sig. |
|---|---|---|---|---|---|
| Between Grp. | 9.433 | 2 | 4.717 | 15.363 | 0.000 |
| Error | 17.500 | 57 | 0.307 | | |
| Total | 26.933 | 59 | | | |

Table 18.   Result of SNK tests of presence of three months.

| Month | N | Means | SNK groups |
|---|---|---|---|
| 1 | 20 | 3.60 | A |
| 2 | 20 | 4.25 | B |
| 3 | 20 | 4.55 | B |

The results of the ANOVA analysis for the three-month responses to the Reinforcement question are presented in Table 19. The table shows a significant difference between the responses for the three months (F = 13.191, p = 0.000), and the results of the SNK post-hoc tests are presented in Table 20. The table shows that both the second and third months were more positive than the first month.

Table 19.   ANOVA table of reinforcement.

| Source of Var. | SS | DF | MS | F | Sig. |
|---|---|---|---|---|---|
| Between Grp. | 6.433 | 2 | 3.217 | 13.191 | 0.000 |
| Error | 13.900 | 57 | 0.244 | | |
| Total | 20.333 | 59 | | | |

Table 20.   Result of SNK tests of reinforcement of three months.

| Month | N | Means | SNK groups |
|---|---|---|---|
| 1 | 20 | 3.75 | A |
| 2 | 20 | 4.20 | B |
| 3 | 20 | 4.55 | C |

The results of the ANOVA analysis of the three-month responses to the Sense of creativity question are presented in Table 21. The table shows that there was a significant difference between the three-month responses (F = 6.544, p = 0.003), and the results of the SNK post-hoc validation are shown in Table 22.

Table 21.   ANOVA table of sense of creativity.

| Source of Var. | SS | DF | MS | F | Sig. |
|---|---|---|---|---|---|
| Between Grp. | 3.100 | 2 | 1.550 | 6.544 | 0.003 |
| Error | 13.500 | 57 | 0.237 | | |
| Total | 16.600 | 59 | | | |

Table 22.   Result of SNK tests of sense of creativity of three months.

| Month | N | Means | SNK groups |
|---|---|---|---|
| 1 | 20 | 4.00 | A |
| 2 | 20 | 4.35 | B |
| 3 | 20 | 4.55 | B |

The results of the ANOVA analysis of the three-month responses to the Sense of freedom question are presented in Table 23. The table shows a significant difference between the three-month responses (F = 4.661, p = 0.013), and the results of the SNK post-hoc validation are shown in Table 24.

Table 23.   ANOVA table of sense of freedom.

| Source of Var. | SS | DF | MS | F | Sig. |
|---|---|---|---|---|---|
| Between Grp. | 2.633 | 2 | 1.317 | 4.661 | 0.013 |
| Error | 16.100 | 57 | 0.282 | | |
| Total | 18.733 | 59 | | | |

Table 24.   Result of SNK tests of sense of freedom of three months.

| Month | N | Means | SNK groups |
|---|---|---|---|
| 1 | 20 | 3.95 | A |
| 2 | 20 | 4.30 | B |
| 3 | 20 | 4.45 | B |

Overall, the results of the questionnaire analysis showed that the three items of sense of health, continuity, and reinforcement had the highest improvement, and the data continued to improve for three months.

From the data of love feeling of the study questionnaire, the value of 4.15 in the first month, 4.55 in the second month, and 4.70 in the third month, showed significant meaning, from A in the first month to B in the second month, and slightly increased to the same B level in the third month. From the health perception data of the study questionnaire, the value of 3.65 in the first month, 4.15 in the second month, and 4.50 in the third month, showed significant meaning in each month, from A in the first month to B in the second month, and to C in the third month. In addition, according to the creativity data of the research questionnaire, the value of the first month is 4.00, the second month is 4.35, and the third month is 4.55. The first month A is obviously progressing to the second month B, showing significant meaning, and the third month is slightly higher than the same B level.

The analysis of the questionnaires and data of the participants in this study shows that painting has a significant effect on emotions. The analysis of the factors of concentration and creativity showed that painting made the inner mind and emotions visible; the analysis of the factors of freedom and strengthening showed that painting practice was beneficial to emotional relief and physical and mental well-being. Therefore, the results of the study showed that regular participation in the process and experience of painting practice has a positive effect on emotional regulation and relaxation.

## 5 CONCLUSIONS AND RECOMMENDATIONS

As a method of painting understanding and knowledge research, art can be transformed, symbolized, and constructed. As a special method of painting research, art creation can fully express emotions and explore the process and products of imagination (Rieger K., Schultz ASH, 2014). Artistic painting allows people to transform their inner emotions and perceptions. Through the practice and process of painting, imagination, and creativity become active ways to express emotions and spiritual perceptions.

In the art painting courses of community colleges, students participating in the painting courses can have a sustainable painting experience, from the creation of materials, experimentation, and non-material spiritual feelings, to the experience of expressing inner perception and self-soothing emotional painting is a self-knowledge. It is a cycle of perception opening, emotional thinking expression, transformation, and balance that allows for self-knowledge. The design and philosophy of the drawing course understand the sustainable cycle of physical, mental, and emotional regulation through the practice of drawing.

The research results confirm that painting practice helps to relieve people's inner emotions; balance between perception and emotion regulation; the process of painting becomes a way of expressing emotions; painting practice is conducive to emotional relief and physical and mental balance. It is hoped that in the future society, the spirit of art can be promoted more, and the aesthetic sense can be practiced in life. We recommend that all people promote and participate in painting activities, enhance the inner spirit and vitality of individuals, balance physical and mental health, and promote a better life for people in the future.

## REFERENCES

### 1. ENGLISH LITERATURE

Allen, P. B. *"Art is a Way of Knowing,"* Mr. Zhang Cultural Enterprise Co., Ltd., Living Psychology Publishers, (2012).
Christina H. West, Debra L. Dusome, Joanne Winsor, Andrea Winther Klippenstein, and Lillian B. Rallison Dialoguing With Images: An Expressive Arts Method for Health Research Qualitative Health Research

2022, Vol. 32(7) 1055–1070© https://doi.org/10.1177/10497323221084924
Dobelli, R. *"The Art of Thinking Clearly,"* Taipei: Weekly Business Publications, Inc., (2012).
Gonçalves, M. Design Studies Volume 72, January 2021, 100988 1 , Milene Gonçalves https://doi.org/10.1016/j.destud.2020.100988
Hickman, R. *Why We Make ART and Why it is Taught in the USA in 2010 by Intellect*, The University of Chicago Press.
Lee, Y.; Kim, M. "The Poetics of Service: Making in the Age of Experience ⟩, 2020 Design Issues 3 #4 2021/06/23 The Poetics of Service: Creation in the Age of Experience (2021) 37 (3): 44–58. https://doi.org/10.1162/desi_a_00647
Lowen, A. MD, *Pleasure: A Creative Approach to Life.* New York, Penguin Books, 1970.
Moon, B. L. (2007) Dialoguing with dream images in existential art therapy. *Art Therapy: Journal of the American Art Therapy Association* 24, 128–133.© AATA, Inc. 2007 https://doi.org/10.1080/07421656.2007.10129428
Moon, B. L. ⌐ Dialoguing with Dreams in Existential Art Therapy ⌐ Bruce L. Moon Ph.D., ATR-BC, LPC Pages 128-133 | Published online: 22 Apr 2011, from https://doi.org/10.1080/07421656.2007.10129428
Olson, R. *"Creation and Life,"* Publisher: Yuanliu Publishing Co., Ltd., (1990).
Payne, B. W. *"How ART Can Make you Happy,"* Publisher: Outflow Edition Enterprise Co., Ltd., (2018).
Rieger K., Schultz ASH (2014). Exploring art-based knowledge transfer: sharing research findings by executing models, rehearsing results, and synthesizing them. *Evidence-Based Nursing Worldview*, 11(2), 133–139. https://doi.org/10.1111/wvn.12031

### 2. CHINESE LITERATURE

Aristotle (2011) *Poetics, Publisher: CITIC Culture Publishing House.*
Fu, P. (2002) *Transfer to the Peak of Life*, Publisher: Taipei, Tianxia Culture Co. Ltd.
Jiang, X. (2011) *Beauty, Invisible Competitiveness*, Publisher: CITIC Culture Publishing House.
Kandinsky (2013), translated by Yu Minling, *"Spirit in Art,"* Reliance Cultural Marketing Co. Ltd.
Moon, B. L. (2011) *Using Paintings as Mirrors—Existential Art Therapy*, Publisher: Mr. Zhang Cultural Enterprise Co., Ltd.
Olson, R. (1982) *Creation and Life*, Publisher: Yuanliu Publishing Co., Ltd.
Peng, L. H. (2008) Using Third Space Theory to Understand Sonia Delaunay's Design Practice and to Facilitate Taiwan's New Cultural Identity, *International Journal of Art Education*, from: https://ed.arte.gov.tw/uploadfile/periodical/1989_arts_education61_173188.pdf
Wang, X. (2016) *Theory and Practice of Art Therapy,"* Publisher: Hongye Culture Co., Ltd.
Wu, M. (2010) *From Art Therapy to Art Educational Therapy in "Into the Door of Hope,"* Publisher: Teacher Zhang Cultural Affairs Industry Co., Ltd.,.
Xu, W. (2021) *Jungian Approach to Art Therapy-Therapeutic Principles and Effects*, Hongye Cultural Enterprise Limited company.
Zhu, G. (2011) *Talking about Beauty*, Publisher: CITIC Culture Publishing House,.

System Innovation for a Troubled World – Lam et al. (Eds)
© 2024 the Author(s), ISBN: 978-1-032-60846-4

# Computer generated art: Exploring the application of artificial intelligence in digital art

Lin Xian
*School of Design, Fujian University of Technology, Fuzhou, Fujian, China*

En-Wu Huang*
*School of Design, Fujian University of Technology, Fuzhou, Fujian, China*
*College of Innovative Design, City University of Macau, Macau, China*

ABSTRACT: This article explores the intersection of computer-generated art and artificial intelligence (AI), discussing the application of AI in digital art creation. This paper examines how AI is being utilized in digital art, including its ability to generate unique, abstract, and diverse art forms. This paper highlights the benefits and limitations of AI-generated art, emphasizing the role of human input in shaping and guiding AI-generated creativity. Additionally, this study discusses the ethical implications of AI-generated art, including issues related to ownership, authenticity, and the potential for AI-generated art to replace human artists. The article concludes by noting that while AI-generated art is a promising field, it is important to recognize the limitations of AI and the need for continued human input and creativity in the digital art world. The article's novel contribution lies in its exploration of the application of AI in digital art creation, including its benefits, limitations, and ethical implications.

## 1 INTRODUCTION

Computer-generated art is an emerging form of digital art that uses computer algorithms and programming techniques to generate artwork. In recent years, the development and popularity of artificial intelligence (AI) technology have led to the increasingly widespread use of computer-generated art. This article attempts to explore the application of AI in digital art, especially in computer-generated art. First, the article reviews the origins, development history, and current situation of computer-generated art. Then, the article discusses the analysis of examples of applications of AI techniques in digital art, including generative adversarial network (GAN) techniques, convolutional neural network image generation algorithm Deep Dream, deep learning image generation technique Mid Journey and diffusion model image generation tool stable diffusion in digital art. The article then analyses the strengths and weaknesses of the practical use cases of computer-generated art, considering and discussing the issues they raise. Finally, the article looks at the future trends and applications of computer-generated art. By analyzing and summarizing the applications of computer-generated art and AI in digital art, this article provides new perspectives on

the integration of digital art and AI, which have positive implications for the future development of digital art.

## 2 THE DEVELOPMENT OF COMPUTER-GENERATION ART

Computer-generated art is a subset of generative art. It refers to any art created by a computer or computer-assisted creation, including images, sound, animation, video, games, websites, or interactive artworks that are generated using a computer. It is characterized by its random nature, with the creator having partial, but not total, control over the outcome of the presentation of the artwork. The main forms of computer-generated art include fractal art based on fractal mathematics, algorithmic art that uses programming and algorithms to generate images and graphics, visual mapping that transforms data into visual art forms through computer programs and visualization techniques, interactive art that combines computer programs and digital technology, virtual reality art, 3D printing art and art forms such as AI-generated art.

The chronology of computer-generated art has its roots in the 1960s, when, due to the high cost and size of computers, only universities and corporate laboratories had large computers for scientific computing and data processing. Some of the first attempts at computers and art were collaborations

*Corresponding Author: n5huang@foxmail.com

DOI: 10.1201/9781003460763-34

between engineers, scientists, and artists. Some of the landmark works of this period were Desmond Paul Henry's invention of the Henry Plotter in 1960, which drew early computer-generated artworks, and A. Michael Noll's application of programming for digital computers to generate visual art in 1962, with Georg Nees, Frieder Nake, Manfred Mohr, and Vera Molnár designed the first computer-generated art algorithm that allowed computers to create artworks based on chance. Informationsverarbeitung' (1974) remains a crucial text in the interdisciplinary field of digital media discussing the links between aesthetics, computing, and information theory. Computer-generated art of the period primarily emphasized the collaborative relationship between artists and scientific institutions, a collaboration that fostered innovation and the development of computer-generated art practices.

The rapid development of computer technology from the 1970s to the 1980s led to an increasing number of scenarios in which computers have become ubiquitous in offices and homes. Computer-generated art continued to diversify and take on various forms and varieties, influenced by technological developments, artistic movements, and cultural contexts. During this phase, artists began to explore the use of computers in areas such as 3D modeling, animation, and virtual reality, using mass technical means such as parametric design, evolutionary algorithms, randomness algorithms, and neural networks to generate a diverse range of computer-generated artworks. These works have attracted widespread attention and have also been applied to other fields. At the same time, the artist's dependence on scientific institutions is gradually decreasing, and more and more individual artists can participate in the generation of computer art.

From the 1990s onwards, artists discovered interactive media and virtual reality technologies, while computer animation and CGI techniques began to show in films, such as the sci-fi spectacular Avatar (2009). With the development of deep learning and neural network technologies, AI and machine learning began to be used in computer-generated art, making computer-generated artworks increasingly artistic and original. These include automatically generated digital art, music, and literature, among others.

From a design perspective, computer-generated art transforms the traditional process of making handmade art into a computer program generation based on code and algorithms. Artists use programming languages and software tools to create a 'digital seed' or set of rules and then manipulate these 'seeds' to program various complex, unique, and abstract art forms. Unlike traditional handcrafted art, computer-generated art emphasizes the importance of code and algorithms, requiring the artist's design and manipulation skills. As a result, computer-generated art breaks away from the creative limitations of traditional handcrafted art to create more experimental and innovative works of art. Today, computer-generated art is widely used in a variety of fields such as animation, film, games, virtual reality, and advertising, bringing new forms of artistic expression to these fields.

## 3 THE APPLICATION OF AI IN DIGITAL ART

In recent years, with the continuous improvement of AI technology, various new computer-generated art techniques have been introduced on the trot. Among them, technologies such as GAN, Deep Dream, Mid Journey, and Stable Diffusion have received widespread attention and popularity. Based on deep learning and neural network algorithms, these techniques can automatically generate highly complex, unique, and even surreal images and videos. These computer-generated artworks are not only aesthetically valuable but also highly technical, demonstrating the immense potential of AI technology and marking the dawn of a new era in digital art. A few typical AI-generated art tools are briefly described below.

### 3.1 *Generative adversarial network*

Generative adversarial network (GAN) has received much attention in academia and industry since its introduction by Ian Goodfellow in 2014. GAN is a deep learning model whose principle based on the adversarial training process of two deep neural network models, Generator (G) and Discriminator (D). The basic idea of GAN is to have the generator G generate some fake data and then have the discriminator D determine whether the data is real or fake; the training of G and D is a dynamic game in which they compete and cooperate with each other. When G and D reach Nash equilibrium, the generator G is able to recover the actual distribution of the data. The discriminator D can not distinguish between true and false samples, i.e., the false data generated by G is close enough to the accurate data as D can not accurately judge the difference between correct and incorrect data. It means that after the GAN training is completed, the generator G can generate fake data that is very similar to the truthful data.

GAN has the advantage of generating high-quality, diverse, and continuous data. It can utilize any differentiable function as the structure of G and D, and is not restricted to a specific distribution or factorization, and can also train classifiers in a semi-supervised manner in combination with deep neural networks to improve classification performance using large amounts of unlabelled data. However, GAN also has some drawbacks like an unstable training process, difficulty or failure in convergence, difficulty in handling discrete data, and pattern collapse, which need to be addressed by various techniques and methods.

There are two stages of current research on GAN: theory and application. The theoretical aspect focuses on solving instability and pattern collapse problems on GAN from the perspective of mathematical theory or reformulating the relevant theories of GAN, such as information theory and energy-based models. The application side is devoted to applying GAN to computer vision, using GAN for image generation and transformation (e.g., specifying image synthesis, text-to-image, image-to-image, video, etc.), and applying GAN to NLP and other fields.

### 3.2 *DeepDream*

DeepDream is an image generation algorithm based on convolutional neural networks. By iteratively optimizing specific layers of neurons, DeepDream can turn an ordinary image into a work of art full of illusion and psychedelic sensations. Originally released as a computer vision program by a team of Google researchers in 2015, DeepDream is a model consisting of 10–30 layers of artificial neurons stacked on top of each other. DeepDream is a "machine that can draw automatically", recognizing images and creating them on its own. The works it creates have been auctioned off at several art exhibitions for high prices.

Although DeepDream is artistically creative and artistic, its applications are still relatively limited. It is used more as a research tool. The reason is that the DeepDream algorithm is prone to overfitting when processing large-scale images, resulting in images that are too similar or repetitive and lack diversity. Moreover, the quality of the generated results of the DeepDream algorithm is unstable and requires a lot of experimentation and parameter tuning to obtain satisfactory results. At the same time, due to the high computational complexity of the DeepDream algorithm, it requires a large number of computational resources or the utilization of high-performance computing devices such as GPUs to accelerate the computation to process large-scale images, which requires high computational and time costs.

### 3.3 *Mid-journey*

The Mid-journey technique was presented by American computer scientist and Google engineer Jeff Dean and his team in 2015. The technology aims to speed up the training process of large machine-learning tasks by splitting the machine-learning model into multiple smaller models. During training, each small model takes a portion of the input data and computes an intermediate result, which is combined to produce the final output. The mid-journey technique is widely used within Google and has been used to train large-scale machine learning models, such as the face recognition model in Google Photos.

Mid-journey technology gives the advantage of training in parallel, increasing the speed of training and processing larger-scale data, thus helping machine learning engineers to practice more accurate models faster. Through adaptive difficulty training, Mid-journey can automatically adjust the difficulty of the generated images to make the resulting images more appealing and unique. In addition, Mid-journey can control the features of the generated image, such as color, shape, and texture, by controlling the input vector, unique and innovative works.

Of course, Mid-journey also has some disadvantages. First, the technique requires more computational resources to support the training process, which may lead to higher costs. Second, the technique needs more advanced programming skills to implement complex decomposition and reassembly operations. For large-scale machine learning tasks, debugging may become more difficult because of the need to consider the interaction of multiple small models. In addition, in the Mid-journey technique, different mini-models pass information between different machines, which may lead to communication overheads that affect training speed and require higher network bandwidth and lower network latency. Although the Mid-journey technique is promising for a wide range of applications, it needs further refinement and development.

### 3.4 *Stable diffusion*

Stable Diffusion was proposed by a research team at the University of California, Berkeley (UC Berkeley) in the USA. The group consisted of Dustin Tran, Matthew Hoffman, and David Blei. They published a paper entitled 'Stable Flows: Sampling Long and Stable Paths in Flow-Based Generative Models' in 2020, where they introduced the concept of Stable Diffusion.

Stable Diffusion is a generative model based on flow-based models, where the main idea is to generate data by randomly sampling it during a random walk. In this model, the data considers a probability density function in a high-dimensional space, and the random walk can be regarded as sampling over this probability density function. Stable Diffusion has been widely used in the domain of image generation, speech synthesis, and natural language processing, and has made considerable progress.

The advantages of the Stable Diffusion Model include its ability to handle complex data distributions, generate credible results with high quality and clarity, be more stable compared to traditional GANs, and be interpretable. At the same time, compared to other image generation methods based on the diffusion process, the stable diffusion model takes advantage of deep neural networks to learn high-level features of images and generate more realistic and clearer images. The method also provides a new perspective for understanding the internal working mechanism of neural networks.

The autoregressive model requires iterative computation and is therefore expensive to train and reason about. Despite its good performance in generating high-quality images, the diffusion model still suffers from high computational complexity, difficulties in handling large-scale data, challenges in dealing with unstructured data, and the possibility of the generated results being affected by noise and perturbations. These limitations and problems make their use in practical applications limited and may require post-processing or adjustment to obtain better generation results.

## 4 THINKING TRIGGERED BY THE ART OF AI

AI-generated art brings new possibilities for generative art and has multiplied in computer vision, natural language processing, and human-computer interaction. More and more digital artists are using AI-generated art to generate plentiful imaginative paintings and create a lot of unique artworks through manual processing. The understanding and appreciation of AI-generated artworks can be considered from technical and humanistic perspectives. From a technical perspective, AI-generated artworks are generated through algorithms and computer programs, bringing new forms of artistic expression and visual effects. From a humanistic perspective, AI-generated artworks contain human wisdom and creativity behind them, showing the ways of human thinking and culture. These two perspectives complement each other and contribute to the development and progress of AI-generated artworks.

At the heart of AI-generated art is the concept of the computer as an artist by fostering the 'creativity' of the computer. Machine Learning (ML) is the key to making computers intelligent, and the foundations of machine learning are neural networks and deep learning. Neural Networks (NNs) are early approaches to machine learning, which perform distributed parallel information processing by mimicking the behavioral characteristics of animal neural networks. Deep Learning (DL) is a more recent approach to machine learning, which combines multi-layer structural neural networks with layer-by-layer information extraction and filtering of big data to give machines powerful representational learning

capabilities, and moves machine learning from the realm of technology to the realm of 'ideas'. By invoking an expert system containing a large amount of artistic expertise and experience, it is possible to cultivate the artistic thinking patterns of the machine, thus forming an artificially intelligent "artist" with "artistic self-awareness" and "creativity".

With the continuous advancement of computer processing power and machine learning algorithms, the application of AI technology in digital media art has become an important research direction in the current digital art field. In the light of image processing, AI technology can help artists process image data more efficiently and accurately. In image generation, AI technology can help artists to generate images in various styles. In music composition, AI technology can use neural networks to create new music pieces, and even automatically generate smooth melodies and rhythms. In interactive media, AI technology can be applied to the development of interactive artworks, helping artists with natural language processing and emotion analysis, making interactive media more emotional and interactive. In short, AI technology plays a significant role in digital art, helping artists to achieve more creativity and inspiration.

However, there are some challenges and problems with AI-generated artwork. For example, copyright issues and ethical concerns may arise, as the generated works may be similar or identical to existing works. In addition, as its generation is through algorithms and datasets, there are algorithmic and dataset biases that affect the quality and diversity of the generated works. In addition, AI-generated artworks may lack human emotion, intuition and intent, making them difficult for human viewers to assess, understand, and appreciate. It requires specialized skills and applications and resources to address these issues and challenges. Professor Filippo Fabrocini, an expert in the field of AI, particularly machine learning and the ethics of AI, points out that technology can be both rational and poetic, and that AI as a technology can be an aid to human progress or a "poison". He, therefore, argued that there is now a need to build sustainable AI that is responsible, transparent and fair, and serves the well-being of humanity. He also emphasized that AI should be defined and developed to enrich human life and work.

Overall, the use of AI technology has opened up many new opportunities and challenges for digital art. Digital artists need to continuously learn and apply the latest AI technologies to better more creative and interesting artworks. To improve AI-generated artworks, we can explore more refined algorithms and data sets to improve the quality and diversity of generated works. At the same time, we should also pay attention to the selection and design of algorithms and datasets to avoid the presence of bias and discrimination as much as possible. In addition, we can also combine AI-generated artworks with those of human artists to achieve more innovative and personalized artistic expressions.

## 5 THE DEVELOPMENT TREND OF AI GENERATION ART

As AI technology keeps on developing, AI-generated art will become more intelligent, creative, and unique. Some hold shortly, computer-generated art will become more popular and personalized. More and more people will use computer programs to create their artwork. It will lead to more democratization and diversity in digital art. The following are some of the possible perspectives:

First, computer-generated art will become more widespread and personalized. Thanks to the spread and development of AI technology, more and more people will be able to use computer programs to create their artworks, which will lead to greater democratization and diversification of digital art. As AI technology develops, computer-generated art will increasingly integrate with other technologies to create more diverse and innovative art forms. For example, by combining techniques, such as virtual reality, augmented reality and blockchain, computer-generated art can produce richer forms of artistic experience and interaction. It may even be possible to achieve deep interaction or customizability, enabling viewers to experience and explore artworks in greater depth.

Second, computer-generated art will become more artful and aesthetically pleasing. Although computer programs can generate many complex and abstract images, only works that are aesthetically and artistically pleasing can be regarded as works of art. Therefore, the future of computer-generated art will focus more on aesthetics and artistic expression. As the technology of computer-generated art continues to be refined and improved,

it will make extensive use of fields. For example, computer-generated art will apply in a broad range of domains such as architectural design, advertising design, and game development.

Third, computer-generated art will integrate human culture and history in greater depth. With the development of AI technology and the accumulation of history and culture, computer programs will understand human culture and history in greater depth, thus creating artworks with more cultural and historical connotations. Computer-generated art will also face several challenges, for instance, how to protect the copyright and intellectual property rights of computer-generated artworks, and how to find a balance between art and technology so that technology does not become overly dominant at the expense of artistry.

In conclusion, the future of AI-generated art is full of endless possibilities and challenges, and we can expect it to bring even more enrichment and innovation to the art field. As technology continues to develop and people become aware of digital art, computer-generated art will play an even more crucial role in digital art and contribute to artistic innovation and the development of human culture.

## REFERENCES

Goodfellow I, Pouget-Abadie J, Mirza M, *et al.* Generative adversarial networks[J]. *Communications of the ACM*, 2020, 63(11): 139–144.

Jiaqin J, Cuijuan X. The application frontier of digital humanities in the field of visual art: Image art analytics and computer generative Art[J]. *Libraly Journal*, 2021, 40(6): 101.

Noll, A.M. 1966. Human or machine: A subjective comparison of piet mondrian's "composition with lines" and a computer-generated picture. *The Psychological Record*, 16(1): 1–10.

Rosado P, Fernández R, Reverter F, GANs and Artificial facial expressions in synthetic portraits. *Big Data Cogn. Comput.* 2021, 5, 63.

*System Innovation for a Troubled World – Lam et al. (Eds)*
© 2024 the Author(s), ISBN: 978-1-032-60846-4

# How to apply inundation potential maps in disaster drills

Meng-Cong Zheng
*Department of Industrial Design, National Taipei University of Technology, Taipei, Taiwan*

I-Wen Yen*
*Doctoral Program in Design, College of Design, National Taipei University of Technology, Taipei, Taiwan*

Ching-I Chen
*Department of Industrial Design, National Taipei University of Technology, Taipei, Taiwan*

Yen-Yu Chang
*Department of Design, Division of Creative Engineering, Chiba University, Chiba, Japan*

Chih-Yung Chen
*Department of Industrial Design, National Taipei University of Technology, Taipei, Taiwan*

ABSTRACT: Inundation potential maps show an area's risk over time and with rainfall. However, how they can be used for disaster preparedness exercises and planning evacuation strategies is still being determined.

This study invited 20 participants from Taiwan and Japan to view inundation potential maps of a specific area and conduct route planning under different scenarios. They were asked to make evacuation plans over time when they were stranded in a particular place due to a disaster. We allowed participants to practice their plans in multiple situations and used a self-assessment questionnaire to understand the difference between before and after the use of inundation potential maps. Paired sample t-tests revealed agreement that question "I do not have much disaster risk in my living environment ($p = .014 < .05$)" was significantly lower than in the pre-test. Most participants may have initially overestimated their understanding of disaster risk. Agreement for two questions on the post-test, "I know the inundation potential maps ($p = .014 < .05$)" and "I have used the inundation potential map ($p = .006 < .01$)", increased significantly compared to the pre-test, indicating that practice on each task contributed to understanding the inundation potential maps. The route-planning scenario tasks showed that the inundation potential maps help users change the route planning according to the rainfall condition to avoid high-risk areas. The timeline planning task also allows the participant to list in advance the items that should be prepared for the disaster. The use of task scenarios and timelines can be effective in helping people understand the application of inundation potential maps.

## 1 INTRODUCTION

"Take urgent action to combat climate change, and its impacts" is one of the key goals under the Sustainable Development Goals (SDG) agenda. According to the International Strategy for Disaster Reduction, UNISDR (UNDRR, 2016), "climate change" will change the character of natural hazards and increase the risk of future disasters and losses. As climate change is considered the greatest threat to human society in the coming decades, different regions have different vulnerabilities and demographic characteristics.

Global natural disaster statistics show that over the past 50 years, more than 100 disasters have occurred annually. Most of these natural disasters are hydro-meteorological disasters such as typhoons, tropical cyclones, floods, and landslides (Ritchie & Data 2014). According to the Emergency Events Database (EM-DAT), Asia is the region with the highest number of major natural disasters in 2021, with floods being the most significant disaster. Floods are one of the world's most severe hydro-meteorological disasters causing socio-economic, environmental, and physical damage (Atta-ur-Rahman & Khan 2011; Atta-ur-Rahman & Shaw 2015; Mahmood *et al.* 2019). These impacts will directly affect some vulnerable areas and populations. Extreme climates are so destructive and catastrophic that countries worldwide are taking a

*Corresponding Author: leslie.yen@gmail.com

DOI: 10.1201/9781003460763-35

proactive approach to disasters. In all efforts, identifying and assessing potential hazards in the surrounding environment is essential and challenging, providing decisive information for disaster preparedness and relief planning (Gilbert 2008; Lindell & Perry 2012; Minciardi *et al.* 2009). Constructing climate change based on local events and geography will help bring the issue into sharper focus (Lorenzoni & Pidgeon, 2006). Also, it will promote emotional and cognitive engagement with climate change (Lorenzoni *et al.* 2007; Weber 2006) and will make the benefits of responding to climate change more tangible (Rayner & Malone 1997).

Many countries have produced hazard maps to raise awareness of natural disaster risks. Still, little is known about communicating these maps to the public to facilitate disaster preparedness awareness and response (Maidl & Buchecker 2015). Although most people have heard of disaster prevention maps, few understand the content and application of disaster prevention maps. Lindell and Prater (K. & S. 2000) suggest that the frequency of thinking about, discussing, and receiving passive messages about disasters can alert people to take action to reduce their vulnerability to disasters. Research shows citizens act rationally in the face of disaster and tend to make informed decisions based on the information they receive (Helsloot & Ruitenberg 2004).

This study chooses the inundation potential map as the theme. With the help of its ability to display regional risk and flexible presentation of risk information over time and rainfall, it is possible to understand the possibility of using it in disaster prevention drills and planning evacuation strategies. The public is used as an object to understand the difference in attitudes between the two places before and after using the potential map.

## 2 METHOD

This experiment aimed to understand people's risk perception of disaster prevention and avoidance, their understanding of inundation potential maps, and the influence of Inundation Potential maps on their avoidance strategies. The one-group pretest-posttest design was used to recruit 20 participants from Taiwan and Japan. The following materials were used: 1) disaster risk self-assessment questionnaire, consisting of a 5-point Likert scale (one being "strongly disagree" and five beings "strongly agree.") It was used to assess the change in attitude before and after using the inundation potential maps. 2) 3D Disaster potential maps from Taiwan's National Science and Technology Center for Disaster Reduction (https://dmap.ncdr.nat. gov.tw/1109/map/#), and Kumamoto City Hazard Map (https://hazard.kumamoto-city.jp/sphone. html#) in Japan Collect relevant maps for test

subjects to view the disaster potential map of a specific area and plan the path under different scenario tasks. Tasks included planning for evacuation if trapped in a location due to heavy rainfall and evacuation if trapped in a location due to a long-term heavy rainfall disaster (Figure 1). 3) The Daily Disaster Preparedness Planning Timeline task asked participants to plan for items and plans to be prepared before evacuation according to the timeline and to plan for items to be prepared in a "personal disaster kit." The complete experiment took approximately 15 minutes to complete.

Figure 1. Inundation potential maps which contain the task for participants marking the route planning.

## 3 RESULTS AND DISCUSSION

The paired sample T-test of the pre-and post-test questionnaires shows that the participants in Taiwan and Japan are all significant in the following items. In Q4, "There is no significant disaster risk in my living environment (t = 2.342. df = 19, p = .03 < .05), the post-test agreement (M = 2.9) was lower than the pre-test agreement (M = 3.45). It means that Taiwanese and Japanese participants improved their perception of disaster risk and the possibility of natural disasters after using the inundation potential map. In addition, in Q1, "I know the inundation potential map (t = −2.930, df = 19, p = .009 < .01)," the posttest agreement (M = 3.75) increased compared to the pretest agreement (M = 2.6). Q3, "I have used the inundation potential map (t = −4.188, df = 19, p = .000 < .001)", the post-test agreement (M = 2.55) increased compared to the pre-test agreement (M = 1.35). It indicates that each task's rehearsal helped improve the participants' knowledge and understanding of the inundation potential map.

However, people's attitudes before and after using the inundation potential maps differed from region to region. Taiwanese participants' pre-and post-tests were significant for the following questions: Q1 "I know the inundation potential map (M = −1.70, SD = 1.77, p = .014 < .05)", with a higher agreement on the post-test (4.2) than on the pre-test (2.5). Q3 "I have used the inundation potential map (M = −1.60, SD = 1.43, p = .006 < .01)", with a higher agreement on the post-test (4.2) than on the pre-test (2.5). Q3 "I have used inundation potential maps (M = −1.60, SD = 1.43, p = .006 < .01)", the post-test agreement (3.0) was higher than the pre-test agreement (1.4). The results showed that before and after using the inundation potential map, the participants understood the concept of the inundation potential map and increased their experience in using it.

Figure 2. Shortly after the rainfall started, participant J10 chose the SHORTEST PATH for evacuation path planning.

Figure 3. After three hours of rainfall, participant J10 chose a higher terrain path for evacuation path planning.

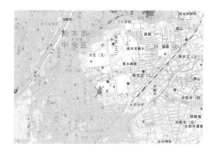

Figure 4. After Seven hours of rainfall, Participant J10 chose to STAY IN PLACE for evacuation path planning.

The Japanese participants were significant in the pre-test and post-test for the following questions.

Q4 "I do not have much risk of disasters in my living environment (M = 0.70, SD = 0.82, p = .025 < .05)", with a lower agreement on the post-test (2.9) than on the pre-test (3.6). Q7 "I know the method of disaster prevention and avoidance (M = 0.40, SD = 0.52, p = .037 < .05)", the post-test agreement (M = 2.5) was lower than the pre-test agreement (M = 2.9). The result indicates that using the inundation potential map increased the risk awareness of the participants. At the same time, the situational tasks reflected disaster preparedness and avoidance activities and made the participants understand the importance of participating in disaster preparedness drills.

Q3 "I have used an inundation potential map (t = −2.449, df = 9, p = .037 < .05)", the post-test agreement (M = 2.1) was higher than the pre-test agreement (M = 1.3), indicating that the experiment helped to improve the participants' understanding of the inundation potential map.

The inundation potential map was learned in the path scenario task to help users change the path planning according to the rainfall condition to avoid high-risk areas. Most participants chose the fastest route to their destination when there was recent rainfall and minor flooding (Figure 2). In the case of prolonged rain and extensive flooding, they would take a detour and choose a higher terrain route to their destination to avoid the risk (Figure 3) or even stay in place (Figure 4).

In addition, the timeline planning task allowed participants to list the items they could prepare in advance (Figure 5). Regarding personal disaster preparedness backpacks, Taiwanese participants would prepare ambulance supplies/drugs, food, water, and flashlights. In contrast, Japanese participants would prepare power, dry food, water, and cell phones, highlighting the difference in the disaster preparedness items that Taiwanese and Japanese people are concerned about during emergency evacuation.

In addition, Japanese participants' agreement in Q8, "I understand the importance of time planning

Figure 5. Tasks demo for timetable planning. The timetable template is from "有備無患" which is the emergency evacuation kit interview result report (AGUA Design & Matinal Design, 2020).

for evacuation (t = −2.714, df = 9, p = .024 < .05)." It is significantly higher in the post-test (M = 3.3) than in the pre-test (M = 2.7). It indicates that the task of time planning positively affects Japanese participants. The result shows that the schedule planning task positively affects Japanese participants.

## 4 CONCLUSION

The "Inundation Potential Map" plays a vital role in disaster risk reduction and adaptation planning in the face of extreme weather caused by climate change and the need to understand how disasters may threaten one's environment. Despite the efforts made by Taiwan and Japan (the government) to promote risk communication for disaster preparedness and avoidance, it is still challenging for people to understand how to receive relevant information.

The results of this study show a general lack of risk awareness among Taiwanese and Japanese people about possible disasters. Therefore, a situational task to simulate disaster conditions can highlight the importance of inundation potential maps. Since participants had to develop their avoidance paths based on several hypothetical scenarios and time lapses, they deepened their understanding of the potential map and practiced its use. The timeline planning task presents a reference to a disaster scenario, prompting participants to think about possible responses and preparedness items and reminding people to prepare a list of personal disaster kits that can last up to 72 hours in advance.

The results of this study confirm the inundation potential maps for use in disaster preparedness drills. The drills are the most effective way to communicate disaster preparedness knowledge to the public, and they are effective in enabling the public to understand the knowledge and application of inundation potential maps. In the future, it is recommended that more exercises on inundation potential maps be conducted to help the public develop disaster preparedness and response capabilities to enhance disaster knowledge and risk awareness for all.

## ACKNOWLEDGEMENT

Special Thanks to The Sumitomo Foundation for supporting investigations of this study.

## REFERENCES

AGUA Design, & Matinal Design. (2020). 有備無患. https://www.matinaldesign.com/ohhhh

Atta-ur-Rahman, & Khan, A. N. (2011). Analysis of flood causes and associated socio-economic damages in the Hindukush region. *Natural Hazards*, 59(3), 1239–1260. https://doi.org/10.1007/S11069-011-9830-8/TABLES/9

Atta-ur-Rahman, & Shaw, R. (2015). *Floods in the Hindu Kush Region: Causes and Socio-Economic Aspects*. 33–52. https://doi.org/10.1007/978-4-431-55242-0_3

Gilbert, R. B. (2008). *Our Role as Engineers in Mitigating Natural Hazards*. 1–16. https://doi.org/10.1061/40971(310)1

Helsloot, I., & Ruitenberg, A. (2004). Citizen response to disasters: a survey of literature and some practical implications. *Journal of Contingencies and Crisis Management*, 12(3), 98–111. https://doi.org/10.1111/J.0966-0879.2004.00440.X

K., L. M., & S., P. C. (2000). Household Adoption of seismic hazard adjustments: a comparison of residents in two states. *International Journal of Mass Emergencies and Disasters*, 18(2), 317–338. http://www.safetylit.org/citations/index.php?fuseaction=citations.viewdetails&citationIds[]=citjournalarticle_55981_4

Lindell, M. K., & Perry, R. W. (2012). The protective action decision model: theoretical modifications and additional evidence. *Risk Analysis*, 32(4), 616–632. https://doi.org/10.1111/J.1539-6924.2011.01647.X

Lorenzoni, I., Nicholson-Cole, S., & Whitmarsh, L. (2007). Barriers perceived to engaging with climate change among the UK public and their policy implications. *Global Environmental Change*, 17(3–4), 445–459. https://doi.org/10.1016/J.GLOENVCHA.2007.01.004

Lorenzoni, I., & Pidgeon, N. F. (2006). Public views on climate change: European and USA perspectives. *Climatic Change* 2006 77:1, 77(1), 73–95. https://doi.org/10.1007/S10584-006-9072-Z

Mahmood, S., Rahman, A. ur, & Sajjad, A. (2019). Assessment of 2010 flood disaster causes and damages in district Muzaffargarh, Central Indus Basin, Pakistan. *Environmental Earth Sciences*, 78(3), 1–11. https://doi.org/10.1007/S12665-019-8084-8/TABLES/6

Maidl, E., & Buchecker, M. (2015). Raising risk preparedness by flood risk communication. *Natural Hazards and Earth System Sciences*, 15(7), 1577–1595. https://doi.org/10.5194/NHESS-15-1577-2015

Minciardi, R., Sacile, R., & Trasforini, E. (2009). Resource allocation in integrated preoperational and operational management of natural hazards. *Risk Analysis*, 29(1), 62–75. https://doi.org/10.1111/J.1539-6924.2008.01154.X

Rayner, S., & Malone, E. L. (1997). Zen and the art of climate maintenance. *Nature* 1997 390:6658, 390(6658), 332–334. https://doi.org/10.1038/36975

Ritchie, H., & Data, M. R. (2014). Natural disasters. *Ourworldindata.Org*. https://ourworldindata.org/natural-disasters?fbclid=IwAR2C1uQR2N1_jegLjxUHjMuLP_ClFJMz5CHdLuSf5ce9L46yQxe9Ls0H1OE

UNDRR. (2016). *UNISDR Annual Report 2015*. https://reliefweb.int/report/world/unisdr-annual-report-2015?gclid=CjwKCAiAxP2eBhBiEiwA5puhNQFbygOBpWBHDXeQN8KwXNg5Ld-zIacm8mvsrHsprjuS9Rj1mzJGsRoC7foQAvD_BwE

Weber, E. U. (2006). Experience-based and description-based perceptions of long-term risk: Why global warming does not Scare us (Yet). *Climatic Change* 2006 77:1, 77(1), 103–120. https://doi.org/10.1007/S10584-006-9060-3

*System Innovation for a Troubled World – Lam et al. (Eds)*
© 2024 the Author(s), ISBN: 978-1-032-60846-4

# HoloLens project for job teaching made for LeadWell CNC machines Mfg., Corp.

Liang-Yin Kuo*
*Smart Machinery and Intelligent Manufacturing Research Center, National Formosa University, Hu-Wei, Yunlin, Taiwan*
*Department of Multimedia Design & Institute of Digital Content and Creative Industries, National Formosa University, Hu-Wei, Yunlin, Taiwan*

Jheng-Kai Ciou*
*Department of Multimedia Design & Institute of Digital Content and Creative Industries National Formosa University, Huwei Township, Yunlin, Taiwan*

ABSTRACT: The purpose of this thesis is to use HoloLens2 to develop interactive employee training content by taking advantage of the opportunity for LeadWell machinery company to entrust project production. HoloLens2 is a mixed reality tool developed by Microsoft, which can interact with virtual objects by grabbing, clicking, and dragging without any auxiliary props. HoloLens can quickly scan the user's surrounding environment and create a virtual space environment with spatial information, allowing users to combine virtual objects with natural objects through HoloLens2 while visualizing the surrounding environment and capturing any virtual object place it on the desktop of reality. Mixed reality technology can help to use a simple space environment to cooperate with virtual reality to generate objects, and achieve the purpose of using equal-scale virtual tools and machinery in open spaces for staff training, thereby reducing space and energy consumption.

*Keywords*: Mixed reality, Hololens2, virtual space, virtual reality

## 1 INTRODUCTION

Since 2020, I have been exposed to the fields of mixed reality and augmented reality such as AR, VR, XR, etc., and during this time I have been exposed to Microsoft HoloLens (HoloLens).

During the research process of HoloLens, I learned that this equipment is capable of simulating and presenting objects and interacting with virtual scenes. LeadWell CNC Machines Mfg., Corp. (LeadWell) also saw this part and contacted me through the Professor of the National Formosa University Multimedia Design Department Kuo, Liang-Yin. This started the development of a project to build a virtual staff training facility using HoloLens2 experimental results provided further evidence for our proposed mechanism.

## 2 LITERATURE REVIEW

Mixed reality is an important trend in the development of science and technology in the future.

Through the cooperative development of mixed reality equipment and industry, the functions required by the industry are developed, the requirements required by the industrial field are known, and the complete function development process is obtained with experience stacking, so as to obtain important development information needed in the field of mixed reality,

This study, through cooperation with LeadWell, records the information and design rules obtained in the development process of the mixed reality staff training virtual field developed by the company.

### 2.1 *Mixed reality*

Merge the real world with the virtual world to create a new environment and a virtual image that conforms to general visual cognition, in which objects in the real world can coexist with objects in the digital world and be generated in real-time interactive.

### 2.2 *Visual system*

Three types of cone cells stimulated by light generate an impulse that travels to the visual cortex of the brain. The three kinds of cone cells have

*Corresponding Authors: g9330808@gmail.com and 30948131@gm.nfu.edu.tw

different photosensitive curves, so they can combine a variety of different feelings in the visual cortex, and different feelings lead to the perception of different colors.

Color is purely a perception of the eye; that is, color is a perception produced by the brain, not in our environment.

The cognition of color is learned from acquired learning, not innate.

Stereoscopic vision is derived from binoculars or dynamic information.

Stereoscopic vision is also acquired, not innate. [1]

## 2.3  Visual blind spot

The blind spot is where the optic nerve crosses the retina to connect to the brain. The tubes of nerve cells that make up the optic nerve create a "hole" in the retina where there are no photoreceptors to detect light, so there is a small portion of our visual field that we cannot perceive. This retinal design, which creates a blind spot in our field of vision, is known by experts as an inverted eye.

The blind spot is located approximately 15 degrees nasally from the fossa.

Healthy people usually don't notice this lack of visual information, as our brain fills in the blind spot based on surrounding details, information from the other eye, and various image calculations produced by eye movements [2].

## 2.4  Mixed reality devices

Microsoft HoloLens is an augmented reality (AR)/ mixed reality (MR) headset developed and manufactured by Microsoft. HoloLens runs the Windows Mixed Reality platform under the Windows 10 operating system. Some of the positional tracking technology used in HoloLens can trace its lineage to the Microsoft Kinect, an accessory for Microsoft's Xbox game console that was introduced in 2010 [3].

## 2.5  Mixed reality development tools

Unity is a cross-platform game engine developed by Unity Technologies, first announced and released as a Mac OS X game engine at the Apple Worldwide Developers Conference in June 2005. The engine has been gradually extended to support various desktop, mobile, console, and virtual reality platforms.

It is especially popular for iOS and Android mobile game development, is considered easy to use for beginner developers, and is popular for indie game development.

The engine can be used to create three-dimensional (3D) and two-dimensional (2D) games, as well as interactive simulations and other experiences [5–7].

## 2.6  Common virtual interface components

A button gives the user a way to trigger an immediate action. It is one of the most foundational components in mixed reality.

MRTK provides various types of button prefabs.

**PressableButtonHoloLens2**

HoloLens 2 shell-style button with a backplate supports various visual feedback such as border light, proximity light, and compressed front plate [8].

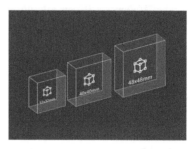

Figure 1.  (Microsoft Build, Buttons—MRTK2, May 23–25, 2023).

**PressableButtonHoloLens2_32x96**
Wide HoloLens 2 shell-style button 32 × 96mm

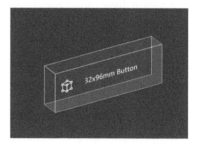

Figure 2.  (Microsoft Build, Buttons—MRTK2, May 23–25, 2023).

**PressableButtonHoloLens2Bar3H**
Horizontal HoloLens 2 button bar with shared backplate

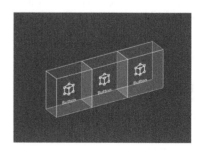

Figure 3.  (Microsoft Build, Buttons—MRTK2, May 23–25, 2023).

**PressableButtonHoloLens2Bar3V**
Vertical HoloLens 2 button bar with shared backplate

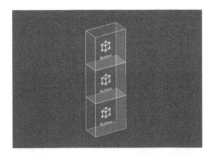

Figure 4. (Microsoft Build, Buttons—MRTK2, May 23–25, 2023).

**PressableButtonHoloLens2ToggleCheck
Box_32x96**
HoloLens 2 shell-style checkbox 32 × 96mm

Figure 5. (Microsoft Build, Buttons—MRTK2, May 23–25, 2023).

**ButtonHoloLens1**
HoloLens 1st gen's shell-style button

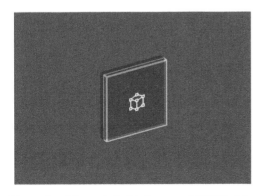

Figure 6. (Microsoft Build, Buttons—MRTK2, May 23–25, 2023).

*2.6.1  Interaction states*
In the idle state, the button's front plate is not visible. As a finger approaches or a cursor from gaze input targets the surface, the front plate's glowing border becomes visible. There is additional highlighting of the fingertip position on the front plate surface.

When pushed with a finger, the front plate moves with the fingertip. When the fingertip touches the surface of the front plate, it shows a subtle pulse effect to give visual feedback of the touch point.

In HoloLens 2 shell-style button, there are many visual cues and affordances to increase the user's confidence in interaction.

The subtle pulse effect is triggered by the pressable button, which looks for ProximityLight(s) that live on the currently interacting pointer. If any proximity lights are found, the ProximityLight. Pulse method is called, which automatically animates shader parameters to display a pulse. [8]

**Proximity light**

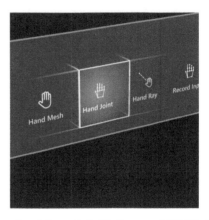

Figure 7. (Microsoft Build, Buttons—MRTK2, May 23–25, 2023).

**Focus highlights**

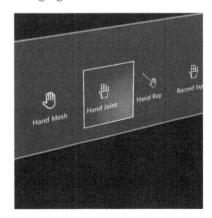

Figure 8. (Microsoft Build, Buttons—MRTK2, May 23–25, 2023).

**Compressing cage**

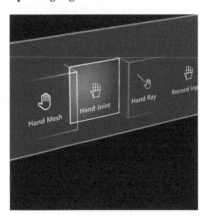

Figure 9. (Microsoft Build, Buttons—MRTK2, May 23–25, 2023).

**Pulse on trigger**

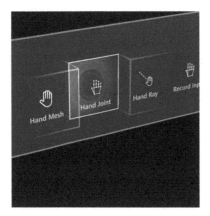

Figure 10. (Microsoft Build, Buttons—MRTK2, May 23–25, 2023).

### 2.6.2 *Hand menu*

Hand menus allow users to quickly bring up hand-attached UI for frequently used functions.

To prevent false activation while interacting with other objects, the hand menu provides options such as "Require Flat Hand" and "Use Gaze Activation." It's recommended to use these options to prevent unwanted activation [8].

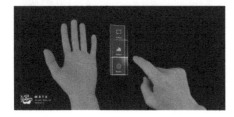

Figure 11. (Microsoft Build, Buttons—MRTK2, May 23–25, 2023).

### 2.6.3 *Scrolling object collection—MRTK2*

The MRTK scrolling object collection is a UX component that enables the scrolling of 3D content through a contained viewable area. The scrolling movement can be triggered by near or far input interaction and by discrete pagination. It supports both interactive and non-interactive objects [8].

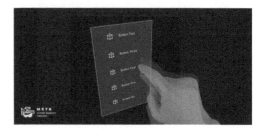

Figure 12. (Microsoft Build, Buttons—MRTK2, May 23–25, 2023).

### 2.6.4 *Near menu—MRTK2*

Near Menu is a UX control that provides a collection of buttons or other UI components.

It is floating around the user's body and easily accessible anytime. Since it is loosely coupled with the user, it does not disturb the user's interaction with the target content. The user can use the "Pin" button to world-lock/unlock the menu. The menu can be grabbed and placed at a specific position [8].

Figure 13. (Microsoft Build, Buttons—MRTK2, May 23–25, 2023).

**Interaction behavior**

Tag-along: The menu follows you and stays within a 30–60 cm range from the user for near interactions.

Pin: Using the "Pin" button, the menu can be world-locked and released.

Grab and move: The menu is always grabbable and movable. Regardless of the previous state, the menu will be pinned (world-locked) when grabbed and released. There are visual cues for the grabbable area. They are revealed on hand proximity.

Figure 14. (Microsoft Build, Buttons—MRTK2, May 23–25, 2023).

### 2.6.5 Bounds control—MRTK2

BoundsControl is the new component for manipulation behavior, previously found in BoundingBox. Bounds control makes several improvements and simplifications in setup and adds new features.

This component is a replacement for the bounding box, which will be deprecated.

The BoundsControl.cs script provides basic functionality for transforming objects in mixed reality.

A bounds control will show a box around the hologram to indicate that it can be interacted with.

Handles on the corners and edges of the box allow scaling, rotating, or translating the object.

The bounds control also reacts to user input. On HoloLens2, for example, the bounds control responds to finger proximity, providing visual feedback to help perceive the distance from the object.

All interactions and visuals can be easily customized.

Figure 15. (Microsoft Build, Buttons—MRTK2, May 23–25, 2023).

## 3 RESEARCH METHODS

### 3.1 Data collection

Through Internet inquiries, book searches, past case analysis, and customer discussions, we can obtain information on the method and type of the required function to confirm that the program is complete, use the information provided by the official website to find the direction of function development, and confirm the required prepared software plugins.

### 3.2 Environment

This project uses Unity to build the project environment, put the MRTK kit into Unity to create the environment required for transcoding HoloLens in Unity, use VisualStudio to transfer out the HoloLens input file after completing the project, connect HoloLens to the computer and use VisualStudio to put the input file into HoloLens.

### 3.2.1 Create project

Use Unity3D to create a new project folder

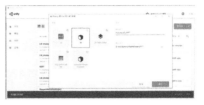

(Source: this study)

### 3.2.2 Put MRTK Kit in the project

In this project, we chose to use Legacy XR to make the whole Project.

(Source: this study)

### 3.2.3 Convert platform to universal windows platform (UWP)

The UWP platform is a dedicated input platform made by Windows developed specifically for HoloLens.

(Source: this study)

181

### 3.3 Modeling

Use Blender to make the scale model of the field, prepare the six-sided texture of the model in Adobe Photoshop, use the UV map and Blender to paste the texture on the simple model, and create a low-polygon model with a complex visual sense to replace the hard surface model provided by the customer, reducing HoloLens performance consumption.

#### 3.3.1 UV Texture

Use Photoshop to draw a six-angle plane map.

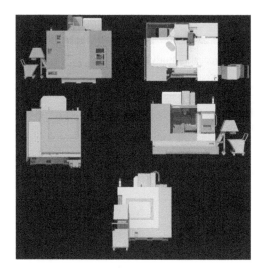

(Source: this study)

#### 3.3.2 Low poly model coloring

Use low-polygon models with coloring and light source calculations to create a deep visual sense of the model.

(Source: this study)

#### 3.3.3 Comparison of model modelling results

When we put the hard surface model provided by the customer into the HoloLens running, HoloLens will not be able to afford it due to the high number of points, lines, and surfaces, therefore, we decided to replace the hard surface model

with a simple low-poly model to reduce the calculation of HoloLens low energy consumption, using light sources and depth calculations to create visual effects

The hard surface model provided by the customer (Source: this study)

Low-poly model remake results (Source: this study)

### 3.4 Scenes switcher

In this project, it is necessary to switch between different scenes in HoloLens through buttons.

We write a script to catch the sequence number of scenes in Unity and use the method of catching scene number information to specify the scene that can be jumped to by the button.

#### 3.4.1 Select a button to open properties

(Source: this study)

### 3.4.2 *Specify scenesswitcher in the property bar to capture the conversion script of the specified scene*

(Source: this study)

### 3.4.3 *Script explanation*

The following is one of the scripts in ScenesSwitchers:using System.Collections;

using System.Collections.Generic;
using UnityEngine;
using UnityEngine.SceneManagement;

public class ScenesSwitcher: MonoBehaviour
{
    public void ShowData()
    {
        SceneManager.LoadScene(SceneManager.GetActiveScene().buildIndex + 1);
    }
}

Through the code, we can see that we use addition and subtraction to increase or decrease the displayed number.

When more than two or more scenes are switched to each other, you can use the button to choose the number of additions and subtractions to obtain the addition and subtraction results and represent the scene represented by the answer.

## 4 RESULTS AND DISCUSSION

Through this experience, we have gained the following experience:

1. HoloLens has a complete function database, and you can find the required functions through the webpage during the development process.

2. Since most of the time customers do not know the amount of information that HoloLens can bear, it is necessary to discuss with customers a lot to understand customer needs, provide customer suggestions according to the results we can foresee, and discuss results that can be produced and accepted by customers.

3. Since HoloLens lacks functional codes, such as scene conversion, model depth calculation, and light source calculation, it can be put into HoloLens through the light source and depth calculation data provided by Unity itself, but it must be produced in the traditional XR environment (Legacy XR).

4. Even with simple button functions combined with Unity model animation, an amazing virtual model look-around function can be created in the HoloLens environment.

5. The virtual staff training manual made by HoloLens can reduce the actual consumption of paper, increase the convenience of repeated use and portability, and can be used following various fields and user habits.

## REFERENCES

[1] Prof. Din-Chang Tseng Inst. CSIE, Nat'l Central Univ. (Sep.2021 ~ Jan.2022) "*Image Processing*".

[2] Zeiss(Oct.16, 2017) "Mysteries of the Human Eye – From Blind Spot and Macular Spot to Central and Peripheral Vision" Edme Mariotte (1620~1684, Dijon, France)

[3] Mcbride, Sarah (May 23, 2016). "With HoloLens, Microsoft aims to avoid Google's mistakes". *Reuters*. Retrieved May 23, 2016.

[4] Dealessandri, Marie (Jan 16, 2020). "What is the best game engine: is Unity right for you?". *GamesIndustry.biz*. Gamer Network.

[5] Axon, Samuel (Sep. 27, 2016). "Unity at 10: For better—or worse—game development has never been easier". *Ars Technica*. Archived from the original on October 5, 2018. Retrieved October 17, 2018.

[6] Takahashi, Dean (Sep 15, 2018). "John Riccitiello Q&A: How Unity CEO views Epic's Fortnite success". VentureBeat. Archived from the original on September 17, 2018. Retrieved October 17, 2018.

[7] Microsoft Build, Buttons — MRTK2(Microsoft Build, Buttons — MRTK2, May 23–25, 2023)

*System Innovation for a Troubled World – Lam et al. (Eds)*
*© 2024 the Author(s), ISBN: 978-1-032-60846-4*

# Mobile learning use of smartphones in the post-pandemic era

Siu-Tsen Shen*
*Department of Multi-media Design, National Formosa University, Hu-Wei, Yunlin, Taiwan*

Stephen D. Prior
*Aeronautics, Astronautics and Computational Engineering, The University of Southampton, Hampshire, Southampton, United Kingdom*

ABSTRACT:   Mobile learning in higher education is relatively new and has only been studied over the last 15 years. The outcomes of the existing literature (2007–22) are scattered in several directions: Self-Regulated Learning (SRL), Open Educational Practices (OEP), and Open Educational Resources (OER). During the COVID-19 pandemic, educational institutions were forced to adopt mobile learning strategies when schools, colleges and universities were closed. The authors have established what they term the $A^6$ use metric to measure students' and teachers' performance in higher education based on their experiences and observations of: (i) Accessibility – representing the capacity of network technology; (ii) Affordability – representing the cost of ownership of smartphones/tablets; (iii) Adoptability – representing the individual's buying, downloading, installing, and starting to learn and use; (iv) Adaptability – representing the individual who needs to be able to deal with the unexpected and that which is beyond their experience; (v) Acceptability – representing individualistic acceptance and use of new technology; (vi) Appropriateness – referring to the course design model. The results showed that the majority of the participants (90%) had used their smartphones in an online learning situation. It indicated that three-quarters of the participants (75%) adapted and adopted well in terms of using their smartphones/tablets for learning and teaching. The reasons given included that they could save time and money by traveling to the campus. However, the disadvantages were the unexpected disruption of unstable networks, and the screen size of the smartphones/tablets that was rather small compared to their laptops. The reluctance to download the required reading materials for students was due to the limited memory of their smartphones or if the files were too large. Furthermore, half of the participants (50%) considered the online learning environment to be the same as the real classroom setting. Future research may involve building a new meta-verse classroom with the use of virtual reality and augmented reality sets to facilitate mobile learning and teaching pedagogy that will be employed in the context of a subject area within the Department of Multimedia Design at National Formosa University in Taiwan.

## 1   INTRODUCTION

According to Statista (2023), the number of internet users in Taiwan was 21.7 million (91% penetration rate) for this small island population. Taiwanese people, on average, spend over eight hours per day using the internet (Statista 2023). This will serve as an interesting starting point to investigate smartphone teaching and learning in higher education.

This study investigated the use of smartphone devices in the post-pandemic era in terms of teaching and learning within higher education in Taiwan. The study hypothesis (H1) states that Taiwanese university students' reliance on their own smartphone devices for learning has had a positive effect

on their campus life. The study hypothesis (H2) states that Taiwanese university students and teachers will adapt well to teaching and learning through their smartphones. The study hypothesis (H3) states that Taiwanese university students and teachers will have a wide acceptance of mobile teaching and learning as pedagogical tools in higher education with their smartphone devices.

The study hypothesis (H4) states that all university courses are appropriate for mobile teaching and learning. The user trial consisted of 331 students (UG, MSc, and PhD) and 7 teachers in higher education, with an equal number of males and females.

The $A^6$ user metric model will be carefully measured and analyzed. Based on the results of the studies, adaptable design methods and general design guidelines will be proposed. Future research may use a new meta-verse classroom to facilitate

*Corresponding Author: stshen@nfu.edu.tw

DOI: 10.1201/9781003460763-37

mobile learning and teaching pedagogy that will be employed in the context of a subject area within the Department of Multimedia Design at National Formosa University (NFU) in Taiwan.

## 2 LITERATURE REVIEW

Several researchers have discussed how to keep learners motivated and engaged during this long period of online learning. Huang, Liu, Tlili, Knyazeva, Chang, Zhang, Burgos, Jemni, Zhang, and Zhuang (2020) proposed the use of open educational practices (OEP) and open educational resources (OER) to provide engaging and interactive experiences (Huang, Liu *et al.* 2020). In their handbook, they talked about the use of OEP and OER during the COVID-19 outbreak through global vivid stories and experiences, in line with the five UNESCO objectives, namely: (i) building the capacity of stakeholders to create access, re-use, adapt, and redistribute OER; (ii) developing supportive policies; (iii) encouraging inclusive and equitable quality OER; (iv) nurturing the creation of sustainability models for OER; and (v), facilitating international cooperation (UNESCO 2019). They also talked about OER competencies for OEP. This handbook provided guidelines to both teachers and learners to facilitate OEP and OER applications (Huang, Liu *et al.* 2020). Corbeil and Corbeil (2007) did a survey regarding mobile learning readiness amongst students and faculty in their online programs and found that 94% of the students (107) who were frequent users of mobile devices did get ready for mobile teaching and learning, while 62% of the faculty members (29) confirmed their readiness (Corbeil and Valdes-Corbeil 2007). Four years later, Corbeil and Corbeil (2011) did the same survey and discovered that a majority of students (82%) and faculty members (80%) felt ready for mobile learning. Nevertheless, there were 18% of the students and 19.7% of the faculty members who had reservations about their and/or the platform's readiness for mobile learning. It was interesting to note that student readiness dropped by 12%. The reasons to explain these were that some students were concerned with the limitations of the hardware (i.e., small screen size, limited power, high cost, etc.), as well as restrictions on the delivery of some types of content (i.e., Flash, large text files, etc.). Others expressed concerns over the lack of pedagogy and best practices in designing instruction suitable for mobile teaching and learning. Yet, despite these concerns, a significant majority of faculty and students expressed a willingness to explore mobile learning and its potential for enhancing instruction, both in and out of the classroom (Corbeil and Corbeil, 2011).

## 3 EXPERIMENTAL

The rising use of so-called smart devices, with people reporting using them for up to eight hours per day on average, raises concerns about whether these devices are liberating or inhibiting people's productivity. This study will investigate the ownership of smartphones, accessibility, affordability, adoptability, adaptability, and acceptability of using smartphones in learning and teaching in higher education.

The user trial consisted of 338 students and teachers in higher education. After interviewing the potential participants, the selected participants who agreed to share personal information on their smartphones for this research completed a series of questionnaires. Part 1: General Online Questionnaire: 14 Questions; Part 2: Online Learning for Students: 14 Questions; Part 3: Online Teaching for Teachers: 14 Questions).

This research conducted a series of formative studies, including two online questionnaires, both for students and teachers, and interviews, to observe and record users' cognitive behavior and preferences on smartphone learning and teaching in a year-long timeframe.

After interviewing the potential participants, the selected participants who agreed to share personal information on their smartphone learning and teaching for this research were carefully documented.

After an initial analysis of the users' feedback, selected members were called back for further interviews; this was an opportunity to discuss their feelings and overall experience of smartphone for learning and teaching before and after the research.

The $A^6$ user study metric was carefully measured, analyzed, and evaluated. Based on the results of the studies, adaptable design methods and general design guidelines were proposed. Future research may involve building a new metaverse classroom with the use of virtual reality and augmented reality sets to facilitate mobile learning and teaching pedagogy that will be employed in the context of a subject area within the Department of Multimedia Design at NFU.

## 4 RESULTS AND DISCUSSION

Figure 1 shows that, as anticipated, a significant portion of the participants (over 1/3) are using their mobile devices for 5–6 h/day. The Apple iPhone is most prevalent (63%), with the Samsung phone in second place (29%).

In terms of the negative effects of using a mobile device, participants, when asked, stated eye strain (82%), followed by hand/arm strain (33%). Interestingly, participants then mentioned poor

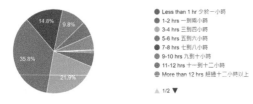

Figure 1.   Mobile   device   use   amongst   study participants.

educational attainment (32%). Clearly, the users are aware of the problems associated with extensive use of mobile devices and their addictive effects when playing games and other apps. The participants then stated the effects of anxiety (18%), stress (15%), and depression (11%).

In terms of the Part 2 questionnaire, almost all the participants (94%) had access to and were using the online learning platform provided by the educational institution. The participants also supplemented the use of these packages with other platforms, such as Google Meets, Teams, Zoom, and Discord (see Figure 2).

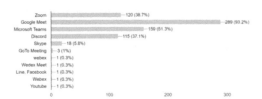

Figure 2.   Supplementary   use   of   other   learning platforms.

Students and staff also used other Social Media platforms both before, during, and after learning sessions. Of particular, such platforms are Line, Discord, and Facebook (see Figure 3).

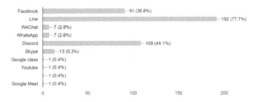

Figure 3.   Use of other social media platforms.

When asked if a network connection problem had occurred during an online learning session, 79% stated that it had. When asked if they thought that this was a platform problem or the participant's own network issue, 70% blamed the platform, with only 58% blaming their own network.

In terms of the participant's network, when asked if the user knew their own network's internet speed, almost 56% stated that they did not. Those that did generally had fast connections with high bandwidth.

For those who didn't know this, a link was provided whereby they could test their network's upload and download speeds. As you might expect, the results were quite interesting and varied widely from over 200 Mbps (upload) and 229 Mbps (download) to just 1.2 Mbps (upload) and 1.6 Mbps (download). This shows the variability of networks, even within a first-world country such as Taiwan.

When asked if they thought that they could concentrate better in an online classroom rather than in a real classroom, the participants responses were very mixed, with 43% stating that it was the same, 26% stating that it was better, and 31% stating that it was worse.

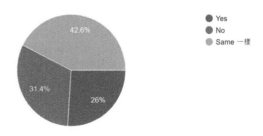

Figure 4.   Preference of the virtual classroom over the real classroom environment in terms of ability to concentrate.

In terms of privacy and engagement, 80% of the survey participants preferred not to turn on their cameras during online learning sessions. This could be due to the desire not to reveal their personal circumstances to the world, a desire for privacy due to their attire at home, or indeed just as a means of avoiding the attention of the teacher. Whether this is for the purpose of not wishing to engage or avoidance of being engaged, i.e., being able to do something else whilst still actively appearing to be paying attention, it is impossible to say.

When asked if their virtual learning experience was the same or different than the real-world classroom experience, 50% stated that it was the same, 18% said it was better, and 32% stated that it was worse.

To highlight three major issues with online learning: connectivity of the network in three ways (i.e., the student's, the teacher's, and the platform's ends), smoothness of online instant interaction, personal engagement such as meeting online on time, and sustained attention over the course of a class.

It is interesting to note that in the UK, a student group civil action is currently taking place, which aims to force universities to pay back a proportion of the student fees due to the so-called lack of engagement and the poor quality of teaching that was given to the students during the COVID-19 lockdown of 2020–21. The outcome of this legal case will have a profound effect on the education sector around the world (Tidman 2020) (Hall 2021).

The majority of the survey participants were happy with their own performance and that of their teachers during online learning.

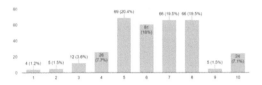

Figure 5.   Judgement of own online performance (Scale 1-10).

Clearly, this was a difficult time for all concerned, and people made the best of it since there were few alternatives. We are now much better placed to learn from this experience and improve things in the future.

## 5   CONCLUSION

This paper has outlined the problems faced by students and teachers during and after the COVID-19 pandemic in terms of teaching and learning.

The virtual online learning environment clearly suits some people better than others. We might label these individuals as insular, introverted, or loners. As humans, we are generally social creatures who engage with and thrive in the company of others.

The COVID-19 pandemic has had a devastating effect on the health and well-being of millions of people all around the globe. The effects of this are only now starting to be seen, with learners lacking primary skills and the ability to socially engage with others.

There is no doubt that the online learning environment has been propelled to the fore due to the crisis; however, there is much to learn from this to enable better engagement and learning interaction.

## REFERENCES

Corbeil J.R. and M.E. Corbeil (2011). "Are we ready for mobile learning now? 2007 Mobile learning predictions revisited." *Issues in Information Systems* **12**(2): 142–152.

Corbeil J.R. and M.E. Valdes-Corbeil (2007). "Are you ready for mobile learning?" **30**(2): 51.

Hall R. (2021). UK students want tuition fees refunded as they face third year online. *Guardian*. United Kingdom, Guardian News & Media Limited.

Huang R., Liu D., Tlili A., Knyazeva S., Chang T., Zhang X., Burgos D., Jemni M., Zhang M. and Zhuang R. (2020). *"Guidance on open educational practices during school closures: Utilizing OER under COVID-19 pandemic in line with UNESCO OER recommendation."* Beijing: Smart Learning Institute of Beijing Normal University.

Statista. (2023). "Number of internet users in Taiwan from January 2012 to January 2023." Retrieved Apr 3, 2023, from https://www.statista.com/statistics/1296415/taiwan-online-population/.

Tidman Z. (2020). University students call for tuition fee refunds amid government 'mistreatment' during pandemic. *Independent*. United Kingdom, Independent.

UNESCO. (2019). "Recommendation on Open Educational Resources (OER)." Retrieved August 8, 2022, from https://www.unesco.org/en/legal-affairs/recommendation-open-educational-resources-oer.

*System Innovation for a Troubled World – Lam et al. (Eds)*
© 2024 the Author(s), ISBN: 978-1-032-60846-4

# AR interactive auxiliary teaching software application-digital basketball basic movement teaching

Liang-Yin Kuo*
*Smart Machinery and Intelligent Manufacturing Research Center, National Formosa University, Hu-Wei, Yunlin, Taiwan*
*Department of Multimedia design and institute of Digital Content and Creative Industries, National Formosa University, Hu-Wei, Yunlin, Taiwan*

Ching-Chun Chen*
*Department of Multimedia Design and Institute of Digital Content and Creative Industries National Formosa University, Huwei Township, Yunlin, Taiwan*

ABSTRACT: In view of the concept of integrating assistive technology into daily life applications and practice in the 108 new curriculum of the Ministry of Education in 2019, and the limitations of traditional textbooks on students' independent learning, this research aims to develop "AR interactive auxiliary teaching software application-digital basketball basic movements "Teaching", and use this software to assist teachers in classroom teaching, and study the differences in its benefits and effects on students' knowledge learning. It is hoped that the application of software can enhance students' interest in learning, learning motivation, learning efficiency, concentration, and memory. In order to make the basic movement teaching of basketball more accurate, this research invites the basketball team students of the National Huwei University of Science and Technology to wear Xsens motion capture equipment to capture the standard movements when playing basketball, and apply them to the 3D character model, and then develop "AR interactive assistance Teaching software application – digital basketball basic movement teaching".

## 1 INTRODUCTION

In recent years, Taiwan's 12-year national basic education has been implemented, and the new curriculum has also been officially launched in 2018. The core qualities of the curriculum include: "autonomous action", "communication and interaction", and "social participation", which are no longer limited to the previous ones. Scientific knowledge, expanding and cultivating students' soft power as the educational goal, developing the spirit of "whole person education", with the concepts of "spontaneity", "interaction," and "community".

Recently, the popularization and convenience of mobile devices have caused many augmented reality (AR) applications to be applied in the educational field. Asai *et al.* (2005) pointed out that AR has become a kind of teaching that can stimulate learning motivation and new trends. It has unlimited development space and potential for the future. If AR technology is used as an auxiliary teaching material in classroom teaching, it will have a very good effect on the learning process and learning effect.

### 1.1 *Research background and motivation*

The dilemma encountered in teaching is that traditional textbooks are usually a one-way tool for transmitting knowledge, and students cannot interact with the them, discuss, or ask questions. Moreover, because of the time it takes to produce, print, and distribute them, the content may be outdated or inaccurate by the time they are published. In addition, it cannot be read electronically or in other formats, providing limiting learning flexibility for students as each student's learning style and learning requirements are different. Traditional textbooks cannot provide video, sound, or interactive elements such as multimedia content, providing insufficient interactivity, flexibility, update, and variety. It can be observed in the teaching site that students often lack learning motivation when they encounter unfamiliar content. On the contrary, students who have experienced the content are usually better able to integrate the content. Improving and enhancing students' learning in response to the above-mentioned difficulties can increase their interest and learning motivation.

In recent years, with the development of AR technology, AR interactive auxiliary teaching

*Corresponding Authors: g9330808@gmail.com and kingyo00147@gmail.com

DOI: 10.1201/9781003460763-38

software has been widely used in the field of education. The characteristic of AR technology is that it can integrate virtual objects into the real environment, and make students more intuitive and vivid in the learning process, improving their interest and enthusiasm for learning. Therefore, this research aims to develop "AR interactive teaching assistant software application-digital basketball basic movement teaching", and use this software to assist teachers in classroom teaching and study the differences in its benefits and effects on students' knowledge learning. Therefore, this study has two purposes:

1. Researching and developing "AR interactive auxiliary teaching software application-digital basketball basic movement teaching".
2. Exploring the application of the functions of "AR interactive auxiliary teaching software application-digital basketball basic movement teaching" such as learning interest, learning efficiency, concentration, memory, and enthusiasm.

## 2  LITERATURE REVIEW

In the era of information technology, traditional books are not as convenient as they used to be. To better attract students to focus on learning, deepen the interest, memory, and efficiency of the subject matter in the learning process, using AR interactive auxiliary application software will be the future trend of classroom teaching. Interesting animations derived from the screens of physical books can be seen on the screen. This study reviews and discusses relevant literature on the research design of AR interactive-assisted teaching applications.

### 2.1  *Augmented reality definition*

AR is a virtual-reality integration technology that adds virtual objects to the real scene, without actually adding them to a real space. Through the camera's image recognition technology and sophisticated image analysis technology, it allows virtual objects to combine and interact with real scenes.

Azuma (1997) defined three characteristics of AR including combining virtual objects with the real world, real-time interaction, and operating in a 3D environment. AR technology can superimpose virtual objects into the real world for real-time interaction and feedback, enhancing real feelings and fun. Combining AR technology with traditional textbooks can subvert the previous teaching methods, making students more lively and interesting in class, and can also improve the learning motivation and learning motivation of low-achieving students. Things such as dangerous

processing plants, special geographical environments, medical anatomy classrooms, historical events, and other things that are not easily accessible can be presented to students through AR technology. As an auxiliary material for the classroom, AR technology can increase the learning effect which helps students to better understand abstract concepts.

### 2.2  *Combining Augmented Reality and Motion*

AR-based sports games use mobile phones, tablet computers, and other devices to capture images of the real world with cameras, and then add virtual game elements to them so that the real world and virtual game elements are integrated to give an immersive gaming experience. The following are some common AR-based sports game:

1. Boxing games: It captures the player's boxing action through the camera of the mobile phone or tablet computer, and place the virtual boxing opponent in the real world, allowing the player to experience the real boxing experience.
2. Rope skipping games: It uses the camera of the mobile phone or tablet to capture the player's rope skipping action, allowing the player to jump on the virtual rope, and at the same time, it can also be matched with the rhythm of the music to increase the fun of the game.
3. Running games: Through the GPS positioning of mobile phones or tablets, players can run in the real world, and at the same time, they can search for treasures or perform tasks on the virtual map.
4. Tennis games: It uses the camera of the mobile phone or tablet to capture the player's swinging action, and place the virtual tennis opponent in the real world so that the player can feel the real tennis experience.
5. Rhythm sports games: It captures the player's body movements through the camera of the mobile phone or tablet computer, let the player dance on the virtual stage, allowing to play the game with the rhythm of the music.

In short, AR sports games usually take the real world as the background, capture the player's actions through the camera of the mobile phone or tablet computer, and then add virtual game elements to allow the player to experience a real sports experience.

The AR production program with the theme of basketball needs to follow the following principles:

1. Realism: The production program needs to reproduce the actual basketball scenes and actions in the virtual world so that players can experience a realistic basketball experience. Through AR technology, virtual objects can be

combined with real scenes to enhance the sense of reality.

2. A sense of precision: Basketball requires precise movements and hand control, so the AR production program needs to ensure precision, allowing players to perform various skills and tactics in the virtual world.
3. Interactivity: The AR production program needs to provide rich interactivity, allowing players to interact with other players or NPCs in the game, increasing the fun and challenge of the game.
4. Adaptability: Basketball involves a variety of scenes and venues. The AR production program needs to be able to adapt to different scenes and allow players to play basketball in different venues.
5. Educational: Basketball is also a kind of physical education. The AR production program needs to combine games and education so that players can learn basketball skills and tactics in the game.

Therefore, in the AR production program with the theme of basketball, it is necessary to reproduce the actual basketball scenes and actions in the virtual world to ensure accuracy and realism, provide rich interactivity and adaptability, and integrate educational elements that allow players to learn basketball knowledge in the game and improve the effect of physical education.

## 3 RESEARCH METHODS

### 3.1 *Gather information*

Collect relevant research from both local and international sources, organize, and focus on analyzing the literature, and develop a research plan in accordance with this.

### 3.2 *Project production and research design*

1. 3D portrait character model production: We used Iclone8 to make 3D character models.
2. Basic basketball motion capture production: National Huwei University of Science and Technology basketball team members are invited to wear Xsens motion capture equipment to capture standard movements when playing basketball.
3. Post-production animation parameters and UI interface design: Adjust action details, dribble animation, and design APP interface and fluency.
4. Design AR interactive auxiliary software applications: Materials were imported into Unity to create AR interactive APPs.

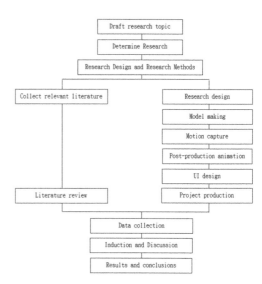

Figure 1.   Research flow chart.

Action Classification Table

| No. | Action name | Iclone scene name | Picture |
|---|---|---|---|
| 1 | Dribble | 005 | |
| 2 | Cross-leg dribble | 006 | |
| 3 | Behind-the-back dribble | 007 | |

*(continued)*

190

Continued

| No. | Action name | Iclone scene name | Picture |
|---|---|---|---|
| 4 | Turn dribble | 008 | 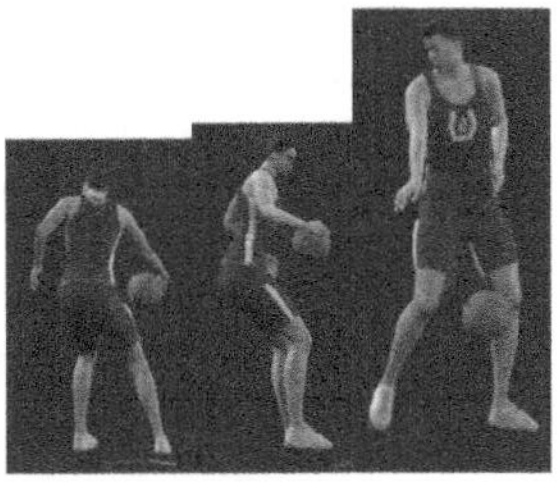 |
| 5 | Lay up | 009 | 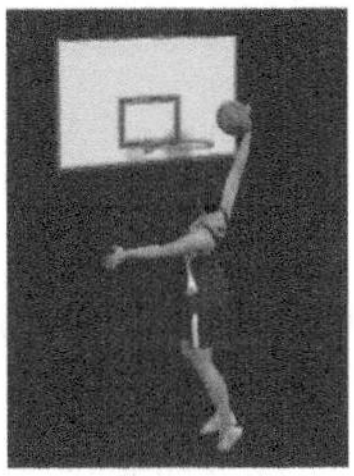 |
| 6 | Dunk | 010 | 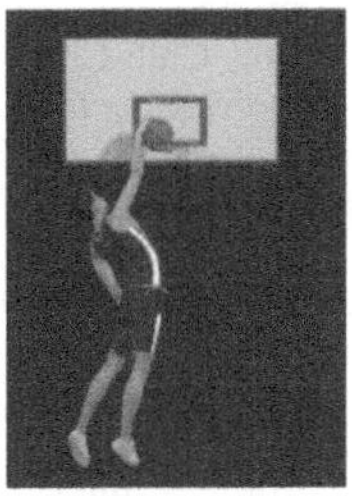 |
| 7 | Free throw | 012 | 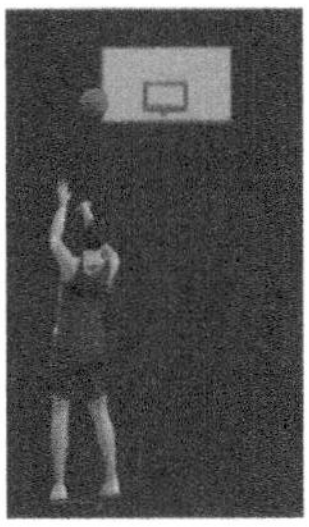 |
| 8 | Defense | 013 | 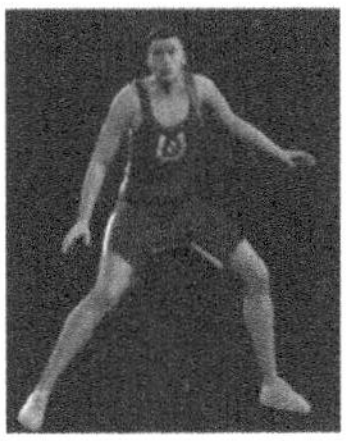 |
| 9 | Pass | 014 | |

(*continued*)

Continued

| No. | Action name | Iclone scene name | Picture |
|---|---|---|---|
| | | | 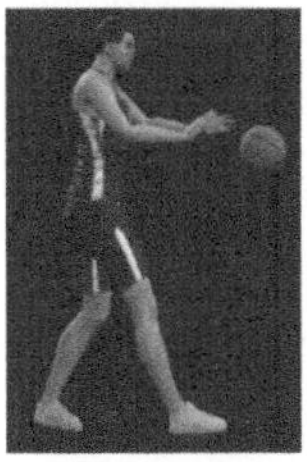 |
| 10 | Rebound | 015 | 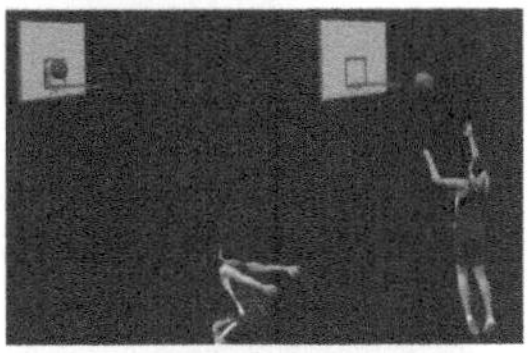 |
| 11 | Catch | 016 | 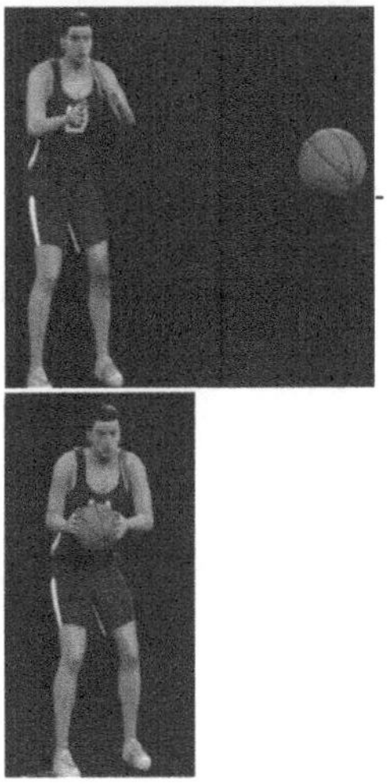 |

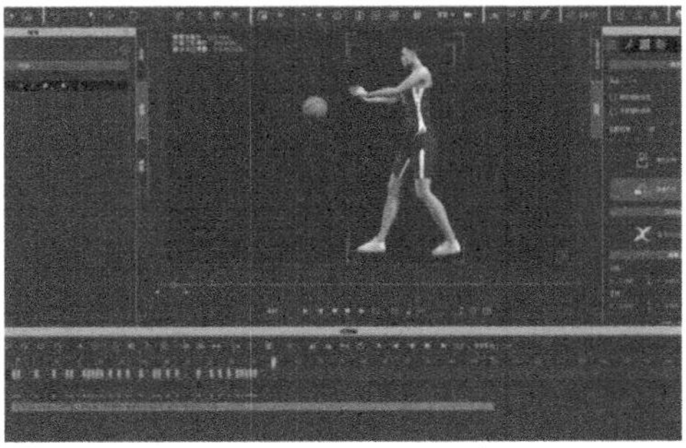

Figure 2. Iclone production screen.

Figure 3.    Motion capture screen.

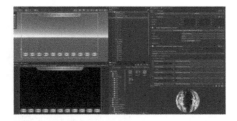

Figure 4.    Unity project production.

Figure 5.    AR interactive assisted teaching application.

## 4    RESULTS AND CONCLUSIONS

With the rapid development and maturity of information technology, the integration of technology into education has become the current development trend. Teachers can use multimedia teaching materials to assist in teaching. Through immediate feedback, image analysis, text, video and audio, animation simulation, etc., abstract objects can be displayed more concretely. In front of students, they are no longer limited to the content of textbooks but can see more detailed pictures and concepts, which will deepen their impression of knowledge and generate learning motivation and interest.

## REFERENCES

Azuma R., A Survey of Augmented Reality, Presence: Teleoperators and Virtual Environments, pp. 355–385, August 1997.

Chao, Wen-Hung, "The Study of Development of Augmented/Virtual Reality Software to Math Volume Study in Elementary Schools", in press.

Chen, Yu-An, "*The Effect of AR & VR Assisted Instruction on Learning Achievement & Attitude in Social Science for Taiwanese Elementary School Students*", in press.

Chiu-Hsia Huang, Chih-Chiang Yang, *To Investigate the Effects of Applying the Interactive Volume AR Assisted Learning Software in Elementary Mathematics Learning*, ISSN(Print), A70, pp.17–34, December 2020.

Chiu-Hsia Huang, Chih-Chiang Yang, Yi-Wen Tsai, *A Survey on User Satisfaction with Interactive AR Assisted Learning Software*, ISSN(Print), A73, pp. 33–56, June 2022.

Huang, Shin-Min, "*A Study of Environmental Education by Integrating AR/VR Multimedia Materials*", in press.

Hung-Wen Ma, 比較虛擬實境及擴增實境的發展趨勢 - 以社群媒體探勘分析" in press.

System Innovation for a Troubled World – Lam et al. (Eds)
© 2024 the Author(s), ISBN: 978-1-032-60846-4

# Design custom 3D VTuber avatar framework based on VRM

Hong Yi Pai* & Cha Yi Lin
*Department of Multimadia Design, National Formosa University, Hu-Wei, Yunlin, Taiwan*

ABSTRACT: With the rapid development of VTuber, VR live streaming provides new services for interactive storytelling and brings business opportunities to Metaverse. However, due to the existing VTuber character generation system, most are based on Japanese art forms. The lack of diverse art design types has caused many drama performances to fail to run smoothly on the VTuber platform. Therefore, this project proposes a framework for generating customized 3D avatars. Based on the perspective of storyteller role-playing in story teaching, the framework defines a 3D model in Virtual Reality Modeling (VRM) format so that the character can be widely used in service platforms that support VTuber roles, such as VRchat or VSeeFace. Taking the character development in the story of "The Little Prince" as an example, this study defines the design process a 3D virtual avatar should have. We hope this research will inform storytellers about creating avatars in parenting education or language learning.

*Keywords*: Virtual reality modeling, Virtual avatar, VTuber, Storyteller

## 1 INTRODUCTION

In recent years, virtual role-plays and interactive narratives have gained immense popularity, and virtual avatars are primarily designed for e-commerce advertising. Successful storytelling requires a harmonious relationship between the storyteller, the story, and the audience (Turner et al. 1997). To address this issue, we have developed the role of a virtual storyteller as a spokesperson from the perspective of "story teaching" for parent-child education. This role is distinct from an internet celebrity or brand endorser for e-commerce product promotion as it establishes a psychological process for story mapping and recognition while effectively conveying the story's meaning (Wu *et al.* 2005).

This paper explores the use of role-playing in real-time by VTubers, focusing on the fairy tale of "The Little Prince". The four main characters from the story include the pilot (natural human), the little prince (natural human), the fox (animal), and the rose fairy (mutant). Those are used as case studies to develop real-time interactive storytelling characters suitable for the fairy tale's content. These characters are distinct from the current Japanese-style VTubers and showcase the quality of artistic creation in illustration design.

To showcase the developed "Virtual Character Live Interactive System," we will use it to present the story. This interactive narrative application differs from traditional game learning, allowing viewers and storytellers to engage in bi-directional

(player/author) interactions through dialogue and real-time interactions within 3D scenes. In addition, we will conduct user satisfaction research to analyze the interests and preferences of viewers in virtual role-playing, empathy, and role preference.

This project presents a framework for creating customized 3D virtual avatars that cater to the development of multiple characters, including monsters or non-comic characters, and conform to the Virtual Reality Modeling (VRM) format. These avatars can be widely used to support the service platform of the VTuber role (VR Chat or VSeeFace).

The process framework of customized 3D virtual avatars is based on the theoretical basis of visual perception (Zell et al. 2019). The process framework of this design mainly includes the following six modules: character concepting module, character design module, character modeling module, character shading module, character rigging module, and VRM formatting module. Figure 1 shows the production framework process for customized 3D virtual avatars

Figure 1. The production framework for creating customized 3D virtual avatars.

---

*Corresponding Author: hpai@ms38.hinet.net

DOI: 10.1201/9781003460763-39

## 2 RESEARCH

In recent years, VTubers have become a popular and mainstream method of online interaction, utilizing appearance materials provided on live streaming platforms to create characters that match users' preferences. These characters can then interact with others online through motion capture technology, promoting emotional communication and audience engagement. As VTuber streaming services gain popularity, the significance of storytellers in captivating audiences through storytelling has increased (Lufkin 2019). In traditional face-to-face storytelling, the speaker's presence and emotional connection with the audience result in a memorable experience. Similarly, in the digital realm, the presence and emotions of the speaker are vital to creating engaging stories (Zhao et al. 2019).

Interactive storytelling can increase the audience's understanding of a story. Interactive games are no longer just a source of entertainment, they now significantly impact society and culture, and they are playing an increasing role in education. Games that encourage interaction have enhanced students' creativity and engagement and provided opportunities to acquire knowledge (Costa et al. 2021).

VRM includes VR, 3D models, 3D space, and timely data entry and archiving. VRM is revolutionizing digital workflow from field to lab postprocessing and timely visualization. Most data sets generated during fieldwork are in a digital format and can easily be migrated between digital platforms. This makes them highly compatible with virtual reality applications (Forte, 2018).

## 3 CHARACTER CONCEPTING

Our customized 3D VTuber avatar framework is designed based on Egri's "bone structure" (1972) for building a three-dimensional character, which consists of physiology, sociology, and psychology. The physiology aspect of our avatar framework includes gender, age, posture, skin, and distinct features, with a focus on posture and unique features. The sociology aspect includes race, religion, occupation, social status, and hobbies, which are primarily reflected in dressing and accessories. The psychological aspect emphasizes personality and emotion, which are mainly expressed through facial expressions and body language.

## 4 CHARACTER DESIGNING

The character design module includes the definition of realism and cartoon, body and facial expression, posture, facial emotion, dressing, appearance, accessories, Props, skin color, and defects. We first analyze the character's art style in the character design process. Next, we focus on their posture and facial expression. Then, we plan the character's accessories, clothing, and other details. By following these steps, we can create a complete character design.

### 4.1 Realism and cartoon

Appearance design style can be largely divided into two directions: realism and cartoon. Realism aims to create a natural and realistic look, while the cartoon exaggerates some features to highlight the character's identity.

At present, most virtual characters on the market are of Japanese origin, and their appearance tends to be more realistic. However, according to a study by Fleming et al. (2016) on body perception, the most attractive appearance style lies between realism and cartoon stylizations. The study sampled virtual characters with various levels of style, from 0% to 100% ranging from realism to cartoon. The results showed that the most attractive look was achieved at 33% styling, followed by 66%.

### 4.2 Character designing

Our character images consist mainly of cartoons that utilize various features to convey the personalities and distinctions of the four characters.

The pilot has dark skin, sharp lines, a narrow upper body, and a wider lower body, emphasizing his convincing and melancholic personality.

The little prince's free-spirited personality is expressed through his disheveled hair, flowing scarves, and well-dressed clothes.

The fox retains its original features such as fur and long ears but wears human costumes to demonstrate that each aspect of the character has been modeled after human traits.

The rose, with its human appearance enhanced by the addition of flowers and leaves, conveys an arrogance, and her phoenix eyes exude confidence. The overall image of four avatars is shown in Figure 2.

Figure 2. The overall image of the four avatars.

# 5  CHARACTER MODELING

The character modeling module explores the relationship between the head-body proportion, skin and gender relationship, level of detail function, dramatic and exaggerated function. We will first discuss the importance of head-body proportions to character, the relationship between character types and discrimination, then introduce the details of character modeling, then finally introduce the methods of character expression and settings.

## 5.1  Categories

In our story framework, characters are divided into three categories: natural people, animals, and mutants. Human characters allow the audience to connect with a realistic portrayal of a person, while animal characters are less likely to promote prejudice such as racial or body discrimination. Mutant characters have metaphorical properties that reflect the relationship between humans and other species. This type of character combines the advantages of the first two, enabling the viewer to eliminate prejudices and better connect with the story. In this particular story, the pilot and the little prince are human characters, representing adult and juvenile males, respectively. The roses are mutant characters, portraying minor females, while the foxes are animal characters with neutral traits.

## 5.2  Head-Body proportions

Artist Polycrites proposed the ideal head-to-body height ratio of seven heads based on his head-to-body ratio theory. Using the head as a reference point to determine the overall height and proportions can confirm that the character's proportions meet this standard (Fleming et al. 2016). Toddlers typically have a ratio of about 4 heads, while children grow up with a ratio of 5 heads. For adults, there is a ratio of 6.5 to 8 heads. Taking advantage of this feature, we changed the pilot proportion to 4 heads, with a top-to-bottom ratio of around 6:4, which makes him look mature and friendly.

## 5.3  Skin and gender

As mentioned earlier, human characters help create a sense of connection with the viewer, while animal characters can eliminate bias issues that can be associated with human characters. In humans, obesity is often associated with laziness, whereas in animals is considered cute and approachable, indicating that animals have a charm that humans lack. For this study, consider the case of roses. Consider the example of the rose in this study. The viewer may not find her attractive if she is designed as an ordinary flower. However, if she is designed as a fairy with flower characteristics, the viewer might perceive her as an elf and find her more intriguing. This approach can help focus the viewer's attention on the character's personalities and dialogue, better understanding their unique qualities.

## 5.4  Level of detail

3D models are typically divided into three levels based on their requirements to achieve optimized performance. In this study, we created a high-polygon model, extracted the details of the high model, baked them into a texture map, and then used the texture map to display the details and effects of the high model. This approach allows us to preserve the sculpted details of the high-polygon model while maintaining the low-polygon model's efficiency. By doing so, we can achieve a high-quality appearance for the model while optimizing performance simultaneously.

## 5.5  Dramatic and exaggerated

People are used to interpreting information about each other from facial expressions. As a result, viewers typically focus on changes in the character's eyes and mouths to understand their emotions. Facial expressions should be adjusted to be realistic. For example, we set phrase values for pilot and fox at 60% and 100%, respectively. Initially, the pilot's expression was set to 100%, which had a dramatic and exaggerated effect but made the person appear unrealistic. The fox is different from the pilot, requiring more over-regulation to effectively convey its emotions. The effects of facial changes at different levels are illustrated in Table 1.

Table 1.  The effects of facial changes at different levels.

| Level | 40% | 60% | 80% | 100% |
|---|---|---|---|---|
| Pilot/ fun expressions | | | | |
| Fox/ fun expressions | | | | |

# 6  CHARACTER SHADING

The character shading module includes the influence of Lighting on visual cognition, the comparison between toon shading and realism, and the understanding of related PBR texture knowledge, such as texturing, detail (PBR), normal, roughness, sculpting, and baking.

## 6.1  Lighting

The lighting effect varies depending on the character's style, and the direction of the light source creates different emotions in people. When the light is positioned in front, the character looks positive, but when viewed from below, it appears more serious and melancholic. To prevent insufficient lighting when the character is in motion, we will incorporate a self-illuminating light source on the character to eliminate moving shadows.

## 6.2 *Toon shading or realism*

The lighting effect varies with the character's style, and the direction of the light source creates a variety of emotions in people ( Rademacher et al. 2001). For example, when the light is in front, the character looks optimistic, but more severe and melancholic when viewed from below. To prevent insufficient lighting when the character is in motion, we will incorporate a self-illuminating light source for the character to eliminate moving shadows.

## 6.3 *Texture*

PBR texture is crucial for achieving authenticity and consistency in objects. It comprises six components: base color, roughness, normal, ambient occlusion, height, and metallic. To refine the finished work on the character's texture map, we use base color, roughness, and normal as control elements. Base color refers to the primary color of an object, while normal mapping simulates concavity details on a plane using light and shadow. Another type, known as a Bump map, only creates a bump effect without the normal deviation caused by uneven surfaces. On the other hand, roughness expresses the degree of light scattering on the surface. We collect the final output maps of the multi-pass channels with the following table in Figure 3.

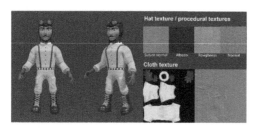

Figure 3. The final output maps of multi-pass channels of the PBR.

## 7 CHARACTER RIGGING

The character rigging module includes binding and skinning analysis, morphing and blend shape definition, and software analysis.

### 7.1 *Binding and skinning*

To save time from manual bone binding, we utilize bone binding software called "AccuRIG" and adjust weights and details according to the character's required action level.

### 7.2 *Morphing and blendshape*

To customize the expressions, we adjusted them through Blender, which mainly includes five types: A, E, I, O, and U, and additional expressions such as joy, surprise, fun, blink, anger, sorrow, neutral, up and down, left and right looks. We then output these expressions to the VRM format. The images below illustrate the blend shape generated results of the facial expressions shown in Figure 4.

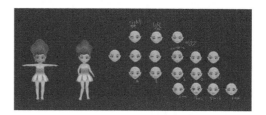

Figure 4. The blend shape generated results of the facial expressions.

### 7.3 *Software analysis*

To complete the customized 3D VTuber avatar framework, we sculpted the character details using ZBrush and exported the textures, which we applied in 3ds Max and Blender. We then exported the model in VRM format to Unity. The final step involved motion capture using VSeeFace, and this completed the entire framework production process.

## 8 VRM FORMATTING

VRM formatting modules include bones setup, blending shape setup, material setup, and animation setup. VRM is a 3D model format that has gained strong recommendation in Japan's VR and VTuber fields in recent years. Based on the 3D standard format glTF2.0, VRM includes specifications and extensions for handling humanoid models. It is intended to be a simplified, interoperable format for 3D assets, with a focus on minimizing file size and processing difficulty for applications.

In the previous chapter on character rigging, we have already explained the bones setup and blending shape setup and will not discuss them again here. Thanks to the VRM standardization of consistent naming and connection methods for the skeleton and expression blend shape, we can now use AI software, such as motion capture (VseeFace), to transmit animation data in real-time and achieve a real-time animation display.

## 9 CONCLUSION

We mainly discuss customized 3D VTuber avatar framework and storytelling and design a different style for the appearance of the virtual characters, hoping that this framework can provide a different suggestion to the community and effectively increase the diversity of the virtual characters. Story teaching is still an area that needs to be developed. In the future, we hope that by playing different roles, we can effectively relate to the characters and accurately convey their emotions and feelings to the audience. Although VRM technology is mature, we must be cautious about subjective features based on our experimental results. These features should be cross-evaluated to demonstrate that the artist has achieved the desired goal. Nonetheless, the customized 3D virtual avatar framework has significantly enhanced many aspects of character design. This framework enables virtual storytellers to offer various learning channels through context integration and increased learning interest.

## ACKNOWLEDGEMENTS

The authors thank the Ministry of Science and Technology for the grant support and to all personnel involved in developing and experimenting with this project in 2022. Project number: MOST 111-2637-H-150-001.

## REFERENCES

Costa M.C., Santos P., Patrício J.M., & Manso A. (2021). An interactive information system that supports an augmented reality game in the context of game-based learning. *Multimodal Technologies and Interaction*, 5(12), 82.

Egri L. (1972). *The art of dramatic writing: Its basis in the creative interpretation of human motives.* Simon and Schuster.

Fleming R., Mohler B.J., Romero J., Black M.J., & Breidt M. (2016, February). Appealing Female Avatars from 3D Body Scans: Perceptual Effects of Stylization. In *VISIGRAPP* (1: GRAPP) (pp. 335–345)

Forte M. (2018). Virtual reality modeling. *The Encyclopedia of Archaeological Sciences*, 1–4.

S.K.M. Jönsson, Birgerson J., Crispin X., Greczynski G., Osikowicz W, Denier van der Gon A.W., Salaneck W. R., Fahlman M., 2003. *Synyh. Met.* 139 1–10.

Lufkin B. (2019). From japanese anime characters to barbie, virtual YouTubers talk and act just like people and they could change the way we all interact forever. Retrieved March, 13.

Pai H.Y. (2019, October). Texture designs and workflows for physically based rendering using procedural texture generation. In *2019 IEEE Eurasia Conference on IOT, Communication and Engineering (ECICE)* (pp. 195–198). IEEE.

Rademacher P., Lengyel J., Cutrell E., & Whitted T. (2001). Measuring the perception of visual realism in images. *In Rendering Techniques 2001: Proceedings of the Eurographics Workshop in London*, United Kingdom, June 25–27, 2001 12 (pp. 235–247). Springer Vienna.

Raiturkar P., Farid H., & Jain E. (2018). Identifying computer-generated portraits: an eye tracking study. *Technical Report*, University of Florida.

Sloan R.J.S. (2015). *Virtual character design for games and interactive media.* CRC Press.

Sungeun Park, Sung Ju Tark, Donghwan Kim, Curr., 2011. Appl. Phys. 11 1299–1301.

Turner T.N., & Oaks T. (1997). Stories on the spot: Introducing students to impromptu storytelling. *Childhood Education*, 73(3), 154–157.

Wu Y.T., & Tsai C.C. (2005). Development of elementary school students' cognitive structures and information processing strategies under long-term constructivist-oriented science instruction. *Science Education*, 89(5), 822–846.

Zell E., Zibrek K., & McDonnell R. (2019). Perception of virtual characters. In *ACM Siggraph 2019 Courses* (pp. 1–17).

Zhao Z., Han F., & Ma X. (2019, December). A live storytelling virtual reality system with programmable cartoon-style emotion embodiment. In *2019 IEEE International Conference on Artificial Intelligence and Virtual Reality (AIVR) (pp. 102–1027)*. IEEE.

# Exploring the efficiency and usability of pet adoption website

Min Wei*
*Department of Industrial Design, National Taipei University of Technology, Taipei, Taiwan (R.O.C.)*

Li-Jen Wang
*Department of Industrial Design, National Taipei University of Technology, Taipei, Taiwan (R.O.C.)*
*Doctoral Program in Design, College of Design. National Taipei University of Technology, Taipei, Taiwan (R.O.C.)*

Meng-Cong Zheng
*Department of Industrial Design, National Taipei University of Technology, Taipei, Taiwan (R.O.C.)*

ABSTRACT: This study analyzed the efficiency and usability of two longstanding pet adoption websites in the United States. We examined users' operational processes through task scenarios, the SUS, AttrakDiff, NPS, and semi-structured interviews. The study found that both websites had errors when using filters to find pets due to unclear prompts and processes. Additionally, the filter options were only categorized based on appearance, not matching people's internal needs for a pet companion, resulting in more time searching. The survey results showed that the SUS scores of both websites did not pass the usability standards, and the NPS scores were negative. In semi-structured interviews, 84.3% of the participants reported that an animal's personality and behavior would affect their willingness to adopt. Therefore, future design optimizations should focus on the usability of filters to improve the efficiency of finding an ideal pet companion.

## 1 INTRODUCTION

The U.S. Pet Statistics 2022 report showed 189.6 million cats and dogs would be in 2023 (IBISWorld, 2022). In 2021–2022, 70% of U.S. households will have a pet, with most cats and dogs in shelters and rescue groups (APPA, n.d.). According to ASPCA, approximately 6.3 million animals are placed in shelters annually. However, due to limited space and care resources, animals were humanely euthanized when they aged or had specific medical problems. Statistics showed that approximately 100,000 cats or dogs were euthanized annually (ASPCA 2019).

Fortunately, studies have found that the number of euthanized animals decreases as the number of animals adopted increases (Rowan & Kartal 2018). This highlighted the importance of pet adoption for animals in shelters. 30% of cat adopters and 36% of dog adopters cited the Internet as an essential source for adopting animals (Weiss et al. 2012).

In Workman & Hoffman's study, it was found that approximately one-third of adopters adopted their pets through Petfinder (a pet adoption website), and half of them had viewed information about their adopted cats on the website (Workman & Hoffman 2015).

In Becerra's study, it was found that website recommendations should consider the human needs of a pet, such as matching personalities and lifestyles. For those who already have pets, attention should be paid to the personality and size of the new pet as it relates to the existing pet (Becerra et al. 2021).

However, the usability of pet adoption websites has yet to be explored. Therefore, this study aimed to analyze the efficiency and usability of pet adoption websites through tasks, questionnaire research, and interviews with existing websites and suggested directions for future optimization.

## 2 EXPERIMENTAL

This study evaluated two pet adoption websites, Website A (Figure 1) and Website B (Figure 2), which have been operating for over 20 years.

The Animal Foundation created website A and has rehomed approximately 200,000 pets between 2017 and 2022. Website B has been operating the largest pet adoption website in North America.

Both websites utilized responsive web design, which means that regardless of the operating system used for browsing, the URL remains the same, and the interface design and interaction remain consistent.

---

*Corresponding Author: zmcdesign@gmail.com

DOI: 10.1201/9781003460763-40

Figure 1.   Website A.

Figure 2.   Website B.

The experimental process conducted the task, questionnaires, and a semi-structured interview with the participants. The experiment occurred in a private and quiet meeting room in a business office in Taipei.

The 32 participants were between the ages of 20 and 60 years old. They were randomly and evenly assigned to use the two websites. Participants were provided with an Apple smartphone (iPhone 12) with a resolution of $2532 \times 1170$ pixels or an Android smartphone (Pixel 6) with a resolution of $2400 \times 1080$ pixels, based on their usual smartphone system.

The experiment consisted of four stages: (1) Participants were asked to provide basic information and share their experiences related to pet ownership. (2) Then, they were asked to complete the specific task. (3) After completing these tasks, participants were asked to fill out the SUS (System Usability Scale), AttrakDiff, and NPS (Net Promoter Score) in that order. (4) Finally, during semi-structured interviews, participants were asked to describe their challenges and problems while interacting with the interfaces.

A task required participants to find a particular pet on the websites and match the task information. The four tasks were: (1) Finding a small-sized, white adult dog. (2) Finding a cat that is friendly with children. (3) Finding a dog that enjoys exercise. (4) Finding a pet that gets along well with cats.

Participants could browse or use filters to find the pets. A reminder would be given if the task was not completed after 1 minute and 30 seconds. If they were unsuccessful within 3 minutes, the task would be considered as failed. During the semi-structured interviews, the participants were needed to browse and interact with another website not used in the tasks. All the interactions observed during the studies and discussions in the interviews were recorded through video and audio. It further aided the researchers in documenting the findings.

In addition, the experiment also assessed the usability of the filters on these two websites. The process lasted approximately 30–50 minutes to evaluate the efficiency and usability of the two websites, helping in future design improvements.

## 3   RESULTS

The results of task operation time indicated that Website B spent less time (Table 1). The average time for Task 2 was lower on Website B than on Website A, with a significant difference (p = 0.034); Task 4 also had a more down average time on Website B compared to Website A, with a significant difference (p = 0.041).

Participants reported in semi-structured interviews that Website B had ten filter options, but Website A only had five options, effectively reducing the time spent finding pets.

In task operations, Website A had only 57.84 % success rate, while Website B had an average success rate of 78.13 %. In Task 1, the number of failures on Website B was lower than on Website A, with a significant difference (p = 0.006)

Table 1. Task performance in all tasks.

| Task performance | Website | Average time (seconds) | M | SD | p |
|---|---|---|---|---|---|
| Task 1 | A | 01.31 | 91.19 | 39.53 | 0.760 |
| | B | 01.35 | 95.69 | 42.96 | |
| Task 2 | A | 02.09 | 129.06 | 51.99 | 0.034* |
| | B | 01.31 | 91.00 | 44.55 | |
| Task 3 | A | 02.10 | 129.06 | 34.71 | 0.452 |
| | B | 01.56 | 116.25 | 57.45 | |
| Task 4 | A | 02.04 | 124.00 | 47.79 | 0.041* |
| | B | 01.27 | 87.31 | 49.24 | |
| Total duration | A | 07.54 | 473.25 | 88.52 | 0.052 |
| | B | 06.29 | 390.25 | 137.80 | |

*Significance is for the following levels: *p<0.05; **p<0.01

(Table 2). Similarly, in Task 2, the number of failures on Website B was also lower than on Website A, with a significant difference (p = 0.036).

During semi-structured interviews, participants who used Website A reported that the options could not be edited when using the filters. They had to perform a new search instead of making edits to the selected options. To make matters worse, clicking the filter options would directly generate search results on Website A instead of using a "Submit" button. This behavior was unpredictable and caused difficulties in operation, requiring additional learning. These factors resulted in spending more time and ultimately led to failures.

Table 2. The number of failures per participant in all tasks.

| Failed tasks | Website | Participant | M | SD | p |
|---|---|---|---|---|---|
| Task 1 | A | 8 | 0.50 | 0.52 | 0.006** |
| | B | 1 | 0.06 | 0.25 | |
| Task 2 | A | 6 | 0.38 | 0.50 | 0.036* |
| | B | 1 | 0.06 | 0.25 | |
| Task 3 | A | 7 | 0.44 | 0.51 | 0.733 |
| | B | 8 | 0.50 | 0.52 | |
| Task 4 | A | 6 | 0.38 | 0.50 | 0.462 |
| | B | 4 | 0.25 | 0.45 | |

*Significance is for the following levels: *p<0.05; **p<0.01

The SUS scores were 49 (grade F) for Website A and 60 (grade D) for Website B, which was a significant difference (p = 0.039). The NPS scores were −41 for Website A and −31 for Website B. People were less likely to recommend these websites to their family and friends.

Table 3. SUS & NPS score for the two websites.

| SUS& NPS score | Website | Score | M | SD | p |
|---|---|---|---|---|---|
| SUS | A | 49 | 49.53 | 14.87 | 0.039* |
| | B | 60 | 60.00 | 12.38 | |
| NPS | A | −41 | 6.00 | 2.28 | 0.314 |
| | B | −31 | 6.69 | 1.40 | |

*Significance is for the following levels: *p<0.05; **p<0.01

According to the AttrakDiff score, Website B performed better in two items (Figure 3). In Table 4, item ATT showed a significant difference (p = 0.005) and PQ (p = 0.013), indicating that participants perceived Website B as more attractive and usable (Hassenzahl et al. 2003).

Table 4. AttrakDiff scores of two websites.

| AttrakDiff score | Website | Score | M | SD | p |
|---|---|---|---|---|---|
| ATT(Attractiveness) | A | −0.31 | −0.31 | 0.68 | 0.005** |
| | B | 0.59 | 0.59 | 0.97 | |
| HQ-I(Hedonic Quality-Identification) | A | −0.38 | −0.38 | 0.59 | 0.193 |
| | B | −0.03 | −0.03 | 0.85 | |
| HQ-S (Hedonic Quality-Stimulation) | A | −0.06 | −0.06 | 1.17 | 0.066 |
| | B | 1.09 | 1.09 | 2.09 | |
| PQ (Pragmatic Quality) | A | −0.77 | −0.77 | 0.62 | 0.013* |
| | B | −0.20 | −0.20 | 0.59 | |

*Significance is for the following levels: *p<0.05; **p<0.01

This study concluded with semi-structured interviews with the participants, which focused on the problems encountered during the website operation process. This aimed to discuss their real-life experiences further and provide insights for analyzing the experimental data.

The participants from both websites expressed that the filters did not have a return or edit function. Additionally, the absence of prompts for single or multiple selections added to the difficulty of operation. The participants from Website A further expressed that it is unpredictable and challenging to learn the design of the filter by clicking on it and then running the results directly.

Additionally, 65.6% of participants indicated that they would have liked to have pictures attached to the animal species to choose their favorite pet more quickly. Furthermore, 84.3% of the participants reported they expected more pet personality and behavior options on the filter.

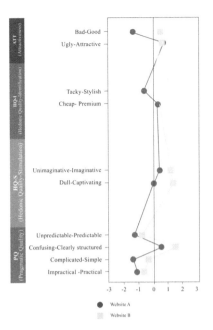

Figure 3. AttrakDiff score chart. * 1 ~ 3 for positive evaluation, 0 is the middle value, −1 ~ −3 is negative evaluation.

The interview content was categorized into topics based on the participants' common feedback, focusing on user experience, pet information, and visual design (Figure 4).

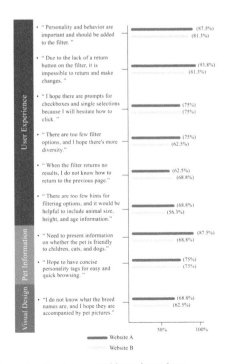

Figure 4. Semi-structured interviews chart.

## 4 DISCUSSION

Based on the results of this study, Website B performed Website A in terms of SUS score, item ATT, PQ in AttrakDiff score, and NPS score. In addition, Website B demonstrated better task operations time and success rate performance than Website A.

However, participants reported dissatisfaction with finding their ideal pet on both websites due to the unclear operational process of the filters and the unsuitable filter options that did not meet their needs. The SUS score showed that both websites did not pass the usability standards (grade A-) (Sauro & Lewis 2016). The NPS score also received negative numbers. The questionnaire results showed that people might not recommend it to others, indicating that the design of both websites needed to meet people's actual usage needs.

Additionally, participants hoped that the website could have more options related to the personality and behavior of pets, which was consistent with Becerra et al.'s findings (Becerra et al. 2021).

## 5 STUDY LIMITATIONS

This study recruited people aged 20 to 60 for research but did not limit the participants' experience in pet ownership, gender, or experience using mobile websites. Future studies should further analyze these factors to determine whether they influenced the experimental results.

## 6 CONCLUSION

This study reported the usability and efficiency of the website through tasks and explored reasons behind participants' behaviors through interviews. The result showed that the flow of operations and clear prompts are essential for users.

In particular, the content of the filters should have included options related to pet personality, as it would have influenced people's willingness to adopt a pet. Especially for those with pets at home, choosing only based on appearance did not satisfy their requirements.

Overall, some experiences need improvement in usability and satisfaction for both websites. In conclusion, the study recommended that future design optimization focuses on improving the usability of the filters to enhance the efficiency of finding an ideal pet companion.

## REFERENCES

American Pet Products Association (APPA). (n.d.). *Pet Industry Market Size, Trends & Ownership Statistics.* Retrieved January 16, 2023, from https://www.americanpetproducts.org/press_industrytrends.asp

American Society for the Prevention of. Cruelty to Animals (ASPCA). (2019). *Pet Statistics*. January 23, 2023, from https://www.aspca.org/helping-people-pets/shelter-intake-and-surrender/pet-statistics

Becerra Z. M., Parmar S., May K., & Stuck, R. E. (2021). Exploring user information needs in online pet adoption profiles. *Proceedings of the Human Factors and Ergonomics Society Annual Meeting*. https://doi.org/10.1177/1071181320641311

Hassenzahl, M., burmester, M., & koller , F. (2003). AttrakDiff: Ein fragebogen zur messung wahrgenommener hedonischer und pragmatischer qualität. *Mensch & Computer*, *57*,187–196. https://doi.org/https://doi.org/10.1007/978-3-322-80058-9_19

IBISWorld. (2022). *Number of Pets (Cats & Dogs)* Retrieved January 25, 2023, from https://www.ibisworld.com/us/bed/number-of-pets-cats-dogs/75/

Rowan A., & Kartal T. (2018). Dog population & dog shel. tering trends in the united states of america. *Animal*, *8*(5), 68. https://doi.org/10.3390/ani8050068

Sauro J., & Lewis, J. R. (2016). *Quantifying the user experience: Practical statistics for user research*, 2nd ed. Cambridge, MA: Morgan-Kaufmann.

Weiss E., Miller, K., Gibbons, H. M., & Vela, C. (2012). Why Did You Choose This Pet?: Adopters and pet selection preferences in five animal shelters in the united states. *Animal*, *2*(2), 154. https://doi.org/10.3390/ani2020144

Workmana, M.K., & Hoffman, C. L. (2015). An evaluation. of the role the internet site petfinder plays in cat adoptions. *Journal of Applied Animal Welfare Science*, *18*(4), 8–9. https://doi.org/10.1080/10888705.2015.1043366

*System Innovation for a Troubled World – Lam et al. (Eds)*
© 2024 the Author(s), ISBN: 978-1-032-60846-4

# Research on the construction of unmanned store environment experience with Virtual Reality (VR)

Chien-Yu Kuo*
*Department of Education, National University of Tainan, West Central District, Tainan City, Taiwan, ROC*

Chun-Ping Wu*
*Associate Professor, Department of Education, National University of Tainan, West Central District, Tainan City, Taiwan, ROC*

ABSTRACT: Artificial Intelligence (AI) has penetrated our daily lives such as robots, drones, autonomous cars, unmanned stores, etc., which arouses students' curiosity. However, students are not able to understand the above AI concepts by only watching videos or listening to teachers' lectures. Therefore, this study, grounded on Dale's Learning Pyramid, aims to develop a virtual reality (VR) for elementary school students to explain the AI concepts, which are used in unmanned stores. Specifically, a virtual unmanned supermarket will be created, allowing students to experience buying groceries and checking out without clerks. Hopefully, the immersive and interactive VR experience could help students to understand the concepts by observing the operating process of the unmanned stores. This study designed an immersive and interactive VR for primary school students to experience the new mode of a supermarket and to learn the concept of computer vision.

*Keywords*: Artificial Intelligence, Virtual Reality, Immersive Experience, Unmanned Store

## 1 INTRODUCTION

Due to the advancement of science and technology, AI has gradually changed our way of life. For example, AlphaGo defeated the king of Go in 2016 (Pan Wenzhong, 2019). Furthermore, the most common mobile phone voice assistant, SIRI, uses big data to calculate customer preferences and provides product advertisements that are suitable for the customers. The world's first unmanned convenience store "Amazon Go" opened in 2016 (Wang Zhixuan, 2020). The development of AI technology has brought more possibilities for improving teaching and learning, such as Learning systems, tablets and computers, virtual reality (VR), and so on.

Feng Tang, the Minister of Digital Development of Taiwan, stated in 2017 that regardless of age, we all need to learn to live with AI and learn to understand the method of AI. The most important thing is to "Treat AI as a part of life" (Feng, 2017). Facing the new trend of AI, Bingzhang Ye said that the current education reform focused on cultivating children's ability to solve problems and learn to face new things and

technologies (Ye, 2017). Therefore, it is important to let our students to have a basic understanding of AI.

The Ministry of Education in Taiwan has launched the artificial intelligence courses in the "Artificial Intelligence Technology Application and Talent Cultivation Plan Primary and Secondary School Subitems: Primary and Secondary School Promotion Education Plan", and planned a series of "Make Friends with AI-Artificial Intelligence Teaching in elementary and junior high Schools Example teaching plan", but the Taiwan Internet Science and Education Center also stated that there is lots of ArtiAI course materials and teaching aids on the market, but most of them are designed for college students or professionals who specialize in artificial intelligence. There are few relatively teaching materials for elementary courses (Zeng).

Therefore, this research designed a VR to teach elementary school students AI concepts by having students interact with the virtual unmanned stores.

## 2 THEORETICAL BASIS

Dale's "Experience Pyramid" theory pointed out that knowledge is obtained from direct (personal

---

*Corresponding Authors: sally901027@gmail.com and learning@mail.nutn.edu.tw

DOI: 10.1201/9781003460763-41

activities) or indirect (through text, language, pictures, and other media) experience (Chen, 2014). This pyramid is divided into 10 layers (as shown in Figure 1).

Figure 1. Dale's experience pyramid.

This study is based on the Dale experience pyramid with Piaget's cognitive development theory. Piaget believes that the development of children between the ages of seven and eleven is to solve problems based on concrete experience. (Lin, 2020) The immersive experience of VR can be used to arouse students' learning motivation, and the embedded tasks may guide students to purposefully interact with the learning concepts embedded in the VR.

## 2.1 Definition of VR

VR is through computer simulation to construct a 3D virtual environment (Liao, 2016). People need to wear special equipment, and through the stimulation of various senses, let our bodies think that we are in another real environment (Liao, 2016). Creating or recreating these situations in VR may be used to reduce experimental errors or visualize abstract concepts through the manipulated situation, or it may be reparation that learners cannot go to the place to learn in person. VR has the nature of simulation, which can make operational teaching activities more immersive, interactive, and safer so that learners can have opportunities by themselves and deepen the learning effect (Zhang 2006).

Furthermore, it also allows students to learn by doing (Wallace & Weiner 1998: quoted from Ke Zhixiang & Lin Shuchun 2003).

## 3 DESIGN OF VR

### 3.1 VR script

This research designed a VR of the unmanned store. When learners operate the VR unmanned store, they first act as the customers, entering the unmanned store entrance from the gate.

At the same time, several cameras in the unmanned store automatically detect the identity of customers.

Customers can pick up the goods they want from the shelves. The camera and the weight detectors automatically record what have been taken by the customers.

While the customers go to the checkout counters, the screen shows the products and the total expenses.

While the customers agree and go out of the store, the money will be deducted from the bank account.

The difference between the unmanned store and the general convenience store is that it does not require cashiers. In addition to the need for product replenishment staff and remote monitoring personnel to deal with emergencies, all other shopping processes are based on induction, detection, and self-service conduct (Xu Zongxi, 2019).

## 4 CONCLUSION

In conclusion, this research designed a VR program to teach elementary school students about the concept of AI. Based on Dale's experience pyramid theory and Piaget's cognitive development theory, the VR program aims to provide an immersive and interactive learning experience for students. The unmanned store scenario in the VR program provides a practical application of AI technology, allowing students to have a better understanding of its role in our daily lives. This research responds to the call of the Ministry of Education to introduce AI education to elementary and junior high school students. The design of this VR program can serve as a reference for developing other AI-related teaching materials and aid in promoting AI education in primary and secondary schools. Overall, this study contributes to the cultivation of students' AI literacy, which is essential for their future development in a world where AI technology is becoming increasingly prevalent.

## REFERENCES

Feng Tang 2019. United Daily News (From: 2023/1/31) To Haoyu 2016.IThome (From: 2023/1/31)

Jianshu Li, Hongling Chen, Ruiling Chen, Zhaolingshi, Jianhong Chen, Li Yilin and Meiyu Peng. 2019. Making Friends with AI – Encounter (first edition). Ministry of Education.

Jianxing Liao, 2016. Introduction to the Development and Application of Augmented and Virtual Reality (AR/VR). Education in Taipei Junior and Primary Schools. (From: 2023/1/31)

Jianxing Liao, 2016. *Introduction to the Development and Application of Augmented and Virtual Reality (AR/VR)*, 67 IECQ Annual Report

Meng Jielin, 2020. *Comparing Orff and Ke Dayi's music teaching methods based on Piaget's cognitive development theory [published in 2018]*. Master's thesis of National Tsing Hua University.

Ting Ai Zhang, 2008. Research on e-learning Instructional Design of Internet Inquiry Teaching Strategies Developing History Courses with Virtual Reality Technology [Published in 2008]. Master of Science and Technology Education Department of National Taiwan Normal University.

Xun Yizhang, 2018. Possible problems in the application of virtual reality in the field of education. *Taiwan Educational Review Monthly*. 7 (11). 120–125.

Yanhui Li, Yanjie Wang, 2019. VR, Broaden the vision of learning—integrating information technology into chinese teaching. *Teaching Site*. 2 (1)

Yifeng Ruan, 2009. Research on the Impact of Elementary School Innovation on Educational Quality [Published in 2009]. Master of Department of Educational Policy and Administration, National Jinan International University

Yueru Chen, 2014. Learning effects of integrating information technology into elementary school visual art curriculum – taking pinglin elementary school as an example IECQ Annual Report. 67–72

Zhen Fu Zeng. Taiwan Internet Science and Education Museum: Promotion of Artificial Intelligence (AI) [Published in 2014]. Master of Cultural and Creative Business Management Department of Nanhua University.

Zhixuan Wang 2020. Carat Media Weekly (From: 2023/1/31)

Zi Wenchen. *Basic Theoretical Discussion on Learning Satisfaction* (Extracted from: 2023/2/9)

Zong Xu, 2019. *A Comparative Study on the Innovative Operation Mode of Unmanned Stores – A Case Study of Unmanned Stores in Northern Taiwan [Published in 2019]*. Master Thesis of the Institute of Business Management, Universal University of Science and Technology.

*System Innovation for a Troubled World – Lam et al. (Eds)*
*© 2024 the Author(s), ISBN: 978-1-032-60846-4*

# The invention of traditional children's folk game into virtual reality game: An example of Yunlin Re-toy House

Chia-Fang Hsu*
*Ph.D of Institute of Education, University of Warwick, Da'an Dist., Taipei City, Taiwan*

Liang-Yin Kuo
*Associate Professor, National Formosa University, Hu-Wei, Yunlin, Taiwan*

ABSTRACT: Traditional children's folk games represent certain lifestyles and values of culture of a certain period of time. Unfortunately, as time goes by, some of them have faded away from the memory of society especially from the young generation, and lost popularity in the educational realm, as digital and online games have rapidly grown nowadays and captured the preference of children. Despite the fact mentioned above, the values of folk games are worth to be preserved and introduced to the young generation by being transformed into the forms that suit today's trend. As a result, this research provides an attempt to transform 1 traditional children's folk games into virtual reality (VR) games by adopting VR technology. This study is not very extensive, but the findings suggest that with moderate application of modern technology, the traditional folk games are possible to be innovated as more attractive and accessible to today's children. The objective of this research is to explore an innovative way and the most suitable design content in turning traditional folk games into VR games, in hope to open a new approach of preserving, inheriting and innovating traditional children's folk games in the future.

*Keywords*: Traditional Children's folk game Virtual Reality Technology

## 1 INTRODUCTION

### 1.1 *Traditional children's folk game*

Traditional children's folk games are valuable assets, as they are part of the history and represent lifestyles and values of the culture of a certain period of time. Thus, it is important for us to learn, preserve, and transmit traditional folk games. Samovar, Porter, and McDaniel (2012) defined children's folk games as cultural symbols that can enable a culture to preserve what is important and worthy of transmission. Unfortunately, the preference of today's children towards online or computer games endangered the existence of traditional folk games, they gradually fade away from people's life nowadays. However, with the help of modern technology, the preservation of folk games as well as other cultural heritages, is no longer difficult, as these folk games can be transformed into new forms that suit today's trends, such as the screen-based applications. Yunlin Re-toy House, a local toy museum, has been devoted to preserving traditional children's folk games for many years and exploring strategies to transform old games into new modern looks via which values and skills can be learned indirectly.

Thus, this research aims to apply virtual reality (VR) technology to transform a traditional folk game into an interactive and animated game, in the hope that the new approach to folk games can be more appealing to the young generation. It is also hoped that this research will shed light on the possibility that the digitizing form of these traditional treasures, not only folk games but also various cultural heritages, can be a timeless and holistic learning way in the educational realm in the future.

In this study, a Japanese traditional folk game "Hagoita" (Japanese Badminton) is chosen. It is a popular traditional children's folk game and is usually played during New Year; this game stands on a cultural belief that playing this game can drive away evils and attract good luck. Hagoita is chosen due to the reason that it is similar to Badminton which combines characteristics of sports and folk game; it is fun and easy to play; additionally, the rule of this game requires physical coordination and skill learning whereby players need to catch, aim and pitch, and is suitable to be transformed and playing with VR equipment.

---

*Corresponding Author: edpfs8533@gmail.com

DOI: 10.1201/9781003460763-42

Figure 1. Hagoita.

Figure 2. Hagoita game.

## 1.2 *Virtual reality*

VR is a computer-generated environment with scenes and objects that appear to be real, making the user feel they are immersed in the surroundings as one of the characters. This environment is created with VR software and perceived through a device known as a VR headset or helmet. For games, VR supersedes the surroundings, taking the user to any places where physical presence is no longer important. These features provide numerous possibilities for VR games, as the player is free of the boundary of time and space and can have realistic experiences of the world from different historical or even future eras. This is the main difference between VR and AR. The characteristics mentioned above make the incorporation of VR technology into the game industry on the rise in recent years, and increasingly found their way into museums, exhibitions, and the educational field.

## 2 RESEARCH DESIGN

The research design in this study is to transform a traditional children's folk game "Hagoita" into a VR

game. The purpose is not only to create a new approach to traditional folk games but more importantly, to make them appealing and motivating to youngsters as a creative learning tool. As a result, the design of this research is built on the VR game production procedure with consideration of the learning model. For the whole project, the methodology applies the ADDIE model (i.e., Analysis, Design, Development, Implementation, and Evaluation). ADDIE model is a suitable method for game design development as a learning tool.

Figure 3 shows the framework for this research. In the development phase, the software Unity 2019.3.0f6 is used for developing the game.

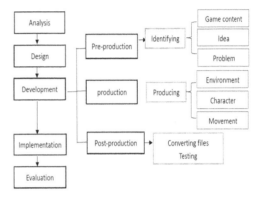

Figure 3. ADDIE model and research framework.

## 3 RESULTS AND DISCUSSION

This section consists of two parts including the analysis and design phases, and the development phase of the VR game production process. The implementation and evaluation phases will be discussed in future studies.

## 3.1 *Analysis and design*

In this research, before starting to develop a VR game, two phases—namely analysis and design—were conducted as necessary pre-stage for the researcher to build an in-depth understanding as well as make a preliminary sketch of the game. During the analysis phase, the researcher collected information and the background which enhanced the knowledge of Hagoita. As for designing VR games related to exercise or a great amount of physical movement, it is crucial to identify knowledge with regard to the player's body mobility, rackets, shuttlecocks, flexibility, etc., as detailed as possible. The overall goals well as learning objectives of the game were also discussed at the later stage via mind-mapping and brainstorming.

At the design phase, issues such as the goals of the game and the learning objectives were decided;

the style and content of the game, the targeted players, whether it's single player game or multiplayer game, were discussed; the procedure to produce the game was outlined and tools to be used were specified.

## 3.2 Development

The development phase includes three stages: preproduction, production, and postproduction. Three stages integrate the materials planned and collected in the previous phase and bring the game to life.

### 3.2.1 Preproduction

At the preproduction stage, the key procedure is to identify the most suitable content in design and gameplay that can be developed into a VR game based on the physical game of Hagoita. The prototype of the elements and environments of the game was also designed. The workflow chart of the process of gameplay was clarified and proposed; problems of the design of gameplay were also explored and modified. Figure 4 shows the script of the workflow chart of the gameplay process. Figure 5 shows the prototype of the racket and shuttlecock design.

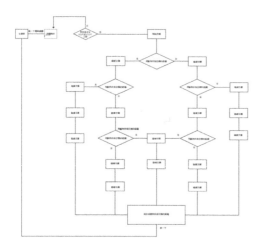

Figure 4.   Flow chart of the gameplay process.

Figure 5.   Prototype of racket and shuttlecock.

### 3.2.2 Production

At this stage, it requires a lot of work and creativity to transform the ideation from a physical game into an interface design. The interface design is conducted with the software Unity 2019.3.0f6. In developing the digital game, processes such as character design, motion capture, and 3D modeling, are undergone in order to make the simulated world as natural as possible. There are also other crucial aspects to make the game design successful, for example, the application of Physics engine technology was involved to provide a simulation of a physical system and make the VR simulation in real-time. Scene design and level design are also carefully undertaken to enhance the visual sensual perception, playfulness and thus influence the overall qualify of the gameplay experience. The number of players and the size of the players needs to be designed (or scaled) as well. Many more issues and aspects needed to be considered and designed.

Figure 6.   Prototype of Hagoita VR game.

### 3.2.3 Postproduction

In this phase, other elements also need to be confirmed and imported such as sound effects to enhance the game's environmental value and encourage for outstanding gameplay experience. Plus, the researcher has come out with continuous testing on the game prototype in order to identify any problems regarding the scripting and programming. Producing a game is never a one-way process, it requires continuous testing, adjustments, and performance optimization, which are the key ingredients to ensure comfort, safety, and a great VR player experience.

## 4   CONCLUSION

As mentioned previously, in recent years, the application of VR technology has been gaining

Figure 7. Testing.

popularity and developing in the fields of museums, exhibitions, and educational realm. In this paper, a case of how VR technology turns a traditional children's folk game into a new look and thus reveals its value with the transformation of cultural heritage, is presented. In this research, the use of VR has shown many advantages, including helping players in exploring places without actually being there; its creativity and sensory stimuli encourage players' learning motivation; it provides a realistic

world experience that is free of time and space boundaries. The new approach of traditional folk games builds easier access to the educational realm and be used as a multi-functional learning tool.

Despite many advantages, some challenges need to be discussed as well. Cost is one of the disadvantages when transforming traditional folk games into VR games as the implementation of VR is an expensive procedure. Second, the VR technology is complex. There are various types of folk games with different rules and requirements, and unfortunately, there is no fixed SOP for game implementation. Therefore, the transformation procedure will be complicated and time-consuming. Third, the concern that VR games might have an impact on player's body, and such addiction, can never be ignored. With regard to the implementation and evaluation of VR, it needs to be further investigated in future research.

## REFERENCES

Gillam Scott. "*Spotlight VR/AR: Innovation in Transformative Storytelling – MW17: Museums and the Web 2017*," February 28, 2017. https://mw17.mwconf.org/paper/spotlight-vrar-innovation-in-transformative-storytelling/

Haugstvedt A.C. and J. Krogstie. "Mobile augmented reality for cultural heritage: A technology acceptance study." In *2012 IEEE International Symposium on Mixed and Augmented Reality (ISMAR)*, 247–55, 2012. https://doi.org/10.1109/ISMAR.2012.6402563.

Prasanna, Virtual Reality Advantages And Disadvantages | What is Virtual Reality (VR)?, Benefits, Drawbacks, Pros and Cons-Aplus Topper June 20, 2022. https://www.aplustopper.com/virtual-reality-advantages-and-disadvantages/#Advantages_of_Virtual_Reality

Samovar, L. A., Porter, R. E., Mcdaniel, E. R.: *Communication Between Cultures (8th edition)*. Belmont, CA: Wadsworth, Cengage Learning, 2012.

Yeong Chong. (2012) "*Then and Now: Games Children Play*", [Retrieved November 28, 2015], Then and Now_ Games Children Play.html

System Innovation for a Troubled World – Lam et al. (Eds)
© 2024 the Author(s), ISBN: 978-1-032-60846-4

# A bibliometric study of SDG 5 gender equality by using text mining methods

Chia-Lee Yang*, Yi-Hao Hsiao, Meng-Chi Huang & Mei-Ya Chung
*National Center for High-performance Computing, National Applied Research Laboratories, Hsinchu, Taiwan*

ABSTRACT: The United Nations 2030 agenda for sustainable development, with its 17 Sustainable Development Goals (SDGs), is increasingly being adopted by countries globally and is transforming our society. SDG 5, which specifically targets gender equality, is a fundamental human right and a key enabler for achieving sustainability across all SDGs. As the deadline for the 2030 agenda approaches, having a roadmap to translate gender equality promises into action is essential. However, the current state of research on SDG 5 gender equality remains unclear. This paper presents a bibliometric study that implements a novel framework to assess gender equality research trends and associative content based on SDG 5. The bibliometric database for SDG 5 research projects was built by employing contextual text mining to extract relevant research projects from a vast collection of government research databases in Taiwan. The study found that research projects on gender equality have increased from 1993 to 2022 and academic grants are the main funding source, and universities are the main executing agencies with a tendency for research to focus on a single topic. This research provides insights into the measures required to facilitate progress towards SDG 5 and is an important foundation for future studies aimed at achieving gender equality and sustainable development by 2030.

*Keywords*: Sustainable Development, Gender equality, bibliometric analysis, Contextual text mining

## 1 INTRODUCTION

The adoption of the 2030 Agenda for Sustainable Development Goals (SDGs) by the United Nations in 2015 provided a universal framework for achieving economic, social, and environmental sustainability. Among the 17 SDGs, UN Sustainable Development Goal 5 (SDG 5) is gender equality, which seeks to empower all women and girls and eliminate all forms of discrimination and violence against them (U. N. UN, 2015a). Despite the global commitment to achieving gender equality, it is crucial to assess the extent of progress made in translating the SDGs into measurable outcomes for women and girls. This evaluation is particularly significant given the impact of the COVID-19 pandemic, which has further exacerbated gender inequality in various countries, resulting in setbacks to the advances made thus far (Clemente-Suárez *et al.* 2022).

As a complex and multidisciplinary field, the development of gender equality research requires a re-examination of the historical progression of research in this area, including current research focus and direction. Such an examination is crucial in bridging the gaps that still exist between rhetoric and reality. Therefore, this paper aims to provide an overview of the current state of gender equality research and highlight areas that require further exploration to bridge the gap between policy and practice. Given the complex nature of gender equality, it is imperative to critically examine the existing research on gender equality research. To achieve this objective, the study adopts quantitative techniques which involve the use of contextual text mining to process the textual data and construct the SDG 5 database. Building a gender database is crucial for inclusive global development and aligns with UN policies (Baptista & Seck 2023). Data helps identify marginalized groups and craft effective policy responses to measure progress and accountability. Leveraging gender data during the midpoint of the SDG timeline can accelerate progress toward gender equality and achieving SDG targets.

In Taiwan, the Government Research Bulletin (GRB) (STPI 2023) is the official platform for disseminating information on government-funded science and technology research projects, and it contains comprehensive and influential data about research projects in Taiwan. This study uses the GRB as the primary data source and employs a mixed-methods approach to build a gender database and analyze the data. The findings of this study will provide significant input for the

*Corresponding Author: joy.yang@nchc.org.tw

DOI: 10.1201/9781003460763-43

development of a local research strategy for continuous improvement in the domain of gender equality.

## 2 LITERATURE REVIEW

### 2.1 Gender equality and sustainable development

Gender equality is a critical factor in achieving the SDGs (U. N. UN, 2015b). Achieving gender equality is not only a matter of Gender equality (SDG 5) but also essential for other sustainable development goals, such as ending poverty (SDG 1), ensuring access to quality education (SDG 4), promoting decent work and economic growth (SDG 8), reducing inequalities (SDG 10), and promoting peace, justice, and strong institutions (SDG 16) (Esquivel & Sweetman 2016). Women are often responsible for the well-being of their families and communities and are often the most vulnerable to the effects of poverty, climate change, and other challenges. However, there still have many barriers to achieve gender equality toward SDG. Several studies highlight the existing barriers to achieving gender equality, including discrimination, gender-based violence, limited access to education, and lack of economic opportunities.

To achieve SDG 5, it is essential to have high-quality, reliable, and disaggregated data that captures the diversity of experiences and perspectives of women and girls. Such data can inform evidence-based policies and programs that address the root causes of gender inequality and empower women and girls to realize their rights and aspirations. However, the United Nations Statistics Division (2017) highlights that there are significant gaps in the data availability and quality to monitor progress in developing countries (W. UN, 2018). This may be due to the limited resources, weak statistical systems, and inadequate attention to gender-sensitive data collection and analysis. To address these gaps, partnerships and collaboration among governments, civil society, and other stakeholders are needed to ensure that data is effectively collected, analyzed, and used to achieve SDG 5 and promote gender equality more broadly.

### 2.2 Bibliometric analysis

Bibliometric analysis, originally defined by Alan Pritchard in 1969 as "the application of mathematics and statistical methods to books and other media of communication," provides valuable insights into the patterns and trends of scientific research (Lawani, 1981). Bibliometric analysis is widely used as a tool for evaluating academic impact and interdisciplinarity by analyzing citation relationships between papers and journals

(Leydesdorff & Rafols, 2011). Bibliometric studies employ several important laws and principles to analyze patterns in scientific publications, citations, and author productivity. For example, Bradford's law arranges scientific journals in a given field based on decreasing productivity (Brookes, 1969). The number of articles in each group of journals is approximately proportional to the reciprocal of the group number. Lotka's law suggests that the number of authors who have published k papers is approximately proportional to $1/k^2$ (Rousseau & Rousseau, 2000). Zipf's law predicts word frequencies in language processing and information retrieval. Zipf's law predicts word frequencies in language processing and information retrieval by stating that the frequency of a word is inversely proportional to its ran (Hood & Wilson, 2001). Price's law describes the distribution of scientific productivity across institutions, and the Law of concentration describes the concentration of scientific publications among a small number of countries.

Researchers from different disciplines are motivated to work on various facets of bibliometrics due to its potential. For example, Donthu et al. conducted a meta-analysis and systematic literature review of the bibliometric methodology in business research (Donthu, Kumar, Mukherjee, Pandey, & Lim, 2021). Emich et al. assess the 50-year-old Small Group Research journal corpus using clustering and network analysis to evaluate its context and content (Emich, Kumar, Lu, Norder, & Pandey, 2020).

### 2.3 Government research bulletin (GRB) in Taiwan

GRB was established in 1997 as the official platform for disseminating current information on government-funded research projects in Taiwan. Its content comprises research findings from diverse government agencies, frequently encompassing significant national policies, economic trends, social concerns, and scientific advancements. Since its inception in 1993, GRB has evolved into a data warehouse for collecting and storing research information from various research institutes, with over 630,000 cumulative projects recorded. For each project, GRB collects not only its metadata, but also its final report and research output information. Several research and analysis applications related to GRB have been proposed in recent years.

The GRB serves as a vital resource for scholars seeking to stay abreast of cutting-edge research across a broad range of fields related to government policy, social issues, and scientific developments. For example, Hsiao et al. (2022) used contextual Text Mining and Ontology Methods to Establish an associative analysis framework for SDG 7 (Hsiao, Chuang, Huang, Yang, & Wu,

2022). Lee (2022) analyzed nearly 6000 government-funded climate change research projects in Taiwan from 1993 to 2020 based on data in the Government Research Bulletin (GRB) (Lee *et al.*, 2022).

## 3 METHODS

### 3.1 *Contextual text mining*

Text mining, also known as text data mining or knowledge discovery from text database, is an artificial intelligence technology that employs natural language processing (NLP) to transform unstructured text found in documents and databases into structured, normalized data that is suitable for further analysis (Kao & Poteet, 2007). In recent times, text mining research has gained widespread acceptance in innovation research (Antons, Grünwald, Cichy, & Salge, 2020). However, due to the diverse nature of the available unstructured documents, text mining has become a challenging task. Contextual text mining is the process of extracting valuable information from textual data by considering the context in which the data was generated (Qiaozhu Mei & Zhai 2006). By comparing and analyzing the variations of themes over different contexts, interesting theme patterns can be revealed. Since the topics covered in a document are usually related to the context of the document, analyzing topical themes within context can provide valuable insights. Some studies consider different types of context information, such as time trends, authorship analysis, and sub-collection (Hsiao *et al.* 2022).

### 3.2 *Bidirectional encoder representation from transformers (BERT)*

The Bidirectional Encoder Representation from Transformers (BERT) is a deep learning model that uses transformer-based architectures to generate deep bidirectional representations of language from unlabeled text. Unlike recent language representation models, BERT is designed to pre-train deep bidirectional representations from unlabeled text by joint conditioning on both the left and right context in all layers. (Emich *et al.* 2020). The BERT model is trained using a combination of two objectives: masked language modeling (MLM) and next sentence prediction (NSP). MLM randomly masks words in the input text, and the model is trained to predict the masked words based on the surrounding context. NSP is designed to help the model understand the relationship between two sentences. The model is trained to predict whether two input sentences are consecutive in the original text or not. As a result, the pre-trained BERT model can be fine-tuned with just one additional output layer to create state-of-the-art models for a wide range of tasks,

such as question answering and language inference, without substantial task-specific architecture modifications.

Despite its impressive performance, BERT requires high computational overhead and the inability to perform semantic similarity searches for both sentences are fed into the network. To address these challenges, researchers have developed modifications of the BERT model. Reimers and Gurevych developed the Sentence-BERT (SBERT), which employs siamese and triplet network structures to produce semantically meaningful sentence embeddings for each sentence (Reimers & Gurevych, 2019). These embeddings can be used for various NLP tasks, including sentence similarity, paraphrasing, and clustering.

## 4 RESULTS AND DISCUSSION

This study uses contextual text mining methods based on SBERT to build Taiwan SDG 5 database from GRB in Taiwan and applies bibliometric analysis methods to analyze the data.

### 4.1 *Data collection and text mining*

We collected 634,283 research projects related to GRBs from 1993 to October 2022 and extracted descriptions of SDG 5 goals, targets, and indicators from the United Nations website. We then utilized the SBERT method to compare project names and abstracts from the GRB database for similarities. Similarity scores were calculated based on the semantic textual similarity analysis algorithm in SBERT. We applied expert-set threshold values to the results, resulting in the extraction of 1011 GRB projects that are concerned with the interrelation on SDG 5.

Figure 1 displays the high-frequency words in the keywords of the SDG 5 research projects. Among the 3,060 words in the keyword list, the most popular words are "gender," "sexual," "education," "equality," "health," "technology," "women," "discrimination," "rights," "social," "female," "sex," "violence," and "legal."

Figure 1.   High-frequency words.

### 4.2 Research projects growth in gender equality

The result of the yearly distribution of research projects focused on gender equality is displayed in Figure 2. To investigate the growth trend of such research projects over a 30-year period, we conducted a regression analysis. Our findings revealed a positive and significant relationship between time and the growth of research projects, as indicated by the standardized coefficient $B$ of 0.787 and an R-squared value of 0.62. These results imply that the number of research projects on gender equality has increased from 1993 to 2022. The gender equality projects publication trend can be characterized by three phases. The first phase spans from 1993 to 2006 and is characterized by a low number of studies per year. The second phase spans from 2007 to 2018 and is marked by a considerable increase in the number of studies, with a peak of 78 studies in 2009. Finally, the third phase spans from 2019 to 2022 and is characterized by a decrease in the number of studies, with a minimum of 4 studies in 2019.

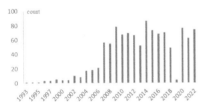

Figure 2.   Year-wise research project stats.

The research types in gender studies can be classified into five categories: applied research, commercialization, fundamental research, others, and technological development (Figure 3). Fundamental research accounts for 53%, followed by applied research (36%), although the latter has decreased in quantity since 2018. The limited focus on applied research in gender studies may be due to various reasons, including most funding from academic grants, methodological challenges, and a focus on theoretical frameworks and critical analysis of social structures, which may not always be compatible with applied research. Additionally, conducting applied research in gender studies may involve working with vulnerable populations and addressing sensitive issues, requiring specialized knowledge and skills.

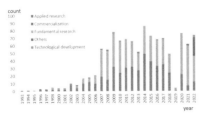

Figure 3.   The SDG 5 projects research types.

### 4.3 Founding distribution of Research projects on gender equality

Government funding for SDG research projects in six fields includes institutionally funded research, academic grants, commissioned research, grant-funded research, commissioned handling, and contractual collaboration between public and private sectors (Figure 4). Academic grants account for 84% of all projects, with commissioned research following. Gender studies research may have limited funding opportunities beyond academic grants due to a lack of funding priorities and limited awareness among potential funders. The lack of funding sources for gender studies research may be attributed to a combination of these and other factors, highlighting the need for increased awareness and advocacy for this important area of research.

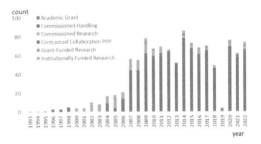

Figure 4.   The SDG5 project funding types.

The supervising agencies of SDG 5 projects can be classified into 11 government departments, with 84% of the projects coming from the National Science and Technology Council (NSTC), followed by 7% from the Ministry of Health and Welfare (MOHW), 3% from the Council of Agriculture (COA), and other departments having a proportion of less than 1% (Figure 5). NSTC is the main unit promoting gender studies in science in Taiwan. Meanwhile, MOHW primarily focuses on biomedicine and healthcare, conducting gender-related research on women's gynecological diseases or the gender issues of lung cancer.

Figure 5.   The SDG 5 projects supervising agencies.

The executing agency of SDG 5 projects is mainly universities, accounting for 84%, while health institutes only account for 4%, and the proportion of research institutions is relatively low (Figure 6). This may be because SDG 5 aims to achieve gender equality and enhance the status of women and girls in all aspects, which requires efforts in various fields such as education, employment, and health. Universities typically have strong expertise and experience in these areas, making it reasonable for them to take a dominant position in SDG 5 projects.

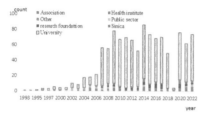

Figure 6. The SDG5 projects executing agency.

## 4.4 Principal investigators distribution of Research projects on gender equality

In addition, health research institutions play an important role in conducting SDG 5 projects related to health. This study examined 1011 bibliometric records from 2208 principal investigators, finding that 57% of projects had a single principal investigator and only 30% had 2 to3 co-principal investigators (Figure 7), indicating a tendency for research to focus on a single topic rather than interdisciplinary studies. Possible reasons for this trend include limited research resources, researcher preference for deepening personal interests, and the specialization of scientific fields that promote research on a single topic. Interdisciplinary studies may require more collaboration and resources, increasing project complexity and cost.

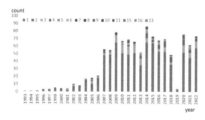

Figure 7. The number of principal investigators.

## 5 DISCUSSION

In 1995, the United Nations hosted the Fourth World Conference on Women and adopted the Declaration on the Elimination of Discrimination Against Women, which called on governments to take measures to promote women's social, economic, and political development, and to enhance women's participation and contribution to peace and security. Since then, the United Nations has continuously developed and promoted international legal and policy documents related to gender equality, such as the "Convention on the Elimination of All Forms of Discrimination against Women and the Beijing Declaration and Platform for Action", which have advanced global gender equality. The United Nations also established the UN Women in 1996.

The Taiwanese government felt pressured by international evaluations of its progress toward gender equality, and women's groups in Taiwan raised awareness of gender inequality through protests and other actions, leading to increased research in the field. In 2012, the Gender Equality Committee of the Executive Yuan in Taiwan was established to promote gender mainstreaming policies, education, and research funding, which drew more researchers to the field. The Gender Statistics Working Group, created in 2005, developed frameworks and indicators for gender statistics, providing open data for researchers to analyze. Scholars began exploring the connections between gender equality and other issues, such as foreign spouses, transnational marriage, and gender-based violence, mainly in the fields of social sciences and biomedical research.

In 2019, significant policies related to gender equality, such as the "Gender Equality Education Act" and same-sex marriage, sparked social controversy, but there were few actual research studies on these topics. Of the 17 same-sex marriage-related research projects, 16 were in basic science research, and only one involved actual surveys. After 2019, there was an increase in cross-disciplinary research on gender equality, particularly in fields such as science and engineering, which is to address the issue of low representation of women in science, which has been promoted by the UN. However, there is still a significant lack of research on the impact of COVID-19 in the intersection of medical, health, and social sciences. Further examining COVID-19-related research with respect to gender, out of 8 identified projects related to COVID-19 in their abstracts, none specifically address the impact of COVID-19 on women or attitudes toward vaccines.

## 6 CONCLUSIONS

This study has three main contributions. First, this study proposes a novel framework for analyzing gender equality in GRB research projects related to SDG 5 in Taiwan, leveraging the SBERT contextual text mining and bibliometric analysis methods. By considering contextual and semantic information, the SBERT method can effectively mitigate word ambiguity and polysemy, leading to more accurate analysis results. Integrating SBERT with bibliometric analysis enables the extraction of precise feature vectors from textual data, and provides comprehensive and efficient insights into the development trends and key topics in the research field. The main advantage of this approach is the significant reduction in the workload and time required for researchers and experts to read and analyze large volumes of literature. Furthermore, the results can serve as a valuable reference for policy-making and decision-making processes in Taiwan.

Second, the findings of this study on the distribution and characteristics of gender studies research projects in Taiwan over a 30-year period provide important insights and implications for future research and policy. The positive and significant relationship between time and the growth of research projects indicates a growing recognition and importance of gender equality issues in Taiwan. The dominance of academic grants as the main funding source for gender studies research projects, and the limited opportunities for applied research, suggest a need for greater awareness and advocacy for this important area of research. Furthermore, the fact that universities account for the majority of executing agencies of SDG 5 projects, with health institutes playing a smaller role, suggests the need for more interdisciplinary collaboration and involvement of health research institutions in addressing gender-related health issues. The tendency for research to focus on a single topic rather than interdisciplinary studies also highlights the need for more resources and support for interdisciplinary research. Finally, the lack of COVID-19-related research specifically addressing the impact of the pandemic on women or attitudes towards vaccines underscores the need for continued attention to gender equality issues in all areas of research and policy. The findings provide guidance for future research and policy initiatives aimed at promoting gender equality in Taiwan.

Finally, we build a gender database. Research grants are crucial in promoting gender equality, but to determine the effectiveness of policies, hard data is essential. By using data, policies can be transformed into a cohesive strategy to determine.

## ACKNOWLEDGMENT

We thank the Ministry of Science and Technology, Taiwan for their generous support through grant number MOST 111-2629-M-492-001-MY2.

## REFERENCES

Antons D., Grünwald E., Cichy P. & Salge, T. O. (2020). The application of text mining methods in innovation research: current state, evolution patterns, and development priorities. *R&D Management*, 50(3), 329–351.

Baptista, K. J., & Seck, P. (2023). *Gender Data can Reinvigorate the SDGs*, from https://data.unwomen.org/features/gender-data-can-reinvigorate-sdgs

Brookes B.C. (1969). Bradford's law and the bibliography of science. *Nature*, 224, 953–956.

Clemente-Suárez V.J., Rodriguez-Besteiro S., Cabello-Eras J. J., Bustamante-Sanchez, A., Navarro-Jiménez, E., Donoso-Gonzalez, M., . . . Tornero-Aguilera, J. F. (2022). Sustainable development goals in the COVID-19 pandemic: A narrative review. *Sustainability*, 14(13), 7726.

Donthu N., Kumar S., Mukherjee D., Pandey N. & Lim, W.M. (2021). How to conduct a bibliometric analysis: An overview and guidelines. *Journal of Business Research*, 133, 285–296.

Emich K. J., Kumar S., Lu L., Norder K., & Pandey N. (2020). Mapping 50 years of small group research through small group research. *Small Group Research*, 51(6), 659–699.

Esquivel V., & Sweetman C. (2016). Gender and the sustainable development goals. *Gender & Development*, 24(1), 1–8.

Hood W. & Wilson, C. (2001). The literature of bibliometrics, scientometrics, and informetrics. *Scientometrics*, 52(2), 291–314.

Hsiao Y.-H., Chuang C.-Y., Huang M.-C., Yang C.-L., & Wu, J.-H. (2022). *Using Contextual Text Mining and Ontology Methods to Establish a Novel Technology Trend and Associative Analysis Framework for Sustainable Energy Development in Taiwan*. Paper presented at the 2022 IEEE International Conference on Big Data (Big Data).

Kao A., & Poteet S.R. (2007). *Natural language processing and text mining*: Springer Science & Business Media.

Lawani, S. M. (1981). Bibliometrics: Its theoretical foundations, methods and applications. *Libri*, 31 (Jahresband), 294–315.

Lee, C.-C., Huang K.-C., Kuo S.-Y., Cheng C.-K., Tung, C.-P., & Liu, T.-M. (2022). Climate change research in Taiwan: beyond following the mainstream. *Environmental Hazards*, 1–19.

Leydesdorff L., & Rafols, I. (2011). Indicators of the interdisciplinarity of journals: Diversity, centrality, and citations. *Journal of Informetrics*, 5(1), 87–100.

Qiaozhu Mei, & Zhai, C. (2006). *A Mixture Model for Contextual Text Mining*. Paper presented at the Proceedings of the 12th ACM SIGKDD International Conference on Knowledge Discovery and Data Mining.

Reimers, N., & Gurevych, I. (2019). Sentence-bert: Sentence embeddings using siamese bert-networks. *arXiv preprint arXiv:1908.10084*.

Rousseau B., & Rousseau, R. (2000). LOTKA: A program to fit a power law distribution to observed frequency data. *Cybermetrics: International Journal of Scientometrics, Informetrics and Bibliometrics* (4), 4.

STPI. (2023, 2023.4.13). Government Rearch Bulletin, from https://www.grb.gov.tw/

UN, U. N. (2015a). Achieve gender equality and empower all women and girls Retrieved 4.11, 2023, from https://sdgs.un.org/goals/goal5

UN, U. N. (2015b). Transforming our world: the 2030 Agenda for Sustainable Development, from https://sustainabledevelopment.un.org/post2015/transformingourworld

UN, W. (2018). Gender equality and big data: Making gender data visible.

System Innovation for a Troubled World – Lam et al. (Eds)
© 2024 the Author(s), ISBN: 978-1-032-60846-4

# Improving transportation industry corporate sustainability reporting effects based on a new hybrid fuzzy dynamic MRDM Model

Fu-Hsiang Chen*
*Department of Accounting, Chinese Culture University, Taipei, Taiwan*

Kuang-Hua Hu
*Finance and Accounting Research Center, School of Accounting, Nanfang College, Guangzhou*

ABSTRACT: Corporate sustainability reporting can help investors assess a company's governance, business risks, and ability to seize opportunities. The issues related to the influencing factors of information disclosure of corporate sustainable development are more complex and are classified to multi-objective/attribute decision-making problems. To address such problems, this study adopts a new hybrid fuzzy dynamic multi-rule decision-making model, which combines the Two-Stage Filter-Wrapper Feature Selection Method, fuzzy Decision Making Trial and Evaluation Laboratory, to identify key influential factors to achieve optimal aspiration levels. The improvement priority of dimensions is given as environment (A), social capital (B), business model and innovation (D), leadership and governance (E), and human capital (C). Based on the results, the best design scheme is proposed as an important basis for information disclosure of corporate sustainability reporting in the future.

## 1 INTRODUCTION

Corporate sustainability reporting performance disclosure by companies is an important tool for communication between companies and investors. Investors need to have a shared understanding of the main risks and investment opportunities to make effective investment allocations. The Sustainability Accounting Standards Board (SASB) was specifically designed for investors and defines materiality consistently with the standards required by the U.S. Securities and Exchange Commission (SEC) for financial reporting, to help investors use the same judgment standards in interpreting both financial and non-financial information on corporate sustainability reporting performance by companies. Companies can also use their sensitivity to financial information disclosure in preparing non-financial information, to disclose non-financial indicators of corporate sustainability reporting performance. After the launch of SASB guidelines, US and other international companies began to adopt SASB guidelines to reflect the financial impact of Corporate sustainability reporting performance, such as global semiconductor manufacturer Intel, which has adopted SASB guidelines and integrated SASB's quantitative indicators (Accounting Metrics) into its sustainability report.

Although in recent years, some large companies have implemented corporate sustainability reporting based on frameworks such as the Global Reporting Initiative, many governments are gradually requiring companies to modify and submit their corporate sustainability reporting based on the SASB framework (Jørgensen et al. 2022). However, the framework proposed by SASB involves five dimensions and various standards (SASB 2017). A key issue for organizations is how to introduce the setup process based on such a complex framework and investigate the key determinants of sub-standards in each of the five sustainable development dimensions. Meeting the transformational demands of such applications is a daunting challenge that relates to the future growth and value creation of the enterprise.

The objective of this study was to construct a comprehensive view of a sustainable framework suitable for enterprises under the SASB framework. That is, this research gives a holistic perspective on sustainability reporting (SR) for a group MRDM problem, which corresponds with the expectation of investors at large specifically. Despite the importance of corporate sustainability reporting practices in academic research, there are few empirical analyses on comprehensive frameworks and, in particular, for SASB topics. Moreover, we can't seem to find the consideration of the dependence and feedback between multiple factors that impact the implementation of corporate sustainability reporting frameworks. The disentanglement of the complex relations among factors influencing corporate sustainability

---

*Corresponding Author: chenfuhsiang1@gmail.com

DOI: 10.1201/9781003460763-44

reporting information disclosure can give a more appropriate solution for SR practical framework. To overcome this sustainability issue, an integrated evaluation framework based on the fuzzy dynamic MRDM model was proposed. This hybrid approach combines the Two-Stage Filter-Wrapper Feature Selection Method (TSFWFSM), fuzzy decision-making trial, and evaluation laboratory, in order to provide practical insights to senior executives and support the improvement of corporate sustainability reporting performance.

Briefly, the TSFWFSM (Chaudhuri *et al.* 2021) is a combination of the high-efficiency algorithm by the Filter method and the high quality of the Wrapper method that was used to diminish the length of sustainability features based on SASB standards and related literatures. Fuzzy DEMATEL (Hasheminezhad *et al.* 2021; Hu *et al.* 2021) is utilized to clarify the complex problems and determine the causal relationships among sustainability dimensions/criteria based on selected elements by TSFWFSM in fuzzy environment. By doing so, we expect that the produced metrics can enable the prioritization of improvement plans to reach a sustainability goal.

## 2 EXPERIMENTAL

Efforts and improvement reports on corporate sustainable development need to be continuously evaluated, but selecting which factors to use as sustainable development metrics needs to be more comprehensive. The effectiveness and robustness of sustainability reporting are crucial and depend on a variety of complex factors. In this article, the evaluation criteria for sustainability reporting are based on SASB principles and the relevant literatures and are to be categorized in five sustainability dimensions: environment (A), social capital (B), human capital (C), business model and innovation (D), and leadership and governance (E).

### 2.1 Environment

Given the concerns of environmental conservation and corporate social responsibility, environmental management by global corporations has been widely accepted as one of the pillars of SR. Goel (2021) is of the view that corporates are responsible for the influence initiated by their strategy and operations on the natural environment, but the information disclosure of SR practices is one useful means of honoring such responsibility.

### 2.2 Social capita

Social capital refers to the multiple connections and social ties gradually established through social interaction. Corporations have an obligation to provide various public welfare activities for the public to fulfill their social responsibility and meet the creation and consolidation of social capital. Despite this, social capital has received more attention lately due to its impact on sustainability reporting through social interactions (Millar and Searcy, 2020).

### 2.3 Human capita

SR relates to the investment that human capital contributes to the business, which includes labor relations, fair labor practices, diversity and inclusion, employee health, safety, well-being, etc. In the age of the rising of labor awareness, fair labor practices have been widely considered and recognized in the real world and are also a necessary requirement for corporate employees. To fill the workforce gaps, many companies are attempting to overcome environmental evolutions and achieve corporate sustainability goals through the effective implementation of workforce diversity and inclusion strategies (Kincaid and Smith, 2021).

### 2.4 Business model and innovation

More and more companies are forced to disclose information on the environmental impact of their business models and product innovations, as shown in the annual report. In addition, as pointed out by Karaman *et al.* 2018, an appropriate corporate operational strategy will capture the expectations of investors and SR quality, for arriving at social acceptance, for establishing a favorable image.

### 2.5 Leadership and governance

From the perspective of environmental development, the generation of SR for corporates is pushed by investors rather than an unsolicited pre-planned report by senior leaders. Nonetheless, support and governance of the senior leadership is crucial for such transparent and practical initiatives to have high influence and reach (Adams, 2013). Besides that, risk management is an important part of leadership and corporate governance, especially in a crisis situation. However, Corazza *et al.* (2020) argue that good leadership and governance reflect good business ethics, as they can enhance corporate value creation for improving social welfare and align with the construction of corporate SR.

The proposed hybrid fuzzy dynamic MRDM model is based on the combination of TSFWFSM, and fuzzy DEMATEL methods to assist SR strategic decision-making.

### 2.6 Screening key factors

Feature selection is the process of identifying and selecting key features relevant to a specific learning task, and is an inevitable preprocessing step in model building for decision making and prediction.

The techniques of feature selection are mainly divided into three groups: filters, wrappers, and hybrids (i.e., filter + wrapper). Filter techniques achieve feature selection by only considering the inherent attributes of the data. Its advantage is that it is fast and does not require a large amount of computation. Wrapper techniques use embedded classifiers to evaluate the quality of given features. Its advantage is that it has better performance than a filter, but its disadvantage is that it has a higher computational cost. Hybrid techniques combine the advantages of both filters and wrappers. The two-stage filter-wrapper feature selection method (TSFWFSM) is thus conducted herein.

## 2.7 Fuzzy DEMATEL for developing influential network relationship map (INRM)

The technique is based on the INRM, which uses expert opinions to determine the priority level of decision factors in the system. In addition, this method can also help decision-makers implement better plans by analyzing the causal relationships between complex factors through graph analysis. Although DEMATEL is a superior technique in measuring MCDM problems, human evaluations can be influenced by preferences and are often unclear, therefore precise numerical calculations alone are not enough. Therefore, fuzzy set theory has been integrated into the DEMATEL method to address such complex problems. The fuzzy DEMATEL method has been proven to be an effective tool for dealing with the fuzziness and uncertainty of information in real-life environments and has been successfully applied in multiple fields (Chen et al. 2022).

Opricovic and Tzeng (2003) proposed to transform fuzzy data into crisp scores (CFCS). The five linguistic terms corresponding to the linguistic values are shown in Table 1. Based on linguistic metrics from experts, we obtained a fuzzy direct influence matrix $\tilde{Z}$.

$$\tilde{Z} = [\tilde{Z}_{ij}]_{n \times n}, \quad \text{where } \tilde{Z}_{ij} = (Z_{ij}^l, Z_{ij}^m, Z_{ij}^r) \quad (1)$$

Based on the fuzzy direct influence matrix, we can derive a normalized fuzzy direct influence matrix.

$$\tilde{D} = \tilde{Z}/u, \text{ where } u$$

$$= \max_{i,j} \left\{ \max_i \sum_{j-1}^{n} z_{ij}, \max_j \sum_{j-1}^{n} z_{ij} \right\}, = (e_{ij}^l, e_{ij}^m, e_{ij}^r)$$

$$i,j \in \{1,...,n\} \tilde{D} = [\tilde{e}_{ij}]_{n \times n}, \tilde{e}_{ij} \quad (2)$$

The normalized fuzzy direct influence matrix $\tilde{D} = (D^l, D^m, D^r)$ where $D^l = [e_{ij}^l]_{n \times n}, D^m = [e_{ij}^m]_{n \times n}$, and $D^r = [e_{ij}^r]_{n \times n}$.

When considering the identity matrix ($I$), we can obtain the fuzzy total influence matrix ($\tilde{T}$).

$$\tilde{T} = [\tilde{t}_{ij}]_{n \times n}, \quad \text{where } \tilde{t}_{ij} = (t_{ij}^l, t_{ij}^m, t_{ij}^r) \quad (3)$$

Where
$$T^l = [t_{ij}^l]_{n \times n} = D^l(I - D^l)^{-1}, T^m = [t_{ij}^m]_{n \times n} = D^m(I - D^m)^{-1}$$

$$\text{and} \quad T^r = [t_{ij}^r]_{n \times n} = D^r(I - D^r)^{-1}$$

Finally, the CFCS defuzzification method is utilized to develop the total fuzzy relation matrix.

Table 1. The linguistic scale for the influence of criteria.

| Linguistic term | Triangular fuzzy numbers |
|---|---|
| No influence | [0, 0.1, 0.3] |
| Weak influence | [0.1, 0.3, 0.5] |
| Medium influence | [0.3, 0.5, 0.7] |
| Strong influence | [0.5, 0.7, 0.9] |
| Very strong influence | [0.7, 0.9. 1] |

## 3 RESULTS AND DISCUSSION

Based on the SASB framework, existing literature, characteristics of the transportation industry, and the expertise of domain experts, a survey was designed consisting of 5 dimensions and 33 standards for assessment (see Table 2). Too many factors can confuse users and lead to inappropriate solutions. Therefore, to address this issue, the aforementioned survey is considered a predictive test questionnaire and is being distributed among 5 statistical populations (heads of sustainability offices at listed companies). The respondents are invited to rate the importance of the 33 SR standards on a scale of 0 (not important at all) to 10 (extremely important). The data obtained from the experts will then be input into TSFWFSM to define the key factors and provide a new improved questionnaire. As TSFWFSM is a supervised learning algorithm, the conditioning variables need to be identified beforehand. The results of TSFWFSM are shown in Table 3.

The formal questionnaire was developed based on Table 3 and was distributed to 12 domain experts consisting of 3 managers of investment institutions, 6 CPAs from Big 4 accounting firms (KPMG, PricewaterhouseCoopers (PwC), Ernst & Young (EY), and Deloitte), and 3 managers sustainability office at transportation industry companies. During the process of data collection in a survey, we attempt to briefly explain to the respondents the purpose of the study. These respondents are then asked to provide a paired comparison matrix for the selected criteria, which

218

Table 2. Criteria of transportation industry sustainability reporting for the pre-test questionnaire.

| Dimensions | Criteria |
|---|---|
| Environment | $c_1$: GHG (Greenhouse gas) emissions |
| | $c_2$: Air quality |
| | $c_3$: Material efficiency and recycling |
| | $c_4$: Fuel economy |
| | $c_5$: Use-phase emissions |
| | $c_6$: Materials sourcing |
| | $c_7$: Biodiversity impacts |
| Social capital | $c_8$: Human rights |
| | $c_9$: Access and affordability |
| | $c_{10}$: Customer welfare |
| | $c_{11}$: Data security and customer privacy |
| | $c_{12}$: Fair disclosure |
| | $c_{13}$: Fair marketing and advertising |
| Human capital | $c_{14}$: Labor relations |
| | $c_{15}$: Labor practices |
| | $c_{16}$: Employee health, safety, and wellbeing |
| | $c_{17}$: Diversity and inclusion |
| | $c_{18}$: Compensation and benefits |
| Business model and innovation | $c_{19}$: Lifecycle impacts of products |
| | $c_{20}$: Lifecycle impacts of services |
| | $c_{21}$: Environmental and social impacts on assets |
| | $c_{22}$: Environmental and social impacts on operations |
| | $c_{23}$: Product packaging |
| | $c_{24}$: Product quality and safety |
| Leadership and governance | $c_{25}$: Systemic risk management |
| | $c_{26}$: Accident and safety management |
| | $c_{27}$: Political influence |
| | $c_{28}$: Business ethics |
| | $c_{29}$: Competitive behavior |
| | $c_{30}$: Regulatory capture |
| | $c_{31}$: Transparency of payments |
| | $c_{32}$: Materials sourcing |
| | $c_{33}$: Supply chain management |

range from no influence at all (0) to very high influence (4) based on their knowledge. In the end, a total of 12 complete questionnaires were collected as the statistical sample for the empirical investigation in this study.

Table 3 shows the influence relationship matrix of the five dimensions, where Dimension A (Environment) has the highest degree of positive influence ($\tilde{D}_i - \tilde{R}_i = 0.057$), whereas Dimension C (Human capital), Dimension D (Business model and innovation), and Dimension E (Leadership and governance) with negative value to mean influenced by other dimensions.

For criteria, criterion $a_2$ (material efficiency and recycling) has the highest ($\tilde{D}_i - \tilde{R}_i$), indicating

Table 3. The criteria used in the official questionnaire.

(●: selection; ◎: no selection)

| Dimensions | Criteria (Preliminary questionnaire) | New code | Result |
|---|---|---|---|
| | | Official questionnaire received from TSFWFSM | |
| A | $c_1$: GHG (Greenhouse gas) emissions | $a_1$ | ● |
| | $c_2$: Air quality | – | ◎ |
| | $c_3$: Material efficiency and recycling | $a_2$ | ● |
| | $c_4$: Fuel economy | – | ◎ |
| | $c_5$: Use-phase emissions | $a_3$ | ● |
| | $c_6$: Materials sourcing | – | ◎ |
| | $c_7$: Biodiversity impacts | – | ◎ |
| B | $c_8$: Human rights | $b_1$ | ● |
| | $c_9$: Access and affordability | – | ◎ |
| | $c_{10}$: Customer welfare | – | ◎ |
| | $c_{11}$: Data security and customer privacy | $b_2$ | ● |
| | $c_{12}$: Fair disclosure | $b_3$ | ● |
| | $c_{13}$: Fair marketing and advertising | – | ◎ |
| C | $c_{14}$: Labor relations | $c_1$ | ● |
| | $c_{15}$: Labor practices | $c_2$ | ● |
| | $c_{16}$: Employee health, safety, and wellbeing | $c_3$ | ● |
| | $c_{17}$: Diversity and inclusion | $c_4$ | ● |
| | $c_{18}$: Compensation and benefits | – | ◎ |
| D | $c_{19}$: Lifecycle impacts of products | – | ◎ |
| | $c_{20}$: Lifecycle impacts of services | – | ◎ |
| | $c_{21}$: Environmental and social impacts on assets | $d_1$ | ● |
| | $c_{22}$: Environmental and social impacts on operations | $d_2$ | ● |
| | $c_{23}$: Product packaging | – | ◎ |
| | $c_{24}$: Product quality and safety | $d_3$ | ● |
| E | $c_{25}$: Systemic risk management | $e_1$ | ● |
| | $c_{26}$: Accident and safety management | $e_2$ | ● |
| | $c_{27}$: Political influence | – | ◎ |
| | $c_{28}$: Business ethics | $e_3$ | ● |
| | $c_{29}$: Competitive behavior | – | ◎ |
| | $c_{30}$: Regulatory capture | – | ◎ |
| | $c_{31}$: Transparency of payments | – | ◎ |
| | $c_{32}$: Materials sourcing | – | ◎ |
| | $c_{33}$: Supply chain management | – | ◎ |

that this criterion has the strongest influence on other criteria, whereas criterion $a_3$ (Water and wastewater management) had the lowest $(\tilde{D}_i - \tilde{R}_i)$ among criteria, showing that it is easily influenced. From the influence relationship $(\tilde{D}_i + \tilde{R}_i)$ among criteria, criterion $c_2$ (fair labor practices) shows the strongest relation at 1.099, whereas the value of $d_3$ (Systemic risk management) is 0.791 with the weakest relation.

The latitude axis $(\tilde{D}_i + \tilde{R}_i)$ represents the strength of the overall relationship between factors, while the longitude axis $(\tilde{D}_i - \tilde{R}_i)$ represents the causal relationship between factors. Dimension A (environment) affirmed its direct impact on the other dimensions; Dimension B (social capital) also had a significant impact on Dimension C (human capital), D (business model and innovation), and E (leadership and governance). Therefore, this study indicates that if a manufacturing enterprise aims to establish a robust SR, then environment and social capital are the most decisive aspects.

Table 4. Cause ($\tilde{D}_i$) and effect ($\tilde{R}_i$) values of dimensions and criteria.

| Dimensions /Criterions | Row sum ($\tilde{D}_i$) | Colum sum ($\tilde{R}_i$) | $\tilde{D}_i + \tilde{R}_i$ | $\tilde{D}_i - \tilde{R}_i$ |
|---|---|---|---|---|
| Environment (A) | 0.771 | 0.714 | 1.485 | 0.057 |
| $a_1$ | 0.406 | 0.431 | 0.837 | -0.025 |
| $a_2$ | 0.504 | 0.415 | 0.919 | 0.089 |
| $a_3$ | 0.392 | 0.448 | 0.840 | -0.056 |
| Social capital (B) | 0.766 | 0.718 | 1.484 | 0.048 |
| $b_1$ | 0.398 | 0.438 | 0.836 | -0.040 |
| $b_2$ | 0.407 | 0.432 | 0.839 | -0.025 |
| $b_3$ | 0.490 | 0.416 | 0.906 | 0.074 |
| Human capital (C) | 0.675 | 0.735 | 1.410 | -0.060 |
| $c_1$ | 0.515 | 0.521 | 1.056 | -0.006 |
| $c_2$ | 0.585 | 0.514 | 1.099 | 0.071 |
| $c_3$ | 0.508 | 0.537 | 1.045 | -0.029 |
| $c_4$ | 0.512 | 0.536 | 1.048 | -0.024 |
| Business model and innovation (D) | 0.711 | 0.725 | 1.436 | -0.004 |
| $d_1$ | 0.380 | 0.409 | 0.789 | -0.029 |
| $d_2$ | 0.451 | 0.384 | 0.835 | 0.067 |
| $d_3$ | 0.374 | 0.417 | 0.791 | -0.043 |
| Leadership and governance (E) | 0.702 | 0.723 | 1.425 | -0.021 |
| $e_1$ | 0.372 | 0.410 | 0.782 | -0.038 |
| $e_2$ | 0.378 | 0.408 | 0.786 | 0.030 |
| $e_3$ | 0.454 | 0.381 | 0.835 | 0.073 |

Furthermore, Dimensions C, D, and E are clearly located below the latitude axis, indicating that they are the influenced dimensions. Similarly, the investigation of the network relationships that are influential among the standards within the

scope revealed that the standards $a_2$ (material efficiency and recycling), $b_3$ (fair disclosure), $c_2$ (fair labor Practices), $d_2$ (environmental and social impact of operations), and $e_3$ (business ethics) have significant individual dimension influences. In other words, these five standards are the core of their corresponding dimensions and play a significant role in enhancing and improving the SR of the transportation industry.

According to Table 4, the improvement priority of dimensions is given as environment (A), social capital (B), business model and innovation (D), leadership and governance (E), and human capital (C). This means that the environment' (A) is of paramount importance for improving the structural system, as this action goal directly or indirectly affects other potential goals, thereby providing a multiplier effect for problem-solving. Due to long-standing uncivilized human behavior, there has been a strong threat to the natural environment, making environmental sustainability issues a focus of the global market (Othman et al. 2017).

In the era of global warming, the importance of environmental sustainability is increasing, driving companies to disclose their corporate SR through annual reports. In response to the Brundtland Commission's call to protect natural resources in 1989, the environmental dimension was emphasized and thus incorporated into companies' SR. The Brundtland Report had a significant impact on the field of environmental sustainability, and the concept of sustainable business development was subsequently introduced by many international organizations, such as the World Commission on Environment and Development (WCED) and the Global Reporting Initiative (GRI). It seems obvious that environmental awareness has been highlighted in SR, thereby creating a new milestone in the corporate environment sustainability development (Hasan et al. 2022).

For criteria (factors), material efficiency and recycling $(a_2)$ is said to have the highest influence relation $(d_i - \tilde{s}_i = 0.089)$ on other criteria based on Table 4, this means that when a company intends to establish a SR, material efficiency and recycling is the most important factor. Karagiannis et al. (2022) revealed that energy management was identified as the fourth significant aspect among 40 major dimensions, playing a critical role in driving economic activities for the sustainable development of businesses in promoting Industry 4.0. In conceptual terms, sustainability disclosure factors are related to material efficiency and recycling, which is an important component of energy management policies, and therefore, there is a need to enhance the material efficiency and recycling of companies. Clearly, efficient material management can not only promote enterprise value creation but also achieve sustainable development performance.

Fair disclosure ($b_3$) is the main driver of social capital (Dimension B) and the second highest contributor of all criteria. If a sustainable development report is a fair and unquestionable disclosure, it can meet the requirements of stakeholders. High transparency in the sustainability report provided by organizations can have a positive impact, increase company value, and help establish the organization's public image (Gunawan *et al.* 2022). Encouraging companies to prioritize compliance with SASB's sustainability reporting standards is important, as transparent disclosure of sustainability information can instill integrity in decision-makers, thereby increasing public confidence and reducing information asymmetry between companies and investors (Jørgensen *et al.* 2022). Fair and truthful sustainability disclosure should be implemented, along with accountability and responsibility for all stakeholders, to improve the quality of sustainability reporting. Therefore, the results of this study can serve as a useful reference for improving sustainability reporting in the transportation industry.

## 4 CONCLUSION

This paper proposes a fuzzy dynamic MRDM method to evaluate the transportation sector for improving sustainability reporting. The study employs TSFFFSM and fuzzy DEMATEL to investigate the patterns and key criteria of corporate sustainable development reporting. TSFFFSM is used to filter the key factors. Based on fuzzy DEMATEL technology, we capture the causal influences within the system and subsystems. For dimensions, the priorities for improvement include environment, social capital, business model and innovation, leadership and governance, and human capital. "Material efficiency and recycling" is the core of sustainability reporting disclosure for transportation industries and a primary focus for strengthening sustainable development and environmental responsibility in all standards. Furthermore, by focusing on these factors, we can identify the best impact for each subsystem and achieve greater effectiveness for both individual subsystems and the overall framework.

Despite having established a comprehensive evaluation model, there are still some shortcomings that are worth exploring in future work. The evaluation criteria proposed here are based on the SASB framework but can also consider other standards such as the GRI Guidelines. Additionally, applying more diverse samples or optimization techniques based on meta-heuristics, such as the White Shark Optimizer (Braik *et al.* 2022), can improve the effectiveness and reliability of the analysis. Multi-criteria group decision-making techniques, such as the VIKOR method, can reduce conflicts and disagreements among experts and achieve more reasonable consensus.

## REFERENCES

Adams C.A. (2013). Sustainability reporting and performance management in universities: Challenges and benefits. *Sustainability Accounting, Management and Policy Journal* 4(3), 384–392.

Braik M., Hammouri A., Atwan J., Al-Betar M.A. and Awadallah M.A. (2022). White Shark Optimizer: A novel bio-inspired meta-heuristic algorithm for global optimization problems. *Knowledge-Based Systems* 243, 108457.

Chaudhuri A., Samanta D. and Sarma M. (2021). Two-stage approach to feature set optimization for unsupervised dataset with heterogeneous attributes. *Expert Systems with Applications* 172, 114563.

Chen F.H., Hsu M.F. and Hu K.H. (2022). Enterprise's internal control for knowledge discovery in a big data environment by an integrated hybrid model. *Information Technology & Management* 23 (3), 213–231

Corazza L., Truant E., Scagnelli S.D. and Mio C. (2020). Sustainability reporting after the Costa Concordia disaster: a multi-theory study on legitimacy, impression management and image restoration. *Accounting, Auditing & Accountability Journal* 33(8), 1909–1941.

Gunawan J., Permatasari P. and Fauzi H. (2022). The evolution of sustainability reporting practices in Indonesia. *Journal of Cleaner Production* 358, 131798.

Goe, P. (2021). Rising standards of sustainability reporting in India. *Journal of Indian Business Research* 13(1), 92–109.

Hasan A., Hussainey K. and Aly D. (2022). Determinants of sustainability reporting decision: evidence from Pakistan. *Journal of Sustainable Finance & Investment* 12(1), 214–237.

Hasheminezhad A., Hadadi F. and Shirmohammadi H. (2021). Investigation and prioritization of risk factors in the collision of two passenger trains based on fuzzy COPRAS and fuzzy DEMATEL methods. *Soft Computing* 25, 4677–4697.

Hu K.H., Chen F.S., Hsu M.F. and Tzeng G.H. (2021). Construction of an AI-driven risk management framework for financial service firms using the MRDM approach. *International Journal of Information Technology & Decision Making* 20(3), 1037–1069.

Jørgensen S., Mjøs A. and Pedersen, L.J.T. (2022). Sustainability reporting and approaches to materiality: tensions and potential resolutions. Sustainability Accounting, *Management and Policy Journal* 13(2), 341–361.

Karagiannis I., Vouros P., Sioutas N. and Evangelinos K. (2022). Mapping the maritime CSR agenda: A cross-sectoral materiality analysis of sustainability reporting. *Journal of Clean Production* 338, 130139.

Karaman A.S., Kilic M. and Uyar, A. (2018). Sustainability reporting in the aviation industry: worldwide evidence. *Sustainability Accounting, Management and Policy Journal* 9(4), 362–391.

Kincaid C. and Smith, N.M. (2021). Diversity and inclusion in mining: An analysis of indicators used in sustainability reporting. *The Extractive Industries and Society* 100981.

Millar E. and Searcy C. (2020). The presence of citizen science in sustainability reporting", *Sustainability Accounting, Management and Policy Journal* 11(1), 31–64.

Opricovic S. & Tzeng, G. H. (2003). Defuzzification within a multicriteria decision model. *International Journal of Uncertainty, Fuzziness and Knowledge-Based Systems*, 11(05), 635–652.

Othman R., Laswad F. and Nath N. (2017). Local councils' environmental sustainability reporting: who really counts?. *Pacific Accounting Review* 29(4), 469–489.

Sustainability Accounting Standards Board. (2017). *SASB's approach to materiality for the purpose of standards development (Staff Bulletin No. SB002-07062017)*. San Francisco, CA: Author.

System Innovation for a Troubled World – Lam et al. (Eds)
© 2024 the Author(s), ISBN: 978-1-032-60846-4

# Integration of Gaussian process latent variable model in data envelopment analysis for advanced decision making process

Mushang Lee
*Department of Accounting, Chinese Culture University, Taipei, Taiwan*

Guo-Hsin Hu
*Department of Electronic Engineering, National Kaohsiung University of Science and Technology, Kaohsiung, Taiwan*
*Department of Industrial Upgrading Service, Metal Industries Research & Development Centre, Kaohsiung, Taiwan*

Sin-Jin Lin*
*Department of Accounting, Taipei, Taiwan*

Ming-Fu Hsu
*Department of Business Management, National United University, Miaoli, Taiwan*

ABSTRACT: Data envelopment analysis (DEA) has been widely adopted and applied in numerous research domains and reaches superior performance outcomes for-profit organizations as well as for non-profit organizations. Unfortunately, when it comes to handling large amounts of variables with respect to observations, its discriminant ability will be extremely degraded. That is, it cannot tell the differences between efficient and inefficient decision-making units (DMUs). If the performance evaluation model loses its basic evaluation function, it is impossible for decision makers to deploy resources to appropriate places as well as to give quick responses to market dynamics. To combat this, one of the dimensionality reduction techniques, called Gaussian process latent variable model (GPLVM) is considered. It can learn a low-dimensional representation of high-dimensional data via the Gaussian process and represent the inherent messages with less complexities. By joint utilization of GPLVM and DEA, the decision makers can point out some structures hidden behind successful practices. To demonstrate the effectiveness of the proposed decision framework, the pharmaceutical industry is taken. It is because this specific industry recently received a bunch of resources from public and private sectors and receives lots of market participants' attentions, especially in today's pandemic outbreak era. The results indicate that the proposed model reaches superior discriminant ability.

## 1 INTRODUCTION

In today's highly competitive business environment, characterized by limited resources, performance evaluation, and management play an essential role. Data envelopment analysis (DEA) is a non-parametric approach commonly adopted to evaluate the relative efficiency of decision-making units (DMUs) (Amado *et al.* 2012; Hahn *et al.* 2021). According to the production metaphor, this approach evaluates the efficiency of DMUs by considering the input consumed and output produced. The requirement of DEA on which inputs and outputs it should include has been a matter of concern for a long time because the efficiency ranking it provides is affected by the inclusion or exclusion of an input or an output (Jenkins & Anderson, 2003). To combat this and to look beyond any single DEA specification, this study proposes an advanced fusion mechanism—i.e., combining inputs and outputs in different ways— to conclude a much more trustworthy research outcome. However, too many DEA specifications surrounded by decision-makers will confuse them and increase their cognitive burden, and finally lead to improper judgments. To overcome this, the dimensionality reduction technique, called the Gaussian process latent variable model (GPLVM), can represent high-dimensional data into low-dimensional data without losing essential messages, is considered (Li & Chen, 2016; Lawrence 2005). By joint utilization of DEA specifications and GPLVM, the users can uncover some

*Corresponding Author: annman1204@gmail.com

DOI: 10.1201/9781003460763-45

weaknesses hidden in best practices and set up a remedy for performance improvement. The rest of the paper is organized as follows. In section 2, we represent the introduced fusion mechanism. In section 3, we display the experimental outcome. Section 4 concludes this study.

## 2 THE FUSION MECHANISM

The corporation with superior operating performance normally has higher profitability and risk-absorbing ability to survive in a highly turmoil atmosphere. How to evaluate corporate operating performance in a precise manner turns out to be an essential task. Most studies relied heavily on ratio analysis. However, ratio analysis merely considers one input and one output that cannot depict the whole picture of business operation. To combat this, DEA with the advantage of handling multiple inputs and multiple outputs without a pre-decided cost function is proposed (Charnes *et al.* 1978; Hsu *et al.* 2022). Before we receive the performance rank from DEA, the inputs and outputs need to be decided first. That is, different inputs and outputs will lead to different performance ranks. However, most previous studies do not consider different inputs and outputs combination strategies. To combat this, this study considers different combination strategies and further performs GPLVM to determine the corporate's operating performance. By joint utilization of multiple DEA specifications and GPLVM, the decision makers can realize the real situation of business operation.

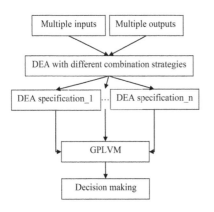

Figure 1.    The fusion mechanism.

## 3 EXPERIMENTAL OUTCOME

We follow previous related researches and choose three inputs (total assets: TA; cost of goods sold: COGS; number of employees: NE) and two outputs

(net sales: NS; earnings before interest and taxes: EBIT) (Hsu *et al.* 2022). To examine the representativeness of chosen variables, the Pearson correlation is considered (see Table 1). We can see that all the chosen variable has a positive correlation. That is, all the chosen variables are representative.

Table 1.    The outcome of the pearson correlation.

| Variable | TA | COGS | NE | NS | EBIT |
|---|---|---|---|---|---|
| TA | 1.00 | | | | |
| COGS | 0.49 | 1.00 | | | |
| NE | 0.48 | 0.70 | 1.00 | | |
| NS | 0.57 | 0.97 | 0.78 | 1.00 | |
| EBIT | 0.62 | 0.69 | 0.67 | 0.81 | 1.00 |

The requirement from the DEA, as to which inputs and outputs it should include, has been a matter of concern for a long period of time, because the performance rank it provides is affected by the inclusion or exclusion of an input or an output. To look beyond one specific DEA model and gain a much more reliable outcome, this study extends one specific model to multiple specifications model. The combination strategies are displayed in Table 2.

Table 2.    Multiple specifications of DEA.

| DEA specification | Inputs | Outputs |
|---|---|---|
| Specification_1 | TA | NS |
| Specification_2 | TA | EBIT |
| Specification_3 | TA | NS, EBIT |
| Specification_4 | COGS | NS |
| Specification_5 | COGS | EBIT |
| Specification_6 | COGS | NS, EBIT |
| Specification_7 | NE | NS |
| Specification_8 | NE | EBIT |
| Specification_9 | NE | NS, EBIT |
| Specification_10 | TA, COGS | NS |
| Specification_11 | TA, COGS | EBIT |
| Specification_12 | TA, COGS | NS, EBIT |
| Specification_13 | TA, NE | NS |
| Specification_14 | TA, NE | EBIT |
| Specification_15 | TA, NE | NS, EBIT |
| Specification_16 | COGS, NE | NS |
| Specification_17 | COGS, NE | EBIT |
| Specification_18 | COGS, NE | NS, EBIT |
| Specification_19 | TA, COGS, NE | NS |
| Specification_20 | TA, COGS, NE | EBIT |
| Specification_21 | TA, COGS, NE | NS, EBIT |

To summarize all the DEA specifications, the GPLVM is considered. By integrating multiple DEA specifications and GPLVM, the decision-makers can realize which company has superior operating performance.

## 4 RESULTS AND DISCUSSION

This study aims to look beyond one DEA specification by considering multiple combination strategies to gain much deeper insights and realize the corporation's overall operation. The introduced mechanism can be viewed as a decision support system to assist managers in deploying resources to appropriate places as well as avoid preventable waste.

## REFERENCES

Amado C.A.F., Santos S.P., Marques P.M. (2012). Integrating the data envelopment analysis and the balanced scorecard approaches for enhanced performance assessment, *Omega*, 40(3), 390–403.

Charnes A., Cooper W.W., Rhodes E. (1978). Measuring the efficiency of decision making units," *European Journal of Operational Research*, 2, 429–444.

Hahn G.J., Brandenburg M., Becker J. (2021). Valuing supply chain performance within and across manufacturing industries: A DEA-based approach, *International Journal of Production Economics*, 240, 108203.

Hsu M.F., Hsin Y.S., Shiue, (2022). Business analytics for corporate risk management and performance improvement. *Annals of Operations Research* 315, 629–669.

Jenkins L., Anderson M. (2003) A multivariate statistical approach to reducing the number of variables in data envelopment analysis, *European Journal of Operational Research*, 147, 51–61

Lawrence N. (2005). Probabilistic non-linear principal component analysis with Gaussian process latent variable models, *Journal of Machine Learning Research*, 6, 1783–1816.

Li. P., Chen S. (2016). A review on Gaussian process latent variable models. *CAAI Transactions on Intelligence Technology* 1, 366–376.

System Innovation for a Troubled World – Lam et al. (Eds)
© 2024 the Author(s), ISBN: 978-1-032-60846-4

# Do firm-level sustainability targets drive financial reporting quality?

Kaile Li
*Accounting School of Nanfang College, Guangzhou, Guangdong, China*

Lu Pan
*School of Accounting, Zhongnan University of Economics and Law, Wuhan, Hubei, China*

Sheng-Hsiung Chiu\*
*Accounting School of Nanfang College, Guangzhou, Guangdong, China*

ABSTRACT: This paper examines the relationship between corporate environmental awareness and its financial reporting quality, using data from Chinese A-share listed companies covering the 2011–2020 period. The results find that if a firm with environmental disclosures, the probability of its financial report restatement would be relatively lower. In addition, ESG practice and performance play an important channel to serve the relationship between corporate environmental awareness and its financial report quality.

## 1 INTRODUCTION

The United Nations Framework Convention on Climate Change (UNFCCC) entered into force on March 21, 1994, and today, it has been ratified by 198 countries and regions, with parties from almost all over the world. Against the backdrop of intensifying global climate change, the recent 27th Conference of the Parties (COP27) of the United Nations Framework Convention on Climate Change (UNFCCC) held in Sharm El Sheikh, Egypt, received a great deal of attention from around the world. The concept of green investment, green growth, and green consumption has quietly emerged (Nekmahmud *et al.* 2022; Xu *et al.* 2022), and more and more enterprises have spontaneously put forward their own environmental protection philosophy or set clear environmental protection targets. However, we do not know whether the positive performance of companies in terms of social responsibility, such as environmental protection, is "true" to protect the earth and practice the concept of sustainable development, or "false" to attract the attention of investors and consumers to build a good image.

Research on the credibility of corporate social responsibility has a long history, drawing the attention of researchers since the early 1980s, and many studies have found that corporate social responsibility disclosures do not always maintain a positive correlation with their true social responsibility performance (Pattern 2002, Wang *et al.* 2004), and that the motivation of companies to

voluntarily undertake social responsibility is closely related to the quality of their financial reports. Corporate social responsibility is to generate profits (Friedman 1970), the pursuit of short-term performance can cause managers to be short-sighted and thus neglect or even have to abandon programs that are beneficial in the long run. Therefore, companies that have developed an environmental protection philosophy or set environmental goals may be more aggressive in their financial statements. On the other hand, companies that have a positive corporate culture and sincerely practice their environmental protection targets may avoid such short-sighted behavior and be more transparent in their statement disclosures.

We use financial restatements to test the link between firms' environmental behavior and the quality of their financial reports to determine whether firms' environmental declaration is symbolic slogans or substantive actions. Firms that initiate environmental ideas or set environmental goals are part of their overall corporate culture, and this positive corporate culture generally leads to more transparent disclosure and less earnings management [6], and the less likely their statements should be restated. Conversely, if firms use environmental protection only as an impression management tool, which may involve the use of false information to present an environmentally responsible image (Kim 2011; Griffin 2006), this motive to greenwash is likely to be reflected in the financial statements as well, thus increasing the likelihood of future restatements by the firm.

Today, ESG is widely used in investment and regulatory fields, and more and more investors

---

\*Corresponding Author: mika.bear0809@gmail.com

DOI: 10.1201/9781003460763-46

rely on ESG ratings to obtain information about corporate performance in social responsibility (Berg 2022), and more and more academic studies rely on ESG ratings for empirical analysis (Flammer 2015; Servaes 2013). We select the Bloomberg ESG Rating Index as a proxy variable for corporate sustainability practices, and further examine whether companies with an environmental protection philosophy or clear environmental protection targets are effectively fulfilling their ESG-related obligations, proactively enhancing communication with stakeholders, and thus improving the transparency of their financial reports.

## 2 THEORETICAL ANALYSIS AND RESEARCH HYPOTHESES

Agency theory suggests that a firm's investment in environmental protection is an excessive investment behavior, which is inconsistent with the goal of profit maximization, and therefore a firm's environmental action will only add additional burden to the original business and bring more business risks (Chang *et al.* 2015), and management, forced by short-term performance pressure, may take more aggressive measures in the disclosure of financial information, thus reducing the financial statement transparency and increase the likelihood of future financial restatements. Therefore, our first hypothesis is as follows:

Hypothesis 1: Companies that present environmental protection philosophy or environmental protection targets are more likely to have restatements in their financial reports.

Contrary to the above view, some researchers have found a positive relationship between corporate environmental performance and information disclosure. Voluntary disclosure theory suggests that for firms with high environmental performance, it is important to differentiate themselves from other poor performers by voluntarily disclosing more environmental information (Clarkson 2015). Therefore, our second hypothesis is as follows:

Hypothesis 2: Companies that present environmental protection philosophy or environmental protection targets are less likely to have restatements in their financial reports.

From the available literature, although there is controversy about the relationship between corporate social responsibility and performance, most studies conclude that companies that sincerely fulfill their social responsibility will have better overall performance in all three ESG dimensions, which will help reduce the degree of corporate information asymmetry, enhance corporate value, and reduce corporate internal and external risks, thus effectively improving corporate performance. Therefore, our third hypothesis is as follows:

Hypothesis 3: Companies that present environmental protection philosophy or environmental protection targets improve the quality of financial reports and reduce the probability of restatement through responsible social activities (ESG).

## 3 DATA SOURCES AND STUDY DESIGN

This paper takes Chinese A-share listed companies from 2011 to 2020 as the research sample. The ESG rating data in this article was obtained from the Bloomberg Rating Agency, and other relevant financial data was obtained from the CSMAR database.

Equation (1) is used to test hypothesis 1 and hypothesis 2.

$$Rest = \beta_0 + \beta_1 Envthink/Envtarget + Control_{i,t} + Industry_i + Year_i + \varepsilon_{i,t} \tag{1}$$

The dependent variable of the model is the likelihood of a firm's financial restatement (Rest). Financial restatement is the act of discovering and correcting errors in a firm's prior period financial reports and is a direct measure of statement quality, with no restatement indicating higher quality statements for the current year (DeFond *et al.* 2014; Eisenberg *et al.* 2004). Therefore, in this paper, whether a company restates its financial reports for the year is used as a proxy for the quality of the current year's financial reports, Rest equals 1 in year $t$ if that year's annual financial statements are restated and 0 otherwise.

The independent variables of the model are environmental protection philosophy (*Envthink*) and environmental protection targets (*Envtarget*), respectively. Environmental protection philosophy (*Envthink*) refers to whether the company disclosed its environmental protection concept, environmental policy, environmental management organization structure, circular economy development model, green development, etc. in year $i$. If yes, it is 1, otherwise it is 0. Environmental protection target (*Envtarget*) refers to whether the company discloses the completion of the company's past environmental protection targets and future environmental protection targets in year i. If yes, it is 1, otherwise it is 0. Relatively speaking, the environmental protection concept is a soft indicator of the company's fulfillment of environmental protection because of the lack of clear and quantifiable targets, while the disclosure of environmental protection targets is a hard indicator that better reflects the company's determination to adhere to green development.

In this paper, based on previous studies (Ani 2021, Chepurko *et al.* 2018), we selected firm size

(*Size*), profitability (*Roa*), leverage level (*Lev*), whether the firm is losing money (*Loss*), whether it has overseas operations (*Fore*), growth opportunities (*M/B*), firm investment opportunities (*Growth*), and audit fees (*lnfee*) as control variables. In addition, year and industry effects are controlled in all the regression specifications. Standard errors are clustered at the firm level in all regressions.

To test Hypothesis 3, we constructed (2) and (3) in this paper to verify whether the improvement in the quality of statements of companies with an environmental protection philosophy or environmental goals is due to responsible social activities, thus verifying their environmental motives.

$$Pesg = \beta_0 + \beta_1 Envthink/Envtarget + Control_{i,t}$$
$$+ Industry_i + Year_i + \varepsilon_{i,t} \tag{2}$$

$$Rest = \beta_0 + \beta_1 Envthink/Envtarget + \beta_2 Pesg$$
$$+ Control_{i,t} + Industry_i + Year_i + \varepsilon_{i,t} \tag{3}$$

## 4 EMPIRICAL RESULTS

We first tested whether firms with an environmental protection philosophy (*Envthink*) would have higher financial report quality and the possible mediating role of corporate ESG behavior in this. Hypothesis 2 is verified. The finding also provides preliminary evidence of the motivation of companies to promote environmental protection, as companies that sincerely fulfill their environmental obligations are more inclined to disclose truthful information and value information communication with their stakeholders. Meanwhile, the coefficient of *Pesg* is significantly positive at the 1% level, it proves hypothesis 3 that corporate ESG performance has a mediating effect between environmental philosophy and statement quality, and that companies with environmental protection philosophy will be ethically driven to invest more resources in practicing ESG, which in turn improves the transparency of statement information and mitigates information asymmetry.

We used the same approach to empirically test those companies that proposed an explicit environmental goal (*Envtarget*). In summary, the study shows that more and more companies have become concerned about environmental issues and have begun to take action. However, there are fewer companies with clear environmental protection targets, and more companies are still only proposing environmental concepts, and the environmental cause needs further development.

## 5 CONCLUSION

With climate change and environmental issues becoming increasingly serious worldwide, companies, as an important force for social change and development, are bound to join in the action to protect the environment. What worries us is that the "good actor" enterprises mixed in the green wave do not sincerely fulfill their social responsibility, but consume a lot of social resources, such as cheating the government's green subsidies, obtaining low-interest green loans, etc. However, after our testing, we found that those companies that disclosed their environmental protection philosophy or had clear environmental protection goals tended to have high ESG performance and were recognized by society, and they also made efforts to improve the quality of their statements, enhance information communication with stakeholders, and improve mutual trust, which would be more conducive to further corporate efforts in environmental protection.

## ACKNOWLEDGMENTS

The paper was supported by the 2022 Scientific Research Project of Nanfang College, Guangzhou. [Grant number 2022XK30]

## REFERENCES

Ani M. K. A., "Corporate social responsibility disclosure and financial reporting quality: Evidence from Gulf Cooperation Council countries," *Borsa. Istanb. Rev*, vol. 21, pp. S25–S37, August 2021.

Berg F., Koelbel J.F. and Rigobon R., "Aggregate confusion: The divergence of ESG ratings," *Rev. Financ*, vol.26(6), pp. 1315–1344, May 2022.

Chang Y., Hsieh C.H., Wang T. C. and Hsieh S. Y., "Corporate social responsibility, cost of equity and cost of bank loans," *International Review of Accounting, Banking & Finance*, vol. 6, pp. 99–143, 2015.

Chepurko I., Dayanandan A., Han D. and Nofsinger J., "Are socially responsible firms less likely to restate earnings?" *Glob. Flnanc. J*, vol. 38, pp. 97–109, 2018.

Clarkson P.M., Li Y., Richardson G. D and Vasvari F. P., "Revisiting the relation between environmental performance and environmental disclosure: an empirical analysis," *Account. Organ. Soc*, vol. 33 (4–5), pp. 303–327, May–July 2008.

DeFond M. and Zhang J. "A review of archival auditing research," *J. Account. Econ*, vol. 58(2), pp. 275–326, November–December 2014.

Eisenberg T. and Macey J.R., "Was Arthur Andersen different? An empirical examination of major accounting firm audits of large clients," *J. Emplr. Legal. Stud*, vol. 1(2), pp. 263–300, June 2004.

Flammer C., "Does corporate social responsibility lead to superior financial performance? A regression discontinuity approach," *Manage. Scl*, vol. 61(11), pp. 2549–2824, November 2015.

Friedman M., "The social responsibility of business is to increase its2 profits," *New York Times Magazine*, vol. 32, pp. 173–178, September 1970.

Griffin J. and Weber J., "Industry social analysis: examining the beer industry," *Bus. Soc*, vol. 45(4), pp.413–440, December 2006.

Kim Y., Park M.S., Wier B., "Is earnings quality associated with corporate social responsibility?" *Account. Rev*, vol.87, pp.761–796, July 2011.

Nekmahmud M., Ramkissoon H. and Fekete-Farkas M., "Green purchase and sustainable consumption: A comparative study between European and non-European tourists," *Tour. Manag. Perspect*, vol. 43, 100980, July 2022.

Pattern D.M., "The relation between environmental performance and environmental disclosure: a research note," *Acc. Organ. Soc*, vol. 27 (8), pp. 763–773, November 2002.

Servaes H. and Tamayo A., "The impact of corporate social responsibility on firm value: The role of customer awareness," *Manage. Sci*, vol. 59(5), pp. 1045–1061, Jan 2013.

Wang H., Bi J., Wheeler D., Wang J.N., Cao D., Lu G. F. and Y. Wang, "Environmental performance rating and disclosure: China's greenwatch program," *Environmental. Management*, vol. 71 (2), pp. 123–133, June 2004.

Xu J., Zhao J., She S. and Liu W., "Green growth, natural resources and sustainable development: Evidence from BRICS economies," *Resour. Policy*, vol. 79, 103032, December 2022.

System Innovation for a Troubled World – Lam et al. (Eds)
© 2024 the Author(s), ISBN: 978-1-032-60846-4

# China's heterogenous equity and corporate investment efficiency

Lin Tzu-Yu
*Accounting School, Nanfang College, Guangzhou, China*

Ya Liu*
*Accounting School, Dongbei University of Finance and Economics, Dalian, China*

Chang Cai & Jingyi Zhu
*Accounting School and Academy of Politics & Business Studies, Nanfang College, Guangzhou, Guangzhou, China*

ABSTRACT:   Mixed ownership reform has entered a deepening stage, and it is valuable to study whether the addition of heterogeneous property rights can effectively curb the inefficient investment behavior of state-owned enterprises. This paper selects the A-share listed state-owned enterprises (SOEs) from 2003 to 2020 as a sample to investigate whether mixed ownership can effectively suppress inefficient investment in SOEs. The empirical results show that the mixed ownership structure achieved by introducing foreign ownership and top management team shareholding in mixed ownership reform can effectively suppress inefficient investment in SOEs.

## 1   INTRODUCTION

SOEs still account for two-thirds of the total market capital of all listed companies (Jiang *et al.* 2020). SOEs have long been considered inefficient in terms of productivity and innovation (Zhang *et al.* 2020, Allen *et al.* 2005, H. Che et al 1998, R. Cull et al 2005, J. P. H. Fan *et al.* 2007).

Some scholars believe that the mixed ownership reform can alleviate principal-agent contradiction, reduce information asymmetry and implicit government guarantee by introducing non-state-owned shares in state-owned enterprises (G. Borisova et al. 2011, N. Boubakri *et al.* 2005, D.K. Denis et al. 2003,O. Guedhami *et al* 2009), increase cash holdings (R.Y. Chen *et al.* 2018).

Effective company governance and good internal control can curb the over-investment behavior of enterprises (T. Y. Yu et al. 2013). Taking the A-share listed companies of state-owned enterprises from 2003 to 2020 as a sample, this paper uses regression analysis to empirically explore whether the mixed ownership reform can effectively curb the inefficient investment behavior of state-owned enterprises by "mixing" into heterogeneous property rights.

## 2   THEORETICAL ANALYSIS AND RESEARCH HYPOTHESES

### 2.1   *Mixed ownership reform*

The mixed ownership reform of state-owned enterprises, namely, in response to the actual situation that state-owned enterprises are monopolized by one share, promotes all types of ownership to complement each other and develop together through non-public capital participating in state-owned enterprises, state-owned capital participating in non-state-owned enterprises, initial public offerings (IPO), asset restructuring, and employee stock option program (ESOP) (Tong *et al.* 2019; Wang *et al.* 2019).At present, the relevant research on mixed ownership reform focuses on the change of ownership structure, and rarely involves the efficiency of the board of directors and investment efficiency (Yuan *et al.* 2022).

### 2.2   *Inefficient investment*

Investment activities are an important part of the production and operation of enterprises, investment efficiency is crucial to the survival and development of enterprises, investment efficiency is one of the basic determinants of enterprise value (Ohlson 1995). Neoclassical economics argues that in a perfect capital market, investment efficiency depends entirely on the investment opportunities of the firm (measured by Tobin's Q) (Modigliani *et al.* 1958). However, in the real world, companies may deviate from their optimal investment levels, resulting in over- or under-investment (Fazzari *et al.* 1988; Stein *et al.* 2003; Benlemlih *et al.* 2018). The first research hypothesis of this paper is proposed. Hypothesis 1: The more investment opportunities or the higher the net cash flow from operating activities, the more willing the enterprise is to invest.

---

*Corresponding Author: liuyahnu@163.com

DOI: 10.1201/9781003460763-47

## 2.3 Mixed ownership reform and inefficient investment

By constructing a regression model between ownership structure, investment opportunities and investment, Chen et al. find that state-owned ownership weakens investment-Q sensitivity, which in turn increases investment inefficiency ( R. Chen *et al.* 2017). In the process of mixed ownership reform, through the implementation of a state-owned + foreign + private type mixed equity structure in state-owned enterprises, it was found that the deepening of external nonstate components, and the company was urged to make optimal decisions as far as possible, thus alleviating the phenomenon of inefficient investment in enterprises (Xu *et al.* 2017, Yang *et al.* 2018; Kahn *et al.* 1998). The participation of foreign institutional investors in corporate governance practices can significantly reduce the encroachment of controlling shareholders in emerging markets (Huang *et al.* 2015).

Based on the above theoretical analysis, the second research hypothesis of this paper is proposed.

Hypothesis 2: In terms of equity structure, mixed ownership reform significantly discourages inefficient investment in SOEs by introducing heterogeneous property rights.

## 3 DATA SOURCES AND STUDY DESIGN

### 3.1 Data sources

This paper selects A-share state-owned listed companies from 2003 to 2020 as the sample.

### 3.2 Description of the model and variables

This study adopts Tobin's Q sensitivity to investment and Ocf sensitivity to investment to measure investment efficiency (Bushman *et al.* 2007, S. M. Chen *et al.* 2011, R. D. McLean *et al.* 2012, K. Huang et al. 2022, A. Bhandari *et al.* 2022). The baseline model was constructed as follows.

$$Inv_t = \beta_0 + \beta_1 TQ_{t-1} + \beta_2 Ocf_{t-1} + \beta_3 LNAT_{t-1}$$

$$+ \beta_4 Lev_{t-1} + FirmFE + YearFE + \varepsilon_t \tag{1}$$

Where $Inv_t$ is the firm's investment expenditure in year t, measured by dividing the total cash payments for fixed assets, intangible assets and other long-term assets by the book value of total assets; $TQ_{t-1}$ represents investment opportunities, measured by dividing the sum of the market value of tradable equities and the book value of nontradable equities and liabilities by the book value of total assets; $Ocf_{t-1}$ represents net cash flows

from operating activities. $LNAT_{t-1}$ represents the size of the firm, expressed as the logarithm of total assets; $Lev_{t-1}$ represents the level of leverage.

Hypothesis 1 predicts the sensitivity of investment opportunities, net cash flows from operating activities and investment expenditures. We wish to test the impact of a market-responsive direction of mixed reform, i.e., equity diversification on investment efficiency. Therefore, we modified model (1) to incorporate the "mixed" element of mixed ownership reform from the above direction.

$$Inv_t = \beta_0 + \beta_1 (TQ_{t-1} \times Poe20)$$

$$+ \beta_2 (Ocf_{t-1} \times Poe20)$$

$$+ \beta_3 (TQ_{t-1} \times D\_Fown)$$

$$+ \beta_4 (Ocf_{t-1} \times D\_Fown)$$

$$+ \beta_5 (TQ_{t-1} \times D\_Tmthold)$$

$$+ \beta_6 (Ocf_{t-1} \times D\_Tmthold) + \beta_7 TQ_{t-1}$$

$$+ \beta_8 Ocf_{t-1} + \beta_9 Poe20 + \beta_{10} D\_Fown$$

$$+ \beta_{11} D\_Tmthold + \beta_{12} LNAT_{t-1}$$

$$+ \beta_{13} Lev_{t-1} + FirmFE + YearFE + \varepsilon_t \tag{2}$$

Based on the results of descriptive statistics, it is clear that the mean value of investment expenditure is 5.41%, with a maximum value of 34.7%, indicating a wide variation in investment expenditure between SOEs and a highly uneven level of investment. The mean value of Tobin's Q is 1.806, with a minimum value of 0.850 and a maximum value of 7.957, indicating a wide variation in investment opportunities between SOEs. The mean value of Ocf is 5.2%, the maximum value is only 36.3% and the minimum value is negative, indicating that the net cash flow from operating activities of Chinese SOEs is unevenly distributed and relatively scarce overall. In the Pearson correlation analysis, the coefficients between the variables are less than 0.5, so there is no problem of multicollinearity.

## 4 EMPIRICAL RESULTS

### 4.1 Investment opportunities and the relationship between net cash flow from operating activities and investment expenditure

After fixing the firm and year in both directions and controlling for firm heterogeneity using the clustering criterion error, it can be found that there is a significant positive relationship between Tobin's Q and Inv (0.007, p-value < 0.01), which is consistent with the existing literature [31]. That is, a firm's investment expenditure depends on the firm's investment opportunities. Ocf from operating activities is significantly positively correlated with Inv (0.062, p-value < 0.01), and the empirical results support hypothesis 1. Both LNAT and Lev are significantly negatively correlated with Inv at the 1% level. Specifically, the larger the firm, the stronger its financing capacity, the lower its risk aversion tendency, and the lower the requirement to invest to cope with and prevent future operational risks. Firms with high leverage are usually short of capital, need more cash to service their debt and have financing constraints that limit investment (S. M. Chen *et al.* 2011, H. Wang *et al.* 2021).

### 4.2 The impact of heterogeneous equity inclusion in mixed ownership reform on the investment efficiency of state-owned enterprises

From the estimated coefficients it can be found that Tobin's Q*Poe20 is negatively correlated with Inv at the 5% level, while Tobin's Q*D_Fown and Tobin's Q*D_Tmthold are positively correlated with Inv at the 5% and 10% levels respectively. This suggests that with 20% private ownership, investment decisions tend to be conservative, weakening the investment sensitivity of Tobin's Q. With foreign ownership or top management team shareholding, investment decisions are more aggressive, increasing the investment sensitivity of Tobin's Q. This suggests that the "mixing" of heterogeneous shares in the mixed ownership reform can indeed discourage inefficient investment, and Hypothesis 2 is supported. The investment sensitivity of Ocf is not statistically significant. In mixed ownership reform, it is not only important to "mix" but also to "integrate", so it is particularly important to control the scale of "mixing".

## 5 CONCLUSION

Mixed ownership reform is an important measure to deepen Chinese state-owned enterprises reform. In order to investigate the impact of mixed ownership reform on the investment efficiency of SOEs, this paper conducts a series of tests from the perspectives of whether private ownership has reached 20%, whether there is foreign ownership, and whether there is a top management team shareholding, based on the sensitivity of Tobin's Q and Ocf to investment, combined with the "mixed reform" direction of equity diversification of mixed ownership reform. Empirical studies show that the mixed ownership reform can effectively curb the inefficient investment behavior of state-owned enterprises through the introduction of foreign ownership and top management team shareholding.

## REFERENCES

Allen F., Qian J. and Qian M.J., "Law, Finance, and economic growth in china.," *J. Financ. Econ*, vol. 77 (1), pp. 57–116, July 2005.

Benlemlih M. and Bitar M., "Corporate social responsibility and investment efficiency," *J. Bus Ethics*, vol. 148(3), pp. 647–671, January 2018.

Bhandari A., Kohlbeck M. and Mayhew B., "Association of related party transactions with sensitivity of investments and external financing," *Journal of Corporate Finance*, vol. 72, pp. 1–16, February 2022.

Borisova G., Megginson W.L., "Does government ownership affect the cost of debt? Evidence from privatization," *Rev. Financ. Stud*, vol. 24 (8), pp. 2693–2737, March 2011.

Boubakri N., Cosset J.C., Guedhami O., "Post privatization corporate governance: the role of ownership structure and investor protection," *J. Financ. Econ*, vol. 76 (2), pp. 369–399, May 2005.

Bushman R., Piotroski J. and Smith A., "Capital allocation and timely accounting recognition of economic losses," *J. Bus Finan Account*, vol. 38, pp.1–33, January 2007.

Che J.H. and Qian Y.Y., "Insecure property rights and government ownership of firms," *Q. J. Econ*, vol. 113 (2), pp.467–496, May 1998.

Chen R., El Ghoul S., Guedhami O. and Wang H., "Do state and foreign ownership affect investment efficiency? Evidence from privatizations," *J. Copr. Financ*, vol. 42(1), pp. 408–421, February 2017.

R.Y. Chen, S. EI Ghoul, O. Guedhami, R. Nash, "State ownership and corporate cash holdings," *J. Financ. Quant. Anal*, vol. 53 (5), pp. 2293–2334, July 2018.

Chen S.M., Sun Z., Tang S. and Wu D.H, "Government intervention and investment efficiency: Evidence from China," *J. Copr Financ*, vol. 17, pp. 259–271, April 2011.

Cull R. and Xu L.C, "Institutions, ownership, and finance: The determinants of profit reinvestment among chinese firms," *J. Financ Econ*, vol. 77(1), pp. 117–146, July 2005.

Denis D.K., McConnell J.J, "International corporate governance," *J. Financ. Quant. Anal*, vol. 38, pp. 1–36, January 2003.

Fan J.P.H., Wong T.J. and Zhang T.Y., "Politically connected CEOs, corporate governance and post–IPO performance of China's partially privatized firms," *J. Financ Econ*, vol. 84(2), pp.330–357, May 2007.

Fazzari S.M., Hubbard R.G. and Petersen B.C., "Financing constraints and corporate investment. brook," *Pap. Econ. Act*, vol. 1, pp. 141–195, January 1988.

Guedhami O., Pittman J.A., Saffar W., "Auditor choice in privatized firms: empirical evidence on the role of state and foreign owners," *J. Account. Econ*, vol. 48 (2–3), pp. 151–171, December 2009.

Huang K., Zhu Y., "China's secondary privatization and corporate investment efficiency," *Res. Int. Bus. Financ*, vol. 61, pp. 1–16, October 2022.

Huang W. and Zhu T., "Foreign institutional investors and corporate governance in emerging markets: Evidence of a split–share structure reform in China," *J. Corp. Finan*, vol. 32, pp. 312–326. June 2015.

Jiang F. and Kim K.A., "Corporate governance in china: A Survey," *Rev. Financ*, vol. 24, pp. 733–772, July 2020.

Kahn C. and Winton A., "Ownership structure, speculation, and shareholder intervention," *J. Financ*, vol. 53(1), pp. 99–129, February 1998.

McLean R.D., Zhang T. and Zhao M., "Why does the law matter? Investor protection and its effects on investment, finance, and growth," *J. Financ*, vol. 67 (1), pp. 313–350, January 2012.

Modigliani F. and Miller M.H., "The cost of capital, corporation finance and the theory of investment," *Am. Econ. Rev*, vol. 48, pp.261–297, June 1958.

Ohlson J.A., "Earnings, book values, and dividends in equity valuation," *Contemporary Accounting Res*, vol. 11(2), pp. 661–687, Spring 1995.

Stein J.C., "Agency, information and corporate investment," *Handbook of the Economics of Finance*, vol. 1, pp. 111–165, January 2003.

Tong S.Y. and Yin X., "Mixed ownership reforms of china's state–owned enterprises," *East. Asian. Policy*, vol. 11, pp.104–116, April 2019.

Wang H., Wang W. and S. E. A. Alhaleh, "Mixed ownership and financial investment: Evidence from Chinese state–owned enterprises," *Economic Analysis and Policy*, vol. 70, pp. 159–171, June 2021.

Wang J.Y. and Han T.C, "Mixed ownership reform and corporate governance in china's state–owned enterprises," *Vanderbilt Journal of Transnational Law*, vol.53, pp.1055–1107, July 2019.

Xu W.B., Zhou J., Management S.O and University G. "Mixed Ownership, the check–and–balance of ctock ownership and the over investment of state–owned enterprises: An explanation based on the view of politics and managers," *Journal of Guangdong University of Finance & Economics*, 2017.

Yang Z. and Li Z., "Mixed ownership structure, environmental uncertainty and investment efficiency: A perspective of specialization of property rights," *Journal of Shanghai University of Finance and Economics*, vol. 40, pp. 4–24, April 2018.

Yu T.Y. and Chen C.C., "Corporate governance, internal control and over investment under insider control: evidence from listed manufacturing companies in china," *Research Journal of Applied Science, Engineering and Technology*, vol.22, pp. 4247–4253, December 2013.

Yuan R., Li C., Cao X, Li N. and Khaliq N., "Research on the influence of mixed–ownership reform on exploratory innovation of SOEs: The mediation effect of agency conflict and financing constraint," *SAGE. Open*, vol. 12(2), April 2022.

Zhang X.Q., Yu M.Q., and Chen G.Q., "Does mixed–ownership reform improve SOEs' innovation? evidence from state ownership." *China. Econ. Rev*, vol. 61, pp. 1–22, June 2020.

*System Innovation for a Troubled World – Lam et al. (Eds)*
*© 2024 the Author(s), ISBN: 978-1-032-60846-4*

# Does privatization of state-owned enterprises matter for stock price synchronicity?

Sheng-Hsiung Chiu, Xiaorui Zhang*, Zhiyuan Zhang & Haotong Lin
*Accounting School, Nanfang College, Guangzhou, Guangzhou, China*

ABSTRACT: This paper explores the impact of the control transfer of SOEs on the synchronicity of stock prices of A-share listed SOEs from 2003 to 2021 using a multi-period DID model with exogenous shocks from a quasi-natural experiment of split share structure reform starting in 2005. It is found that the stock price synchronicity of SOEs that have completed privatization is significantly lower than that of enterprises whose ultimate controllers remain the state capital after undergoing privatization.

## 1 INTRODUCTION

For more than 30 years, the reform around the ownership of SOEs has been an important part of China's economic reform. SOEs have gradually diversified their shareholding structure from wholly state-owned to state-controlled to cross-shareholding. The process can be divided into three reform phases: the "retreat of the state-owned capital and advance of the non-state-owned capital" wave, the spilt share structure reform, and the reform of the mixed ownership system.

During the transition from a planned economy to a market economy in China, most of the companies formed were wholly SOEs, and they shouldered important responsibilities for the country's livelihood, which was also an important stage in the rapid development of SOEs in China [1]. However, due to the unavoidable policy burden of SOEs' supportive role in economic and social development [2] and the agency conflict worsened by the absence of owners [3], some scholars have proposed the theory of complete privatization in the process of deepening reform of SOEs [4]. Some scholars point out that SOEs have earnings management behaviors such as reducing earnings before privatization [5]. Some point out that privatization can significantly promote enterprise technological innovation [6], but some scholars hold the opposite view [7]. Others draw a conclusion that privatization reduces internal information transmission costs and improves information asymmetry [8]. According to the existing literature, it is known that a sound corporate governance structure can improve the quality of information disclosure [9], which in turn improves the allocation efficiency of the overall capital market [10]. Thus, how will the information content of capital market stock prices change after the privatization of SOEs? Existing studies do not provide an answer.

Based on the above, this paper examines whether Chinese SOEs' stock price synchronicity from 2003 to 2021 decreased after control transfer caused by split share structure reform. In addition, this paper adopts fixed effects including industry and year fixed, individual and year fixed, and enterprise individual clustering standard error setting. The results of the study indicate that, in general, the stock price synchronicity of SOEs undergoing split share structure reform significantly decreases, which means that the amount of firm heterogeneity information contained in stock prices increases and the ability and efficiency of capital market pricing is enhanced.

## 2 THEORETICAL ANALYSIS AND RESEARCH HYPOTHESIS

### 2.1 *The split share structure reform*

Before the reform, 2/3 of the listed stocks were non-liquid, mainly held by the state or legal entities, while the remaining stocks were held by individuals and institutional investors, and the pattern of shareholding division led to serious problems in corporate governance. Existing research about split share structure reform focuses on two aspects. On one hand, the corporate governance effect is based on agency theory. On the other hand, some

*Corresponding Author: 1747145116@qq.com

DOI: 10.1201/9781003460763-48

research explores its market effects based on information theory.

## 2.2 The information content of the stock price

The information content of the stock price characterizes the degree and efficiency of the company's heterogeneous information delivered to investors and is a comprehensive indicator that reflects the pricing efficiency of the capital market. Compared with market and industry information, the higher the degree of explanation to stock returns by company heterogeneous information, the more the stock price can reflect the fundamental value of the company, which also means the capital market pricing efficiency is higher [11]. The high frequency of trading also led to a more diversified shareholding structure of SOEs. An empirical study found that the higher the shareholding ratio of state-owned capital, the lower the value relevance of accounting information. [12]. Therefore, what would be the effect on stock price synchronicity if SOEs undergo split share structure reform and the control of SOEs is transferred to non-state capital? The answer is not available in the existing literature.

Based on the above theoretical analysis, the hypothesis of this paper is proposed:

Hypothesis 1: After going through the split share structure reform, fully privatized SOEs have lower stock price synchronicity than partially privatized SOEs.

## 3 STUDY DESIGN

### 3.1 Sample description and data sources

This paper selects China's A-share SOEs data from 2003 to 2021 as a sample. Specifically, the data were selected according to the following principles: (1) excluding financial and public utility companies, (2) excluding *ST and ST companies, and (3) excluding companies with missing values. Finally, 17,057 observations were obtained. The financial data and stock price data of listed companies are obtained from the CSMAR database. To remove the influence of outliers, we winsorize all continuous variables at the top and bottom 1% levels. And multi-period DID approach is used to conduct the study.

### 3.2 Model setting and variable definition

To test hypothesis one, the regression model shown below is constructed in this paper:

$$SYN_{i,t} = \alpha_0 + \alpha_1 \times Private + Controls$$

$$+ Year + Firm + \varepsilon \qquad (1)$$

### 3.2.1 Dependent variable

The dependent variable in this paper is stock price synchronicity. Drawing on Durnev et al.'s [13] studies, the goodness-of-fit R2 of individual stocks is estimated by equation (2); then, synchronicity which conforms to normal distribution is estimated by equation (3) with R2. The higher the stock price synchronicity, the less the company heterogeneous information. In equation (2), $RET_{i,w}$ is the stock return of company I in week w. $MarketRET_w$ is the market return rate in week w. $IndustryRET_{j,w}$ is the industry return rate (excluded company i) in which company I is in week w. The industry is followed the 2012 SEC industry classification criteria. And R2i, t in equation (3) is the equation (2)'s regression goodness-of-fit.

$$RET_{i,w} = \alpha_0 + \alpha_1 \ MarketRET_W$$

$$+ \alpha_2 \ IndustryRET_{j,w} + \varepsilon_{i,w} \qquad (2)$$

$$SYN_{i,t} = \ln\left[R^2_{i,t}/\left(1 - R^2_{i,t}\right)\right] \qquad (3)$$

### 3.2.2 Independent variable

The subjects of this paper are SOEs which the nature of ownership of the ultimate controllers changed after the split share structure reform. Therefore, the dummy variable Private is set. The dummy variable Private equals one if the ultimate controller of the enterprise changes from state-owned capital to non-state-owned capital after the reform, and zero otherwise. Since there may be cases of privatization followed by nationalization, this study only examines changes in the synchronicity of share prices of firms that are initially privatized.

### 3.2.3 Control variable

Controls in this paper refer to control variables. Drawing on the studies of Gul et al. [14], this paper introduces the following control variables: (1) Lev, defined as total debt divided by total assets; (2) Size, defined as the natural logarithm of total assets; (3) Growth, defined as the annual change of sales for a firm; (4) Ocf, defined as net cash flow from operating activities; (5) Big 4, defined as whether the company is audited by international Big 4 or domestic Big 4 accounting firms; (6) M/B, defined as market value by book value of equity; (7) Taturnover, defined as total asset turnover ratio; (8) Analyst, defined as a number of analyst research reports; (9) Volume, defined as an annual number of individual stock transactions; (10) Volatility, defined as the standard deviation of weekly idiosyncratic returns; (11) Instu, defined as institutional investor shareholding ratio; (12)

Bigholder, defined as major shareholder shareholding ratio.

# 4 EMPIRICAL RESULT AND ANALYSIS

## 4.1 *Descriptive statistic results*

The mean value of the dependent variable SYN is 0.48 with a standard deviation of 0.196. The independent variable Private has a mean value of 0.158 and a standard deviation of 0.365, which means that 15.8% of listed SOEs have completed privatization and restructuring after the reform. Lev has a mean value of 0.504 and a standard deviation of 0.203, with a minimum value of 0.009 and a maximum value of 4.026, which shows that SOEs have a lower asset-liability ratio and more adequate own funds. Bigholder has a mean value of 38.57% and a standard deviation of 15.825, which can be seen as the shareholding ratio of major shareholders of SOEs varies greatly. The maximum value is 89.99%, however, the minimum value is only 3.89%. It reflects that SOEs have the characteristics of state-owned equity dominance and excessive concentration of equity.

## 4.2 *Analysis of regression results*

The estimated coefficient on Ln_SYN is $-0.141$, significant at a 1% level. When the year and individual fixed effects are controlled, the estimated coefficient on Ln_SYN is $-0.137$, significant at the 1% level. The above results are consistent with the hypothesis H1.

# 5 ROBUSTNESS TEST

## 5.1 *Adding possible omitted variables*

The existing literature suggests that privatization of SOEs is not a random choice [15]. This article adds the addition of omitted variables: the number of board of directors (board), the number of independent directors (Ind_board), the number of supervisors (Sup), the number of executive team (Tmt), and the proportion of women in the board of directors(F_board) and in the executive team (F_tmt). The regression results show that the coefficient of private is significantly negative and still supports H1. It is also found that with year-fixed effect and industry-fixed effect, supervisors and female executives significantly reduce stock price synchronicity and enhance stock price information content at the 5% and 1% levels, respectively. It shows that the reform can enhance the role of directors and supervisors' mechanisms and improve the governance structure of SOEs.

## 5.2 *One-period lag of variables*

Considering the lag of information transmission, this paper adopts a one-period lag of the independent variable and the dependent variable for testing. The coefficient of private is still significantly negative, although it is lower than the coefficient of the main regression. However, insignificant coefficient after year fixed effects and individual fixed effects are controlled, probably because some factors that do not vary over time and individuals have not been removed and need further analysis.

# 6 CONCLUSION

Privatization of listed SOEs affects the company-specific disclosure behavior and ultimately affects the information content of stock prices. Using A-share SOEs from 2003 to 2021 as the sample, this paper finds that the synchronicity of stock prices of SOEs also significantly decreases if the ultimate controller changes from state-owned to non-state-owned capital after the split share structure reform. The result still exists after the robustness test with additional omitted variables and a one-period lag of variables.

# ACKNOWLEDGEMENTS

This study was supported by the 2022 Scientific Research Project of Nanfang College, Guangzhou [Grant number 2022XK33]

# REFERENCES

[1] Luo H.H., Wu X. and Wu Y., "Mixed ownership reform of state-owned enterprises and R&D investment," *Math. Probl. Eng*, pp. 1–14(1), August 2022.

[2] Ye S., Zeng J., Liao F. and Huang J., "Policy burden of state-owned enterprises and efficiency of credit resource allocation: Evidence from china," *SAGE. Open*, 11(1), 2021.

[3] Laffont J.J. and Tirole J., *"A theory of incentives in procurement and regulation,"* Mit Press Books, 1993.

[4] Sanders R. and Chen Y., "On Privatisation and Property Rights: Should China Go Down the Road of Outright Privatisation?" *J. Chin. Econ. Bus. Stud*, 3:3, pp. 231–245, February 2007.

[5] Chen C.J.P., Du J. and Su X., "A game of accounting numbers in asset pricing: Evidence from the privatization of state-owned enterprises," *J. Contemp. Account. Ec*, pp. 115–129, August 2014.

[6] Castelnovo P., "Innovation in private and state-owned enterprises: A cross-industry analysis of

patenting activity," *Struct. Change. Econ. D*, Vol. 62, pp. 98–113, September 2022.

[7] Maria E., Rocha P.D., Araújo M. and Ferreira T., "Analysis of Brazilian technological innovation indicators: assessing the impact of privatization on innovation," January 2001.

[8] Bös D. and Peters W., "Privatization, internal control, and internal regulation," *J. Public. Econ*, Vol. 36, Issue 2, pp. 231–258, July 1988.

[9] Shleifer A. and Vishny R. W., "Large Shareholders and Corporate Control," *J. Polit. Econ*, 94(3), pp. 461–438, 1986.

[10] Healy P.M. and Palepu K.G., "Information Asymmetry, Corporate Disclosure, and the Capital Markets: A Review of the Empirical Disclosure Literature," *J. Account. Econ*, 31 (1–3), pp. 405–440, 2001.

[11] Morck R., Yeung B. and Yu W., "The information content of stock markets: Why do emerging markets have synchronous stock price movements?" *J. Finance. Econ*, pp. 215–260, 2000.

[12] Li J.M., Wang H.B. and Wang Z.H., "An empirical study on the relationship between corporate ownership structure and quality of accounting information of china's listed companies in the manufacturing industry," *2008 4th Int. Conf. Wirel. Commun, Netw. Mob. Comput*, pp. 1–4, 2008.

[13] Durnev A., Mrck R. and Yeung B.Y., "Value enhancing capital budgeting and firm-specific stock returns variation," *J. Financ*, Vol. 59, pp. 65–105, 2003.

[14] Gul F.A., Kim J. and Qiu A.A., "Ownership concentration, foreign shareholding, audit quality, and stock price synchronicity: evidence from china," *J. Financ. Econ*, 95(3), 2010.

[15] Parker D., "Privatization of state-owned enterprises," *Oxford Research Encyclopedia of Business and Management*, September 2021.

System Innovation for a Troubled World – Lam et al. (Eds)
© 2024 the Author(s), ISBN: 978-1-032-60846-4

# An integrated data transformation, cluster determination, and data envelopment analysis for advanced decision making

Te-Min Chang
*Department of Information Management, National Sun Yat-sen University, Kaohsiung, Taiwan*

Sin-Jin Lin
*Department of Accounting, Taipei, Taiwan*

Ming-Fu Hsu*
*Department of Business Management, National United University, Miaoli, Taiwan*

ABSTRACT: Data Envelopment Analysis (DEA) is a sort of non-parametric linear programming approach for measuring the relative efficiency of homogeneous decision-making units (DUMs). Because it poses the ability to handle multiple inputs and outputs simultaneously without a predetermined cost function, it has gained numerous attention in recent years, especially in the domain of performance measures. However, when it comes to handle a large amount of assessing measures with respect to DMUs, its discriminant ability will be decreased largely. To overcome this obstacle, data transformation and cluster determination are adopted to refine the data so as to enhance its discriminant quality. The data transformation is applied to disentangle the interaction between assessing measures so as to give suitable responses to changing human behavior and evolving social situations. The cluster determination is adopted to realize the sub-patterns of assessing measures in order to assist users in inferring the inherent and valuable data structure. To demonstrate the effectiveness of the introduced framework, the publicly listed companies in Taiwan's IT industries are considered. The result indicates that the introduced model reaches superior discriminant ability over the model without data preprocessing steps.

## 1 INTRODUCTION

With the competition in the 1990s intensified and the market became international and diversified, the challenges and disturbances associated with getting a product and service to a suitable place at the right time at a lower cost turn out to be an essential driving force for corporate success. Corporate began to understand that it is not enough to improve the inherent efficiency within its operation, but the whole interconnected up- and downstream partners have to be made competitive (Li et al. 2006; Yu et al. 2021). The practice and realization of supply chain management (SCM) has become a critical and inevitable element for corporations to maintain and stay competitive in this highly fierce and turbulent economy (Childhouse and Towill 2003; Hahn et al. 2021).

Council of the Supply Chain Management Professionals (CSCMP, 2013) also indicated that SCM deals with the planning, steering, and controlling of internal operations and the

coordination of related business activities with supply chain partners. It represents a main performance driver and contributes considerably to shareholder value generation. In today's competitive business situation characterized by limited resources, accurate performance evaluation and management gradually attracts considerable attention from academicians and practitioners. Data envelopment analysis (DEA) is a non-parametric approach commonly adopted to measure the relative efficiency of comparable units called decision-making units (DMUs) (Lozano and Khezri 2021; Wu et al., 2023) by considering the inputs consumed and the outputs produced, and it has been widely adopted in many fields, such as education, accounting, banking and others (Emrouznejad and Yang 2018; Zhou et al. 2018; Hsu et al. 2022) with satisfactory successes.

Even though the DEA has many advantages, it still encounters some flaws. The discriminant ability of DEA often fails when there is an excessive number of inputs and outputs in relation to the number of DMUs. When it occurs, the Pareto frontier may be determined by a considerable amount of DMUs that are deemed as efficient. Even if the dimensionality reduction

*Corresponding Author: hsumf0222@gmail.com

DOI: 10.1201/9781003460763-49

technique is taken to reduce the dimensions of inputs and/or outputs, this refinement may still be inefficient in generating an appropriate ranking of the DMUs (Adler and Golany 2002). To overcome the mentioned obstacle, this study aims to strengthen the model's discriminatory power by considering the data transformation and clustering technique.

Most of the data adopted in performance analysis by DEA are derived from financial statements. The financial data are social data, which are usually dominated by many complicated and interconnected latent factors and those factors are prone to influence by external evolving and changing environment over time. Furthermore, most of the financial data are correlated, and even autocorrelative, that is, these elements affect each other mutually and finally lead to an unsatisfactory outcome (Li et al. 2022). To combat this, random Fourier (RF) transformation is considered to eliminate the effect of multimodel distribution. Rao's quadratic entropy takes both the size of clusters and the distance between clusters into consideration to determine the suitable number of groups. The result (i.e., the best number of groups) can be taken as the dependent variable and equips it with independent variables and then fed all of the variables into rough set theory (RST) to determine the essential variables for DEA as well as strengthen its discriminant ability. The rest of the paper is organized as follows. In section 2, we describe the model we adopted. In section 3, we present the experimental results. In section 4, we make concluding remarks and discuss future work.

## 2 THE HYBRID DECISION MECHANISM

Figure 1 displays the introduced hybrid decision mechanism. To alleviate the influence of multimodel distribution within the data, the data transformation is taken. The transformed data are inserted into Rao's quadratic entropy to determine the best number of groups with the data. The outcome can be viewed as a dependent variable. By doing this, we can transform the problem into a classification task. The dependent variable and independent variables (i.e., transformed data) are fed into RST to point out the most representative variables. The selected variables are inserted into DEA to describe the corporate operating performance. By doing so, the DEA's discriminant ability will improve and calculation complexity will reduce. The decision-makers can receive much more reliable and trustful decision support to assist them in deploying limited resources to appropriate places as well as avoid preventable waste

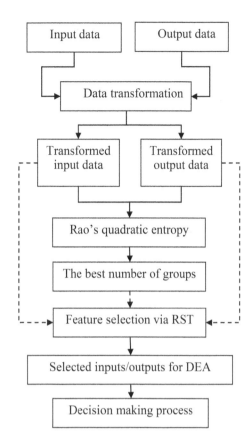

Figure 1. The hybrid decision mechanism.

## 3 EXPERIMENTAL RESULTS

Financial indicators have been widely applied in selecting the DEA model's inputs and outputs to evaluate the corporate operating performance. However, most of the financial indicators' distribution is multimodel. That is, the data contain more than two distributions. Figure 2 displays the data with and without transformation. We can see that the data after transformation can be much easier to be clustered. Thus, data transformation is required.

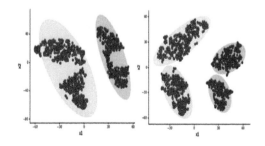

Figure 2. The data with (right) and without (left) transformation (Li et al. 2022).

According to previous researches, we take fixed assets (FA), operating expense (OE), number of employees (NE), cost of goods sold (COGS), total equity (TE) as inputs, and net sales (NS), gross margin (GM), earnings before interests and taxes (EBIT) as outputs. To ensure the selected variables are representative, the Pearson correlation is considered. Table 1 displays the outcome. We can see that all of the variables show a positive relationship. That is, all the adopted variables are representative of DEA application.

Table 1. The outcome of Pearson correlation.

| Variable | FA | OE | NE | COGS | TE | NS | GM | EBIT |
|---|---|---|---|---|---|---|---|---|
| FA | 1.00 | | | | | | | |
| OE | 0.84 | 1.00 | | | | | | |
| NE | 0.38 | 0.70 | 1.00 | | | | | |
| COGS | 0.43 | 0.74 | 0.96 | 1.00 | | | | |
| TE | 0.98 | 0.91 | 0.55 | 0.59 | 1.00 | | | |
| NS | 0.58 | 0.83 | 0.94 | 0.98 | 0.72 | 1.00 | | |
| GM | 0.98 | 0.85 | 0.36 | 0.42 | 0.97 | 0.57 | 1.00 | |
| EBIT | 0.98 | 0.77 | 0.26 | 0.32 | 0.94 | 0.48 | 0.99 | 1.00 |

However, DEA with too many inputs and outputs will decrease its discriminant ability. To combat this challenge, Rao's quadratic entropy is considered to group the data into suitable clusters. The outcome derived from Rao's quadratic entropy and the transformed inputs and outputs are fed into RST to determine the best features for DEA. Table 2 shows the selected outcome.

Table 2. The selected variables via RST.

| Variable | Selected | Non-selected |
|---|---|---|
| FA | ■ | |
| OE | | ☐ |
| NE | | ☐ |
| COGS | ■ | |
| TE | | ☐ |
| NS | ■ | |
| GM | | ☐ |
| EBIT | ■ | |

To demonstrate the effectiveness of feature selection, we divide the experimental design into three scenarios: (1) no data transformation and no feature selection; (2) with data transformation and no feature selection; (3) with data

transformation and feature selection (see Table 3). We can see that the DEA with feature selection process poses higher discriminant ability (i.e., lower mean and higher variance values). The decision-makers can take this hybrid mechanism as a roadmap to modify their business operating strategy as well as provide an appropriate and quick reaction to consumers' requirements.

Table 3. The outcome.

| Scenario | Mean | Variance |
|---|---|---|
| 1. No transformation and no feature selection | 0.72 | 0.08 |
| 2. With transformation and no feature selection | 0.58 | 0.11 |
| 3. With transformation and feature selection | 0.47 | 0.14 |

## 4 CONCLUSION AND FUTURE WORKS

This paper introduces a hybrid decision mechanism that integrates data transformation, the best number of cluster selections, RST, and DEA for advanced decision-making tasks. The result indicates that the data going through each procedure can reach a satisfactory outcome. The decision-makers can consider the potential implications of the outcome and adjust their business strategies to fit into the current and future business environment.

Despite its contributions, this study is subject to some limitations that provide directions for future studies. First, the network DEA that opens up the black box of DEA can be considered to dig out much more meaningful outcomes. Second, advanced feature selection architecture, such as feature selection ensemble, can be adapted to initially screen essential elements as well as eliminate the course of dimensionality.

## REFERENCES

Adler N., Golany B. (2002). Including principal component weights to improve discrimination in data envelopment analysis. *Journal of Operational Research Society*, 53(9), 985–991

Childerhouse P., Towill D.R. (2003). Simplified material flow holds the key to supply chain integration, *Omega*, 31(1), 17–27.

Emrouznejad A., Yang G. (2018). A survey and analysis of the first 40 years of scholarly literature in DEA: 1978–2016, *Socio-Economic Planning Sciences*, 61, 4–8.

Hahn G.J., Brandenburg M., Becker J. (2021). Valuing supply chain performance within and across manufacturing industries: A DEA-based approach, *International Journal of Production Economics*, 240, 108203.

Hsu M.F., Hsin Y.S., Shiue F.J., (2022). Business analytics for corporate risk management and performance improvement. *Annals of Operations Research* 315, 629–669.

Li S., Ragu-Nathan B., Ragu-Nathan T.S., Rao S.S. (2006). The impact of supply chain management practices on competitive advantage and organizational performance, *Omega*, 34(2), 107–124.

Li T, Kou G., Peng Y., Philip S.Y. (2022). An integrated cluster detection, optimization, and interpretation approach for financial data, *IEEE transactions on cybernetics* 52 (12), 13848–13861

Lozano S., Khezri S. (2021). Network DEA smallest improvement approach, *Omega*, 98, 102140.

Wu J., Pan Y., Zhou Z. (2023). Assessing environmental performance with big data: A DEA model with multiple data resources, *Computers & Industrial Engineering*, 177, 109041.

Yu A., Shi Y., You J., Zhu J. (2021). Innovation performance evaluation for high-tech companies using a dynamic network data envelopment analysis approach, *European Journal of Operational Research*, 292(1), 199–212.

Zhou Z., Xiao H., Jin Q., Liu W. (2018). DEA frontier improvement and portfolio rebalancing: An application of China mutual funds on considering sustainability information disclosure, *European Journal of Operational Research*, 269(1), 111–131.

System Innovation for a Troubled World – Lam et al. (Eds)
© 2024 the Author(s), ISBN: 978-1-032-60846-4

# Survey on users' acceptance and intention of using ChatGPT

Wen-Yang Yan
*Department of Digital Multimedia Arts, Shih Hsin University, Taipei, Taiwan*

ChenJiun-Ting*
*Department of Information and Communication/Department of Digital Multimedia Arts, Shih Hsin University, Taipei, Taiwan*

ABSTRACT: In recent years, Taiwan has been following the global trend of Artificial Intelligence (AI) technology development, and the use of AI technology in daily life has become popular. In November 2022, the Chat Generative Pre-trained Transformer (ChatGPT) launched by OpenAI can interact with users in conversational dialogue forms and perform QNA, programming, and copywriting functions. ChatGPT has reached 100 million users worldwide as of January this year and is currently available for free and continues to expand its application. It is expected ChatGPT or similar AI technologies will be closely bound to daily life in the future, and there are already discussions on the understanding, use, and ethics of this new tool among the general public. Therefore, this study aims to investigate users' acceptance and intention of using ChatGPT to understand the current status of this technology tool in their minds. A questionnaire survey will be conducted among adults over 18 years old in Taiwan. The facets of the survey are "willingness to use", "intent to use", "information trust", and "stickiness to use". The results are expected to inform user attitudes for industries that will be integrated with AI, provide insight into the research and education of AI technology from the perspective of user needs, and remind society and government to pay more attention to this issue and establish regulations.

## 1 INTRODUCTION

Research Background and Motivation
Currently, the global trend of AI is changing rapidly, and the technology is becoming more and more popular in daily life applications. Many companies, academic research institutions, and government agencies are committed to research and development in AI-related fields in order to enhance the competitiveness of Taiwan's related industries in the world.

In response to this trend, OpenAI launched an artificial intelligence chatbot program called "ChatGPT" in November 2022, which has reached 100 million users worldwide as of January this year and is still available for free. According to a report published by OpenAI 2022, ChatGPT has demonstrated its powerful language generation capabilities by performing well in various natural language understanding tasks, including language translation, question and answer systems, and article generation. In addition, the study shows that ChatGPT has a wide range of promising applications in everyday life, such as in the customer service industry, the medical field, and

education. However, the rapid development of artificial intelligence also brings corresponding problems and challenges, such as security and privacy issues, the impact on the job market, and so on. Therefore, in addition to exploring technology enhancement and developing applications, researchers should also pay attention to the impact of artificial intelligence on society and users.

### 1.1 Purposes

The purpose of this study was to investigate the association between users' acceptance of ChatGPT and their intention to use it, to investigate users' attitudes and usage behaviors toward this tool, and to explore the factors that may influence users' behaviors. Through the questionnaire method, this study will analyze the acceptance, trust, behavioral intention, and adhesion of ChatGPT from the users' perspective to further understand the status and influence of this emerging AI technology tool in their minds. The research question contains the following three points:

1. With the increasing maturity of AI technology, what is the acceptance of ChatGPT by users?
2. Do users' background factors (e.g., age, education, occupation, etc.) affect their acceptance of ChatGPT and their intention to use it?

*Corresponding Author: andy@mail.shu.edu.tw

 DOI: 10.1201/9781003460763-50

3. Do the constructs of information trust and stickiness of ChatGPT have any significant impact on the intention to use?

## 2 LITERATURE REVIEW

### 2.1 *Artificial intelligence*

AI is a technology that describes the use of computers to simulate the behavior and thinking abilities of human intelligence. Initially, AI research focused on logical reasoning, knowledge representation, and problem-solving. Now, AI has developed into a comprehensive discipline that includes many sub-fields such as machine learning, deep learning, speech recognition, image recognition, and natural language processing. The core of AI technology is machine learning, a method based on data analysis, which allows machines to learn by analyzing large amounts of data and continuously optimizing their performance. Deep learning is one of the most popular machine learning methods in recent years, which enables efficient processing and analysis of large amounts of unstructured data by constructing multi-layer neural network models.

Currently, AI is moving from single-task models to models with multiple capabilities. For example, a model can perform speech recognition, natural language processing, and sentiment analysis simultaneously, thus enabling a wider range of applications and capabilities (Bacciu et al. 2020).

According to a survey conducted by Taiwan Network Information Center in 2022, more than half of Taiwan's population had used at least one AI service and product in the month prior to the survey (52.48%). Nearly half of them have used digital voice assistants (42.75%), the highest percentage of AI technology among all AI services and products, while chatbots account for 14.64% of the survey's usage rate. At present, the use of AI services and products by Taiwanese people is still not widespread, indicating that there is still considerable room for the development of AI technology in the Taiwanese market (TWNIC 2022).

### 2.2 *ChatGPT*

On November 30, 2022, OpenAI launched a free web preview version of its new human intelligence chatbot, ChatGPT, which reached 100 million monthly active users just two months after its launch, setting a record for the fastest growing consumer app in history. (Bianke, 2023; OpenAI 2022).

ChatGPT is a new state-of-the-art chatbot developed by the OpenAI team based on GPT-3, which can understand and interpret user requests through extensive data storage and efficient design, and then generate appropriate responses in human language with high naturalness and

fluency, and can be customized for different scenarios and needs. Beyond practical applications, ChatGPT's ability to generate humanlike language and perform complex tasks makes it a major innovation in the field of natural language processing and artificial intelligence (Lund 2023).

The emergence of ChatGPT has promoted the development of chat robot technology and provided new ideas and methods for implementing human-computer conversations. However, ChatGPT also faces some challenges and problems, for example, the machine-generated responses may have unclear semantics, unreasonable flow, and misleading and erroneous content of the generated conversations. In general, ChatGPT has wide application prospects and room for development. In future research and application, model optimization and personalized design need to be enhanced to improve conversation quality and user experience. It is expected that as natural language processing technology continues to develop, ChatGPT will continue to become more intelligent and user-friendly and provide better experiences and services for people in real-world applications.

Unified Theory of Acceptance and Use of Technology (UTAUT)

UTAUT was developed by Venkatesh et al. (2003) after combining the Theory of Reasoned Action (TRA), Theory of Planned Behavior (TPB), Social Cognitive Theory (SCT), Technology Acceptance Model (TAM), Innovation Diffusion Theory (IDT), Model of PC Utilization (MPCU), Motivational Model (MM), Combined TAM and TPB; C-TAM-TPB (C-TAM-TPB), and other eight theoretical models for comparative validation. An integrated theory was then developed.

The aim is that future research in this area can use the integrated model as a basis to identify more ideas that influence users' behavioral intentions, and further improve the explanatory power and understanding of the model (Lin 2022).

The theory consists of four core components, namely, "Performance Expectancy", "Effort Expectancy", "Social Influence" and "Facilitating Conditions", and four moderating variables: gender, age, experience, and voluntary use, as shown in Figure 1. In this study, this model is used as a framework for analyzing users' behavioral intentions.

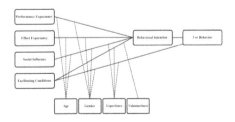

Figure 1. Unified theory of acceptance and use of technology, UTAUT.

### 2.3 Technology trust

Glikson and Woolley (2020) pointed out that user trust is a key factor affecting the acceptance of new technologies. Trust is an important factor to be considered in the study of human-computer interaction because the presence or absence of trust has an impact on the outcome of interaction. Trust and emotion may be considered important factors in Human-Computer Trust (HCT) based on cognition when users do not have sufficient knowledge of cognition and decision-making.

Madsen and Gregor (2000) argue that users' behavioral intentions may originate from their trust in the system and that when users have sufficient evidence to judge the reliability of the system, they will act toward the system. The scholar also compiled a Human-Computer Trust Scale for human-computer interaction, which has the following five components: "Perceived Reliability", "Perceived Technical Competence", "Perceived Understandability", "Faith", and "Personal Attachment", as shown in Figure 2.

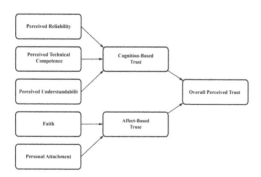

Figure 2.  Human-Computer Trust, HCT.

### 2.4 Stickiness

Stickiness is "the sum of all site qualities that induce visitors to stay on a site and not switch to another site". In other words, site stickiness is what encourages customers to stay on a site longer, to visit it more deeply, and to return more often (Holland & Baker, 2001). As a result, many scholars have explored why Internet users stick to a particular website, defining stickiness as a user's commitment to a preferred website that is so deep-rooted that he or she will continue to use it again and again, no matter where they are in the future. The study's many findings point to trust and satisfaction as key factors influencing stickiness, as users are more likely to continue using a website when they feel trust and satisfaction with it. In addition, the value that a website provides to users also affects their stickiness. If the perceived value that users receive from a website exceeds the transaction cost, they are more likely to be sticky to the website. Therefore, websites should focus on

improving user trust and satisfaction and providing value to users to promote the formation of stickiness and thus increase the success rate of the website.

As for how to measure the stickiness of web users, Holland and Baker (2001) proposed three metrics to measure stickiness, namely Uration of Visit, Depth of Visit, and Repeat Visits. They are the length of stay and the frequency of return to the software, which indicates the degree of continuous or frequent use of the software or service by users.

### 3  RESEARCH METHODS

This study will use a questionnaire survey to study the population of ChatGPT users in Taiwan who are 18 years old or older. The purpose of this study is to investigate the influence of user background on the acceptance, trust, and intention to use the artificial intelligence chat robot. The integrated technology acceptance model combined with technology trust and user adhesion will be used to investigate the user behavior and feelings of the web board ChatGPT. This chapter will explain the design and implementation steps of this study, presented in a flowchart, Section 1: Research structure diagram; Section 2: Research Hypotheses; Section 3: Operational Definition and Measurement; Section 4: Questionnaire; Section 5: Scope and Limitations of the Study Subjects.

### 3.1 Research structure diagram

This study is based on the Unified Theory of Acceptance and Use of Technology (Venkatesh et al. 2003), in which the components of "Performance Expectancy", "Effort Expectancy", and "Social Influence" are extracted as the basis for the study of users' expectations and social influence on ChatGPT. In addition, we combined the "Faith" and "Personal Attachment" components of the Human-Computer Trust component model (Madsen & Gregor 2000) as the basis for assessing users' perceptual psychological influence on ChatGPT, and finally, we combined them with the "Stickiness" perspective (Holland & Baker 2010). The conceptual framework of this study was developed using the above-mentioned literature, as shown in Figure 3.

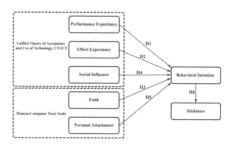

Figure 3.  Research structure diagram.

## 3.2 Research hypotheses

Based on the above research objectives and the conceptual framework of the study, the following hypotheses were developed for this study.

H1: Performance Expectancy positively influences users' behavioral intention to use ChatGPT.

H2: Effort Expectancy will positively affect users' behavioral intention to use ChatGPT.

H3: Social Influence positively influences users' behavioral intention to use ChatGPT.

H4: Faith positively influences users' behavioral intention to use ChatGPT.

H5: Personal Attachment positively influences users' behavioral intention to use ChatGPT.

H6: Behavioral intention positively affects users' stickiness to use ChatGPT.

## 3.3 Operational definition and measurement

This section discusses the various aspects of the research framework. The main measurement aspects include Performance Expectancy, Effort Expectancy, Social Influence, Faith, Personal Attachment, and Stickiness constructs. The operational definitions for this study are shown in Table 1.

Table 1. Operational definition comparison.

| Dimensions | Details | Operational Definition | Source |
|---|---|---|---|
| Unified Theory of Acceptance and Use of Technology (UTAUT) | Performance Expectancy | The extent to which the user believes that using the system will help improve the performance effectiveness of the work. | Venkatesh et al. (2003) |
| | Effort Expectancy | How easy it is for users to use the system. | Yang (2021) |
| | Social Influence | The extent to which users are influenced by the social environment to use the system. | Lin(2022) |
| Human-Computer Trust(HCT) | Faith | The extent to which the user is confident in the capabilities of the technology. | Mercieca (2019) |
| | Personal Attachment | The extent to which the user has a strong preference and possible attachment to the technology. | Hsieh (2019) |
| Stickiness | Stickiness | The extent to which users are interested in the technology on an ongoing basis. | Cheng et al. (2019) |

## 3.4 Questionnaire

In this study, the questionnaire design was based on the above-mentioned literature, and a structured questionnaire with a five-point Likert scale was used for each variable, and Respondents were asked to fill in the questions according to their level of agreement, ranging from strongly disagree to strongly agree. The test questions for each research dimension variable are explained in the following Table 2.

Table 2. Test item table.

| Dimensions | Test Topic Content |
|---|---|
| Performance Expectancy | 1. I think using ChatGPT is helpful to me. |
| | 2. Using ChatGPT helps me to solve problems quickly. |
| | 3. Using ChatGPT helps me to improve my work effectiveness. |
| | 4. Using ChatGPT helps me to improve my learning ability. |
| Effort Expectancy | 1. ChatGPT is easy to understand for me. |
| | 2. The first time I use ChatGPT, I can get familiar with the system functions and interface in a short time. |
| | 3. ChatGPT is very easy to use. |
| | 4. It is easy for me to learn how to operate ChatGPT. |
| Social Influence | 1. I think using ChatGPT is up to date. |
| | 2. The support of my friends and family will increase my willingness to use ChatGPT. |
| | 3. I know that others who have used ChatGPT have generally given positive feedback. |
| | 4. I am a pioneer in using ChatGPT in my circle of friends. |
| | 5. I don't need help to understand how ChatGPT works. |
| | 6. I decided to use ChatGPT with input from others. |
| | 7. My decision to use ChatGPT is based solely on the opinions of others. |
| Faith | 1. Even though the information given by ChatGPT is not always correct, I still follow its advice because I trust it. |
| | 2. When making a decision, I choose to listen to ChatGPT over my own original thoughts. |
| | 3. When I am unsure of a decision, I trust ChatGPT to provide me with the best and most accurate advice. |
| | 4. When ChatGPT offers an unreasonable recommendation, I still believe it is the right one. |
| | 5. Even though there is no reason to do so, I still choose ChatGPT and trust that it will solve my problem. |
| Personal Attachment | 1. If ChatGPT ever breaks down or disappears, I will feel lost because I can no longer use it. |

(continued)

Table 2. Continued

| Dimensions | Test Topic Content |
|---|---|
| | 2. I feel like I rely on ChatGPT to exist. |
| | 3. I find that ChatGPT's decision-making style works well for me. |
| | 4. I enjoy interacting and communicating with ChatGPT. |
| | 5. I prefer to use ChatGPT to help me decide on things. |
| Stickiness | 1. I use ChatGPT almost every day. |
| | 2. I use ChatGPT several times a day. |
| | 3. I use ChatGPT for a long period of time each time. |
| | 4. When I have a question, I use ChatGPT to seek an answer first. |
| | 5. Using ChatGPT has become an integral part of my life. |

### 3.5 Scope and limitations of the study subjects

According to the terms of use published on the official website of OpenAI, you must be at least 13 years old to use the services (including ChatGPT) of the affiliated company. If you are under 18 years old, you must obtain permission from your parents or legal guardians to use the service. Therefore, the target population of this study was web-based ChatGPT users in Taiwan who were 18 years old or older.

Limitations: This study mainly used the questionnaire method for data collection, and therefore may be limited by issues such as sample selection and sample size, which may further affect the generalizability of the study results. In addition, because users' attitudes toward accepting new technologies may vary depending on factors such as cultural background, socio-economic status, and educational level, the results of this study may not be applicable to users in other countries or regions. Finally, this study adopted a cross-sectional research design, so it was not possible to examine the effect of time factor on users' acceptance and intention to use ChatGPT.

## 4 EXPECTED RESULTS

The expected results of this study can be used to explore the impact of ChatGPT, an emerging technology, on the perceptions and behaviors of users in Taiwan, to understand the background information of this user group in terms of age group, gender, and education level, and the impact of background variables on the acceptance, trust, intention to use, and adherence to ChatGPT. Among them, the survey on performance expectancy and expectation of payment can reflect

users' feelings about the process of using ChatGPT and their expectations of the tool after using it. The survey on faith and personal attachment reveals the users' sentimental attitude towards ChatGPT in the past six months since the free web version was launched, even though the tool is new but still has a lot of room for improvement. In addition, the results of the stickiness study can further explore the level of dependence of users on ChatGPT.

ChatGPT is a more convenient, efficient, and personalized conversational experience generated by its natural language processing capability than the chat robots of the past, which required artificially designed conversation rules and conditions, as evidenced by the enthusiastic responses from around the world. Therefore, the research on ChatGPT user feedback can, on the one hand, promote the development of natural language technology and improve the language understanding and generation capability of AI, especially in the fields of natural language processing, machine translation, and speech recognition. On the other hand, more relevant research on the social controversies caused by the abuse of this tool when the masses are exploring its capabilities and limits, such as legal and ethical issues of being cheated, cheating, baiting, and inciting hatred, can promote the community to pay attention to the influence of ChatGPT and develop corresponding policies and measures to safeguard public interests and social values.

## REFERENCES

Bacciu D., Errica F., Micheli A. & Podda M., 2020. *Multi-Task Learning with Deep Neural Networks: A Survey.* https://doi.org/10.48550/arXiv.1912. 12693

Bianke N., 2023. *Chatgpt Breaks Record with 100 Million Users and Investors Come Flocking.* https://dailyinvestor.com/world/8520/chatgptbreaks-record-with-100-million-users-and-investors-come-flocking/

Cheng F.F., Wu C.H., Chang J.F. & Lin C.P., 2019. Stickiness on a mobile instant messaging service: Perspective of consumption value theory, flow, and social influence theory. *Journal of E-Business*, 21 (1), 1–27. https://doi.org/10.6188/JEB.201906_21 (1).0001

Glikson E. & Woolley A.W., 2022. Human trust in artificial intelligence: Review of empirical research. *Academy of Management Annals*, 14(2). https://doi. org/https://doi.org/10.5465/annals.2018.0057

Holland J., & Baker S.M., 2001. Customer participation in creating site brand loyalty. *Journal of Interactive Marketing*, 15(4), 34–45. https://doi.org/10.1002/ dir.1021

Hsieh T., 2019. The influence of voice assistant's personality traits on user's trust and behavior. *National Digital Library of Theses and Dissertations in Taiwan.* https://hdl.handle.net/11296/rzcxt7

Lin H.S., 2022. Using UTAUT model to investigate university students using applications of artificial intelligence in education. *National Digital Library of Theses and Dissertations in Taiwan*. https://hdl.handle.net/11296/uu7bwm

Lund B. & Wang T. 2023. *Chatting About ChatGPT: How May AI and GPT Impact Academia and Libraries?* Library Hi Tech News, 40. https://doi.org/10.1108/LHTN-01-2023-0009

Madsen M. & Gregor S., 2000. *Measuring Human-Computer Trust.*

Mercieca J., 2019. *Human-Chatbot Interaction - Assessing Technology Acceptance, Confidence and Trust in Chatbots Within Their Application Areas.* https://doi.org/10.13140/RG.2.2.28452.09600.

Taiwan Network Information Center., 2022. *Taiwan Internet Report 2022*. Retrieved from https://report.twnic.tw/2022/index.html

Thomas F., Sebastian S. & Sven O., 2019. The impact of social commerce feature richness on website stickiness through cognitive and affective factors: An experimental study. *Electronic Commerce Research and Applications*, 36, 100861. https://doi.org/10.1016/j.elerap.2019.100861

Venkatesh V., Morris M.G., Davis G.B. & Davis F. D. 2003. User acceptance of information technology: Toward a unified view. *MIS Quarterly*, 27(3), 425–478.

Zhang C., Zhang C., Li C., Qiao Y., Zheng S., Dam S., Zhang M., Kim J., Kim S.T., Park G.M., Choi J., Bae S.H., Lee L.H, Hui P., Kweon I., & Hong C. S., 2023. *One Small Step for Generative AI, One Giant Leap for AGI: A Complete Survey on ChatGPT in AIGC Era*. https://doi.org/10.13140/RG.2.2.24789.70883

System Innovation for a Troubled World – Lam et al. (Eds)
© 2024 the Author(s), ISBN: 978-1-032-60846-4

# A pose retrieval system based on skeleton contrastive learning

Yen-Chun Liao & Tz-Yu Liao
*Industrial Engineering and Management, National Kaohsiung University of Science and Technology*
*Department of Computer Science and Information Engineering, National Pingtung University*

I-Fang Su
*Department of Computer Science and Information Engineering, National Pingtung University*

Yu-Chi Chung*
*Industrial Engineering and Management, National Kaohsiung University of Science and Technology*

ABSTRACT: This study proposes a human pose retrieval system that can retrieve images with similar poses to a pose provided by users. This technology has a wide range of applications, such as providing illustrators and artists with poses to imitate, or for use in the fields of video understanding and AI-generated content (AIGC). Existing research on pose retrieval can be divided into two categories: (1) describing poses with text, or (2) manually extracting pose features, converting them into a low-dimensional space, and searching for similar poses in this space. As the text is imprecise in describing poses and manually extracted features cannot capture the rich semantics of poses, both techniques result in inaccurate search results. In this study, we propose a research method based on graph neural networks (GNNs) and contrastive learning for human pose retrieval. We use GNNs to model human posture and leverage contrastive learning techniques to learn the GNN representation. In this paper, we will explain the design principles of our method and conduct experiments to verify its effectiveness and efficiency.

## 1 INTRODUCTION

In recent years, human pose recognition has become a popular research field for its practical application in real-world scenarios. In this study, we propose a "human pose retrieval system" in which users can input a pose or image, and our system can find similar poses from a collection of images or video output. Human pose retrieval is one of the tasks in content-based information retrieval (CBIR) [19]. It is a rich way to retrieve images and videos and has important applications in sports and dance fields. In practical applications, our study can be useful for illustrators, artists, and AI drawing. For example, as the image is difficult to describe in words, detailed human pose references are necessary to create a realistic image. Our system can provide assistance in such cases.

In previous methods, Google provided an image search service where users could input an image, and the system would return similar images. However, the output results often do not meet the requirement of "the same pose" because Google's image search is not designed to search for the same pose, but rather to search for similar features. In

that case, it is often affected by background and clothing [1], and cannot provide accurate results.

Therefore, we believe that several areas in human pose retrieval research need improvement. First, the primary step of pose retrieval is to transform the pose information in the image into a feature vector. Common methods include using an encoder-decoder architecture [2] to obtain pose features, while Deep Poselet uses a convolutional neural network (CNN) to extract features from RGB images, and then uses SVM to learn skeletal information [3]. In recent years, the rise of graph neural networks (GNNs) and contrastive learning has sparked a trend in representation learning, with many research results showing that better data features can be learned through graph convolution and contrastive learning. Since the pose skeleton itself is a graph, we believe that incorporating a contrastive learning mechanism will result in better feature vectors than previous methods.

Second, if the time it takes to return search results is too long, the system becomes meaningless. Most current research focuses on search accuracy but pays less attention to efficiency issues. Studies [3], [4], [5], [6] used one-to-one matching to find similar poses. However, this method is time-consuming. When the database has a large amount of data, one-to-one comparison

*Corresponding Author: ycchung@nkust.edu.tw

DOI: 10.1201/9781003460763-51

will obviously waste a lot of time and may even be unable to return results to the user within a reasonable time. Comparing each feature vector in the database with the query vector one by one may find a large number of useless results, leading to a decrease in the recall rate.

In summary, the human pose retrieval field has not only practical applications but also many research issues that are worth exploring. Therefore, in this study, we propose a research called *"A Pose Retrieval System Based On Skeleton Contrastive Learning."*

## 2 RELATED WORK

### 2.1 *Graph neural networks*

The expressiveness of GNN [7] has shone in various fields due to the ability to obtain topological information in graphs during training [8,9]. The structure represented by graph data consists of nodes (vectors) and edges, with each node having corresponding features and edges connecting nodes to one another.

A graph $G = (V, E)$ can be represented by $V$ and $E$, where $V$ is a set of nodes and $E$ is a set of edges, $(v_i, v_j) \in E$ represents the connection between node $v_i$ and $v_j$. $A \in \mathbb{R}^{N \times N}$ is the adjacency matrix, which is a symmetric matrix with values belonging to {0,1}. The graph data structure solves the problem of non-Euclidean structures in data, where the data may have unconventional structures such as social network data, biological data, chemical data, and so on.

GNN is a deep learning method that operates on the graph domain and learns to generate new node features through the propagation and aggregation processes between the nodes in the graph. During this process, nodes transmit their features to their neighboring nodes and aggregate the features of neighboring nodes to update their own features. As the number of GNN layers increases, the nodes update their features more times, and their receptive fields become larger.

Kipf *et al.* [16] proposed a new semi-supervised learning method for graph-structured data, based on an efficient variant of convolutional neural networks that can operate directly on graphs. Their [16] paper introduced a novel semi-supervised learning method that uses ChebConv for convolutional operations on graph-structured data. ChebConv is based on Chebyshev polynomials and uses a local first-order approximation of spectral graph convolution to compute convolutional patterns. This allows the model to learn a hidden layer representation that encodes the local graph structure and node features. The authors demonstrated the superior performance of ChebConv through experiments on citation networks and knowledge graphs. ChebConv outperformed other related methods in these experiments. The contribution of this method lies in two aspects: first, it introduces a simple and well-behaved layer-wise propagation rule for neural network models that operate directly on graphs and demonstrates how to derive it from the first-order approximation of spectral graph convolution; secondly, it demonstrates how to use this graph-based neural network model to perform semi-supervised classification on nodes in a graph quickly and in a scalable manner.

### 2.2 *Graph representation learning*

Graph representation learning is a research field that has emerged in recent years with the aim of transforming graph data into low-dimensional vector representations for ease of learning. In many practical applications, data is often represented as graph structures, which are usually sparse and high-dimensional. Converting these graph data into low-dimensional vector representations can not only improve computational efficiency, but also achieve better performance on many tasks. The focus of this study is to represent the human skeleton using graphs and to represent each pose as a vector, which is the process of graph representation learning. The goal is to learn the vector representation of the graph, which is to represent the nodes or edges in the graph as low-dimensional vectors so that they can be efficiently trained in the model. Similar methods include Node2vec [15], which is a method for learning node features on a graph, used to learn continuous feature representations of nodes in a network. The algorithm aims to map nodes to a low-dimensional space to maximize the preservation of node network neighbor features. The algorithm can effectively explore diverse neighborhoods and learn richer representations than previous strictly conceptual network neighbor-based work. In this study, the entire skeleton graph representation is required, so a pooling layer is used to aggregate the feature vectors of all nodes in the graph to obtain the representation of the entire graph.

### 2.3 *Human pose retrieval*

Jammalamadaka *et al.* [13] improved on previous research by proposing a new human pose search method that uses pose as a query. This research introduces two new deep-learning methods for representing human pose that can be used for image retrieval. This means that users can search images and videos faster and more accurately using poses, rather than just using keywords or tags. The article proposes two methods: the Deep Poselet Method and the Deep Pose Embedding Method. The first method can divide pose space into "Pose-Sensitive" deep poses, which are used as the basic building blocks for constructing pose feature representations using state-of-the-art CNN [14] features. In the second method, images are directly mapped to a lower-dimensional, pose-sensitive space. However, the drawback of this paper [13] is that it is limited to deep learning techniques, including CNNs, linear support vector machines, and other methods, while this research uses graph neural networks, which can more intuitively represent the human skeleton's pose.

Jennifer J. Sun *et al.* [18] proposed a new method called Pr-VIPE for identifying similar human poses from multiple viewpoints using only 2D joint key points. This method models the inherent ambiguity of projecting poses from 3D space to 2D by using probabilistic embeddings, allowing the method to learn a compact, view-invariant embedding space only from 2D joint keypoints, without explicitly predicting 3D poses. During training, this paper applies three losses: triple margin loss, positive pair loss, and prior loss with a unit Gaussian applied before embedding. Experimental results show that the proposed embedding model retrieves similar poses more accurately from different viewpoints compared to 2D-to-3D pose lifting models. The authors also demonstrate the effectiveness of applying their embedding to view-invariant action recognition and video alignment.

## 2.4 *Contrastive learning with data augmentation*

Contrastive learning is a method of learning features from unlabeled data by grouping similar data together and separating different data. This is achieved by projecting the data into a feature space. Recently, more and more research has also applied graphs to contrastive learning tasks. The main goal of contrastive learning is the design of the loss function. Prannay Khosla *et al.* [17] proposed a new loss function based on label information for a deep image model, which can cluster points of the same category together while separating clusters of samples from different categories. By conducting experiments on the ImageNet dataset, the researchers demonstrated that the model achieved state-of-the-art performance in image classification tasks.

## 3 EXPERIMENTAL

In this study, a GNN-based framework is used to conduct experiments on the human pose retrieval task. First, NTU RGB+D [20] is used as the experimental data, of which 60% is for training and 40% is for testing, and it is converted into a graphical data representation. Then, we use GCN to represent each pose as a vector. Next, we compare these vectors using a contrast learning framework to find similar poses.

## 3.1 *GCN*

GCN [16] is an effective graph embedding model designed to learn low-dimensional representations

(i.e., embeddings) of nodes. In the experiment, features are extracted by convolutional operations on the graph and then used to represent the nodes. Specifically, GCN normalizes the neighborhood matrix and feature matrix and then multiplies them to calculate the embedding of nodes. In this way, the embedding of each node contains information about its neighboring nodes, which better represents the structure of the graph data.

In the experiment, each human skeleton has 25 nodes as $N$, and each node has 3 features as $F$. The size of the feature matrix $X$ is $N \times$ , and the neighbor matrix $A$ represents the connection relationship between the nodes in the graph data, and the size is $N \times N$.

$$((l+1), A) = \sigma(AH(l)W(l))$$

where $H(l)$ is the node representation of layer $l$, $A$ is the neighboring matrix, $W(l)$ is the weight matrix of layer $l$, and $\sigma(\ )$ is a nonlinear activation function such as ReLU. In the first layer, (0) will be equal to the feature matrix $F$. By multi-layer GCN, the embedding vector representation $z$ of each node can be obtained.

## 3.2 *Data*

NTU-RGB+D [20] is a multimodal dataset containing multiple action categories, mainly used for skeleton-based action recognition. These action categories include daily-life actions, interactions, and health-related actions. We conducted experiments based on the NTU-RGB+D[20] dataset and referred to top-1 accuracy reports. In the experiments, we randomly sampled each pose and used 60% of the poses for training and 40% for validation.

## 3.3 *Loss function*

Contrastive loss is a loss function used for training models, which aims to make data from the same class closer in feature space and data from different classes more separated. This function calculates the contrastive loss of feature vectors, which includes features from multiple perspectives and is used to compare the feature representations of the same sample from different angles. By minimizing the loss function, we can make the representation of data from different classes in feature space as dispersed as possible while keeping samples from the same class together. For each sample, we treat it as an anchor point and select a set of positive samples from the same class and negative samples from other classes. We hope that the anchor point and positive samples are as close as possible in feature space, and as far away as possible from negative samples. Specifically, we use the logarithmic softmax loss function to measure the similarity between the anchor point and positive samples and compare it with the similarity between the anchor point and negative samples, so that the similarity between the anchor point and positive samples is maximized while the similarity between the anchor point and negative samples is minimized. This can cluster samples from the same class together and separate samples from different classes.

$$\mathcal{L} = \sum_{i \in I} \frac{-1}{|P(i)|} \sum_{p \in P(i)} \log \frac{\exp(z_i \cdot z_p / \tau)}{\sum_{n \in N(i)} \exp(z_i \cdot z_n / \tau)}$$

The above is a loss function formula, where $i \in I$ represents the sample $i$ in the dataset, $P(i)$ is the set of other samples belonging to the same class as sample $i$, and $N(i)$ is the set of samples belonging to different classes as sample $i$. $z_i$ and $z_p$ are the embedding values of each human skeleton posture, and $\tau$ is the temperature parameter. This formula maximizes the similarity between the feature vectors of similar posture samples $i$ and $p$. When training the model, for samples $i$ and $n$ from different classes, it is desired that their representations in the feature space are as far away from each other as possible, making them easier to distinguish and achieve the purpose of contrastive learning.

### 3.4 Model

In this study, we use the Chebyshev polynomial approximation of the Laplacian operator to construct a network that can accept node features, edge indices, and batch-processing information to output a fixed-dimensional node representation for classification or other tasks. The network consists of four ChebConv layers and one linear layer, where each ChebConv layer takes the output of the previous layer as input and updates node representations by extracting information from neighboring nodes using Chebyshev polynomials with K (order) of 3. ReLU activation functions are used for nonlinear transformation between each ChebConv layer.

After the ChebConv layers, the global_max_-pool function is used to pool all node representations into a fixed dimension, which is further reduced by a linear layer. To reduce overfitting, dropout functions are applied for regularization. This design effectively captures the relationships and features between nodes, allowing for accurate classification or other tasks by distinguishing nodes from different classes.

| Model | Accuracy |
|---|---|
| GATv2Conv | 87% |
| GATConv | 86% |
| **ChebConv** | **91%** |
| GraphSAGE | 86% |
| GCNConv | 86% |

## 4 RESULT

In this experiment, we applied our method to five common models including GATv2Conv, GATConv, ChebConv, GraphSAGE, and GCNConv. We trained each model with various parameters and obtained the best results for these five models. Among these models, ChebConv achieved the highest test accuracy of 0.9141, while GraphSAGE had the lowest test accuracy of 0.86, as shown in Table 1.

According to multiple experiments conducted in this study, global_max_pool performed the best on this data, as it is believed to better capture key information and is less likely to be affected by noise or outliers. Specifically, global_max_pool selects the maximum value from each node"s feature vector, which helps the model focus on the most representative features.

ChebConv layer uses the Chebyshev polynomial approximation of the Laplace operator, which can better capture the relationships and features among nodes, and differentiate nodes of different classes. This may be one of the reasons why ChebConv performs better than other models.

Table 1 shows that in the task of classifying the similarity of human skeletons among different models, ChebConv performed best, achieving an accuracy rate of 91%, whereas the accuracy rates of other models ranged from 86% to 89%.

## 5 CONCLUSION

The aim of this experiment is to explore the effectiveness of extracting embeddings for each skeleton and training them using multiple common convolutional models in the NTU-RGB+D [20] dataset based on skeleton action. The results show that the use of embeddings can effectively reduce training costs and improve training efficiency. Further research is needed to explore more methods.

## REFERENCES

[1] Laptev I. and Pérez P., "Retrieving actions in movies," *Proceedings of the IEEE International Conference on Computer Vision*, 2007, doi: 10.1109/ICCV.2007.4409105.

[2] Kim H., Zala A., Burri G. and M. Bansal, "FixMyPose: Pose correctional captioning and retrieval," *35th AAAI Conference on Artificial Intelligence, AAAI 2021*, vol. 14B, pp. 13161–13170, Apr. 2021, doi: 10.48550/arxiv.2104.01703.

[3] Jammalamadaka N., Zisserman A. and J. C.V., "Human pose search using deep networks," *Image Vis Comput*, vol. 59, pp. 31–43, Mar. 2017, doi: 10.1016/j.imavis.2016.12.002.

[4]     Hamanishi N. and Rekimoto J., "Poseasquery: Full-body interface for repeated observation of a person in a video with ambiguous pose indexes and performed poses," *ACM International Conference Proceeding Series*, Mar. 2020, doi: 10.1145/3384657.3384658

[5]     Jammalamadaka N., Zisserman A., Eichner M., Ferrari V. and Jawahar C.v., "Video retrieval by mimicking poses," in Proceedings of the 2nd ACM *International Conference on Multimedia Retrieval*, ICMR 2012, 2012. doi: 10.1145/2324796.2324838.

[6]     Ferrari V., Marin-Jimenez M. and Zisserman A., "Pose search: Retrieving People Using Their Pose," pp. 1–8, Mar. 2010, doi: 10.1109/CVPR.2009.5206495.

[7]     Zhou J., Cui G., Zhang Z., Yang C., Liu Z., Wang L., Li C., Sun M., Graph neural networks: A review of methods and applications, *arXiv preprint arXiv:1812.08*. 2018.

[8]     Zhou J. et al., "Graph neural networks: a review of methods and applications," *arXiv. arXiv*, Dec. 20, 2018. Accessed: Dec. 30, 2020. [Online]. Available: http://arxiv.org/abs/1812.08434

[9]     Zhang Z., Cui P. and Zhu W., "Deep learning on graphs: A survey," *arXiv. arXiv*, Dec. 10, 2018. doi: 10.1109/tkde.2020.2981333.

[10]    Zafarani R. and Liu H.. Social computing data repository at ASU, 2009.

[11]    Breitkreutz B.-J., Stark C, Reguly T., Boucher L., Breitkreutz A., Livstone M., Oughtred R., Lackner D.H., Bähler J., Wood V., et al. The BioGRID interaction database. *Nucleic Acids Research*, 36:D637–D640, 2008.

[12]    Debnath A.K., Lopez de Compadre R.L., Debnath G., Shusterman A.J. and Hansch C.. Structure-activity relationship of mutagenic aromatic and heteroaromatic nitro compounds. Correlation with molecular orbital energies and hydrophobicity. *J Med Chem*, 34:786–797, 1991.

[13]    Jammalamadaka N., Zisserman A., Eichner M., Ferrari V. and Jawahar C.v., "Video retrieval by mimicking poses," in *Proceedings of the 2nd ACM International Conference on Multimedia Retrieval*, ICMR 2012, 2012. doi: 10.1145/2324796.2324838.

[14]    Donahue J., Jia Y., Vinyals O., Hoffman J., Zhang N., Tzeng E., Darrell T., "DeCAF: a deep convolutional activation feature for generic visual recognition", 2013. *arXiv preprint* arXiv:1310.1531

[15]    Grover A. and Leskovec J., "node2vec: Scalable Feature Learning for Networks," *Proceedings of the ACM SIGKDD International Conference on Knowledge Discovery and Data Mining*, vol. 13-17-August-2016, pp. 855–864, Jul. 2016, doi: 10.48550/arxiv.1607.00653.

[16]    Kipf T.N. and Welling M., Semi-supervised classification with graph convolutional networks. *arXiv preprint arXiv*:1609.02907, 2016.

[17]    Khosla P., et al., Supervised contrastive learning. *Advances in Neural Information Processing Systems*, 2020. 33: p. 18661–18673.

[18]    Sun J.J., et al. View-invariant probabilistic embedding for human pose. in *Computer Vision–ECCV 2020: 16th European Conference*, Glasgow, UK, August 23–28, 2020, Proceedings, Part V 16. 2020. Springer.

[19]    Li X., Yang J. and Ma J., "Recent developments of content-based image retrieval (CBIR)," *Neurocomputing*, vol. 452, pp. 675–689, Sep. 2021, doi: 10.1016/J.NEUCOM.2020.07.139

[20]    Shahroudy A., et al. Ntu rgb+ d: A large scale dataset for 3d human activity analysis. in *Proceedings of the IEEE Conference on Computer Vision and Pattern Recognition*. 2016.

System Innovation for a Troubled World – Lam et al. (Eds)
© 2024 the Author(s), ISBN: 978-1-032-60846-4

# Mortality prediction for total joint arthroplasty by machine learning

Wei-Huan Hu
*College of Computer Science, National Yang Ming Chiao Tung University, Hsinchu, Taiwan*

Feng-Chih Kuo
*Department of Orthopaedic Surgery, Kaohsiung Chang Gung Memorial Hospital, College of Medicine, Chang Gung University, Kaohsiung, Taiwan*

Yuh-Jyh Hu\*
*College of Computer Science, National Yang Ming Chiao Tung University, Hsinchu, Taiwan*
*Institute of Biomedical Engineering, National Yang Ming Chiao Tung University, Hsinchu, Taiwan*

ABSTRACT: Total Joint Arthroplasty (TJA) is a surgical procedure that significantly improves patients' quality of life. However, periprosthetic joint infection (PJI) after TJA procedures is a devastating complication associated with increased morbidity. In this study, we conducted a retrospective analysis to investigate the overall 30-day mortality rate for primary and revision TJA using the stacked generalization approach of machine learning. We limited the structures to 2 or 3 levels and tested only widely used learning algorithms. Ultimately, a three-level stacked generalization architecture was optimal compared with three commonly used mortality scorings, the Charlson Comorbidity Index (CCI), the American Society of Anesthesiologists Scores (ASA Scores) and the Elixhauser Comorbidity Index (ECI). Results indicate that the proposed stacked generalization technique is a promising approach for predicting 30-day mortality after TJA and outperforms the conventional mortality scoring systems.

## 1 INTRODUCTION

Although total joint arthroplasty (TJA) remains one of the most successful surgeries and can improve the quality of life for patients, periprosthetic joint infection (PJI) after TJA procedures is a devastating complication that is associated with increased morbidity (Leta et al. 2019; Pugely et al. 2015; ). It even carries a risk of mortality, particularly in the peri- and early post-operative periods due to the surgical operation and to patient factors such as age, gender, and comorbidities (Belmont et al. 2014; Hunt et al. 2014).

Several midterm and long-term studies of mortality rate after revision total knee arthroplasty (Choi et al. 2020; Yao et al. 2019) have been done; nevertheless, other evidence reveals that the first 30 postoperative days after surgery may be the most critical to the investigation into the risk of mortality (Harris et al. 2019). Most of the previous works applied standard statistical analysis with the aim to estimate mortality rate and identify significant patient factors that impact the mortality rate of TJA. Unlike earlier research, in this study, we conducted a retrospective analysis to investigate the overall 30-day mortality rate for primary and revision TJA, using machine learning approaches.

With the advancements in its technology, machine learning (ML) has been widely employed in medicine (Cruz and Wishart 2007; Hu et al. 2018; Samad et al. 2018). To total joint arthroplasty specifically, ML has been applied for outcome predictions, including medical costs (Navarro et al. 2018), complications and mortality (Harris et al. 2019), length of stay (Gabriel et al. 2019), and PJI treatment with irrigation and debridement (Shohat et al. 2020). We developed a data-driven ML approach to TJA mortality prediction that involves many factors of various types. Unlike classical statistic approaches that are typically hindered by large numbers and mixed types of variables, ML is able to efficiently and effectively investigate large and different variable spaces to create accurate predictive models (Handelman et al. 2018, Obermeyer and Emanuel 2016). In addition, as the availability of patient data increases, a data-driven ML approach can utilize, and take advantage of increased data flexibly and adaptability to refine current predictive models or to generate new models.

To verify the feasibility of applying ML to PJI mortality prediction, we tested the proposed ML approach on more than 4000 TJA patients and compared it with two scoring methods commonly practiced in orthopedics. The results show that the proposed ML system outperforms the widely used scoring methods significantly.

---

\*Corresponding Author: yhu@cs.nycu.edu.tw

DOI: 10.1201/9781003460763-52

## 2 MATERIALS AND METHODS

We conducted a retrospective study with the approval of the Institutional Review Board at Chang Gung Memorial Hospital (CGMH) in Kaohsiung City, Taiwan. We collected the records of patients who underwent primary or revision total joint arthroplasty (hips and knees) between January 2000 and December 2022 for analysis. After discarding incomplete patient records with missing but not imputable feature values, we obtained a final cohort of 4338 patients. Each patient is represented by 25 features. Table 1 presents a summary of patient features, which were divided into four categories: (a) demographic features, (b) biomedical features, (c) comorbidities, and (d) operation-related features. These 4338 patients were categorized into two classes, die within 30 days after arthroplasty (Death) and otherwise (Others). We conducted stratified $k$-fold cross-validations (CV) to evaluate the predictive performances of ML and compared it with the Charlson Comorbidity Index (CCI), the American Society of Anaesthesiologists Scores (ASA), and Elixhauser Comorbidity Index (ECI), which are commonly used in orthopedics to predict patient mortality after surgery (Menendez et al. 2014).

We used six measures for comparison: (1) percentage accuracy (ACC), (2) F1-score, (3) Precision, (4) Recall, (5) Matthews correlation coefficient (MCC), and (6) area under the receiver operating characteristic curve (AUC). They are defined as follows:

$$ACC = (TP + TN) / (TP + TN + FP + FN)$$
$$\text{F1-score} = 2 \times TPR \times \text{Precision} / (TPR + \text{Precision})$$
$$\text{Precision} = TP / (TP + FP)$$
$$\text{Recall} = TP / (TP + FN)$$

$$MCC = \frac{TP \times TN - FP \times FN}{\sqrt{(TP + FP) \times (TP + FN) \times (TN + FP) \times (TN + FN)}}$$

$$AUC = \text{Area under the ROC curve}$$

where TP, TN, FP, and FN represent true positive, true negative, false positive, and false negative, respectively.

Different learning algorithms explore different hypothesis spaces and consequently obtain different results because they employ different knowledge representations and search heuristics. We propose combining multiple prediction methods to achieve superior performance compared with that achieved using a single predictor. Stacked generalization (aka stacking), as shown in Figure 1, is an ensemble learning method of combining the predictions of multiple learning models that have been trained for a classification task (Ting & Witten 1997; Wolpert 1992).

Table 1. Summary of patient features.

| Features | Alive (n = 4196) | Death (n = 142) |
|---|---|---|
| **Demographic** | | |
| Age | 58.4 (± 19.0) | 69.2 (± 14.9) |
| Gender (F/M) | F (43%), M (57%) | F (41%), M (59%) |
| **Biomedical** | | |
| WBC (103/µL) | 9.6 (± 4.6) | 12.5 (± 7.2) |
| RBC (106/µL) | 4.2 (± 0.8) | 3.4 (± 0.8) |
| Hg (g/dL) | 11.8 (± 2.3) | 9.8 (± 2.3) |
| MCV (fL) | 86.9 (± 7.8) | 87.8 (± 10.2) |
| Platelet (103/µL) | 282.0 (± 121.0) | 229.5 (± 151.7) |
| BUN (mg/dL) | 20.2 (± 15.7) | 43.8 (± 34.1) |
| Creatinine (mg/dL) | 1.2 (± 1.3) | 2.7 (± 2.5) |
| Na (mEq/L) | 137.2 (± 5.7) | 135.2 (± 5.4) |
| K (mEq/L) | 4.1(± 0.7) | 4.1 (± 0.8) |
| ESR (mm/hr) | 63 (± 36.2) | 73.7 (± 36.1) |
| Bacteria (No/Yes) | N (25%), Y (75%) | N (13%), Y (87%) |
| Gram-positive (No/Yes) | N (44%), Y (56%) | N (35%), Y (65%) |
| Gram-negative (No/Yes) | N (83%), Y (17%) | N (60%), Y (40%) |
| Polymicrobial infections (No/Yes) | N (82%), Y (18%) | N (63%), Y (37%) |
| Blood bacterial infections (No/Yes) | N (87%), Y (13%) | N (44%), Y (56%) |
| Culture negative sepsis (No/Yes) | N (68%), Y (32%) | N (90%), Y (10%) |
| **Comorbidity** | | |
| Hypertension (No/Yes) | N (61%), Y (39%) | N (69%), Y (31%) |
| Diabetes (No/Yes) | N (77%), Y (23%) | N (72%), Y (28%) |
| Renal Failure (No/Yes) | N (95%), Y (5%) | N (70%), Y (30%) |
| Coagulopathy (No/Yes) | N (98%), Y (2%) | N (83%), Y (17%) |
| Fluid and Electrolyte Disorders (No/Yes) | N (94%), Y (6%) | N (77%), Y (23%) |
| **Operation-related** | | |
| Acute PJI (No/Yes) | N (64%), Y (36%) | N (50%), Y (50%) |
| Blood Trans (No/Yes) | N (41%), Y (59%) | N (6%), Y (94%) |

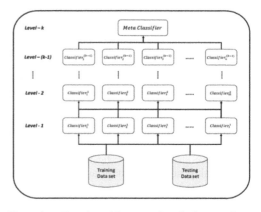

Figure 1. Generic architecture of stacked generation.

Unlike other ensemble learning approaches, stacked generalization operates as layered processes that aim to deduce the biases of the base classifiers. In the stacked learning framework, each base classifier in a set is trained on a dataset, and their predictions are assembled as the metadata. Successive layers of meta classifiers receive the metadata as the input for training the meta-models in parallel, then pass their outputs to the subsequent layer. A single classifier at the top level plays the role of an arbiter and makes the final prediction.

Stacked generalization is considered a form of meta-learning because the transformed training data for the current layer contain the predictive information of the preceding learners, which constitutes a form of meta-knowledge. The hierarchy of stacked generalization can affect the predictive performances. It is computationally impossible to evaluate all possible hierarchical architectures with all types of learning algorithms. Therefore, we limited the structures to 2 or 3 levels and tested only widely used learning algorithms. We evaluated their predictive performances using 5-fold CV and finally settled on a three-level stacked generalization architecture, which was later compared with three widely used mortality scorings in practice, CCI, ASA, and ECI.

## 3 RESULTS AND DISCUSSION

In the final cohort of 4338 patients, 142 patients died within 30 days after TJA, and the remaining 4196 survived over 30 days. The 142 patients were positive examples and labeled as *Death*; the other 4196 were negative examples and labeled as *Others*. The cohort of patients for the study is an imbalanced dataset, and the imbalance of classes can severely affect the performance of machine learning. To mitigate the class imbalance problem, we undersampled the negative examples and tested 8 representative ML algorithms based on three times 5-fold CV with different ratios of positives and negatives. Table 2 shows that when the positive-to-negative ratio is set to 1:5, the predictive performances are the highest for these learning algorithms, which suggests that 1:5 is a proper ratio for training to alleviate the effects of imbalanced data. Therefore, we set the ratio to 1:5 for ML training in the remaining experiments.

We tested different 2-level and 3-level hierarchical structures for stacked generalization by varying the learning algorithms at different levels in the hierarchies. The hierarchies are described in Table 3. We compared their predictive performances, using a stratified 5-fold CV, and show their predictive performances in Table 4. In comparison, the 3-level architectures outperform the 2-level structures. The results show Meta-2-6 is the

Table 2. Performance results of representative classifiers with different positive-to-negative ratios.

| Method | Ratio (+:−) | ACC | F1 | Precision | Recall | MCC | AUC |
|---|---|---|---|---|---|---|---|
| Decision Tree | 1:1 | 0.706 | 0.146 | 0.081 | 0.762 | 0.180 | 0.733 |
| | 1:3 | 0.800 | 0.176 | 0.102 | 0.648 | 0.199 | 0.727 |
| | 1:5 | 0.840 | 0.198 | 0.119 | 0.603 | 0.216 | 0.726 |
| Nearest-Neighbor | 1:1 | 0.845 | 0.219 | 0.135 | 0.652 | 0.245 | 0.830 |
| | 1:3 | 0.870 | 0.237 | 0.153 | 0.598 | 0.253 | 0.817 |
| | 1:5 | 0.893 | 0.252 | 0.164 | 0.554 | 0.260 | 0.805 |
| Logistic Regression | 1:1 | 0.747 | 0.188 | 0.106 | 0.873 | 0.248 | 0.894 |
| | 1:3 | 0.767 | 0.200 | 0.113 | 0.873 | 0.262 | 0.898 |
| | 1:5 | 0.774 | 0.205 | 0.117 | 0.873 | 0.267 | 0.898 |
| Support Vector Machine | 1:1 | 0.763 | 0.191 | 0.108 | 0.840 | 0.246 | 0.889 |
| | 1:3 | 0.767 | 0.193 | 0.109 | 0.842 | 0.249 | 0.895 |
| | 1:5 | 0.780 | 0.204 | 0.116 | 0.844 | 0.261 | 0.896 |
| Naïve Bayesian | 1:1 | 0.771 | 0.198 | 0.113 | 0.833 | 0.252 | 0.877 |
| | 1:3 | 0.776 | 0.197 | 0.112 | 0.833 | 0.252 | 0.878 |
| | 1:5 | 0.774 | 0.197 | 0.112 | 0.835 | 0.252 | 0.879 |
| Random Forest | 1:1 | 0.839 | 0.223 | 0.134 | 0.687 | 0.254 | 0.875 |
| | 1:3 | 0.906 | 0.297 | 0.202 | 0.585 | 0.304 | 0.889 |
| | 1:5 | 0.931 | 0.321 | 0.243 | 0.493 | 0.312 | 0.897 |
| Linear Discriminant Analysis | 1:1 | 0.765 | 0.192 | 0.108 | 0.845 | 0.248 | 0.892 |
| | 1:3 | 0.783 | 0.207 | 0.118 | 0.845 | 0.264 | 0.898 |
| | 1:5 | 0.767 | 0.200 | 0.113 | 0.873 | 0.261 | 0.900 |
| Extra Tree | 1:1 | 0.871 | 0.264 | 0.166 | 0.685 | 0.293 | 0.898 |
| | 1:3 | 0.931 | 0.354 | 0.261 | 0.568 | 0.353 | 0.908 |
| | 1:5 | 0.944 | 0.351 | 0.292 | 0.467 | 0.338 | 0.908 |

Table 3. Hierarchy of stacked generalization.

| | | Level-1 | Level-2 | Level-3 |
|---|---|---|---|---|
| 2-level Meta | Meta-2-1 | kNN, NB, LDA, XTree, SVM | LR | – |
| | Meta-2-2 | kNN, NB, LDA, LR, SVM | Xtree | – |
| | Meta-2-3 | kNN, NB, LDA, XTree, LR | SVM | – |
| | Meta-2-4 | LR, NB, LDA, XTree, SVM | kNN | – |
| | Meta-2-5 | kNN, LR, LDA, XTree, SVM | NB | – |
| | Meta-2-6 | kNN, NB, LR, XTree, SVM | LDA | – |
| 3-level Meta | Meta-3-1 | kNN, NB, LDA | XTree, SVM | LR |
| | Meta-3-2 | kNN, NB, LDA | LR, SVM | XTree |
| | Meta-3-3 | kNN, NB, LDA | XTree, LR | SVM |
| | Meta-3-4 | LR, NB, LDA | XTree, SVM | kNN |
| | Meta-3-5 | kNN, LR, LDA | XTree, SVM | NB |
| | Meta-3-6 | kNN, NB, LR | XTree, SVM | LDA |

top 2-level meta-learner for F1, MCC, and AUC, and Meta-3-1 is the best among the 3-level meta-learners. In Meta-3-1, the bottom level comprises

Table 4. Performance results of different architectures.

| Method | ACC | F1 | Precision | Recall | MCC | AUC |
|--------|-----|-----|-----------|--------|-----|-----|
| Meta-2-1 | 0.879 | 0.282 | 0.178 | 0.713 | 0.314 | 0.908 |
| Meta-2-2 | 0.922 | 0.348 | 0.242 | 0.629 | 0.358 | 0.910 |
| Meta-2-3 | 0.880 | 0.288 | 0.183 | 0.713 | 0.319 | 0.902 |
| Meta-2-4 | 0.896 | 0.295 | 0.201 | 0.624 | 0.310 | 0.874 |
| Meta-2-5 | 0.899 | 0.312 | 0.201 | 0.697 | 0.338 | 0.910 |
| Meta-2-6 | 0.938 | *0.381* | 0.308 | 0.554 | *0.378* | *0.912* |
| Meta-3-1 | 0.943 | **0.388** | 0.324 | 0.540 | **0.383** | **0.914** |
| Meta-3-2 | 0.765 | 0.192 | 0.109 | 0.845 | 0.249 | 0.884 |
| Meta-3-3 | 0.943 | 0.346 | 0.353 | 0.472 | 0.351 | 0.833 |
| Meta-3-4 | 0.941 | 0.323 | 0.302 | 0.452 | 0.323 | 0.894 |
| Meta-3-5 | 0.952 | 0.176 | 0.133 | 0.283 | 0.178 | 0.912 |
| Meta-3-6 | 0.944 | 0.385 | 0.338 | 0.517 | 0.380 | 0.914 |
| | | | | | | |
| ASA | 0.959 | 0.207 | 0.291 | 0.163 | 0.197 | 0.750 |
| CCI | 0.819 | 0.121 | 0.072 | 0.388 | 0.103 | 0.650 |
| ECI | 0.851 | 0.146 | 0.090 | 0.387 | 0.130 | 0.730 |
| | | | | | | |
| P-value[a] | <0.05 | **<0.005** | 0.280 | <0.005 | **<0.005** | **<0.005** |
| P-value[b] | <0.005 | **<0.005** | <0.005 | <0.005 | **<0.005** | **<0.005** |
| P-value[c] | <0.005 | **<0.005** | <0.005 | <0.005 | **<0.005** | **<0.005** |

[a]The P-value of the paired t-test between Meta-3-1 and ASA
[b]The P-value of the paired t-test between Meta-3-1 and CCI
[c]The P-value of the paired t-test between Meta-3-1 and ECI

three base classification algorithms, the Nearest-Neighbor (kNN) (Cover & Hart 1967), the naïve Bayesian classifier (NB) (Rish 2001) and the linear discriminant analysis (LDA) (Gaber et al. 2017); the support vector machine (SVM) (Steinwart & Christmann 2008) and the extra tree (XTree) (Geurts et al. 2006) serve as the second-level meta classifiers in the stacked architecture. At the third level, logistic regression (LR) (Dayton 1992) is present as the top meta classifier that arbitrates between the lower-level meta classifiers, and makes the final prediction. We show the architectures of Meta-2-6 and Meta-3-1 in Figures 2 and 3.

In Meta-3-1, the base classifiers—kNN, NB, and LDA—are trained from a set of feature vectors of patients prelabeled as *Death* or *Others*. The predictions of kNN, NB, and LDA provide the metadata, which are used to train the second-level

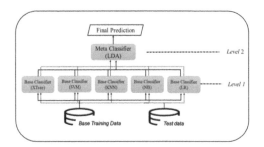

Figure 2. Hierarchy of meta-2-6.

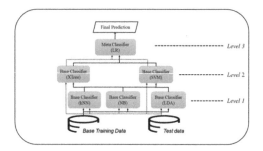

Figure 3. Hierarchy of Meta-3-1.

meta classifiers, SVM and XTree. The outputs of SVM and XTree are successively passed to the top to train LR. To classify a new patient, we first feed the feature vector derived from the patient records to the trained base classifiers—kNN, NB, and LDA. The predictions of the three base classifiers are then uploaded to the trained meta classifiers, SVM and XTree, and successively their outputs are passed to LR at the top to make the final prediction of PJI mortality for the new patient.

To maintain fairness and consistency in comparison, we conducted three times 5-fold CVs, using the same data, to evaluate the performances in mortality prediction between meta-learners and three commonly used indices, CCI, ASA, and ECI scores. It is noteworthy that because this diagnosis prediction task is class-imbalanced, the reasonable performance measures are F1, MCC, and AUC. The percentage accuracy (ACC) is not an appropriate measure. We included ACC solely for reference purposes. The results in Table 4 indicate that the proposed machine learning approach Meta-3-1 outperforms CCI, ASA, and ECI Scores for F1, MCC, and AUC by a marked positive difference. The results demonstrate the feasibility of applying ML to PJI mortality prediction.

The flexibility and adaptability of machine learning can be the key factors to the improvement over the commonly practiced mortality prediction criteria. What distinguishes ML approaches from the scoring criteria is that the features considered by the scorings were prespecified and remained the same for different patients with different characteristics, possibly due to race or region heterogeneity. By contrast, important features identified by ML depend on the patients to diagnose. Consequently, the important features can vary accordingly, and the trained models for PJI mortality prediction using these features will fit the data better than the scoring criteria.

## 4 CONCLUSION

We developed an ensemble machine meta-learning system for PJI mortality prediction and compared it with three commonly applied mortality scorings in medicine. The results show that machine learning approaches significantly outperformed the medical scoring systems for MCC, AUC, and F1 scores. In addition, treating PJI mortality prediction as an inductive learning task enables us to learn predictive models adaptably from the data available, which provides the flexibility that is missing in the medical scoring indices.

# REFERENCES

Belmont P.J. Jr, Goodman G.P., Waterman B.R., Bader J.O., Schoenfeld A.J, 2014. *J. Bone and Joint Surgery*, 96(1), 20–26.

Cover T., Hart P., 1967, *IEEE Transactions on Information Theory*, 13(1), 21–27.

Choi H.G., Kwon B.C., Kim J I, Lee J.K. 2020. *J. Orthopaedic Surgery*, 28(1), 1–8.

Cruz J.A., Wishart D.S., 2007. *Cancer Inform*, 2, 59–77.

Dayton C., 1992. *Stat*, 474: 574.

Gaber T., Tharwat A., Ibrahim A., Hassanien A.E., 2017. *AI Communications*, 30(2), 169–190.

Gabriel R.A., Sharma B.S., Doan C.N., Jiang X., Schmidt U.H., Vaida F., 2019. *Anesth Analg*, 129, 43–50.

Geurts P., Ernst D., Wehenkel L., 2006. *Machine Learning*, 63, 3–42.

Handelman G.S., Kok H.K., Chandra R.S., Razavi A.H., Lee M.J., Asadi H., 2018. *J Intern Med*, 284, 603–19.

Harris I.A., Hatton A., de Steiger R., Lewis P., Graves S., 2019. *ANZ J. Surgery*, doi: 10.1111/ans.15529.

Harris A.H.S., Kuo A.C., Weng Y., Trickey A.W., Bowe T., Giori N.J., 2019. *Clin Orthop*, 477, 452–460.

Hu Y.J., Ku T.H., Yang Y.H., Shen J.Y., 2018. *IEEE J Biomed Health Inform*, 22, 265–75.

Hunt L.P., Ben-Shlomo Y., Clark E.M.et al., 2014. *Lancet*, 384, 1429–36.

Leta T.H., Lygre S. H.L., Schrama J.C., Hallan G., Gjertsen J.-E., Dale H., Furnes O., 2019. *J. Bone and Joint Surgery*, 7(6), e4.

Menendez M.E., Neuhaus V., van Dijk C.N., Ring D., 2014. *Clin Orthop Relat Res.*, 472(9), 2878–2886.

Navarro S.M., Wang E.Y., Haeberle H.S., Mont M.A., Krebs V.E., Patterson B.M. et al., 2018. *J. Arthoplasty*, 33, 3617–23.

Obermeyer Z., Emanuel E.J., 2016. *N Engl J Med*, 375, 1216–1219.

Pugely A.J., Martin C.T., Gao Y., Schweizer M.L., Callaghan J.J., 2015. *J. Arthoplasty*, 30, Suppl 1, 47–50.

Rish I., 2001. *IBM Research Report*, RC 22230 (W0111-014) November 2.

Samad M.D., Ulloa A., Wehner G.J., Jing L., Hartzel D., Good C.W.et al., 2018. *JACC Cardiovasc Imaging*, 12, 681–689. https://doi.org/10.1016/j.jcmg.2018.04.026

Shohat N., Goswami K., Tan T.L., Yayac M., Soriano A., Sousa R. et al., 2020. *J. Bone and Joint*, 102-B:11–19.

Steinwart I., Christmann A. 2008. *Springer*, ISBN 978-0-387-77241-7.

Ting K.M., Witten I.H., 1997. *IJCAI*. Hamilton: Department of Computer Science, University of Waik.

Wolpert D.H., 1992. *Neural Netwm* 5, 241–259.

Yao J.J., Hevesi M., O'Byrne M.M., Berry D.J., Lewallen D.G., Maradit K.H., 2019. *J. Arthoplasty*, 343(3), 542–548.

*System Innovation for a Troubled World – Lam et al. (Eds)*
*© 2024 the Author(s), ISBN: 978-1-032-60846-4*

# Design and manufacture of a device that can capture particulate matter

Meng-Hui Hsu* & I-Kuan Chuang
*Department of Mechanical Engineering, Kun Shan University, Yongkang, Tainan , Taiwan*

ABSTRACT: Although the industry has contributed to a prosperous economy, it has also brought increasingly polluted air and water. Although there are many factories, but only a very small number of them have complete pollution prevention and control equipment. Therefore, there are many pollutants in the air, especially particulate matter (PM) like dust particles. $PM_{2.5}$, a fine particle with a particle size less than or equal to 2.5 microns ($\mu m$), is larger than viruses and smaller than bacteria, and it is easy to carry toxic substances into the human body. Therefore, particulate matter seriously damages human health. Although manufacturers can regard pollution prevention and control as a part of production management and eliminate pollution through industrial upgrading, the environment we live in will not deteriorate rapidly. But how will people protect themselves in this environment of air pollution. Therefore, the purpose of this research is to establish a device design and production method for capturing particulate matter $PM_{10}$ and $PM_{2.5}$ with a high cost-performance ratio that can be made by oneself and used at home. The design feature of this device is to use a water film to capture suspended particles. The way to form a water film is to guide the deflector to the gauze, let the water flow through the mesh, and form a water film through the holes in the gauze, so that the film captures the suspended particles. In addition, the gauze frame can be equipped with different layers of water film to obtain different effects of capturing suspended particles. The result of this research is to build a device to capture particulate matter $PM_{10}$ and $PM_{2.5}$ according to the established method, and it is indeed effective in capturing particulate matter through practical operation.

## 1 INTRODUCTION

The results of these researches (Yao et al. 2022; Liu. et al. 2022) showed particulate matter $PM_{10}$ and $PM_{2.5}$ seriously damage human health. A. L. Print et al. (2022) believe that additional epidemiological investigations are needed to examine the causality and severity of particulate air pollution and COVID-19 cases.

Liu. et al. 2022 reinforced the importance of air quality improvement. Therefore, many pollution prevention technologies have been developed. M., Tyle et al. (2020) developed an active wet scrubbing filtration system to filter pollutants. J. Laslo et al. (2016) proposed a method to clean a flue gas and/or cooling a flue gas with a dispersed finely divided absorption liquid.

However, ordinary people do not have the anti-pollution technology that the industry has. How can they protect themselves in this air-polluted environment?

Therefore, the purpose of this research is to establish a device design and production method for capturing particulate matter $PM_{10}$ and $PM_{2.5}$ with a high cost-performance ratio that can be made by oneself and used at home.

## 2 CAPTURING PARTICULATE MATTER DEVICE

The design feature of this device is to use a water film to capture suspended particles. The way to form a water film is to guide the deflector to the gauze, let the water flow through the mesh, and form a water film through the holes in the gauze, so that the film captures the suspended particles. In addition, the gauze frame can be equipped with different layers of water film to obtain different effects of capturing suspended particles.

Figure 1 shows the diagram of the designed capturing particulate matter device. This design consists of two subsystems, namely the air constant flow device and the air filter device.

The water film generated in the air filter device, which can catch the suspended particulate matter in the air. Air constant flow devices can control the steady-state air flow to obtain accurate experimental results and confirm that water membrane filtration is effective and feasible.

Air constant flow device shown in Figure 2 has the following:

1. One incense burning device that burns sandalwood powder to generate suspended particles.
2. Some sponges that can filter suspended particles to maintain an appropriate particle concentration.

---

*Corresponding Author: mhhsu@mail.ksu edu.tw

DOI: 10.1201/9781003460763-53

3. Two fans that guide the flow direction of suspended particles.
4. One sensor for sensing suspended particles.

The blue lines shown in Figure 2 are the flow direction of suspended particles.

The air filter device shown in Figure 3 has the following:

1. Some sponges that can filter suspended particles to maintain an appropriate particle concentration,

2. Three PMS5003T sensor sensors for sensing suspended particles.
3. Some water filtration module (Figure 4) that can form water films and capture suspended particles
4. One A-039-2000 pumping motor pumps water into water filtration module and form water films.
5. One Arduino Mega 2560 board drives the motor and fan and captures the concentration of suspended particles from the sensor.

Figure 3 (a) and (b) represent the schematic diagrams of the Flow direction of suspended particles and the Flow direction of water respectively.

Tables 1 and 2 show the specifications of the PMS5003T sensor and A-039-2000 pumping motor respectively.

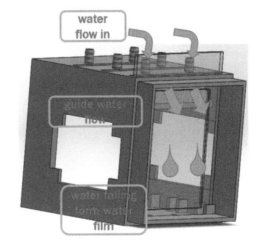

Figure 4. Water filtration module.

Figure 1. Capturing particulate matter device.

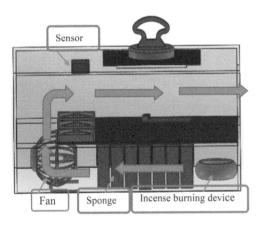

Figure 2. Air constant flow device.

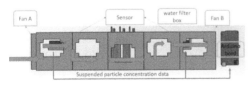

(a) Flow direction of suspended particles

(b) Flow direction of water

Figure 3. Air filter device.

Table 1. PMS5003T sensor specifications.

| Measuring range | 0.3~1.0 μm |
|---|---|
| | 1.0~2.5 μm |
| | 2.5~10 μm |
| Effective range | 0~500 μg/m^3 |
| Maximum range | 1000μg/m^3 |
| Working humidity range | 0~99% |
| Standard volume | 0.1 L |
| Working humidity range | 0~99% |
| Sensor size | 50 × 38 × 21 mm |
| Weight | approx. 40 g |

Table 2. A-039-2000 pumping motor specifications.

| Size | 11.5 × 7 × 9cm |
|---|---|
| Voltage | 110V |
| Frequency | 60HZ |
| Power | 35W |
| Lift | 2.2 m |
| Traffic | 2000 L/H |
| Outlet size | 1.9/2.2 cm |

## 3  EXPERIMENT

Based on the design of a capturing particulate matter device, the study establish a protype of capturing particulate matter device as shown in Figure 5. The prototype was used for experiments, and the experimental results are shown in Figures 6 and 7.

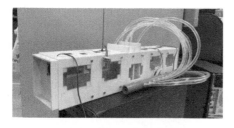

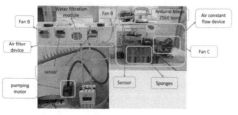

Figure 5.  A protype of capturing particulate matter device.

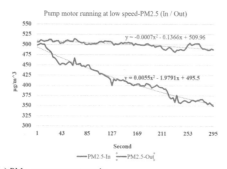

(a) PM$_{2.5}$ measurement results

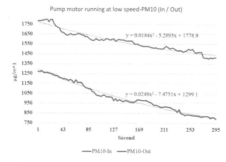

(b) PM$_{10}$ measurement results

Figure 6.  Pump motor running at low speed.

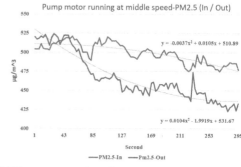

(a) PM$_{2.5}$ measurement results

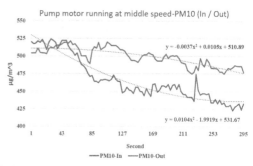

(b) PM$_{10}$ measurement results

Figure 7.  Pump motor running at middle speed.

## 4  DISCUSSION

When the pumping motor is running at low speed, after 5 minutes, it is found that this experimental device can effectively reduce the high concentration of PM$_{10}$ and PM$_{2.5}$ produced by burning sandalwood powder at the entrance, and the water film of the water filtration module will also effectively absorb PM$_{10}$ and PM$_{2.5}$ particles.

When the pumping motor is running at a medium speed, after 5 minutes, it is found that this experimental device can indeed reduce the high concentration of PM$_{10}$ and PM$_{2.5}$ particles produced by burning sandalwood powder at the entrance. Within 45 seconds after the start of the experiment, the concentrations of PM$_{10}$ and PM$_{2.5}$ were higher than at the entrance. However, after 45 seconds, the high concentrations of PM$_{10}$ and PM$_{2.5}$ lower than the inlet were measured instead. The reason for this may be that the speed of the pumping motor was too high within 45 seconds after the start of the experiment, and it was too late to effectively form the water film in the Water filtration module, so PM$_{10}$ and PM$_{2.5}$ particles could not be effectively absorbed.

# REFERENCES

Laslo D.J., Mile T., Hakansson R., Brogaard F.J., Forsgren K.M. and Hognef K., Method and apparatus for wetdesulfurization spray towers, *United States Patent*, Patent No.: US 9,468,885 B2, Oct. 18,2016.

Liu Q., Huang K., Liang F.C, Yang X.L. Li J.X, Chen J.H., Liu X.Q., Cao J., Shen C., Yu L., Zhao Y.G., Deng Y., Li Y., Hu D.S., Lu X.F., Liu Y., Gu D.F, Liu F.C., and Huang J.F., Long-term exposure to fine particulate matter modifies the association between physical activity and hypertension, *Journal of Sport and Health Science* 00 (2022) 1–8.

Prinz A.L. and Richter D.J., Long-term exposure to fine particulate matter air pollution: An ecological study of its effect on COVID-19 cases and fatality in Germany, *Environmental Research* 204 (2022) 111948.

Tyle M., James B., Thomas L. and John C.G., Active wet scrubbing filtration system, International Application Published under the Patent Cooperation Treaty (PCT), *International Publication Number WO* 2020/131309 A1.

Yao Y., Wang K. and Xiang H., Association between cognitive function and ambient particulate matters in middle-aged and elderly chinese adults: Evidence from the china health and retirement longitudinal study (charls), *Science of the Total Environment* 828 (2022) 154297.

System Innovation for a Troubled World – Lam et al. (Eds)
© 2024 the Author(s), ISBN: 978-1-032-60846-4

# Design and build a device that can generate an ellipse

Meng-Hui Hsu* & Jing-Jing Chen
*Department of Mechanical Engineering, Kun Shan University, Yongkang, Tainan, Taiwan*

ABSTRACT: Ellipses can be used to focus energy waves, study the motion of celestial bodies, elliptical gears with different speed ratios, football, design elliptical bridge arches or whispering galleries, and assist in processing operations to draw elliptical marking lines. Based on the many applications above, it can be known that drawing a standard ellipse is a very important part of the application of ellipse technology. Therefore, the purpose of this study is to design and manufacture a device that can generate a standard ellipse. However, an ellipse is a plane curve such that the sums of the distances of each point in its periphery from two fixed points, the foci, are equal. According to this characteristic, a six bars and seven joints mechanism with four connecting links, two sliders, two prismatic joints, and five revolute joints can be designed. This mechanism has a cross-shaped four-bar loop, and the cross-shaped loop will form two congruent triangles. In this mechanism, there is a revolute joint connecting two sliders at the intersection point of the cross-shaped loop, and the two sliders slide on a connecting link respectively. Then an ellipse can be drawn at the intersection point where the rotary joint is located. The research results are to design and build a device that can generate an Ellipse.

## 1 INTRODUCTION

In the 4th century BC, conics were known to include ellipses, hyperbolas, and parabolas. These three kinds of conic sections are all symmetrical patterns and have a symmetrical aesthetic feeling. Ellipses are used in life, such as the focus energy waves, elliptical gears with different speed ratios, football, elliptical bridges, etc.

Apollonius (Apollonius, about 262 BC-190 BC) was the first scientist who put forward the definition of conic section based on the difference of conic section, surface intersection space, and projection (Apollonius 1956; Apollonius & L. T. Health 2013; Allen 2009; Eves 1990).

F. V. Schooten (1650, 1656) discussed various mechanism patterns from drawing perfect circles to ellipses, pushing hyperbolas to parabolas, and demonstrations of drawing tools.

The above basic research results are the foundations for modern mathematics and technology. Schooten (1650) designed the elliptical mechanism as shown in Figure 1. The link length relationship of the four-bar linkage is:

$$\overline{HI} = \overline{FG}, \ \overline{FI} = \overline{HG} \qquad (1)$$

Then the path of the intersection E of lines HG and FI is an ellipse. These research results are applied to design an elliptical gearset (Ali 2019).

The application of the principles of elliptical mechanism design to the elliptical gears design is interesting.

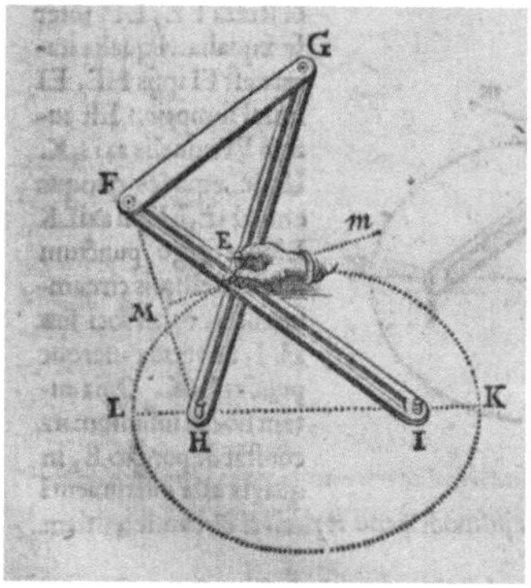

Figure 1. An elliptical mechanism (Schooten1650).

Figure 2. An elliptical gearset (Ali 2019).

Hence, the purpose of the research is to study the design principles of basic mechanisms like elliptical mechanisms and apply these principles to innovative designs of a new elliptical mechanism.

---

*Corresponding Author: mhhsu@mail.ksu edu.tw

DOI: 10.1201/9781003460763-54

## 2 PRINCIPLES

As shown in Figure 1, H and I are the focal points of the ellipse, and LK is the long axis of the ellipse. H, I, E, F, and G in the figure satisfy the principle of drawing an ellipse, that is, the intersection point E of the two connecting lines is the drawing point E of the ellipse. The sum of points E to H and I is a constant, and the major axis of the ellipse is:

$$\overline{EF} + \overline{EG} = \overline{EH} + \overline{EI} = \text{constant} \qquad (2)$$

The path of point E shown in Figure 1 is an ellipse.

As shown in Figure 1, the trajectory of point E is an ellipse, then point E needs to meet two conditions:

1. Point E can move along the direction of link HG and link IF at the same time,
2. There is a relative rotation between the link HG and the link IF at point E.

According to condition 1, point E is on a slider that slides relative to the link HG, and point E is also on a slider that slides relative to the link IF. According to condition 2, these two sliders have a rotation relative to point E so the two sliders are connected by a rovolut joint $J_R$.

Hence, an elliptical mechanism as shown in Figure 3 is different from the elliptical mechanism shown in Figure 1. It is a six links and seven joints mechanism with four connecting links ($K_{L1}$, $K_{L2}$, $K_{L3}$, $K_{L4}$), two sliders($K_{P1}$, $K_{P2}$), two prismatic $J_P$joints, and five revolute joints $J_R$.

## 3 RESULTS

The results of this research are as follows:

1. This research studies the design principles of elliptical mechanisms, and applies these principles to innovatively design a new elliptical mechanism, as shown in Figure 3.
2. Two ellipses, shown in Figure 3, are attached to link 1 and link 4, respectively. The ellipse attached to link 4 will move with it as link 4 moves. The two relatively moving ellipses are also the theoretical basis for designing the elliptical gears.
3. Figure 4 shows the designed elliptical mechanism with two different positions.
4. Figure 5 is an exploded view of the designed elliptical mechanism components.
5. Figure 6 shows a designed elliptical mechanism with different geometry.

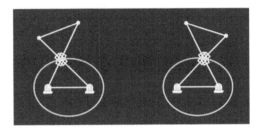

Figure 4. Designed elliptical mechanism with two different positions.

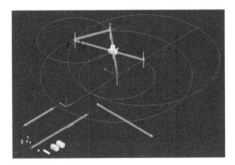

Figure 5. Exploded view of the designed elliptical mechanism components.

Figure 6. An designed elliptical mechanism with different geometry.

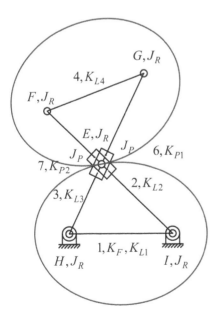

Figure 3. A planar elliptical mechanism with six links and seven joints.

6. Figure 7 shows the real device of the designed elliptical mechanism shown in Figure 6.

Figure 7.   Real device of designed elliptical mechanism.

REFERENCES

Ali N.E., Yildirim N., Erdoğan F., Karba B. and Şahin B., *Non-Circular Gear Design, Elliptical Gears as an Example, Ejons VI – International Conference On Mathematics - Engineering - Natural & Medical Sciences*, March 8-10, 2019 Adana/ TURKEY, pp.624–641.

Allen A., *Apollonius of Perga: Historical Background and Conic Sections*, Master's Thesis, U.S.A., Liberty University, 2009.

Apollonius and Health L. T., *Treatise on Conic Sections-Edited in Modern Notation*, Carruthers Press, UK, 2013.

Apollonius, *Treatise on Conic Sections*, Cambridge University Press, UK, 1956.

Eves H., *An Introduction to the History of Mathematics*, Cengage Learnin Press, U.S.A., 1990.

Maanen J.V,. *Seventeenth instruments for drawing conic sections. The Mathematical*, Vol.76, No 476, July 1992, pp.222–230.

Schooten F.V., *Exercitationum Mathematicarum* (1656), Kessinger Publishing, LLC, U.S.A., 2010.

Schooten F.V., *Exercitationvm Mathematicarum Liber Primus*. Ex Officina Johannis Elisevrii,Academic Typographi, Netherlands, 1650.

*System Innovation for a Troubled World – Lam et al. (Eds)*
© 2024 the Author(s), ISBN: 978-1-032-60846-4

# Exploring the current status and future trends of batteries in Taiwan

Po-Hsun Lai & Tai-Shen Huang*
*Department of Industrial Design, Chaoyang University of Technology, Taichung, Taiwan*

ABSTRACT: With the rapid development of technology in recent years, our lives have become increasingly convenient, and as a result, the number of electronic products continues to grow. Many electronic products rely on batteries to operate, and when these batteries run out of energy, they are often carelessly thrown into trash cans or soil by humans, causing serious environmental damage. The purpose of this study is to investigate the issue of poor waste battery energy recovery rates in Taiwan and use a literature analysis method to identify differences in waste battery energy recovery policies between the United States, the European Union, Japan, China, and Taiwan. Based on these differences, relevant questionnaires will be formulated to develop more precise experimental processes to identify the issue of poor battery energy recovery rates in Taiwan and provide reference materials for future researchers on Taiwan's battery energy recovery rates.

## 1 INTRODUCTION

### 1.1 Research background

In recent years, with the continuous development and progress of technology, the variety of electronic products we use in our daily lives is increasing. As a result, the demand for batteries in these electronic products is also increasing year by year. However, when batteries lose their value, most people simply throw them into the trash, which poses a great threat to the environment and human health. Therefore, battery recycling education is an important research direction.

Most batteries contain many harmful substances such as lead, mercury, nickel, acid, and alkali. When batteries are discarded in soil or water, they can cause environmental pollution and harm. If humans consume animals or plants that have been contaminated with harmful substances from batteries, it can cause harm to human health. Therefore, battery recycling education can increase public awareness and understanding of the importance of battery recycling, so that more people can improve their awareness of environmental protection and reduce the harm to the environment and human health.

### 1.2 Research objectives

The purpose of this study is to explore the issue of poor battery recycling rates in Taiwan and to analyze and compile recommendations for improving battery recycling rates in Taiwan. The findings and recommendations of this study will be useful for future scholars and researchers to reference and build upon.

## 2 LITERATURE REVIEW

### 2.1 The impact of green consumption

Liu Jie-xin et al. synthesized relevant literature on the impact of green consumption both domestically and internationally and found that green consumers generally have the following characteristics: young, highly educated, from higher income households, female, and have higher occupational status [1]. In reviewing six articles on green consumption behavior among university students and six articles on the general public, conducted by Lin Xin-pei and Chao Yu-long, it was found that women tend to have higher behavioral intentions and are more likely to purchase green products compared to men [2]. Dietz, Stern, and Guagnano found that women are more likely than men to engage in green consumption behavior. Domestic and foreign scholars have also pointed out that gender factors have an impact on resource recycling behavior, with women accounting for a higher proportion of those involved in environmental behavior, and having better attitudes and behavioral intentions [3]. Hines et al.'s meta-analysis also found that variables such as education, income, age, and gender are significantly correlated with responsible environmental behavior [4].

### 2.2 Future trends of lithium batteries

According to the Industrial Technology Research Institute's Industrial Economics and Knowledge

---

*Corresponding Author: ss105218050@gmail.com

DOI: 10.1201/9781003460763-55

Center, in 2011, the largest application of consumer lithium batteries globally was still in 3C products. Among them, the highest application area for lithium batteries was mobile phones, accounting for 42%, followed by notebook computers, accounting for 32%, digital cameras accounting for 4%, camcorders accounting for 1%, electric hand tools accounting for 5%, and other devices such as portable game consoles and cleaners accounting for 16%. In the future, the development of lithium battery applications and technology will shift towards base stations and electric vehicles, creating a more environmentally friendly green energy source [5]. Since 2010, the global manufacturing capacity of lithium-ion batteries has soared. According to a report by the International Energy Agency (IEA), the total manufacturing capacity of electric vehicle and energy storage lithium-ion batteries is expected to reach 200 GWh in 2017. It is estimated that there are more than 200 lithium battery factories worldwide in operation, with the majority of production capacity concentrated in China since 2015 [6]. According to a report by INSIDE, the biggest challenge for lithium battery recycling may not be the technological aspect, but the market driving factors. Currently, there are no detailed statistics on lithium battery recycling rates on a global scale [7].

### 2.3 Current status of battery recycling in taiwan

According to the statistics of the Taiwan Environmental Protection Administration, Taiwan uses about 11,000 tons of dry batteries annually, but only about 4,000 tons are collected for recycling. The recycling rate has remained stable at around 40%, indicating that some dry batteries have not yet entered the recycling system [8]. According to statistics from the Taiwan Environmental Protection Administration, in 2021 the recycled amount of secondary lithium batteries (including electric cars, 3C products, and commodities with secondary lithium batteries) was approximately 600 tons, accounting for about 15% of the overall recycled amount of waste dry batteries. With a focus on the million electric vehicle market, which has accumulated a total of 8,000 electric cars and sold 500,000 electric motorcycles, the Environmental Protection Administration estimates that the amount of waste secondary lithium batteries in Taiwan will be around 1,100 tons per year in 2025 [9]. According to statistics from the Taiwan Ministry of Transportation and Communications, the number of registered electric vehicles in Taiwan has been increasing year by year. In 2016, there were only 737 registered electric vehicles (including pure electric, electric/gasoline, electric/diesel, and range-extended electric vehicles). However, in 2020, the number of new registered electric vehicles surged to 13,364, which is about 18 times the number from five years ago

[10]. According to the "Investigation, Analysis and Evaluation of the Recycling and Disposal System for Waste Dry Batteries and Waste Lighting Sources and Implementation Effect Review Project Plan, 2012" by the Taiwan Environmental Protection Administration, the sources of waste dry battery recycling in Taiwan mainly come from households, companies, schools, the military, prisons, and sales points. According to the survey results of the project plan, in 2012, the majority of waste dry battery recycling sources were from the public, accounting for about 35% of the total [11]. After six years since the 39.74% battery recycling rate in 2014, the recycling rate has still not reached 50% in 2020. This suggests that there is still much room for development in battery recycling in Taiwan, particularly with the advent of the lithium-ion battery era. For example, there is a lack of comprehensive measures in place to regulate this area under current policies.

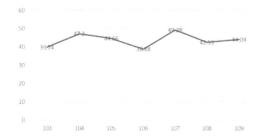

Figure 1. Recycling rate of waste batteries in Taiwan in recent years.

### 2.4 Recycling and current status of waste lithium batteries

Currently, there hasn't been a wave of electric vehicle battery replacement, as the average lifespan of lithium batteries is typically seven to ten years. With the global trend of promoting electric vehicles, Taiwan will eventually have to face issues such as the disposal of fossil-fuel vehicles and secondary batteries. Therefore, it's important to explore how other countries regulate lithium batteries, which will aid Taiwan in developing corresponding regulations in the future.

1. American lithium battery: Lithium-ion batteries in the US: The current status of the recycling of automotive lithium-ion batteries by the US government and recycling companies is not clearly described. Although several facilities in the US are capable of processing lithium-ion batteries, the demand is not yet sufficient, which affects the processing cost. Although there are no specific laws regarding the recycling of automotive lithium-ion batteries, the concept of extended producer responsibility is well-established, and all stakeholders in the product life cycle are responsible for reducing environmental hazards.

2. EU: In March 1991, the EU issued Directive 91/157/EEC on "batteries and accumulators containing certain hazardous substances." In February 2003, the European Environment Agency reviewed the battery system.

| |
|---|
| 1. EU member states have the obligation to collect all types of batteries, and the collection rate should reach 25% in 2012 and 45% in 2016. |
| 2. The collected batteries should all be properly recycled and disposed of, excluding those that contain hazardous substances. |
| 3. The disposal of industrial or automotive batteries by landfill or incineration is prohibited. |
| 4. "Mercury and cadmium are prohibited from being used during manufacturing." |
| 5. The individual recycling rates for different types of batteries are set as follows: lead-acid batteries should achieve 65% of their average weight, nickel-cadmium batteries should achieve 75% of their average weight, and other batteries (including automotive lithium-ion batteries) should achieve 50% of their average weight. |
| 6. The costs related to the collection, treatment, and reuse of waste batteries are borne by the manufacturers. |

Figure 2. Establishment and evaluation of vehicle lithium battery recycling system/this research system.

3. China: China has not yet faced a large amount of discarded lithium-ion batteries from electric vehicles, but the "Technical Policy for the Prevention and Control of Waste Battery Pollution" was formulated in 2003, which includes regulations for the disposal of waste batteries. Regarding battery recycling, the types of batteries that should be recycled and the responsible industry players have been determined.

4. Japanese: The Japanese government revised the enforcement regulations of the Automobile Recycling Law on February 1, 2012, to ensure proper recycling of nickel-hydrogen and lithium-ion batteries used in electric vehicles. The revised regulations added "lithium-ion batteries" and "nickel-hydrogen batteries" to the list of items that should be recycled before dismantling. Japanese car manufacturers have also fulfilled their social responsibility by providing safety dismantling instructions for their models' lithium and nickel-hydrogen batteries to dismantling companies. After removing the batteries, dismantling companies declare the battery model, serial number, and appearance and apply it to the vehicle manufacturer for dismantling fees.

5. Taiwan: In Taiwan, the standard for the recycling, storage, and disposal of waste dry batteries is regulated by the "Standards for Methods and Facilities for Recycling, Storage, and Disposal of Waste Dry Batteries." There

are currently no newer regulations in place. However, Taiwanese manufacturers of lithium batteries have a great advantage in terms of their technology and expertise, as each part of the production process has its own specialized area of focus, resulting in a highly competitive value." [12]

### 2.5 Recycling and current status of waste non-lithium batteries

1. American: Mercury-Containing and Rechargeable Battery Management Act. This law was jointly developed and implemented by the federal government and state governments. It regulates the labeling, production, collection, transportation, and storage of waste cadmium-nickel batteries, waste small-sealed lead-acid batteries, and other waste rechargeable batteries. The law was enacted on May 13, 1996, and went into effect in the United States [13]. For example, California's AB 1125 (Battery Recycling Act) requires retailers to charge a recycling fee for the sale of batteries and requires manufacturers to provide methods for recycling batteries. Manufacturers who do not comply with the battery recycling law may face fines of up to $25,000. Many states in the United States have also passed similar laws to establish a system for battery recycling through this sales model [14].

2. The European Union (EU) issued the Battery Directive in 2006, mainly to prevent the harm of batteries to the environment and human health. The directive also requires member states to establish battery recycling systems within their countries and mandates battery manufacturers to be responsible for the recycling and treatment of the batteries they produce [15].

3. China: In 2004, the People's Republic of China issued the Solid Waste Pollution Control Law, which mainly manages electronic waste by regulating environmental monitoring of designated disassembly and processing companies, ensuring that recycled waste appliances are safely disassembled and processed in an environmentally friendly manner. Other related regulations include the Environmental Protection Law, the Waste Management Regulations, and the Management Measures for Waste Battery Recycling [16].

4. Japan: Japan began implementing the Resource Recycling Promotion Law in 2001, with the goal of promoting the 3Rs: waste reduction, reuse of parts, and resource recycling. This law is part of a comprehensive effort to promote efficient use of resources, and there are other related laws, such as the Law for the Promotion of Effective Utilization of Resources [17]

5. In Taiwan, the management of waste batteries is primarily regulated by the Waste Disposal Act. Since 1990, there have been ongoing updates to the regulations, and the current standard for the management of waste dry batteries is the "Standard for the Collection, Storage, Clearing, and Disposal of Waste Dry Batteries." This standard specifies the requirements for the collection, storage, transport, treatment, and disposal of waste dry batteries in Taiwan [18].

In literature, it can be found that green consumption behavior is significantly correlated with gender, educational level, age, etc. Regarding the disposal of waste lithium batteries, the waste disposal projects in various countries' policies are not yet fully planned. Currently, the trend of lithium batteries is growing globally, but the planning for the subsequent disposal of secondary lithium batteries is not yet complete. Many countries' policies are also not well planned. In the future, electronic products will become more diversified. In recent years, Taiwan's waste battery recovery rate has been only 40%. If future policies are not well planned, the impact on Taiwan's future battery recovery rate will be significant.

## 3 RESEARCH METHOD

### 3.1 Research methodology and description

The present study aims to explore the issue of the battery recycling rate in Taiwan. First, a literature review will be conducted to identify the factors that contribute to the low recycling rate of batteries in Taiwan. Subsequently, a questionnaire will be designed to investigate the issue further. The study will focus on the policy aspects of the problem, exploring the areas of education, regulation, and promotion to determine the reasons behind the low battery recycling rate in Taiwan. In Chapter 3, the experimental procedure focuses on exploring the issue of the battery recycling rate in Taiwan. Based on the literature review, it is known that gender can affect recycling behavior, indicating that different genders may exhibit different recycling behaviors under the same educational system. In terms of regulations, the existing laws and regulations in Taiwan do not set a limit on the maximum number of batteries that individuals can purchase, which may result in some individuals hoarding batteries at home. Additionally, the penalties for violations are relatively light compared to other countries, leading to a lack of public awareness and attention. Regarding promotion, the lack of incentives can easily result in a low level of importance attached to batteries by Taiwanese people, leading to behaviors such as littering, non-separation, and burying, which can cause issues such as poor battery recycling rates, pollution, and global warming. Currently, Taiwan's battery recycling rate is lower

than the European Union's standards. However, in the coming years, the replacement of secondary lithium batteries will pose a significant challenge to Taiwan's battery recycling efforts.

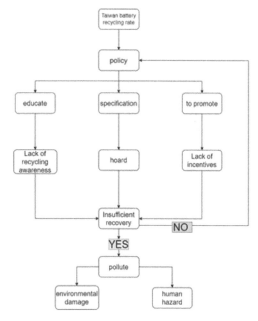

Figure 3. Establishment and evaluation of vehicle lithium battery recycling system/this research system.

### 3.2 Experiment process

The research scope can be limited to a specific region, and the research subjects can be selected through simple random sampling. Data can be obtained by using a questionnaire. Before the survey, the research content and privacy principles will be explained and permission will be obtained to fill out the questionnaire. The survey will start by asking for basic information from the participants to ensure that they fall within the research's constraints. The following topics will be explored in the questionnaire: (1) Gender: Does the motivation to recycle batteries at home differ between genders in Taiwan, and are the gender roles of male breadwinners and female homemakers a factor? (2) Occupation: How aware are different occupational groups of Taiwan's battery recycling issues? (3) Education level: Is there a difference in awareness of Taiwan's battery recycling rate among people with different education levels? (4) Environmental issues: How concerned are people about environmental issues, both domestic and international? (5) Policy: Are people aware of the regulations and fines related to the Environmental Protection Administration's Waste Disposal Act, and do they understand the consequences of improper battery disposal?

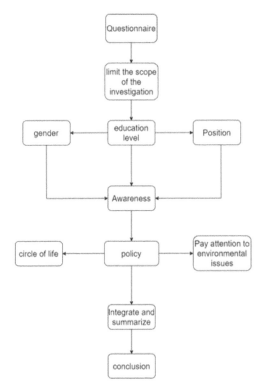

Figure 4. Experimental procedure, this study draws.

## 4 RESEARCH RESULT

It can be concluded from the literature that the situation of battery recycling in Taiwan is different from that in other countries, with the United States as an example.

| Promotion of policies and regulations | ✗ | ○ |
|---|---|---|
| recycling pathway | ✗ | ○ |
| Knowledge | ✗ | ✗ |
| cost | ✗ | ○ |

Figure 5. This study draws.

The main issues contributing to poor battery recycling in Taiwan are as follows:

1. Lack of policy and regulatory promotion: Compared to other countries in Europe and America, Taiwan's battery recycling policy and regulations are still not complete, lacking clear policy objectives, and regulations are relatively light compared to those in Europe and America.

2. Lack of recycling channels: There is insufficient incentive for battery recycling channels in Taiwan.

3. Lack of knowledge: Taiwanese people lack knowledge of battery recycling and environmental awareness, making it difficult to raise the recycling rate. They lack understanding of the importance of battery recycling and how to recycle them properly.

4. High cost: In the battery recycling process, high investment and technology are required for the post-processing equipment. When companies make choices between economic benefits and social responsibility, they often prioritize economic benefits, resulting in low recycling rates.

## 5 CONCLUSION AND SUGGESTION

The experimental process outlined above can reveal the shortcomings of battery recycling in Taiwan, as well as the reasons why the recycling rate of batteries in Taiwan cannot be further improved. However, we must now strive to achieve a virtuous cycle of battery recycling within the constraints of limited resources. How to achieve cradle-to-cradle sustainable development is the issue that we humans will have to face. It is hoped that this study will provide subsequent scholars with a reference for Taiwan's battery energy recycling program.

## REFERENCES

[1] Liu J.-X., Yan H.-W., Liu G.-Y., Chiu S.-Y., & Li, J.-R. (2000). A study on community residents' green consumption behavior and related information dissemination. *Journal of Health Education*, 13, 189–212.

[2] Lin H.P. & Chao Y.L. (2003). Meta-analysis of influencing factors on green consumer behavior among college students and general public. *The 13th Symposium on Urban Regeneration and Development Strategies and Environmental Management*, Kaohsiung City Government Construction Bureau.

[3] Paul C, Stem, Thomas Dietz,Gregory A. Guagnano (1995). The New Ecological Paradigm in Social-Psychological Context

[4] Hines J.M., Hungerford H.R. & Tomera A.N. (1986). Analysis and synthesis of research on responsible environmental behavior: A meta-analysis. *The Journal of Environmental Education*, 18(2), 1–8.

[5] Lin T.-H. (2014). *Establishment and Evaluation of Recycling System for Lithium-ion Batteries in Electric Vehicles*. Master's thesis, Graduate Institute of Natural Resources and Environmental Management, National Taipei University, New Taipei City, Taiwan.

[6] Techorange Juheng.com 2021/10/22 https://buz-zorange.com/techorange/2021/10/22/tesla-chinese-battery-lfp/

[7] INSIDE, Chris, 2021/06/01 https://www.inside.com.tw/feature/electric-car-generation/23817-electric-vehicles-and-battery-recycling

[8] *Environmental Sanitation Management Section*.2022/08 https://www.hccg.gov.tw/ch/hotkey_print.jsp?mtitle=%E5%B8%82%E6%94%BF%E6%96%B0%E8%81%9E&contentlink=ap/municipalnews_view.jsp&dataserno=202108020002&mserno=201601300307&id=48&contentid=48&page=null

[9] *Executive Yuan Protected Resources Recycling Network*.2022/05 https://recycle.epa.gov.tw/News/NewInfo/1165

[10] CSR@, NTU Risk Center, 2022/01/05 https://csr.cw.com.tw/article/42336

[11] Environmental Protection Department of the Executive Yuan - 110A017110 annual waste dry battery and waste lighting source recycling system review and management strategy refinement project work plan https://www.epa.gov.tw/Page/3E265A75FE433BE4/314d6c3f-8ff8-42dc-8ff2-92c3f1a486be

[12] Huaxin News2023/02/22 https://newmediamax.com.tw/article/1ipuin61dl5x0.html.

[13] Shenzhen Institute of Standard Technology A. B.2901/1125, admin, 2019/03/13 https://tbt.sist.org.cn/zdcp_75/omydzdcpsczr/mgydzdcsczrzd/hbyq_3809/201903/t20190313_2239329.html

[14] Liu Xiaohua (2006). Preliminary research on the European Union's Directive on Restricting the Use of Hazardous Substances in Electrical and Electronic Equipment and the Directive on Waste Electrical and Electronic Equipment. Thesis. Chung Yuan University Taiwan doctoral and master thesis knowledge value-added system.

[15] *Central People's Government of the People's Republic of China, Ministry of Environmental Protection.* http://big5.www.gov.cn/gate/big5/www.gov.cn/test/2012-04/10/content_2110054.htm

[16] *Shenzhen Institute of Standards and Technology-Environmental Protection Regulations and Measre.* lzk.2020/10/20https://tbt.sist.org.cn/zdcp_75/dc/rbsc_214/hbfghcs_1031/200807/t20080715_163427.html

[17] *Taiwan Executive Yuan Environmental Protection Agency* 2022/10/16 https://oaout.epa.gov.tw/law/LawContent.aspx?id=FL021002&kw=%e5%bb%a2%e9%9b%bb%e6%b1%a0

System Innovation for a Troubled World – Lam et al. (Eds)
© 2024 the Author(s), ISBN: 978-1-032-60846-4

# Stress, depression, and sleep management: Through an integrated smartphone application

Ya-Chien Chan & Cheng-Jung Yang*
*Program in Interdisciplinary Studies, National Sun Yat-sen University, Kaohsiung, Taiwan*

ABSTRACT:  Modern people commonly experience psychological problems owing to their environment, work, and social intercourse. According to a 2019 survey by the Global Burden of Disease (GBD), mental disorders are gradually being considered one of the main causes of the global disease burden. Moreover, stress causes psychological problems. During the COVID-19 pandemic, the prevalence of psychological problems, including depression, stress, and sleep problems, has increased. In addition to the positive correlation between stress and depression, insomnia has been shown to be a precursor to depression. If the relationship among the three can be identified, disease occurrence can be prevented in advance. Therefore, we designed an integrated application program that included depression assessment, stress assessment, and sleep time records. Eventually, it presents the historical records of these three factors to users in charts, allowing them to observe the relationships between their own stress, depression, and sleep. When one of the indicators is unusual, it serves as a reminder to users to promptly review their own mental state. Thus, this application achieves the purpose of managing the user's physical and mental health and preventing the occurrence of psychological problems.

*Keywords*: stress, depression, sleep, application

## 1  INTRODUCTION

Modern people often experience psychological problems because of their changeable lives, workplaces, and social occasions. Recently, society has been increasingly focusing on psychological problems every year, and an increasing number of people are concerned about their mental health. According to a 2019 survey by the Global Burden of Disease (GBD), mental disorders are gradually being recognized as one of the main causes of the global disease burden, and the most common occurrence is psychological problems caused by excessive stress, such as depression and insomnia (Lakhan *et al.* 2020). Stress is positively correlated with depression, whereas insomnia has also been shown to be a precursor to depression (Çelik *et al.* 2018; Mahmood *et al.* 2021). In addition, Li *et al.* observed that depression and insomnia are linked to total mortality and the worsening of depression leads to higher mortality (Li *et al.* 2022). Dedovic *et al.* identified that the human brain is the primary target of psychological stress because the human brain is responsible for perceiving situations such as threats and stress (Dedovic *et al.* 2005). Therefore, if the brain is under severe depression for a long time, the hippocampus,

which is in charge of memory, and the amygdala, the center of negative emotions, shrink (McEwen 2022), eventually leading to atrophy of the entire brain. Psychological stress is not as shallow as previously imagined. If this stress value can be immediately identified, the subsequent harmful effects can be greatly reduced. Understanding stress in real time and properly managing it can prevent the physical effects of worsening mood and sleep. In addition, if insomnia can be treated at an earlier stage, the symptoms of depression can be prevented or reduced. One method is sleep restriction in cognitive behavioral therapy for insomnia (CBT-I) which improves sleep motivation and quality by reducing the time spent in bed. If total sleep deprivation is regarded as a type of sleep restriction, it would be a rapid and short-term treatment to improve depression (Riemann *et al.* 2020). Apparently, sleep management is more important than previously thought; hence, an increasing number of sleep-related apps and devices are available in the market. According to research statistics in 2020, 3,287 apps in the Google Play Store used health and stress as keywords, of which 1,009 were related to stress health and management. Most of them conducted self-intervention effects through mindfulness thinking and less use of mental health analysis for stress management (Lau *et al.* 2020). One study evaluated the effectiveness of using apps for stress and

*Corresponding Author: cjyang0521@mail.nsysu.edu.tw

DOI: 10.1201/9781003460763-56

depression management. The experimental group was asked to use the app for four weeks, twice a week, for more than 10 min each time. The results showed that the stress in the experimental group was significantly different. However, although depression and anxiety decreased, no significant difference was observed: approximately 70% of the users believed that the app was helpful for stress management, and approximately 60% of the users had enhanced anti-stress and increased motivation to seek treatment (Hwang *et al.* 2019). In addition to apps, many people who want to monitor their sleep use wearable devices. Certain studies observed sleep and depression levels through subjects who used wearable devices and observed that total sleep time or bedtime is significantly related to depression, but none of the indicators were significantly associated with stress (Moshe *et al.* 2021).

According to the aforementioned aspects, this study developed an integrated record of stress, depression, and sleep status by designing a mobile phone application called "SDS Recorder." This App helps users to detect their own physical and mental changes through trends deduced from statistical data to manage personal, physical, and mental states and prevent mental health deterioration.

## 2 METHODOLOGY

SDS is an abbreviation for stress, depression, and sleep. As the name suggests, the SDS Recorder was designed to help users record and manage their stress, depression, and sleep. This App uses the MIT App Inventor for programming and human-machine interface (HMI) design and utilizes the Firebase database to access user data. The summary chart uses the App Inventor's extension component CharMakerPlus to present a record line chart.

### 2.1 *MIT App Inventor and CharMakerPlus*

The App Inventor is an online programming environment developed by the Massachusetts Institute of Technology (MIT). It can be used to design fully functional applications for Android and iOS mobile devices, such as mobile phones and tablets. The coding method is based on simple module dragging and dropping. This simple and easy-to-use method is extremely friendly for beginners who have no experience in editing code. Just as their team said on the webpage "'Those new to MIT App Inventor can have a simple first app up and running in less than 30 minutes," both adults and children have the opportunity to design their own apps in a short time.

CharMakerPlus is a free extension of App Inventor Beta (AI2). Users can quickly generate Google charts by calling the data, including line charts, pie charts, bar charts, histograms, and tables. Charts are dynamically updated as data

change; therefore, developers do not have to update them manually.

### 2.2 *Firebase*

Firebase is an application development platform for Google. Users can apply to Firebase projects for their own applications. Firebase is compatible with iOS+, Android, and Web apps. In addition, Firebase provides user data analysis and app complete functions, including construction, publication, monitoring, and cloud communication. This study used the real-time database in Firebase data analytics as the access database for all user data.

## 3 APP INTERFACE

The HMI of an SDS Recorder includes seven tabbed screens: Login, Sign up, Home, Stress, Depression, Sleep, and History. A detailed introduction of each screen is sequentially provided in the following sections.

### 3.1 *Login and sign up screens*

The Login screen is the home page (Figure 1) that users view after opening the App; it provides users with registration and login button to the registered account. A user can enter the account number and password and click the *Log in* button to log in. Once the *Log in* button is clicked, the program automatically validates the account number and password in the background (Figures 2 and 3). If the user has not yet registered, the user can click *Go to sign up* to go to the Sign up page. The Sign up screen requires the user to fill in the following information (Figure 4): Nickname, Account, and Password. If the user account has been registered,

Figure 1. Login screen.

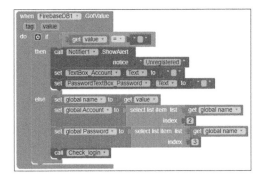

Figure 2.   Database comparison account and password.

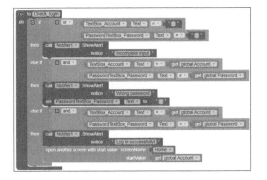

Figure 3.   Check user account registration status.

Figure 4..   Sign up screen.

"This account has been registered" is displayed; otherwise, "Successful registration" is displayed. The program structure of the background discriminant is shown in Figure 5. After the registration is complete, the Login screen is automatically displayed.

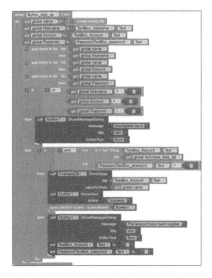

Figure 5.   Access user registration information.

## 3.2   Home screen

After a successful login, the Home screen is displayed, as shown in Figure 6. The user nickname is displayed on the upper-right corner of the screen, and the user can click on the Stress, Depression,

Figure 6.   Home screen.

273

Sleep, or History to enter the respective screen. If users have any ideas regarding the App, they can contact the developer through *Contact us*. To log out of the system, the user can click on *Log out*.

### 3.3 Stress and depression screens

The Stress screen provides a Perceived Stress Scale (PSS scale), as shown in Figure 7(a) (Cohen *et al.* 1983). The scale includes 14 multiple choice questions, and each question is scored from 0 to 4 — "Never": 0 points, "Occasionally": 1 point, "Sometimes": 2 points, "Often": 3 points, and "Always": 4 points. The higher the score, the greater is the pressure. Notably, 0–28 points of pressure indicates within the normal range; 29–42 points of pressure indicates high; 43–56 points of pressure indicates significantly high. After the user checks all question options, the user can click the *Count* button to automatically calculate the score. The system provides a description of different stress situations according to the scores obtained by the user, as shown in Figure 7(b). Finally, the user can choose whether to upload the survey record to the cloud storage. When the user no longer uses the functions of this page, the *Back to Home* button in the lower-right corner of the page can be clicked to return to the home page and continue to browse other items.

The Depression screen is similar to the Stress screen in that it provides a Beck Depression Inventory (BDI) scale for assessing depression, as shown in Figure 8(a). The scale consists of 21 multiple-choice questions, and the scores for each question are 0, 1, 2, and 3 points in sequence, according to the options. Notably, 0–13 points belong to the normal range of depression, 14–19 points to mild depression, 20–28 points to moderate depression, and 29–63 points to severe

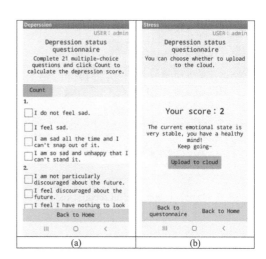

Figure 8. (a) Depression screen, (b) Melancholy score description.

depression. After the user has checked all options, the user can click the *Count* button to calculate the score. The system provides descriptions of different depression states according to user score, as shown in Figure 8(b). Finally, the user can decide whether to upload the filled record to the cloud. The advantage of continuously uploading records to the cloud is that, in the future, this information can be linked with healthcare institutions, and the professionals can track any user who has worsening symptoms of stress and depression in real-time. After the user completes filling in, the user can click the *Back to home* button in the lower right corner of the page to return to the Home page to browse other items.

### 3.4 Sleep screen

The Sleep screen allows the user to input the sleep state, including date, bedtime, wake-up time, and total sleep hours, as shown in Figure 9. Because the total sleep hours may be affected by the user's daily schoolwork and the user is expected to wake up early, in addition to recording the total sleep hours, the user's bedtime can also be recorded to evaluate a more complete sleep condition of the user. However, this App is still in the experimental stage, and currently, it only records total sleep hours. In the future, using bedtime will be better than using total sleep hours to remind users.

### 3.5 History screen

The History screen displays the user's stress, depression, and sleep history line chart records, as shown in Figure 10(a). The information provided on this screen is among the most important parts of an SDS Recorder. After entering this screen, the three records are displayed first such that the user

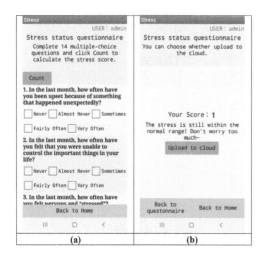

Figure 7. (a) Stress screen PSS, (b) Stress score description.

Figure 9.   Sleep screen.

Figure 10.   (a) History screen, (b) Single information record-stress.

can simultaneously understand all the states in the shortest time. To view the detailed information of one of the records, the user can click the pink sub-button, as shown in Figure 10(b). To return to the general information item screen, the user can click the *Renew page* button at the bottom of the screen. This page provides a system for users to observe

their past records and make the following inferences: when the sleep is reduced and the stress curve is high and the similarity between the stress curve and the depression curve. When users summarize a set of rules for their stress, depression, and sleep curves, they can perceive their physical and mental conditions and detect potential dangers early.

## 4   DISCUSSION

Using the SDS Recorder, users' past stress, depression, and sleep records are presented in line charts on the History screen, achieving the purpose of simultaneously detecting the three types of information. By introducing these charts, users can examine their physical and mental conditions early. However, certain restrictions still exist on the use of the App. First, the records of stress, depression, and sleep are limited to one record per day, and new records on the same day will overwrite old records. Second, the uploaded records cannot be deleted; thus, users must think twice before uploading them.

The results of using the App, as described in Section 3, revealed that User A's stress had a significant relationship with depression, and depression had a significant relationship with sleep duration. Unexpectedly, no significant relationship existed between stress and sleep duration, and neither stress nor depression showed a significant relationship with sleep duration. However, according to User A, the wake-up time depended on the schedule for the next day, implying the difficulty in delaying the wake-up time. The bedtime was delayed as the pressure increased, and depression appeared to not affect it, resulting in "possible" workday sleep hours reduction. In contrast, rest days involved a marginal delay in waking up. Based on User A's feedback, we can assume that this may be one reason for stress to have no significant relationship with sleep duration. Future research may be able to observe this at bedtime.

Therefore, future improvements to the SDS Recorder will first add regular tracking and send reports to users. Second, the user status will be summarized based on this report. Third, a user will receive a reminder if their bedtime is unusual. This saves the user's time and improves the occurrence of the aforementioned problems. Finally, we will attempt to combine cutting-edge AI technology—such as ChatGPT—and the role of a smart assistant with this App to achieve greater benefits.

## 5   CONCLUSION

In this study, we designed an integrated mobile phone application called an SDS Recorder. It was developed and programmed using App Inventor which aims to integrate and provide users with stress, depression, and sleep records. This App presented long-term record results in the form of a line graph, allowing users to observe their physical and mental conditions and summarize potential rules. Through this rule, they could detect physical and mental abnormalities early and seek professional assistance to overcome psychological problems when necessary.

# REFERENCES

Beck A.T., Steer R.A., Brown G.K. *Beck Depression Inventory – Second Edition: Manual.* San Antonio, TX, The Psychological Corporation, 1996.

Çelik, Neşe; Ceylan, Burcu; Ünsal, Alaettin; Çağan, Özlem (2018). Depression in health college students: Relationship factors and sleep quality. *Psychology, Health & Medicine.* DOI:10.1080/13548506.2018.1546881.

CharMakerPlus. Retrieved from https://community.appinventor.mit.edu/t/free-chartmakerplus-an-extension-to-make-google-charts/36473.

Cohen S., Kamarck T., & Mermelstein R. (1983). A global measure of perceived stress. *Journal of Health and Social Behavior*, 24(4), 385–396. https://doi.org/10.2307/2136404.

Dedovic K., Renwick R., Mahani N.K., Engert V., Lupien S.J., & Pruessner J. C. (2005). The Montreal imaging stress task: using functional imaging to investigate the effects of perceiving and processing psychosocial stress in the human brain. *Journal of psychiatry & neuroscience: JPN*, 30(5), 319–325.

*Firebase.* Retrieved from https://firebase.google.com/

GBD 2019 Mental Disorders Collaborators (2022). Global, regional, and national burden of 12 mental disorders in 204 countries and territories, 1990-2019: A systematic analysis for the Global Burden of Disease Study 2019. *The lancet. Psychiatry*, 9(2), 137–150. https://doi.org/10.1016/S2215-0366(21)00395-3

Hwang W.J., & Jo H.H. (2019). Evaluation of the effectiveness of mobile app-based stress-management program: a randomized controlled trial. *International Journal Of Environmental Research And Public Health*, 16(21), 4270. https://doi.org/10.3390/ijerph16214270.

Lakhan R., Agrawal A., & Sharma M. (2020). Prevalence of depression, anxiety, and stress during COVID-19 pandemic. *Journal of Neurosciences in Rural Practice*, 11(04), 519–525.

Lau N, O'Daffer A, Colt S, Yi-Frazier J, Palermo T, McCauley E, Rosenberg A. Android and iPhone Mobile Apps for Psychosocial Wellness and Stress Management: Systematic Search in App Stores and Literature Review. *JMIR Mhealth Uhealth*. 2020, 8 (5):e17798. URL:https://mhealth.jmir.org/2020/5/e17798. DOI:10.2196/17798.

Li W., Chen D., Ruan W., Peng Y., Lu Z., & Wang, D. (2022). Associations of depression, sleep disorder with total and cause-specific mortality: A prospective cohort study. *Journal of Affective Disorders*, 298, 134–141.

Mahmood A., Ray M., Dobalian A., Ward K.D. & Ahn, S. (2021). Insomnia symptoms and incident heart failure: a population-based cohort study. *European Heart Journal*, 42(40), 4169–4176.

McEwen B. S. (2022). Protective and damaging effects of stress mediators: central role of the brain. *Dialogues in clinical neuroscience.*

MIT App Inventor. Retrieved from https://appinventor.mit.edu/

Moshe I., Terhorst Y., Opoku Asare K., Sander L. B., Ferreira, D., Baumeister H., Mohr D. C. & Pulkki-Råback, L. (2021). Predicting symptoms of depression and anxiety using smartphone and wearable data. *Frontiers in Psychiatry*, 12, 625247. https://doi.org/10.3389/fpsyt.2021.625247.

Riemann D., Krone L.B., Wulff K., & Nissen C. (2020). Sleep, insomnia, and depression. *Neuropsychopharmacology: Official publication of the American College of Neuropsychopharmacology*, 45 (1),74–89. https://doi.org/10.1038/s41386-019-0411-y.

System Innovation for a Troubled World – Lam et al. (Eds)
© 2024 the Author(s), ISBN: 978-1-032-60846-4

# Application of concurrent design strategy to the design for assembly of flood gate

Chu-Hsuan Lee*
*Department of Culture Creativity and Digital Marketing, National United University, Miaoli, Taiwan*

ABSTRACT: The Pacific Northwest is one of the regions with the highest frequency of typhoons, and Taiwan is located in this area. During the flood season, many heavy rains or typhoons threaten people's lives and property, and the damage caused by flooding is countless. Therefore, how to prevent disasters before they face them will indeed prevent unfortunate accidents from happening. In view of this, flood barrier has become one of the main ways to solve the problem. Although there are already many flood control products with excellent flood control effects on the market, their high price and large size make them difficult to collect, and many of these products often take time to assemble. Therefore, at present, the control flood method of many people is still based on sandbags to block water. However, sandbags' flood-blocking effect is limited and cannot block excessive water volume. It cannot achieve substantial benefits in preventing flooding and reducing damage. This study focuses on the design for assembly flood gates that are easy to store and have an excellent flood-blocking effect. In addition to reducing the number of assembly steps, other materials will be considered for the easy-to-assemble parts to reduce the product's weight and achieve the goal of easy assembly. This study uses the systematic concurrent design methodology to obtain product design results. First, conduct market research and select products from different manufacturers for analysis and comparison. Through functional analysis and sorting out the problem points, the TRIZ theory and morphological chart method are used to find the best solution to the problem. Then, the best design scheme is obtained by the PUGH method. Besides, a 3D model to construct and present the design concept that meets the design goals. The research results are hoped to be used as a reference for designing and developing related products, thereby increasing the design for assembly of flood gates' market share.

*Keywords*: Design for assembly, Concurrent design, Morphological chart method, PUGH method, TRIZ theory

## 1 INTRODUCTION

Three types of natural disasters most harm Taiwan: typhoons, earthquakes, and floods. Among them, the typhoon is the most noticeable disaster in Taiwan because Taiwan is located on the path of typhoons in the Northwest Pacific Ocean. From June to September, tropical low-pressure cyclones are active and often develop into typhoons (Li et al. 2020). According to statistics from the Statistics Bureau of the Ministry of the Interior, the agricultural losses caused by typhoons from 1975 to 1986 amounted to NT$4.8 billion. Typhoons can be said to be the number one natural disaster in Taiwan. Therefore, how to prevent disasters is a problem that must be solved. This research intends to design a floodgate. In addition to effectively controlling water, this device also improves the convenience of its storage and assembly to solve the problem that it is too large and complex to store and

too heavy to assemble. At the same time, further thinking about how to reduce the assembly steps to improve the prevention effect.

A successful product should be able to solve consumers' problems. Thus, designers and planners must look for problems, implement practical solutions, and develop high-quality products that benefit consumers (Kwaku & Wei, 2011). However, many products still need to be improved even though they have been mass-produced. Many consumers tend to learn to accommodate and adapt to the problem of products based on long-term use inertia. Hence, in addition to designing a new product that can solve consumer problems, the designer's job should also be to modify and redesign the defective products sold.

According to Cooper and Kleinschmidt (2011), the key to the success of a product that is about to come out should be considered: the design of the product itself, the characteristics of the product, the production method, and the technology to produce a quality finished product as the goal, and the

*Corresponding Author: hsuan6389@nuu.edu.tw

DOI: 10.1201/9781003460763-57

implementation can be achieved collaborative production and design, the benefits of products to users, in addition, a good product should carefully evaluate every detail in the development stage. For the industry, the purchase rate of a product can be seen from whether it is competitive. Therefore, the study of product competitiveness must first start with market performance, analyze cost price, quality, brand, and other direct factors, then analyze resources, materials, funds, technology, and other indirect factors, and finally find out the specific reasons and ways to improve competitiveness.

This study uses concurrent design methodology as the primary policy for designing a floodgate. It will use different research methods to analyze various problems and propose solutions through a systematic design process. The selected design solutions are expected to improve the product's performance effectively.

## 2 BACKGROUND AND MOTIVATION

Affected by global warming and global climate change in recent years, typhoon disasters in Taiwan have tended to expand. Significantly, the frequency of destructive torrential rains has gradually increased since 2000, causing devastating and even compound disasters to be more common (Chen 2013). Because of the immeasurable loss of life and property due to flood disasters every year, this study considers how to use existing resources or develop better equipment to minimize damage, which is the primary research motivation of this design project. In the early days, sandbags were mainly used to block the external water to prevent heavy rain, but the effect of blocking floods was not noticeable. Therefore, the advent of floodgates played an effective role at this critical moment. However, after the actual assembly of this product, it was found that there were still some restrictions on its operation, loading and unloading, and storage. Therefore, this proposal attempts to redesign the waterproof gate to make it closer to the needs of consumers. The research objectives of this study are as follows:

- Because most floods surge instantly, assembling currently available gates on the market is relatively time-consuming. Therefore, the main goal of this study is to reduce the loading and unloading time, hoping to achieve "more safety and less assembly time."
- The disassembled flood control gate is too large and there are too many assembly parts to make storage difficult. Therefore, improving the storage problem is also the goal of this research.

### 2.1 Objectives tree method

The development of the objectives tree method is one of the most critical links in helping designers clarify the main goals of design and organize consumer needs effectively. It can provide a clear and concise method, point out the real needs of consumers, and make the design process more smooth. It also minimizes the point of ambiguity between the consumer and the design team. The objectives tree method is presented as a diagram, and the interrelationships between primary and secondary goals are also clearly presented (Haik & Shahin 2010).

### 2.2 Function analysis method

Functional analysis is a method used to analyze detailed work procedures in the initial stage of design ideas. It analyzes product functions from input and output. In order to identify the relationship between each component, the overall components of the product are disassembled and confirmed. The function of each element is a main function or a sub-function. Since functional analysis is a dynamic process, if any stage's function is deficient, it can be re-analyzed in the previous step (Mansfield & Mitchell 1996). Although the functional analysis method plays a vital role in solving the function of the problem, Altshuller (1997) believes that it only focuses on the starting point of the analysis problem and does not focus on the attribute. Therefore, if we want to explore the core issues in depth, we should expand the attributes and rely on Teoriya Resheniya Izobreatatelskikh Zadatch (TRIZ) theory to solve the core issues.

### 2.3 TRIZ theory

Since the TRIZ theory summarizes 39 parameters and 40 inventive problem-solving rules and emphasizes that invention or innovation can be carried out according to specific procedures and steps, the problems encountered in the process should also clarify the contradictions in the system as much as possible so known as a theory that comprehensively and systematically solves invention problems and can realize technological innovation.

### 2.4 Morphological chart method

Synthesizing the arguments of many scholars (Roozenburg & Eekels 1995; Cross 1989), the morphological diagram is a method to analyze and systematize all the generated concepts, and the generation of this method is based on functional analysis. The functional analysis method is mainly to examine the product structure and possible types and try to find all the possibilities to combine components. Therefore, functional analysis is also regarded as a method for systematically analyzing and solving problems.

### 2.5 PUGH method

Although there are many design evaluation methods, the decision-matrix method or PUGH method has been proven to be a simple and effective method (Hsiao 1998). The PUGH method is accomplished by correlating comparisons with many question options. All question options have a weight factor used to compare with the datum solution (Ullman 1996; Pugh1990).

If the question option is better than the datum solution, it will be represented by "+"; on the contrary, if it is worse than the datum solution, it will be represented by "-"; if the two are equivalent or incomparable, it will be represented by "S." The number of "+" and "-" is obtained by comparing the problem options and the datum solution. Through the PUGH method, better designs can be screened out, and poorer solutions can be eliminated. Therefore, this method can be effectively used in judging and comparing the quality of products.

## 3   CASE STUDY

Most of the users of this design are the affected households in the disaster area. Due to the sudden flood caused by the heavy rain, the gate must not only completely control water but also be able to be quickly assembled to block the sudden flood. Firstly, select the products provided by different companies for analysis and comparison, summarize the problem points of the flood gate through functional analysis, and use TRIZ theory and morphological chart method to find out the solution to the problem, and finally, use the PUGH method to find the best Design (Figure 1).

### 3.1   Existing product analysis

Conduct market research and analysis on products through data collection to accurately understand the market demand for floodgates at the initial stage of design. Besides, after collecting data and compiling the results, in addition to grasping the functional structure of the existing waterproof gates, design and improvement criteria can also be obtained from the summarized problems. The floodgates that have been launched in the market today have mostly stayed the same in appearance except for slightly different materials. In addition, their functions are mainly to prevent floods and foreign objects from entering, and no other additional parts are available. Hence, the study only collects flood gates with different materials, structures, and usage methods. The collected data shows that the floodgates developed and produced by current manufacturers lack the characteristics of easy storage and assembly. In addition to the fixed electric flood gate that does not need to be assembled and the fixed one-piece stainless steel flood gate that has no assembly and storage problems, it can be inferred that the other flood gates may generally be too large, the assembly steps are

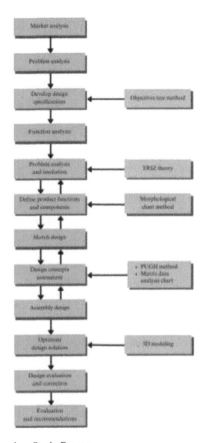

Figure 1.   Study Process.

complicated, the water-blocking board is too heavy, and once there are problems such as blocking entry and exit after the sluice gate is erected. Given this, the follow-up of this case will focus on improving these problems.

### 3.2   Design specification

The results of market research, product analysis, and personal experience were drawn into the objectives tree method with a hierarchy (Figure 2). The habit and process of assembling a floodgate for the affected households use the black box method to analyze possible problems in the operation process. Then they use the TRIZ method to determine the parameters to be improved and the parameters to avoid deterioration. In addition, the functional analysis and use of the floodgate process are as follows: first, lift the bottom grooves, install fixed support members, insert the water-blocking boards, and tighten the screws. The actions in this process will repeat the cycle.

Draw up a set of design specifications (as shown in Table 1) through the above actions, and use D (Demand) to indicate that the design requirement

Figure 2.    The objectives tree of flood gates.

Table 1.    Design specifications of floodgates.

| Main goal | Sub-goal | Attribute |
|---|---|---|
| Assembly | Reduce time | D |
| Assembly | Simplified steps | D |
| Storage | Improved parts storage | D |
| Storage | Reduce storage space | D |
| Additionality | Appearance | W |
| Additionality | Anti-stress function | D |
| Additionality | Extended use period | W |
| Additionality | Blocking function | D |

is a necessary function, while W (Wish) is a non-essential function.

### 3.3  Development Strategies

The product is still in the development stage, so this study uses different design strategies to try to improve the poor design.

### 3.4  TRIZ theory

At this stage, use the Function and Attribute Analysis (FAA) method of TRIZ theory to discuss the deficiencies of the retaining gate and the accompanying problems in operation. The problem-solving model according to TRIZ theory and the steps are as follows:

• Analysis of problem points: This study draws up the design specifications through functional analysis and uses the process and also analyzes four problems: (1) Too many assembly parts make the loading and unloading process complicated and time-consuming; (2) The water-blocking boards and other components are relatively heavy, and the user needs to spend a lot of physical strength to assemble; (3) Once the assembly is completed, it cannot be freely entered and exited; (4) There are too many parts and components and the large

size of the water-blocking boards make flood gate difficult to store.

• TRIZ Inventive problem solving: After the problem analysis, the improvement goals were summarized as reducing the assembly time and simplifying the steps while reducing the number of parts and excessive weight of the fender were the features to be improved and to avoid deterioration, respectively. These two features must be translated into the context of various engineering parameters of TRIZ theory. Next, go to the contradictions matrix and select the contradictions from the list of 39 that best fit the conflict statement. According to the TRIZ contradictions matrix, parameter 1 "Weight of moving object" is introduced into the vertical axis (Feature to improve) and parameter 25 "Waste of time" is introduced into the horizontal axis (Undesired result). According to the matrix, the invention is derived as Principle 10 "Prior action", Principle 20 "Continuity of useful action", Principle 28 "Mechanics substitution" and Principle 35 "Transformation of properties". In this case, after a comprehensive evaluation of the above invention principles, Principle 35 "Transformation of properties" was used as the basis of the design specification. We attempt to solve the problems brought by the floodgates to users by changing the product's material properties (changing the physical state, degree of elasticity, pressure, length, and volume).

#### 3.3.1  Component development

The product of this study is considered in terms of practicality, ease of operation, durability, and price. Therefore, in the component development stage, the results obtained by referring to the TRIZ matrix will be used to complete the morphological chart method, as shown in Figure 3.

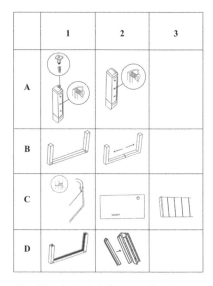

Figure 3.    Morphological diagram of each component.

280

This study collects and defines the problems through the abovementioned theoretical methods, adopts a systematic design method to develop design concepts, and produces three concept sketches after preliminary evaluation, which is used for subsequent screening of the best plan. The product's primary function in this design case is to block flood, so it is necessary to consider whether it can ultimately withstand the water pressure. Since it cannot be tested in practice, only the formula is used for hydrostatic pressure analysis. Taking the water depth of 1.5 meters as an example, the hydrostatic pressure ($P_H$) on the bottom of the gate is equal to the product of the water weight per unit volume (r) and the water depth (H). Therefore, assuming that the water depth of this test program is 1.5 meters, The water pressure at the bottom is 1.5(t/m²).

$$P_H = \gamma H$$
$$= 1000 \times 1.5$$
$$= 1500(kgw/m^2) = 1.5(t/m^2)$$

If the total force (F) of water pressure acting on the gate is desired, it is 1/2 the water weight per unit volume multiplied by the square of the water depth and then by the gate width (B). This design assumes that the gate width is 3 meters and the total force the gate can control water is 3375 (kgw).

$$F = \frac{1}{2}\gamma H^2 B$$
$$F = 0.5 \times 1000 \times 1.5^2 \times 3 = 3375(kgw)$$

The design of Concept 1 (A1_B2_C1_D1) is based on reducing the number of parts for the fixing function. Therefore, only one bolt is installed on the top of the side column, and three bolts are installed on each side. This device can tighten the bolt and the pressure frame. The side column and the bottom frame are combined into positive and negative L-shaped, and a strong magnet is added at the joint point to connect the two structures tightly. In addition, the bottom frame can also be stored in the side column after the equipment is removed. To reduce the storage space, reduce the weight and facilitate disassembly; the material of the water-blocking board is replaced by aluminum alloy with rubber as the expansion part. Compared with other materials, although rubber is not the strongest, considering its lightweight and wear resistance and toughness are also better (Figure 4), this design uses it as the main water-retaining gate material. Use inflatable expansion parts to block flood and pressure, and use magnet-made abutment pieces to absorb canvas-made water-repelling cloth on both sides of the frame. Once the expansion part is inflated, it squeezes the water-retaining fabric to

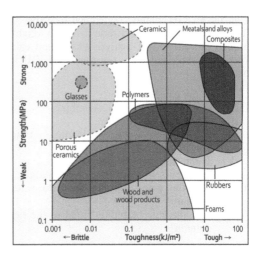

Figure 4. Strength versus toughness graphs for different types of materials (A.M. Lovatt, H.R. Shercliff and P.J. Withers (2000), "Material selection and processing").

bond the two tightly. In the design of Concept 2 (A2_B1_C2_D1), three bolts are arranged on both sides of the frame, and the side column and the bottom column are combined by three frame bars to form a ⊠-shaped. Compared with Concept 1, Concept 2 uses the water-filled expansion part as the flood-blocking device, and the two sides use the abutment sheet to absorb the water-retaining cloth made of canvas to make it close. The most significant difference between Concept 3 (A2_B1_C2_D1) and Concepts 1 and 2 is that the flood-blocking member is made of aluminum alloy. Although this concept is roughly the same as the general market-produced flood gates, it uses reinforcing ribs to increase the strength of the water barrier to resist water pressure and fixes the water barrier with two positive and negative L-shaped frames. Three sketches as shown in Figure 5.

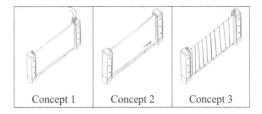

| Concept 1 | Concept 2 | Concept 3 |

Figure 5. Three concept sketches.

### 3.3.2 Concept selection and evaluation
The design criteria for each evaluation are clearly defined, and the weighted weights are obtained by the tabular method (as shown in Table 2). Then the optimal decision-making scheme is evaluated

using the PUGH method (as shown in Table 3). First, use the eight design criteria to obtain weights through a Matrix data analysis chart, and each criterion is represented by the number I-VIII as follows:

(I)    Is the gate too heavy?
(II)   Are the gates easy to assemble?
(III)  Is the gate easy to store?
(IV)   Is loading and unloading time-consuming?
(V)    Is the gate material durable?
(VI)   Is the custom-made gate cost too high?
(VII)  Are the gates fully resistant to water pressure?
(VIII) Can the gate be tightly fitted to the side column?

Table 2. The Weight of each design criteria.

|      | I | II | III | IV | V | VI | VII | VIII | Score | Weight |
|------|---|----|-----|----|---|----|-----|------|-------|--------|
| I    |   | 6  | 3   | 6  | 2 | 4  | 6   | 6    | 33    | 0.147  |
| II   | 2 |    | 3   | 4  | 2 | 3  | 5   | 6    | 25    | 0.112  |
| III  | 5 | 5  |     | 6  | 4 | 4  | 6   | 6    | 36    | 0.161  |
| IV   | 2 | 4  | 2   |    | 2 | 2  | 5   | 5    | 22    | 0.098  |
| V    | 6 | 6  | 4   | 6  |   | 3  | 6   | 6    | 37    | 0.165  |
| VI   | 4 | 5  | 4   | 6  | 5 |    | 7   | 7    | 38    | 0.170  |
| VII  | 2 | 3  | 2   | 3  | 2 | 1  |     | 4    | 17    | 0.076  |
| VIII | 2 | 2  | 2   | 3  | 2 | 1  | 4   |      | 16    | 0.071  |
| Score |  |    |     |    |   |    |     |      | 224   | 1      |

Table 3. The Weight of each concept.

|       |       | Concept |     |        |        |
|-------|-------|---------|-----|--------|--------|
|       |       | 1       | 2   | 3      | Weight |
| I     | DATUM | +       | +   | S      | 0.147  |
| II    |       | +       | +   | −      | 0.112  |
| III   |       | +       | S   | S      | 0.161  |
| IV    |       | S       | +   | S      | 0.098  |
| V     |       | −       | −   | S      | 0.165  |
| VI    |       | +       | +   | S      | 0.170  |
| VII   |       | −       | −   | +      | 0.076  |
| VIII  |       | S       | S   | S      | 0.071  |
| +     |       | 4       | 4   | 1      |        |
| −     |       | 2       | 2   | 1      |        |
| Score |       | 0.349   | 0.286 | −0.036 |      |

The weighted weights calculated for each design criterion are applied to the PUGH method to screen and evaluate the three concepts. A comparison is made with datum, a floodgate sold by a certain company. The material of this datum is similar to that of Concept 3, both are SMC boards and aluminum alloy frames. There are five movable screws on both sides of the frame to strengthen the fixation. Each board is about 30cm high. If the water depth is 1.5 meters, as an example, about 5 baffles are needed. After evaluation by the PUGH, Concept 1 has the highest overall score, and this research will use it as the sketch for the final product development. However, in the criterion IV " Is loading and unloading time-consuming", only Concept 2 is better than datum. The main difference is that the water-blocking function of Concept 1 is an inflatable expansion part, while Concept 2 is a water-filled expansion part, and the inflatable type needs another pumping equipment; the pumping time is also longer. Hence, based on this factor, the final change is the inflatable expansion part of sketch one to water-filled.

### 3.3.3 3D modeling
After the model is generated based on the above evaluation, take Concept 1 as the main concept and combine the water-filled expansion part of Concept 2 for 3D modeling. There will be a water injection hole on the expander, as shown in Figure 6. Figure 7 is a positive and negative L-shaped frame, with strong magnets at the connection to make the structure more tightly bonded. Compared with the three bolts on the side frames, larger bolts are installed on the top for tightness and fixation (Figure 8).

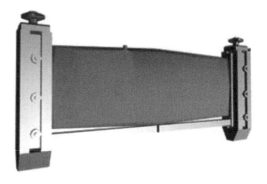

Figure 6. 3D modeling.

Figure 7. L-shaped frame.

Figure 8.    Top bolt.

## 4    CONCLUSION

This study mainly applies the simultaneous design strategy to the development and redesign process of the floodgate. In the early stage of development, the objectives tree method is used to make decisions, and the design specifications are drawn up through functional analysis and the black box method. Through the TRIZ theory and morphological chart method, the problems and solution principles of the use of floodgates are summarized. In the entire design process, personal experience is added, and the optimized final version is screened with the PUGH method. Finally, the design proposal is presented in detail through the 3D construction of the computer-aided design. The method of concurrent design can effectively save product development and design time and is also closer to the real needs of users. Overall, this design proposal only uses methods and data to analyze its water pressure resistance, and the calculated data results are within the allowable range.

However, whether it can achieve the effect of water blocking still needs to be tested.

## REFERENCES

Altshuller G., 1997. *40 Principles: TRIZ Keys to Technical Innovation.* Technical Innovation Center: Worcester.

Chen C.K., 2013. A retrospect and discussion on major natural disasters in taiwan during 1951–2010. *J.TW. Disaster Prev. Soc.* 5 1–20.

Cooper R.G., Kleinschmidt E.J., 2011. *New Products: The Key Factors in Success.* Marketing Classics Press: USA.

Cross N., 1989. *Engineering Design Methods.* Chichester: Wiley.

Haik Y., Shahin T.M.M., 2010. *Engineering Design Process.* Cengage Learning: USA.

Hsiao S.W., 1998. Fuzzy logic based decision model for product design. *Int. J. Ind. Ergon.* 21 103–116.

Kwaku A.G., Wei Y., 2011. The vital role of problem-solving competence in new product success. *J. Prod. Innov. Manage.* 28 81–98.

Li Z.T., Xu Y.J., Jian Y.Y., Chen, 2020 S.H.. Typhoon trajectory clustering and disaster statistical testing in Taiwan region. *J. Data Anal.* 15 41–58.

Lovatt A.M., Shercliff H.R.and P.J. Withers, 2000. *Material Selection and Processing.* Technology Enhancement Programme.

Mansfield B., Mitchell L., 1996. *Towards a Competent Workforce.* Gower Publishing: UK.

Pugh S., 1991. *Total Design: Integrated Methods for Successful Product Engineering.* Addison Wesley: UK.

Roozenburg N.F.M., Eekels J., 1995. *Product Design : Fundamentals and Methods.* Utrecht: Lemma.

Ullman D.G., 1996. A taxonomy for classifying engineering decision problems and support systems. *Artif. Intell. Eng. Des. Anal. Manuf.* 9 427–438.

*System Innovation for a Troubled World – Lam et al. (Eds)*
© *2024 the Author(s), ISBN: 978-1-032-60846-4*

# Integration of flipped teaching into the professional practice courses of department of multimedia design with action research

You-Shan Zhou*
*Graduate School of Design, National Yunlin University of Science and Technology, Yunlin, Taiwan*

Chang-Franw Lee
*Professor, Graduate School of Design, National Yunlin University of Science and Technology, Yunlin, Taiwan*

ABSTRACT: This research explored the integration of flipped teaching into professional practice courses of multimedia design based on an action research model, with the goal of improving the performance of undergraduate students' basic design professional skills. Moreover, it investigated the learning process and results of basic design subjects by freshmen to junior students in the Department of Multimedia Design at National Houbi Senior High School. One class was chosen from each grade, and three lessons were offered each week over an 18-week period. In total, 54 lessons were taught, and 60 students were engaged in the study. This research took the recent concept of flipped teaching courses advocated by the Ministry of Education as the main axis and used the self-developed flipped interactive teaching model by the author who has many years of teaching experience. Teaching was carried out with relevant teaching activities such as group work, presentations, and post-class tests. The research methods include participation observation, questionnaire survey, interview and inductive analysis of students' works. The research results are as follows: (1) flipped teaching can quickly enhance students' interest in learning; (2) students feel a high sense of participation through on-stage operation and group exercises; (3) frequent practice of painting techniques in groups and on-stage enable students to review or remember more efficiently during exams; (4) this teaching method is proven to be highly effective according to the results of the post-test; (5) this teaching method provides a reference for relevant research on flipped teaching design, so that more teachers can understand the advantages and limitations of flipped teaching and apply it to their teaching sessions.

## 1 RESEARCH BACKGROUND AND MOTIVES

In the history of design education in Taiwan, it can be seen from "A Study of Oral History on the Design Education in Taiwan during the years of 1960s" published by Lai (2001) that the design-related courses can be traced back to 1951, when "Basic Design", "Pattern Techniques" and other courses were included in the courses of the Department of Art Design of National Taiwan Academy of Arts (Lin 2009). The content objectives of the "Basic Design" course for decades have been "to help students to understand the basic knowledge and concepts of design, and be familiar with the basic design principles, and apply them to various design activities" (Lee 2019). Therefore, the source of all design departments is the subject of "Basic Design", which is a "Fundamental Design" today and also known as "Fundamental Design Practice" in the new syllabus of 2019. Since 2002, the Ministry of Education has stipulated that

vocational students need to take the "Unified Entrance Tests for Four-year Technology Universities and Two-year Junior Colleges" for admission to higher education, and the professional subject examinations are divided into two parts, namely "Professional Subjects (1)" and "Professional Subjects (2)" in addition to the subjects of Chinese, English, and Mathematics. Professional Subjects (1) include Color Principle, Principle of Form, and Introduction of Design; Professional Subjects (2) include the three subjects of Basic Design Practice, Basic Painting and Painting, and Basic Painting Practice (Testing Center for Technological & Vocational Education 2021). As learned from the exploration of design theories and past test questions, there are logical rules to be explored for the problem-solving steps in the basic design test questions. Therefore, in order to help undergraduates to thoroughly understand the subject of fundamental design and use a faster and more efficient method in the face of a short-term big test, it is necessary to design and develop a set of unit teaching materials and innovative teaching strategies for basic design practice courses. The innovation of teaching plans, teaching

---

*Corresponding Author: chaoysan@gmail.com

DOI: 10.1201/9781003460763-58

materials, and teaching strategies cannot be achieved overnight, so this study began to explore the "basic design" subject that the author himself has taught for many years. In fact, the establishment and construction of the curriculum is a growing process of continuous circulation between teachers and students. Ralph W. Tyler (1902–1994) believed that the early curriculum development tradition is based on goal orientation and that curriculum is a tool to achieve goals (Tsai 2015). Teachers faithfully implement the curriculum plan and perform evaluations based on the curriculum selection and design of curriculum experts to understand whether students have achieved their learning goals. Teachers are positioned as instructors who have no mastery of the curriculum and face the problem of skill abolition (Apple 1982). The overall curriculum development history compiled in this study is divided into several development stages: (1) teacher-led curriculum teaching before the 1960s, (2) a focus on the participation of teachers and students since the 1960s, (3) emphasizing personal learning experience since the 1980s (Tsai 2014). As found from the literature review, it is believed by the teaching method of postmodernism that teachers are not only the initiative researchers of curriculum design, but also the initiators of students' capacities (Rau 1999). Therefore, based on the concept of flipped teaching curriculum development of postmodernism, this research used action research methods to verify whether students can produce learning results faster and more efficiently through the curriculum materials and teaching methods designed and compiled by the researcher. This research attempted to integrate basic design subject theoretical knowledge and technical operations of performance techniques to allow students to quickly achieve the learning goals of basic design performance techniques during their three-year study in high school.

## 2 RESEARCH PURPOSE

This study took the high school vocational students as the subjects, aiming to understand their learning process of basic design professional performance techniques and develop a set of course units and innovative teaching strategies for professional basic design practice. First, a pre-test questionnaire was prepared before the formal teaching of the term to diagnose the students' performance technique concepts for basic design as an understanding of the students' prerequisite knowledge; second, relevant curriculum units were designed to assist students in understanding and constructing the basic knowledge of professional technique performance for basic design. At the same time, a formative assessment was carried out in the classroom supplemented by the action research method to explore whether the flipped

interactive teaching model established by the author is effective. There are three research purposes, which are described as follows:

1. Develop a set of innovative, flipped, and interactive teaching modes so that multimedia students can quickly understand the subject theory, construct basic design professional knowledge, and finally practice performance techniques of the Professional Subjects (2) of the unified test.
2. Apply the action research model to develop appropriate strategies for teachers' teaching and students' learning in technical high schools, and explore whether there are specific changes in the basic design performance technique concept and technical operation performance of the students before and after receiving the teaching.
3. Reflect and sort out the teacher's professional growth process and practice of teaching concepts in the teaching process.

## 3 LITERATURE REVIEW

### 3.1 Overview of the development of basic design course

The history of design education can be traced back to the founding of Bauhaus in 1919 (1919~1933). The teaching in Bauhaus focused on the training of the combination of making and thinking in workshops, allowing students to use visual elements to construct or express design patterns or shapes with the beauty of form principles such as repetition, balance, unity, symmetry, rhythm, proportion, order, contrast, and harmony (Anandasivam 2005; Chu 1999; Lin 1990). Therefore, this set of design education templates developed from "Modernism" has been followed by most schools both at home and abroad over the years (Yang 2007). The name of the course has also been changed from "Design Basics" and "Basic Design" to the term "Fundamental Design" formulated by the Ministry of Education. Today, by comparing the contents of the certified version of the basic design textbook of the Ministry of Education, we have found that the content of basic design courses has hardly changed since Bauhaus. According to the "Group Subject Syllabus for Twelve-year National Basic Educational Technology-based Senior High Schools" of the Ministry of Education, the learning content of "Fundamental Design Practice" subject mainly includes eight major items (Ministry of Education 2018), as shown in Table 1.

It can be seen from Table 1 that the scope of fundamental design practice course covers a variety of knowledge, and this study learned from literature review and interviews with experts and scholars that most colleges or high school teachers who teach this subject are "following the procedures" according to the units set by Ministry of Education supported

Table 1. Eight major learning indicator items for fundamental design.

| Eight indicators of fundamental design practice | |
| --- | --- |
| A. Basic concept of fundamental design | E. Formal principle of beauty |
| B. Elements of fundamental design | F. Visual effect presentation |
| C. Plane composition method | G. Graphic-aided design |
| D. Principle and implementation of visual illusion | H. Graphic and text visual composition |

with personal practical operations. The process includes (1) classroom lectures, (2) homework reviews, and (3) end-of-term overviews (Hwa *et al.* 2012) (Yang 2007). Therefore, how to compile a set of teaching materials and teaching methods with a logical system to enable students to acquire the knowledge of basic design professional performance techniques more quickly is the ultimate goal of this research. And because this subject covers a wide range, this research only took "H. Graphic and Text Visual Composition" as the main discussion category. Table 2 contains the key points of "H. Graphic and Text Visual Composition" of the only two versions of "TKD Books" (Chen *et al.* 2019) and "Chuan Hwa" Books" (Mo *et al.* 2019) approved by Ministry of Education in 2021summarized by this article:

Table 2. Eight major learning indicator items for fundamental design.

| H. Graphic and visual composition | | |
| --- | --- | --- |
| Latest textbook version and syllabus 2021 | | |
| Chuan Hwa Books | 4-1 Design Procedure 4-2 Analysis of design theme characteristics 4-3 Development of creative ideas | 4-4 Layout and planning 4-5 Graphic design and painting 4-6 Graphic and text composition |
| TKD Books | 8-1 Programs for graphic and text integrated design<br><br>1. Design theme feature analysis<br>2. Creative thinking<br>3. Layout planning | 4. Graphic design and painting<br>5. Font design and drawing<br>6. Graphic and text integration and composition |
| | 8-2 Appreciation of works of graphic and text integration<br><br>1. Text-based graphic design<br>2. Graphic design of plane structure | 3. Illustrated graphic design<br>4. Image-based graphic design |

Looking at the content of textbooks from two publishing houses, there are two key points for the basic design poster presentation techniques: patterns and text, and H. Graphic and Text Visual Composition. This is one of the most important teaching units in making a poster. However, questions arise about how can a professional teacher teach this scattered design theory knowledge to students so that they are able to produce technical works. What methods should the teacher use for teaching? Such questions are the focus of this study.

### 3.2 *Teaching action research*

"Action research" is an effective way for educational practitioners to clarify and solve practical problems (Chen 1998). If educational practitioners conduct research during educational practice and take practical innovation actions in the research process, they can not only solve practical educational problems, but also gain professional growth in education from the experience in educational research, comprehensively carry out educational innovation from the bottom up, and obtain overall progress and development (Tsai 2000b). When teachers are implementing courses and designing a course, they must be able to consider students' life experiences, help students in combining knowledge and experience, and develop appropriate courses (Tsai 2015). In the education system, education action research has long been a prominent study, and there are a lot of various related research papers. According to Yang *et al.* (2001), the action research method was quite attractive to practitioners, and it was regarded as one of the strategies to strengthen professionalism. However, there are still few teachers in the design world who conduct classroom observations with action research and construct an independent design teaching system. Therefore, this research attempts to use the action research model as a framework to explore the basic design curriculum development and teaching process and construct a set of teaching methods for basic design performance techniques with the cycle of students' feedback and teachers' reflection and correction.

### 3.3 *Concept of flipped teaching*

"Twelve-year National Basic Education" of the Ministry of Education has been implemented year by year since the 2019 school year. From the perspective of the spirit of the syllabus, the educational concepts of "achieving every child" and "spontaneity", "interaction" and "mutual good" coincide with the connotation of the flipped classroom (Chen 2015). Flipped teaching has been a very popular teaching mode in recent years. The main core concept is to meet the individual learning needs of students and enhance the best value of

Table 3. Comparison of flipped classrooms, empowerment classrooms, and traditional classrooms.

|  | After 1980s Flipped class-room | After 1960s Empowerment classroom | Before 1960s Traditional classroom |
|---|---|---|---|
| Source of knowledge | Objective knowledge defined by the field of expertise | Personal experience turning into knowledge | Objective knowledge defined by the field of expertise |
| Teacher's role | Guider and facilitator | Inspirer | Knowledge imparter |
| Student's role | Active participant and inquirer | Active participant and inquirer | Passive receiver |
| Teacher-student relationship | Interaction, exploring together | Interaction, exploring together | One-way, top-to-bottom relationship |
| Teaching methods | Blended learning, autonomous learning, peer cooperation | Dialectical dialogue | Hoarding teaching |
| Equipment requirements | Technology equipment, internet | No equipment required | No equipment required |
| Educational purpose | Use technology to promote students to learn independently, and everyone has equal competitiveness | Education is a critical practice, with the goal of achieving a democratic society. | Cultivate talents that meet the needs of society |

the physical classroom. The teaching design is based on the approach of preparing for class beforehand at home to participate in the discussion at school (Teng 2016). Its founders Sams and Bergman believe that the focus of "flipped classroom" is that teachers must really think about how to use the time of classroom interaction more effectively. As experts in the field of knowledge, teachers allow students to learn on their own those parts of one-way teaching, and use face-to-face time to solve individual problems. Only by enabling students to take the initiative to understand, we can explore problems and have in-depth thinking during the entire teaching process, which can really deepen their learning; and the self-learning attitude cultivated is also the foundation of all innovative research (Sams & Bergmann 2013). Tsai (2014) proposed the three-stage teaching concept of the curriculum development history, as shown in Table 3:

## 4 RESEARCH METHOD

### 4.1 Research process

This research took the structure of an actual action research model to solve the problems faced by teachers in practical situations. In postmodern teaching, teachers are researchers, curriculum designers, and implementers, which is similar to the participatory research proposed by Kemmis and McTaggart (1988) that combined action research with curriculum reform. The operation of its research methods includes: (1) participation observation method, (2) questionnaire survey method, (3) interview method, (4) inductive analysis of student's works, or other research process. Although this research was based on qualitative research, it still used structured questionnaires to collect quantitative data for reference. This model was used to construct a set of flipped teaching systems. At the beginning of this research, a literature review, interviews with scholars and experts, and the researcher's experience in teaching this subject for many years were used to discuss the current situation, difficulties, and limitations of students' learning of basic design performance techniques. At the same time, we entered the stage of curriculum preparation, teaching arrangement, and actual teaching operation. Finally, the students' learning questionnaire survey, post-class interviews, works, etc. were organized and analyzed. The action research implementation strategies include the three strategies of (1) constructing pre-knowledge before class, (2) group on-stage performances in class, and (3) post-class exam scoring to reflect and adjust teaching actions through the action research circulation process. In addition, students' study and reflection on study sheets, post-class works, classroom observations, peer reviews, and other qualitative data for analysis were collected to understand the results of the teaching practice research. The research process is shown in Figure 1.

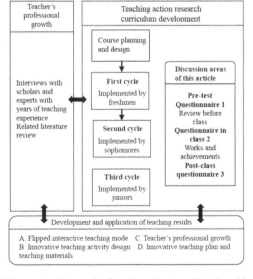

Figure 1. Research flowchart 2 (compiled by this study).

### 4.2 Research site and subjects

This study employed the action research model as the structure and chose three classes in the Department of Multimedia Design at National Houbi Senior High School as the implementation field. The total number of students in multimedia design in the school was 60 (enrolled in 2018–2019), so the number of questionnaires returned was 28 from the freshmen, 19 from the sophomores, and 13 from the juniors. The questionnaires were distributed before, during, and after the study, and then the questionnaires were collected for survey and analysis to understand the student's learning status. The research process is shown in Figure 2.

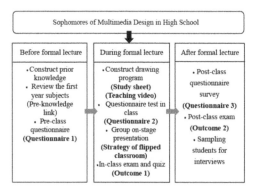

Figure 2. Research flowchart1 (compiled by this study).

### 4.3 Research tools

Different research tools and data analysis methods were adopted in this study to collect data according to the process of each stage. Due to the limited length of the paper, the research process and results for the second-year students are explained first, as shown in the simplified table of Table 4.

Table 4. Explanation of purposes of questionnaire and interview.

| Sophomores of multimedia design in high school | |
| --- | --- |
| Research purposes | Research steps |
| Understand the fundamental design professional theoretical knowledge before formal learning | A semi-open questionnaire survey was used to collect students' understanding of fundamental design disciplines, and qualitative data sorting and analysis were conducted. |
| Explore students' knowledge and | Semi-open questionnaire surveys and intra-class |

*(continued)*

Table 4. Continued

| Sophomores of multimedia design in high school | |
| --- | --- |
| Research purposes | Research steps |
| understanding of fundamental design performance techniques after formal learning | technical tests were employed to collect students' understanding of the after-class teaching materials provided by teachers after learning, and qualitative data analysis was conducted. |
| Test the proficiency and results of fundamental design performance techniques after formal learning | Final quizzes and post-test questionnaire surveys were adopted, practical works were collected and semi-open questionnaires were adopted to investigate students' proficiency in the application of fundamental design performance techniques after class and actual results. |

### 4.4 Recording and analysis of action research results

#### 4.4.1 Literature survey and analysis results
Based on the relevant literature data and the results of the analysis and survey of the works with the full score, the basic design performance technique poster composition has the following elements and definitions, as summarized in Table 5.

Table 5. Poster composition elements, compiled by this study.

| Professional Subjects (2) of Unified Tests-Fundamental Design | |
| --- | --- |
| Image | Text |
| Concrete shape, abstract shape Figures, animals, and other concrete pictograms often appear; followed by abstract shapes, such as elements composed of dots, lines, and planes. Arrange the position of each element according to the degree of importance. | Heading, middle heading, subheading, body text Arrange the position according to the visual focus and importance, and choose the font and bold according to the importance. Arrange the position of each group of words according to the degree of importance. |
| Fundamental design composition principle | Fundamental design composition principle |

In this study, the above-mentioned scattered fundamental design theories were summarized and analyzed with the concept of layers and the principle of grouping, and a set of fundamental design expression techniques—Standard Operating Procedure (SOP) for painting posters was constructed.

It can be seen from the literature theories that in the first year of high school, teachers will teach students the subject knowledge in "basic design theory" on how to complete a graphic composition and arrangement. But, for students, subject theory is a separate and fragmented individual knowledge, and is difficult for students to construct a logical learning system on their own without teachers' instructions and guidance. Therefore, the teacher's job should be to integrate these separate and fragmented individual knowledge and form a teaching system that can be effectively taught to students. The development of the conceptualization process of the SOP of basic design performance technique by this study is shown in Figure 3 (Figure 4 illustrates how to make the program into teaching materials, and Table 6 shows the teaching videos recorded by teachers before class).

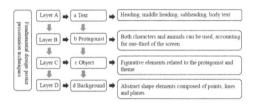

Figure 3. Sop for basic design poster performance technique (compiled in this study).

Figure 4. Teaching materials designed by researcher.

Table 6. Teachers recording instructional videos before class

The teacher recorded the video for the basic design performance technique of Professional Subjects (2)

### 4.2 Questionnaire survey analysis results

There were three tests for the questionnaire in this study, which were the pre-class test, in-class test, and after-class test. A questionnaire and a technical test were given each time, and a total of 57 copies of questionnaires were issued for three tests. While 57 copies were recovered with a recovery rate of 100%, 55 copies of the questionnaires were valid. As found in the basic statistics, 98% of the students did not understand at the beginning of class and did not know how to start painting posters. After they were taught by the teacher, 75% of the students believed that they knew the order of painting the posters clearly while 25% of the students considered themselves to somewhat know the process with 0% of the students being not clear about the steps of painting a poster. As can be seen from the results of questionnaire surveys and interviews, students can apply the theoretical knowledge learned in the first year of high school to the performance techniques in the second year of high school more quickly after the teacher's teaching of the SOP for basic design performance technique to face the "Unified Entrance Examination for Four-year Technology Universities and Two-year Junior Colleges" in the third year.

### 4.3 Scene of on-stage presentation of groups of students

In the process of action research, it is a very important job to record the teaching site truthfully while observing the feedback. In addition to the paper records, every lecture in this research was recorded with photos and videos, and the students' on-site demonstrations in groups were observed. Table 7 shows students being invited to work in groups on stage after the teacher provided video viewing and theoretical teaching of the SOP for basic design performance technique.

Table 7. Interactive on-stage exercises for students in groups.

Recording of the Flipped Teaching Site

Students working in groups on stage for poster painting exercises, with four students in a group (four layers)

### 4.4 Students' after-class learning outcomes and analysis

The basic teaching process model of this study is: A. Teachers record posters and make instructional videos before class → B. Teachers provide videos for students to preview before class → C. Teachers give theoretical prior knowledge reviews in class → D. Students have on-stage group exercises in class → E. After-class learning test → F. Display of students' works. The students' learning achievements are shown in Table 8.

Table 8. Display of students' after-class works.

Achievements and analysis of students' after-class works
Layer A protagonist → Layer B text → Layer C object → Layer D background

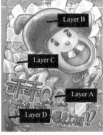

5. The students said in the questionnaires and interviews that because the teacher asked them to watch the video first, and invited them to work in groups in the classroom, they were able to effectively review the SOP of basic design performance techniques given by the teacher during the post-test and exam, and smoothly follow the steps to complete the works.

6. This teaching method can provide a reference for the design of flipped teaching in related research. When more design teachers understand the advantages and limitations of the flipped teaching method through this study, they can apply the method to design their own teaching practice through the action research method.

## 5 CONCLUSION AND SUGGESTIONS

### 5.1 Conclusion

After the research has gone from theoretical discussion, and curriculum planning to the actual operation of the entire action research teaching process, the results are as follows:

1. The design of this subject is different from other subjects in that it focuses on practice with theory as the supplement. Therefore, it is very suitable for teachers to use flipped interactive teaching for the design practice of Professional Subjects (2) as students will have a high classroom participation which rapidly enhances their interest in learning and achieving learning goals.

2. The development concept of the flipped classroom is that the teacher records the content of the class in advance and allows the students to browse the learning online at home, while interactive teaching is carried out in the classroom to improve the learning motivation and test scores of the students (Hao 2015). The teaching mode of the basic design performance technique of this study conforms to the postmodernism concept of a flipped classroom and achieves a high degree of teaching effectiveness.

3. Because the teacher in this study has already organized a set of teaching procedures for the scattered theoretical knowledge of the basic design before teaching, and all are coherent teaching from recording videos, and preparing textbooks to formal lectures, so that teachers can not only integrate knowledge but also guide students to integrate fragmentary knowledge into a logical system.

4. The questionnaire surveys and pre-class and post-class interviews have all confirmed that students believed that this interactive teaching method could quickly arouse their personal metamemory when having exams and tests and lead to substantial results.

### 5.2 Suggestions

1. Educational action research is relatively fragile in terms of "theory". The validity of educational action research depends on the skills of the investigator. It seems that it is not as rigorous as the methodology of basic research (Tsai 2000a). As this study is a preliminary exploration of curriculum action research on "fundamental design practice", the reliability and validity of practical operations still need to be further considered and checked, and the number of questionnaire samples is still insufficient. So, this study will continue to implement the curriculum teaching model developed by the author every school year, and provide real-time course corrections and feedbacks.

2. It takes a long time for the actual implementation of the entire research process in this study to obtain truly effective results and complete the teaching action research. In the future, this research concept will continue to be implemented in related research projects.

3. Jonathan Bergmann, the founder of flipped classroom, proposed the four flipping Ts: Thinking, Training, Time, and Technology. Teachers must break through these four elements to complete the flip (Lin 2015).

Therefore, it is recommended that teachers who want to operate the flipped classroom action research in the future to first understand these four operating concepts as they will have the opportunity to flip their students' learning after flipping their own thinking.

### REFERENCES

Anandasivam, K. (2005). Thinking with hands: Intuitive structural design. *Proceedings of the 2005 IDSA National Education Conference*[CD ROM]. Alexandria: Industrial Designers Society of America.

Apple M.W. (1982). *Education and power*. Boston, MA: Routledge & Kegan Paul.

Chen H. (2015). On the Book "Promoting active learning through the flipped classroom model". *Pulse of Education*, 1, 185–189. Retrieved from http://ericdata.com/tw/detail.aspx?no=285628.

Chen H.B. (1998). *Educational Action Research*. Taipei: Shta Books.

Chen M.Y., Lee M.L. Lin H.Y. (2019). *Fundamental design Internship Volume II*. Taipei: TKD Books.

Chu S.C. (1999). The current problems and responses of basic education in creative creation. *Proceedings of the Fourth Academic Research Achievement Symposium of the Design Society of the Republic of China*, 113–116.

Hao Y.W. (2015). A flipped classroom: The Study of Students' Perspectives. *Pulse of Education*, 1, 34–52. Retrieved from https://epaper.naer.edu.tw/edm.php?grp_no=2&edm_no=111&content_no=2511.

Hwa K., Chen S.J., Hsieh S.L. (2012). The study of appropriateness for the teaching of the course of basic architectural and interior design-taoyuan innovation institute of technology as an example. *Journal of Taoyuan Innovation*, 32, 213–231.

Kemmis S., & McTaggart R. (1988). *The Action Research Planner* (3rd ed.). Geelong, Australia: Deakin University Press.

Lai, C. D., (2001). A study of oral history on the design education in taiwan during the years 1960s. *The Journal of Advertising Research*, 17, 149–174.

Lee M.L., (2019). *Fundamental design Internship (I)*. Taipei: TKD Books.

Lin H.T. (2015, August 17). The creator of the flipped classroom coming to Taiwan to teach the new "4T" method. *Reading a good book*. Retrieved from May 10, 2021, from https://books.cw.com.tw/blog/article/620.

Lin P.C. (1990). *Basic Design Education*. Taipei: Artist Magazine.

Lin P.C. (2009). Overview of Research on Taiwan Design History. *Humanities and Social Sciences Newsletter Quarterly*, 11(1-06) Retrieved from: https://www.most.gov.tw/most/attachments/2a843d80-8c66-4bb2-807c-1f1c71d8ab78?.

Ministry of Education. (2018). *Group Subject Syllabus for Twelve-year National Basic Educational Technology-based Senior High Schools -Design Group*,

Retrieved May 21, 2021, from https://www.k12ea.gov.tw/Tw/Common/SinglePage?filter=11C2C6C1-D64E-475E-916B-D20C83896343

Mo J.B., Sun S.H., Weng C W. (2019). *Fundamental design Internship Volume II*. Taipei: CHWA books.

Rau J. W. (1999). Supporting implementation strategies for the nine-year consistent curriculum and professional development of teachers. Published in Association for Research & Development of Teaching Materials (ed.). *Proceedings of the nine-year consistent curriculum seminar—marching towards a new era of curriculum*, 305–323.

Sams A. & Bergmann, J. (2013). *Flip your students' learning*. *Educational Leadership*, 70(6), 16–20.

Teng, W. C., (2016). The teaching design of applying flipped teaching to the higher vocational mathematics, *Taiwan Education Review*, 700, 42. Retrieved from http://lawdata.com.tw/tw/detail.aspx?no=265281.

Testing Center for Technological & Vocational Education Retrieved May 16, 2021, *Announcement on Scope of Unified Entrance Examination for Four-year Technology Universities and Two-year Junior Colleges in 2021 School Year*. from: https://www.tcte.edu.tw/download/110year/110Range_4y_20210209/

Tsai C.T. (2000a). *Action research and its application in educational research*. Graduate Institute of Education, National Chung Cheng University (ed.): Qualitative research methods. Kaohsiung: Liwen Publishing.

Tsai, C. T. (2000b). *Educational Action Research*. Taipei: Wu Nan Books.

Tsai R.C. (2014). The significance and critical issues in the 'flipped classroom' in the digital Age. *Journal of Educational Research and Development*, 10 (2), 115–138.

Tsai, R. C. (2015). The past, present and future of the "Flipped Classroom" approach, *Pulse of Education*, 1, 17–29. Retrieved from: https://epaper.naer.edu.tw/edm.php?grp_no=2&edm_no=111&content_no=2510

Yang, M. E. (2007). Designing the fundamental: contemporary concepts and applications of college basic design curriculum. *Journal of aesthetic education*, 158, 14–21. Retrieved from https://ed.arte.gov.tw/ch/content/m_periodical_content.aspx?AE_SNID=1621.

Yang R.J., Chen M.Y., Huang L.H. (2001). Action research concepts and nursing application. *The Journal of Health Science*, 3 (3), 244–254.

*System Innovation for a Troubled World – Lam et al. (Eds)*
*© 2024 the Author(s), ISBN: 978-1-032-60846-4*

# An analysis of innovative thinking of the color of Kuki Shuzo's Iki and chinese ink painting

Chung-Ho Tien & Wei-Jiang She*
*Dongguan City University, Liaobu Town, Dongguan City, Guangdong Province, China*

Xia-Na Ma
*Guangzhou College of Technology and Business, Huadu District, Guangzhou City, Guangdong Province, China*

ABSTRACT: Based on the book The Structure of Iki by Kuki Shuzo, this paper analyzes the innovative thinking behind the color of the artistic expression of Iki. This paper discusses the color of Iki through the basic principles of color and, in addition, compares the color of traditional Chinese ink painting with that of the famous paintings of three Ukiyo-e masters of the Edo period. The emotional expression of color used in the works reflects their national emotion, spiritual aspirations, and deep feelings for the land. Through the artistic expression of color, this paper allows students who are new to the field of art to understand that color has the role of emotional change and association; it is also a means for the author to express his inner feelings and spiritual thoughts, create an atmosphere, and so on.

*Keywords*: Kuki Shuzo, Iki, three Ukiyo-e masters, Chinese Ink Painting

## 1 INTRODUCTION

China and Japan have been in close contact for more than two thousand years, and the cultural exchanges have imperceptibly influenced each other, especially the Japanese culture during the Tang and Song dynasties when Japanese culture was most significantly influenced. In 1868, the Meiji Restoration was implemented in Japan, which led to a new reform in the economy and modernization. Living in a different era, people unconsciously developed the so-called spiritual aspirations of life.

People often give symbolic meaning to the era through color to adapt to the life of that era, so this kind of color with special meaning and infectious power was born. Under the impact of Western modernization, the distinguished Japanese philosopher Kuki Shuzo tried to awaken the national sentiment of the Japanese people in his introspection by using personal examples as subjects and the opera, architecture, costume patterns, and novels of the Edo period as examples.

The use of folk colors in the Edo period, as mentioned in the article The Structure of Iki, is similar to the use of traditional Chinese ink painting. Both of them reduce the purity and saturation of colors, making the colors in the picture grayish so that they appear simple and soft visually and can

calm down the mind. This is why it is also called high-quality gray. Color is now a conceptual interpretation of symbols, not just a simple visual sense. Therefore, I use the basic principles of color to analyze and compare the colors of Iki and then interpret the various emotions between individuals and nations implied by color with the works of Chinese and Japanese artists.

## 2 LITERATURE REVIEW

Mentioned by Kuki Shuzo, Tameinai Gaxiusi (1790–1843), a late Edo playwright, wrote in his book Spring Color Loves White Waves: "The mouse gray crumpled silk of the Imperial Court is embroidered with the fine thread of color of the yellow stalked tea, and the tiny checkerboard top is embroidered. The belt is made of a dark blue vajra pattern of Hakata with the old-fashioned national style of weave, and the two Tawny threads are woven together to form a different belt inside and out. The cuffs of the dress, like the blouse and the undergarment, are made of satin in the color of Onando, like the color of Pine Leaf Tree, which is perfect.

The colors in this description belong to three systems similar to those in Chromatics. The first is the mouse gray, the second is the brown system of the yellow tea color and the tawny color, and the third is the cyan system of the indigo color and the

---

*Corresponding Author: 114605808@qq.com

DOI: 10.1201/9781003460763-59

onando color. In addition, after the description in Haruga Tori: Dyeing the bellyband with different colors such as onando, tawny, and mouse gray, and dyeing it with a half handset, it says, "What a graceful dress" [1]. From this, the color of Iki can be judged as having three color systems: mouse gray, tea color, and cyan and green, while the color of Iki has different degrees of gray.

Since ancient times, China has had the concept of five colors, known as the five primary colors: green, red, yellow, white, and black. In ancient China, dynasties were changed and replaced by the principle of the five elements. Before Wang Mang founded the new dynasty, the change of dynasties was called the Five Virtues, according to Zou Yan, a scholar of the Five Elements [2]. It can be seen that both eastern and western colors are obtained in principle by using the three primary colors with different degrees of 'gray'.

## 3 RESULTS AND DISCUSSION

### 3.1 *Discussion on Iki and the basic color of chromatics*

The colors mentioned in the book The Structure of Iki are gorgeous and negative, affirming colors but implying negativity and the book is full of tension based on dualism. The colors of the Edo period described in the book The Structure of Iki are the most artistic expressions of Iki: the simple and smooth vertical stripes in the striped patterns; the colors that can express Iki most are the three colors of mouse gray, tawny, and cyan, while red and purple, red flowers and green leaves, gaudy colors, and fabrics are not "Iki" [3]. The text shows a negative attitude towards bright colors. The following is an analysis of Iki and the basic colors of chromatics, which are red, yellow, blue (cyan), black, and white.

The mouse gray is similar to black and white, which are colorless in chromatics, while there is the concept of grayscale in computer graphics and sketches. The image of grayscale is different from that of black and white. In the field of computer graphics, the image of black and white has only two colors. There are many levels of color depth between black and white in the grayscale image.

The mouse gray is gray and has been admired since the Edo period, as the color of the Rikyu mouse, the silver mouse, the blue wind, the tea mouse, the budonezumi, and so on have appeared. All kinds of colors are considered the color of Iki in terms of rhythm. The gray of the Edo period was an elegant grayscale color with the addition of a small amount of color. In the Edo period, due to the policy of emphasizing agriculture over commerce and the fact that Japan was under a state of self-seclusion, many colors on clothes were forbidden by the people at that time, so these gray

colors with different layers were widely used in Ukiyo-e, tile plates (printed materials that recorded current events), and the amusement parks that were popular at that time. The following chart shows the RGB code for the mouse color system.

Figure 1.    The RGB code for the mouse color system.

### 3.2 *Tawny of Iki and red and yellow*

The tawny color mentioned in the book "The Structure of Iki" is close to brown, red, and yellow, which are the basic colors of chromatics. They are all warm colors. Tawny is a color system between red and yellow that is close to the earth and gives people a warm feeling.

Just to mention the names of Tawny used in the Edo period, there are kincha, Ding Zi tea, Iris tea, Lu Kaocha tea, kogecha, Mei tea, etc. Named after the figurative nature of the color of the object, they range from red through orange to yellow, which is magnificent, together with mouse gray to reduce its saturation; all are colors produced as a result of luminosity reduction. In another book, The Wandering Soul, written by Kuki Shuzo, it is mentioned that, at the age of six, I cried, listening to lullabies, and at the age of thirty, I wet my pillow with tears. I am always sad when I think of my parents, and I ask for forgiveness for forgetting my sins. I learned that the white tea color was popular, and I am happy with the love of my loving mother [4]. The color tawny is particularly symbolic of the color associated with his and his mother's unfortunate fate, a color that belongs to his mother, implying a sense of warmth and desolation. The following chart shows the RGB code of Tawny.

### 3.3 *Onando of Iki and green and blue*

In the Edo period, Onando was the title of a samurai. It was not a high-official position, but a position in clothing management.

In the book "The Structure of Iki," it is mentioned that "Onando" is the same as the basic colors green and blue, belonging to cold colors. It is mentioned in the article that when the blue color gets close to the green color, it is the color of Iki, so it is generally related to saturation. The color of Onando, the color of the pine leaves, the color of Equisetaceae, the color of the warbler, the color of the willow, and so on, have the nature of Iki, all due to the reduction of saturation. The most important factor is the addition of the appropriate mouse gray color.

In chromatics, blue and green help people feel comfortable and empty while holding a high degree of saturation and color. Therefore, in a sense, tiny amounts of black must be added to achieve the meaning of Iki; it is similar to the color used in Chinese ink painting, adding a little bit of the ink color to make the picture achieve a unified and harmonious tone. The chart below shows the RGB code for the Onando color system.

Figure 2. The RGB code for the Onando color system.

## 4 RESULT

The comparison of Iki and the color used in traditional Chinese ink painting

In different eras, they have their own colors, which have developed an inherent or distinctive color over time. The pigments of traditional Chinese ink are generally natural and made from mineral or vegetable materials, which are similar to those used in Japan during the Edo period. This section compares the color and emotion of traditional Chinese ink painting with the works of the three masters of the Ukiyo-e' in Japan.

The mouse gray of Ukiyo-e of Iki and the ink color of Chinese ink painting

Ink color is often mentioned in Chinese paintings, but it does not only refer to the blending of water and ink; 'ink' itself has the connotation of color. In this section, ink color refers only to ink in the blend of water and ink.

The mouse gray of Iki is the same as the ink color. There is a Chinese tradition of using ink as a substitute for color, giving rise to the saying that ink is divided into five color, as Zhang Yan Yuan of the Tang Dynasty says in his Record of Famous Paintings of All Ages, the five colors can be obtained if the ink is used perfectly. The five colors, such as black, thick, heavy, light, and clear, are each divided by different levels of dry, wet, thick, and light ink. It is also said in his book that the distance of the landscape can be painted with light and thick ink, as can the age of the branches and leaves. Ink can be used as a substitute for color when painting the blossoming of grass and trees, the rain and snow, and green for the mountains. The following is a comparison between the mouse gray of ukiyo-e and the ink colors of Chinese ink painting.

Kitagawa Utamaro (1753–1806) is known as a master of beauty paintings, and one of his masterpieces—Three Beauties of the Edo Kansei Period (Figure 1)—shows the unique beauty of women by using a soft mouse gray color to present the picture as soft, simple, and graceful.

In the three women's costumes, different shades of gray are used to match different ornaments, so that the three are distanced but reconciled by the shades; the gray costumes match the skin of the three beauties to show their skin color. In particular, he uses the technique of Nishiki-e, which is a technique used in printmaking, to print on the paper called Fengshu (Japanese paper), and because Fengshu is thick and ductile, it can show a three-dimensional texture. Therefore, it can appear with multi-layered color gradations. The multi-layered colors can be seen in the light.

Figure 3. Three Beauties of the Edo Kansei Period, 1793, Kitagawa Utamaro,25 x 37 cm, printmaking, Toledo Museum of Art, America.

Xu Beihong (1895–1953) painted the scenery of Li River in Yangshuo, Spring Rain in Li River (Figure 2), one of his masterpieces of landscape painting, using splash-ink to render the masterpiece, fully demonstrating the theory of five colors in ink of the traditional Chinese ink painting through the multi-layered changes in ink color to show the misty light and shadow, the combination of mountain and water, ink and water, making the quiet and tranquil fishermen's life more interesting. The Qing dynasty calligrapher and painter Li Shan, one of the Eight Wonders of Yangzhou, said: "The brush and ink are fundamental, but the water is the key factor" and "the vividness of the paintings depends on the smart use of water in Chinese ink painting". Both Xu Beihong and Kitagawa Utamaro use the characteristics of paper to highlight the hierarchy of color gradations in their works. Xu Beihong's brushwork is full of intelligence and rhythm, and he makes full use of paper to present the countryside between the rain and the mountains.

Mouse gray and ink color are used as the main colors in these two works, with different shades of color to give a sense of the tonal hierarchy of the work, showing that the world of black and white can still be charming.

E3896A  DC9B7D  563F43  3C4749  503D42

Figure 5. Kameido Ume Yashiki (Figure 3), 1857, Utagawa Hiroshige, 36.8 cm × 25 cm, printmaking, Hiyakomachi, Hagi, Yamaguchi.

CDD3D3  E7E8E0  BBC1BD  45494C  A3ACA8

Figure 4. Spring Rain in thr Li River, 1937, Xu Beihong,73.8cm × 113.8cm, Chinese Ink Painting, China Artists Association.

The Tawny of Ukiyo-e of Iki and the Brown Color of Chinese ink painting

The tawny in Iki is like the warm colors in Chinese ink colors such as magenta, cinnabar, gamboge, ochre, and so on. Although it has bright colors, the saturation is reduced, just like the dark red and rouge colors. Both of them add a small amount of ink (mouse gray) to the use of color so that the colors in the picture present a sense of harmony.

The master of landscape painting, Utagawa Hiroshige, whose original name was Ando Hiroshige (1797–1858), Kameido Ume Yashiki (Figure 3) describes a private plum garden near Tokyo, which is often crowded with people enjoying the blossoms when the owner opens the garden to the public. With a reddish Tawny background, the most striking part of the picture is a famous plum tree, Wolong Plum, whose branches are mainly brownish in color, and which are matched with the blue purple-sky that reduces the color intensity and purity of the night and the deep warbler green of the grass, forming a color palette with a sense of warmth and a sense of seclusion.

Li Keran (1907–1989), a master of Chinese ink painting, painted the series of the Red Mountains (Figure 4) in three colors: red, black, and white, of which red is made of the finest cinnabar pigment, which has a bright red color and a sense of calm and steady. The use of layers of iterative ink and color in the application of color gives the picture a lot of power. Cinnabar and ink are used in the work, allowing the colors and ink to blend naturally and the distinctive layers to form naturally. The magnificent red mountains occupy the center of the picture, showing the breathtaking mountains together with the white waterfalls, streams, and white tile walls among the mountains, allowing the visual sense to indulge in the picture leisurely with the aerial perspective, and the southern late-autumn scene immediately appears.

Both works are colored with warm colors, giving people a warm psychological feeling. One is a close-range description, using soft colors to make people feel the connection of social harmony and warmth of human nature; the other has a sense of the mountains looming over them, with a waterfall cascading straight down from the mountains, using a high-reaching method to give the mountains a sense of looming.

The cyan of Ukiyo-e of Iki and the blue and green of Chinese ink painting

The colors used in Chinese ink painting and Japanese ukiyo-e are mostly the colors of mountains, rocks, and water, presenting a literati's state of mind, which has been sought after by literati for generations. As in the case of Kuki Shuzo, under the impact of modern Western civilization, the

2B0D06   541607   951510   C57563   3C110F

Figure 6.   Red Mountains All Over (Figure 4), 1962, Li Keran, 69cm × 45cm, Chinese paintings, private collection.

source of the aesthetic sense of Iki was rediscovered in traditional Japanese culture.

Katsushika Hokusai, a landscape master (1760–1849), paints a print of ukiyo-e, the Great Wave off Kanagawa (Figure 5), which is one of the thirty-six views of Mount Fuji. The main color in the picture is blue, and the background, tawny with some mouse gray, stabilizes the picture and highlights the great waves. The rich color layers and asymmetrical composition result in a visual shock. The dynamic waves contrast with the static Mount Fuji; the blue waves contrast with the tawny sky and the ship's board, forming a contrast between warm and cold colors.

B9D1BD   182838   284058   C0B898   3D6271

Figure 7.   The Great Wave off Kanagawa (Figure 5), 1831, Katsushika Hokusai, 26 cm × 38.5 cm, printmaking, Kanagawa, Japan.

Wang Ximeng, a painter of the Northern Song Dynasty (1096–) painted "A Thousand Li of Rivers and Mountains," (Figure 6) which is a silk scroll with cyan and green colors. In this work, the mountains and rocks are first outlined with ink, then colored with cyan and green, and the peaks and the mountains are colored with lime green to show the layers of the mountains. The picture is composed of layers of mountains and peaks, woods and countryside, small boats, bridges and arches, people, houses, and pavilions, creating a beautiful and productive living environment.

Dr. Wang Zhongxu, a research curator at the Department of Painting and Calligraphy of the National Palace Museum of China, mentioned in his book A Thousand Li of Rivers and Mountains: Green Landscapes and Rivers and Mountains at the Court of Emperor Huizong that Wang Ximeng integrated the empty imagery of feasible, desirable, tourable, and liveable based on the traditional rivers and mountains, which changed the picture from a simple theme to a poetic and thoughtful painting [5]. It can be seen that the author's state of mind is harmonious, calm, and serene, so the picture can be constructed with an extraordinary Zen, with the brilliant and implicit features of Chinese ink painting, and the admirer is like indulging in a paradise in the green landscape.

8B803A   7AA167   6AADBD   54836D   5A624C

Figure 8.   A Thousand Li of Rivers and Mountains, 1113, Wang Ximeng, 51.5cm × 1191.5cm, silk scroll, the National Palace Museum of China.

The two works, one dynamic and one static, in which color plays a varied role under the artist's intelligent arrangement, each have a unique color. The contrast of warm and cold colors can make people feel dazzled and shocked. One is that the picture gives a sense of gorgeous but elegance, and the colors are interwoven between green and ochre, with a strong sense of decoration and magnificence. The other is that the strong contrast between dynamic and static and color makes the picture harmonious, and both have a unique dualism.

## 5 CONCLUSION

Xunzi, a Chinese thinker at the end of the Warring States period, had a famous phrase: "without richness and typicality, art cannot be said to be beautiful." When applied to the beauty of art, it means that art should be extremely rich in the comprehensive expression of life and nature, but also select the essence and discard the gross. It means that art should be improved and express life and nature in a more typical and universal way.

The popular colors of the Edo period and Chinese ink painting are expressed through the colors of the negative visual afterimage of the magnificent experience, and the picture offers viewers multiple visual feelings of colors through the slight warmth with gray or black colors, which can touch the hearts and arouse spiritual aspirations. It can be seen that color gives a quick visual impression, which can increase recognition and memory; color has the element of unique emotional expression and can express rich thoughts through the creative thinking of the artist's emotion. Through the use of color, artists can not only describe the people and the land but also show the beauty of the country's mountains and rivers.

## REFERENCES

[1] Kuki Shuzo, annotated by Masakatsu Fujita Hara, translated by Jin-Rong Huang/Wen-Hong Huang/Kang Uchida, (2016), *The Structure of Iki*, Taipei: Lianjing Publishing co., Ltd, P94–95

[2] 2021 *Annual Conference on Chinese Traditional Color Science, Institute of Fine Arts*, Chinese National Academy of Arts, (2021), P5

[3] Kuki Shuzo, Abe Jiro, translated by Wang Xiangyuan, (2020), *Japanese Coloring*, Beijing: Beijing United Publishing co., Ltd, P25

[4] Kuki Shuzo, translated by Guo Yongen,Fan Liyan, (2015), *Wandering Souls*", Beijing: China Book Press, P52

[5] Wang Zhongxu, (2018), *"A Thousand Li of Rivers and Mountains: Green Landscapes and Rivers and Mountains at the Court of Emperor Huizong"*, Beijing: People's Fine Arts Press, P238

*System Innovation for a Troubled World – Lam et al. (Eds)*
*© 2024 the Author(s), ISBN: 978-1-032-60846-4*

# Study on the size of the intra-oral tongue pressure sensor for the elderly based on anthropometry

Shu-Yi Qin*
*School of Design, Straits Institute of Technology, Fujian University of Technology, Fuzhou, China*

Jeng-Chung Woo
*School of Design, Straits Institute of Technology, Fujian University of Technology, Fuzhou, China*
*Design Innovation Research Center of Humanities and Social Sciences Research Base of Colleges and Universities in Fujian Province, Fuzhou, China*

Zi-Xian Lin, Kang-Lin Liao & Wen-Qian Young
*School of Design, Straits Institute of Technology, Fujian University of Technology, Fuzhou, China*

ABSTRACT: Oropharyngeal Dysphagia (OD) is a geriatric syndrome that prevents the elderly from swallowing food safely. Tongue muscle resistance training can effectively improve the swallowing function of the elderly, but it is difficult to quantify accurately. The flexible sensor placed at the hard palate can accurately collect tongue pressure during natural swallowing and tongue muscle resistance training. By collecting the key points and stress points of the hard palate during tongue muscle resistance training for the elderly, it is conducive to the accurate design of sensor placement points. However, there is little research on the hard palate size data of the elderly, and this study is designed to provide a reference for the intra-oral tongue pressure sensor. In this study, hard palate dental casts were collected from 110 elderly subjects (valid sample = 76) with an average age of $67.30 \pm 9.78$ years for males and $65.78 \pm 7.74$ years for females, and were examined with a camera, tripod and 5mm standard grid shot. Through literature collection and questionnaire analysis, the required palate point for sensor design was obtained. Then, the sampling results were processed by Digimier Version 5.4.4 software to extract the required palate point data, and the final data were analyzed with SPSS 27. Based on the results of this study, it is recommended that the 5th, 50th, and 95th percentiles of this statistical result be used as a size reference for the intra-oral tongue pressure sensor.

*Keywords*: Tongue pressure sensor, elderly, anthropometry, Oropharyngeal Dysphagia

## 1 INTRODUCTION

The aging population is a common global challenge. According to the 7th National Census, the proportion of senior citizens over 65 years old in China is 13.50%. According to the World Health Organization, the number of people over the age of 60 will reach 1.4 billion in 2030. How to provide the elderly with a healthy life in their later years is a widespread concern for the current society and academic circles.

The aging of the human body is an irreversible process that cannot be prevented. It is also an inevitable trend that the muscle content of the human body decreases with age. Studies have shown that the muscle mass of humans will decline at a rate of about 1%–2% per year after the age of 50 (Vandervoort 2002), and the decrease in muscle mass will accelerate to 3% per year after the age of 60. Among the elderly aged 65 or older, 5% to 13% have low muscle mass (Rolland *et al.* 2008).

Low muscle mass affects swallowing ability in the elderly and even leads to swallowing dysphagia (Fujishima *et al.* 2019). Swallowing in the human body is the whole process of food intake through the mouth and transmission into the stomach through the pharyngeal cavity and esophagus (Cook & Kahrilas 1999). Normal swallowing requires accurate coordination of more than 30 muscles in the oral cavity, pharynx, larynx, and esophagus (Shaw & Martino 2013). Problems in coordination or strength of muscles involved in swallowing may cause Oropharyngeal Dysphagia (OD).

OD is a common geriatric syndrome (Baijens *et al.* 2016; Speyer *et al.* 2022). In view of the

---

*Corresponding Author: Shuyi-Qin@outlook.com

DOI: 10.1201/9781003460763-60

current aging rate of the population, dysphagia of the elderly will be an increasingly serious healthcare problem.

OD is mainly manifested as difficulty in the process of forming food pellets in the mouth and in the process of safely moving the formed food pellets from the mouth to the esophagus (Cook & Kahrilas 1999). Tongue plays a key role in swallowing. During swallowing, the tongue is mainly responsible for allowing food to form a pellet, which is then transmitted from the oral cavity to the pharynx by extrusion (Youmans & Stierwalt 2006). Tongue pressure is an indicator of tongue muscle strength, and a decrease in tongue pressure also represents a decrease in tongue muscle strength. Tongue pressure decreases with age (Nagashima et al. 2021). A statistical study shows that the average tongue pressure of people under 60 years old is 52.2Kpa, while the average tongue pressure of people aged 60 and over is 34.9Kpa (Arakawa et al. 2021). Therefore, the measurement of tongue pressure is very important for assessing swallowing function.

Tongue muscle resistance training is considered to be of positive significance in improving tongue pressure and swallowing ability (Iyota et al. 2022; C.-J. Lin et al. 2022; Yano et al. 2021). Tongue-palate resistance training (TPRT) is one of the tongue muscle resistance training, which trains the tongue muscle with the continuous squeeze of the tongue on the palate, and can improve the tongue strength, thus helping to improve the OD caused by muscle atrophy (C.-H. Lin et al. 2021; Namiki et al. 2019).

The tongue pressure of different tongue segments and the time of tongue pressure generation are different (Ono et al. 2004). According to a previous study, after the anterior tongue fixes and moves the food pellet, the posterior tongue is responsible for squeezing the pellet toward the pharynx and maintaining the airway unobstructed (Gingrich et al. 2012). Therefore, accurate measurement of the tongue pressure and its generation time in different tongue segments is of great significance for the diagnosis of OD, which can help physicians to better understand the oropharyngeal swallowing process of patients and the causes of OD.

In many studies, researchers used devices to observe tongue pressure, such as Iowa Oral Performance Instrument (IOPI) and JMS (TPM-02E), to measure tongue pressure and conduct tongue muscle resistance training (Kim et al. 2017; Plaza & Ruviaro Busanello-Stella 2022). However, the tongue pressure measured by such a device is not the pressure under natural swallowing. In contrast, the flexible film pressure sensor can provide accurate information about the functional movement of the tongue during swallowing (Ono et al. 2004). In addition, the flexible film pressure sensor can be placed at any position to observe the state of tongue-palate contact and the change in time and intensity of contact with the palate when tongue movement occurs.

Until now, many researches have applied flexible pressure film sensors to the field of tongue pressure measurement. Such a sensor is used to measure the tongue pressure of a person in different postures (Yu & Gao 2019), swallowing objects with different textures (Furuya et al. 2012), and normal swallowing (Hori et al. 2006). In addition, it's also used in tongue pressure measurement research for patients with Parkinson's disease (Fukuoka et al. 2019) and muscular dystrophy (Hamanaka-Kondoh et al. 2014). Due to the thin and soft characteristics of such sensors, it is possible to record tongue pressure and other data generated by a person under real swallowing conditions with minimal influence when the sensor is fixed on the hard palate, which is not possible with the traditional balloon tongue pressure detection devices. In order to better observe the natural tongue pressure of the elderly, it's important to design a sensor chip that meets the palate size of the elderly for collecting and analyzing the palate data of the elderly.

Similarly, the flexible pressure film sensor can also measure the tongue pressure of a person during tongue pressure resistance training. A latest study has applied such a sensor to tongue pressure measurement during tongue pressure resistance training (Fukuoka et al. 2022), but the sensor used in such an article is not specially designed for the contact points of tongue pressure resistance training. Therefore, in order to better understand the recovery process of elderly patients with OD, it is important to design a reasonable recovery plan and a sensor chip suitable for tongue pressure resistance training that meets the palate size of the elderly. On account of this, this study collects and analyzes the palate data of the elderly.

At present, few researches are on the hard palate data of the elderly. This study analyzes the hard palate dental casts of the elderly and summarizes the reference size for designing the sensor.

According to ergonomics, anthropometric data play an important role in the products designed and improved for different users, and poorly designed and ill-fitting products are one of the factors that increase the risk of musculoskeletal pain and discomfort. Conducting an anthropometric survey before design can provide basic reference data for designing ergonomic equipment, tools, products, or environment, thus improving the usability, suitability, comfort, and safety of products (Dianat et al. 2018). Ergonomics is also applied in the design of medical products. For example, researchers analyzed the perineal anthropometric characteristics of young women in China by statistics, which provided a basis for the design of the opening shape of a female urination device (Wang et al. 2015). Through statistical analysis of the anthropometric characteristics of the human body, the researchers provided reference dimensions for the spinal plate stretcher for rescue. The use of anthropometric data in the design process ensures the safety and comfort of the spinal plate, as well as the flexibility and speed of the rescue evacuation process (Zadry et al. 2017).

Based on the advantages of anthropometric data in the design, this study uses an anthropometric method to sample and analyze the palate plaster of the elderly, which will provide a reference for the sensor design for the elderly.

## 2 OBJECTIVE

The objective of this study is to determine the human measurement features of the palate of the elderly, which is used for the ergonomic design of the intra-oral tongue pressure detection sensor.

## 3 METHODS

### 3.1 Determination of sample size

The sample size for this study is determined based on the standard formula in ISO15535:2012. The calculation formula is shown in (1).

$$n = \left( \frac{Z \times CV}{\alpha} \right)^2 \times 1.534^2 \qquad (1)$$

$$CV = SD\bar{x} \qquad (2)$$

n – minimum sample size;
CV –coefficient of variation; $\alpha$–relative accuracy;
Z – standard normal value;
SD – standard deviation; –average

To ensure the confidence of the minimum sample size (n), the value of Z is determined to be 1.96 (1.96 is the critical value of the standard normal distribution at 95% confidence). Due to the lack of reference of available data in this sample survey, the CV value cannot be directly obtained. Therefore, this study adopts the methods of phased sampling and phased assessment of the effectiveness of the sample size. Based on the analysis of the sensor system designed by the present study (Hori et al. 2009), $\alpha$ is identified as 15% in this study.

Finally, 110 samples were collected, of which 76 were valid.

### 3.2 Measuring tools

Canon 850d camera, Canon EF 50mm F/1.8 lens, camera holder, T-square, and 5mm standard grid were used to take photos and sample the palate of the elderly (Fig. 1). A standard grid of 5mm was placed under the plaster model to calibrate the photo size.

### 3.3 Determination of measurement point on the hard palate

A literature search was conducted at Google Scholar and articles were obtained using the following keywords and phrases "tongue pressure", "flexible sensor" and "palate", with no time limit until February 2023. After screening, representative articles were obtained, and the point information of sensor placement and the size of the sensor measurement area in the articles were summarized Table 1). After extraction and analysis, it is concluded that for the size design of the tongue pressure detection flexible pressure film sensor attached to the palate, the confirmation of the distance between the following points is important: the incisive papillae, posterior edge of the palate, the first molar on the left side, and the first molar on the right side.

In this study, 45 volunteers were recruited to record the range of contact between tongue and palate during tongue pressure resistance training in front, left, right, and back directions. The

Table 1. Design of sensors in past research.

| Data source | Key Point | diameter |
|---|---|---|
| (Yu & Gao, 2019) | Ch.1(anterior) was placed at the incisive papilla, palatal side of a contact area of maxillary central incisors Ch.2(posterior) was placed at the intersection point of the palatal vault and the last molars Ch.3 and Ch.4(lateral) were placed at the left and right palatal gingival margin of the upper first molars respectively | 9.53mm |
| (Hori et al. 2006) | (Ch.1) Position 5 mm posterior to the incisive papilla (Ch.2) One-third anterior between incisive papillae and posterior edge of the palate (Ch.3) One-third posterior between incisive papillae and posterior edge of the palate (Ch.4) One-third anterior between incisive papillae and Hamuller's notch on the habitual masticatory side (Ch.5) One-third posterior between incisive papillae and Hamuller's notch on the habitual masticatory side (Ch.6) One-third anterior between incisive papillae and Hamuller's notch on the non-habitual masticatory side (Ch.7) One-third posterior between incisive papillae and Hamuller's notch on the non-habitual masticatory side | 6mm |

(continued)

Table 1. Continued

| Data source | Key Point | diameter |
|---|---|---|
| (Chiba et al. 2003) | The loop of the TPA was positioned at the middle of the second premolars (P) The first molars (M1), or the second molars (M2) | |
| (Sardini et al. 2013) | Two measurement points (P1-P4) are placed along the midline, two (P5-P6) are in the back-side and two (P2-P3) laterally | 3.2mm |
| (Hori et al. 2009) | Three measuring points (Chs.1–3) were placed along the median line Ch. 1 was set at the anterior median part Ch. 2 was set in the mid-median part Ch. 3 was set at the posterior-median part Two (Chs.4 and 5) were in the posterior-lateral part of the hard palate Ch. 4 was set at the left side Ch. 5 was set at the right side | 3mm |

determination range is that the incisive papillae (point P) is the point touched when the tongue touches the anterior palate, the canine teeth are the point where the tongue touches both sides of the palate, and the point where the tongue touches the posterior palate is at the intersection of the connecting line of the first premolar teeth on both sides and the midline of the palate. The sensor position that is more suitable for the tongue pressure resistance training can be determined with the above points.

This study measures and analyzes the distance of 6 points on the palate of the elderly as shown in the figure below. In addition, human dental arches can be classified into tapered dental arches, ovoid dental arches, and square dental arches according to their shapes (Yang et al. 2021). The angle from point P of the square dental arch to both sides of the posterior end of the palate is the largest, followed by the ovoid dental arch and the tapered dental arch. The shape of the dental arch may also affect the sensor design. In this study, the angle from the point p of the dental arch to the outside of the posterior end of the palate is also counted Figure 1)

The hard palate dental casts of 110 senior citizens were randomly collected from villages and towns in Heilongjiang and Hubei provinces of China (male (n = 51) and female (n = 59)). All participants for whom the palate plaster model was collected completed the consent form.

Photos taken were processed with Digimier Version 5.4.4 software.

## 3.4 Statistical tests

The anthropometric data were analyzed by SPSS version 27 software. Descriptive statistics (maximum, minimum, mean, standard deviation, and percentile ) of human body dimensions were output, and the extent of gender-induced differences in palate data in the elderly was examined by ANOVA analysis, and the relationship between the angle $\beta$ and each measured dimension was examined by Spearman analysis. Statistical significance was considered when P-value $< 0.05$.

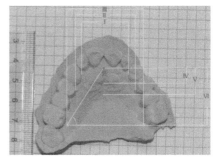

Figure 1. Graphic representation of palate measurement data.

I: Horizontal distance between canine teeth on both sides of the palate
II: Horizontal distance between the first premolar teeth on both sides of the palate
III: Width of the palate
IV: Vertical distance from p to I
V: Vertical distance from p to II
VI: Vertical distance from p to III
$\beta$: Angle between p and the outside of IV

For convenience of explanation, this article will use this serial number as an abbreviation for the measurement name.

## 4 RESULT

The result shows that the average age of the senior citizens participating in this study is $67.30 \pm 9.78$ years old for males and $65.78 \pm 7.74$ years old for females.

The CV% is obtained by calculating the average and standard deviation of the statistical table (Table 2) of the hard palate data collected from the male senior citizens in this study with the formula (1.2). Taking the maximum value of CV% as 21% and the sample size as 41, $a\% = 10.28\%$ is obtained from formula (1.1).

The CV is obtained by calculating the average and standard deviation of the statistical table (Table 3) of the oral cavity data collected from the female senior citizens in this study with the formula. Taking the maximum value of CV%

Table 2. The hard palate data of male.

|  | N | min | max | M | SD |
|---|---|---|---|---|---|
| I | 41 | 20.088487 | 32.370812 | 25.81984590 | 3.17291407 |
| II | 41 | 24.334797 | 38.755963 | 31.66752295 | 3.55599135 |
| III | 41 | 30.637575 | 48.318954 | 39.25387724 | 4.79163775 |
| IV | 41 | 3.641834 | 8.037158 | 5.70709680 | 1.25127870 |
| V | 41 | 7.395455 | 16.645783 | 11.91183066 | 2.04405443 |
| VI | 41 | 19.004226 | 38.327928 | 26.91052807 | 3.81660754 |
| β | 41 | 43.472235 | 62.430857 | 54.34961627 | 4.38324229 |

Table 3. The hard palate data of female.

|  | N | min | max | M | SD |
|---|---|---|---|---|---|
| I | 35 | 20.069394 | 20.069394 | 31.567953 | 2.633351487 |
| II | 35 | 25.070678 | 25.070678 | 36.900594 | 3.223174136 |
| III | 35 | 31.596153 | 31.596153 | 49.333739 | 4.139098776 |
| IV | 35 | 3.735588 | 3.735588 | 7.725418 | 1.173647598 |
| V | 35 | 9.042596 | 9.042596 | 15.680991 | 1.758791268 |
| VI | 35 | 22.606489 | 22.606489 | 37.925583 | 3.267681652 |
| β | 35 | 46.178056 | 46.178056 | 61.873014 | 3.664107012 |

as 15% and the sample size as 35, $\alpha\% = 7.64\%$ is obtained from formula (1.1).

The value of $\alpha$ calculated from the hard palate data of both male and female senior citizens is not more than 10%, which is within the acceptable range. Therefore, the sample size of this study meets the minimum sample size requirement.

Gender differences may result in differences in palate measurement data. The degree of difference determines whether the difference in size caused by gender difference should be considered when designing the intra-oral tongue pressure detection sensor.

In order to determine the degree of data difference between men and women, we performed One-Way ANOVA on the joint activity data collected, which was used to test the degree of gender-induced differences in the palate data of the elderly. The principle is that the difference between the mean values of different treatment groups is due to the experimental conditions and random errors. By analyzing the contribution of the variation from different sources to the total variation, the influence of controllable factors on the results can be known. This study grouped the male and female data to establish a test assuming that H0: the overall means of the multiple samples were equal and the test level was 0.05. If the significance is greater than 0.05, it means that the H0 hypothesis is accepted, indicating that there is no significant difference in data between men and women; Otherwise, the difference is significant.

The results of ANOVA analysis showed that there was no significant difference in the distance between the palate data of male elderly and female elderly except for II ($p>0.05$). Therefore, gender differentiation is not required in the development of the intra-oral tongue pressure detection sensor for the elderly. However, when designing, the sensor referred to in II should be able to meet the minimum size requirements.

The results of ANOVA analysis (Table 4) showed that there was no significant difference in the distance between the palate data of male elderly and female elderly except for II ($p>0.05$). Therefore, gender differentiation is not required in the development of the intra-oral tongue pressure detection sensor for the elderly. However, when designing, the sensor referred to in II should be able to meet the minimum size requirements.

Among the elderly people who participated in this study, 11% have the tapered dental arch (Tapered group), 43% have the ovoid dental arch (Ovoid group), and 46% have the square dental arch (Square group) Figure 2).

Table 4. ANOVA analysis results of hard palate data for male and female elderly individuals.

ANOVA

|  |  | Sum of Squares | df | Mean Square | F | Sig. |
|---|---|---|---|---|---|---|
| I | Between Groups | 21.076 | 1 | 21.076 | 2.443 | .122 |
|  | Within Groups | 638.470 | 74 | 8.628 |  |  |
|  | Total | 659.545 | 75 |  |  |  |
| II | Between Groups | 78.408 | 1 | 78.408 | 6.754 | .011 |
|  | Within Groups | 859.024 | 74 | 11.608 |  |  |
|  | Total | 937.432 | 75 |  |  |  |
| III | Between Groups | 15.355 | 1 | 15.355 | .757 | .387 |
|  | Within Groups | 1500.884 | 74 | 20.282 |  |  |
|  | Total | 1516.240 | 75 |  |  |  |
| IV | Between Groups | .145 | 1 | .145 | .098 | .755 |
|  | Within Groups | 109.461 | 74 | 1.479 |  |  |
|  | Total | 109.606 | 75 |  |  |  |
| V | Between Groups | .970 | 1 | .970 | .264 | .609 |
|  | Within Groups | 272.300 | 74 | 3.680 |  |  |
|  | Total | 273.270 | 75 |  |  |  |
| VI | Between Groups | 24.423 | 1 | 24.423 | 1.911 | .171 |
|  | Within Groups | 945.703 | 74 | 12.780 |  |  |
|  | Total | 970.126 | 75 |  |  |  |
| β | Between Groups | 36.394 | 1 | 36.394 | 2.199 | .142 |
|  | Within Groups | 1224.986 | 74 | 16.554 |  |  |
|  | Total | 1261.380 | 75 |  |  |  |

According to the results of Spearman correlation analysis (Table 5), the angle $\beta$ is significantly correlated with II, III, IV, V VI. Among them, it is positively correlated with IV V VI, and negatively correlated with II and III, and not correlated with I.

302

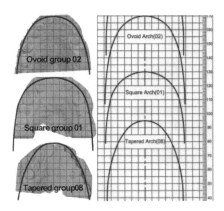

Figure 2. Three different dental arch classifications.

Table 5. ANOVA analysis results of hard palate data for male and female elderly individuals.

| | | | β | I |
|---|---|---|---|---|
| Spearman's rho | β | Correlation Coeficient | 1.000 | -.174 |
| | | | . | .133 |
| | | Sig 2-tailed) | 76 | 76 |
| | | N | | |
| | I | Correlation Coeficient | -.174 | 1.000 |
| | | | .133 | . |
| | | Sig 2-tailed) | 76 | 76 |
| | | N | | |

| | | | β | II |
|---|---|---|---|---|
| Spearman's rho | β | Correlation Coeficient | 1.000 | -.228* |
| | | | . | .047 |
| | | Sig 2-tailed) | 76 | 76 |
| | | N | | |
| | II | Correlation Coeficient | -.228* | 1.000 |
| | | | .047 | . |
| | | Sig 2-tailed) | 76 | 76 |
| | | N | | |

| | | | β | III |
|---|---|---|---|---|
| Spearman's rho | β | Correlation Coeficient | 1.000 | -.372** |
| | | | . | .001 |
| | | Sig 2-tailed) | 76 | 76 |
| | | N | | |
| | III | Correlation Coeficient | -.372** | 1.000 |
| | | | .001 | . |
| | | Sig 2-tailed) | 76 | 76 |
| | | N | | |

| | | | β | IV |
|---|---|---|---|---|
| Spearman's rho | β | Correlation Coeficient | 1.000 | .507** |
| | | | . | .000 |
| | | Sig 2-tailed) | 76 | 76 |
| | | N | | |
| | IV | Correlation Coeficient | .507** | 1.000 |
| | | | .000 | . |

(continued)

Table 5. Continued

| | | | β | IV |
|---|---|---|---|---|
| | | Sig 2-tailed) | 76 | 76 |
| | | N | | |

| | | | β | V |
|---|---|---|---|---|
| Spearman's rho | β | Correlation Coeficient | 1.000 | .418** |
| | | | . | .000 |
| | | Sig 2-tailed) | 76 | 76 |
| | | N | | |
| | V | Correlation Coeficient | .418** | 1.000 |
| | | | .000 | . |
| | | Sig 2-tailed) | 76 | 76 |
| | | N | | |

| | | | β | VI |
|---|---|---|---|---|
| Spearman's rho | β | Correlation Coeficient | 1.000 | .649** |
| | | | . | .000 |
| | | Sig 2-tailed) | 76 | 76 |
| | | N | | |
| | VI | Correlation Coeficient | .649** | 1.000 |
| | | | .000 | . |
| | | Sig 2-tailed) | 76 | 76 |
| | | N | | |

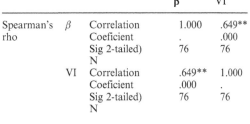

Figure 3. VI and β scatter plot of distribution table.

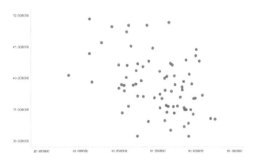

Figure 4. III and β scatter plot of distribution table.

303

Table 6. Anthropometry measurements of the hard palate in the elderly percentile.

|    | I | II | III | IV | V | VI | β |
|----|----|----|----|----|----|----|----|
| 5  | 20.54056860 | 25.28816270 | 32.08312055 | 3.78557550 | 9.05433535 | 21.62430245 | 46.44596240 |
| 10 | 21.85752160 | 25.95059030 | 33.28575760 | 3.97452060 | 9.29470670 | 23.69554930 | 49.93682200 |
| 25 | 23.22027575 | 28.05504025 | 35.34537300 | 4.86293475 | 10.46670775 | 24.68178600 | 51.85413900 |
| 50 | 25.08311950 | 30.22472200 | 38.58990700 | 5.76412700 | 12.24549350 | 27.40311150 | 55.94450750 |
| 75 | 27.02011075 | 33.21631475 | 41.99731150 | 6.40911550 | 13.07060775 | 29.23444500 | 58.38326375 |
| 90 | 30.07889240 | 36.08959890 | 45.18084660 | 7.53946700 | 14.35911930 | 31.96885900 | 59.75356860 |
| 95 | 31.49982975 | 37.03879155 | 48.31112805 | 7.79109645 | 15.55695955 | 34.13081865 | 60.50624530 |

The angle $\beta$ should be taken into account when designing the aspect ratio of the sensor. The larger the angle, the longer and narrower the sensor as a whole, and the smaller the angle, the shorter and wider the sensor as a whole Figure 3–4).

## 4 DISCUSSION

This subject actually collected and measured the plaster model of the palate of the elderly, and collated and analyzed the measured data to determine the human measurement features of the palate of the elderly and provide data reference for the ergonomic design of the intra-oral tongue pressure detection sensor Percentile Table of Palate Size for the Elderly).

Generally, measuring the human size of the palate is overlooked by ergonomics experts when compared to other anthropometric data. However, the current research makes the palate more than just a body part that assists in forming food pellets. The sensor placed on the palate can not only be used to detect the tongue pressure, but also assist the quadriplegia patients in controlling the intra-oral mechanical arm with the tongue to perform some daily activities (Andreasen Struijk, Egsgaard, et al. 2017). It can also assist the severely disabled in completing computer text typing with the oral cavity, enabling the severely disabled to control the computer even if they lose both hands (Andreasen Struijk, Bentsen, et al. 2017).

For people who need special care, a better sensor size design can help them to touch the sensor with their tongue more accurately, reduce the discomfort that the sensor may bring, and increase comfort and safety (Hori et al. 2009). In that study, the sensor was divided into three sizes for better measurement data, which is also agreed in this study. Through data analysis, it is concluded that the magnitude of angle $\beta$ affects the proportion of the sensor. Sensors that are too long, too wide, too short, or too narrow may increase the measurement error. In particular, sensors that are too long or too wide may bring discomfort to the wearer.

## 5 CONCLUSION

In this study, the size of the elderly in the 5th, 50th, and 95th percentiles is recommended as a reference for preliminary design Table 6).

## REFERENCES

Andreasen Struijk L. N. S., Bentsen B., Gaihede M., & Lontis, E. R 2017). Error-free text typing performance of an inductive intra-oral tongue computer interface for severely disabled individuals. *IEEE Transactions on Neural Systems and Rehabilitation Engineering*, 25(11), 2094–2104. https://doi.org/10.1109/TNSRE.2017.2706524

Andreasen Struijk L. N. S., Egsgaard L. L., Lontis R., Gaihede, M., & Bentsen, B 2017). Wireless intraoral tongue control of an assistive robotic arm for individuals with tetraplegia. *Journal of NeuroEngineering and Rehabilitation*, 14(1), 110. https://doi.org/10.1186/s12984-017-0330-2

Arakawa I., Igarashi K., Imamura Y., Müller F., Abou-Ayash, S., & Schimmel, M 2021). Variability in tongue pressure among elderly and young healthy cohorts: A systematic review and meta-analysis. *Journal of Oral Rehabilitation*, 48(4), 430–448. https://doi.org/10.1111/joor.13076

Baijens L. W., Clavé P., Cras P., Ekberg O., Forster A., Kolb, G., Leners J. C., Masiero, S., Mateos del Nozal, J., Ortega, O., Smithard D. G., Speyer R., & Walshe M 2016). European society for swallowing disorders &ndash; european union geriatric medicine society white paper: oropharyngeal dysphagia as a geriatric syndrome. *Clinical Interventions in Aging*, Volume 11, 1403–1428. https://doi.org/10.2147/CIA.S107750

Chiba Y., Motoyoshi M., & Namura S 2003). Tongue pressure on loop of transpalatal arch during deglutition. *American Journal of Orthodontics and Dentofacial Orthopedics*, 123(1), 29–34. https://doi.org/10.1067/mod.2003.51

Cook I. J., & Kahrilas P. J 1999). AGA technical review on management of oropharyngeal dysphagia. *Gastroenterology*, 116(2), 455–478. https://doi.org/10.1016/S0016-5085(99)70144-7

Dianat I., Molenbroek J., & Castellucci H. I 2018). A review of the methodology and applications of anthropometry in ergonomics and product design. *Ergonomics*, 61(12), 1696–1720. https://doi.org/10.1080/00140139.2018.1502817

Fujishima I., Fujiu-Kurachi M., Arai H., Hyodo M., Kagaya, H., Maeda K., Mori T., Nishioka S., Oshima F., Ogawa S., Ueda, K., Umezaki T., Wakabayashi H., Yamawaki, M., & Yoshimura Y 2019). Sarcopenia and dysphagia: Position paper by four professional organizations: Dysphagia due to sarcopenia. *Geriatrics & Gerontology International*, 19(2), 91–97. https://doi.org/10.1111/ggi.13591

Fukuoka T., Ono T., Hori K., & Kariyasu M 2022). Effects of tongue-strengthening exercise on tongue strength and effortful swallowing pressure in young healthy adults: A pilot study. *Journal of Speech,*

*Language, and Hearing Research*, 65(5), 1686–1696. https://doi.org/10.1044/2022_JSLHR-21-00331

Fukuoka T., Ono T., Hori K., Wada Y., Uchiyama Y., Kasama, S., Yoshikawa H., & Domen K 2019). Tongue pressure measurement and videofluoroscopic study of swallowing in patients with parkinson's disease. *Dysphagia*, 34(1), 80–88. https://doi.org/10.1007/s00455-018-9916-5

Furuya J., Nakamura S., Ono T., & Suzuki T 2012). Tongue pressure production while swallowing water and pudding and during dry swallow using a sensor sheet system: Tongue pressure production during swallowing. *Journal of Oral Rehabilitation*, 39(9), 684–691. https://doi.org/10.1111/j.1365-2842.2012.02319.x

Gingrich L. L., Stierwalt J. A. G., Hageman C. F., & LaPointe, L. L 2012). Lingual propulsive pressures across consistencies generated by the anteromedian and posteromedian tongue by healthy young adults. *Journal of speech, Language, and Hearing Research*, 55(3), 960–972. https://doi.org/10.1044/1092-4388 (2011/10-0357)

Hamanaka-Kondoh S., Kondoh J., Tamine K., Hori K., Fujiwara S., Maeda Y., Matsumura T., Yasui K., Fujimura H., Sakoda S., & Ono, T 2014). Tongue pressure during swallowing is decreased in patients with duchenne muscular dystrophy. *Neuromuscular Disorders*, 24(6), 474–481. https://doi.org/10.1016/j.nmd.2014.03.003

Hori K., Ono T., & Nokubi T 2006). Coordination of tongue pressure and jaw movement in mastication. *Journal of Dental Research*, 85(2), 187–191. https://doi.org/10.1177/154405910608500214

Hori K., Ono T., Tamine K., Kondo J., Hamanaka S., Maeda Y., Dong J., & Hatsuda M 2009). Newly developed sensor sheet for measuring tongue pressure during swallowing. *Journal of Prosthodontic Research*, 53(1), 28–32. https://doi.org/10.1016/j.jpor.2008.08.008

Iyota K., Mizutani S., Kishimoto H., Oku S., Tani A., Yatsugi H., Chu T., Liu X., & Kashiwazaki H 2022). Effect of isometric tongue lifting exercise on oral function, physical function, and body composition in community-dwelling older individuals: A pilot study. *Gerontology*, 68(6), 644–654. https://doi.org/10.1159/000518270

Kim H. D., Choi J. B., Yoo S. J., Chang M. Y., Lee S. W., & Park J. S 2017). Tongue-to-palate resistance training improves tongue strength and oropharyngeal swallowing function in subacute stroke survivors with dysphagia. *Journal of Oral Rehabilitation*, 44(1), 59–64. https://doi.org/10.1111/joor.12461

Lin C.-H., Chung S.-Y., Lin C.-T., & Hwu Y.-J 2021). Effect of tongue-to-palate resistance training on tongue strength in healthy adults. *Auris Nasus Larynx*, 48 (1), 116–123. https://doi.org/10.1016/j.anl.2020.07.014

Lin C.-J., Lee Y.-S., Hsu C.-F., Liu S.-J., Li J.-Y., Ho Y.-L., & Chen H.-H 2022). Effects of tongue strengthening exercises on tongue muscle strength: A systematic review and meta-analysis of randomized controlled trials. *Scientific Reports*, 12(1), 10438. https://doi.org/10.1038/s41598-022-14335-2

Nagashima K., Kikutani T., Miyashita T., Yajima Y., & Tamura, F 2021). Tongue muscle strength affects posterior pharyngeal wall advancement during swallowing: A cross-sectional study of outpatients with dysphagia. *Journal of Oral Rehabilitation*, 48(2), 169–175. https://doi.org/10.1111/joor.13120

Namiki C., Hara K., Tohara H., Kobayashi., Chantaramanee A., Nakagawa K., Saitou T., Yamaguchi K., Yoshimi K., Nakane A., & Minakuchi

S 2019). Tongue-pressure resistance training improves tongue and suprahyoid muscle functions simultaneously. *Clinical Interventions in Aging*, Volume 14, 601–608. https://doi.org/10.2147/CIA.S194808

Ono T., Hori K., & Nokubi T 2004). Pattern of tongue pressure on hard palate during swallowing. *Dysphagia*, 19(4), 259–264. https://doi.org/10.1007/s00455-004-0010-9

Plaza E., & Ruviaro Busanello-Stella A 2022). Effects of a tongue training program in Parkinson's disease: Analysis of electrical activity and strength of suprahyoid muscles. *Journal of Electromyography and Kinesiology*, 63, 102642. https://doi.org/10.1016/j.jelekin.2022.102642

Rolland Y., Czerwinski S., van Kan G. A., Morley J. E., Cesari M., Onder G., Woo J., Baumgartner R., Pillard F., Boirie Y., Chumlea W. M. C., & Vellas B 2008). Sarcopenia: Its assessment, etiology, pathogenesis, consequences and future perspectives. *The Journal of Nutrition Health and Aging*, 12(7), 433–450. https://doi.org/10.1007/BF02982704

Sardini E., Serpelloni M., & Fiorentini R 2013). Wireless intraoral sensor for the physiological monitoring of tongue pressure. 2013 Transducers & Eurosensors XXVII: *The 17th International Conference on Solid-State Sensors, Actuators and Microsystems* (TRANSDUCERS & EUROSENSORS XXVII), 1282–1285. https://doi.org/10.1109/Transducers.2013.6627010

Shaw S. M., & Martino R 2013). The Normal Swallow. *Otolaryngologic Clinics of North America*, 46(6), 937–956. https://doi.org/10.1016/j.otc.2013.09.006

Speyer R., Cordier R., Farneti D., Nascimento W., Pilz W., Verin E., Walshe M., & Woisard V 2022). White paper by the european society for swallowing disorders: screening and non-instrumental assessment for dysphagia in adults. *Dysphagia*, 37(2), 333–349. https://doi.org/10.1007/s00455-021-10283-7

Vandervoort. A. A 2002). Aging of the human neuromuscular system. *Muscle & Nerve*, 25(1), 17–25. https://doi.org/10.1002/mus.1215

Wang L., He X., Wang C., Wang Z., & Zhou X 2015). Anthropometric measurements of the female perineum for design of the opening shape of urination device. *International Journal of Industrial Ergonomics*, 46, 29–35. https://doi.org/10.1016/j.ergon.2015.01.004

Yang H.-X., Li F.-L., & Li L.-M 2021). Comparison of maxillary anterior mathematical proportions among 3 dental arch forms. *The Journal of Prosthetic Dentistry*, S0022391321006594. https://doi.org/10.1016/j.prosdent.2021.11.025

Yano J., Nagami S., Yokoyama T., Nakamura K., Kobayashi M., Odan Y., Hikasa M., Hanayama K., & Fukunaga, S 2021). Effects of tongue-strengthening self-exercises in healthy older adults: A non-randomized controlled trial. *Dysphagia*, 36(5), 925–935. https://doi.org/10.1007/s00455-020-10216-w

Youmans S. R., & Stierwalt J. A. G 2006). *Measures of Tongue Function Related to Normal Swallowing*. *Dysphagia*, 21(2), 102–111. https://doi.org/10.1007/s00455-006-9013-z

Yu M., & Gao X 2019). Tongue pressure distribution of individual normal occlusions and exploration of related factors. *Journal of Oral Rehabilitation*, 46(3), 249–256. https://doi.org/10.1111/joor.12741

Zadry H. R., Susanti L., & Rahmayanti D 2017). Ergonomics intervention on an alternative design of a spinal board. *International Journal of Occupational Safety and Ergonomics*, 23(3), 393–403. https://doi.org/10.1080/10803548.2016.1156843

*System Innovation for a Troubled World – Lam et al. (Eds)*
*© 2024 the Author(s), ISBN: 978-1-032-60846-4*

# A study on the strategies of integrating traditional chinese toad motifs into visual design

En-Wu Huang
*School of Design, Straits Institute of Technology, Fujian University of Technology, Fuzhou, China*
*Faculty of Innovation and Design, City University of Macau, Macau, China*

Bai-Yu Liu*, Chen Wang & Ya-Ling Yu
*School of Design, Straits Institute of Technology, Fujian University of Technology, Fuzhou, China*

ABSTRACT: Chinese excellent traditional culture has a long history. A Chinese traditional toad pattern is a kind of idealized image that has been deified and beautified by human beings. The application of this pattern shows the changing path of people's worship. With the innovation and development of the Chinese visual design industry, more and more attention is paid to the application of traditional toad patterns. Through the effective integration of Chinese traditional patterns and visual arts, we can carry forward and inherit Chinese excellent traditional culture and improve its artistic value. Based on this, from the perspective of design, the Chinese traditional toad pattern is taken as the research object, and the image analysis and induction methods are used to discuss and analyze the connotation and artistic characteristics of the Chinese traditional toad image. The analysis is carried out from the media carrier form, composition form, modeling angle, shape angle, theme creation, and style characteristics. And summarize the symbolism of the Chinese toad pattern. With visual design as the core, packaging design and clothing texture materials were classified, and cases were analyzed. Finally, innovative design strategies were proposed to make an effective combination of Chinese traditional toad patterns and visual designs and to provide referable suggestions for related industrial workers.

*Keywords*: Chinese traditional culture, Iconography, Toad pattern, Visual design

## 1 INTRODUCTION

By studying the cultural relics unearthed in China at this stage, it is not difficult to find that toad patterns appeared earlier because toad worship has a long history. Toad worship was popular in Guanto, Guanzhong, Bashu, and other areas, and toad patterns spread around the world. In Chinese tomb art, there are a large number of forms related to toad patterns, such as picture stones, silk paintings, and utensils, and the characteristics of toad patterns in Chinese culture mainly focus on modeling and pattern. Guide-toad designs are the best of them. The unique times and artistic charm make the toad pattern the cultural symbol of the Chinese nation in the history of Chinese decorative art, which is worth carrying forward and inheriting later generations.

## 2 CONNOTATION AND ARTISTIC CHARACTERISTICS

Under the influence of Chinese culture, toad patterns were infused by people's subjective ideas and

promoted the worship of spiritual images, and the culture of advocating immortals and Taoism also followed them. In the past dynasties, the toad pattern, as a representative of the auspicious animal, has been carrying people's yearning for a better world.

(1) In the form of media carriers, toad patterns are no longer limited to books and documents but are extended to different styles of sculpture and painting. The toad image on various products has its own characteristics due to different materials.
(2) In terms of composition form, toad patterns are usually arranged in accordance with the characteristics of symmetry and balance, dynamic and rhythmic, and dynamic and static combinations. In stone, the same decorative elements are arranged and aligned through symmetry, and balance is more representative of the stability and balance of patterns. Compared with symmetry and balance, it is characterized by different shapes on both sides. Dynamic refers to the dynamic shaping of the image in the portrait; while the picture itself is static, the dynamic images it creates

*Corresponding Author: BaiYuLiu8@outlook.com

DOI: 10.1201/9781003460763-61

echo each other. Rhythm refers to the dynamic images of the portrait with a certain sense of rhythm. The toad pattern seems to appear as a single pattern, but in fact, the motion effect produced by the rich movement changes can bring an impressive sense of rhythm to the picture, making the picture more vivid and multi-faceted.

(3) From the perspective of modeling, because of the different dynasties, each toad image has obvious characteristics. The toad image is widely spread in Chinese folklore; from the normal four-legged toad to the common three-legged toad image, it should be said that it is in line with the so-called strange evolution process created by humans. The characteristics of three-legged modeling are also the unique artistic image given to it by people to achieve the homogeneity and heterogeneity of its totemic semantics. [1] The three-legged Golden Toad is also called "Golden Toad" in the book, which has the meaning of prosperous wealth. [2]

(4) From the perspective of morphology, toads can be divided into two classes: upright and hopping. The former has more posture, both side and back, and a more positive side image and complex changes. The front side includes the image of a complete toad formed by holding a weapon on the back side and a respectful serving or holding a medicine pestle. The latter is more on the positive side, but the side image is relatively stiff.

(5) From the theme creation analysis, most of the ancient people had the love of eternal life because the toad pattern is often regarded as the messenger role of the West Queen Mother in myths and legends, so the toad pattern often appeared as a foil, most of the time to bless the owner of the tomb ascension into the immortal role. [3]

(6) From the perspective of style characteristics, the idea of immortality was popular in the Han Dynasty, which had an impact on the social culture at that time, resulting in the subconscious deepening of the immortal thought of Han culture. [4] Under the influence of this thought, the image of a toad began to break away from its "ugly physical appearance" and was endowed with an interesting soul.

Through the vicissitudes of many dynasties, the forms, pictographs, and abstractions of toad patterns in Chinese culture blend together, resulting in the formation of two types of toad patterns: realistic and abstract. Refers to the realistic modeling used to reproduce its general shape features; abstract toad patterns are transformed into points, lines, and surfaces on the premise of realism and then recombined with other objects. But both are highly symbolic, as the fairy beasts that people believe in assist them in their ascension, symbolizing a better vision.

## 3 VISUAL DESIGN AND APPLICATION ANALYSIS

### 3.1 The field of packaging design

Modern packaging design shows the cultural connotation through its packaging products to convey the designer's design concept, so that excellent packaging designers design overall packaging, pay more attention to national cultural connotations and ideas, in the packaging design, input innovative elements, and promote the overall packaging design from multiple angles to show the integration of new and old culture under the design development law. Only the traditional pattern and artistic concept, talent characteristics, cultural environment, and other factors actively applied in the packaging design will be enough to express the depth. In terms of packaging design, the image characteristics of the toad pattern and the use of color are re-created and applied. The toad pattern is integrated into different subjects, colors, materials, and other aspects, which can mostly reflect different styles of design. While highlighting the national cultural spirit, modern people often choose design and packaging containing auspicious characteristics. Once again, deeply feel the emotional experience brought by traditional culture.

Xiao Creative used to be known as Lucky Toad Packaging Design. Xiao Creative is a design brand in Taiwan with the cultural connotation of the design to meet the needs of the public in modern life. The founder of the brand is committed to integrating Western culture or design thinking with Chinese culture and integrating traditional culture into the packaging design. This group of packaging designs is based on the traditional charm toad, simplified from a modern aesthetic point of view, consisting of two geometric shapes: The hemispherical shape formed by the overlooking circle and the semicircle of the profile begins to develop, connecting the curve of tai chi with a continuous corner line and running through the surface of the streamline, forming a simple and symmetrical shape full of traditional charm and organic life. This set of packaging designs combines the elements of a toad pattern. Based on the designer's imagination and social sensitivity, the toad pattern is integrated, which has an obvious modern style. The metallic color highlights the wealth implied by a toad.

### 3.2 Clothing texture design field

As people pay more and more attention to culture, traditional culture has gained the favor of more and more people, and those patterns and patterns with auspicious meanings in traditional culture can be found in the shadow of the current fashion design, through modern improvement and deformation, showing a new trend of development. The appearance of traditional toad patterns in clothing is mostly in groups or as a small pattern in the whole group of patterns. Today, the toad pattern in clothing has long been separated from the original style, but abstracted design elements are extracted from the concrete toad elements. However, the design concept of modern clothing emphasizes the characteristics of patterns. To better meet the aesthetic requirements of modern people, the modern version of the toad pattern is typical and more recognizable, based on the traditional toad pattern to convey the deep meaning and connotation of the pattern.

(Figure 1) The whole picture is divided into upper and lower parts, and the upper part is divided into the pattern of the toad and jade rabbit tile in the Han Dynasty. By extracting the elements of the toad pattern, it can be seen that the back of the toad pattern extracted has many dots, which are cleverly in line with the special fabric designed by Rosanna Bishop. Rosanna Bishop, a London-based printed textile designer and graduate of the Royal College of Art, is keen to combine traditional culture with printed fabrics. Ten years ago, Rosanna Bishop saw a video of an endangered toad hatching its young through the skin on its back in a lecture, which deeply touched her. Therefore, she took it as inspiration, narrated the natural reaction between nature and herself, infused her thoughts on nature, and completed her design. The resonance from the design thinking of traditional Chinese toad patterns and Western printing textile designers both pays attention to the egg-like dots of different sizes on the back of the toad. However, in modern clothing printing culture, designers are better at discovering and absorbing its elements, applying the elements of

toad eggs to fabric art and bionic design to clothing design. The bionic factor is closely combined with the clothing design to produce special fabric with a toad pattern, which is no longer limited to the basis of discovery and further pattern exploration.

## 4 INNOVATIVE DESIGN STRATEGY

The above two categories of packaging design and clothing texture design are discussed, and the excellent cases involving toad patterns are analyzed. It is also concluded that the toad pattern in modern design applications is more a use of the toad pattern left over in ancient China to carry on the implied extension of modern things and even extend the new connotation. To some extent, this "new", which is a form of innovation, is the continuation of the traditional meaning based on the original culture to achieve the continuation of toad pattern culture. The innovative pattern should emphasize cultural information transmission and cultural continuity of pattern. [5] Based on the continuation of patterns, almost the bionic concept is applied throughout the whole design application, no matter in the West or the Chinese side, no matter in the packaging design or the clothing texture design. From the perspective of bionics, it is clearly found that it is expressed in terms of form, color, and composition. Then the innovation combined with the traditional Chinese toad pattern is to re-conceive the original toad pattern characteristics and continue the traditional toad pattern meaning and connotation. Starting from the analysis of aesthetic characteristics, it summarizes the innovative strategy analysis into three levels: "form", "color" and "structure".

### 4.1 Precise refining of "form"

Pattern in the application of "shape", should be taken as "shape" but should not be subject to "shape". "Shape" represents the unique Chinese traditional toad pattern, and the artistic modeling of the toad pattern is the artistic concentration of the toad pattern. When the pattern is innovative, it should avoid simple application, make a high summary of the traditional toad pattern according to its actual characteristics, and pay attention to the appropriate combination of popular styles in contemporary design in the refining process. In terms of specific steps and processes, first of all, the toad shape of the toad pattern should be extracted and extracted into linear characteristics, and the "shape" of the toad pattern formed by linear characteristics can promote the toad pattern to burst out and release the new light of life.

From the perspective of packaging design, morphological bionics have been one of the most

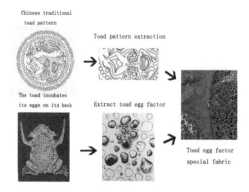

Figure 1. Comparison of elements extraction of a pattern of toad between Chinese and foreign animals.

important means of expression to convey the product concept. This kind of morphological bionics thought is given to packaging design to realize the unity of design concepts and art. More importantly, it is demonstrated by concrete forms of expression, imitating the external characteristics of natural creatures and following the style trend of industrialization. Moderate innovation and change in style and concept, such as modern style, industrial style, and minimalist style, to extend the new development trend of packaging design. Similarly, bionic design is also very common in clothing texture design. This innovation in design method not only saves cost but also integrates with nature better, becoming more artistic, decorative, and practical. Of course, the refinement of toad patterns is not a simple copy but a precise refinement of traditional Chinese modeling. Based on the original shape, traditional toad modeling techniques and contemporary forms of expression are combined into modern design to show the concept of design to advocate the characteristics of Chinese national culture.

## 4.2 *The innovative auxiliary color of "color"*

Color bionics is the use of natural colors to convey product information, arouse people's related emotions, and meet people's psychological needs. Therefore, in today's design, color bionics has visual aesthetic, decorative, symbolic, and other features. The strongest is the visual impact, which is relatively direct and quick to attract people's attention and promote the formation of the aesthetic conception of the design. The decorative and symbolic are mainly the combination of natural material colors and the use of such colors in the design to show the rich connotation of the product. [6] Combined with relevant historical documents and other materials, it is found that the pattern of toads on cultural relics does not have clear iconic colors to be divided, and only yellow, blue, white, dark green, dark brown, and other colors are common, which is not much.

Both in terms of packaging design and clothing texture design, the original colors can be inherited based on traditional Chinese toad patterns, and the Han toad patterns can be innovatively supplementary colors combined with new design characteristics. Taking inheritance as the starting point, the coordination and foil function of toad patterns in supplementary colors can be kept. The color change of the toad can only be adjusted for the specific contemporary practical application, and the aesthetic perspective can be added to highlight the aesthetic characteristics. Through the psychological feelings of modern people about color and the feedback factors of the external environment, different colors can be used to directly express the color beauty of a design product, to make people feel physically and mentally

happy, and to produce visual enjoyment. To ensure the uniformity of color, it is applied to contemporary packaging and clothing texture design to achieve the inheritance and continuation of the Han toad pattern.

## 4.3 *The design reorganization of "structure"*

The concept of "structure" refers to the reconstruction and extraction of traditional toad patterns. In fact, it is very characteristic of Chinese culture and art to derive new aesthetic meaning by conforming to toad patterns through this design concept. Specifically, the "structure" of the toad pattern refers to the division according to the law of symmetry and balance, dynamic and rhythm, which is inseparable from the decomposition of the composition angles of points, lines, and planes, which can be decomposed and new elements can be found to extract the detachment and deformation of elements, and the distribution elements can be recombined. It is precisely because of this accurate separation that the extracted essence can be obtained. Thus, a new toad pattern is integrated and reorganized. The extracted new toad pattern has become a new pattern after undergoing deformation and abstraction. When it is applied to the texture design of packaging and clothing, it is necessary to highlight the characteristics of reconstruction and convey the traditional meaning at the same time, so that it has more contemporary freshness. The innovative reorganization and application method conveyed by "structure" also requires designers in terms of relevant ability, which can not only do a good job in visual design but also build on the understanding of the traditional toad pattern meaning. Under the premise of innovation and reorganization, it presents the contemporary cultural implications of the toad pattern applied to packaging and clothing texture.

## 5 CONCLUSION

On the whole, in the current era of globalization and integrated development, people are required to explore, analyze, summarize, and innovate national culture, which requires us to absorb the essence, discard the bad components, and not copy the traditional image culture. It is necessary to extend the toad pattern, inherit and develop from multiple perspectives of history and art, and integrate with contemporary culture. Based on image data, literature, and books, this paper aims to explore the unique toad pattern in Chinese history and culture and analyze the innovative ideas of patterns for modern design strategies, which is to provide valuable suggestions for toad patterns in various fields of contemporary design in the future. In today's contemporary design of toad patterns, there is a deep analysis of traditional pattern culture to build new elements, design products to give depth of art and culture content, enhance the cultural value of modern design, and promote the economic development of modern design. Every innovative integration of the toad pattern provides a new idea for the inheritance and development of the toad pattern and creates more possibilities.

## REFERENCES

[1] Wu Wei, Zhang Xiaohua. Interpretation of The art symbol of the three-legged golden toad [J]. Decoration, 2008(02):120–121.

[2] Cui Chaoqun, Xu Lei. A brief analysis of the semantic symbol of Jinchan's art symbol [J]. *Popular Literature and Art*, 2011(01):130–131.

[3] Wen Leping, Zhou Guangming. *Analysis Of Seal Shape Of "Liu He" Jade Seal Unearthed From Haihunhou Tomb [J]*. Cultural Relics of Southern China, 2020(06):167–179.

[4] Liang Y. *Image of Toad In Ancient China And Its Symbolic Significance [J]*. Journal of Zhuzhou Institute of Technology, 2002(02): 70–72 + 76. (in Chinese with English abstract)

[5] Xu C. Study on Virtual Restoration Method of Ancient Architecture – Taking Tang Palace Cluster as an example [J]. *Art of Design Research*, 2019, 54(06):89–94.

[6] Liang Jinming. Research on the Application of Bionic Concept in Modern Packaging Design [J]. *Design*, 2021, 34(21):38–40.

*System Innovation for a Troubled World – Lam et al. (Eds)*
© 2024 the Author(s), ISBN: 978-1-032-60846-4

# Research on the construction of service design elements system for rural homestays

Ya-Ling Yu*
*School of Design, Straits Institute of Technology, Fujian University of Technology, Fuzhou, China*

Xiang-Yuan Zeng
*School of Design, Straits Institute of Technology, Fujian University of Technology, Fuzhou, China*
*Regional Intangible Cultural Heritage and Design Research Center, Fujian Institute of Technology,*
*Fuzhou, China*

Bai-Yu Liu & Chen Wang
*School of Design, Straits Institute of Technology, Fujian University of Technology, Fuzhou, China*

ABSTRACT: This paper applies service design thinking and methods to thoroughly explore the formation mechanisms of rural homestays. Based on this exploration, the paper analyzes the rural homestay design system under the paradigm of service design, focusing on the three elements of stakeholders, service system, and service process. Through analyzing these three elements, a theoretical model of service design for rural homestays is constructed, providing theoretical support and reference for the service design and planning of rural homestays, ultimately improving the service quality of rural homestays and promoting the sustainable development of the rural homestay industry.

*Keywords*: Rural homestays, Service design, Service experience

## 1 INTRODUCTION

Since China entered the era of mass tourism, people's travel demands have gradually shifted towards generalization, diversification, and personalization. To cope with the new development trends of the tourism industry, the concept of "holistic tourism" has been officially introduced at the national level. Rural areas have become the best experimental ground for holistic tourism, which refers to using the rural environment as a basis and involving various industries, sectors, and residents in rural tourism development to promote the smooth development of rural tourism and the effective integration of rural industrial structure. [1] As an emerging product of rural tourism, rural homestays currently face various issues such as poor infrastructure, a lack of cultural connotation, and limited leisure experiences, which do not provide a good service experience for tourists. Therefore, against the backdrop of the widespread development of holistic tourism and the common challenges faced by rural homestays, service design can re-examine products, brands, business models, and operation processes from a holistic and systematic perspective and make adjustments to optimize the service system of rural homestays and improve the quality of homestay services, and meet the increasingly upgraded accommodation needs of consumers.

## 2 CONCEPTUAL ANALYSIS

### 2.1 Rural homestays

According to the current location of homestays, they can be divided into rural homestays and urban homestays. Rural homestays are generally located in rural areas, while urban homestays are typically located in city centers. The focus of this study is on rural homestays located in rural areas. In 2017, the China National Tourism Administration issued the "Basic Requirements and Evaluation for Tourism Homestays", which defined the concept of rural homestays as follows: rural homestays refer to small-scale accommodation facilities established by rural households based on local idle resources, providing tourists with the opportunity to experience local nature, culture, and production modes. [2]

### 2.2 Service design

Service design is a relatively new topic in the field of design, and there is no unified and clear definition for it yet. As Mark Stickdorn mentioned in "This is

*Corresponding Author: ya-lingyu@outlook.com

DOI: 10.1201/9781003460763-62

Service Design Thinking": "If you ask ten people about service design, you will get at least eleven different answers". [3] Although there is no unified definition of service design among scholars, from the perspective of design, the essence of service design research is about the systematic design of people, objects, behaviors, society, and environment in a service context, as well as the service and experience of the entire system. In general, service design is a design activity that takes users as the main perspective, involves effective planning and organization of the systemic relationships between people, objects, behaviors, environment, and society in service, and uses design thinking to achieve systemic innovation in service processes and touchpoints, ultimately improving user experience and service quality.

## 3   FORMATION MECHANISM OF RURAL HOMESTAYS

### 3.1   *Formation conditions*

First, natural conditions are essential for the formation of rural homestays. Rural homestays are located in rural areas, and the quality of the natural environment in rural areas serves as the background and foundation for the development of this economic industry. Rural areas often boast beautiful ecological environments, stunning natural landscapes, unique folk cultures, and idle resident resources, as well as distinctive production activities and ways of life. The main reason for tourists to visit rural areas is the differences between rural and urban areas in terms of the natural environment, way of life, cultural characteristics, social economy, etc. In other words, everything that is different from tourists' own lives in rural tourist destinations is attractive tourism resources, and these resources specifically refer to the unique living environment of the villagers.

Second, social conditions play a role in the formation of rural homestays. With the continuous development of China's economy and the intensification of urbanization, an increasing number of urban residents are eager to visit rural areas and experience natural scenery, and rural homestays have a broad market space for potential customers. As tourists' demands for beautiful environments, localized products, unique experiences, and high-quality services increase during their travels, the intrinsic demand drives the arrival of the era of high-quality tourism, and rural homestays emerge as a new form of upgraded rural tourism beyond traditional farmhouse-style accommodations.

### 3.2   *Reasons for formation*

First, in terms of political policies, under the strategic background of rural revitalization in the new era, the central government of China has recognized tourism as an important industry for rural development and has repeatedly mentioned in its policy documents the need to vigorously develop rural tourism and leisure agriculture. In recent years, rural tourism management departments at all levels have attached great importance to the spirit of the central government's policy documents and have successively issued a series of policy documents to support the development of rural tourism in various aspects, such as land use, finance, public services, brand building, and advertising and promotion. Policy innovation and institutional supply have promoted the formation of rural homestays. Second, in terms of folk customs, as an ancient agricultural country with thousands of years of development, China has rich and distinctive folk customs, ranging from village architecture to farmland orchards, from production methods to living customs, all of which constitute local cultural characteristics. These folk customs themselves have cultural connotations and can be transformed into tourism products with prominent cultural characteristics. [4] Rural homestays rely on these unique cultural characteristics of rural areas, which are the fundamental reasons that attract travelers.

### 3.3   *Design system for rural homestays*

From the perspective of design rationale, the formation of rural homestays is inevitably a result of specific needs in a particular context, involving adaptation to external factors and the rationality of internal factors. [5] It is the result of the joint action of external and internal factors in a specific environment.

By incorporating the thinking of design rationale into the design system of rural homestay products and services, we can explore the design system of rural homestays under the paradigm of service design (Table 1). The external factors of design rationale mainly focus on considering two major categories of stakeholders: people and the environment, which are the service subjects of rural homestays. In addition, there may be external factors such as regulations, politics, and economics that can affect and constrain the design. In service design, it is not just the design of physical "objects". The whole process of factors influencing the design is complex, and external factors need to be fully considered and utilized, which is similar to the "affair" and "reason" in design rationale [6]. Therefore, from external factors to internal factors, it includes both product and service aspects. In terms of products, it mainly includes physical and conceptual aspects, including product principles, structures, materials, etc. In terms of services, it mainly includes service processes, touchpoints, cooperation models, etc., which are the service objects of rural homestays, also known as service content. Design rationale, as a "methodology for

Table 1. Rural homestay service design system.

| Rural Homestay Service Design System | Internal Factors (Service Objects) | Visualized Products | Catering; Homestay Buildings; Furniture and Facilities; Cultural and Creative Products; Hardware and Software for Activities |
|---|---|---|---|
| | | Services | Service Processes; Service Touchpoints; Collaboration Models; Profit Models; Management Level |
| | External Factors (Service Providers) | People | Homestay Operators; Staff; Tourists; Villagers; Collaboration Partners; Suppliers |
| | | Environment | Natural Geography and Environment; Transportation Environment |
| | | Policies and Regulations | Public Transportation-related Policies; Consumer Rights and Interests |

human-made things", focuses on the structure and relationship of things rather than individual elements and grasps the rational context of "affairs". In service design, this is also known as service ecology, which means that in service design, the existing relationships and needs of stakeholders are analyzed, and the service process is the execution path. The research on the service objects of rural homestays and the appropriate relationship between the two is reflected in the service ecology relationship.

## 4 CONSTRUCTION OF THE SERVICE DESIGN THEORETICAL MODEL FOR RURAL HOMESTAY ECOLOGICAL SYSTEM

### 4.1 Stakeholders of rural homestays

The development of the comprehensive tourism model has strengthened cooperation among various industries, with the participation of local residents under the coordination and supervision of government departments, leading to numerous stakeholders in the operation of rural homestays. These stakeholders can be broadly categorized into three types based on core users, internal systems, and cooperative relationships, as summarized by the author through methods such as online questionnaires, interviews, and literature research, from the perspective of comprehensive tourism (Figure 1).

Core users, namely the tourists of rural tourism, are the main service recipients, and their interests are reflected in two aspects. Basic demands include personal and property safety, well-developed road transportation and infrastructure, a clean environment, and sanitation. Advanced demands include experiencing local culture, scenery, and emotions and obtaining high-quality homestay services.

Internal system, including homestay operators, service staff, cleaning personnel, etc., who are responsible for the daily operation of the rural homestay service system. Their demands include a

Figure 1. Stakeholders diagram.

good working environment, fair remuneration, and sustainable development of the homestay.

Cooperative partners, including government departments, suppliers, cooperation partners, online platforms, etc., provide diverse operational possibilities for the rural homestay service system and support the effective completion of the service chain with external resources. The interests of government departments lie in improving the development level of the homestay industry, promoting rural economic development, and realizing rural revitalization. The demands of other stakeholders are unified in participating in benefit distribution and obtaining high investment returns.

### 4.2 Service ecosystem of rural homestays

Based on the analysis of stakeholders' interests in rural homestays, the service ecosystem of the rural homestay service system is depicted using a service ecosystem map, which shows the dynamic mechanisms that support the existence of the system from three aspects: information flow, fund flow, and material flow (Figure 2).

The main components of this system include tourists, the government, partners, homestay hosts, and online platforms. First, in terms of material flow, homestay managers oversee the

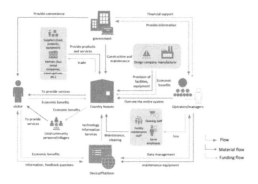

Figure 2.    Service ecosystem.

operation of the entire rural homestay system. Suppliers and partners deliver material flow mainly in the form of food ingredients, cultural and creative materials, and bus transportation to rural homestays. Material flow between government departments and rural homestays includes the construction of homestays, land provision, and business permits. Material flow between rural homestays and tourists includes cultural and creative products, catering, entertainment facilities, and the homestay accommodation itself. Second, in terms of information flow, the platform provides tourists with information such as homestay costs, homestay environment, service items, and user evaluations, and provides homestay managers with information such as total orders and user feedback. The information flow between government departments and homestay managers mainly includes policy support and business conditions. Finally, in terms of fund flow, the main flow of funds is between government departments and homestay operators in the form of loans, taxes, and fees. The flow of funds between homestay managers and cleaning personnel, maintenance personnel, and service personnel is in the form of employment wages. The flow of funds between tourists and the platform mainly involves the payment of fees. The flow of funds between rural homestays and suppliers and partners mainly involves payment of supply costs and the sharing of cooperative benefits. The flow of funds between rural homestays and local villagers mainly involves the flow of funds from increased income and job opportunities.

### 4.3    The service process diagram of rural homestays

Based on Marc Stickdorn's service design process steps (Figure 3), the service process of rural homestays can be divided into four stages: explore, create, reflect, and implement. The main purpose of the explore stage is to gain user insights, gaining a deep and comprehensive understanding of users

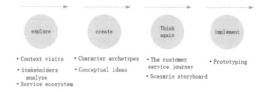

Figure 3.    Service process map.

through context research, stakeholder analysis, and service ecosystem analysis. In the create stage, based on the research from the previous stage, task role models are created, and service design methods are used to generate a large number of service design concepts. In the reflect stage, service scenarios, such as scenario storyboards, are used to present the overall outline and usage details of service concepts, facilitating reflection and discussion. In the implement stage, the previous creative ideas are integrated to create service design prototypes while optimizing the details of touchpoints. Moreover, the structure of the rural homestay service process is iterative, which means that each step in the implementation of the service process may require going back to a previous step for refinement.

### 4.4    Theoretical model of service design for rural homestays

Analyzing the industrial form of rural homestays in the context of comprehensive tourism, based on a clear understanding of the formation mechanism of rural homestays and analyzing its design system from the perspective of design, this theoretical model of service design for rural homestays is derived (Figure 4).

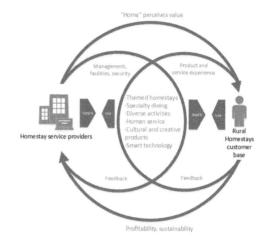

Figure 4.    Theoretical model of service design for rural homestays.

In the theoretical model of service design for rural homestays, there are two main stakeholder groups: the homestay customers and the homestay service providers, which are represented by the stakeholder diagram mentioned above. Rural homestays, influenced and constrained by external factors such as people, environment, and policies, provide products and services to customers (i.e., service content) through the information flow, material flow, and fund flow described in the service ecosystem diagram. The specific service content includes theme homestays, specialty dining, diverse activities, humanized services, cultural and creative products, and intelligent technology, which provide customers with rich product and service experiences based on management, facilities, and security. At this point, the homestay has successfully provided customers with a "home away from home" and achieved perceived value. At the same time, customers provide feedback on their experiences, which is used to supervise and improve services, forming a virtuous cycle. The service process, as the path followed by various parts of the theoretical model, runs through the entire process, promoting the sustainable development of rural homestays.

## 5 CONCLUSION

This article proposes a theoretical model of service design for rural homestays, with the aim of guiding the design practice of rural homestays, optimizing service quality, promoting rural tourism, and ultimately contributing to rural revitalization. Based on a deep analysis of the formation mechanism of rural homestays, the research is conducted using the methods of service design, with the stakeholder diagram analyzing the interests of different stakeholders in rural homestays, the service ecosystem diagram analyzing the operation mechanism of the service system of rural homestays, and the service process diagram analyzing the service design path of rural homestays. Finally, the theoretical model of service design for rural homestays is constructed. However, due to limitations in resource conditions, the theoretical model has not been applied to specific practices. In the future, it is expected to further deepen and refine the model through design practice to verify its applicability.

## REFERENCES

[1] Liu Lianzi. Rural revitalization strategy and whole-region tourism: An analytical framework. *Reform*, 2017, (12): 80–92.

[2] Long Fei, Liu Jiaming, Chang Jingliang. *Research Status and Future Prospects of Domestic Homestays. Urban Studies Journal*, 2019, 40(01): 31–37.

[3] Marc Stickdorn, Jakob Schneider. *This is Service Design Thinking: Basics*, Tools, Cases. Wiley, 2012, 01.

[4] Zhang Jian, Li Shitai. *Research on the Development Path of Rural Tourism under the Background of New Urbanization. Development Research*, 2015, No. 346(06): 49–53.

[5] Liu Guanzhong. *Outline of the Theory of Reasoning*. Hunan: Central South University Press, 2006.

[6] Xu Hongqi. *The Application of Reasoning Theory in Service Design. Industrial Design*, 2020, (02): 64–65.

System Innovation for a Troubled World – Lam et al. (Eds)
© 2024 the Author(s), ISBN: 978-1-032-60846-4

# Research on Lane Deviation Warning System

Jui-Chang Lin*
*Professor, Department of Mechanical Design Engineering, National Formosa University*

Cheng-Jen Lin
*Assistant Professor, Vehicle Engineer of National Formosa University*

Zi-Hao Huang
*MS Scholar, Department of Mechanical Design Engineering National Formosa University*

ABSTRACT: This research combines software to develop an effective vibration warning system for drivers' dangerous behaviors. To effectively reduce the occurrence of vehicle accidents and protect driving safety, this research adopts the driving behavior mode to develop various automobile safety equipment. It is hoped that with the assistance of the warning system, the driver will be able to respond quickly and correctly to avoid car accidents. The directions for this research are as follows: (1) Research and development of the deviation system warning system for intelligent trucks: This research mainly focuses on the research and development of deviation recognition software, which informs driving by voice or vibration. (2) Research and development of an anticollision warning system for intelligent vehicles; general anticollision devices use images to identify the dangerous distance and then use voice to notify the driver in danger. Often, drivers will not accept the signal due to the noisy environment and ignore the danger. (3) Perceived software and hardware system combination design: combine the image system, vibration system, and mechanism design to construct the entire automobile safety system. (4) Mechanism equipment and transmission design: The electromechanical equipment mainly assembles coils, windings, mechanisms, and detection devices. This research will consider the design of perceptual reaction time, perceived reaction speed, braking reaction time, time to collision (TTC), and average acceleration. In terms of vibration force, tested by 3N, the error value is 3%, the offset time is set at 0.5 sec, the error value is 5%, and the overall reliability is more than 95%, which conforms to the original design.

## 1 INTRODUCTION

At present, the lane departure warning system of domestic automobile safety equipment can be roughly divided into two types: (1) image detection type; (2) photosensitive detection type. The sensing principles of the two warning systems are introduced as follows: (1) Image detection type: It is the warning system used by most automobile manufacturers in the world, mainly through the charge-coupled device (CCD), complementary metal-oxide semiconductor (CMOS), sensing lens, real-time detection of forward images, and lane lines. Then, through the precise calculation of the computer system, the position of the lane line can be accurately identified to increase the driving safety of the driver. (2) Photosensitive detection type: Its working principle is to use infrared to detect lane lines, which is different from the CCD/CMOS detection method. There is no need for sensing lenses and computer systems to process

complex images and signals to determine whether the lane is offset. The system is mainly installed in the car chassis or bumper and uses the infrared light source of the detector to illuminate the road surface, and the auxiliary light source sensor captures the color difference to determine whether the vehicle deviates from the lane line.

In 1999, Batavia [1–5] *et al.* mentioned that audible warnings are not the only way to warn drivers, and tactile warnings may be another helpful way. It is possible that tactile warnings will be more advantageous than sound warnings, which needs to be explored. Others use visual signals, voice messages, and a vibrating steering wheel to warn the driver. Among them, it is found that the combination of the three warning signals significantly shortens the reaction time. In 2001, the method proposed by Jeong Kim and Lee [6] first enhanced the entire image (histogram equalization) and then used the Sobel operator to perform edge detection on the entire image. Then, project these detected edge points onto the ground, and then use the following search procedure to

---

*Corresponding Author: nhit100@gmail.com

DOI: 10.1201/9781003460763-63

find the position of the lane line. In 2007, this type of radar emits square pulse waves to detect target objects. The square pulse waves can be called pulse width, which is the duration of electromagnetic waves emitted by the radar. Time, the amplitude of the pulse wave represents the peak power of the radar emission (peak power), the period between the end of one pulse wave and the next pulse wave is called pulse repetition time, and the number of pulse waves generated per second is called pulse repetition frequency.

## 2 EXPERIMENTAL EQUIPMENT

### 2.1 Vibration system design

The vibration system design includes a body, shaft, winding coil, magnet transmission element, plate spring, electric control, and other electro-mechanical components, as shown in Figure 1–2. Because the magnetic force is affected by the thrust of the spring and produces different vibration frequencies, this study adjusts different parameters to achieve the target design value. Therefore, this research uses the spring, transmission mechanism, and body as the sources of force to analyze and adjust the force. The design is divided into three main points: (1) the body; (2) the required strength of the plate spring; and (3) the strength of the thrust mechanism. To ensure the basic production capacity of the product, after entering the mass production stage, a machine with a certain pro-duction quality is handed over to the customer. Therefore, the establishment of standard proce-dures can reduce the considerable manpower and material resources required for development. Therefore, considering the pressure of cost and fierce market competition, shortening the design time, and reducing the number of tests, we must actively adopt finite element analysis technology to engage in mechanism design.

Figure 1. Vibration system design.

Figure 2. Vibration system.

### 2.2 Image sensing system design

#### 2.2.1 Image grayscale
A color image has quite a lot of pixels; each pixel is composed of three bits, which are red (Red), green (Green), blue (Blue), and other three colors. The range of color distribution is between 0 and 255. The grayscale is to convert a color image into a grayscale image, as shown in Figure 2.6. The grayscale image converts the RGB color space to the Y plane, representing the brightness in the color space, so each pixel value in the grayscale image is The brightness value (luminance) indicates that the brightness range is between 0 and 255, and the conversion formula between the brightness value (Y) and RGB is shown in the formula (1).

$$Y = 0.299 \text{x} R + 0.587 \text{x} G + 0.141 \text{x} B \qquad (1)$$

In the formula, R, G, and B represent the red, green, and blue components of each pixel.

#### 2.2.2 Image filtering
Image quality will be affected by the noise formed by the image-capturing system, insufficient light source uniformity, or insufficient contrast, which affects the accuracy and repeatability of machine vision. Therefore, filters must be used to remove noise in the image or increase the contrast effect.

Image filtering is mainly divided into spatial domain and frequency domain in two ways. The spatial domain only involves the image plane itself, directly processing the pixels in the image, and the processing method in the frequency domain is based on modifying the fourier transform of the image. This research uses the spatial domain method as the image filtering method.

The spatial domain refers to the set of pixels that make up an image. The processing method is to directly perform operations on these pixels. The processing function of the spatial domain can be expressed as (2):

$$g(x, y) = T[f(x, y)] \qquad (2)$$

In the formula, f (x, y) is the input image, g (x, y) is the processed image, and T is an operator acting on f, which is defined in a certain neighborhood of (x, y). The main method to define a neighborhood near (x, y) is to use a square or rectangular sub-image mask centered on (x, y), as shown in Figure 3. Using operators for each (x, y) in the image will generate the image g (x, y) at that position.

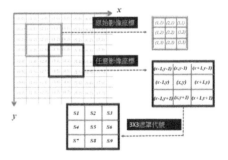

Figure 3. 3×3 filter mask.

The main purpose of designing an image filter is to not only remove noise during the image filtering process but also to maintain the original structure and details of the image. Nowadays, many methods have been developed to eliminate the noise in the image and improve its quality. For image filtering methods in the spatial domain, common methods include smoothing filters, median filters, high-pass filters, and so on. The averaging filter is also called low-pass filtering, which makes the signal change smoother, strengthens the smooth part, and suppresses the faster-changing components. Although this filter can filter some image impurities, it also often causes the image to have some disadvantages. High-pass filtering is a method of increasing the pixel value of its own and reducing the pixel value of adjacent pixels to highlight the high-frequency part. This filter can highlight the high-frequency part of the image but also increases the noise.

## 3 RESULTS AND DISCUSSION

### 3.1 *Vibration force measurement and sensor design*

This research uses Arduino programs to make an electronic scale to measure the vibration force of the motor under different voltages. First, the load cell element, combined with the HX711 weight-sensing amplifier module, is used as the main sensor to measure the vibration force of the motor. And connect the relay to provide the motor signal and drive the motor vibration under each voltage through the power supply. The following Figure 4 shows the motor vibration force test sensor for this experiment.

Figure 4.    Vibration force sensor.

### 3.2 *Connection of motor vibration sensor*

Because the motor is removed from the lane deviation warning system, it cannot be driven directly by power. It is necessary to provide a signal source to the motor to make the motor vibrate. Therefore, this experiment uses an Arduino with a relay to provide a signal source and a power supply to provide a 12V voltage to drive the motor to vibrate. Figure 5 shows the relay connection method; Figure 6 shows the actual connection method.

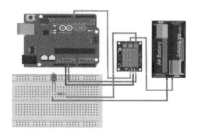

Figure 5.    Relay connection.

Figure 6.    Relay-system connection.

This research needs to measure the vibration force of the motor. Because it is impossible to measure the vibration of the motor simply by driving the motor, it is equipped with an Arduino program to make a scale to measure the vibration force of the motor. This scale needs to be equipped with load cell components and an HX711 amplifier module. Group, relay, Arduino Uno R3 development board, and scale support; the scale support is made by 3D printing. Figure 7 shows the wiring of the HX711 amplifier module; Figure 8 shows the wiring of the load cell components; and Figure 9 shows the vibration force sensor.

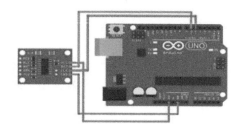

Figure 7.    Enlarged module design.

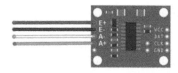

Figure 8.    Load cell component design.

Figure 9.    Vibration force sensor.

### 3.3    *Vibration force test*

Figure 10 shows the e-sensor experiment. This experiment measures the vibration force of 12V, 14V, 16V, 18V, and 20V motors under different voltages. The results are shown below; Figure 11 shows the Arduino monitoring data window, and the data is integrated into Table 1.

Figure 10.    Vibration force measurement machine.

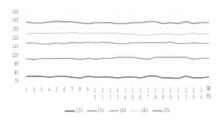

Figure 11.    Vibration force with different voltage.

Table 1.    Vibration force with different voltage.

| sec | 12V | 14V | 16V | 18V | 20V |
|-----|-----|-----|-----|-----|-----|
| 1 | 81 | 101 | 119 | 130 | 143 |
| 2 | 81 | 100 | 119 | 130 | 142 |
| 3 | 81 | 101 | 118 | 130 | 142 |
| 4 | 80 | 101 | 118 | 130 | 143 |
| 5 | 81 | 101 | 117 | 130 | 144 |
| 6 | 81 | 101 | 117 | 130 | 143 |
| 7 | 80 | 101 | 117 | 131 | 143 |
| 8 | 79 | 100 | 119 | 130 | 142 |
| 9 | 81 | 101 | 120 | 130 | 141 |
| 10 | 80 | 100 | 121 | 130 | 142 |
| Ave. | 80 | 101.12 | 118.54 | 129.5 | 141.80 |
| unit: g | | | | | |

The regression equation is (3):

$$F(N) = \alpha Y(V) + \beta \qquad (3)$$

$$\alpha = 10; \quad \beta = 20$$

The error is about 5%.

### 3.4    *Vehicle drift test*

The hardware design specifications of the software and hardware design for path deviation detection are as follows:

(1) Resolution: 640x480 and above (inclusive)
(2) Acquisition frequency: above 30 fps (inclusive)
(3) Photosensitive element: 1/4" or more (including CMOS or CCD)
(4) Power supply: DC5V-12V or DC12V-24V

Path offset detection includes left offset and right offset. The measurement results are shown in Figure 12–13 and Table 2.

Figure 12.    Left test.

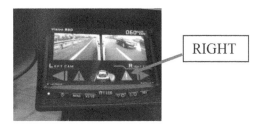

Figure 13.    Right test.

Table 2.    Vehicle drift test.

| Test Item | 1st test | 2nd test |
|-----------|----------|----------|
| Normal test | NO data | NO data |
| | OK | OK |
| Left offset test | Image & vibration force | Image & vibration force |
| | OK | OK |
| Right offset test | Image & vibration force | Image & vibration force |
| | OK | OK |

## 4  CONCLUSION

It is measured from the experimental results that under different voltage values, the vibration force of the motor will produce different vibration forces due to the different magnitudes of the voltage provided. Thus, we can summarize a few points:

(1) The greater the voltage value, the greater the vibration force of the motor, and the experimental error is 3%.
(2) The motor used in this experiment uses the principle of lateral vibration, and its vibration has an obvious sense of direction, and the effect is better than that of an eccentric hammer. In this experiment, the vibration force of the motor is different under different voltage values. Therefore, the data can be used to activate the motor at different vehicle speeds to protect the driving of the vehicle. This experiment is designed to be 30 times/sec, and the experimental error is 5%.
(3) This system is equipped with a dedicated driving recorder, so this system is not only a driving recorder but also a lane deviation system. This device can be mounted not only on small cars but also on large cars, and it is provided to medium and large vehicles that are not equipped with a lane departure warning system. The test offset time of this system is set to 0.5 s, and the experimental error is within 3%.

This study successfully designed a lane deviation warning system that can expand the needs of the automotive market and prevent drivers from being overly fatigued and causing accidents while driving. When the system detects that the vehicle has deviated from the original driving lane, the vibration device will be activated to remind the driver to achieve driving safety.

## REFERENCES

[1]  Batavia P.H., *"Driver Adaptive Lane Departure Warning Systems"*, (The degree of Doctor of Philosophy), Carnegie Mellon University, 1999.
[2]  Houser, Pierowicz, & Fuglewicz, *"Concept of Operations and Voluntary Operational Requirements for Lane Departure Warning Systems (LDWS) On board Commercial Motor Vehicles"* (Technical Report No. FMCSA MCRR 05 005), Federal Motor Carrier Safety, 2005.
[3]  Motoyama, S., Ohta, T., Watanabe, T., & Ito, Y., " Development of lane departure warning system", Proc. 7th ITS World Congress, 2000.
[4]  Keisuke, S., & Hakan, J., "An analysis of driver's steering behavior during auditory or haptic warnings for the designing of lane departurearning system.", *JSAE Review*, 24 (1), pp.65–70, 2003.
[5]  Bertozzi, M. and A. Broggi, "GOLD: a parallel real-time stereo vision system for generic obstacle and lane detection," *IEEE Trans. On Image Processing*, Vol.7, Issue: 1, pp.62–81. 1998.
[6]  Jeong, S.G., C.S. Kim, D.Y. Lee, S.K. Ha, D.H. Lee, and M.H. Lee, "Real-time lane detection for autonomous vehicle," *Proc. IEEE Int. Symposium on Industrial Electronics*, Vol. 3, pp.1466–1471, 2001.

System Innovation for a Troubled World – Lam et al. (Eds)
© 2024 the Author(s), ISBN: 978-1-032-60846-4

# The Design for efficient plastic element splitting

Bing-En Liu, Gadi Ashok Kumar Reddy, Jun-Jie Liao & Kuang-Chyi Lee*
*Department of Automation Engineering, National Formosa University, Hu-Wei, Yunlin, Taiwan*

ABSTRACT: A plastic element is produced using the injection molding technique. Various methods are available to detach the barrel from the gates, such as cutting with a blade, hot wire, or laser. However, these methods generate heat and take more time to complete. In contrast, ultrasonic machining can break off the barrel without producing heat and with minimal machining time. This research aims to create an ultrasonic horn that produces longitudinal vibrations at an optimized frequency while maintaining low-stress concentration in finite element analysis (FEA). The optimized design is compared with the SJ-26a ultrasonic machine horn, and it shows lower stresses, directional deformation, and total deformation. The maximum principal stress was reduced almost four times compared to the old design, from 0.44 MPA to 0.12 MPA. Upon fine-tuning the ultrasonic horn in the machine, the research successfully attained a vibration duration of 0.29 seconds and a rest duration of 0.48 seconds on the workpiece. The total machining time for a single pass is 1.25 seconds. By utilizing tuning parameters, our ultrasonic horn effectively detached all plastic elements from the gates of the workpiece within one cycle.

## 1 INTRODUCTION

Ultrasound technology has found extensive use in various industries for multiple machining applications, including ultrasonic cleaning, welding, cutting, material removal, and others, tailored to meet specific industrial needs. The ultrasonic horn is particularly interesting to many industries, whose size and shape determine the type of vibration motion produced (longitudinal, vertical, torsional, etc.). The ultrasonic horn's principal benefit is that it concentrates and focuses vibrational energy at its tip (bottom surface). When in contact with the machining workpiece's surface, the tip can transfer the vibration from the horn to the workpiece (Mtiinstruments 2017). The ultrasonic machine's performance is significantly influenced by the shape and size of the horn (M. nad'a 2010). The resonant frequency and resonant length are the essential parameters for ultrasonic horn design. Modal analysis can help to calculate the mode shapes and natural frequencies of the ultrasonic horn (Rai *et al.* 2020). Typically, ultrasonic horns are manufactured using titanium, aluminum, and steel materials, selected based on their acoustic properties, fatigue strength, and the machining material being used. The primary aim of this project is to employ harmonic analysis in finite element analysis (FEA), using 15 KHz as the input

frequency, to design an ultrasonic horn that can generate longitudinal vibrations at the specified frequency.

ANSYS is a software platform designed for engineering simulation and analysis. It provides a comprehensive suite of tools for engineers and designers to simulate and evaluate the behavior of complex systems, ranging from small-scale components to large-scale structures. In this study, ANSYS software is used to analyze ultrasonic horn design.

## 2 ULTRASONIC HORN DESIGN

In the case of a stepped horn, the sudden reduction in diameter results in an increase in both stress and amplitude values. However, this machining method is unreliable due to the peak stress, which significantly reduces the horn's lifespan. On the other hand, the exponential-shaped horn gradually decreases in diameter, resulting in uniformly increased stress, as shown in Figure 1. While the amplitude of the exponential-shaped horn is lower than that of the stepped horn, it is a more reliable option for machining operations. The catenoidal horn shape is considered to be more reliable than both the step horn and exponential horn shapes. The catenoidal horn contains the advantages of both the step and exponential horns, according to Dipin et al., (2014). Finally, the catenoidal horn shape was chosen in the ultrasonic horn design.

*Corresponding Author: kclee@gs.nfu.edu.tw

DOI: 10.1201/9781003460763-64

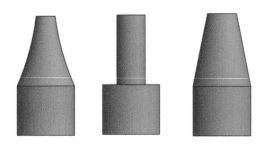

Figure 1. Difference types of shapes.

As shown in Figure 1, from left to right, they are catenoidal shape, step shape, and exponential shape.

The fourth step is the production of an ultrasonic horn. The first step is to choose the appropriate vibrational frequency. For this study, a frequency of 15 KHz was selected due to the limitations of the SJ-26a ultrasonic machine and the delicate nature of the plastic element's barrel material. Another reason is that the barrel of the plastic element is a fragile material and susceptible to damage. Using a frequency of 15 KHz is the most appropriate for processing delicate materials, as it minimizes the risk of damage to the product when compared to higher-frequency machines such as 20 KHz or 30K Hz. Typically, higher-frequency ultrasonic machines are reserved for ultrasonic spot welding.

The second step involves selecting the material for the ultrasonic horn. This decision is based on the material's acoustic properties and fatigue strength. In this case, aluminum was chosen for its good acoustic properties and lower surface hardness compared to steel and titanium. An ultrasonic horn made of aluminum alloy is considered, given its material properties. The alloy has Poisson's ratio of 0.33, a Young's modulus of 71GPA, and a density of 2770 kg/m$^3$.

The third step involves designing the ultrasonic horn, which can be done using other authors' citations (Hayiegan et al., 2015). The other parameters were adjusted to produce longitudinal vibration motion and low stress at a frequency of 15 KHz for the ultrasonic. These parameters included the input surface diameter, output surface diameter, radius, input length, and output length of the ultrasonic horn. The head and tail were used to adjust the parameters based on the results obtained through FEA. Other parameters were changed while keeping the length of the horn constant until the ultrasonic horn produced longitudinal vibration at 15 KHz. It was important to maintain a tolerance of ±5 Hz frequency in FEA, as different frequencies could produce different vibrational motions, such as vertical or torsional vibrations or a combination of longitudinal and torsional vibrations. As this study required the ultrasonic horn to produce longitudinal vibration

motion at a frequency of 15 KHz, there were infinite possibilities for achieving this outcome through adjustments to the parameters.

The process of designing an optimal ultrasonic horn involves several steps, which are shown in Figure 2.

Figure 3 illustrates that, to fit within the 100 × 100mm base holder area, a 65mm output surface radius was selected, resulting in a diameter of 120 mm that covers the base holder surface. To accommodate the smaller output face diameter

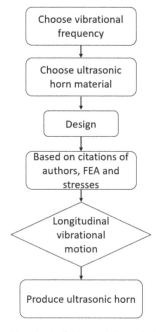

Figure 2. Flowchart of ultrasonic horn design.

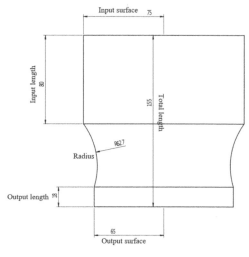

Figure 3. Dimension of designed ultrasonic horn (mm).

compared to the input face diameter, analytical experience was utilized, and the input surface radius was chosen at 75 mm, equivalent to a 150mm diameter. The input length is 80mm and has a radius of 62.71, while the output length is 18mm. At this size, the ultrasonic horn produces longitudinal motion with a frequency of 15 KHz. Dipin et al. (2014) recommended adjusting the radius between the input and output lengths to reduce stress concentration on the ultrasonic horn. All dimensions were analyzed multiple times to achieve optimal results and increase the radius to produce a smoother curve.

Table 1 displays the modes and frequencies of ultrasonic horn design as determined by modal analysis. Specifically, it lists the 20 modes and their corresponding frequencies, ranging from 648.16 Hz to 19625 Hz. However, some frequencies from mode 12 to mode 14 between 1500 Hz and 1600 Hz, such as 15123 Hz, 15130 Hz, and 15793 Hz, fall outside of the acceptable range.The given vibration frequency is 15 KHz with a tolerance limit of ±5 Hz, meaning that frequencies within the range of 14995 Hz to 15005 Hz are acceptable. Unfortunately, the frequencies listed in Table 1 are outside of this range. To determine the vibrational motion at a frequency of 15 KHz, a harmonic analysis was performed by inputting the 15 KHz frequency and checking the resulting vibrational motion at that frequency. The vibrational motion at 15 KHz is shown in Figure 4, which shows longitudinal vibrational motion that satisfies both conditions in the harmonic analysis.

For the longitudinal vibration at the desired frequency of 15 KHz for the ultrasonic horn design, harmonic analysis is performed by inputting 15 KHz as the frequency value, as shown in Figure 4. Unlike in modal analysis, where the number of modes provided determines the frequencies generated, harmonic analysis produces vibrational motion at a specific input frequency.

The ultrasonic horn fabricated after design and analysis is depicted in Figure 5. It meets the requirements of generating low-stress vibration along the axes of forward and backward motion with directional and total strains considered.

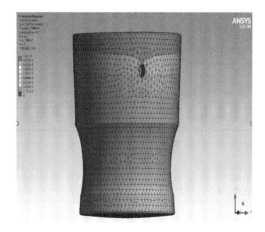

Figure 4. Ultrasonic horn harmonic analysis at 15 KHz.

Figure 5. Product of ultrasonic horn design.

## 3 RESULTS

The ultrasonic horn was designed and simulated using longitudinal harmonic analysis to produce

Table 1. Model analysis of ultrasonic horn design.

| Models | Frequency (HZ) |
| --- | --- |
| 1 | 648 |
| 2 | 648 |
| 3 | 912 |
| 4 | 3524 |
| 5 | 5880 |
| 6 | 5883 |
| 7 | 10379 |
| 8 | 12603 |
| 9 | 12607 |
| 10 | 13776 |
| 11 | 13808 |
| 12 | 15123 |
| 13 | 15138 |
| 14 | 15793 |
| 15 | 16347 |
| 16 | 16358 |
| 17 | 16926 |
| 18 | 16939 |
| 19 | 19150 |
| 20 | 19625 |

nearly half a wavelength (155 mm) of 15 kHz longitudinal vibration motion with the lowest stress. After adjusting the parameters, the optimized ultrasonic horn was compared with the SJ-26a ultrasonic horn in Table 2, which showed that the former had lower stress and deformation. FEA analysis has proven that the optimized ultrasonic horn is the optimal design and provides better results than the SJ-26a ultrasonic horn. The optimized ultrasonic horn has a longer lifespan compared to the SJ-26a ultrasonic horn due to significantly lower stress acting on it. Where the maximum deformation ($\delta_m$) is 19 nm, the maximum longitudinal deformation (in the Z-axis) ($\delta_Z$) is 17 nm, the maximum principal stress ($\sigma_P$) is 0.12 MPA, the equivalent stress ($\sigma_E$) is 0.50 MPA, and the normal stress frequency response ($\sigma_N$) is 0.03 MPA.

Table 2. Harmonic analysis.

| Ultrasonic Horn | Optimized | SJ-26a |
|---|---|---|
| $\delta_m(nm)$ | 19 | 83 |
| $\delta_z(nm)$ | 17 | 69 |
| $\sigma_P(MPA)$ | 0.12 | 0.44 |
| $\sigma_E(MPA)$ | 0.50 | 0.71 |
| $\sigma_N(MPA)$ | 0.03 | 0.04 |

When the ultrasonic begins machining, the ultrasonic horn attaches to the molded plastic element base holder and remains on the base holder for a duration of 0.48 seconds ($T_b$). Subsequently, the ultrasonic machine vibrates for a period of 0.29 seconds ($T_v$). Finally, the horn rests on the base holder again for 0.48 seconds ($T_a$) before returning to its original position. The total machining time for a single pass is 1.25 seconds ($T_t$). This ultrasonic horn design is faster than the SJ-26a ultrasonic horn, which has a total machining time of 1.45 seconds.

Table 3. Machining tunning parameters of the ultrasonic horn.

| Ultrasonic Horn | Optimized | SJ-26a |
|---|---|---|
| $T_{before}$(seconds) | 0.48 | 0.50 |
| $T_{vibration}$(seconds) | 0.29 | 0.45 |
| $T_{after}$(seconds) | 0.48 | 0.50 |
| $T_{total}$(seconds) | 1.25 | 1.45 |

## 4 CONCLUSION

In this paper, the researchers have successfully developed a separation method and scaffold for ultrasonic machining. Specifically, an ultrasonic horn has been designed to facilitate perfect longitudinal vibration at a frequency of 15 KHz. The processing vibration time is brief, and after setting and adjusting the processing parameters, all plastic elements can be crushed at once, with a total processing time of 1.25 seconds. The stresses acting on the ultrasonic horn design are low compared to those experienced by SJ-26a ultrasonic horns, and the ultrasonic horn design offers perfect longitudinal vibrational motion at 15 KHz frequency. Additionally, deformation is lower than that experienced by SJ-26a ultrasonic horns. As a result of these factors, the ultrasonic horn design can perform ultrasonic machining operations consistently over a long period of time. Experimental trials have demonstrated that the ultrasonic horn design requires less vibrational machining time than SJ-26a ultrasonic horns, indicating that vibrational frequency travels more quickly in the ultrasonic horn design. The ultrasonic horn design features a circular catenoidal shape, which helps reduce stresses to an optimum level.

## REFERENCES

Dipin K.R., Roopa R.M., & Elangovan S. (2014). Design and analysis of slotted horn for ultrasonic plastic welding. *Applied Mechanics and Materials, 592* (594), 859–863.

Hayiegan C., Nedeloni M., Micliuc D., Pellac A., Bogdan S.L., & Pelea I.M. (2015). *Simulation Study with SolidWorks Software of an Ultrasonic Horn of Different Materials and Dimensions to Obtain the Natural Frequency of 20 KHz*. University of Târgu-Jiu, Engineering Series.

Mtiinstruments. (2017, August 7). *Ultrasonic Horn Vibration*. https://mtiinstruments.com/applications/ultrasonic-horn-vibration/

nad'a M. (2010). Ultrasonic horn design for ultrasonic machining technologies. *Applied and Computational Mechanics, 4*(1), 79.

Rai P.K., Patel R.K. & Yadava, V. (2017). Modal analysis of horns used in ultrasonic machine", elk asia pacific journals. *ELK Asia Pacific Journals*.

*System Innovation for a Troubled World – Lam et al. (Eds)*
© 2024 the Author(s), ISBN: 978-1-032-60846-4

# Exploring the roles of Taiwan's Yuan-Li rush-weaving industry members in the cultural value chain

Wei-Ken Hung*
*Department of Industrial Design, National United University, Miaoli, Taiwan*

ABSTRACT: This study investigates the relationships and market positioning of the four types of rush-weaving industry members in Yuan-Li from an industry-level perspective, using industry clustering and cultural value chain theories. Through multiple case interviews, the study found that weavers are a vital "shared resource" and that there is a "buyer-supplier relationship." However, the "commercial competition and cooperation relationship" is not evident and should be better explained by the "complementarity" of the cultural value chain. By analyzing the five segments (creation, production, dissemination, exhibition, and consumption) of the cultural value chain, this study reveals the differentiated and complementary roles played by the four types of industry members: the Taiwan Yuan-Li Handwork Association, SunnyRush (a start-up), the Yuan-Li Town Farmers' Triangle Rush Exhibition Hall, and traditional Hat and Mat Shops. The results illustrate why Yuan-Li's rush-weaving industry is more resilient and recognizable and how it can continue to be a cultural and craft revival model in Taiwan.

*Keywords*: Design Creativity, Cultural and Craft, Industry Clustering, Regional Revitalization

## 1 INTRODUCTION

Yuan-Li's rush-weaving industry is one of Taiwan's representative examples of handicraft revival. However, after the 1970s, the industry declined for over 30 years due to various factors, including the development of the petrochemical industry, the replacement of hand-made fabrics with plastic products, and the entry of inexpensive straw weaving products from abroad. According to Chang and Wang (2017), the industry's renaissance began in 1993 with the establishment of the Shan-Chiao Community Development Association (SCDA). Retired elementary school teacher Wen-Hui Yeh took over the chairmanship of the SCDA in 1997 and gradually recruited a dozen aunts to reintroduce rush-weaving. In 2009, the Taiwan Yuan-Li Handwork Association (TYHA) was established to preserve the culture of rush-weaving and restore the work of women with rush-weaving skills to their past glory. In 2014, TYHA launched the "Tshioh Rushcraft" brand, systematically developing and marketing weaving products.

However, the previous study only focused on Yuan-Li's development history before 2014 and the TYHA, lacking an industry perspective on member relations and market positioning, including the traditional hat and mat shops that have been in business for over 60 years, the Yuan-Li Town Farmers' Association that established the

"Triangle Rush Exhibition Hall" in 2005, and the industrial designer who established the "SunnyRush" brand in Yuan-Li since 2016. Additionally, since cultural products have substantial symbolic value that depends on the social and cultural meanings associated with them, and allow consumers to express their personal and social identities through their purchase and use (Ravasi & Rindova 2008), understanding how industry members can innovate to maintain or enhance the symbolic value and meaning of the rush-weaving industry's culture and crafts is crucial. This study aims to explore this aspect further by using industry clustering and cultural value chain theories to investigate the relationships and market positioning of the four types of rush-weaving industry members in Yuan-Li. Through multiple case interviews, the study found that weavers are a vital "shared resource," and there is a "buyer-supplier relationship." However, the "commercial competition and cooperation relationship" is not evident and should be better explained by the complementary nature of the cultural value chain. By analyzing the five segments of the cultural value chain (creation, production, dissemination, exhibition, and consumption), this study reveals the differentiated and complementary roles played by the four types of industry members mentioned earlier, illustrating why Yuan-Li's rush-weaving industry is more resilient and recognizable and how it can continue to be a cultural and craft revival model in Taiwan.

*Corresponding Author: hungweiken@nuu.edu.tw

DOI: 10.1201/9781003460763-65

# 2 LITERATURE REVIEW

## 2.1 *Relationships and market positioning of industry members*

According to Anderson (1994), there are three patterns of relationships among members of the cluster industry that can be used to examine the relationships among members of the rush-weaving industry: 1) Buyer-Supplier Relationships, which refer to the supply and demand relationships between those who provide products or services to end consumers, those who process intermediate products and supply raw materials, and those who distribute goods or services, resulting in cost savings and economies of aggregation; 2) Competitor-Collaborator Relationship, which exists when companies producing the same or similar products share resources, information, and opportunities between industry clusters, resulting in competitive relationships and the possibility of cooperation; and 3) Shared Resource Relationship, which refers to the accumulated infrastructure, knowledge, different human and technical resources, and information when manufacturers and related industries gather in a specific area, and these resources are shared among the manufacturers, thus generating cost advantages and economic benefits of clustering.

Furthermore, Saqib's (2021) market positioning study views the relationship between different industry members from the perspective of competition and differentiation. It includes the following: 1) Competition, which is a characteristic that differentiates from competitors and appeals to the public to occupy an influential and unique competitive position in the minds of buyers in the target market; 2) Competitive Advantage, which is a value creation strategy that contributes to a competitive advantage, and it differs from the above view of "competition" in that it is not an item implemented by a potential current competitor; 3) Differentiation, which focuses on specific product differences; 4) Empty Slot/Mind, which fills the gap in the minds of potential buyers (target customers); and 5) Consumers' Perception, which refers to the perceptual space that consumers perceive as geometry and the change of product perceptions that consumers purposefully create or evoke. This research can be used to examine the types of relationships and market positioning among the members of the rush-weaving industry.

## 2.2 *The role of industry members in the cultural value chain*

The key to assessing the value of creative industries is understanding their value chain (Henry 2007). The perspective of the "cultural value chain" can be used to emphasize the small-scale service economy of the arts and crafts industry and to explore the value provided by industry members and the division of labor in the market (Potts *et al.*, 2008). Landry (2000) refers to the cultural value chain as consisting of five stages: initiation, production, distribution, delivery mechanisms, and reader reception and feedback. This is distinctly different from the value chain of industrial products, which emphasizes physical manufacturing, logistics, marketing, and supporting activities such as management, technology development, and procurement (Porter 1985).

According to UNESCO's (2009) "The 2009 UNESCO Framework for Cultural Statistics," the value chain of culture is defined as having five key components (Figure 1), which are well-suited to analyzing the role of rush-weaving industry members:

1 Creation: the origination and authoring of ideas and content, and the making of one-off productions;
2 Production: the reproducible cultural forms, as well as the specialist tools, infrastructure, and processes used in their realization;
3 Dissemination: the bringing of generally cultural products to consumers and exhibitors;
4 Exhibition/Reception/Transmission: refers to the place of consumption and providing live and/or unmediated cultural experiences by granting or selling access to consume/participate in festivals or museums. Transmission relates to the transfer of knowledge and skills that may not involve any commercial transaction and often occurs in informal settings.
5 Consumption/Participation: the activities of audiences and participants in consuming cultural products and participating in cultural activities and experiences.

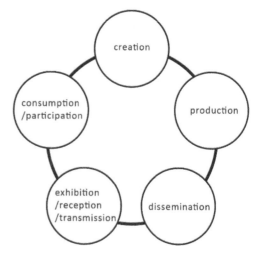

Figure 1. Cultural value chain (adapted from UNESCO, 2009).

## 3 RESEARCH METHODS

This study uses a qualitative "multiple case study" approach to conduct in-depth interviews with four types of industry members. The multiple case study approach is a qualitative and case-based research method that combines extensive research and secondary data. Especially when the researcher has little control over events and is concerned with real-world phenomena, case studies are the preferred strategy. They can increase the reliability of findings and explore questions related to the "how" and "why" (Yin 2003). The interviewees were managers from the Taiwan Yuan-Li Handwork Association (TYHA) and the Yuan-Li Town Farmers' Triangle Rush Exhibition Hall, as well as those in charge of the startup SunnyRush and one of the traditional Hat and Mat Shops. The questions asked included: 1) the relationship with other industry members, 2) the market position of the organization and its focus on the cultural value chain, and 3) the main activities and government projects applied in recent years.

## 4 RESULTS

The results of the study indicate that "rush-weavers" are a "shared resource" among the four types of industry members, and there is a "buyer-supplier relationship" within the industry, with the Hat and Mat Shops supplying some of the traditional rush-weaving products to the TYHA, SunnyRush, and the Triangle Rush Exhibition Hall. However, there is no clear commercial "competition and cooperation" within the industry. A more appropriate explanation is to use the cultural value chain to differentiate the market positioning and the "complementary" relationship.

### 4.1 Industry structure and relationships

It is difficult to estimate the total number of rush-weavers, but there are at least a hundred of them who are mainly aged 70–80 and live in Yuan-Li and the neighboring areas of Dajia and Tungshiau. The four types of industry members have regular collaborators: a dozen from the TYHA, two dozen from SunnyRush, a dozen from the Triangle Rush Exhibition Hall, and the rest with the three Hat and Mat Shops. The traditional procurement process of "paid on a piecework basis" is used, with industry members placing orders for regular rush-weavers and collecting from them regularly. Only the TYHA offers a monthly salary for regular work, with four rush-weavers currently being subsidized through a government program. As most rush-weavers work with different industry members simultaneously, it can be considered a "shared resource."

Regarding the "buyer-supplier" relationship, the traditional Hat and Mat Shops are suppliers to the other three industry members, offering traditional rush-weaving products. For example, the largest supplier is the Mei-Tian Hat and Mat shop, which offers a wide range of products, including hats, cushions, bags, and slippers, while the Jian-Cheng Hat and Mat Shop focuses on mats and helmet liners made of rush. Since "hand-making time" is the most critical cost factor, the hats and mats are usually woven from whole rushes, which are rough, stiff, and affordable.

TYHA and SunnyRush develop and produce their brand rush-weaving products, which are more expensive, such as hats and bags, and the lowest priced products, such as coasters. The highest-priced items are woven at higher densities, using a sewing needle to cut a single piece of rush into two or three finer pieces before weaving. When the weaving is denser, the finished product is softer but more labor-intensive and time-consuming. Conversely, novice community residents often make the lowest-priced coasters as an introductory exercise.

The TYHA interviewees mentioned that the quality of "good" rush-weaving is evaluated using three standards from the Japanese era. First, the thickness of the selected rush must be uniform; second, there must be no color difference because the color of each rush varies, with the new rush being brighter and the old rush being darker; even the same piece of rush may be more yellow at the head and greener at the end; and third, the weaving edges must be straight. It is essential to hide the rushes' ends and keep the edges straight when weaving the rush one by one from thread to surface and three-dimensional shape. In addition, because the source material is so vital to the quality of the finished product, each industry member grows its rush for use by weavers. Although the size of the rush field is much smaller (less than one hectare) than it was in its heyday, it is a crucial part of Yuan-Li's cultural value to preserve the original rush field so that even visitors can understand and experience the process of planting, cutting, and drying the rush.

On the other hand, there are very few art collector buyers for the rush-weaving craft. This is primarily due to the symbolic cultural value of a rush-weaving craft being the functional, moisture-wicking wearable product that wears out with use and is prone to mold and mildew due to humidity, affecting its durability and making it unsuitable for long-term collector's requirements.

### 4.2 Complementarity of Yuan-Li Rush-Weaving industry

Based on the results of the interviews, there appears to be no clear commercial competition or collaboration within the rush-weaving industry chain. The differences in product form, function, and meaning may not be intuitive or quickly identifiable to the average consumer. Therefore, using the competition-oriented perspective suggested by Saqib (2021) to differentiate market positioning is inappropriate. Instead, the cultural value chain is more suitable for explaining the complementary relationships and position differences among the four industry members at the commercial and cultural levels, as shown in Table 1.

Table 1. Role weighting of rush-weaving industry members in the cultural value chain.

| Industry Members / Cultural Value Chain | TYHA : Taiwan Yuan-Li Handwork Association/ SCDA:Shanchiao Community Development Association | Triangle Rush Exhibition Hall (supported by Yuan-Li Town Farmers' Association) | SunnyRush (young startup) | Traditional Hat and Mat Shops |
|---|---|---|---|---|
| 1. Creation | high | low | high | low |
| 2. Production | low | low | medium | high |
| 3. Dissemination | high | medium | medium | low |
| 4. Exhibition/ Reception/ Transmission | high | high | medium | low |
| 5. Consumption/ Participation | high | low | high | low |

Of the five cultural value chains, TYHA and SunnyRush have the most "creation" activities and regularly develop branded products such as rush-weaving hats and bags. The difference is that TYHA is more suitable and willing to experiment with more weaving patterns and customize its products. For example, one of the bags has a rattan-like weave on the side and a bamboo-like weave pattern on the bottom, which provides a texture that is not easily seen in the rush. This technique can be explained by "collage." The key to taking on custom-made products is the fact that weavers are paid a monthly salary and do not have to compete on volume, so they are more willing to challenge and try new patterns.

In contrast, SunnyRush's products are created based on various styles and accessories to meet users' needs. For example, in the company's early days, SunnyRush launched a "crowdfunding" campaign to purchase a cap press machine and develop new molds of its design. They also developed over a dozen color patterns for hat bands and unique accessories to differentiate the style. In response to customer feedback that the tops of the hats are prone to damage, some of the hat collections have been shaped with eco-friendly silicone on the inside of the top to improve durability. Additionally, the new design is different from the

original composite weave, which was not washable in the washing machine in the past. The bag is entirely canvas, with a detachable rush weave around the exterior. This approach makes it easier to mass-produce and clean while maintaining cultural authenticity, making it an example of user-driven design. On the other hand, SunnyRush has a socially innovative approach, as some of the older grandmothers who have lost their eyesight but still want to continue weaving or community mothers who are new to weaving may have minor defects in their weaving products that traditional quality control would consider unacceptable. However, SunnyRush encourages the continued participation of weavers by making smaller purses signed by the craftsman and helping to sell them.

Figure 2. TYHA's hats and bags are available in various experimental patterns.

The "production" section is compared in terms of the number of cooperating weavers, emphasizing repetitive production. The Hat and Mat Shops have the largest share in this section, supplying not only traditional items to other members of the Yuan-Li industry but also distributing them to tourist attractions in other counties. This is essential for maintaining the basic scale and capacity of the industry.

Figure 3. The hat, various accessories developed by SunnyRush, and a coin purse signed by the senior weaver.

The "dissemination" section compares the frequency of proactive outreach culture activities to consumers and external media. The TYHA, which has been promoting the revival of the rush-

Figure 4. Hats and Mats Shops supply the traditional rush-weaving hats, slippers, helmet liners, and mats.

weaving culture for 20 years, plays a crucial role in key events, such as the 10-year Rush-Weaving Award since 2006, the publication of rush-weaving instructional books, and the co-organization of the weaving festival. Furthermore, TYHA is often featured in external media and has made documentary films, which have helped to spread the visibility of the culture. In 2019, the certification of the rush-weaver was the first time a private non-profit organization initiated a successful certification in Taiwan. In addition, the two-in-one approach of the TYHA and the SCDA is an essential strategy that allows the TYHA to simultaneously promote the culture from the perspective of cultural commodities and local community development, as evidenced by the National Sustainable Development Award of the Executive Yuan in 2020 and the Gold Medal Village award in 2021.

In the "exhibition/reception/transmission" section of the local exhibition, all of the respondents mentioned that the Triangle Rush Exhibition Hall is often the first stop for visitors to Yuan-Li, and it plays a crucial role in the initial cultural understanding and transmission because of its ample indoor space for more than 100 people. The TYHA exhibits its award-winning works on holidays in the Shan-Jiao Elementary School's Japanese-style dormitory (county-designated historic site), and weaving is done by rush-weavers on-site on weekdays, complementing the exhibition for Triangle Rush Exhibition Hall. In 2022, TYHA further renovated its three-section compound as an exhibition and sales center. Furthermore, SunnyRush has been complementing the industry by occasionally holding small exhibitions in the store space in recent years. Only Hat and Mat Shops are wholesalers and do not deliberately target general consumers for promotion and exhibition.

The "consumption/participation" section found that both the TYHA and SunnyRush have independent exhibition and sales stores, and dozens of other sales channels in department stores, hotels, and cultural centers throughout Taiwan. They also regularly participate in the Cultural and Creative Park's invitational exhibitions and flash stores and offer tours and DIY courses, making them easily accessible to the general public. The difference is that the TYHA has a larger space and can accommodate more than 40 people, whereas SunnyRush can only accommodate small groups of 10 or fewer interviewees. Respondents also mentioned that local sales through self-operated stores are still indispensable due to the high commission (usually over 30%) from external channels, and that a three-hour DIY experience is more beneficial for profit per unit of time to facilitate visitor participation and cultural understanding.

### 4.3 Support from government programs

The TYHA has been active and proactive in all four segments of the overall cultural value chain. Its close integration with SCDA has been critical in gaining support for government programs in various ways. In particular, the longer-term "Multiple Employment Promotion Program and Empowering Employment Program" supported by the Ministry of Labor has enabled the TYHA to employ rush-weavers on a monthly basis to work on-site and to hire young managers who have returned to their hometowns to work on brand promotion, experimental product development, and cultural preservation. The "Rural Regeneration Program" supported by the Soil and Water Conservation Bureau of the Council of Agriculture supports the production, ecology, and living activities of the SCDA by providing support for site planning and renovation, as well as the costs of community education programs. In addition, the Taiwan Craft Research and Development Institute of the Ministry of Culture has assisted in organizing the certification of rush-weaving and the "One Township One Product" program, which helps nurture the new generation of weaving craftsmen and develop experimental new products needed for "creation" respectively. In the last two years, TYHA has continued to promote community-based industries through the "Accelerated Regional Revitalization program," for which the National Development Council encourages applications.

SunnyRush is a new venture. In the early stages of the company's development, the Ministry of Culture's "Youth Village Cultural Development Project," the Council of Agriculture's Soil and Water Conservation Bureau's "Youth Returning to Rural Areas Program," and the "Rural Community Business Counseling Program" were used to research rush-weaving patterns, establish the company, build the brand, and support operations. In the past two years, SunnyRush has been developing new products for commercialization, mainly through the Ministry of Economic Affairs' "Small Business for Township Revitalization (SBTR) Program and further establishing a new directly operated branch at the National Taichung Theater, focusing more on presenting the value chain related to "creation" and "consumption/participation" on the economic level.

The Yuan-Li Town Farmers' Triangle Rush Exhibition Hall and the traditional Hat and Mat Shops have not yet applied for external programs. The Yuan-Li Town Farmers supported the Exhibition Hall because the cultivation and weaving of rush were one of the most important businesses in the early days. Although the main focus of the operation has changed in the past 30 years to the sale of Yuan-Li's specialties such as rice, vegetables, and fruits, (for example, in 2002, the first exhibition of the "Painted Rice Field," which uses different-colored rice ears to create a 3D pattern in visual perspective, was developed) the Yuan-Li Town Farmers' Association was concerned about the emotional responsibility of history and the desire to preserve the precious pieces of rush-weaving crafts left behind from the early days. Therefore, in 2005, the Triangle Rush Exhibition Hall was established with partial subsidies from the Council of Agriculture.

In contrast, wholesalers such as Hat & Mat Shops have the largest number of cooperating rush-weavers. Despite the low profitability, they continue to operate to maintain their established friendships with the cooperating weavers. However, since the operators of these shops are old and the next generation is not willing to take over, it may become a gap for the industry in the future.

## 4  DISCUSSION

The previous results illustrate why Yuan-Li has become a model for Taiwan's community industry and cultural revitalization. More than a plurality of industry members contributes to the five segments of the cultural value chain: creation, production, dissemination, exhibition, and consumption. Thus, despite the small size of the industry members and the lack of apparent commercial cooperation or competition, they complement each other and are resilient to the commercial and cultural values of the rush-weaving industry. Complementarity in the commercial aspect is a matter of value creation in terms of market positioning, from low-price to high-price models, from fully customized to mass-produced products, from the division of labor to large orders, and from large and small group tours. The cultural aspects of communication and exhibition are complemented by the educational promotion of the TYHA, exhibitions at the local exhibition hall, youth entrepreneurship, continuous exposure through various government programs, regular and irregular events, and exhibitions in local and foreign counties to facilitate consumer recognition.

During this study, the author identified several concerns regarding the five cultural value chains of the rush-weaving industry. In the "creation" segment, it was found that half of the products currently sold are functional products made entirely of rush, such as hats. Consumers' perceptions of prices are already anchored, making it difficult to increase purchase prices and economic incentives for rush-weavers. It is also challenging to enter the market of high-priced art and collectibles because of the non-durable nature of the material. Therefore, it is essential to consider improving the value and cultural authenticity through design while also considering mass production and cost reduction.

In the "production" segment, there is still a severe aging trend among weavers and operators in charge of producing hats and mats. Newly certified rush-weavers are more of a hobby than a job, and this production gap still needs to be filled.

In the "exhibition" segment, the Triangle Rush Exhibition Hall display has aged after 20 years and needs to be updated to attract visitors.

In the "consumption" segment, with the current high commission rate (over 30%) from external distributors, promoting in-depth local experiences and direct sales is still essential. Therefore, at this stage, a cultural preservation perspective is still needed to support the commercial viability of the Yuan-Li rush-weaving industry.

Furthermore, despite the small size of the industry, there are still over a hundred rush-weavers, and different weavers specialize in different types of patterns and products, which do not meet the Ministry of Culture's definition of uniqueness or the ability to integrate all weaving skills required for the "Living National Treasure" certification. Giving senior weaving experts appropriate honor is also an issue to consider in cultural asset preservation policies.

## 5  CONCLUSION

This study utilizes industry clustering and cultural value chain theories to examine the relationships, market positioning, and innovative practices of the four types of rush-weaving industry members in Yuan-Li. The study found that the weavers are vital "shared resource," and there is a "buyer-supplier relationship," but the commercial competition and cooperation are not apparent. In addition, the cultural value chain explains the complementarity and differences between the commercial and cultural values of Yuan-Li's rush-weaving industry members, illustrating how this industry can continue to serve as a cultural and craft revival model for the Taiwanese community. The study also discusses the hidden problems and demand gaps identified during the study, which can serve as a reference for government policies and local universities to engage the community in promoting industrial cooperation.

## ACKNOWLEDGEMENTS

Thanks to the respondents of the rush-weaving industry and the Ministry of Science and Technology of Taiwan for the grant (MOST 111-2410-H-239-017).

# REFERENCES

Anderson G. (1994). Industry clustering for economic development. *Economic Development Review*, *12*(2), 26–32.

Chang B.-J., & Wang H. (2017). Taiwan Yuan-Li Handiwork Association: The beauty of small or the fullness of big? *Management review*, *36*(2), 89–90. [in Chinese, semantic translation]

Henry C. (2007). *Entrepreneurship in the Creative Industries: An International Perspective*. Cheltenham, UK: Edwin Elgar Publishing.

Landry C. (2000). *The Creative City*. London: Earthscan Publications.

Porter M.E. (1985). *Competitive advantage: creating and sustaining superior performance*. New York, NY: FreePress.

Potts J., S. Cunningham, J. Hartley & P. Ormerod (2008). Social Network markets: A New Definition of the Creative Industries. *Journal of Cultural Economics*, *32*(3), 166–185.

Ravasi D. and V. Rindova. (2008). A Cultural Perspective on Value Creation. In *Handbook of Emerging Approaches to Organization Studies*. Eds.D. Barry and H. Hansen. Sage Publications.

Saqib N. (2021). Positioning – a literature review. *PSU Research Review*, *5*(2), 141–169.

UNESCO (2009). *The 2009 UNESCO framework for cultural statistics (FCS)*. Quebec, Canada: UNESCO Institute for Statistics. Retrieved from http://uis.unesco.org/sites/default/files/documents/unesco-framework-for-cultural-statistics-2009-en_0.pdf

Yin R.K. (2003). *Case Study Research: Design and Methods*. Thousand Oaks, CA: Sage.

System Innovation for a Troubled World – Lam et al. (Eds)
© 2024 the Author(s), ISBN: 978-1-032-60846-4

# A case study to discuss the sensibility and rationality of design: "SOUL" branding of lock's cultural and creative products as an example

Chen-I Huang*
*Department of Visual Communication Design, Southern Taiwan University of Science and Technology, Tainan, Taiwan*
*Graduate School of Design, Master & Doctoral Program, National Yunlin University of Science and Technology, Yunlin, Taiwan*

C.F. Lee
*Graduate School of Design, Master & Doctoral Program, National Yunlin University of Science and Technology, Yunlin, Taiwan*

ABSTRACT: This study uses the case study method. And design practice to present the visual extension and redesign of cultural concepts, using innovative design to simplify and integrate visual graphics into the conceptual meaning of sensibility thinking. In rationality operation, taking usability design is an investigation to solve the problem of user universality, so that the finished product design has more diverse and complete design values.

In addition, after design development and mass production to finish the products, it has been affirmed by IF design award and K-design award in international competitions, which also shows the exquisite design and brand value of SOUL products, so through the research, the design process will be exposed and design thinking will be shared with the design industry, which definitely provides a reference to the design industry, which is really valuable.

## 1 INTRODUCTION

The word "design" is both a verb and a noun, which highlights the essential need to take into account both processes and final results.

Therefore, recording the "design process" to show the design thinking context can not only strengthen the reader's understanding of the core value of the product but also provide the budding designers to think about design transformation.

### 1.1 Motivation and purpose

From the past to the present generation, locks have always existed and played an indispensable role in life, only the appearance of locks and the way they are used vary according to history, but the meaning and value of locks have not changed, the material from the past generations of wooden locks, metal locks, to the present electronic locks, all have their significance from the history of generations.

The biggest difference between cultural and creative goods and ordinary goods is the selection of the theme, through the integration of intangible cultural assets, the process of acquiring, reading, and evaluating goods is full of different and deep

stimulation. The interactive relationship between products and people will be closer, and the "soul" of the product will be found to be visible, allowing the owner to cherish it more.

This study takes "ancient locks" as the topic, and designs and develops cultural and creative products with the commercial market in mind. In addition to extracting and presenting the meaning of "locks", the design must also be able to master the visual beauty, so that the finished product can be loved by the public and gain more attention in the market.

## 2 LITERATURE REVIEW

### 2.1 Lock

"Lock" is a product extended by the concept of "protection", and the explanation of "lock" in "Cihai" is: "The key must be used to open the device of silence. In Shuowen Jiezi, the word "lock" is interpreted as: "Lock, iron lock, door key. It can be clearly read that "metal" was the main material of door locks at that time, and "lock" also has the action relationship of "open and close".

Chinese locks have a long history, from wooden locks, metal locks, three-reed locks, leaf locks, etc., to the current electronic locks, the central concept of the product value is the same, all to protect the concept

---

*Corresponding Author: zay@stust.edu.tw

DOI: 10.1201/9781003460763-66

of precious objects, the key to open to take out, when then also developed the "mechanism lock", in addition to increasing the complexity of opening, but also to generate the fun of the concept of wit.

Since a lock is a security device, it is a device that can only be opened with a key, invented by man to protect his property. However, in modern times, a lock is a device of silence that is opened by a key, code, circuit, or other devices to prevent the opening or removal of objects, and has a protective, management, or even decorative role. The explanation of the word "lock" is: "A device of silence that must be opened by a key."

### 2.2 *Problem-solving*

"Problem-solving" has always been an important concept in people's minds. In order to survive, people have to feed and protect themselves, which leads to products and solutions, such as food, shelter, and other products with protection mechanisms.

Although problems are often complex and varied, we depend on our ability to find solutions.

### 2.3 *Sensibility and rationality*

Mituo Nagamachi (1989) defines rationality in terms of the association between humans and objects, from the senses and sensibility to the association of motives, and this association is the process of human reaction after contact with objects. Yen Hsu and Wu, Tsung-Han (2012) have interpreted rationality to mean "rational function" or "using rational motivation" to achieve the purpose of action within the effective range. The ability to use past experiences to select and plan current or future actions.

Jfeng Shie (2002) has also proposed that sensibility is defined in terms of the "association between humans and things", from the sensory, sensual, and perceptual to the motivational association of humans to things.

Conclusion: Through design transformation, the old culture will be given a new costume, so that more people can understand the uniqueness, history, and function of culture because of the beauty of design, and then cherish it and preserve it. In turn, it can be accepted by today's innovative and diversified market, while intangible cultural assets can be preserved and passed on.

### 3 RESEARCH PROCESS

In order to make the design development meet the marketability requirement, the design is considered in multiple aspects.

First of all, the theme of "antique locks" is used to identify the advantages and disadvantages of "antique locks" recognized by consumers, and then the problem is solved by "emotional" and "rational" orientation.

After the design concept is complete, the commercial market is the target, and the operation steps are specified in the following steps:

1. Brand construction: Branding involves the perceptual value and rational evaluation of goods, so the construction of a complete design brand will be able to establish a good market positioning for consumers.
2. Product design: The concept of "rolling" revision is run, and the products produced by the design are completed in accordance with the stage tasks to ensure the smoothness of the concept extension and then refined according to the design revision.
3. Packaging Design: Branded packaging increases the perception of a product, so a range of packaging designs can make the marketing process smoother.
4. Commercial photography: Professional visual presentation to make the value of brand products more fluent and can be fully applied to the advertising of marketing channels.

With the above four steps, we will build a complete "ancient lock" product plan, and then continue to compete for awards in international design competitions, hoping to be more convincing in marketing and display.

### 4 DESIGN RESULTS

#### 4.1 *Branding*

SOUL is pronounced like the Chinese word and means "lock". The meaning of SOUL is "soul".

SOUL is a lock that protects the heart and soul, and this concept is used to design and develop the brand, combining culture, aesthetics, and engineering with "heart" and "thinking".

Figure 1. SOUL logo.

#### 4.2 *Product design*

The main purpose of a "lock" is to protect precious or collectible things, and also to wish good luck to the things that are important in life and life, and it has become one of the important decorations for home or personal.

For example, a "Longevity Lock" or "Ruyi Lock" is worn in the hope that the child will have a long and prosperous life, good fortune, peace of mind, etc. The symbolic meaning is that good things can be firmly locked and treasured inside.

In ancient times, the "lock" was extended in appearance with many shapes and patterns, and the record shows that there were designs with creatures such as unicorns, butterflies, tigers, leopards, etc. However, the "fish" has the visual feature of not closing its eyes all day long, and the open eyes look like they are guarding the owner's treasure.

Figure 2.    The restoration of the ancient lock pattern.

Figure 3.    Lock and key.

Figure 4.    The lock elements.

Through the design of the old lock, we understand the advantages and disadvantages of the operation of the mechanism, and then consider the possibility of "commercialization" with the market

demand, so that the meaning of daily necessities and decorative items is deeper than the practical value.

Figure 5.    The first stage of the fish lock design, from the fish's mouth to open the necklace.

Figure 6.    The second stage of the fish lock design is visual design to present the concept of fish corresponding to the collection (five cakes and two fish).

In the second stage, the abstract presentation of the design reduces the idea of the lock, so the design decision returns to the rational operation axis of the lock, making the operation of the lock an important reading thread for brand products.

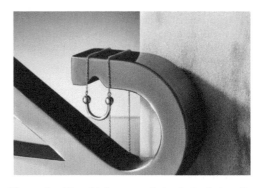

Figure 7.    The third stage of the lock design (for marketing), from the chest embellishment, rotate to open the necklace.

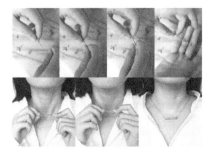

Figure 8. The lock design and how to use it.

The third stage of the product has become more mature, in addition to the concept of the lock, but also to solve the common problems of use that the necklace is easy to hook the hair, the lock is easy to fall to the chest because of the weight, in order to interpret the product focus and user experience design.

Figure 9. The fourth stage of the lock design (for marketing) is by the chest embellishment clasp and open the necklace.

After the fourth stage of the product, the core concept and commonality of the design can be grasped, and the beauty of the design can be more and more easily presented.

### 4.3 Packaging design

This project presents the complete brand products in series to make the brand more visible, and the items of the products "start from the heart" and surround the user's soul, so that the feeling of loving and cherishing the products is locked in the heart.

Figure 10. SOUL packaging design.

Figure 11. SOUL whole products.

### 4.4 Commercial photography

This project used commercial photography to present the beauty of the products and present the

Figure 12. SOUL product photos 1.

Figure 13. SOUL product photos 2.

Figure 14. SOUL product photos 3.

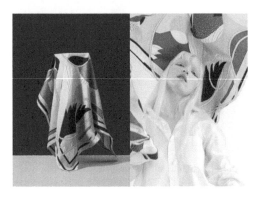

Figure 15.   SOUL product photos 4.

whole series of products: necklaces, scarves, ties, hand creams, etc., with more attractive images so that consumers can see them.

### 4.5   *International design awards*

The team led by Leader Huang, Chen I had a good experience in planning and designing "SOUL", which won the iF Design Award 2021 and the K-Design Award 2021!

SOUL is one of the Winners of the iF DESIGN AWARD 2021 and the K-Design AWARD 2021!!!!

Web site news is:

https://ifworlddesignguide.com/entry/301071-soul-brand-identity-design

Brand Spirit:

SOUL, pronounced like the Chinese word "lock", represents the meaning of "soul".

"SOUL is a lock that protects the heart and soul, and this concept is used for brand design and development, combining culture, aesthetics, and engineering with "heart" and "thinking".

#A good design is one that allows you to read the soul of the product

#Make you want to own it and cherish it

## 5   CONCLUSIONS

The use of emotional and rational thinking combined to produce psychological coordination, more able to achieve a sense of complete satisfaction. In the process of design, designers need to take more into account, because the work of designers is not only "creative design", should carry the "target market demand to achieve" the heavy responsibility, so if designers can design process while measuring the emotional and rational needs, then the production of goods will be more perfect!

By using design development to realize the transformation and reproduction of intangible cultural assets, the cultural depth of the diversified market can be enhanced, and the products will not only be a battle of prices but also show the core value and presentation of design. Through participation in international design competitions, the visibility of the international market can be expanded, so that the award-winning mark can add value to the products and be recommended for culture.

## REFERENCES

Jfeng Shie, 2002, *"The Influence of Product Forming Attributes on Users' Sensory Imagery: The Case of Mobile Phones"*, National Yunlin University of Science and Technology, Graduate Institute of Industrial Design, Master's Thesis

Mituo Nagamachi, 1989, *Sensual Engineering*, Tokyo, Japan, Haibundo Publishing Co.

Wu, Tsung-Han 2012 *"A Study on User-Oriented Design Methodology Combining Emotion and Rationality,"* Master's Thesis, Institute of Industrial Design, Ming Chi University of Technology

Yan, Hong-Sen and Huang, Hsing-Hui, 2001, *Understanding Early Chinese Locks*, Collection.com, National Taiwan Museum of History, YAN-hs/2001.0411.

Yan, Hong-Sen, 1999, The Beauty of Ancient Chinese Locks, Chinese Ancient Machinery Cultural and Educational Foundation, Tainan, Taiwan, ISBN 957-97374-9-5.

System Innovation for a Troubled World – Lam et al. (Eds)
© 2024 the Author(s), ISBN: 978-1-032-60846-4

# Nyanggit Nggathok patterned batik in clothing as an alternative to increasing production efficiency in the batik industry

Urip Wahyuningsih*, Indarti Yulistiana & Ratna Suhartini
*Fashion Study Program, Vocational Faculty, Surabaya state university, Surabaya*

Niken Purwidiani
*Culinary Education, Surabaya State University, Surabaya*

Andang Widjaja
*Civil Engineering, Faculty of Engineering, Surabaya state university, Surabaya*

ABSTRACT: Currently, batik craft continues to grow according to the times. The development of this batik art gave rise to a variety of batik industries, both in the form of Small and Medium Enterprises (SMEs) or on a large scale. The increase in the number of batik industry players automatically increases the competitiveness of each batik industry, to compete for local and global batik market share. This situation gave rise to the idea of making batik motif patterns that could increase the cost efficiency and the production time of batik cloth, to reduce production costs and time without leaving quality, creativity, and product innovation. This research is a study that examines or critically reviews knowledge, ideas, or findings contained in the body of academic-oriented literature and formulates theoretical and methodological contributions for certain topics. The making of Nyanggit Nggathok patterned batik is a pattern of batik motifs where the motif is incomplete and is placed in certain locations only based on the pattern of the parts of the garment so that after it becomes a garment, it will later be Nggathok (Javanese) or meet the pattern of the motif. This Nyanggit Nggathok batik pattern can reduce costs and production time for batik clothing. Research on the development of patterned batik motifs (Nyanggit Nggathok) on this clothing is to develop batik motifs on clothing, provide technical knowledge of patterned batik making to the industry to realize production and time efficiency of batik clothing so that the batik industry can continue to grow and create innovations that ready to be commercialized in global and local markets.

## 1 INTRODUCTION

Batik is an original Indonesian culture that was recognized by UNESCO as an Intangible Cultural Heritage (ICH) in 2009 and is recognized by the international community as a fabric of the history of human civilization. It is known that the art of batik during the royal era in Indonesia can be interpreted as the art of drawing on cloth for clothing or clothing which became a culture in the royal family. Initially, batik was only limited to the palace and the results were for the clothes of the king and his family and followers. Because many of the king's followers lived outside the palace, the art of batik was brought by them outside the palace.

Currently, batik continues to develop according to the times with all its consequences, adjusting to technological advances and the development of fashion forms that change every time. The development of this batik art gave rise to a variety of batik industries, both in the form of Small and Medium Enterprises (SMEs) or on a large scale. The emergence of the batik industry to meet the needs of the market for batik clothing is increasing and growing. In fact, according to the Ministry of Industry in its press release on the website https://kemenperin.go.id/ on Tuesday, October 4, 2022, it stated that the batik industry is a significant contributor to the national economy. The Ministry of Industry (Kemenperin) continues to strive to encourage this industry which is dominated by small and medium industries (IKM) to continue to be productive and competitive. One of the efforts made is through the facilitation of Batikmark certification as support from the Ministry of Industry to guarantee the quality, quality, and authenticity of Indonesian batik products, so that they can compete, both in local and global markets.

---

*Corresponding Author: uripwahyuningsih@unesa.ac.id

DOI: 10.1201/9781003460763-67

The increase in the number of batik industry players automatically increases the competitiveness of each batik industry, to compete for local and global batik market share. This situation gave rise to the idea of making batik motif patterns that could increase the cost efficiency and production time of batik cloth, to reduce production costs and time without leaving quality, creativity, and product innovation. The making of Nyanggit Nggathok patterned batik is a pattern of batik motifs where the motif is incomplete, and is placed in certain locations only based on the pattern of the parts of the garment so that after it becomes a garment it will later be Nggathok (Javanese) or meet the pattern of the motif. This Nyanggit Nggathok batik pattern can reduce costs and production time for batik clothing.

The objectives of this research are: 1) To produce patterned batik cloth products according to the Nyanggit Nggathok fashion design which is ready for commercialization, 2) To produce batik clothing products with intersecting motif patterns (Nyanggit Nggathok) as one of the innovations in the batik industry, 3) Increasing cost efficiency and production time in the batik industry by making the Nyanggit Nggathok batik pattern.

## 2 LITERATURE REVIEW

### 2.1 Nyanggit nggathok patterned batik fabric

Batik cloth whose motifs are not full, and are placed in certain locations only based on the pattern of the parts of the clothing, are often called Patterned Batik Materials. Parts of clothing are usually given motifs or decorations, for example, necklines, sleeve patterns, skirts, collars, front and back body patterns, and so on. Patterned batik cloth is basically a batik cloth that has pattern lines of clothing parts that are arranged efficiently, so there is no need to bother designing the layout of the pattern of the clothing parts on the batik cloth to be cut (Enny Zuhni Khayati 2009, in Sri Wening et al. 2013).

Batik cloth generally has a composition of motifs which results in the motifs not meeting in the clothing pattern. Nyanggit is a condition in which the batik motifs meet one another, and are not cut off. Patterned batik cloth is often found for the manufacture of men's shirts. Patterned batik cloth is a batik cloth that is made specifically for materials according to clothing designs. Patterned batik cloth with batik motifs will help in the process of cutting materials to be used as clothing. The composition of motifs on patterned batik influences the placement of clothing patterns so that the final result of the clothing will have an impact according to the design.

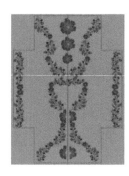

Figure 1.   Examples of Tektona batik cloth motifs and batik clothing Tektona motifs patterned according to clothing designs (Nyanggit Nggathok) (source: private collection).

### 2.2 Efficiency

Efficiency is a measure of success that is assessed in terms of the number of resources/costs to achieve the results of the activities carried out. In other words the relationship between what has been completed. Therefore, according to the statement mentioned above, the concept of efficiency will be created if the desired output can be optimally produced with only relatively fixed inputs, or if the smallest possible input can produce optimal output. These definitions will not always be the same but will generally include all ideas that can only be achieved with available resources. An efficient economic system can provide more goods and services to society without using more resources (Taufik H et al. 2021).

Along with the development of businesses that are growing rapidly, the competition in the business environment is getting tougher, especially in similar businesses. Therefore, companies must be able to survive and are required to be ready to face market competition. Especially small companies that must have efficient production cost control efforts in order to produce quality products at low costs (Palupi et al. 2016).

Mulyadi (2009, p. 14) production costs are costs incurred to process raw materials into finished products that are ready for sale. These costs are raw material costs, auxiliary material costs, employee salary costs, machine depreciation costs, and other costs, both directly and indirectly related to the production process.

Production efficiency is the relative amount of input used to achieve a certain level of output. The less input quantity used to make a number of products or the more products made with a certain input quantity, the higher the efficiency (Horngren et al. 2008, p. 279). Production cost efficiency is cost efficiency or reducing costs used for raw materials, labor, and overhead for the production process. The efficiency of production costs is important for companies to achieve optimal profit.

The efficiency level of a company's production costs can be measured by the cost of raw materials, direct labor, and factory overhead used to produce certain outputs (Palupi *et al.* 2016).

Production cost control can be seen by comparing the results achieved with the results expected by the company. One of the benchmarks used to control production costs at the company is the standard cost. "Standard cost is a predetermined cost to produce one unit or a certain number of products in a certain period" (Carter 2009, p. 158).

### 2.3 *Indonesian batik industry*

Research conducted by Abi Pratiwa Siregar, *et al.* In 2020, 27 provinces in Indonesia used a descriptive-analytical method using primary data and secondary data. Based on research results, it is estimated that the number of batik industries in Indonesia has reached 6,120 units with a workforce of 37,093 people and is capable of achieving a production value of around 407.5 billion rupiahs per month or the equivalent of 4.89 trillion rupiahs per year. The problems faced by the batik industry consist of printing, raw materials, labor skills, local fabric business development, waste management, guidance and assistance by Regional Apparatus Organizations (OPD), and competition with batik printing.

Furthermore, Abi Pratiwa Siregar *et al.* (202) state that the status of batik-producing areas is still attached to Java. Eighty-seven percent of the batik industry in Indonesia is spread across West Java (38.42%), Central Java (26.22%), Yogyakarta Special Region (DIY) (19.52%), East Java (2.66%), Banten (0.23%), and the Special Capital Region (DKI) Jakarta (0.05%), while outside Java the largest batik industry is in Jambi Province

As part of the textile industry, the batik industry is one of the priority sub-sectors in the implementation of the Making Indonesia 4.0 roadmap. This is because the batik industry is considered to have great leverage in boosting national economic growth. The batik industry is also one of the industrial sectors that creates many job opportunities. This sector, which is dominated by Small and Medium Industries (IKM), absorbs a workforce of more than 200 thousand people in 47,000 business units spread across 101 centers in Indonesia. Based on data from the Ministry of Industry, batik exports in 2020 reached US $532.7 million. In the first quarter of 2021, it reached US$157.8 million. This shows that the batik industry has played an important role in the national economy and has succeeded in becoming a market leader in the world batik market (Ministry of Industry in a press release on the website https://kemenperin.go.id/ on Tuesday, October 4, 2020).

The status of batik-producing areas is still attached to Java Island. Eighty-seven percent of the batik industry in Indonesia is spread across West Java (38.42%), Central Java (26.22%), Yogyakarta Special Region (DIY) (19.52%), East Java (2.66%), Banten (0.23%), and the Special Capital Region (DKI) Jakarta (0.05%), while outside Java, the majority of the batik industry is in Jambi Province. West Java province is ranked first with the largest number of batik industries. This is inseparable from the status of Cirebon which is one of the centers of batik and has made a long journey to date (Handayani 2018). In this area, several batik artisans even have branches in other big cities, such as Jakarta and Yogyakarta, so their marketing is expanding. In addition, several large written batik artisans have successfully exported (Wahyuningsih & Fauziah, 2016). The development of the batik industry in Cirebon is also influenced by orders for typical motifs from other regions such as South Sumatra due to limited human resources in the region (Suryani 2017).

## 3 DISCUSSION

The process of making patterned batik motifs begins with finding ideas for batik motifs that are of course in accordance with or following the wishes of consumers or market share and it would be better if explored from local regional values or local natural wealth. Batik motifs greatly determine the journey of batik cloth or clothing after it is later released to the market, although the quality of the cloth, the coloring, and the pattern also determine it. Therefore, on an industrial scale, the production of certain batik motifs needs in-depth study.

Making batik motifs is done before the batik process. The initial stage of making batik motifs is to determine the idea or choose the desired motif. The design is done before drawing the pattern on the cloth. The design is made on paper complete with coloring. The batik paintings that we make are tailored to the design of the motif. The fabric to be used should be ironed before the surface is given a pattern image. The smooth and even surface of the cloth will make it easier to make motifs and the process of reading them.

The steps for making patterned batik motifs in outline are as follows: 1) drawing of designs based on existing ideas, 2) making fashion designs, 3) Laying designs on clothes, 4) making dress patterns, 5) transferring motifs to patterns, 6) laying patterns on materials by tracing motifs on materials, 6 ) whined, 7) fun, 8) poking, 9) wall, and 10) sagging.

Based on the 2018 SKKNI, the swaying batik motifs are motifs that meet at the appearance of the final product, and the gunshot batik motifs are batik motifs that are symmetrical left and right in the appearance of the final product. The depiction of this batik motif is done manually and or using a computer application for drawing.

The making of the Nyanggit Nggathok patterned batik motif begins with the first step of determining the design, then the design that has been obtained is applied to the pattern image according to the pattern per piece of clothing. Furthermore, it is then applied to the cloth so that the final result of the clothing produces a pattern of batik motifs that are not cut.

This patterned batik cloth will help in the process of cutting the material to be used as clothing. The composition of the motifs on patterned batik influences the placement of clothing patterns so that the final result of the clothing will have an impact according to the design and this will increase the economic and aesthetic value of the batik.

In addition to producing new products that match the pattern, it is also more time-efficient to work on this because the batik process will only be in accordance with the pattern that has been designed and the existing pattern designs can be directly applied to many fabrics and clothing as needed so that future work will be faster. Efficiency is also obtained in terms of costs because it can minimize the remaining unused cloth. The Nyanggit Nggathok pattern will only cut the cloth according to the design needs of the clothing.

This, when applied to the batik industry in the manufacture of patterned batik cloth motifs on a large scale or in large quantities, will clearly have an impact on cost efficiency and the production time of ready-to-wear patterned batik cloth and batik clothing. This is in accordance with what was conveyed by Halimatus Sa'dyah *et al.* (2013) that the production process of batik clothing consists of three stage: the stage of preparing the layout of the dress pattern, the stage of cutting the cloth and the stage of sewing the dress. The stage of preparing the layout of the clothing pattern aims to adjust the shape of the pieces of batik cloth to match the desired fashion model, the stage of cutting the cloth aims to cut the batik cloth according to the position and shape of the pattern of clothing that has been placed on the batik cloth, while the sewing stage aims to sew pieces of batik cloth to get ready-made clothes. Among the three stages, the stage that determines the optimal use of raw materials is the stage of preparing the layout of the clothing pattern. The more optimal the layout of the clothing pattern, the more optimal the use of raw materials.

In the production function, the factors that directly affect the amount of product produced are the production factors (inputs) used. These factors are raw materials, auxiliary materials, and labor. In addition to these direct factors, some factors do not directly affect the amount of product produced. These factors are related to management tips in the batik production business. One of the efforts to reduce product selling prices is by

Figure 2. An example of a bird motif batik cloth with a Nyanggit-Nggathok pattern. (source: private collection).

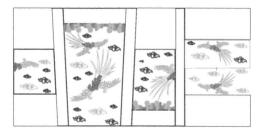

Figure 3. Placement of the cutting pattern on the Batik Batik cloth with the Nyanggit Nggathok pattern (source; private collection).

Figure 4. The clothing design is a bird batik motif with the Nyanggit Nggathok pattern. (source: private collection)

increasing technical efficiency. Based on empirical observations, these factors are closely related to the characteristics of batik entrepreneurs such as age, educational level of the batik entrepreneur/ producer, level of skills, and knowledge.

In making batik motifs with the Nyanggit Nggathok pattern, efficiency will occur on direct factors (efficiency in the use of raw materials for cloth, efficiency of batik materials, and efficiency of production time) and indirect factors (required additional knowledge on the skills and knowledge of batik entrepreneurs regarding batik motifs). As previously stated, the production of the Nyanggit Nggathok patterned batik motifs in the batik process will only be in accordance with the patterns that have been designed and the existing pattern designs can be directly applied to as many fabrics and clothing as needed so that future work will be faster. Efficiency is also obtained in terms of costs because it can minimize the remaining unused cloth. This is coupled with if the knowledge and skills of batik craftsmen about the Nyanggit Nggathok pattern motif open and increase, efficiency values will be applied properly.

The characteristic of the batik industry is the existence of a high level of competition, which causes the batik industry to be very dependent on consumers, where product prices are determined by the market. This is caused by the short life cycle of a product, where the types of products marketed are very diverse. Thus, the management of the product launch strategy needs to be carried out precisely and carefully so that the company can meet consumer demands quickly and be able to compete for profits. Therefore, the batik industry, which focuses on fulfilling time to market quickly and precisely, requires an accurate, targeted, and effective product launch strategy.

According to Indra Cahyadi (2017), the most appropriate alternative marketing strategy for Batik SMEs based on existing limitations is the people network strategy. This strategy is a new strategy for Batik SMEs, where Batik SMEs can pay more attention to the criteria that are the builders of this marketing strategy, namely positive image, expanding network, number of customers, costs, customer loyalty, and business volume. From this opinion, it can be further that the manufacture of Nyanggit Nggathok patterned batik products is a creativity and innovation of batik clothing products that match the desired design patterns so that consumers have many choices of tastes and this clearly increases and expands the selling value of these batik clothes.

## 4 CONCLUSION

This Nyanggit Nggathok patterned batik product will assist in the process of cutting the material and the composition of the motifs will affect the placement of the clothing pattern so that the final result of the clothing will have an impact in accordance with the expected design.

Regarding the production efficiency of the batik industry, this is reflected in the innovation of batik cloth products that match the desired design patterns so that consumers have many choices of tastes, and savings in fabric materials thereby reducing production time and costs.

Nggathok nyanggit patterned batik cloth products will be able to penetrate today's very global consumer tastes and increase the competitiveness of the existing batik industry.

## REFERENCES

Abi Pratiwa Siregar. 2020. Upaya Pengembangan Industri Batik Di Indonesia. *Dinamika KErajinan dan Batik.* Kemenperin RI. Vol. 37 No. 1, Juni 2020, Hal 79–92

Assauri Sofjan. (2016). *"Strategic Management Sustainable Competitive Advantages"* Edisi 2. Jakarta: Rajawali Pers

Carter W. K. (2009). *Akuntansi Biaya.* Jakarta: Salemba Empat.

Council, D. (2019). *What is the Framework for Innovation? Design Council's Evolved Double Diamond.* Retrieved from Design Council: https://www.designcouncil.org.uk/news-opinion/what-framework-innovation-design-councils-evolved-double-diamond.

Dwinda P.E.. & Rahdriawan M. (2013). *"Peran Perempuan Dalam Pengembangan Industri Batik Tulis Di Kabupaten Pamekasan (Studi Kasus Di Desa Klampar, Kecamatan Proppo, Kabupaten Pamekasan)".* Disertasi. Universitas Diponegoro

Halimatus Sa'dyah dkk (2013). *Framework Optimalisasi Tata Letak Pola Busana Pada Kain Batik Dengan Mempertimbangkan Keserasian Motif.* Scan Vol. VIII Nomor 3 Oktober 201. ISSN: 1978–0087

Handayani, W. (2018). Bentuk, Makna Dan Fungsi Seni Kerajinan Batik Cirebon. *Jurnal Atrat,* 6 (1), 58–71

Horngren, C.T., Datar M., & Foster, G. (2008). *Akuntansi Biaya, Penekanan Manajerial.* Jakarta: Erlangga.

Ika Anggun dan U. Wahyuningsih. *"Pengaruh Peletakan Motif Pada Pola Zero Waste terhadap Hasil Jadi The Chinese Square Blouse".* Volume 8, issue 1

Indra Cahyadi, Ika Deefi Ana. 2017. Penentuan strategi pemasaran batik madura dengan pendekatan multi criteria decicion making. *Journal Industrial Services* Vol. 3 No. 1 Oktober 2017

Irfa Rifaah. (2020). "Analisis komposisi motif kain batik yang berefek pada visual kemeja pria. *Prosiding Seminar Nasional Industri Kerajinan dan Batik* 2020, eISSN 2715-7814. Yogyakarya 6 Oktober 2020.

Karta, Abdul Azis, D. C. (2019). "Strategi Diversifikasi Konsentris Tenun Sutera Wajo." *Jurnal Desain Komunikasi Visual Fakultas Seni Dan Desain UNM,* 6 (118–127)

Ledbury, J. (2017). *Design and Product Development in High-Performance Apparel. In High-Performance Apparel: Materials, Development, and Applications.* Elsevier Ltd. https://doi.org/10.1016/B978-0-08-100904-8.00009-2

Lisbijanto, Herry. 2013. *"Batik".* Yogyakarta: Graha Ilmu.

Menurut Moh. Takdir & Moh. Hosnan (2021). Revitalisasi kesenian batik sebagai destinasi wisata berbasis budaya dan agama: peran generasi muda dalam mempromosikan kesenian batik di pamekasan madura. *MUDRA Jurnal Seni Budaya* Volume 36, Nomor 3, September 2021. P- ISSN 0854-3461, E-ISSN 2541-0407

Mia Ayu Wardani, dkk. 2017. *"Analisis Daya Saing dan Faktor-Faktor yang Memengaruhi Ekspor Ban Indonesia ke Kawasan Amerika Latin. Jurnal Ekonomi dan Kebijakan Pembanguan",* hlm. 81-100 Vol 6 No 1 Edisi Juli 2017.

Mudrajad, Kuncoro, *"Ekonomika Industri Indonesia Maju Negara Industri Baru 2020",* (Yogyakarta: Penerbit Andi, 2007), h.82

Mulyadi. (2009). *Akuntansi Biaya. Edisi 5.* Yogyakarta: YKPN

Nihayah Nurul, dan U. Wahyuningsih. *"Analisis Pemanfaatan Tepung sebagai bahan baku perintang warna pada rekayasa kain batik,"* vol 10 No.02

Novi D.B. Tamami dkk (2021. Strategi peningkatan pemasaran batik madura berdasarkan customer value. *Seminar Nasional Politeknik Pertanian Negeri Pangkajene Kepulauan "Sustainability and Environmentally of Agricultural System for Safety, Healthy and Security Human Life"*

Palupi T.A., Z.A, Z., & NP., M. W. (2016). Analisis Biaya Standar untuk Mendukung Efisiensi Biaya Produksi Perusahaan (Studi pada Pabrik Gula Lestari, Patianrowo, Nganjuk). *Jurnal Administrasi Bisnis (JAB)*, Vol. 36 No. 1, 80–85

Priyambodo, Miftakhul (2020). *"Perancangan Aplikasi Marketplace Penjualan Batik Klampar Berbasis Android."* Undergraduate thesis, UPN "Veteran" Jatim.

Syamwil R., Nurrohmah S. and Wahyuningsih U. 2013. *"Pemberdayaan Pengrajin Batik Kendal,"* no. 1, pp. 44–52. 2013.

R.A Sekartaji Suminto, (2015). *"Batik madura: menilik ciri khas dan makna filosofinya." CORAK Jurnal Seni Kriya* Vol. 4 No.1, Mei-Okteber 2015

Rani Sulistyorini, dan U. Wahyuningsih, 2021. *"Eksplorasi Perintang Warna Alami Pada Kualitas Motif Batik,"* vol.10 No.02. 2021

Sri Ira Suharwati. (2019). *"Pengembangan Industri Batik Tulis Sebagai Potensi Daerah ( Studi Kasus Di Desa Klampar Kabupaten Pamekasan)".* Jurnal Pendidikan Ilmu Pengetahuan Sosial. P-ISSN: 2355 – 8245 E-ISSN: 2614 – 5480. *Permalink/DOI:* 10.18860/jpips. v6i1.7822

Sri Wening, Enny Zuhni Khayati, Sri Emy Yuli Suprihatin. 2013. *"Pengembangan Produk Dan Strategi Pemasaran Busana Batik Bantulan Dengan Stilasi Motif Ethno Modern". Jurnal Penelitian Humaniora*, Vol. 18, No.1, April 2013: 70–81

Suryani, I. (2017). Terpesona Lembaran Kain Sumatera Selatan. https://travel.detik.com/dtravelers_stories/u-3673319/terpesona-lembarankain-sumatera-selatan diakses 25 Januari 2023.

Tambunan, Tulus. (2001). *"Industrialisasi di Negara Sedang Berkembang, Kasus Indonesia".* Jakarta: Ghalia Indonesia

Taufik H. dkk. (2021). Penerapan Prinsip Efektif dan Efisien dalam Pelaksanaan Monitoring Kegiatan Penelitian. dan Perencanaan Pembangunan, *Penelitian dan Pengembangan Kota Bandung.*

Tis'aini, N. (2010). *"Analisis Faktor-Faktor yang Mempengaruhi Perkembangan Industri Batik Madura di Pamekasan (Studi Kasus Pada Industri Batik di Dusun Banyumas, Desa Klampar, Kecamatan Proppo, Kabupaten Pamekasan)".* Skripsi Jurusan Ekonomi Pembangunan-Fakultas Ekonomi UM

Tjiptono. 2019. *"Strategi Pemasaran Prinsip & Penerapan".* Edisi 1. Yogyakarta. Andy.

Wahyuningsih, N., & Fauziah, N. (2016). Industri Kerajinan Batik Tulis Trusmi dan Dampaknya Terhadap Pendapatan Pengrajin Batik Tulis Trusmi di Desa Trusmi Kulon Cirebon. 4(2), 124–132

*System Innovation for a Troubled World – Lam et al. (Eds)*
© 2024 the Author(s), ISBN: 978-1-032-60846-4

# A study on the benefits of long-term care services setting community interaction spaces and service models

RuYuh You*, Heng Zhang & ChiPang Lu
*Department of Architecture, National Cheng Kung University, Tainan, Taiwan*

LiangJu Chen
*Department of Health Business Administration, Hungkuang University, Taichung City, Taiwan*

ABSTRACT: In Taiwan, there has been a push toward long-term care policies and the development of related institutions for elderly care, but there has been less exploration of the space and service models for institutions to interact with communities. This study draws on Japan's experience in promoting community interaction and believes that if long-term care service units can improve or reserve communication spaces that connect with the community in spatial design, they can provide diverse informal care services to promote intergenerational communication in the community. It can also provide more networks and support for residents' lives (Jinnai 2018). The study takes the YMCA community center and care cafe' in Tainan, Taiwan, as the research objective, where a relatively diverse mix of volunteers and employees provide formal and informal care services. The study found that the space design and service model for community interaction can inadvertently create a sense of comfort for users in the space, and four factors, including "appropriate communication level," "social role," "imagination of aging," and "healthy eating and knowledge," showed significant benefits.

## 1 INTRODUCTION

In Taiwan, the long-term care policies and the elderly care institutions both focus on the spatial design and the needs of care providers and aim to improve the quality of life for the elderly. However, there is relatively less attention given to the spaces for interaction between institutions and communities. Drawing from Japan's experiences, incorporating community interaction spaces in spatial design can provide diverse informal care services, promote intergenerational communication, and enhance care support.

In response to the challenges of an aging society, collaboration between local governments and local units is crucial. The White Paper on Aged Society points out that the construction and strengthening of community networks directly affect the well-being of the elderly. The Long-Term Care 2.0 Strategy emphasizes the establishment of a community-based care service system. By integrating resources from various levels and sectors, the elderly can be provided with community participation, life support, and disability prevention services, improving the efficiency and convenience of service space utilization and supporting their autonomous lives in the community.

The open-care housing design experience in Japan shows that reserving spaces for community interaction can facilitate integration (Haruhiko *et al.* 2020; Su & Chao 2022). Research has found that autonomy in life

and a friendly environment within communities can enhance the quality of life for the elderly. Previous studies on social participation and community spaces for the elderly have mainly focused on barrier-free facilities, with little exploration of the sense of comfort experienced by the elderly in these spaces.

This study takes the Tainan YMCA community care center as an examples providing both formal and informal care services. The research aims to investigate how spatial environment planning and care service design can make the elderly feel comfortable and maintain autonomy in life within institutions, as well as the impact of the institutional spatial environment and care services on the elderly's sense of comfort and autonomy.

## 2 LITERATURE REVIEW

### 2.1 *Sense of autonomy*

Individuals' ability to choose and maintain their preferred lifestyle, as well as the friendliness of the community environment, greatly influence whether the elderly can continue to participate in society, which in turn affects their quality of life (Levasseur *et al.* 2017). Past research has found that the higher the autonomy of the elderly, the higher their life satisfaction and social activity participation (Hertz & An-schutz 2002), and maintaining high autonomy leads to greater well-being in old age (Wahl *et al.* 2012).

Even in long-term care institutions, the elderly who can autonomously participate in activities and

*Corresponding Author: akirayoutatsu@hotmail.com

DOI: 10.1201/9781003460763-68

control their environment have better psychological and physical adaptation. Autonomy is an expression of the need for freedom, providing the elderly with more opportunities to actively establish good relationships with others and potentially receive higher social support. Lee, Chen *et al.* (2015) studied the correlation between elderly well-being, the degree of freedom needed for fulfillment, and social support, finding that the "degree of comfort and fulfillment," "social companionship support," and "instrumental support" in "social support" can effectively predict happiness. Among these factors, social support has a greater strength for happiness than the degree of freedom that needs fulfillment.

Based on the above discussions, this study believes that the sense of comfort for the elderly in community centers or institutions stems from individual autonomy and the social support provided by the spatial environment. To achieve higher life satisfaction and happiness, it is necessary to maintain a higher level of autonomy, while social support and a friendly environment are the key factors in supporting autonomy.

## 2.2  *Friendly environment with social support*

In terms of community care and home services, social support can be provided through interactions with family members, relatives, friends, or other informal social networks, making the senior people feel respected, intimate, and secure. As they age, these informal network connections become closely intertwined with their lives, helping them gain social support and face difficulties encountered in life (Bowling 1997).

Suen (2018) used the Self-Determination Theory to discuss the autonomy of elderly people in daycare centers based on the three basic psychological needs of autonomy, competency, and relatedness (Deci & Ryan, 2002). The study found that in daycare centers, elderly individuals exhibit varying levels of autonomy during meals, rest, and activities. Moreover, in their daily lives, the elderly's ability to live independently affects the improvement of their daily life competencies. Additionally, the center must assist in establishing new social relationships for the elderly, providing opportunities for them to participate in social activities and to live independently, which can help them affirm their abilities, take control of their destiny, and face the experience of loss in life, avoiding learned helplessness.

The institutional spatial environment plays a role in providing social support for the elderly. In the Japanese community-integrated service center experience, institutions embodying the concept of "intergenerational interaction spaces (places)" enable the elderly to achieve "moderate communication," "social roles," "protection," "imagination of aging," "regular life activation," and "healthy knowledge" (Megumi *et al.* 2012). These conditions and impacts contribute to a sense of freedom and comfort, referred to as "ご ちゃまぜ感 (mixed-up feeling)" (Jinnai 2018).

In summary, the community-oriented institution is an essential living resource for local elderly communities. By considering the design of spatial environment planning, care service functions, elderly people's independent living, competency, and assisting them in building social relationships, institutions can maintain the elderly's autonomy while allowing them to experience a sense of freedom and comfort, known as "ごちゃまぜ感 (mixed-up feeling)" within the institutional environment.

## 3  METHOD

### 3.1  *Research field and participants*

The research field is the YMCA Community Care Center in Tainan City, which is a community-integrated service center and a senior learning center located in the East District of Tainan City. Informal care services in the surrounding area include cafes, hair salons, volunteer lounges, etc. The YMCA Community Care Center is staffed with a relatively diverse team of employees and volunteers to provide related services.

The center is located on the first floor of the Tainan Accessible Home, with other social welfare units on the other floors. In addition, the center location is in the Houjia school district, surrounded by Xiaodong, Zhuangjing, and Dongming neighborhoods, and adjacent to National Cheng Kung University. As a result, the population visiting the center includes not only the original service participants but also employees and the public from other floors of the Tainan Accessible Home, local community residents, as well as teachers and students from National Cheng Kung University.

Figure 1.  Tainan YMCA Community Center floor plan.

### 3.2  *Research method*

This study is cross-sectional research conducted from May to June 2020, conducting a combination of quantitative questionnaire surveys and qualitative individual interviews. The survey participants were attendees of community health courses at the center. A total of 100 questionnaires were distributed, with 71 valid responses collected. The questionnaire included personal basic information, space usage status, overall comfort with space usage, and perceived benefits of community interaction spaces. Personal basic information comprised gender, age, education, financial situation, living situation, and self-perceived health; space usage status included transportation mode and travel time, vis frequency, duration of stay, time of participation, most frequently used spaces, most frequently contacted individuals, most frequently participated activities, and volunteering in other organizations. The mixed-up feeling in space usage was assessed using a Likert 5-point scale (1–5 points) to measure the degree of comfort, with options ranging from very poor, poor, average, good, and excellent. The investigation of perceived benefits of community interaction spaces included the degree of adequate interaction (5 items), social role (4 items), imagination of aging (4 items), knowledge of healthy eating (3 items), feeling of being protected (2 items), and regular life activation (4 items); each item has binary choices.

Qualitative interviews were conducted individually with those willing to participate in the interviews, with a total of 7 interviewees. The interview content included reasons for using the interaction space, differences in life and mental state before and after using the space, and feelings about using the multifunctional space of the care cafe.

Figure 2. Research Framework.

### 3.3 Analysis

After the questionnaire data was collected, SPSS version 17.0 was used for analysis. Descriptive statistics and inferential statistics were conducted to analyze the influencing factors.

## 4 RESULT AND DISCUSSION

### 4.1 Concept of establishment and users' sense of comfort

In response to the super-aged society, the goal is to support the elderly to live independently and autonomously in the community, allowing them to receive more social support in their lives, and to engage community residents of different generations in taking collective action to address the challenges of the times. Therefore, in terms of care service functions, in addition to long-term care services and elderly vitality teaching services, spaces have been designed for general public use, providing informal care services such as coffee, nail art, and social interaction. As Jinai (2018) suggests that a sense of place in the integrated community space is essential: (1) space design allows anyone to enter and exit freely, and anyone can imagine; (2) community participants are diverse and cross-generational, with diverse staff; and (3) providing a variety of services.

The aim is to make the various services provided more closely related to community life rather than being limited to "care." "Care" should not be simplified to just caregiving but should also include the everyday life experiences that everyone has. This study found that, for the respondents, the main purpose of the space was to provide courses, with the majority of respondents participating in the elderly vitality classes (93%), making the vitality classroom the most frequently used space (77.5%). However, the café also played an important role, with 33.8% of respondents using it as their free time space after class and as a free area. The sense of comfort had an average score of 4.2 (standard deviation: 0.73). Further analysis using logistic regression showed that, after controlling for other factors, the influencing factor for "space comfort " was the frequency of space visiting, particularly for those visits 2–3 times a week, whose sense of comfort was significantly lower. It can be inferred that, compared to the frequency of space participation, the participants' contact with the space may be a more important factor in enhancing their sense of comfort.

Table 1. Logistic regression analysis for influencing factors of comfort of the space.

| Variable (Reference Group) | OR | 95% | C.I of OR |
|---|---|---|---|
| Participation Time (Joined this month) | | | |
| 1–6 months | 1.307 | 0.197 | 8.690 |
| More than 6 months | 2.093 | 0.421 | 10.399 |
| Number of Participating Spaces (Single) | 1.144 | 0.317 | 4.134 |
| Two or more | | | |
| Space Participation Frequency (1 time/week) | | | |
| 2–3 times/week | 0.250* | 0.064 | 0.977 |
| 4 or more times/week | 0.809 | 0.217 | 3.013 |
| Number of Participated Activities (Single) | | | |
| Two or more | 1.862 | 0.496 | 6.992 |
| Participating in volunteer activities outside of the café (None) | | | |
| Yes | 0.689 | 0.203 | 2.336 |
| Living Situation (Living alone) | | | |
| Living with children | 1.096 | 0.295 | 4.068 |
| Living with husband/wife | 1.838 | 0.367 | 9.202 |

*:p<0.05

### 4.2 Social support

#### 4.2.1 Diverse human resources for social connections and a variety of formal and informal service activities

In the center, the roles and responsibilities of volunteers and staff are differentiated and complemented, and through the training of diverse human resources, more appropriate community life services can be provided. Diverse human resources may include staff, social welfare cases, volunteers, students, residents, and others who can better meet the diverse needs and interests of community residents and attract more people to visit. In the interview summary, Interviewee 1 (the supervisor) said: "*Sometimes, storytelling activities that children would enjoy would attract community mothers to bring their children to participate in.*" They can also naturally interact with the elderly volunteers. In addition, the instructors would bring their own children to participate in the class. Teachers, children, and the elderly would naturally blend together. It can be seen that the volunteers, course teachers, and students in the venue would be the interaction objects for the elderly when they come to the institution. Therefore, in terms of service, it can be seen that integrating informal care services with formal care services, emphasizing cross-disciplinary cooperation, can complement each other. It overcomes the limitations of setting up long-term care units with only legally mandated spaces and manpower, which are not easily expandable. This also achieves the principle of diversity among community participants proposed by Jinnai (2018).

Allowing the elderly to receive social support through spontaneous and autonomous interactions with various people (as shown in the table below). In the community care center, the elderly can not only interact with formal staff but also with other elderly students, café volunteers, general community members, and students from National Cheng Kung University. At the same time, according to the wishes of the elderly, they can be general visitors who come to taste coffee, or they can sign up as senior students or serve as café volunteers or care volunteers. Moreover, the roles can change depending on the time, place, and task. Not leaving anyone behind in the community, making it mixed up, and not identifying who is a visitor and who is a care client, whether he is strong or vulnerable, everyone is an important member. *"I feel that the cases coming to this open space to participate in activities have a different life pattern than when they are at home because no one here cares who has dementia, and they can come if they want to, without having to apply in advance"* (Interviewee 2). Furthermore, the results of the community interaction space show that almost all respondents agree that they can have conversation partners, mutual care, concern, and assistance in this space.

### 4.2.2 *Reserving ample informal care services and communication spaces*

The YMCA Community Center is situated in Tainan's Barrier-Free Home, making its spatial environment an accessible and friendly space. Furthermore, the spatial planning and design concept allows for ambiguous zones between distinct areas, such as the intermediary space between the entrance hall and the café, the corridor space between the café and the classroom, and the waiting space between the parking lot and the building. These spaces provide opportunities for the public to linger and interact, reducing the distance between the institution and the community.

In addition to architectural planning and design, the center actively connects with the community on a software level. For example, it organizes and cooperates with neighboring churches, community organizations, and other units in interactive action plans,

Table 2. The roles and functions of the elderly Autonomy

| Autonomy | The roles and functions of the elderly |
| --- | --- |
| Choosing community courses autonomously and planning time independently | Dynamic and static course activities (youth and elderly activities, intergenerational interaction) Café space activities, interactive activities Non-routine community movie screenings |
| Choosing one's own role and fulfilling one's own functions | Care plan office staff can also come out to the counter to help make coffee; Staff with course expertise can serve as the teacher Students can serve as office volunteers to help with data organization |
| Choosing one's own space regardless of the rules | Care plan office staff can come out to the coffee area to adjust their mood or meet with clients at the café. Students don't have to go home immediately after class. Not necessarily having to order food or drinks at the café. |

providing and developing informal activities, which allows the elderly to autonomously or inadvertently participate in and integrate with other people of different ages, genders, and cultural backgrounds, such as in the café seating area, hair salon, intergenerational creative space, volunteer lounge, and a farming garden.

Figure 3.   Tainan YMCA Community Center informal space.

### 4.3 *Regarding the key factors influencing the sense of comfort*

Using logistic regression to analyze the factors influencing the sense of ease in space, after controlling for other factors, the results show that compared to those who visit once a week, those who visit two to three times a week have a significantly lower chance of having a very good sense of comfort (OR = 0.25, 95% CI = 0.064–0.977, and p<0.05). It was also found that the average number of contacts in this group is related (p<0.05), suggesting that, compared to the frequency of spatial visits, the contacts visiting in the space may be a more critical factor in enhancing the sense of comfort.

There is a significant relationship between different levels of spatial ease and the benefits of en-gawa spaces. The results show that different levels of spatial comfort are significantly related to the degree of adequate interaction (F = 18.676, P<0.001), the degree of social roles (F = 3.898, P<0.05), the degree of imagination of aging (F = 7.168, P<0.01), and the degree of knowledge of healthy eating (F = 11.341, P<0.001). For those who feel more comfortable in the space, the benefits of community interaction are significantly higher than for those who feel an average level of comfort.

## 5 CONCLUSION

In Taiwan, long-term care policies for the social participation and community space of older adults have mostly focused on universally designed barrier-free facilities and equipment, with little exploration of the sense of comfort felt by older adults in these spaces.

This study believes that integrating community exchange elements (engawa) into the multifunctional design of the spatial environment in long-term care service institutions can enhance the sense of comfort and autonomy in the lives of older adults. In addition to participation frequency, it is inferred that the contact of the study subjects in the space may be a more critical factor in enhancing the sense of comfort, or "spatial comfort."

Therefore, providing diverse informal care services in institutions can increase the contact and social support between older adults and their linkage with the space, thus enhancing the sense of comfort for older adults within the institution. These contacts can include volunteers, community residents, and family members of older adults who can provide various forms of care and support, such as companionship, conversation, and assistance in caregiving.

Moreover, the institutional space should allow all users to care for, support, and assist each other. Autonomous planning time, choosing one's role, and selecting the desired space have a significant relationship with different levels of spatial comfort and the benefits of community exchange spaces.

## 6 LIMITATION

This study was conducted one year after the establishment of the center's spatial layout, and various space activities were gradually being implemented;

thus, the use of the space has not yet reached its full potential.

This study is a cross-sectional analysis, and the causal relationship between the benefits and the sense of ease remains uncertain. In the future, long-term tracking data will be required to understand this causal relationship.

## REFERENCES

Bowling A. (1997). *Measuring Health: A Review of the Quality of Life Measurement Scales* (2nd Ed.). Philadelphia: Open University Press, Buckingham.

Chin-Yi S. and Shiau-Fang C. (2022). "aging in place factors, external continuity and quality of life among older adults in cities: taipei city taken as an example." *NTU Social Work Review*(46): 83.

Deci E.L., & Ryan R.M. (2002). Self-determination Research: Reflections and future directions. In E. L. Deci & R. M. Ryan (eds.), *Handbook of Self-determination Research* (pp. 431–441). Rochester, NY: University of Rochester Press.

Haruhiko, G., *et al.* (2020). "Spatial configuration and management of serviced housing for the elderly with spaces open to the neighboring communities." *Journal of the City Planning Institute of Japan* 55(3): 1342.

Hertz, J. E., & Anschutz, C. A. (2002). Relationships among perceived enactment of autonomy, self-care, and holistic health in community-dwelling older adults. *Journal of Holistic Nursing*, 20(2), 166–186. https://doi.org/10.1177/08910102020002006

Levasseur M., Dubois M.-F., Généreux M., Menec V., Raina P., Roy M., Gabaude C., Couturier Y., & St-Pierre C. (2017). Capturing how age-friendly communities foster positive health, social participation and health equity: A study protocol of key components and processes that promote population health in aging Canadians. *BMC Public Health*, 17, 502. https://doi.org/10.1186/s12889-017-4392-7

Haruhiko G., *et al.* (2020). "Spatial configuration and management of serviced housing for the elderly with spaces open to the neighboring communities." *Journal of the City Planning Institute of Japan* 55(3): 1342.

Lee, M.-C., *et al.* (2015). "Relationships of matching degree of need for freedom, social support and well-being in the elderly." *Tajen Journal*(46): 75.

Megumi, K., *et al.* (2012). "Effects of 'en-gawa service' which involves the elderly with the local community A case study on the community restaurant by the non-profit organization." *Journal of Architecture and Planning* 77(680): 2399.

Su C.-Y. and Chao S.-F. (2022). "Aging in place factors, external continuity and quality of life among older adults in cities: taipei city taken as an example." *NTU Social Work Review*(46): 83.

Suen J.-C. (2018). "Elderly people's basic psychological needs satisfaction at day-care centers: an analysis based on self-determination theory." *Taiwanese Journal of Social Welfare*(2): 115.

Wahl H.-W. Iwarsson S., & Oswald F. (2012). Aging well and the environment: Toward an integrative model and research agenda for the future. *The Gerontologist*, 52(3), 306–316. https://doi.org/10.1093/geront/gnr154

*System Innovation for a Troubled World – Lam et al. (Eds)*
*© 2024 the Author(s), ISBN: 978-1-032-60846-4*

# A study of exploring the impact of academic misconduct to the society

Zhihong Luo* & Kuo-Hsun Wen*
*School of Design, Fujian University of Technology, Min-Hou, Fuzhou, Fujian*

ABSTRACT: In recent years, the media have repeatedly broken out reports of academic misconduct which is extremely common, and has become a hot issue of general concern to society. Most domestic research relating to academic misconduct focuses on scholars engaged in academics, and research usually centered on the adverse effects of academic misconduct in the academic world. Among those, there is less literature on the specific effects of academic misconduct on society. Through a series of literature reviews and discussions, the paper explores the negative effects of academic misconduct on different groups in order to provide a more comprehensive understanding of the harm it causes to society. Based on these arguments, several feasible strategies are suggested by the study where a healthy and sustainable academic environment can be achievable.

## 1 INTRODUCTION

Academic misconduct is the act of plagiarism, plagiarism, and falsifying the results of academic research for one's own benefit and knowingly (Cao 2005; Xu 2004). In recent years, the media has exposed academic misconduct, and the feedback from the media has shown that groups concerned about academic misconduct are not only those engaged in academic work but also those not engaged. While citizens may seem to be "eating the melon", they are more upset about the damage to their rights and interests. Academic work should be a stepping stone to social development, not a hindrance to it. As a result, it is very important to consider how academic misconduct can harm society and how it can be prevented.

## 2 THE IMPACT OF ACADEMIC MISCONDUCT ON CITIZENS' RIGHT TO EQUAL ACCESS OF EDUCATION

The right to equal access to education means that all citizens regardless of age, gender, geographical location, etc., have equal access right to educational resources provided by the state and society (Xu 2004). Once citizens have fulfilled their obligations, they have the right to access education equally. The process of realizing equal rights and interests in education is the process of citizens' balanced access to education provided by the state without discrimination. At the same time, the

equality of the right to education is also achieved by whether citizens can pass the examination and meet certain criteria during their various studying periods (Xu 2019). The sensational " Tianlin Zhai incident" in 2019 was met with public outrage because of the breaking of this rule. Consequently, the belief in the fairness of education in the country was shaken, resulting in a very bad social impact.

The indulgence of academic misconduct undermines the public's right to equal access to education (Xu 2019). Therefore, educational resources must not be tilted toward "money" and "power". If the rules can be easily broken, then no one will want to follow them. And if such academic misconduct goes unpunished, the end result will be chaos in education and the violation of citizens' right to receive education. Second, the right to receive education depends on decent teachers who could contribute to the education right. However, there is also academic misconduct happening at some universities, for example, postgraduate supervisors may not have distinguished academic performance as well as the professional practice experience. Most importantly, such inappropriate norm is derived from students' teacher-oriented nature demonstrating the irresponsible situation to students and society.

Academic misconduct often results in academic plagiarism. The academic stagnation of new ideas and thoughts caused by plagiarism makes academic achievements increasingly un-innovative citizens do not receive new knowledge intake, and there is a lack of new culture which largely detrimentizes citizens' education rights (Xu 2019). As a final point, China's educational resources have been balanced as much as possible by the

---

*Corresponding Authors: 1791566378@qq.com and khwen@fjut.edu.cn

DOI: 10.1201/9781003460763-69

efforts of the state. Academic misconduct is a sign of both personal corruption and unruly behavior. At the same time, it is a blow to the fair enjoyment of a student's education right to obtain an education that does not belong to him or her by taking a crooked route.

## 3 THE IMPACT OF ACADEMIC MISCONDUCT ON INNOVATION IN SCIENCE AND TECHNOLOGY

Technological innovation is further divided into continuity innovation and disruptive innovation in terms of innovation. Science and technology innovation in China is mainly continuity innovation, which is a creative and breakthrough development based on the original science and technology. Subsequently, science and technology innovation largely drive the development of society (Li 2020;Ye 2007). In 2012, domestic scholars Yandong Zhao and Dasheng Deng conducted a questionnaire survey on academic misconduct among 30,000 science and technology workers nationwide. The survey covered various groups of science and technology workers, distributed in research institutes, higher education institutions, enterprises, rural areas, and medical and health institutions (Zhao et al. 2012). The results show that the majority of science and technology workers engage in academic misconduct and are not severely punished. In addition, the academic climate was muddy, with nearly half of the science and technology workers not caring whether academic misconduct would cause bad publicity and being more tolerant (Zhao et al. 2012).

In 2013, domestic scholars Fajian Miao and Xiaoyun Wang studied the academic misconduct impact of science and technology editors on society. The academic misconduct of scientific workers was explored in groups according to the content of their work. Through the study, scholars analyzed the external and internal factors that lead to academic misconduct in their groups and the harm of academic misconduct to society. In fact, there is no hope for academics who falsify, plagiarize, and do not practice integrity. Besides, academic misconduct can further develop into academic corruption, breeding a grey economy of dissertations and trading in dissertation power and color. These ugly behaviors are like a cancer in society, and if left unchecked, the dark side of academia will spread unchecked, thus hindering the development of science and the progress of society.

Surveys of the impact on academics show that many academics are familiar with academic misconduct by their peers. However, those involved in academic misconduct are not severely punished, which has a very negative impact on academic teams, often resulting in lower attendance and less motivated staff (Xiong 1997). This not only makes the rest of the team think opportunistically as well but also undermines those workers who are strangely committed and compliant. Further linking to the social level, Hongjun Wang, a member of the Academy of Social Sciences and director of the Social Science Literature Publishing House, believes that "academic misconduct has, to a certain extent, created a false prosperity in academia". Unrealistic academic results reduce the innovation of science and technology and undermine the financial and human resources that the country has invested in scientific and technological innovation strategies.

## 4 THE IMPACT OF ATTITUDES TO ACADEMIC MISCONDUCT ON THE SAFETY OF PUBLIC HEALTH CARE

A cross-sectional, quantitative, and analytical study was conducted by foreign scholars Dorea Bandeira and Oliveira to investigate medical students' attitudes toward academic misconduct. Based on a hypothetical situational analysis behavioral model of the code of ethics, a virtual, semi-structured, anonymous, self-administered questionnaire was used to investigate the perceptions of 240 medical students evaluating five medical courses in Salvador de Bahia, Brazil, and to record socio-demographic and academic variables. Research studies have shown that academic misconduct is widespread among Brazilian medical students and that high frequencies of academic misconduct occur despite their perception that it is unethical. The author argues that this academic misconduct is likely to lead to future misconduct in clinical care settings (D. B. et al. 2022). Meanwhile, Dorea Bandeira and Oliveira summarized what Brazilian academics think about the causes and solutions to academic misconduct. It was concluded that Brazilian medical practitioners believe that academic misconduct is common. Also, it was assumed that there is a necessity to include lessons on the regulation of ethical academic behavior in the curriculum.

Korean scholars Chung Eun Kyung, Lee Young-Mee, *et al.* conducted a study on the attitudes of third-year medical students toward academic misconduct in seven Korean medical schools. The study found that students demonstrated strict attitudes toward cheating on exams as part of academic misconduct and more tolerant attitudes toward other academic misconduct (Kyung et al. 2019). Scholars such as Chung Eun Kyung and Lee Young-Mee have therefore argued this tolerance of academic misconduct is likely to pose a potential threat to their professional lives and result in adverse effects such as irresponsibility, poor initiative, and motivation in their subsequent medical careers. In addition, Chung Eun Kyung, Lee Young-Mee, and other scholars have their own insights on how to strengthen academic integrity and avoid academic misconduct for medical students. They believe that academic integrity should be strengthened at an institutional level, and the existing curriculum structure of medical schools should be changed so that education on academic ethics is not limited to one academic year but is transformed into a longitudinal curriculum in which students receive the code of conduct promoted by academic ethics continuously and repeatedly during their studies.

To avoid academic misconduct leading to a lack of professionalism among students, academics suggest a system with screening, monitoring, and remediation to prevent such incidences from happening. The teaching of ethics in medical training therefore remains a topic of global concern, and research has shown that academic misconduct is potentially harmful to the professional behavior of future doctors. If these potential harms affect the medical profession, then there is a danger to the health treatment of citizens, which can then cause a negative impact on society.

## 5 THE LINK BETWEEN ACADEMIC MISCONDUCT AND ANTI-SOCIAL BEHAVIOUR

Foreign scholar Marguerite Ternes *et al.* studied the link between academic misconduct and anti-social behavior through a questionnaire. All students sampled in the study were enrolled in school, and plagiarism, plagiarism of thesis and examination cheating were defined as academic misconduct (Ternes et al. 2019). The study defines physical aggression, rule-breaking, and social aggression as anti-social behavior. Marguerite Ternes *et al.* argue that academic misconduct can easily attract those who want to acquire something without any effort. Thus, it could produce primary psychopaths that lead those people to have non-criminal and anti-social behavior. Therefore, academic misconduct, if not properly prevented and regulated, can potentially lead to anti-social behavior affecting seriously the development and progress of society.

## 6 CONCLUSION

A study of individual cases in the domestic and international literature shows that academic misconduct has become a very common problem in academia, and if it is not properly addressed, it can jeopardize citizens' education rights, hinder the construction of an innovative nation, endanger health of the population and lead to a series of social problems such as anti-social behavior. This undoubtedly has a negative impact on the development of society.

Therefore, it is particularly necessary to take the required measurements to stop this behavior, by analyzing the causes of academic misconduct in the following ways:

1) driven by the current evaluation mechanism;
2) those who are taking a chance on academic misconduct without severe punishment;
3) the lack of education on academic ethics and not realizing the depravity of academic misconduct.

These measurements taken are summarized as follows: firstly, the evaluation mechanism should be readjusted so that it is not only the number of academic results being evaluated but also the quality of the results must be put first for comprehensive evaluation. Secondly, there should be a joint responsibility and implementation at all levels to create an academic atmosphere of collaborative supervision. It is also crucial to open up channels for complaints and reporting and to strive for a clean academic climate. Finally, there should be greater efforts to educate about academic ethics and regular science. In addition, the punishment mechanism should be clearly stated and explained, and the punishment needs to be precise and severe. The publicity role of the media must be brought into play, and the results of punishments for incidents of academic ethics violations are vital to be released to the public in a timely manner to curb academic misconduct in its cradle.

## REFERENCES

Chung Eun Kyung, Lee Young-Mee, Chae Su Jin, Yoon Tai Young, Kim Seok Yong, Park So Youn, Park Ji-Young; Park Chang-Shin, 2019. *Korean Journal of Medical Education*. 4 309–317.
Dorea Bandeira I, Oliveira V, Araújo Pereira M, Andrade B.B., Nazar A.N., Quintanilha L.F., de Avena K.M., 2022. *Problems of Education in the 21st Century*. 3 426–437.
Jimin Xu 2004. *Hebei Law Science*. 02 19–23.
Marguerite Ternes, Coady Babin, Amber Woodworth, Skye Stephens, 2019. *Personality and Individual Differences*. 138 75–78.
Qiantong. Xu 2019. *Legal System and Society*. 12 144–145.
Shengzhu Ye 2007. *Social Science Edition*. 06 6–9.
Shuji. Cao, 2005. *Tribune of Social Sciences*. 03 36–40.
Wansheng Xiong 1997. *Studies in Philosophy of Science and Technology*. 03 43–47.
Xia Li 2020. *People's Tribune*. 08 132–135.
Yandong Zhao, Dasheng. Deng, 2012. *Science Research Management*. 08 90–97.

*System Innovation for a Troubled World – Lam et al. (Eds)*
© 2024 the Author(s), ISBN: 978-1-032-60846-4

# Establish personal information risk management in university

Shaio-Yan Huang & Po-Sen Huang*
*Department of Accounting and Information Technology, National Chung Cheng University, Minhsiung, Chiayi, Taiwan*

ABSTRACT: Information technologies bring users much convenience as well as risks and threats. According to statistics from IBM Security in 2020, the number of data breaches in the year increased by 10% compared to that in the past five years. Universities represent a special, open environment. The Internet at universities is open and can be accessed by anyone, which is different from strict control of the Internet by enterprises. As a result, the personal data of students are likely to be exposed in this high-risk environment. In addition, universities have insufficient manpower and funds to maintain information security. Therefore, universities face greater risks in the protection of personal data. In view of the above, this study built a risk management mechanism to identify potential personal data breach risks for universities and the corresponding measures. This study sorted out common risk factors for personal data breaches in organizations through a literature review and adopted ISO 27001 and ISO 27701 to form a risk management mechanism for universities to improve their internal personal data management. This study also distributed questionnaires to experts to identify risk factors and control measures for universities. According to the research result, this study obtained 45 risk factors and the control measures corresponding to these risk factors for reference by universities in implementing personal data security protection practices.

## 1 INTRODUCTION

Information technologies bring convenience as well as risks and threats. When customers use software to access online shopping malls, social media, or online banking, large amounts of personal data are retained. Enterprises also need to prevent breaches when using such data. In 2013, the credit card data and payment data of 40 million clients of Target Corporation, an American retailer, were stolen, indirectly causing breaches of the personal data of 70 million clients. This incident also caused a decrease in turnover as well as layoffs at the headquarters of Target Corporation. One report estimates that the cost of data breaches reached USD 200 million [1]. After reviewing major personal data breaches that occurred from 2012 to 2014, Tripathi and Mukhopadhyay (2019) found that personal data breaches can have a negative impact on the market value of an enterprise and cause an average annual financial loss of USD 200 million.

According to the *Cost of a Data Breach Report*, released by IBM Security in 2020, data breaches are becoming increasingly serious. The number of reported breaches in 2020 increased by 10% as compared with that in the previous five years, and the global average annual loss was approximately USD 364 million. The average loss caused by data

breaches among different industries was USD 3.86 million. The education industry is the only non-profit organization that has a higher cost of a data breach than the global average as compared with other profit-making organizations, as shown in Figure 1.

Personal data represent a valuable information asset for an organization. In recent years, personal data breaches have occurred frequently, resulting in serious damage and heavy losses to organizations. Many countries have attached importance to personal data protection and have enacted related laws. Universities should also recognize the

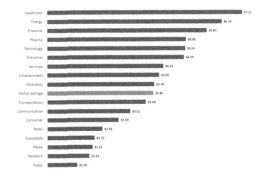

Figure 1. The cost of a data breach by industry.
Source: IBM Security, Cost of a Data Breach Report 2020

*Corresponding Author: jason@ccu.edu.tw

DOI: 10.1201/9781003460763-70

351

importance of personal data protection and focus on how to effectively reduce the risks facing personal data in information systems. In the free network environments of universities, information security risks arising from breaches of students' personal data must be strictly controlled, and effort must be made to build a complete and effective security management mechanism. Therefore, this study aimed to build a personal information management system (PIMS) for universities pursuant to international information security standards ISO 27001 and ISO 27701 to provide universities with more reference directions in implementing a personal data risk management mechanism.

## 2 THEORETICAL BACKGROUND

### 2.1 Personal data breaches

#### 2.1.1 Personal data breaches in enterprises

Tim Cook, CEO of Apple Inc., often says that "personal data privacy is a fundamental human right". Massive amounts of customer data are adopted for promoting enterprise businesses; therefore, maintaining customer data privacy is a corporation's responsibility and obligation, especially for the technology companies in which the majority of the operation revenue comes from push ads. Since they often widely collect the personal data of customers on platforms to present personalized advertisements, such companies can become a target for hackers. Intact, a software company, ran statistics on corporate data breaches from 2004 to 2020. They found that Facebook was at the top of the list, with five major personal data breaches. AOL Inc. and Citigroup Inc. were also on the list, as shown in Figure 2. As shown in the figure, technology and finance companies are often targeted by cybercriminals because they have massive amounts of data [2].

Some transnational enterprises have been penalized under GDPR. GDPR compulsively applied to all enterprises in the European Union on May 25, 2018. Any enterprise that violates GDPR can be fined up to EUR 20 million or 4% of its annual gross revenue. Google, a representative American technology company, was the first transnational company to be penalized under GDPR. This case has resulted from complaints from None of Your Business (NOYB) and La Quadrature du Net (LQDN) received by France's National Commission on Informatics and Liberty (Commission Nationale de l'Informatique et des Libertés; CNIL), which claimed that Google failed to process the personal data of users pursuant to the French Data Protection Law and GDPR. In other words, Google used user data without obtaining the specific consent of the user. Eventually, Google was fined EUR 50 million.

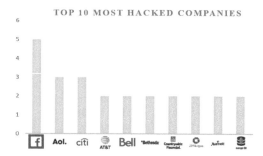

Figure 2. Top 10 most data breaches companies. Source: Intact (2021)

#### 2.1.2 Personal data breaches in universities

As technology companies with strong technical resources cannot prevent data breaches, breaches of students' personal data in schools are emerging endlessly. Since the outbreak of COVID-19, universities have implemented remote teaching in response to epidemic prevention and control measures, and such teaching patterns have increased the risk of student personal data breaches. The U.S. Government Accountability Office (GAO) analyzed the data security reports of K-12 students (from kindergarten through grade twelve) from 2016 to 2020 and found that student cyber incidents increased by 18%, with an average incidence of two or more student cyber incidents occurring per school day. Student data breaches have always been the gravest cyber incidents, as shown in Figure 3 [3].

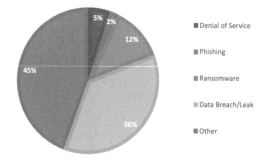

Figure 3. Top 5 cybersecurity threats for schools. Source: Levin (2021)

### 2.2 Personal data risk management

#### 2.2.1 BS 10012

The BS 10012 Personal Information Management System (PIMS) was a personal information management standard released by the British Standard Institute (BSI) in 2009, as shown in Figure 4. It was established under *The Data Protection Act of 1998* and the European Union's Personal Data

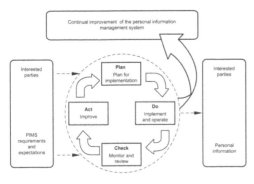

Figure 4.    PDCA model of standard BS 10012.
Source: Standard BS 10012: 2009

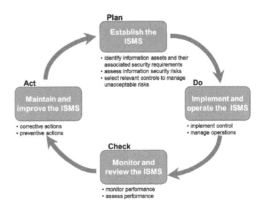

Figure 5.    PDCA model of standard ISO 27001.

Protection Directive of 1995. BS 10012 was further revised to make it consistent with the GDPR that was officially passed by the European Parliament in 2016. In the revised BS 10012, the original eight principles were replaced by six data protection principles in Article 5 of the GDPR, and cross-border transmission requirements were included in the information security issue.

### 2.2.2  *ISO 27001*
The ISO 27001 Information Security Management System (ISMS) was released by the International Organization for Standardization (ISO) in 2005. Appendix A of the revised international information security management standard in 2013 [12] contains 14 control domains, 35 control objectives, and 114 controls in total. Table 1 lists the 14 control domains.

ISO27001 adopted the Plan-Do-Check-Act (PDCA) methodology to establish the standards in the ISMS. An information security system should be constantly reviewed and improved to reduce the information security risk to an acceptable scope and protect the confidentiality, integrity, and availability of information, as shown in Figure 5.

Table 1.    List of ISO 27001 control domains.

| Annex A | Control domains |
|---|---|
| A5 | Information security policies |
| A6 | Organization of information security |
| A7 | Human resource security |
| A8 | Asset management |
| A9 | Access control |
| A10 | Cryptography |
| A11 | Physical and environmental security |
| A12 | Operations security |
| A13 | Communications security |
| A14 | System acquisition, development, and maintenance |
| A15 | Supplier relationships |
| A16 | Information security incident management |
| A17 | Information security aspects of business continuity management |
| A18 | Compliance |

Source: Standard ISO 27001: 2013

### 2.2.3  *ISO 27701*
The ISO 27701 Privacy Information Management System (PIMS) is an extension of ISO 27001 and ISO 27002. It is an international PIMS standard released by the ISO in 2019. ISO 27701 provides guidance on personal privacy information protection. It aims to reduce the risks facing privacy information by adding additional control requirements to establish, implement, maintain, and constantly improve privacy information management in the ISMS scope. It refers to the specific requirements of ISO 27001 and ISO 27002 and provides additional implementation guidance on Personally Identifiable Information (PII) controllers and PII processors. Table 2 compares ISO 27001 and ISO 27701.

Table 2.    Comparison table between ISO 27001 and ISO 27701.

|  | ISO 27001 | ISO 27701 |
|---|---|---|
| System | Information Security Management System (ISMS) | Privacy Information Management System (PIMS) |
| Certification Body (CB) | International Organization for Standardization (ISO) | International Organization for Standardization (ISO) |
| Content | Focus on information security controls. | Strengthen the control of personal data management on the basis of ISO 27001. |
| Outlines | 1. Scope | 1. Scope |
|  | 2. Normative references | 2. Normative References |
|  | 3. Terms and definitions | 3. Terms, definitions, and abbreviations |
|  | 4. Context of the organization | 4. General |
|  | 5. Leadership |  |

*(continued)*

353

Table 2. Continued

| ISO 27001 | ISO 27701 |
|---|---|
| 6. Planning | 5. PIMS specific |
| 7. Support | requirements |
| 8. Operation | related to ISO/ |
| 9. Performance | IEC 27001 |
| evaluation | |
| 10. Improvement | 5.1 General |
| | 5.2 Context of the |
| | organization |
| | 5.3 Leadership |
| | 5.4 Planning |
| | 5.5 Support |
| | 5.6 Operation |
| | 5.7 Performance |
| | evaluation |
| | 5.8 Improvement |
| | 1. PIMS-specific |
| | guidance related |
| | to ISO/ |
| | IEC 27002 |
| | 2. Additional ISO/ |
| | IEC 27002 gui- |
| | dance for PII |
| | controllers |
| | 3. Additional ISO/ |
| | IEC 27002 gui- |
| | dance for PII |
| | Processors |

#### 2.2.4 *Personal data breach risk factors*

Through a literature review, this study organized personal data breach risk factors proposed in prior literature (18 papers from organizations, universities, government agencies, and other fields). The 45 risk factors are listed as follows:

(1) Internal staff fail to comply with related information security rules.
(2) Internal staff's system operation errors indirectly cause loss of data confidentiality and integrity.
(3) Internal staff intentionally leak personal data on the Internet.
(4) Internal staff unintentionally cause breaches of personal data on the Internet.
(5) Internal staff access confidential data without authorization.
(6) Internal staff carry out confidential files using portable devices without authorization.
(7) Internal staff send data to non-relevant personnel by mistake.
(8) Internal staff lack information security awareness when using e-mail (using a private e-mail address to send official information or clicking on insecure sources and phishing programs in e-mails).
(9) Personnel mistakenly send confidential data to personnel or departments with a lower security level.
(10) Internal staff fail to regularly maintain and update the log files generated by data flows and the retention period.

(11) No checking for the unauthorized access of internal personnel to organizational devices or web servers.
(12) Internal staff lose hardware devices storing confidential data by accident.
(13) Internal staff steal or damage internal software in an organization without authorization.
(14) Failing to revoke the system permissions or accounts of internal employees who have been suspended or dismissed.
(15) An organization lacks effective information security governance.
(16) An organization lacks punishments or penalties for staff violating information security policies.
(17) An organization lacks the support and promotion of senior management for data protection.
(18) An organization lacks a responsible person for information security.
(19) An organization lacks an effective information security education mechanism.
(20) An organization lacks a process for improving information security deficiency.
(21) When the system is damaged, an organization lacks a complete disaster recovery plan.
(22) No complete information security advocacy act is taken for outsourcing contractors.
(23) No complete information security governance (no exact management plan) is implemented for outsourcing companies.
(24) A company discretionarily accesses and uses data by virtue of its position.
(25) An organization's environmental control resources are faulty (such as an unstable power supply or tripping of a circuit breaker)
(26) A natural or man-made disaster or incident that is uncontrollable occurs.
(27) Hardware devices storing confidential data are stolen.
(28) Output devices are not regulated and controlled strictly or based on permissions (printers that are shared by units)
(29) Hardware devices are connected to insecure public wireless networks.
(30) Data on hardware devices are not cleared when they are used by different persons.
(31) Sensitive data on devices are not destroyed before such devices are replaced or scrapped.
(32) Internal staff place papers containing personal data in the waste paper recovery area or on the printer.
(33) Hackers intrude into an organization's software or servers.
(34) Computer software security protection is not regularly updated.
(35) System passwords are not properly set (passwords are not regularly updated; passwords are shared; passwords have a low-security level).

(36) The programming language or database in the system has errors.

(37) Permissions on system functions are not set and controlled based on rights and liabilities.

(38) Unauthorized software is used to share personal data.

(39) Data encryption protection is not enabled for electronic devices or databases storing massive amounts of data.

(40) Data with different security levels are stored on the same computer or the same hardware device.

(41) An organization improperly manages the keys of encrypted personal data.

(42) An organization fails to implement permission control on e-mails containing personal data.

(43) The storage space is insufficient, indirectly causing the loss of personal data.

(44) Causes of information security incidents are not reviewed and post-incident report analyses are ignored.

(45) No responsible person regularly reviews whether related programs are appropriately running.

# 3 RESEARCH METHODOLOGY

## 3.1 *Grounded theory*

After Barney Glaser and Anselm Strauss published their seminal work The Discovery of Grounded Theory, grounded theory has become an important methodology in social sciences research. This methodology summarizes developing theories by systematically collecting and analyzing qualitative data to understand the behaviors of people and social sciences. Since then, many scholars have extended grounded theory in different research fields and scopes and applied it to various disciplines [5]. The value of grounded theory lies in that it eliminates the need for establishing hypotheses at the beginning of a study and gradually establishes theories after obtaining meaningful concepts in the data collection process [6].

Theoretical sampling is often used in the grounded theory methodology. Theoretical sampling is a process of sampling based on the generation of theories [7]. In other words, theoretical sampling does not determine the purpose and scope of sampling at the beginning to show the generalization result of a study but shows the gradual generation of theories through sampling. The end of the sampling is determined by the theoretical saturation concept proposed by Glasser and Strauss (1967) [7]. Theoretical saturation is decided based on the following three principles:

1. No new data or related data is found in the related scope.

2. The relationship between scopes is well-established and validated to be true.

3. According to the variability presented by the development direction and nature of the scope, the scope is fully developed.

## 3.2 *Delphi method*

This study aimed to establish a personal data operation risk management mechanism for universities and adopted the framework of Gowin's Vee model as the research strategy (as shown in Figure 6) [8]. Through a literature review, this study analyzed, collated, and summarized the data, and then established personal data breach risk factors in universities. After establishing the risk factors, this study applied the Delphi expert questionnaire method to obtain the opinions of industry and academic experts to rectify the risk factors, thereby filling the gap in the literature review.

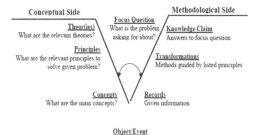

Figure 6. Structure of the vee diagram.
Source: Novak and Gowin (1984)

# 4 ESTABLISHMENT OF A DIGITAL PERSONAL DATA RISK CONTROL MECHANISM

This study aimed to establish a personal data risk management mechanism for universities. This study applied the grounded theory methodology and collected, analyzed, and collated possible personal data breach risk factors from literature related to personal data security and data breach risks. In addition, based on ISO 27001:2013 and ISO 27701:2019, this study used the 14 control domains of ISO 27001:2013 and ISO 27701:2019 as the inductive dimensions to establish the personal data risk management mechanism. Afterward, this study applied the Delphi expert questionnaire method by distributing questionnaires to 13 experts on personal data security-related work for universities and then conducting a statistical analysis of the questionnaire responses.

## 4.1 *Establishment of the risk mechanism*

This study established the personal data risk management mechanism based on the control measures in ISO 27001:2013 and ISO 27701:2019, as listed in Table 3.

Table 3. Mapping of the control measures.

| Risk factors | Controls (Practice Guidelines) | Reference source |
|---|---|---|
| R1.1 An organization lacks effective information security governance | **C1.1 Policies for information security** All organizations processing personally identifiable information (PII) should consider applicable PII protection laws when formulating and maintaining information security policies. | ISO 27701 |
| R1.2 No complete information security governance is implemented for outsourcing contractors | **C1.2 Policies for information security** Organizations should use policies on specific subjects to support information security policies. Generally, such policies should be structured to meet the needs of certain target groups in organizations or to cover certain subjects (such as supplier relations). | ISO 27001 |
| R1.3 An organization lacks the support and promotion of senior management for personal data protection | **C1.3 Policies for information security** Organizations should assign general or specific information security management responsibilities to defined roles when defining information security policies. | ISO 27001 |
| R2.1 An organization lacks a responsible person for information security | **C2.1 Information security roles and responsibilities** Organizations should appoint one or more person (s) to be responsible for formulating, implementing, maintaining, and supervising the governance and privacy plan in the organizations to ensure compliance with all applicable laws on PII processing. | ISO 27701 |
| R3.1 An organization lacks the support and promotion of senior management for personal data protection | **C3.1 Management responsibilities** The management is responsible for motivating employees and contracted personnel to comply with information security policies. Therefore, the responsibilities of the management must be enhanced. | ISO 27001 |
| R3.2 Internal staff fail to comply with related information security rules | **C3.2 Information security awareness, education, and training** An information security awareness program should focus on making employees and contracted personnel aware of information security responsibilities. Information security awareness program activities should be organized regularly to make activities duplicate and cover new employees and contracted personnel. | ISO 27001 |
| R3.3 An organization lacks an effective information security education mechanism | **C3.3 Information security awareness, education and training** Organizations should formulate education and training programs to facilitate the effective implementation of education and training. | ISO 27001 |
| R3.4 Internal staff place papers containing personal data in the waste paper recovery area or on the printer | **C3.4 Information security awareness, education and training** Organizations should take measures (including incident report awareness) to ensure that related employees are aware of possible consequences arising from violations of privacy or security rules and procedures (in particular, such rules and procedures in response to PII processing). | ISO 27701 |
| R3.5 Internal staff lack information security awareness when using e-mail (using their private e-mail address to send official information or clicking on insecure sources and phishing programs in e-mails). | **C3.5 Information security awareness, education, and training** In information security education and training, basic information security procedures and reference control measures should be enhanced (such as malware control measures). | ISO 27001 |

*(continued)*

Table 3. Continued

| Risk factors | Controls (Practice Guidelines) | Reference source |
|---|---|---|
| R3.6 Internal staff unintentionally cause breaches of personal data on the network | C3.6 **Information security awareness, education, and training** Information security education and training should focus more on making employees and contracted personnel familiar and compliant with policies, standards, and laws and regulations, as well as applicable information security rules and obligations. | ISO 27001 |
| R3.7 An organization lacks punishments or penalties for staff violating information security policies | C3.7 **Disciplinary process** Organizations should have an official and communicated penalty and punishment procedure. Progressive punishments should be adopted to take action against employees who violate information security. | ISO 27001 |
| R4.1 Personnel accidentally send confidential data to personnel or departments with a lower security level | C4.1 **Classification of information** In an organization's information classification system, PII should be expressly regarded as part of its implementation scheme. | ISO 27701 |
| R4.2 Data with different security levels are stored on one computer or one hardware device | C4.2 **Handling of assets** An organization should develop information classification-consistent disposal, processing, and storage procedures and consider access controls that support protection requirements for each class. | ISO 27001 |
| R4.3 Output devices are not regulated and controlled strictly or based on permissions (printers are shared by units) | C4.3 **Handling of assets** An organization should develop information classification-consistent disposal, processing, and storage procedures and consider clearly labeling all information copies to remind authorized recipients. | ISO 27001 |
| R4.4 Sensitive data on devices are not destructed before such devices are replaced or scrapped | C4.4 **Disposal of media** If an organization plans to dispose of removable media storing PII, it should specify the secure disposal procedure in writing and implement it to ensure the PII is non-accessible. | ISO 27701 |
| R5.1 Permissions on system functions are not set and controlled based on rights and liabilities | C5.1 **User access provisioning** An organization should specify the configuration process for granting a user ID access permission and check whether the authorized access level meets the access policy and is consistent with other matters such as job divisions. | ISO 27001 |
| R5.2 When internal employees are suspended or dismissed, their system permissions or accounts are not revoked. | C5.2 **User access provisioning** An organization should specify the configuration process for canceling the access permissions granted to a user ID, adjust the access permissions of users whose roles or positions have changed, and immediately cancel or block the access permissions of users who have been dismissed. | ISO 27001 |
| R5.3 Internal staff access confidential data without authorization | C5.3 **User access provisioning** An organization should implement individual users' access IDs and sets a properly configured system to identify which users can access PII and conduct the addition, deletion, and change operations. | ISO 27701 |
| R5.4 System passwords are not properly set (passwords are not regularly updated; passwords are shared; passwords have a low-security level) | C5.4 **Password management system** The password management system should be interactive and employees or contracted personnel should be required to change their passwords regularly. Passwords used by users should be recorded to prevent repeated use. | ISO 27001 |

*(continued)*

Table 3. Continued

| Risk factors | Controls (Practice Guidelines) | Reference source |
|---|---|---|
| R5.5 Internal staff steal or damage internal software in an organization without authorization | C5.5 **Use of privileged utility programs** An identification, discrimination, and authorization procedure should be implemented for shared programs. | ISO 27001 |
| R6.1 Data encryption protection is not enabled for electronic devices or databases storing massive amounts of data | C6.1 **Policy on the use of cryptographic controls** An organization should use an encryption technique in some areas to protect specific PII (such as health data, ID number, and passport number). | ISO 27701 |
| R6.2 Internal staff carry out confidential files using portable devices without authorization | C6.2 **Policy on the use of cryptographic controls** An organization should use information encryption to protect sensitive or key information during storage or transmission. | ISO 27001 |
| R6.3 An organization improperly manages the keys of encrypted personal data | C6.3 **Key management** To reduce the possibility of improper use, keys must have clear effective and expiry dates that can only be used within the period defined in the key management policy. | ISO 27001 |
| R7.1 A natural or man-made disaster or incident that is uncontrollable occurs | C7.1 **Protecting against external and environmental threats** An organization should seek suggestions from experts on how to prevent damages caused by natural or man-made disasters, such as fires, floods, and riots. | ISO 27001 |
| R7.2 Internal staff lose hardware devices storing confidential data by accident | C7.2 **Removal of assets** An organization should record the positions, roles, and organizations of persons who dispose of or use assets in writing, and such records should be returned with devices, information, or software. | ISO 27001 |
| R7.3 Hardware devices storing confidential data are stolen | C7.3 **Equipment siting and protection** An organization should place equipment in places that employees will not necessarily access and take control measures against potential physical and environmental threats, such as theft, fires, and explosives. | ISO 27001 |
| R7.4 Data on hardware devices are not cleared when they are used by different persons | C7.4 **Secure disposal or reuse of equipment** An organization should ensure that all PII in a storage space is non-accessible before re-allocating the storage space. | ISO 27701 |
| R7.5 An organization's environmental control resources are faulty (such as an unstable power supply or tripping of a circuit breaker) | C7.5 **Supporting utilities** An organization should regularly review and test resources to ensure that supporting utilities are running properly. When necessary, it should install an alarm system to detect faults. | ISO 27001 |
| R8.1 Internal staff make system operation errors | C8.1 **Documented operating procedures** An organization should prepare documented operating procedures to deal with errors or other exceptions that may occur during work. | ISO 27001 |
| R8.2 The storage space is insufficient, indirectly causing the loss of personal data | C8.2 **Capacity management** An organization should prepare detection control measures to identify problems in due time and estimate future capacity requirements in view of operational considerations or system requirements. | ISO 27001 |
| R8.3 Hackers intrude into an organization's software or servers | C8.3 **Controls against malware** An organization should install and regularly update malware detection and repair software as a preventive control measure or routine operation. | ISO 27001 |

*(continued)*

358

Table 3. Continued

| Risk factors | Controls (Practice Guidelines) | Reference source |
|---|---|---|
| R8.4 Internal staff fail to regularly maintain and update the log files generated by data flows and the retention period | C8.4 **Event logging** An organization should use a continuous, automatic monitoring and warning process, prepare an event log review process, or manually carry out such reviews as required in writing, to identify violations and propose remedies. When possible, access to PII should be recorded in event logs, including who accessed PII, when PII was accessed, whose PII was accessed, and changes caused by such events. | ISO 27701 |
| R8.5 A natural or man-made disaster or incident that is uncontrollable occurs | C8.5 **Information backup** An organization should provide adequate backup facilities to ensure that all indispensable information and software can be restored after a disaster occurs. | ISO 27001 |
| R8.6 Computer software security protection is not regularly updated | C8.6 **Management of technical vulnerabilities** An organization should define and establish technical vulnerability-related roles and responsibilities, including vulnerability monitoring, vulnerability risk assessments, repair procedures, asset tracking, and all necessary coordination responsibilities. | ISO 27001 |
| R8.7 Unauthorized software is used to share personal data | C8.7 **Management of technical vulnerabilities** An organization should identify the forms of software that are prohibited from installation (such as software for personal use only and software that has similar characteristics of known or potential malware). | ISO 27001 |
| R9.1 Internal staff intentionally leak personal data on the network | C9.1 **Confidentiality or nondisclosure agreements** If an organization is a PII processor, all forms of confidentiality agreements between the organization and its employees and trustees should ensure that its employees and trustees will comply with data processing- and protection-related policies and procedures. | ISO 27701 |
| R9.2 An organization fails to implement permission control on e-mails containing personal data | C9.2 **Electronic messaging** An organization should adopt an information classification scheme to protect electronic messages from being accessed, changed, or blocked without authorization. | ISO 27001 |
| R9.3 Internal staff send data to non-relevant personnel by mistake | C9.3 **Information transfer policies and procedures** An organization should apply cryptography techniques to protect the confidentiality of information. | ISO 27001 |
| R10.1 The programming language or database in the system has errors | C10.1 **Information security requirements analysis and specification** When acquiring a system, an organization should implement an official testing procedure and ensure that functions meet known security requirements. | ISO 27001 |
| R10.2 Hardware devices are connected to insecure public wireless networks | C10.2 **Securing application services on public networks** An organization should apply encryption techniques to transfer PII over untrustworthy data transfer networks. | ISO 27701 |
| R11.1 No complete information security governance is implemented for outsourcing companies | C11.1 **Information security policy for supplier relationships** An organization should identify and specify information security control measures in the information security policies to stipulate the access of suppliers to the information of the organization and keep documentary records. | ISO 27001 |

(*continued*)

Table 3.   Continued

| Risk factors | Controls (Practice Guidelines) | Reference source |
|---|---|---|
| R11.2 A company discretionarily accesses and uses data by virtue of its position | C11.2 **Information security policy for supplier relationships** An organization should define the information access forms allowed for different forms of suppliers and monitor and control the information access of suppliers. | ISO 27001 |
| R11.3 No complete information security advocacy act is taken for outsourcing contractors | C11.3 **Addressing security within supplier agreements** An organization should specify whether to process PII in a supplier agreement and the minimum technical and organizational measures that the supplier must meet for the purpose of fulfilling its information security and PII protection obligations. | ISO 27701 |
| R12.1 An organization lacks a process for improving information security deficiencies | C12.1 **Responsibilities and procedures** An organization should establish responsibilities and procedures for identifying and recording PII violations. In addition, an organization should consider applicable laws and establish requirements for notifying PII violations as well as the responsibilities and procedures for disclosing PII violations to the competent authority. | ISO 27701 |
| R12.2 No action is taken to check for unauthorized access by internal personnel to organizational devices or web servers | C12.2 **Reporting information security events** An organization should establish an official information security event notification procedure and arrange the actions to be taken upon receipt of an information security incident notification based on incident response and reporting. | ISO 27001 |
| R13.1 When the system is damaged, an organization lacks a complete disaster recovery plan | C13.1 **Planning Information Security Continuity** If an organization has no official operational sustainability and disaster recovery plan, the information security management should assume that as compared with normal operations, information security requirements are still at a disadvantage. In addition, an organization should implement an operational impact analysis at the information security level to formulate information security requirements for adverse situations. | ISO 27001 |
| R13.2 When an information security incident occurs, the cause of the information security incident is not reviewed, and post-incident report analysis is ignored | C13.2 **Planning information security continuity** An organization should formulate information security requirements when planning an operational sustainability and disaster recovery plan. | ISO 27001 |
| R14.1 Internal staff fail to comply with related information security rules | C14.1 **Compliance with security policies and standards** The management should regularly review the compliance with security handling and procedures within their scope of responsibility according to applicable security policies, standards, and all other security requirements. If any non-compliance is found, the management should assess whether to take measures to reach compliance. | ISO 27001 |
| R14.2 No responsible person regularly reviews whether related programs are appropriately running | C14.2 **Independent review of information security** The management should initiate an independent review to ensure the constant suitability, appropriateness, and effectiveness of the organization's practices for information security management. | ISO 27001 |

### 4.2 Background information of the experts

In this study, questionnaires were distributed to 13 experts in total, including six information security management personnel in universities and seven experts who executed personal data security policies and used personal data. Table 4 lists the basic information of these experts.

Table 4. Backgrounds of the experts.

| No. | Department | Title | Years of experience |
|---|---|---|---|
| 1 | Information Technology Center | Information Security Manager | 12 |
| 2 | Information Technology Center | Information Security Manager | 13 |
| 3 | Information Technology Center | Information Security Officer | 10 |
| 4 | Information Technology Center | Information Security Officer | 20 |
| 5 | Library | Information Security Officer | 25 |
| 6 | College Admissions Committee | Information Security Officer | 22 |
| 7 | Library | Personal data user and protection executor | 6 |
| 8 | Office of Information Affairs | Personal data user and protection executor | 31 |
| 9 | Office of Academic Affairs | Personal data user and protection executor | 26 |
| 10 | President Office | Personal data user and protection executor | 5 |
| 11 | College Admissions Committee | Personal data user and protection executor | 19 |
| 12 | Office Of Student Affairs | Personal data user and protection executor | 16 |
| 13 | Office of the Secretariat | Personal data user and protection executor | 11 |

### 4.3 Analysis of the questionnaire results

After the questionnaires were recovered, the goodness of fit between the university personal data management risk factors and ISO 27001 and ISO 27701 was identified based on the questionnaire data. In addition, this study discussed the degree of importance of each control measure. The correlation validity analysis and statistical test implemented in this study were as follows:

1. Testing the expert validity according to the content validity ratio (CVR)

   Through the testing method proposed by Lawshe (1975) [9], this study used the content validity ratio (CVR) to determine the appropriateness of each risk factor. This study collected 13 expert questionnaires in total. The CVR was 0.54, representing that the CVR of a risk factor greater than 0.54 can meet the content validity ratio. Risk factors with a CVR less than 0.54 were removed and were not included in subsequent processing for the purpose of maintaining the stringency of this study.

2. Testing the consistency according to the quartile deviation

   This study used the method proposed by Holden and Wedman (1993) [10] to test the consistency of the questions. If the quartile deviation of the expert responses to the questions was below 0.6, the expert opinions would have high consistency. If the quartile deviation was between 0.6 and 1, the expert opinions would reach moderate consistency. If the quartile deviation was greater than 1, the expert opinions would be inconsistent, and related risk factors or control measures would be removed.

3. Testing the degree of importance of the risk factors and control measures according to the mean value

   This study used the five-point scale proposed by Likert (1932) [11] to understand the degree of importance of the risk factors and control measures. The importance was arranged from high to low, with 5 representing very important and 1 representing very unimportant. A higher average score would represent a higher degree of importance attached by the experts.

In view of the above questionnaire analysis method, this study described the statistical results on the CVRs, means, and quartile deviations of the risk factors and control measures in each control domain, as shown in subsequent sections.

#### 4.3.1 Information security policies

Tables 5 and 6 show the statistical results of the risk factors and control measures in the domain of information security policies.

Table 5. CVR value and statistics of risk factors in information security policies.

| Risk factors | University's suitability | | | The importance of risk factors | | |
| | Suitable (N) | Not suitable (N) | CVR | Effective value (N) | Quartile deviation (QD) | Mean |
|---|---|---|---|---|---|---|
| R1.1 | 13 | 0 | 1 | 13 | 0 | 4.84 |
| R1.2 | 12 | 1 | 0.84 | 12 | 0.5 | 4.5 |
| R1.3 | 13 | 0 | 1 | 13 | 0.5 | 4.62 |

**Table 6.** CVR value and statistics of control measures in information security policy.

| Control objectives | Controls (Practice Guidelines) | Solve risk factor suitability | | | The importance of controls | | |
|---|---|---|---|---|---|---|---|
| | | Suitable (N) | Not suitable (N) | CVR | Effective value (N) | Quartile deviation (QD) | Mean |
| Management direction for | C1.1 | 13 | 0 | 1 | 13 | 0 | 4.92 |
| information security | C1.2 | 12 | 1 | 0.84 | 12 | 0.5 | 4.58 |
| | C1.3 | 13 | 0 | 1 | 13 | 0.5 | 4.62 |

**Table 7.** CVR value and statistics of control measures in an organization of information.

| Risk factors | University's suitability | | | The importance of risk factors | | |
|---|---|---|---|---|---|---|
| | Suitable (N) | Not suitable (N) | CVR | Effective value (N) | Quartile deviation (QD) | Mean |
| R2.1 | 13 | 0 | 1 | 13 | 0 | 4.69 |

**Table 8.** CVR value and statistics of control measures in an organization of information.

| Control objectives | Controls (Practice Guidelines) | Solve risk factor suitability | | | The importance of controls | | |
|---|---|---|---|---|---|---|---|
| | | Suitable (N) | Not suitable (N) | CVR | Effective value (N) | Quartile deviation(QD) | Mean |
| Internal organization | C2.2 | 13 | 0 | 1 | 13 | 0.5 | 4.62 |

**Table 9.** CVR value and statistics of control measures in human resource security.

| Risk factors | University's suitability | | | The importance of risk factors | | |
|---|---|---|---|---|---|---|
| | Suitable (N) | Not suitable (N) | CVR | Effective value (N) | Quartile deviation (QD) | Mean |
| R3.1 | 13 | 0 | 1 | 13 | 0 | 4.77 |
| R3.2 | 13 | 0 | 1 | 13 | 0.5 | 4.62 |
| R3.3 | 13 | 0 | 1 | 13 | 0.5 | 4.38 |
| R3.4 | 13 | 0 | 1 | 13 | 0.5 | 4.08 |
| R3.5 | 13 | 0 | 1 | 13 | 0 | 4.69 |
| R3.6 | 13 | 0 | 1 | 13 | 0.5 | 4.54 |
| R3.7 | 12 | 1 | 0.84 | 12 | 0.5 | 3.67 |

**Table 10.** Value and statistics of control measures in human resource security.

| Control objectives | Controls (Practice Guidelines) | Solve risk factor suitability | | | The importance of controls | | |
|---|---|---|---|---|---|---|---|
| | | Suitable (N) | Not suitable (N) | CVR | Effective value (N) | Quartile deviation (QD) | Mean |
| During | C3.1 | 13 | 0 | 1 | 13 | 0.5 | 4.62 |
| employment | C3.2 | 13 | 0 | 1 | 13 | 0.5 | 4.46 |
| | C3.3 | 12 | 1 | 0.84 | 12 | 0.5 | 4.5 |
| | C3.4 | 13 | 0 | 1 | 13 | 1 | 3.92 |
| | C3.5 | 13 | 0 | 1 | 13 | 0 | 4.77 |
| | C3.6 | 13 | 0 | 1 | 13 | 0.5 | 4.46 |
| | C3.7 | 12 | 0 | 1 | 12 | 0.5 | 3.58 |

### 4.3.2 *Organization of information*

Tables 7 and 8 show the statistical results of the risk factors and control measures in the domain of organization of information..

### 4.3.3 *Human resource security*

Tables 9 and 10 show the statistical results of the risk factors and control measures in the domain of human resource security.

Table 11. CVR value and statistics of control measures in asset management.

| Risk factors | University's suitability | | | The importance of risk factors | | |
|---|---|---|---|---|---|---|
| | Suitable (N) | Not suitable (N) | CVR | Effective value (N) | Quartile deviation (QD) | Mean |
| R4.1 | 12 | 1 | 0.84 | 12 | 0.5 | 4.33 |
| R4.2 | 11 | 2 | 0.69 | 11 | 0.25 | 4.09 |
| R4.3 | 12 | 1 | 0.84 | 12 | 0.5 | 3.75 |
| R4.4 | 13 | 0 | 1 | 13 | 0.5 | 4.61 |

Table 12. CVR value and statistics of control measures in asset management.

| Control objectives | Controls (Practice Guidelines) | Solve risk factor suitability | | | The importance of controls | | |
|---|---|---|---|---|---|---|---|
| | | Suitable (N) | Not suitable (N) | CVR | Effective value (N) | Quartile deviation (QD) | Mean |
| Information classification | C4.1 | 11 | 1 | 0.83 | 11 | 0.75 | 4.09 |
| | C4.2 | 11 | 0 | 1 | 11 | 0.5 | 4.27 |
| | C4.3 | 11 | 1 | 0.83 | 11 | 0 | 3.9 |
| Media handling | C4.4 | 13 | 0 | 1 | 13 | 0.5 | 4.61 |

Table 13. CVR value and statistics of control measures in access control.

| Risk factors | University's suitability | | | The importance of risk factors | | |
|---|---|---|---|---|---|---|
| | Suitable (N) | Not suitable (N) | CVR | Effective value (N) | Quartile deviation(QD) | Mean |
| R5.1 | 13 | 0 | 1 | 13 | 0.5 | 4.61 |
| R5.2 | 13 | 0 | 1 | 13 | 0.5 | 4.54 |
| R5.3 | 13 | 0 | 1 | 13 | 0.5 | 4.61 |
| R5.4 | 13 | 0 | 1 | 13 | 0.5 | 4.3 |
| R5.5 | 11 | 2 | 0.69 | 11 | 0.5 | 4.45 |

Table 14. CVR value and statistics of control measures in access control.

| Control objectives | Controls (Practice Guidelines) | Solve risk factor suitability | | | The importance of controls | | |
|---|---|---|---|---|---|---|---|
| | | Suitable (N) | Not suitable (N) | CVR | Effective value (N) | Quartile deviation (QD) | Mean |
| User access | C5.1 | 13 | 0 | 1 | 13 | 0.5 | 4.54 |
| management | C5.2 | 13 | 0 | 1 | 13 | 0.5 | 4.53 |
| System and application | C5.3 | 13 | 0 | 1 | 13 | 0.5 | 4.61 |
| access control | C5.4 | 13 | 0 | 1 | 13 | 0.5 | 4.38 |
| | C5.5 | 11 | 0 | 1 | 11 | 0.5 | 4.45 |

#### 4.3.4 Asset management
Tables 11 and 12 show the statistical results of the risk factors and control measures in the domain of asset management.

#### 4.3.5 Access control
Tables 13 and 14 show the statistical results of the risk factors and control measures in the domain of access control.

**Table 15.** CVR value and statistics of control measures in cryptography.

| Risk factors | University's suitability | | | The importance of risk factors | | |
|---|---|---|---|---|---|---|
| | Suitable (N) | Not suitable (N) | CVR | Effective value (N) | Quartile deviation (QD) | Mean |
| R6.1 | 13 | 0 | 1 | 13 | 0.5 | 4.62 |
| R6.2 | 13 | 0 | 1 | 13 | 0.5 | 4.62 |
| R6.3 | 12 | 1 | 0.84 | 12 | 0.5 | 4.67 |

**Table 16.** CVR value and statistics of control measures in cryptography.

| Control objectives | Controls (Practice Guidelines) | Solve risk factor suitability | | | The importance of controls | | |
|---|---|---|---|---|---|---|---|
| | | Suitable (N) | Not suitable (N) | CVR | Effective value (N) | Quartile deviation (QD) | Mean |
| Cryptographic controls | C6.1 | 13 | 0 | 1 | 12 | 0 | 4.77 |
| | C6.2 | 13 | 0 | 1 | 13 | 0.5 | 4.38 |
| | C6.3 | 12 | 0 | 1 | 12 | 0.5 | 4.58 |

**Table 17.** CVR value and statistics of control measures in physical and environmental security.

| Risk factors | University's suitability | | | The importance of risk factors | | |
|---|---|---|---|---|---|---|
| | Suitable (N) | Not suitable (N) | CVR | Effective value (N) | Quartile deviation (QD) | Mean |
| R7.1 | 10 | 3 | 0.54 | 10 | 0 | 4 |
| R7.2 | 13 | 0 | 1 | 13 | 0.5 | 4.46 |
| R7.3 | 13 | 0 | 1 | 13 | 0.5 | 4.69 |
| R7.4 | 13 | 0 | 1 | 13 | 0.5 | 4.23 |
| R7.5 | 10 | 3 | 0.54 | 10 | 0.375 | 3.8 |

**Table 18.** CVR value and statistics of control measures in physical and environmental security.

| Control objectives | Controls (Practice Guidelines) | Solve risk factor suitability | | | The importance of controls | | |
|---|---|---|---|---|---|---|---|
| | | Suitable (N) | Not suitable (N) | CVR | Effective value (N) | Quartile deviation (QD) | Mean |
| Secure areas | C7.1 | 9 | 1 | 0.8 | 9 | 0.5 | 3.78 |
| Equipment | C7.2 | 11 | 2 | 0.69 | 11 | 0.5 | 4.36 |
| | C7.3 | 13 | 0 | 1 | 13 | 0.5 | 4.54 |
| | C7.4 | 13 | 0 | 1 | 13 | 0.5 | 4.38 |
| | C7.5 | 10 | 0 | 1 | 10 | 0.375 | 3.8 |

### 4.3.6 Cryptography

Tables 15 and 16 show the statistical results of the risk factors and control measures in the domain of cryptography.

### 4.3.7 Physical and environmental security

Tables 17 and 18 show the statistical results of the risk factors and control measures in the domain of physical and environmental security.

Table 19. CVR value and statistics of control measures in operations security.

| Risk factors | University's suitability | | | The importance of risk factors | | |
|---|---|---|---|---|---|---|
| | Suitable (N) | Not suitable (N) | CVR | Effective value (N) | Quartile deviation (QD) | Mean |
| R8.1 | 13 | 0 | 1 | 13 | 0 | 4.07 |
| R8.2 | 10 | 3 | 0.54 | 10 | 0.75 | 3.9 |
| R8.3 | 13 | 0 | 1 | 13 | 0 | 4.77 |
| R8.4 | 11 | 2 | 0.69 | 11 | 0.25 | 4.09 |
| R8.5 | 10 | 3 | 0.54 | 10 | 0.375 | 4.1 |
| R8.6 | 13 | 0 | 1 | 13 | 0.5 | 4.23 |
| R8.7 | 13 | 0 | 1 | 13 | 0.5 | 4.3 |

Table 20. CVR value and statistics of control measures in operations security.

| Control objectives | Controls (Practice Guidelines) | Solve risk factor suitability | | | The importance of controls | | |
|---|---|---|---|---|---|---|---|
| | | Suitable (N) | Not suitable (N) | CVR | Effective value (N) | Quartile deviation (QD) | Mean |
| Operational procedures | C8.1 | 13 | 0 | 1 | 13 | 0 | 4 |
| and responsibilities | C8.2 | 9 | 1 | 0.8 | 9 | 0.5 | 4 |
| Protection from malware | C8.3 | 13 | 0 | 1 | 15 | 0 | 4.8 |
| Logging and monitoring | C8.4 | 11 | 0 | 1 | 11 | 0.25 | 4.18 |
| Backup | C8.5 | 8 | 2 | 0.6 | 8 | 0.5 | 4.375 |
| Technical vulnerability | C8.6 | 13 | 0 | 1 | 13 | 0.5 | 4.38 |
| management | C8.7 | 13 | 0 | 1 | 13 | 0.5 | 4.38 |

Table 21. CVR value and statistics of control measures in communications security.

| Risk factors | University's suitability | | | The importance of risk factors | | |
|---|---|---|---|---|---|---|
| | Suitable (N) | Not suitable (N) | CVR | Effective value(N) | Quartile deviation (QD) | Mean |
| R9.1 | 13 | 0 | 1 | 13 | 0.5 | 4.61 |
| R9.2 | 13 | 0 | 1 | 13 | 0.5 | 4.46 |
| R9.3 | 13 | 0 | 1 | 13 | 0.5 | 4.46 |

Table 22. CVR value and statistics of control measures in communications security.

| Control objectives | Controls (Practice Guidelines) | Solve risk factor suitability | | | The importance of controls | | |
|---|---|---|---|---|---|---|---|
| | | Suitable (N) | Not suitable(N) | CVR | Effective value (N) | Quartile deviation(QD) | Mean |
| Information | C9.1 | 12 | 1 | 0.84 | 12 | 0.5 | 4.58 |
| transfer | C9.2 | 11 | 2 | 0.69 | 11 | 0.5 | 4.36 |
| | C9.3 | 12 | 1 | 0.84 | 12 | 0.5 | 4.58 |

4.3.8 *Operation security*

Tables 19 and 20 show the statistical results of the risk factors and control measures in the domain of operations security.

4.3.9 *Communications security*

Tables 21 and 22 show the statistical results of the risk factors and control measures in the domain of communications security.

Table 23.   CVR value and statistics of control measures in system acquisition, development, and maintenance.

| Risk factors | University's suitability | | | The importance of risk factors | | |
|---|---|---|---|---|---|---|
| | Suitable (N) | Not suitable (N) | CVR | Effective value (N) | Quartile deviation (QD) | Mean |
| R10.1 | 12 | 1 | 0.84 | 12 | 0.5 | 4.25 |
| R10.2 | 13 | 0 | 1 | 13 | 0.5 | 4.3 |

Table 24.   CVR value and statistics of control measures in system acquisition, development, and maintenance.

| Control objectives | Controls (Practice Guidelines) | Solve risk factor suitability | | | The importance of controls | | |
|---|---|---|---|---|---|---|---|
| | | Suitable (N) | Not suitable (N) | CVR | Effective value (N) | Quartile deviation (QD) | Mean |
| Security requirements of information systems | C10.1 | 12 | 0 | 1 | 12 | 0.125 | 4.08 |
| | C10.2 | 12 | 1 | 0.84 | 12 | 0.5 | 4.41 |

Table 25.   CVR value and statistics of control measures in supplier relationships.

| Risk factors | University's suitability | | | The importance of risk factors | | |
|---|---|---|---|---|---|---|
| | Suitable (N) | Not suitable(N) | CVR | Effectivevalue(N) | Quartiledeviation (QD) | Mean |
| R11.1 | 13 | 0 | 1 | 13 | 0.5 | 4.46 |
| R11.2 | 13 | 0 | 1 | 13 | 0 | 4.7 |
| R11.3 | 13 | 0 | 1 | 13 | 0.5 | 4.3 |

Table 26.   CVR value and statistics of control measures in supplier relationships.

| Control objectives | Controls (Practice Guidelines) | Solve risk factor suitability | | | The importance of controls | | |
|---|---|---|---|---|---|---|---|
| | | Suitable (N) | Not suitable (N) | CVR | Effective value (N) | Quartile deviation (QD) | Mean |
| Information security in supplier relationships | C11.1 | 13 | 0 | 1 | 13 | 0.5 | 4.46 |
| | C11.2 | 13 | 0 | 1 | 13 | 0.5 | 4.69 |
| | C11.3 | 13 | 0 | 1 | 13 | 0.5 | 4.15 |

### 4.3.10   System acquisition, development, and maintenance

Tables 23 and 24 show the statistical results of the risk factors and control measures in the domain of system acquisition, development, and maintenance.

### 4.3.11   Supplier relationships

Tables 25 and 26 show the statistical results of the risk factors and control measures in the domain of supplier relationships.

### 4.3.12   Information security incident management

Tables 27 and 28 show the statistical results of the risk factors and control measures in the domain of information security incident management.

### 4.3.13   Information security aspects of business continuity management

Tables 29 and 30 show the statistical results of the risk factors and control measures in the domain of information security aspects of business continuity management.

### 4.3.14   Compliance

Tables 31 and 32 show the statistical results of the risk factors and control measures in the domain of compliance.

Table 27. CVR value and statistics of control measures in information security incident management.

| Risk factors | University's suitability | | | The importance of risk factors | | |
| --- | --- | --- | --- | --- | --- | --- |
| | Suitable (N) | Not suitable(N) | CVR | Effective value(N) | Quartiledeviation(QD) | Mean |
| R12.1 | 13 | 0 | 1 | 13 | 0.5 | 4.69 |
| R12.2 | 12 | 1 | 0.84 | 12 | 0.5 | 4.67 |

Table 28. CVR value and statistics of control measures in information security incident management.

| Control objectives | Controls (Practice Guidelines) | Solve risk factor suitability | | | The importance of controls | | |
| --- | --- | --- | --- | --- | --- | --- | --- |
| | | Suitable (N) | Not suitable (N) | CVR | Effective value (N) | Quartiledeviation (QD) | Mean |
| Management of information security incidents and improvements | C12.1 | 13 | 0 | 1 | 13 | 0.5 | 4.69 |
| | C12.2 | 12 | 10 | 1 | 12 | 0.5 | 4.67 |

Table 29. CVR value and statistics of control measures in information security aspects of business continuity management.

| Risk factors | University's suitability | | | The importance of risk factors | | |
| --- | --- | --- | --- | --- | --- | --- |
| | Suitable (N) | Not suitable (N) | CVR | Effectivevalue(N) | Quartile deviation(QD) | Mean |
| R13.1 | 13 | 0 | 1 | 13 | 0 | 4.92 |
| R13.2 | 13 | 0 | 1 | 13 | 0.5 | 4.69 |

Table 30. CVR value and statistics of control measures in information security aspects of business continuity management.

| Control objectives | Controls (Practice Guidelines) | Solve risk factor suitability | | | The importance of controls | | |
| --- | --- | --- | --- | --- | --- | --- | --- |
| | | Suitable (N) | Notsuitable (N) | CVR | Effectivevalue (N) | Quartiledeviation (QD) | Mean |
| Information security continuity | C13.1 | 13 | 0 | 1 | 13 | 0.5 | 4.54 |
| | C13.2 | 13 | 0 | 1 | 13 | 0.5 | 4.61 |

Table 31. CVR value and statistics of control measures in compliance.

| Risk factors | University's suitability | | | The importance of risk factors | | |
| --- | --- | --- | --- | --- | --- | --- |
| | Suitable (N) | Not suitable (N) | CVR | Effective value (N) | Quartile deviation (QD) | Mean |
| R14.1 | 13 | 0 | 1 | 13 | 0.5 | 4.69 |
| R14.2 | 13 | 0 | 1 | 13 | 0.5 | 4.31 |

Table 32. CVR value and statistics of control measures in compliance'.

| Control objectives | Controls (Practice Guidelines) | Solve risk factor suitability | | | The importance of controls | | |
| --- | --- | --- | --- | --- | --- | --- | --- |
| | | Suitable (N) | Notsuitable (N) | CVR | Effectivevalue (N) | Quartiledeviation (QD) | Mean |
| Information security reviews | C14.1 | 13 | 0 | 1 | 13 | 0.5 | 4.61 |
| | C14.2 | 13 | 0 | 1 | 13 | 0.5 | 4.38 |

## 5 CONCLUSIONS AND SUGGESTIONS

Personal data breaches continue to be an insurmountable problem facing enterprises and governments. Universities are organizations with academic freedom and open networks. As a result, personal data in universities are likely to be exposed in such a high-risk environment. Personal data breaches are frequently seen in universities. However, with limited resources and funds for improving information security, universities still cannot completely eradicate personal data breaches. This study aimed to identify personal data breach risks in universities and further establish a risk management mechanism based on these risks. This study summarized the commonly seen personal data breach risk factors through a literature review and adopted ISO 27001 and ISO 27701 to establish a risk management mechanism for universities to improve their personal information management systems (PIMS). Then, this study distributed questionnaires to experts to identify risk factors and control measures for universities. Lastly, based on the control domains in ISO 27001, this study summarized 14 domains, 45 risk factors, and the control measures corresponding to these risk factors.

Few prior studies have discussed personal data breaches, let alone personal data breaches in universities. This study identified personal data breach risk factors in universities and also established a compliant risk management mechanism, including ISO 27001 and ISO 27701, for the reference of universities in implementing personal data protection practices. This study validated the purpose and result of this study through a literature review and expert questionnaire. This study strived for objectivity and completeness during data collection and in the research methodology and questionnaire design. However, limited by time and manpower, this study did not analyze the implementation effect of this risk management mechanism in organizations. This part can be further discussed in subsequent studies, and the effectiveness of this risk management mechanism can be adjusted based on the results.

## REFERENCES

[1] Clark M. (2014). Timeline of target's data breach and aftermath: How cybertheft snowballed for the giant retailer. *International Business Times*. Retrieved from https://www.ibtimes.com/timeline-targets-data-breach-aftermath-how-cybertheft-snowballed-giant-retailer-1580056

[2] Intact. (2021). *Visualising the Biggest Data Breaches in History*. Retrieved from https://www.intactsoftware.com/blog/visualising-biggest-data-breaches-history/

[3] Levin D. A. (2021). The state of K-12 cybersecurity: 2020 year in review. *K-12 Cybersecurity Resource Center*.

[4] Disterer G. (2013). ISO/IEC 27000, 27001 and 27002 for information security management. *Journal of Information Security*, 4(2), 92–100. doi: 10.4236/jis.2013.42011.

[5] Belgrave L.L. & Seide K. (2019). Grounded theory methodology: Principles and practices. In Liamputtong, P. (Ed.), *Handbook of Research Methods In Health Social Sciences*. Springer. https://doi.org.ezproxy.lib.vt.edu/10.1007/978-981-10-2779-6_84-2

[6] Simmons, O. E. (2006). Some professional and personal notes on research methods, systems theory, and grounded action. *World Futures*, 62(7), 481–490.

[7] Glasser, B. G., & Strauss, A. L. (1967). *The Development of Grounded Theory*. Chicago, IL: Alden.

[8] Novak, J. D., & Gowin, D. B. (1984). *Learning How to Learn*. Cambridge, England: Cambridge Univetsity Press.

[9] Lawshe C.H. (1975). A quantitative approach to content validity. *Personnel psychology*, 28(4), 563–575.

[10] Holden, M. C., & Wedman, J. F. (1993). Future issues of computer-mediated communication: The results of a Delphi study. *Educational Technology Research and Development*, 41(4), 5–24.

[11] Likert, R. (1932). A technique for the measurement of attitudes. *Archives of Psychology*, 22(140), 1–55.

[12] ISO/IEC 27001:2013: Information Technology – SECURITY Techniques – Information security Management Systems – Requirements

[13] ISO/IEC 27701:2019: Information Technology – Security Techniques – Information Security Management Systems – Requirements

System Innovation for a Troubled World – Lam et al. (Eds)
© 2024 the Author(s), ISBN: 978-1-032-60846-4

# Integrating design experience into local brand workshop teaching research: Taking Wanqiao Community, Zhuqi Township, Chiayi County as an example

Huang Hsiao Chien* & Hwang Shyh Huei
*National Yunlin University of Science and Technology, Yunlin, Taiwan*

ABSTRACT: In recent years, in order to enhance the development of the real estate industry, the public sector has carried out the "one community, one characteristic" plan to make full use of local resources to develop rural economic value. The author of this study started to participate in the "Soil and Water Conservation Bureau's Rural Redevelopment Program" as a teacher in 2014 to enter the community, assist in the establishment of local brand and packaging workshops, and create local industrial brand design, Practical actions such as packaging design promote the community to enhance local brand knowledge and aesthetics. The research results show that: 1. The teaching construction of the local brand workshop operates in the mode of 5 frameworks and 20 learning steps; 2. The teachers mainly use the method of "co-creation by both parties, staged drills, and implementation of responsible practice" to plan and implement; 3. Learners mainly gain from "stimulating creative inspiration, enhancing design aesthetics, and interpreting design ability"; 4. Local brand workshops focus on issues such as "design style cannot be escaped, funding problems, reliance on subsidies, and unfinished industrial chains."

*Keywords*: Design experience, local branding, design workshops, adult education

## 1 INTRODUCTION

### 1.1 *Research background motivation*

This study has been studied in academia for more than 10 years and discusses the professional knowledge of the design industry in the practice of community workshop teaching. Since 2014, it has been accompanying the process of community teaching and design practice for many years and has continued to do local design teaching workshop teaching cases. analyze. Based on the theory of participatory action research, teaching research for design practice is mainly due to the rise of local design and social practice in the community in recent years. When designers enter the community for local design, most of them have a limited number of on-site visits, and the follow-up discussion on design is mostly limited to a single discussion with the main person in charge. . There has been relatively little two-way communication with the community for a long time, and the design teaching mode and accompanying method are brought into the community It is even rarer, so I want to use this research to explore the analysis of teaching construction in community place design workshops.

### 1.2 *Research purpose*

This study explores the teaching of community local design workshops, and the following three points are expected to be achieved through the research method as the main purpose:

- To analyze the teaching structure of the local design teaching workshop courses.
- To explore the role of participants in the local design teaching workshops to perform tasks.
- To establish places A design practice empowerment model co-created by design teaching workshops.

## 2 LITERATURE DISCUSSION

### 2.1 *Design experience*

The British Design Council proposed a set of double-diamond design processes in 2005. This set of double diamond design processes and design thinking are used in conjunction with each other, which is a very good tool in the design process. points and thoughts. Through the double diamond design stage "divergence-convergence and then divergence-convergence", five steps of design thinking are included in the divergence and convergence, which are

*Corresponding Author: d10730005@yuntech.edu.tw

Emphathize → Define → Ideate→ Prototype (Prototype)→Test (Test), by using empathy to think from the user's point of view, and clearly defining the key problems, and brainstorming together to quickly come up with solutions, and then start to make a prototype simulation process, and finally determining whether it meets the users' needs through testing, these 5 steps of the design process are repeated and revised until a product is designed more efficiently, which is closer to the user's needs (Figure 1).

Design thinking double diamond process

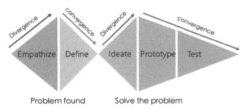

Figure 1. The design process of the double diamond proposed by the british design association.

This researcher enters the community, uses participatory action teaching and design as a method, discusses design projects with local organizations, and uses design thinking methods in community teaching construction and companionship to solve local problems and create local brand designs together and print.

## 2.2 Local brands

The concept of local brand is to plan, construct and manage "the whole place as a brand concept". The integration of personalized local construction is more and more developed toward the local characteristics of this brand planning. Local brands focus more on "local" characteristics, development process, and strategic use. Through the organization or construction methods of various places, they use "local brands" to consider various internal local constructions and various products launched externally, analyzing which local characteristics need to be highlighted under the local brand's identity. Previously, there were four key points to think about "strategic" local cultural resources: 1. Local subjectivity: to strengthen and highlight local cultural themes; 2. Marketability: how to integrate past local culture into current lifestyle; 3. System 4. Recognition: strategic thinking to mobilize local residents to participate together. This researcher has entered the community since 2014. Through local branding workshops, he taught the community the importance of establishing a local brand. It is also an important local representative and symbol. How to excavate local cultural characteristics from

the community as a design element of local brands, making this place easier to be clearly identified in many places, and helping to promote various local products, is one of the key focuses of the local brand workshop.

## 2.3 Design workshop

In recent years, the holding of design workshops has become more and more vigorous and has become a very popular experiential course teaching. The workshop teaching mode introduces the advanced concepts of the workshop into practical teaching, changing the traditional way of "taking the teacher as the main body, centering on the teaching content, and carrying out practical activities as the carrier" to "taking the learner as the main body and taking Interdisciplinary cooperation projects as the core content, with cross-field collaborative innovation activities as the carrier" model. Holding a workshop requires a considerable number of participants, guided by a common goal, to interact to complete a common task. The four key factors for the success of the workshop are: 1. Common themes and common goals, 2. Members are willing to listen to, share, and contribute to each other, 3. Members value their own and others' opinions, 4. Teachers absorb the differences among members viewpoints are then integrated into a consensus (Liu Gongfu 2014).

To promote local brand design workshops, residents from different professions and backgrounds in the community need to create and discuss together. This research uses elements such as common goals, mutual listening, respect, sharing of opinions, and emphasizes commonality throughout the workshop. Subject and goal, with learners as the main body, local brand and packaging design as the core content, and with different drill processes as the carrier, it becomes a way for people in the community to think, discuss, and communicate with each other. Many community learners inspire aesthetic awareness, understand the importance of local brands, and create unique local products and brands.

## 2.4 Adult education

Knowles (1975) believed that the construction design of andragogy should focus on process design because adult learning is mainly "problem-centered" and "task-centered"; The learner is the center of learning, and the role of the teacher is a facilitator, assisting adult learners to solve learning difficulties. Adult education program planning is a process of systematic thinking analysis, which can meet the learning growth or development needs of individuals, organizations, communities, or society. Through the practice of the program to achieve the goal, it is hoped that adults can be encouraged to reflect and improve their problem-solving skills. Therefore, the transformation and internalization of the learning process in the learning process is an important key to whether the learning results can last. The process from improving the cognitive level to changing the behavior can only be achieved through deep personal inner feelings and experiences.

Integrating adult learning and characteristics, adult learners adopt active, needs-satisfied, and goal-directed learning in order to be able to "immediately apply" in the learning process.

## 3 RESEARCH METHODS

### 3.1 Research scope and objects

This study selects "Wanqiao Community, Zhuqi Township, Chiayi County" in 2019 as the research object. Community characteristics and goals: 1. The community plan comes from the county government's "Rural Regeneration Project" 2. Teaching scholars and the community to jointly create community industry revitalization overall development. 3. Promote local industrial brand packaging and enhance community value. 4. Design industrial regional brands and packaging exclusively for local design.

### 3.2 Research methods

This research method adopts qualitative methods, using participatory action research and interview methods as research methods, and using design workshops to actually assist community teaching and accompany them to complete community design output as a research case. In each design workshop, teaching is carried out to solve and produce solutions to the problems encountered by the participants during the actual class teaching discussion. Compared with the "work" after the design is completed, more attention is paid to participation and action in the entire workshop discussion process. Through different stages of teaching courses, in the professional abstract theory thinking, join the workshop to participate in the practical operation and carry out the design thinking process together to complete the activities of different stages, formulate problems and solutions during the whole workshop process, and constantly make corrections and feedback to complete creation and output.

## 4 FINDINGS AND DISCUSSION

### 4.1 Teaching construction and mode of a local brand workshop

The local design teaching workshop is mainly through the courses of the stage department, from scratch to one-stop design. This design workshop is to participate in the brand packaging industry design of the Wanqiao Development Association of Zhuqi Township, Chiayi County in 2019—Rural Regeneration Project. It mainly assists the community in jointly creating the brand image of Wanqiao, basic image design, general fruit gift box, general fruit carton, universal bag, and other brand packaging design, as well as handling community achievement exhibitions and enhancing the aesthetics of community life and the construction of community industry. Product design, through the learning of courses, promotes local industries and cultural resources, enhances the value competitiveness of the community, and looks for the development of industries with unique cultural value and sustainable operation. The time frame is from June 2019 to October 2019; about 5 months, a total of 6 courses during the course, each time is 3 hours, a total of 15 hours.

### 4.2 Local brand workshop teaching plan

The plan was to use the Double Diamond process of the British Design Council in service design to streamline the teaching construction of the local brand workshop-5 aspects (total of 20 stages), as shown in Table 1.

Table 1. Teaching construction of the second round of local brand workshops.

| Architecture: Explore | |
| --- | --- |
| **Learning steps** | **Learning purpose** |
| 1. **Advance planning:** Understanding Community Needs and Planning Courses. | 1. Build relationship |
| 2. **Introduce each other:** Sharing course purpose and mutual introduction. | 2. Learn about the community |
| 3. **Lecture sharing:** Sharing local cultural characteristic courses. | 3. Underst and the industry |
| 4. **Fieldwork:** Engagement in the community and records. | |

| Architecture: Definition | |
| --- | --- |
| **Learning steps** | **Learning purpose** |
| 1. **Consolidated data:** Practical Exercise: Local Industry Analysis | 1. sorting out industry characteristics |
| 2. **Analysis results:** Organize fieldwork records | 2. Establish brand concept |
| 3. **Lecture sharing:** Brand and Packaging Construction Teaching | 3. Induction and analysis |
| 4. **Design proposal:** Practical Walkthrough: Drawing Local Elements | |

*(continued)*

Table 1.   Continued

Architecture: Idea

| Learning steps | Learning purpose |
| --- | --- |
| 1. **Lecture sharing:** elements of brand and packaging presentation<br>2. **Brainstorming:** Practical Walkthrough: Brand Positioning Strategy<br>3. **Integrate creativity:** Practical exercise: creation of brand auxiliary images<br>4. **Selected scheme:** Discussion result: finalized design elements | 1. Inspire creative thinking<br>2. Lots of Proposals<br>3. Choose a design |

Architecture: Solution

| Learning steps | Learning purpose |
| --- | --- |
| 1. **Design presentation:** sketch and color drawing design presentation<br>2. **Adjustment and correction:** practical exercise: joint selection and discussion<br>3. **Proofing design:** complete proofing finished product<br>4. **Reach a consensus:** complete proofing and discuss finalization | 1. Prototyping<br>2. Test adjustments<br>3. Iterate repeatedly |

Architecture: Achievement

| Learning steps | Learning purpose |
| --- | --- |
| 1. **Result announcement:** Practical exercise: display of practice results<br>2. **Feedback:** course experience and harvest feedback<br>3. **Printing finished products:** print out finished products and plan write-off<br>4. **Reflection and Adjustment:** Curriculum Reflection and Adjustment | 1. Results display<br>2. Printed finished product<br>3. Feedback and reflection |

(Source: Organized by this study)

### 4.3   Teaching course execution

Exploration stage: Similar to the first round of teaching, discuss the needs of the community with the community planners in advance to help plan the course content and the results to be produced. The first contact with residents, we will first break the ice and introduce each other together, get to know the participating community leaders and residents, feel the atmosphere of the community, start to introduce the purpose of this plan, and decide what projects we want to create together,

further sharing the local culture. After the characteristic courses, let the community lead the teachers to visit and conduct field research in each scenic spot in the community so that the teachers can have a deeper understanding of the cultural characteristics of the community.

Definition stage: Add two practical drills to the definition. After sorting out the records of the fieldwork, let the learners adopt the strategy of grouping, fill in one piece of landscape and cultural property in each group, and sort out the cultural and landscape property data. Furthermore, share what are the most distinctive places and stories in the community, and then start to share brand design, the content is how to plan a good brand story and positioning, and share the key points of packaging design including shape, pattern, material, color, etc. Planning, and finally began to let the community practice directly, draw up product design projects together, and discuss the box size of the product together.

Conception stage: Enter the course to share the production process of brand planning and packaging design, and then brainstorm with the community to discuss what they think are the characteristics of the community. The actual drill of brand positioning and strategy will allow the community to discuss in groups to find out what the community thinks, share the brand strategy in it, and draw the elements of design together to draw the industrial brand pattern belonging to the community on paper.

Solution stage: After collecting the elements created together by the community, the designer's professional skills will draw sketches and color pictures for presentation, and finally the community will vote together to select the design that finally wins everyone's favorite. Further, this design was adjusted again and samples were modified to complete the final design.

Achievement stage: Same as the first round, after completing the solutions in the solution stage, the design product will be prototyped, the actual output will be made, and the community will be grouped together to learn the product display and planning together. Let the community play a role through the group display and planning more ideas and exchanges. Finally will share experience

Figure 2.   Teaching observation of the second round of local brand workshops.

and feedback, and will also assist in printing and send out plans to write off this project (as shown in Figure 2).

## 4.4 *Workshop teaching course observation and reflection*

The content of the course adopts interactive teaching that is simple, clear, and close to residents' lives. In every class, we focus on teaching one key point at a time remove all technical terms, express and communicate in a language that the community can understand, and make learners feel interesting through simple and clear key-point interactive teaching. It also makes the community feel that design is closely related to their lives.

Increase from three to six physical drills to improve interaction and co-creation to achieve a sense of identity:

In the physical drill, the course theory is used to do the drill to achieve the effect of learning. There are six drills in the whole course, and each actual drill is mostly a group drill, so that the community can discuss creative thinking and co-creation together. During the exercise, we need to focus on a few things: 1. Find out the local elements 2. Learn how to measure the product size 3. Think about the brand name and strategy 4. Create together and belong to the community 5. Jointly select the sketches and color pictures to discuss and finalize the design elements. 6. Display the results of the exercises, etc. (Figures 3 and 4).

All decisions and selections are discussed by the community to achieve resonance with local brands Due to the participation of the community every time, they can clearly share the principles and design concepts of brand design and how to bring the characteristic elements into the community in the later results. The resonance of local brands is even higher.

Figure 3. Community residents create a brand name together.

Figure 4. Community residents create community auxiliary design.

## 4.5 *Characteristics and limitations of the behavior of teachers and learners:*

The content of the local brand workshop is based on "one community, one commodity" (it can be a primary industry or a secondary product), adopts a step-by-step approach, discusses local brand culture in terms of community culture, industry, and residents' lifestyles, and develops a series of characteristic packaging, suitable for a variety of products as the marketing target. The main work characteristics are: 1. The participating students are mainly important community cadres and community residents 2. Lead the community to complete the entire design planning and creation 3. After the finished product is created, a small achievement exhibition will be held to create together from scratch. In our local branding workshops, we explore the behavioral characteristics and limitations of teachers and learners, as shown in Table 2.

Table 2. Traits and constraints of teacher and learner action.

| Traits and constraints of teacher and learner action | | |
| --- | --- | --- |
| Role | Action traits | Movement restrictions |
| Teacher | 1. Pay more attention to the process of co-creation between designers and the community than design results. 2. Staged practical drills enable learners to enhance their unity and help them quickly enter the creative process. 3. Through local brand workshops, we can dig deep into culture and design local characteristics and stories. | 1. Each workshop has different learning effects in co-creation due to the different statuses of the community. 2. The design of local brand workshops can hardly escape the existing style. 3. The high cost of printing funds cannot keep down the cost. |

*(continued)*

373

Table 2. Continued

| Traits and constraints of teacher and learner action | | |
| --- | --- | --- |
| Role | Action traits | Movement restrictions |
| | 4. Create group teams to stimulate learners to achieve cohesion and responsibility practice. | |
| Learner | 1. In local brand workshops, learners have different attitudes towards learning due to their different roles.<br>2. Practical drills increase learners' learning fun and design aesthetics, and then gain creative inspiration.<br>3. The completed design through co-creation and participation in the whole process can give the community a sense of accomplishment and be able to interpret design capabilities. | 1. Long-term government subsidies are prone to dependence.<br>2. The unfinished industrial chain leads to problems such as follow-up channel marketing. |

(Source: Organized by this study)

## 5  CONCLUSION

### 5.1 The teaching structure of the local brand workshop operates

Through participatory action research in the teaching construction of the workshop and the effectiveness of community learning, the final revision is that the local brand workshop has 5 oriented structures, and each structure is divided into 4 learning steps. There are 20 learning steps in total, with "exploration" as the main step. The purpose is to establish relationships and understand the community and industry; the main purpose of "definition" is to sort out industry characteristics, establish brand concepts, induction and analysis; the main purpose of "conception" is to inspire creative thinking, make a large number of proposals, and select designs; Production, testing and adjustment, repeated iterations; the main purpose of "achievements" is to display results, print finished products, feedback and reflection, so that the whole local brand workshop teaching can stimulate creativity and achieve co-creation results through staged practical exercises. The planning course model provides teacher a place to generate relevant course references.

5.2 Teachers mainly use the method of "co-creation by both parties, phased drills, and implementation of responsible practice" to plan and execute. In the local brand workshop, the biggest feature is that all design ideas are guided by the teaching staff, and they are created and produced together with the community residents. Through each phased practical drill and operation, from the interactive drill process to the playing of their respective strengths, the community shared their local cultural heritage and the two-way contribution of designers' professionalism. . They assisted each other in completing the unique local brand design output, and because of the community's participation and selection throughout the process, the community had a practical capacity to participate in responsibility.

5.3 Learners mainly gain by "stimulating creative inspiration, improving design aesthetics, and interpreting design ability": Learners go through every continuous practical exercise in the local brand workshop, from finding out local elements, learning how to measure product size, and collecting and organizing data to inspire learners to create and use Together they create design elements belonging to the community and learn creative ideas and color configurations from them. They draw images belonging to the community and enhance the aesthetics of the design. Afterward, they jointly select sketches and color pictures to discuss and finalize the design and practice the results. The solutions selected throughout the whole process, such as decoration, are the final choice of the community. Because of the whole process of participation and discussion, learners can easily interpret the design ability when producing results.

5.4 Local brand workshops focus on issues such as "design style cannot be escaped, funding problems, reliance on subsidies, and unfinished industrial chains": When completing the local brand workshop, as for the output part, the design cannot be separated from: 1. cuteness 2. realism 3. nostalgic style; in terms of printing, because the government planning book cannot use a large number of printing, it can only A small amount of printing is mainly used, resulting in high printing unit price and high product cost. Most communities are unable to provide more funds for follow-up printing due to insufficient funds and too much reliance on government subsidies; The connection of industries, so that the designed finished products are the difficulties and problems for the

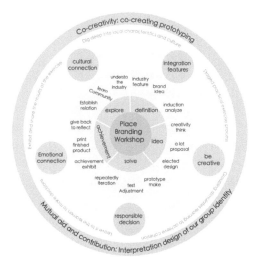

Figure 5. Local brand workshop training model (drawn in this study).

community in the follow-up marketing and distribution.

5.5 The main purpose of the local brand workshop is to jointly create a model for the community to form a sense of self-identity and cultivation of our group.

After the local design workshop is over, the community residents' full participation and contribution have a high degree of recognition and a strong cultural connection to the design products. The deepest emotional side of the community can be revealed through sharing brand packaging, as shown in Figure 12. This

provides expectations for tutoring units or designers to reference, as shown in Figure 5.

## REFERENCES

Cai, Y. P. (2021). *Local design: Extracting The Charm of The Land and Tapping The Value of the Place, Japan's Top Design Team Reveals The Secrets of Operation, and Creates a New Moving Economy! Guoli Culture.*

Gong C.C. (1986). *Develop A New Style Of Overall Community Construction, The Heart Of The People-The Idea and Example of The Overall Construction of Japanese Communities.* Taiwan Provincial Handicraft Industry Research Institute, Nantou City, 27–32.

Huang F.S. (2000). *The Humanistic Meaning of Local Community Leaders Participating in the Conservation of Rural Anc Estral Properties: Take Tainan Madou and Taipei Longpo As Examples.* Doctoral Dissertation, Institute of Geography, National Taiwan University, Taipei City.

Hwang S.H. (2012). Began to change from the community-The humanities and social practice opportunities for innovation. *Humanities and Social Sciences*, 14(1), 17–20.

Hwang, S. H., & Hwang, H. M. (2020). The path analysis of university design majors infiltrating indigenous tribe: a case study of social practice in laiji tribe in alishan township. *Journal of Design*, 25(4), 65–88.

Jhang C.F. (2001). *The Formation and Significance of Local Culture-A Case Study of Anping Area.* Master's thesis of Institute of Rural Culture, Tainan Normal University, Tainan City.

Ru S.J. (2003). *A Study on Brand Image for the Packaging Design of Regional Products.* Ming Chuan University, Taipei City.

Shih S.W.& Chen D.S. (2014). Introduction to the Promotion and Coordination of Humanistic Innovation and Social Practice Projects. *Humanities and Social Sciences*, 15(4), 17–31.

# Author index